The Course of Life

Psychoanalytic Contributions Toward Understanding Personality Development

Vol. II: Latency, Adolescence and Youth

Stanley I. Greenspan
and
George H. Pollock
Editors

MENTAL HEALTH STUDY CENTER
Division of Mental Health Service Programs
National Institute of Mental Health
2340 University Blvd., East
Adelphi, Maryland 20783

U.S. DEPARTMENT OF HEALTH AND HUMAN SERVICES
Public Health Service
Alcohol, Drug Abuse, and Mental Health Administration

ACKNOWLEDGEMENTS

Permission has been granted by the following copyright owners to quote from the works of *Sigmund Freud.* Further reproduction of these materials is prohibited without specific permission of the copyright holders.

Sigmund Freud Copyrights Ltd., the Institute of Psycho-Analysis and The Hogarth Press Ltd.
The Standard Edition of the Complete Psychological Works of Sigmund Freud, translated and edited by James Strachey.

Ernest Benn Ltd.
The Psychopathology of Everyday Life (1901). Translated by Alan Tyson.

George Allen & Unwin (Publishers) Ltd.
Interpretations of Dreams (1882, 1900).
Introductory Lectures (1916–1917).

Routledge & Kegan Paul, Ltd.
Leonardo DaVinci and a Memory of His Childhood (1910).

Alfred A. Knopf, Inc.
Moses and Monotheism (1939, 1934–1938). Translated by Katherine Jones.

Basic Books, Inc. Publishers
The Interpretation of Dreams (1882, 1900). Published in the United States by Basic Books, Inc., New York, by arrangement with George Allen & Unwin Ltd. and The Hogarth Press, Ltd., London.
Three Essays on Sexuality (1905). Published in the United States by Basic Books, Inc., 1962.
Collected Papers of Sigmund Freud, Vols. 1–4. Edited by Ernest Jones, M.D. Published in the United States by Basic Books, Inc., by arrangement with The Hogarth Press, Ltd. and the Institute of Psycho-Analysis, London.
The Origins of Psycho-Analysis: Letters to Wilhelm Fliess, 1887–1902. Translated and edited by Erich Mosbacher and James Strachey. Copyrighted and published by Basic Books, Inc., New York, 1954.

W.W. Norton & Co., Inc. Publishers
The Psychopathology of Everyday Life (1901).
Leonardo DaVinci and a Memory of His Childhood (1910).
On the History of the Psycho-Analytic Movement (1914).
Introductory Lectures (1916–1917).
The Ego and the Id (1923).
An Autobiographical Study (1924–1925).
Civilization and Its Discontents (1930).
New Introductory Lectures (1933).

Liveright Publishing Corp.
Introductory Lectures (1916–1917).

Permission has also been granted to reproduce copyrighted materials from the following works. Further reproduction of these materials is prohibited without specific permission of the copyright holders.

Erikson, Erik. *Childhood and Society* (1950). Copyright 1963, W.W. Norton & Co., New York.

Erikson, Erik. *Identity and the Life Cycle. Psychological Issues,* Monograph #1, Vol. 1. Copyright 1959 by International Universities Press, New York.

Erikson, Erik. *Identity, Youth and Crisis.* Copyright 1968 by W.W. Norton & Co., New York.

Freud, Anna. *Normality and Pathology in Childhood.* Copyright 1965 by International Universities Press, New York.
The Latency Period: The Writings of Anna Freud, Vol. I. Copyright 1974 by International Universities Press, New York.

Mahler, Margaret S. et al. *The Psychological Birth of the Human Infant: Symbiosis and Individuation.* Copyright 1975 by Basic Books, Inc., New York.

Library of Congress Catalog Card Number 79–600150

DHHS Publication No. (ADM) 80–999
Printed 1980

Foreword

Over the past three decades, a diverse group of scientists have extended the frontiers of our understanding of people in their biological, psychological, and social environments.

When one focuses on the impressive advances in each of these broad arenas, it may be difficult—though it is essential—to recall a fundamental purpose that underlies this explosion of knowledge: the search for greater understanding of the development and functioning of the individual throughout the lifespan. Each infant, child, adolescent, adult, and aged person is characterized by distinct biological capacities, psychological tendencies, and social interests that are interactive and cumulative, forming a complex matrix that constitutes a unique personality.

Viewed from this perspective, even such diverse advances as the introduction of psychoactive drugs; refinements of learning theory and its subsequent implementation in behavior therapy; proliferation of psychosocial strategies; and systems theory approaches to human behavior and community psychology come together in terms of their influences on the development of individuals.

It is the challenge, and often the quandary, of behavioral scientists to assimilate a vast variety of influences and forces into a coherent portrayal of the whole person.

A comprehensive model for studying and understanding the process of human development across the lifespan is essential for progress in all areas of understanding mental health and illness. *The Course of Life: Psychoanalytic Contributions Toward Understanding Personality Development* represents a singularly effective attempt to integrate information into a comprehensive approach to human development.

A key strength of the psychoanalytic approach is the study of continuity in development. An adult, interacting with the surrounding world, retains much of the child that person once was. To understand the pathological aspects of a person's functioning—as well as the adaptive aspects—it is necessary to consider the person as a whole rather than as a series of segments. Each phase of development builds upon prior phases, and, unless the totality of that process is somehow taken into account, information is lost.

In these volumes, psychoanalytic approaches, data, and theories related to development are not presented as ends in themselves but as launching points

iii

for development of methodologies and further investigations. Psychoanalytic theory bases its understanding of development and behavior on integrated perspectives gained in naturalistic settings. The clinical lessons of psychoanalytic procedures and direct observation may suggest experimental procedures, but they may also contribute to integrated, rather than narrowly focused, approaches to such investigations.

A comprehensive developmental theory of personality applicable to mental health practice has been both a need and a goal of the field since the late 19th century. Not only research but clinical practice also stands to gain from a sophisticated developmental perspective that avoids compartmentalization of efforts. From clinical interventions to outcome assessment, the total integrated bio-psycho-social person is ideally the object of interest. For example, assessment of the efficacy of a particular treatment strategy demands assessment of related psychopathological conditions or adaptive dimensions that may not have been a treatment objective. Treatment of manifest symptoms in one sector of the personality may lead to progression or regression in other areas of functioning. Planning therapeutic approaches, whether at an individual, family group, or community level, also demands an integrated understanding of the total person lest we add to the fragmentation and compartmentalization from which some of our patients already suffer. Perhaps the most far-reaching contribution of psychoanalytic developmental approaches may be seen in the future development of effective mental health prevention capabilities. In few other areas is the need for a comprehensive understanding of individuals more essential.

The Course of Life: Psychoanalytic Contributions Toward Understanding Personality Development is a major work and should serve as an invaluable reference for years to come. We are honored to have the opportunity to present in this publication original contributions by such authorities as Anna Freud and Erik Erikson and their many colleagues, too numerous to cite in this brief foreword.

I hope that these three volumes will be read not only by psychoanalytically oriented professionals but also by readers whose primary interests lie in biological, behavioral, social, community, and other schools of inquiry. The psychoanalytic developmental perspective provides a framework that encourages one to perceive these many orientations as complementary rather than antagonistic. It offers a unique window on the higher level processes that humanize the individual. Cooperation within such a framework will move the field substantially forward in terms of the breadth of its therapeutic armamentarium, the excitement of its research, and the achievement of its goals of understanding human behavior as fully as possible.

Herbert Pardes, M.D.
Director
National Institute of Mental Health □

Preface

Psychoanalytic developmental psychology is one of the basic foundations for our understanding of how the mind works, how it is organized in its adaptive and pathologic configurations, and how psychological treatment can be used to foster adaptive development. As an indepth psychology, it provides special insights into man's emotional life, including subtleties of wishes, feelings, thoughts, and experiences that influence behavior and are ordinarily outside of awareness (the dynamic unconscious). Psychoanalytic developmental psychology also can be viewed as being the basis of a general developmental psychology, embodying a comprehensive approach to understanding the multiple lines of human development from infancy through the stages of adulthood. For example, the psychoanalytic developmental approach includes the study of genetic and constitutional proclivities and their relationship to the organization of the major dimensions of personality (such as arousal, drive and affect patterns, and regulating, synthesizing, differentiating, and adaptive structures). In studies of early experiences, particularly early relationship patterns, one can observe how these factors are instrumental in molding somatic tendencies. Together with maturation factors, these fundamental experiences form the basis for such fundamental personality (ego) functions as reality testing, impulse regulation, affect regulation and tolerance, a delineated sense of self and of the external world, self-control, self-esteem, the formation of values, ideals, and goals, and continuing patterns of human relationships.

Each of these functions and each line of development (described in Anna Freud's contribution) becomes an area of special analytic, clinical, and investigative interest. For example, central to a psychoanalytic understanding of personality development are the vicissitudes of specific wishes, motives, feelings, attitudes (their related adaptive and social dimensions), conflicts, affects (dysphoric and pleasurable), and anxieties involved in progression from one developmental stage to another. Yet how the various components of the personality form a synthetic whole is equally important and cannot be overlooked. To illustrate, the constructs relating to self and identity (developed in Erik

Erikson's contribution) embody genetic and constitutional proclivities, early relationship patterns, the role of internal and external conflict, individual differences in organization of psychic structure, and the relationship of these to adaptive and maladaptive capacities and opportunities.

Fundamental to psychoanalytic developmental psychology is its scientific approach to the study and understanding of the complexity of human functioning. All variables are considered, and (as is often not recognized) all assumptions drawn about specific contents of experiential organizations (although some findings, such as the oedipal situation as an organizing experience, have stood the test of time) are examined. Emanating from the clinical tradition, the psychoanalytic approach welcomes and searches for complexity, as it attempts to understand how all observations can generate insight about the characteristics of man. Through the use of reconstruction in the clinical situation, direct naturalistic observation, and the data derived from controlled experimental procedures, psychoanalytic developmental psychology studies distinctly human features that include higher level structural personality functions, thought processes, feelings, and wishes, as well as their primitive biological, neurophysiological and emotional substrates.

The psychoanalytic developmental approach is well illustrated by the concept of multiple determination. In the search for ways to further clarify our understanding of human complexity, the psychoanalytic developmental approach has assumed from the outset that specific behaviors, thoughts, wishes, or other mental events might result from the interaction of multiple factors (sets of variables) and that any or all of these may be operative at any one time or become more central at critical periods. One does not look for overly simplified causal links between a given tendency and a wish, symptom, behavior, feeling, thought, or environmental event. Instead, the complex multiple functional interrelationships among a variety of factors are sought.

The chapters in these three volumes reflect the degree to which psychoanalytic psychology has become a truly comprehensive developmental psychology. Historically, the psychoanalytic method of inquiry in the clinical situation led to a relatively focused range of speculations about human development; pathologic symptoms were seen as resulting from singular, traumatic, childhood events. Subsequently, interest in actual "infantile traumas" was replaced by interest in the fantasies of early and later experiences. As our understanding of the defensive and adaptive operations of the ego emerged, the shift from reality to fantasy underwent appropriate rebalancing, and the importance of both the subjective and objective aspects of experience became more central. Formation and organization of personality were considered to be related both to the actual experiences with the early environment and to the perception, organization, and internalization of these experiences. Further developments in the area of ego psychology, and the pioneering psychoanalytic contributions of Anna Freud, Erik Erikson, Heinz Hartmann, and their colleagues, advanced our understanding of human development so that it has evolved into a more comprehensive developmental psychology. Experiences in both objective and subjective dimensions were seen to be associated with specific individual differences in genetic and constitutional factors, social and adaptive opportunities, and the ways in which the developing individual experienced and organized the external and internal world.

Awareness of the plural factors that play roles in human development resulted in new theories, and, as the reports in these volumes demonstrate, the broader perspective has generated new empirical and clinical findings as well as insights about human personality development and functioning throughout the course of life.

The volumes that make up *The Course of Life: Psychoanalytic Contributions Toward Understanding Personality Development,* Volume I—Infancy and Early Childhood; Volume II—Latency, Adolescence and Youth; and Volume III—Adulthood and the Aging Process, represent original contributions by an international group of scientists and clinicians to whom we owe much of our current knowledge about the phases of human personality development. Focused around progressive time frames, the contributions cover the continuum of human development from the prenatal phase through the aging processes. Dimensions of normal development, as well as the emergence of adaptive and pathologic propensities, are discussed for each developmental phase. The reader will find some useful overlapping as each author develops his or her own original concepts.

Anna Freud and Erik Erikson, two of the most influential contributors to current psychoanalytic approaches to understanding human personality development, prepared the introductory papers (to be found in Volume I). Their contributions span the entire course of life and were written especially for these volumes.

In this volume aspects of normal, adaptive, and pathological developments during latency, adolescence, and young adulthood are offered. During early latency, children shift part of their attention from the family of origin to age-peers and to school. Attempts at further resolution of triangular conflicts, stabilization of basic personality functions, and emergence of new phase-specific interests and strategies of defense and coping, in keeping with physical and cognitive growth, occur. We also observe at this time preparations for the biological changes that occur with puberty, providing preadolescents with a new range of experiences to process, differentiate, and organize.

During adolescence, psychological reorganizations occur in almost all sectors of personality development. Coupled with growing social and adaptive needs and opportunities, the maturational processes occurring both physically and cognitively correlate with and may determine the rapid psychological changes that take place. These include shifts in the organization of wishes and affects; self-organization; relationships to internalize representations of early family relationships, as well as to actual ongoing parental relationships; relationships with peers of both sexes; the emergence of new defenses and coping strategies; the development of psychic structures that were present in more informal ways, such as the ego ideal and superego; interests in future planning; consolidation of seemingly prior discordant aspects of personality into an "identity"; and preparation for, working through, a separation from earlier real and fantasized family relationships. To the degree certain tasks are accomplished, they become the basis for entry into adulthood.

Volume III indicates that adulthood is not a relatively static consequence of earlier developmental trends, but may be seen to have its own dynamic processes, developmental tasks, and specific adaptive and pathologic outcomes.

Contents

Melvin Lewis

List of Contributors

Carl P. Adatto, M.D., Training and Supervising Analyst, New Orleans Psychoanalytic Institute; Clinical Professor of Psychiatry, Louisiana State University Medical School, New Orleans.

Helen R. Beiser, M.D., Clinical Professor of Psychiatry, Abraham Lincoln School of Medicine; Faculty, Adult and Child Analysis, Chicago Institute for Psychoanalysis.

Ronald M. Benson, M.D., Clinical Associate Professor, University of Michigan Medical School; Director of the Youth Outpatient Program, Children's Psychiatric Hospital.

Graham B. Blaine, Jr., M.D., Assistant in Psychiatry, Adolescents' Unit, Children's Hospital Medical Center, Boston.

Hilde Bruch, M.D., Professor Emeritus of Psychiatry, Baylor College of Medicine, Waco, Texas.

Edith Buxbaum, Ph.D., Training Analyst and Child Analyst, Seattle Psychoanalytic Institute; Clinical Professor in Psychiatry at University of Washington; Member of The American Psychoanalytic Association.

Lee Combrinck-Graham, M.D., Director of Child Psychiatry Training, Philadelphia Child Guidance Clinic; Clinical Assistant Professor of Psychiatry, University of Pennsylvania, Philadelphia.

Henry P. Coppolillo, M.D., Professor and Director, Division of Child Psychiatry, University of Colorado Medical School, Denver.

Cecil C.H. Cullander, M.D., Founder Member of the Washington Association for Psychoanalytic Education; Supervising and Training Analyst, The Washington Psychoanalytic Institute, Washington, D.C.

Rudolf Ekstein, Ph.D., Clinical Professor of Medical Psychology, UCLA; Training and Supervisory Analyst, Los Angeles and Southern California Psychoanalytic Institutes; Yearly Guest Professor, University of Vienna.

Aaron H. Esman, Chief Psychiatrist, Jewish Board of Family and Children's Services; Faculty, New York Psychoanalytic Institute.

Dana L. Farnsworth, M.D., Henry K. Oliver Professor of Hygiene, Emeritus, Harvard University.

Erna Furman, Member and faculty, Cleveland Center for Research in Child Development; Assistant Clinical Professor in Childtherapy, Case Western Reserve University School of Medicine.

Robert A. Furman, M.D., Director, Cleveland Center for Research in Child Development; Training Analyst, The Cleveland Psychoanalytic Institute.

Stanley I. Greenspan, M.D., Chief, Mental Health Study Center, National Institute of Mental Health; Associate Clinical Professor of Psychiatry and Behavioral Sciences, and Child Health and Development, George Washington University Medical Center, Washington, D.C.

Saul I. Harrison, M.D., Professor of Psychiatry, University of Michigan Medical Center, Ann Arbor, Mich.

James L. Hatleberg, M.D., Supervising Child Analyst, Washington Psychoanalytic Institute; Assistant Clinical Professor of Psychiatry, Georgetown University Medical School, Washington, D.C.

Richard A. Isay, M.D., Associate Clinical Professor, Department of Psychiatry and Child Study Center, Yale University School of Medicine; Faculty, Western New England Institute for Psychoanalysis.

Eugene H. Kaplan, M.D., Faculty, Division of Psychoanalytic Education, SUNY College of Medicine at New York City; Associate Professor of Clinical Psychiatry, SUNY at Stony Brook, N.Y.

Judith S. Kestenberg, M.D., Clinical Professor of Psychiatry and Training Analyst, Downstate Medical Center, Brooklyn, N.Y.; Director, Child Development Research, Sands Point, N.Y.

Selma Kramer, M.D., Professor and Head of Section Child Psychiatry, Medical College of Pennsylvania; Training Supervising Analyst, Philadelphia Psychoanalytic Institute.

Serge Lebovici, M.D. Professeur de Clinique de Psychiatrie de l'Enfant, Universite de Paris-Nord, Faculté de Medecine Experimentale (Professor and Chief, Clinic of Child Psychiatry, University of Paris North, Faculty of Experimental Medicine); Past President of the International Psychoanalytical Association.

Melvin Lewis, M.B., B.S. (London), F.R.C. Psych., D.C.H., Professor of Pediatrics and Psychiatry, Yale University Child Study Center; Editor, Journal of the American Academy of Child Psychiatry.

Irwin M. Marcus, M.D., Clinical Professor of Psychiatry, Louisiana State University Medical School; Adjunct Professor, Tulane University; Director of Child/ Adolescent Program, Psychoanalytic Institute, New Orleans.

Joseph L. Massimo, Ed.D., Chief Psychologist, Newton Public Schools, Newton, Mass.

Joseph D. Noshpitz, M.D., Director of Education and Training, Department of Psychiatry, Children's Hospital NMC; Professor of Psychiatry, George Washington University, Washington, D.C.

Daniel Offer, M.D., Chairman, Department of Psychiatry, Michael Reese Hospital and Medical Center; Professor of Psychiatry, Pritzker School of Medicine, University of Chicago.

Fred Pine, Ph.D., Professor of Psychiatry (Psychology), Albert Einstein College of Medicine, New York City.

Joseph Rudolph, M.D., Clinical Associate Professor of Pediatrics and Psychiatry, Medical College of Pennsylvania; Supervising Analyst in Child Analysis, Philadelphia Psychoanalytic Institute.

Marshall D. Schechter, M.D., Professor and Director of Division of Child and Adolescent Psychiatry, Department of Psychiatry, University of Pennsylvania; Director and Training Director, Irving Schwartz Institute, Philadelphia.

Milton F. Shore, Ph.D., Associate Chief, Mental Health Study Center, National Institute of Mental Health; Adjunct Professor, Catholic University of America, The American University, and the George Washington University Medical School, Washington, D.C.

Morris A. Sklansky, M.D., Training and Supervising Analyst, Chicago Institute for Psychoanalysis; Clinical Professor of Psychiatry, University of Chicago.

Erwin R. Smarr, M.D., Clinical Professor, Department of Mental Health Science, Hahnemann Medical College and Hospital, Philadelphia.

Herman D. Staples, M.D., Chief of Psychiatry, The Media Clinic, Media, Pa.; Past-President, The American Society for Adolescent Psychiatry.

*The Course of Life: Psychoanalytic Contributions
Toward Understanding Personality Development
Vol. II: Latency, Adolescence, and Youth.
S.I. Greenspan and G.H. Pollock, editors.
NIMH 1980*

Early Latency—Normal and Pathological Aspects

Erna Furman

History and Definition of the Concept of Latency

The psychoanalytic concept of the latency period originates with S. Freud. He introduced and formally defined it for the first time in 1905 as a phase in the sexual development of children. From that time on and until the end of his life, Freud essentially maintained his initial view of latency and repeatedly stressed its importance for the understanding of normal and abnormal psychological growth. His many references to the topic of latency also show, however, that he continued to grapple with the concept, adjusting his formulation to clinical findings and weighing the role of biological, phylogenetic, cultural, and individual psychological factors (S. Freud 1905*a*, 1908, 1909*a*, 1911, 1916*a*, 1921, 1923*a*, 1923*b*, 1923*c*, 1924*a*, 1924*b*, 1925, 1926*a*, 1926*b*, 1926*c*, 1939, 1940).

Freud described the latency period as following the phallic-oedipal crest of infantile sexual development and extending until the onset of puberty. Although he several times altered the exact age limits, the indicated span of time coincides roughly with elementary school in this country. Structurally, Freud viewed the latency period as "characterized by the dissolution of the Oedipus complex, the creation or consolidation of the superego and the erection of ethical and aesthetic barriers in the ego" (1926*a*, p. 114). From a dynamic point of view he stressed the role of castration anxiety in bringing about repression and/or dissolution of the Oedipus complex and the increasing importance of guilt emanating from the newly formed superego. He saw the latency child's conflict focus on the struggle against masturbation with its attendant oedipal and pre-oedipal fantasies. Although Freud observed a "halt and retrogression" (1916*a*, p. 326; 1939) in psychic sexual development and hence a relative diminution in drive energy, he pointed out from the start that instinctual breakthroughs do occur and that latency "need not bring with it any interruption of sexual activity and sexual interest" (1916*a*, p. 326). Depending on the cultural setting and individual personality, however, the latency child's adaptation is more usually marked by increasing relationships with peers and adults outside the family, by growth in ego functions, skills, activities, and sublimatory interests, and by conformity to the rules of the family and community.

Freud's metapsychological definition of the latency period has stood the test of later psychoanalytic clinical investigations and theoretical developments. There are only a few additions: A. Freud's (1936) work on defenses paved the way for Bornstein's (1951) suggestion to subdivide latency into two periods. This division is based on differences in the structural equilibrium of the personality and implies technical therapeutic considerations. The early latency period extends roughly from age 6 to 8; the late latency covers the subsequent 2 or 3 years and is characterized by a solidification of the preceding ego and superego developments and greater internal harmony. More recently Williams (1972, p. 600) proposed a triphasic division of latency, again based on theoretical and therapeutic criteria, but

> emphasizing the influence of the preceding phase of prelatency on early latency development, and in delineating the impact of the phase that follows latency—namely, prepuberty. Without trying to schematize, one can roughly describe early latency as lasting from 5 to 7, latency proper from 7 to about 9, and late latency from approximately 9 to 11. It should be understood that this scheme does not represent a strict categorization: In some children the prelatency period, chronologically speaking, extends far into what we would regard as latency proper; others show an early thrust into prepuberty.

Katan (1978) stresses that chronological demarcations of the latency period, and of subdivisions within it, are misleading because of the normally wide variation among children. The child's entry into latency and transition into prepuberty is characterized by the same overlapping of phases as at earlier developmental stages. The actual timing of the beginning and end of latency is therefore difficult to determine and differs greatly from child to child. She notes that some children's onset of latency may normally occur as late as their seventh or even eighth year, depending on factors of endowment, personality development, and environmental influence, e.g., children to whom a father becomes available only at age 6 may experience a delayed oedipal period, followed by a delayed but normal latency and puberty.

Several authors have noted that the clinical picture of latency is sometimes far from calm. Instinctual breakthroughs may be quite frequent; they may occur to a marked degree during the earliest and latest years of latency; there may be no diminution in instinctual interests and activity (Alpert 1941; Sarnoff 1976; Clower 1976). Maenchen (1970) suggests that during recent years in this country latency appears to be less long and its characteristics seem less evident. Such findings help us to understand the many vicissitudes of latency but do not invalidate the concept of latency. S. Freud himself referred to these phenomena and understood them in terms of variations in individual personalities, familial influences, and cultural patterns. It is not the presence or absence of instinctual manifestations that defines latency; rather, it is the emergence within the child's personality of the superego, changes in the ego, and their position vis-a-vis the Oedipus complex and its derivatives.

Freud saw the importance of the latency period in the context of human sexual development which is marked by a diphasic onset. Latency represents a halt to, and interruption of, the progression of infantile sexuality. The child's libidinal attachment to his infantile parental love objects culminates in the Oedipus complex and is repressed and/or dissolved with the onset of latency. Adolescence represents the second onset of sexual development leading to genital maturity and libidinal investment in love objects outside the family. Freud noted that this diphasic onset of sexual life was peculiar to man and that its psychological manifestations were paralleled, and even caused, by comparable physiological and biological phenomena in the maturation of the sexual organs (S. Freud 1905a; 1939). Indeed, he sometimes called it the physiological period of latency (1939).

The causes of the diphasic onset of sexual growth are to be found in biological and historical factors. Following Ferenczi's (1913) suggestion, Freud considered the glacial epoch a key factor. Speaking of the diphasic onset, Freud said, "the last mentioned phenomenon, which seems to be peculiar to man, is a heritage of the cultural development necessitated by the glacial epoch" (1923a, p. 35), and he reiterates this view later (1926a). Whereas this hypothesis of latency may appear strictly Lamarckian in genetic terms and as yet unproven by scientific findings, Lampl (1953) discusses its plausibility. He shows how, more recently, evolutional phenomena have been explained by a combination of Darwinian and Lamarckian theories, and he explores the close interaction of biological and psychological factors in the development of latency and other areas. Sarnoff (1976), by contrast, disputes biological and physiological factors affecting latency and focuses on the cultural-historical development of the human race. Clower (1976) stresses the role of society.

In Freud's view, the historical factor is defined by the lengthy helplessness and dependency of the human infant, by the formation and subsequent repression of the Oedipus complex which are the byproducts of the close extended parent-child relationship, by the superego which is the outcome of the preceding developments, and by the variable cultural utilization and reenforcement of the child's psychological status in the developmental phase of latency (1905a, 1908, 1916a, 1923a, 1923b, 1939). Freud pointed to the important personality achievements during the latency period, especially the emergence of values, ideals, and sublimations, and their positive implications for human cultural development. He stressed, however, that, at the same time, the latency period and its attendant psychological developments constitute "the determining factor for the origin of the neuroses" (1923*b*, p. 246; 1939). The interruption in sexual development and repression or dissolution of the Oedipus complex can be "most propitious culturally" (S. Freud, 1916*a*, p. 326) but also makes man vulnerable to neurotic diseases.

Later psychoanalytic writers have not followed up S. Freud's particular areas of interest in the latency period. In 1959, Fries found that the word "latency" appears in the titles of but a few psychoanalytic publications, although the topic of latency is taken up in many. Her observation still holds true now, almost 20 years later, with some notable exceptions. Psychoanalytic investigators have concerned themselves mainly with the treatment and elucidation of pathology in latency children. Many articles trace the prelatency genesis of latency symptomatology; many others contribute to the technique of therapy with this age group. Relatively few writers have focused on the theory of latency, on normal developmental steps and masteries, and on the multiple pathogenic determinants, internal and external, which operate specifically during the latency period and affect its course and outcome.

The following discussion of normal and pathological development in early latency incorporates many existing psychoanalytic contributions. In addition, it introduces several concepts which, to the best of my knowledge, have not been previously described or whose significance has not been assessed in the context of this developmental phase. For purposes of clarity these concepts are pinpointed below and further amplified in the appropriate sections of the text:

1. The onset of infantile amnesia, characterized by the forgetting of prelatency experiences, causes many children inner disharmony, bewilderment, and distress. The loss of a familiar part of the self—one's past—is sometimes experienced as an inadequacy, leading to dissatisfaction and concern with himself, or as shameful. It may also affect the child's relationships if he is unaware of the source of his discomfort and perceives it as stemming from without or expects it to be alleviated by his loved ones. When the parents recognize this developmental phenomenon, they can extend appropriate educational help to their child by explaining the universal and limited nature of this form of forgetting.
2. The early latency child normally experiences difficulty in recognizing the "voice of conscience" as stemming from within; he can be helped educationally to reach this awareness which, in turn, assists him in integrating and mediating the newly internalized superego demands.
3. Externalization of superego to ward off inner conflict may be regarded as a phase-specific transitional defense in early latency; it becomes pathological only if it exceeds certain limits in intensity and/or becomes so rigid as to

preclude progress toward mature and appropriate integration of superego demands.

4. Partial regression of the libido to the anal-sadistic level is known to be a normal phenomenon in early latency. Observation and clinical material from analytic treatments show that the libidinal regression to the phallic-narcissistic level is equally if not more prominent in normal development. It is linked to the narcissistic hurt of the oedipal rejection and affects the normal course of object relationships in latency: the turning away from the parents, the relative "downgrading" of the parents, the narcissistic object choice of peers, and the defensive attitude to peers of the opposite sex.

5. The post-oedipal regression to the phallic-narcissistic level is more marked and may assume pathological dimensions in cases with a previously established phallic-narcissistic fixation point and in cases where, in early latency, the child experiences a hurt in his relationships with the parents which then constitutes a developmental interference. These latter instances were studied in cases where a satisfactory age-appropriate relationship with father or mother was not available during early latency because of his or her physical absence or emotional unavailability. The effects of earlier fixation and current developmental interference may overlap and reenforce one another.

6. Whereas the father's role during the child's oedipal phase is well recognized, his importance to the child in early latency has not been stressed, as a love object, as a model for identification, and in his attitude to the child's growing up. Even subtle and manifestly minor paternal pathologies constitute very significant developmental interferences at this level.

7. The partial libidinal regression in early latency presents a special diagnostic difficulty in that it makes it hard to distinguish isolated neurotic problems carried over from conflicts at previous levels from those which result from the current regression. This affects the differential diagnoses between phase-appropriate and neurotic conflicts.

8. Early latency is an important time for the differential diagnosis of atypical (borderline and psychotic) disturbances in cases that are not too severe and/or those who responded well to therapeutic intervention in the pre-school years. This applies particularly to the assessment of such ego functions as the capacity to neutralize instinctual energy, to establish secondary autonomy of functions and activities, to mediate structural conflicts, to effect advanced forms of identification, and to take over and independently maintain those functions which, in early years, were vested in the parents.

Some Developmental Characteristics of Early Latency

Superego formation is one of the crucial developmental achievements of the latency child. Since S. Freud (1923a), many writers have contributed to our understanding of the various aspects of the superego. Some have researched the specific mechanisms by which it is built following the dissolution of the Oedipus complex and how this process is related to, or differs from, pre-oedipal precursors (Sandler 1960; Jacobson 1954). A. Freud's (1936) work on the defenses, especially the defense of identification with the aggressor, is a cornerstone to the understanding of the intermediate stage in superego forma-tion which so often characterizes the behavior of the early latency child. At that time in his development, the child's superego is not yet fully internalized or integrated with the rest of the personality, drive pressure is still strong, and the ego functions are often inadequate to the task of mediating to achieve inner harmony.

Intense psychic conflict gives rise to anxiety which in turn is warded off by a variety of defenses. Identification with the aggressor—a combination of intro-jection, projection, and turning passive into active—is phase-appropriately used to avoid guilt feelings. The child's use of this defense may show in unexpected attacks on others by word or deed. Another phase-specific defense is externalization of superego which wards off internal conflict by attributing the superego to another person—usually one in a position of authority. The use of this defense may, similarly, result in unruly aggressive or sexual behav-ior which we customarily expect in much younger children. The casual observer then finds it difficult to appreciate how close such a child is dynami-cally to the responsive obedient latency child whose superego demands regu-late his behavior more effectively. Indeed, these very different behaviors may alternate or manifest themselves in separate settings; for example, the child may be difficult to live with in the family but adapt well at school. As A. Freud said, "If [the teacher] does succeed in representing [the children's] superego, the ideal of the group, the compulsory obedience changes into voluntary submission" (1930, p. 120).

Even when full internalization does take place, the newly formed superego tends to be harsh and uncompromising. Bornstein (1949; 1951; 1953 a; 1953 b) and later Williams (1972) were particularly attuned to the early latency child's heightened sensitivity to criticism, his tendency to experience even the slight-est implied disapproval as a vicious punitive attack and to respond with intensi-fied defensive maneuvers. Both writers described therapeutic techniques to deal with the early latency child's special resistances. Bornstein's work on the interpretation of defenses and affects actually revolutionized child-analytic technique in general and made the earlier use of an introductory phase redundant.

Masturbation

The internal prohibitions, reproaches, and threats of punishment, emanating from the newly formed superego, are of course primarily directed against the instinctual drives and drive derivatives associated with the Oedipus complex.

The diminution of the drives is not a sudden phenomenon. Moreover, as stressed by S. Freud (1916a; 1919; 1926a; 1939), A. Freud (1965), and Bornstein (1951; 1953a), there is a measure of drive regression, partly defensive. As a result, the early latency child's masturbation and accompanying fantasies contain both oedipal and pre-oedipal elements. This further intensifies the conflict with the superego as the latter finds itself particularly opposed to the sadomasochistic regressive aspects.

My own findings in working with children in this phase suggest that the regression from the oedipal to the phallic-narcissistic level (Edgcumbe and Burgner 1975) is especially prevalent. The child's experience of rejection by the oedipal love object leads to a renewed emphasis on the phallic-narcissistic components and revives related conflicts around sexual differences, penis envy, and castration fear.

Since a greater or lesser degree of drive activity continues throughout latency and since the Oedipus complex is usually not fully dissolved but merely kept unconscious, the ego has to channel direct and indirect drive expression. Most writers consider the struggle against masturbation among the latency child's main developmental conflicts. Periodic instinctual breakthroughs are regarded as normal. Some of these occur in the form of displaced activities with pre-oedipal admixtures (such as nailbiting); others involve genital feelings and genital manipulation. There is no consensus as to the exact nature of the latency child's capacity for genital discharge. Especially in girls there appears to be considerable variation within the range of normality. Lampl-de Groot (1950) finds that latency girls masturbate clitorally and do not reach an orgastic climax. Clower (1976) stresses the prevalence of nonmanual clitoral masturbation and the orgastic discharge potential of the clitoris in latency. Bornstein (1953a) and Fraiberg (1972) report cases of vaginal arousal and orgastic experiences. Bernstein (1976) reports on the role of masochistic fantasies of being penetrated in shaping the latency girl's masturbation and related conflict.

The child in early latency usually exhibits in his behavior both the instinctual derivatives and the fight against them, alternately or in combination; for example, his room may be very messy at one time and obsessively tidy at another time; his plea to "stay up late" expresses both his wish to share the parents' evening time and his fight against masturbatory temptations in bed. Bornstein (1953a), A. Freud (1965), and Nagera (1966b) describe these sleep disturbances of the latency period as well as the child's own newly acquired measures of coping with them, for example, by reading in bed.

The latency child finds himself in special difficulty when his struggle against masturbation is too successful, i.e., when his personality allows no voluntary or involuntary episodes of bodily instinctual gratification. A. Freud (1949a) described how, in those cases, the child's sexuality may invade his ego functioning, causing severe disturbances in relationships and activities (see also section on character disorders in this chapter).

Fantasy

The growing ego, however, also makes accommodations with the drives in phase-appropriate activities, provides for indirect discharge, and increasingly converts id energy for use in developing ego functions, such as thought and speech (Kolansky 1967).

Many writers have discussed the development by which the fantasies become separated from the masturbatory activity and undergo changes which disguise their oedipal and pre-oedipal contents (S. Freud 1919; A. Freud 1922, 1949a). Eventually these daydreams and fantasies contribute to the development of thinking and some of its creative aspects, to playing with its attendant skills and social relations, to artistic activities, and to the enjoyment of literature (S. Freud 1911; A. Freud 1922; Friedlander 1942; Burlingham 1945; Blanchard 1946; Lampl-de Groot 1950; Bornstein 1951, 1953a; Peller 1954, 1959; A. Freud 1965; Kaplan 1965; Kramer 1971; Goldings 1974).

The latency child's fantasies, separated from the act of masturbation, do not always lead to ego gains. A. Freud (1949a) showed how they can be transferred from the family to the school and wider community and result in various forms of social maladjustment and/or of interference in ego activities, such as learning inhibitions, feelings of being disliked or persecuted, provocativeness, struggles with the authorities, disruptive exhibitionism.

The fantasies most characteristic of this phase, e.g., the family romance (S. Freud 1909a) and the fantasy of having a twin (Burlingham 1945), crystallize and flourish in late latency. Many children's books dealing with related themes, however, become favorites already in early latency (Friedlander 1942; Peller 1959; Widzer 1977). Kaplan (1965) and Goldings (1974) have shown that some of these fantasies are also expressed in well-known children's rhymes, beloved in latency and chanted rhythmically to accompany the motoric games of this phase, e.g., jump rope.

Motility plays an important part in latency and represents another area where the ego harmoniously includes id derivatives and gradually gains ascendancy over them. Kaplan (1965) and Kestenberg (1975a) particularly have drawn attention to the early latency child's characteristic psychomotor activities. They showed how the normal development of these activities depends on the close interaction of physiological and psychological maturation, how it serves as a vehicle for phase-appropriate instinctual discharge, furthers social relationships, and increases ego skills. Goldings (1974) and Sarnoff (1976) also stress the significance of these rhymes and rhythms for the transmission of cultural traditions, blending individual oedipal and pre-oedipal contents with societal lore and myths. Failure or deviation in this area of ego functioning can be taken as a serious sign of developmental pathology, affecting many aspects of the latency child's personality.

Play

Post-oedipal play in general has received attention as a developmental line in which all parts of the latency child's personality harmoniously interact. Kaplan (1965), Goldings (1974), and especially Peller (1954) traced the oedipal and pre-oedipal contents of social games (e.g., team sports and board games) and individual hobbies (e.g., model building, crafts, collecting). In his charming and instructive autobiographical book, *"Where Did You Go?" "Out." "What Did You Do?" "Nothing,"* Smith (1957) described in detail the many solitary and social games of his latency years, both formal and improvised. He brought out the interaction of fantasy and reality and the extent to which the child deals with them on his own or shares them with peers but, phase-appropriately, keeps them at a distance from the adults.

In early latency the instinctual aspects of these games are often still so poorly integrated with the rest of the personality that they tend to interfere with the enjoyment of playing, e.g., the child can't bear to lose, insists on being the first one, can only collect kings in a card game. At better moments and increasingly with the transition into late latency, the main point of the games is their elaborate defensive nature, such as the insistence on rules and fairness, on the skill of playing as opposed to the thrill of winning, on cooperative effort versus individual rivalry. As a matter of fact, many games never get started or fail to get finished because of interminable discussions about the rules themselves. Even some early latency games focus primarily on defense, such as hopscotch and "Step on the crack, break your mother's back." In games and hobbies, the obsessive ritualistic defenses of this phase tend to stand out, but the overall increase and solidification of reaction-formations and rationalization are also evident.

Defenses and Sublimations

The very onset of latency is associated with the repression of the Oedipus complex. It is primarily the mechanism of repression which the ego uses to ward off the castration anxiety associated with oedipal strivings and to serve as countercathectic measure against the reemergence of infantile sexuality. This brings about the infantile amnesia, the forgetting of the bulk of the prelatency experiences, so characteristic of human mental development. S. Freud (1905b) pointed out that, in the hysteric, the glaring gaps in memory which are caused by the use of repression are gradually filled or bridged so as to produce a conscious continuum of the person's life history. With phase-appropriate repression at the beginning of latency, it is usually a positive sign when it occurs piecemeal over a prolonged period rather than obliterating memories suddenly and totally. The slower selective process indicates better integration and does not make excessive demands on the ego's energies. However, even when repression initially wipes out only some memories, this can be very upsetting to the young latency child. He finds that he can no longer share in the family's conversation about a past happy vacation; he cannot recognize the babysitter who remembers *him* so well, and he struggles in vain to reproduce for himself the continuity of "where I was when" and "what happened next." As they affect the child's synthetic function, these experiences are not only disconcerting but may also be felt as a narcissistic injury which lowers his self-esteem or as an imperfection of which he is ashamed. Some children also worry that their memory is altogether impaired, that they will be unable to remember what they learn at school or experience at home.

The inner disharmony which results from the loss of a familiar part of the self—one's past—is further intensified by having to integrate the new superego— an as yet unfamiliar part of the self. This unsettled and distressing mental state sometimes leads to irritability, excessive demandingness, or withdrawal from love objects when the cause of the painful feelings is perceived to lie in the external rather than internal world. The adults sometimes contribute to the child's discomfort by laughing at his forgetting or by prompting him to remember, as though he could do so if only he were not so lazy, stupid, or uncooperative—"But *surely* you remember Auntie May! Why, she was *so* nice to you when we visited her." I found that, when parents are helped to recognize the phenomenon of infantile amnesia and the puzzlement it causes youngsters at the time of its onset, they can be most helpful to their children. It is very reassuring to children to be told that these lapses of memory are part of growing up, that it happens to everyone and had also happened to all grown-ups when they were young, and that they can learn again about many things in their early lives by looking at photos or home movies or simply by asking the older members of the family to tell them about past events. And, above all, children need to know that they will not go on forgetting and that, from here on in, they will be able to remember what they learn and experience.

Latency is of course best known for the characterological integration of those defenses, such as the reaction-formations of pity, cleanliness, and shame, which aid in socialization and become part of the child's ego-ideal. S. Freud (1905*a*, 1908, 1923*b*, 1926*a*) and other writers have also stressed the concomitant development of sublimations which utilize the newly neutralized energy (Blanchard 1946; A. Freud 1930, 1965; Lampl-de Groot 1950; Bornstein 1953*a*; Panels on Latency 1957, 1965; Fries 1959; Jacobson 1954; Kaplan 1965; Williams 1972).

The child's pleasure in learning is closely linked to sublimations and to the phase-appropriate, teacher-pupil relationship. It is most important for the child's development that this relationship focus on and support these ego activities and serve as a model for identification in this area; by contrast, when the teacher presents himself or herself as a parent substitute and encourages elements of the parent-child relationship in the teacher-pupil interaction this may constitute a developmental interference (Nagera 1966*a*) and lead to pathology in the child (A. Freud 1949*a*; E. Furman 1977). In the past the strictness and rigidity of the school environment sometimes allowed no opportunity for a phase-appropriate relationship with the teacher. The young latency child's libidinal strivings then turned back onto himself, leading to an increase in autoerotic activities, or focused in full force on his peer relations. Such lack of opportunity for a teacher-pupil relationship also discouraged the development of suitable identifications and sublimations and detracted from the joyful investment in learning. More recently, some progressive educational trends have erred in the opposite direction. By encouraging the transfer of family relationships to the teachers and by meeting the child's emotional needs instead of expecting him to work toward the attainment of skills and behavioral norms, the school becomes an arena where prelatency conflicts are perpetuated and progressive latency development is interfered with.

Object Relationships

The intense libidinal attachment to the parents is dissolved and repressed. The parents themselves are no longer considered all-important and almighty. Adults outside the family begin to assume a greater role in the child's life. His oft-repeated "My teacher said. . ." testifies to this and suggests that ego and superego aspects enter into these new relationships to a significant extent (S. Freud 1914). The diminished psychological dependency on the parents and increased importance of relationships with other adults not only contribute to the child's schooling but also affect his performance in the psychotherapeutic setting, especially the transference relationship with the child analyst. Theoretical and technical aspects of the transference in latency analyses have been discussed by several authors. Some of them point to increased transference manifestation; others speak of the development of a transference neurosis in some latency children (Bornstein 1949, 1953b; A. Freud 1965; Harley 1962; Fraiberg 1966, 1967; Maenchen 1970; Novick 1970; Williams 1972; Sandler, Kennedy, and Tyson 1975).

With peers, too, real friendships begin to develop and constitute an important part of the child's life (Pearson 1966). These relationships as well as the many group and social activities are now limited to children of the same sex, while those of the opposite sex tend to be kept at a distance, sometimes despised or teased. The early latency child still struggles with these developmental steps. Remnants of oedipal libidinal interest may show in the boy's love for his woman teacher or play with girlfriends. Commonly we also see the intense defensive measures against such breakthroughs, e.g., the boys' provocative or boisterous defiance with adult women, their abusive and belittling attitudes to girls; with girls we note similar difficulties, e.g., fearfulness of men, tomboyishness, or bossy and "holier than thou" behavior with boys.

The early latency child's retreat to phallic-narcissistic concerns, occasioned in part by the narcissistic hurt of the oedipal rejection and defense against oedipal ties, was referred to earlier. My observation of and therapeutic work with children in the Hanna Perkins Kindergarten[1] suggest that the effects of this regression are particularly noticeable in the area of object relationships. It contributes to the disappointed "downgrading" of the parents, the preference for peers of the same sex, and the defensive attitude to those of the opposite sex. A. Freud (1965) notes that relationships with contemporaries in latency are based on identification, not on object love. Preference for friends of the same sex in this phase is likely to be succeeded by heterosexual object choice in adolescence. The boy who seeks out girls and the girl who seeks out boys are more likely to experience difficulties with heterosexuality later on.

Assessment

These briefly summarized psychoanalytic contributions to the normal development in early latency highlight selected areas. The overall metapsychological assessment of the latency child is facilitated by the use of the diagnostic profile and developmental lines (A. Freud 1965), illustrated in the literature by Meers (1966). R.A. Furman and Katan (1969) utilized the profile in the followup study of youngsters treated in the Hanna Perkins Therapeutic Nursery School and added a "Scheme for Lines of Development and Mastery of Tasks in Latency" to aid in the assessment of latency children.

Latency Pathology

In private psychiatric practice as well as in mental health agencies latency-aged children constitute a large proportion of cases referred and treated. The reasons for this are in part external, i.e., familial and societal. Although emotional difficulties in preschoolers are the rule rather than the exception, the parent-child relationship during the earliest years is so close and exclusive that the child's problems cause the parent especially marked guilt and narcissistic injury (E. Furman 1969). These painful feelings tend to be warded off by defensive measures (e.g., denial, rationalization) against recognizing the child's difficulties and against seeking professional advice for them. The parents' reluctance is helped by the fact that the young child's troubles manifest themselves primarily within the family setting and are largely hidden from the scrutiny of outsiders.

The latency child, by contrast, is less close to the parents (Kestenberg 1975b). They view his maladjustments at a somewhat greater emotional distance, and, moreover, his school attendance exposes him to interaction with, and expectations from, an outside authority. Many referrals of latency children are indeed prompted by the school or occur in consultation with it. Evaluations

---

1. Many of the clinical data and theoretical formulations in this paper derive from my work at the Hanna Perkins Nursery School and Kindergarten (R.A. Furman and A. Katan 1969) and from what I learned there from and with my colleagues.

show that many of the children seen in this age group do not suffer from disturbances which developed with the onset of latency but which were over-looked during the preschool years and now surface undeniably as the children fail to master phase-appropriate tasks.

At the other end of the spectrum, both parents and teachers often wish for psychiatric help for the preadolescent and adolescent youngsters who are caught in the emotional upheaval of growth; but effective referrals and, even more so, treatment programs run afoul of the children's resistances. Unlike the latency child, the adolescent cannot be "taken" to get help.

In addition to these external factors, there are also significant, internal, phase-specific reasons to account for the large numbers and varieties of latency problems. The above review of latency development gives an inkling of the magnitude of the structural changes within the personality, the extent and intensity of new conflicts, and the variety of ego masteries to be achieved. It is not surprising that the early phase of latency, in particular, gives rise to much inner stress with attendant ups and downs in behavioral adjustment and that it also serves as the matrix for the formation of lasting pathology (S. Freud 1926a; A. Freud 1945).

Some presenting difficulties are especially characteristic for the latency child. Among these are learning problems, troubles with peer relations, school pho-bias, and homesickness. But these problems are not necessarily caused by current conflicts. They may represent complex psychic reactions to stresses at several developmental levels and may be indicative of various types of distur-bance (Klein 1945, 1949; Blanchard 1946; Pearson 1952; Sperling 1967). Con-versely, the most diverse complaints may be the outcome of developmental latency conflicts—be they bodily aches, fears, delinquencies, wetting and soil-ing, obsessions, tempers, or maladaptive character traits. A. Freud (1970) has shown that symptoms can be diagnostically revealing of the underlying nature of the pathology if we study them analytically; but even well-understood symp-toms are only one part of a metapsychological assessment. For the purposes of this paper I shall attempt to group latency pathology within the diagnostic categories introduced by A. Freud (1965) and extended for use with young children by Daunton (1969, pp. 213-14):

I. *In spite of some manifest disturbances, the personality growth of the child is essentially healthy.* The earlier description of developmental aspects of latency includes examples of phase-appropriate behavioral difficulties and relates them to conflicts in several areas of personality functioning. Individual varia-tions are so great that it would be impossible to compile an exhaustive list of manifest maladjustments. In each case, however, phase-appropriate signs of inner stress as well as the areas of adequate functioning show that the child has entered latency and is grappling with its developmental tasks—an important indication of emotional progression.

Some phase-specific manifestations cause so much friction in the child's relationships and are so deceptive as to their psychic origin that parents and teachers tend to misinterpret them and to respond in an unhelpful fashion. This is particularly marked with difficulties arising from the initial internalization of the superego.

In observing young children during entry into latency, one is struck with how uneasy they feel with their newly acquired superego, how little it as yet feels like a part of them, and how hard it is for them to understand its signals and to utilize them effectively in their behavior. In the Hanna Perkins Kindergarten there are usually several children who complain that their mothers constantly "yell" at them or that their teachers are "mean" to them. Closer scrutiny shows that these children attribute the harsh voice of conscience to the outside authorities. When it is pointed out that the mother or teacher was actually very encouraging and soft spoken and that perhaps something inside the children is very angry at them, they sometimes listen, half-bewildered, half-thoughtful, with an inward-looking expression on their faces. As they become more aware of what goes on inside them, they learn to distinguish better inner and outer reality, recognize more readily the demands of conscience, and their relationships suffer less interference. Some weeks or months later these children occasionally comment, "My conscience's yelling at me today," or "You like my writing, but I think it's terrible." It seems that, at the earlier stage, attributing the criticism to the outside is not a defense but a sign of unfamiliarity with the new inner agency and lack of its integration into the rest of the personality.

The newly formed superego is indeed hard to integrate because it is usually quite harsh and uncompromising. The slightest mistake is judged to be a major crime. It takes time and educational help for a new conscience to become "liveable" with, and, as we often tell our kindergarten children and first graders, one's conscience has to learn that one does not have to be perfect and that there are big, medium, and little crimes. We also find that the children's superego integration is furthered when we make them more aware of the "loving" inner voice and raised self-esteem at times when they succeed in achieving their ideals; for example, the parent or teacher may comment on the child's pleased expression on completing a hard assignment or conforming to a "difficult" rule. "You look so happy. Perhaps something inside you told you what a good job you did."

Since it is so hard to come to terms with the new superego, it is not surprising that children use a variety of defense mechanisms to ward off the intense anxiety and painful guilt feeling. As mentioned earlier, A. Freud (1936) noted in this connection the defense of identification with the aggressor which can lead to unexpected angry attacks. Projection and denial are also not uncommon, nor are their conscious counterparts of tattling, shifting the blame on others, and lying. Perhaps the most widely used mechanism in this age group is externalization of superego to ward off internal conflict (A. Freud 1965; Brodey 1965; Novick and Kelly 1970), often combined with a need to seek punishment. This combination of mechanisms is similar to the adult criminal's from a sense of guilt described by S. Freud (1916a).

The case of Jimmy illustrates the use of these defenses and how his parents helped him to become more aware of them and to achieve better mastery of his conflicts.

Case

Jimmy was a very "good" first grader, always well behaved in class, somewhat timid, and easily hurt by the least unkind remark, but fairly glowing when praised and appreciated. His work was generally very good, but sometimes he hurried through it to be "the first finished" and then felt guilty and crestfallen when he found that his rush had produced a few mistakes or sloppy writing. At home Jimmy was less concerned with criticism and perfection, enjoyed his activities and relationships with the family. Every now and then, however, Jimmy became quite "naughty" with his parents.

His "naughty" times appeared to start with minor disobediences or mishaps, e.g., playing rambunctiously with a peer and not heeding the first call to come into the house or spilling a dish accidentally. Instead of an apology or effort to put matters right, Jimmy would become inappropriately angry and provocative. He defied the parents' admonitions and requests, loudly proclaimed how little he cared about their expectations, and insisted that he would do just as he pleased. When the parents became very firm and especially when they sent him to his room or instituted a sanction, Jimmy's outburst eventually subsided; but when they tried to reason with him or kindly disregarded his misbehavior, his naughtiness crescendoed as he yelled abusively, sometimes hit out, or caused minor damage to things. Usually these episodes subsided in a few hours, but they could also continue for several days with intermittent outbursts and provocations. At these times Jimmy also became much more tense and worried about school, fearing that he was "dumb" and that the others would not like him.

Jimmy's parents began to tell him that he tried to give them his conscience at these troubled times and wanted them to be angry at him and punish him, perhaps because he felt bad about himself. Would it not be better to be his own boss and let himself know what he felt he had done wrong? They added that then he would be able to get himself in control again, would not have to make others punish him at home or worry about not doing well at school. This helped Jimmy to cut short his "naughty" episodes. Closer observation showed that the incidents which precipitated his outbursts were either displacements from masturbatory concerns or "confessions" of masturbatory indulgence, but this was not discussed with him. In time he was able to cope better with his inner conflict and his behavioral disturbance subsided.

It is tempting for the environment to fall in with the child's defense either by fulfilling the assigned superego role of harsh disapproval and punishment or

by attempting to counteract it by lowered expectations and increased reassur-
ances of love. Both approaches fail to help the child with his developmental
struggle, both tend to perpetuate and intensify the use of the defense mechanism, and both may add further pathological elements, e.g., stimulation of
regressive sadomasochistic strivings in the case of harsh punishments, failure
to develop age-appropriate behavioral self-controls and skills in the case of
permissiveness. In some instances these forms of environmental mishandling
may constitute a developmental interference (Nagera 1966a) and contribute to
pathological exaggerations of developmental conflicts or to the establishment
of maladaptive character traits. A. Freud (1936) noted that identification with
the aggressor too can lead to a specific characterological pathology if the use of
this defense mechanism fails to be supplanted by a more mature internalization of the superego.

II. *Pathological formations (symptoms, defenses, economic factors) are
products of developmental conflicts which are age or phase-appropriate.* Pathological exaggerations of developmental conflicts are rarely explicable in simple
terms. Internal and external, past and present factors interact in complex patterns. Of special significance in their onset and resolution are the child's general personality characteristics—mastery of anxiety, frustration tolerance, sublimation potential, and progressive versus regressive tendencies. Other
important factors include: (1) developmental interferences such as specific
stressful experiences, unhelpful educational handling, and lack of age-
appropriate relationships with the parents. The role of the father in this developmental phase is of particular importance. (2) The conflicts resulting from
the normal, partial libidinal regression may be complicated by fixation points
at the earlier levels, and, by the same token, earlier conflicts may cast their
shadow on the child's management of the internal stresses of latency.

Whereas difficulties in this category may take many forms, an example of
pathological use of the defense of externalization may serve as an illustration
and provide a comparison with the preceding case of Jimmy where the manifestations of the same defense were within the range of normality. With Steven,
described below, the pathological exaggeration of his developmental conflict
was not due to poor educational management; instead it resulted primarily
from the child's failure to mediate pathologically harsh superego demands and
to tolerate the resulting anxiety.

Case

Steven was a handsome, almost-6-year-old boy when he entered Hanna
Perkins Kindergarten. He had been well prepared for this new venture and had
shown by his behavior during the previous year that he was emotionally and
intellectually ready for it, with signs of beginning latency development. It was
therefore quite disconcerting for everyone when Steven, almost from the first
day on, allied himself with the most aggressive and disobedient peer, followed

the latter in disruptive behavior, initiated trouble on his own, and seduced others to join him. He was impervious to the teachers' admonitions, indulged in excited play, and would not apply himself to learning tasks. His reply to reminders was, "There are no rules in kindergarten, and there are no rules inside me."

At home with his mother, however, Steven was well behaved and enjoyed many activities with her and on his own. In treatment-via-the-parent interviews with Steven's mother it was learned that, during the summer, several experiences had served to heighten Steven's anxieties, culminating in a nightmare and a week of severe fears at bedtime just prior to his entry to kindergarten. With the onset of school these worries disappeared, and his uncontrolled school behavior began. The latter warded off the intolerable anxiety by externalizing his conflict and investing the teachers with his superego which he could then defy and/or deny. Other defenses too played a part in his behavior—displacement, isolation, regression in relationships, passive into active, and, as we understood later, identification with the pathology of the paternal model. At first, however, Steven was helped to become aware of his defenses and to face his anxiety. As he improved at school, his night fears returned. His dictum of "no rules for me" could be related to his masturbation and oedipal fantasies; the fear of punishment was linked to his extremely harsh superego.

Steven's latency conflicts were greatly exacerbated by the fact that he had experienced his father's debilitating illness and subsequent death when Steven was 3 years old. He had mastered this major stress in relation to the conflicts of the earlier levels and had been able to progress in his development. During early latency the stressful experiences again represented a developmental interference in the form of a threatening superego introject. With his mother's and school's help Steven could modify his inner turmoil and improve his outward adjustment.

Observers of Steven's school behavior at the start of kindergarten could have been easily misled into thinking that he had either not entered latency or regressed from it instinctually and structurally. Indeed, children who use externalization to a pathological extent are often misdiagnosed as not having achieved latency development and are treated as though they had as yet no superego. Actually, cases of complete arrest or structural regression are quite rare and usually manifest widespread, additional pathology. When a latency-aged child exhibits apparently guiltless aggressive or sexual behavior, it is therefore quite likely that such difficulties are of a defensive nature. The consistent use of externalization brings about a measure of functional ego regression (e.g., in reality testing), of drive regression, and of regression in object relationships (e.g., direction of aggression outward rather than inward). These regressions, however, are of a secondary nature and differ from the more serious conditions of arrest or structural regression.

Steven's experiences with his father's illness, death, and consequent absence during early latency constituted a particularly stressful interference. It highlights the special importance of the father at this stage of development. His physical or emotional absence, his attitude to the child's growing up, the nature of his relationship, his personality as a model for identification—these and a myriad of related aspects deeply affect early latency in children of both sexes. The following case vignettes illustrate some of these vicissitudes.

Case

John had worked through many of his earlier difficulties during his attendance at the Hanna Perkins Nursery School and was anticipating kindergarten with a healthy mixture of pleasure and apprehension. He was keen to further his beginning knowledge of the 3 Rs, regaled his parents with accounts of "My teacher said. . ." and, in line with his new superego development, took all the rules seriously and worried about being criticized for the least imperfection. After some time, however, John's eager work came to a halt and gave way to complaints that work was no fun and that he only wanted to play with nursery school-type toys. His striving for success was replaced by an "I-don't-care" attitude to school activities. He told boastful stories of things he would do or own when he grew up. He often peppered these tales with items of exotic information he had picked up in reading adult science articles with his father and used them to convey an aura of supremacy vis-à-vis his peers. Increasingly his lowered self-esteem and guilt showed in berating other children and inviting the teachers' controls and punishment of his unruly behavior.

In treatment-via-the-parent we explored several factors underlying his trouble; some were internal, e.g., his regression in the face of unattainable ego ideals; some were external, e.g., his mother's reluctance to relinquish the close prelatency relationship with her son. The most crucial aspect, however, proved to be the father's unconscious attitude to his first born's developmental step. The father was very fond and proud of John. He verbalized high hopes for his son's future and supported John's fantasies, for example, that he would become a millionaire if he wanted to. But the father was openly opposed to the mother's and teachers' realistic demands for John in the present. "He is just a child. The hardship of the world comes all too soon. Let him play and dream and have fun." The father failed to see that grandiose fantasies did not bolster John's self-esteem and that neglect of the necessary ego skills jeopardized John's chances of age-adequate achievements. It was possible for the father to gain insight into the fact that, for John, this leniency represented a paternal prohibition against real competition, "You can pretend to be grown up like me or even bigger than me, but in reality I want you to remain little and incompetent." With much honest and painful soul searching the father changed his attitude, discussed it with John, and was able to enjoy his son's resumed application to the daily tasks of a schoolboy.

Case

Brian's early latency difficulties similarly manifested themselves in apparent lack of ambition, unwillingness to work at tasks in the Hanna Perkins Kindergarten, and indulgence in excited cops-and-robbers games with peers. Treatment-via-the-parent revealed Brian's underlying low self-esteem, expectations of scholastic failure, and distrust that anyone would appreciate him as a friend if he offered himself without seductive excitement. Intelligence tests had shown Brian to be of superior intellect, and our knowledge of him in the nursery years had proven his capabilities.

Brian's relationship with his father contained many positive elements but, already during the phallic and oedipal phases, had been weighted by the father's exhibitionistic qualities and tendency to intimidate. With the beginning of latency, Brian showed interest in the father's hobbies which the father greatly welcomed. When Brian wanted to learn something about photography, the father bought him a rather complex camera; when Brian thought he would like to make music, he was given a violin. Brian's own unrealistic standards were thus fostered by what he perceived as the father's expectations for him. His dismal failures with the proffered equipment intensified his inner tensions to an intolerable extent and forced him to give up all attempts at mastery. In addition, and correctly so, Brian understood that father's attitude represented an unconscious scathing mockery and condemnation to defeat: "So you think you can do as I do? Just look how inadequate you are at performing with adult equipment." Brian was greatly helped when the father could more appropriately ally himself with the boy's ego and support its attempts to mediate the internal demands, instead of reenforcing his harsh superego.

Case

Anne, a bright, pretty first grader, was a great source of annoyance to her teacher. Ironically, Anne's interest and fluency in reading were a major hurdle. Absorbed in books, she failed to attend to her other tasks, to hear instructions, or to respond to the requests of children and adults. As a result she never knew what she should do in a given situation, created disruption, and singled herself out by having to be told separately while everyone waited and looked on. She made teacher and peers feel helpless, put upon, and exasperated, but she herself was unaware of her aggressive disregard for them. She met their reproach or protest with feelings of deep hurt and privately took them as proof of her conviction that she was unloved and unlovable, which she voiced to her mother at home.

Among a number of factors contributing to Anne's difficulty, the most significant proved to be her current relationship with her father. During her earlier years he had maintained a stimulating interplay with her which, in spite of its complications, had made her feel loved and appreciated. With the passing of the Oedipus complex this relationship largely ceased, but, unfortunately, nothing positive took its place. The father was unable to relate to Anne in a more neutral manner. Disinterested in her daily life and activities, his brief hours at home were increasingly filled with his work, and he ignored Anne's attempts to interrupt his reading and writing with her approaches. She interpreted his "rejection" of her as a punishment in line with her strict new conscience. Her guilt was further intensified by her anger at him and by her masturbatory activities and fantasies which invaded her loneliness. Anne unconsciously dealt with her conflict by identifying with the father's attitude. With the aid of displacement and turning passive into active, she became the busy reader at school who made others feel helpless and unloved. At the same time she achieved the central position which escaped her at home.

Current stresses and phase-specific conflicts are frequently colored by those of earlier levels of development. With the above children, for example, the father's role in early latency was intricately linked to his part in the child's Oedipus complex. This, in turn, affected the form of its resolution and the nature of the superego internalizations.

The interaction of present and preceding phases is just as evident in those phase-appropriate pathologies which stem from the post-oedipal partial instinctual regression. Fixation points appear to affect the extent of regression and the "choice" of level.

Regression to the anal-sadistic level is cited in the literature (A. Freud 1965; Bornstein 1951, 1953a) and linked to many normal phase-appropriate manifestations as mentioned earlier. The case of Jeremy illustrates a pathological exaggeration and its relation to earlier difficulties.

Case

When Jeremy was almost 3 years old, his mother sought help for his ongoing difficulty in getting toilet trained. He had recently also begun to smear his feces and provoked his mother with his unwillingness to cooperate with the cleanup.

A successful year of treatment-via-the-parent enabled us to learn of several underlying causes, among them Jeremy's reaction to the birth of a brother in his second year and, later, a regression from phallic competition with his father with whom he shared the use of the bathroom. Jeremy then experienced a normal phallic and oedipal development and entered latency.

Around the age of 6, however, he found himself in considerable distress. He had trouble going to sleep and instituted a number of bedtime rituals. During the day he often ruminated about death and plagued his parents with questions about it which they could never answer to his satisfaction. His ambivalence conflict was heightened when his parents were absent for the evening or when he had arranged to sleep over with relatives. He then spent much of the time feeling unloved or unlovable, accused himself of having neglected some or other task, or worried about everyone's safety. Illness in the family exacerbated Jeremy's concerns. With the help of maturation and his parents' educational support, his difficulties subsided in the later phase of latency.

As mentioned earlier, regression to the phallic-narcissistic phase is normally found in boys and girls, but it tends to be marked or pathologically exaggerated with children who have experienced earlier phallic-narcissistic difficulties. Some children's oedipal relationships are foreshortened by an extensive phallic-narcissistic phase. They enter latency almost directly from that level which affects the nature of their superego and characterological development (R.A. Furman 1976) and intensifies their regressive concerns.

Case

Starting in the latter part of her third year, Linda suffered from severe evening fears and nightmares. In treatment-via-the-parent it was learned that Linda's symptoms were caused primarily by her reaction to the discovery of the sexual differences which occurred when she was with a babysitter shortly after her sister's birth. With her parents' help she gained better understanding and mastery and later formed a very close and exclusive oedipal relationship with her father. Her earlier phallic difficulties, however, seemed to heighten her hurt at his "rejection" of her infantile sexual wishes. They also contributed to a harsh superego and to an instinctual regression to the phallic-narcissistic level in early latency. In that period she sometimes looked dejected and withdrew into herself. She refused to wear feminine clothes and avoided girls' games. She followed the boys at school but felt disliked by them. Her interest in schoolwork diminished, and she put out little effort to achieve well scholastically. In spite of very good intelligence, she felt she was stupid. On a few occasions she stole small items from a boy's locker or the teacher's desk. She did not use them, stored them so as to be found out, and readily returned them. But even a gentle confrontation mortified her. Her family's understanding and helpful handling enabled Linda to overcome some of her difficulties, but her feeling of intellectual inadequacy improved only in late latency.

III. *The pathological formations (symptoms, defenses, economic factors) are not phase-appropriate. A latency child placed in this group has some neurotic conflicts which, however, are not incapacitating to further development.* In early latency it is sometimes difficult to differentiate between pathological phase-specific manifestations and isolated neurotic conflicts because the normal libidinal regression in this phase may make a current conflict appear as though it belongs to an earlier level. Some neurotic symptoms are carried over from the preceding developmental levels; others originate during early latency. A very detailed history sometimes helps in determining the exact time of onset. In some cases isolated neurotic conflicts from earlier levels also interact with ongoing conflicts. Fixation points, arrests, and regressions play a part (Nagera

1964). For example, Linda's previously described feeling of intellectual inadequacy in relation to schoolwork (described above) may be viewed as a neurotic symptom related to earlier phallic and oedipal conflicts rather than as a pathological manifestation of conflicts during early latency. Her apparently normal intervening oedipal period suggests that the latency conflicts primarily caused her learning difficulty. However, the symptom may represent an interaction of phallic and early latency conflicts. The following case illustrates more clearly how conflicts stemming from previous developmental levels may manifest themselves during early latency.

Case

Billy suffered from projectile vomiting as a baby. This was a stressful experience for him and for his mother. It necessitated his always being fed twice—the first feed was thrown up; the second one was digested. Although the physical condition subsided without corrective surgery by the end of his first year, oral manifestations accompanied his subsequent development and, at each level, linked up with phase-specific conflicts. Billy was an unusually messy eater throughout his preschool years and maintained a very close link between food and mother so that his eating or not eating reflected his ambivalence. In early latency he felt very guilty about lapses in table manners and worried that his eating too much caused a slight overweight. From toddlerhood on he chewed at his clothes in anger and distress. This difficulty too became connected with his masturbation conflict: Periodic recurrence of clothes chewing came to represent both confession of masturbation and displacement of it. In his earlier years Billy always reacted to new situations with episodes of vomiting, e.g., at the start of nursery school. In kindergarten he suffered only slight stomach aches at such times, but his characterological equivalent of ejecting the first feeding and taking in the second was still marked: When faced with a new experience, he would always angrily berate and reject it and declare his total unwillingness to have any part of it; following such vehement protest he could then attempt to deal with it and usually achieved mastery. Billy's very loud voice and flow of verbal abuse in anger could, in part, also be traced back to early oral elements. Whereas all these manifestations distressed Billy and others at times, they did not affect his overall progressive development.

IV. *Neurosis and character disorder represent the outcome of conflicts which are rigidly internalized within the child's personality.* S. Freud (1909b, 1918, 1923b, 1926a, 1939) considered latency the determining factor for the origin of the neuroses and linked the onset of obsessional neurosis in particular to early latency. Whereas neurotic disturbances occur frequently in preschoolers and the crest of the infantile neurosis is associated with the oedipal phase, early latency is the time when childhood neuroses and character disorders can be seen to crystallize into lasting pathologies. In these cases a metapsychological assessment of all aspects of the child's personality (A. Freud 1965) shows that the neurotic manifestations are not isolated areas in a maturing personality, but, rather, that the regression and fixation of the libido have become so widespread and so rigid as to preclude forward movement and that the compromise formations (symptoms and character traits) constitute the child's main instinctual gratification. Owing to the relative strength of the ego in latency and, especially, its intense defensive measures, the child's manifest behavior may show less turmoil than during the earlier phases, and he may also suffer less as anxiety is warded off more effectively. However, since the conflicts within and between the different structures of the personality are now unconscious, they can no longer be modified either by the child's own endeavor or by environmental measures. There is always a chance that the pubertal upsurge of instinctual strivings may correct the inner balance and force libidinal progression (A. Freud 1945), but even in such instances the improvement may be only temporary and the pathological libidinal constellations may become reestablished after adolescence. For these reasons, and in contrast to the disturbances in the preceding diagnostic categories, with neuroses and character disorders in early latency therapeutic intervention is indicated, and psychoanalysis is the treatment of choice.

The psychoanalytic literature contains many accounts of the treatment of such cases, most of them focused on special technical or theoretical problems, but all of them illustrate various types and forms of neurotic and characterological disturbances. The following is a sample of articles from the most readily available publications: Bernstein 1976; Bornstein 1946, 1953 *b*; Daunton 1967; Evans 1975; E. Furman 1967; R.A. Furman 1967; Fraiberg 1967; Hall 1946; Hamm 1967; Harley 1962; Novick 1970; Scharfman 1976; Shane 1967.

V. *Arrests and regression of drives are paralleled by arrests or regression in ego and superego development, i.e., disturbances of a delinquent or atypical nature.* For present purposes I shall discuss the disturbances in this category under two headings: (1) delinquent or psychopathic pathology; (2) atypical disorders.

Delinquent or Psychopathic Pathology. When the child reaches early latency, he is expected to exercise a considerable amount of behavioral self-control within and without the family. It is assumed that he is capable of respecting the rules of his environment not only with the help of a supervising adult but, to an extent, through the guidance of his own conscience. When the child's development has failed in this respect or suffers internal interference, early latency is the time for these disturbances to become manifest.

Starting with Aichhorn (1925), psychoanalytic investigators of dissociality have stressed certain features of the antisocial character. According to Friedlander (1945, 1947) it "shows the structure of a mind where instinctive urges remain unmodified and therefore appear in great strength, [and] where the ego, still under the dominance of the pleasure-principle and not supported by an independent super-ego, is too weak to gain control over the onrush of demands arising in the id" (1947, p. 94). Internal and external factors in the earliest years of emotional development are responsible: A disturbance in the mother-child relationship during the first 5 years, particularly disruptions through separation, rejection, or inconsistency, interfere with the young child's developing ability to modify his instinctual urges, to fuse libidinal and aggressive drives and to acquire the capacity for identification (Bowlby 1944; A. Freud 1949a, 1949b). A. Freud (1965) also stresses quantitative factors, i.e., the variable relative strength of the ego vis-à-vis the id, and she notes the causative connection between "failure in higher ego development. . . and. . . the large number of delinquents and criminals who. . . are found to be of primitive, infantile mentality, retarded, deficient, defective, with low intelligence quotients" (p. 178). All authors, in addition, stress the crucial role of both parents as models for identification. ". . . dissociality and criminality on the part of the parents are incorporated into the child's superego. . ." (A. Freud 1965, p. 178).

With the beginning of latency, the potentially delinquent character formation becomes consolidated and "it will depend on the various factors exerting their influence in the latency period and puberty, whether delinquent behavior becomes manifest or not" (Friedlander 1947, p. 94). Among these secondary factors Friedlander lists school, companionship, use of leisure, poverty, but she stresses that these influences do not of themselves bring about dissocial behavior. Friedlander's (1947) case examples well illustrate these points.

Delinquent and psychopathic disorders of this characterological nature have to be distinguished from other disturbances with manifest dissocial behavior.

Aichhorn (1925) points out that in early latency, even children with a normal psychic apparatus, unimpaired relationships, and capacity for identifications can become delinquent when the superego takes over the parent's delinquent features. In early latency we see this quite often to a minor extent in otherwise well-developed children. They do not show delinquent behavior in prelatency and the parents' delinquencies are usually hidden from the view of outsiders to the family. Only close scrutiny reveals that the child's difficulties in early latency represent an identification.

Case

Danny is a case in point. He had been known to us since he was a toddler and had attended Hanna Perkins Nursery School for 2 years. Although he exhibited a number of developmental difficulties at each stage, he progressed satisfactorily. Early superego precursors were noted to be rather harsh and contributed to Danny's low self-esteem. During early latency, in the Hanna Perkins Kindergarten, Danny showed some new behavior patterns. He lied in order to cover up minor wrongdoings; he made up tall tales in order to impress his peers; he occasionally stole small objects from other children's lockers and disregarded school rules. He felt no guilt about these acts and resented reprimands, although at other times his superego was very much in evidence.

When, in treatment-via-the-parent, we explored possible reasons for his troubles, Danny himself drew his mother's attention to his father's almost identical delinquencies. The mother knew them well but had tried to ignore her husband's failings and hoped they went unnoticed by the children. Discussion with both parents brought the matter into the open. The father felt bad about his delinquencies. The parents, from then on, acknowledged father's difficulties, and the father told Danny that he hoped his son would take on only his good qualities, not his troubles. This helped Danny a great deal in modifying his as yet fluid inner standards, and his dissocial episodes subsided.

Delinquent behavior stemming from a sense of guilt was referred to earlier in the context of the developmental conflicts and defenses of early latency. The difficulty in these cases is caused by a structural conflict within the personality and is therefore essentially of a neurotic nature. In latency it is particularly related to the child's masturbation conflict (A. Freud 1965). It may manifest itself as a pathological exaggeration of a developmental conflict or form a part of a neurosis or character disorder. As such, it has been discussed by several authors (S. Freud 1916; Aichhorn 1925; Friedlander 1947).

A. Freud (1949a) described two particular types of dissocial behavior which not infrequently manifest themselves in early latency and result from a pathological resolution of the struggle against masturbation and its attendant oedipal and preoedipal fantasies.

In the milder form of these maladjustments, the child may be "moody, anxious, resentful, inhibited, and apparently unresponsive" (p. 199). He may complain of being "picked on" by teachers and peers or withdraw into his own fantasy world and fail to utilize social and intellectual opportunities. In these cases the child's attitude to the school stems from his oedipal and preoedipal fantasies which now distort his view of the teacher as they earlier colored his picture of the parents. His unhappy emotional life and maladaptive behavior at school represent both defensive and gratifying aspects of the transferred primitive fantasies.

A much more severe form of this type of social maladjustment results when the child's fantasies are not merely thought and felt but acted out. This happens when the child's struggle against the bodily act of masturbation and against the content of the attendant fantasies is too successful. Deprived of all bodily gratification, the full force of the masturbatory fantasy is displaced "from the realm of sex-life into the realm of ego-activities" (A. Freud 1949a, p. 203) and leads to dissocial and psychopathic behavior. Its specific form depends on the nature of the masturbation fantasy which they dramatize: Children with passive-feminine or masochistic fantasies succeed in getting bullied, attacked, and persecuted; sadistic fantasies tend to be acted out by torturing the helpless or watching their maltreatment by others, if scopophilic fantasies also play a part; exhibitionistic fantasies are gratified by means of compulsively taking center stage as hero or, negatively, as the fool. Particularly disruptive are those children whose fantasies derive from observations of intercourse which, at earlier levels of development, they had perceived in the light of their own crude pregenital urges. Such children revel in constant fights with peers, provocations of adults and defiance of rules and are most successful in engaging adults and children alike in battles at their own level. Whatever the fantasy, "the monotony and repetiveness of the child's behavior correspond to the endless monotony of the crude fantasies which accompany masturbatory acts; the compulsive and periodic character of the acting out corresponds to the periodic need for masturbation which arises from the id and appears in the child's ego as an unrelated foreign body" (p. 203).

These disturbances do not subside with maturation nor can they be alleviated by changes in the child's environment. Psychoanalysis is the treatment of choice.

Atypical Disturbances. A. Freud (1965) and Daunton (1969)[2] use the terms "borderline" and "psychotic" in this diagnostic category. I prefer to substitute the term "atypical" because I consider the other terms misleading in the context of childhood disorders—"borderline" because it cannot be clearly distinguished from "psychotic" (Pine 1974) and "psychotic" because it suggests an identity with the quite dissimilar adult psychoses which do not occur before prepuberty. Rosenfeld (1977) recently expressed a similar opinion. By any name, however, children in this diagnostic category show serve disturbances. In spite of extensive and intensive research, it is as yet not possible to define them fully in metapsychological terms. Since it is well beyond the scope of this paper, I shall not cite any of the numerous contributions or discuss divergencies of scientific opinion but limit the description to a few widely accepted factors.

Thus, Daunton (1969, p. 214) notes that, in addition to arrests and regression of drives, ego, and superego, "children in this group show a lack of the usual progression in drive development (co-existence of all pregenital drives in almost equal measure). In the area of ego functioning they show particular impairment in the synthesizing and reality-testing functions and in the capacity for secondary-process thinking." Analysts are generally agreed that the genetic factors are to be found in the first 2 to 3 years of a child's life and that the disturbance, however varied in individual manifestations, causation, and severity, affects all parts of the personality.

It is not a disorder that originates in latency, nor do latency conflicts contribute to the basic nature of the disturbance. Early latency does, however, sometimes serve as a crucible in revealing more clearly some pathologies of personality functioning which may have been difficult to assess during the earlier

---

2. Daunton used the terms "borderline" and "psychotic" with the consent of our Hanna Perkins Nursery research group of which I am a member. None of us, however, felt satisfied with this terminology at the time, and our entire group has since then adopted the descriptive term "atypical."

years. This concerns particularly such areas as the capacity of the ego to neutralize energy for functional use, to sublimate, and to achieve secondary autonomy. In relation to the superego it concerns the capacity for advanced, as opposed to primitive, forms of internalization and the ego's capacity to mediate tensions vis-à-vis the new structure. These aspects are not the only ones, nor can they be isolated from other internal and external factors. However, latency development is characterized by so many ego tasks that failures and deficiencies stand out more starkly than in the preschool years when the parental figure legitimately complemented the child's personality, when it was normal for some ego regression to occur, and when functions were still expected to be labile. Early latency becomes the period for differential diagnostic assessment, especially in the milder atypical cases and in those which responded well to treatment during the earlier years and showed improvement, as was the case with Vivienne, described below.

Case

Vivienne, whose birth her parents anticipated with pleasure, was good looking, physically well developed, and intellectually well endowed. She experienced, however, a great deal of difficulty at every emotional level, and her mastery of developmental tasks was impaired.

The parents received professional help with Vivienne's upbringing from the time she was a toddler. With much effort, Vivienne's troubles with eating, sleeping, toileting, fears, aggressive behavior, etc. subsided sufficiently to allow progressive development, but the manifestations of earlier levels persisted along with new conflicts. Typically, anxiety situations of old retained full force for her in the present and could never be overcome. Motility and speech, however, started somewhat early; she was quite adept at age-appropriate play and skills, and there were signs of special gifts, particularly in music. She always functioned much better when she could rely on the full attention of a loved adult. She could never bear to be alone and found the turmoil of a group of people equally distressing. At such times she would become uncontrollably excited and/or aggressive. Vivienne enrolled in a small, structured, and individually attuned kindergarten group where she did quite well and showed signs of ego strength in better tolerating stimulation, frustration, and anxiety and where she also made good strides in academic learning.

The following year Vivienne left this sheltered and supportive school environment to attend public school while coping internally with the beginnings of latency development. Within a short time the stress proved too much. She was beset by fears of imaginary attackers, fiercely criticized everyone, and could not tolerate or respond to reprimands while her behavior constantly invited punishment. When these defensive measures failed to enable her to deal with her instinctualized and poorly integrated superego, she regressed structurally and instinctually. Reaction-formations of cleanliness, pity, and modesty gave way to messiness, sadistic attacks on others, and crudely exhibitionistic behavior. She ate greedily but was also finicky in her choice of foods and overwhelmed with disgust at times as thinly disguised cannibalistic fantasies threatened to force their way into consciousness. Schoolwork lost interest for her. She tried to impress others and bolster her own self-esteem with items of pseudoknowledge, tall tales, and self-aggrandizing fantasies. She often had difficulty in knowing where her own person ended and that of others began, as she barged or melted into people or confused what she or others did and said. Her speech was incorrect, indistinct at times, full of mispronounced words and some neologisms. Reality-testing became instinctualized, as she keenly observed selective aspects for sexual or aggressive gratification and shut out or altered anything that would have caused unpleasure. Similarly, all other ego functions lost secondary autonomy at times of stress as did her many beginning sublimations, e.g., reading which she had earlier enjoyed for ego gains was now neglected or used for instinctual stimulation with certain comic strips.

Vivienne's personality could maintain itself in the earlier years with the help of the adults' ego but proved unequal to the tasks of latency which required more internal stability and independence.

There are three remaining diagnostic categories: psychosomatic disorders; primary organic deficiencies or very early deprivations leading to defective or retarded personalities; and destructive processes at work (organic, toxic, psychological, and so on) effecting a disruption of mental growth. None of these is related to the phase of latency or affected by it, except in the case of psychosomatic disorders where the nature of the psychic factors is individually so variable that generalizations are inevitably inaccurate.

Closing Statement

The above detailing of early latency conflicts and pathology may leave the reader with the impression that this developmental phase is particularly fraught with hazards and hardships and must be difficult for children to enjoy, not to mention the adults who, by choice or necessity, associate with them. Such assumptions would be quite erroneous. Latency is usually, and with justification, the part of childhood which is rather fondly remembered—though this is perhaps more true of middle and late rather than early latency. It is a time of relative inner and outer mastery, with energy to spare for exploring the new horizons of reality and for playing, with newly won ease, with the derivatives of the inner world because it no longer threatens to take over. It is a time when a child can be an easy friend and congenial companion for peers and adults without the heart-rending heights and depths of emotion which tend to accompany the earlier infantile and later adolescent relationships.

References

Aichhorn, A. *Wayward Youth* (1925). New York: Viking Press, 1935.

Alpert, A. The latency period. *American Journal of Orthopsychiatry*, 2(11):126–133, 1941.

Bernstein, I. Masochistic reactions in a latency-age girl. *Journal of the American Psychoanalytic Association*, 24(3):589-608, 1976.

Blanchard, P. Psychoanalytic contributions to the problems of reading disabilities. *The Psychoanalytic Study of the Child*, 2:163-187, 1946.

———. Masturbation fantasies of children and adolescents. *Bulletin of the Philadelphia Association for Psychoanalysis*, 3:25-38, 1953.

Bornstein, B. Hysterical twilight states in an eight-year-old child. *The Psychoanalytic Study of the Child*, 2:229-240, 1946.

———. The analysis of a phobic child: Some problems of theory and technique in child analysis. *The Psychoanalytic Study of the Child*, 3/4:181-226, 1949.

———. On latency. *The Psychoanalytic Study of the Child*, 6:279-285, 1951.

———. Masturbation in the latency period. *The Psychoanalytic Study of the Child*, 8:65-71, 1953 a.

———. Fragment of an analysis of an obsessional child: The first six months of analysis. *The Psychoanalytic Study of the Child*, 8:313-332, 1953 b.

Bowlby, J. Forty-four juvenile thieves. *International Journal of Psychiatry*, 25:19-53, 1944.

Brodey, W.M. On the dynamics of narcissism: I. Externalization and early ego development. *The Psychoanalytic Study of the Child*, 20:165-193, 1965.

Burlingham, D.T. The fantasy of having a twin. *The Psychoanalytic Study of the Child*, 1:205-210, 1945.

Clower, V.L. Theoretical implications in current views of masturbation in latency girls. *Journal of the American Psychoanalytic Association*, 24(5):109-125, 1976.

Daunton, E. Some aspects of ego and super-ego resistance in the case of an asthmatic child. In: Geleerd, E.R., ed. *The Child Analyst at Work*. New York: International Universities Press, 1967. pp. 206-228.

———. Diagnosis. In: Furman, R.A., and Katan, A., eds. *The Therapeutic Nursery School*. New York: International Universities Press, 1969, pp. 204-214.

Edgcumbe, R., and Burgner, M. A differentiation between preoedipal and oedipal aspects of phallic development. *The Psychoanalytic Study of the Child*, 30:161-180, 1975.

Evans, R. "Hysterical materialization" in the analysis of a latency girl. *The Psychoanalytic Study of the Child*, 30:307-340, 1975.

Ferenczi, S. Stages in the development of the sense of reality (1913). In: *Sex in Psychoanalysis*. New York: Basic Books, 1950. pp. 213-239.

Fraiberg, S. Further considerations of the role of transference in latency. *The Psychoanalytic Study of the Child*, 21:213-236, 1966.

———. The analysis of an eight-year-old girl with epilepsy. In: Geleerd, E.R., ed. *The Child Analyst at Work*. New York: International Universities Press, 1967. pp. 229-287.

———. Some characteristics of genital arousal and discharge in latency girls. *The Psychoanalytic Study of the Child*, 27:439-475, 1972.

Freud, A. Beating fantasies and daydreams (1922). In: *The Writings of Anna Freud*. Vol. I. New York: International Universities Press, 1974. pp. 137-157.

———. "The latency period" (1930). Lecture 3 of 4 lectures on psychoanalysis for teachers and parents. In: *The Writings of Anna Freud*. Vol. 1. New York: International Universities Press, 1974. pp. 105-120.

———. *The Ego and the Mechanisms of Defense* (1936). New York: International Universities Press, 1946.

———. Indications for child analysis (1945). In: *The Writings of Anna Freud*. Vol. 4. New York: International Universities Press, 1968. pp. 3-38.

———. Certain types and stages of social maladjustment. In: Eissler, K.R., ed. *Searchlights on Delinquency*. New York: International Universities Press, 1949 a. pp. 193-204.

———. Aggression in relation to emotional development: Normal and pathological. *The Psychoanalytic Study of the Child*, 3/4:37-42, 1949 b. Also in: *The Writings of Anna Freud*. 4:489-497, 1968.

——. *Normality and Pathology in Childhood.* New York: International Universities Press, 1965.

——. The symptomatology of childhood. *The Psychoanalytic Study of the Child*, 25:19-44, 1970.

Freud, S. Three essays on the theory of sexuality (1905*a*). *Standard Edition.* 7:130-243. London: Hogarth Press, 1953.

——. Fragment of an analysis of a case of hysteria (1905*b*). *Standard Edition.* 7:3-124. London: Hogarth Press, 1953.

——. Character and anal eroticism. *Standard Edition* (1908). 9:167-176. London: Hogarth Press, 1959.

——. Family romances (1909*a*). *Standard Edition.* 9:235-241. London: Hogarth Press, 1959.

——. Notes upon a case of obsessional neurosis (1909*b*). *Standard Edition.* 10:153-250. London: Hogarth Press, 1955.

——. Formulations on the two principles of mental functioning (1911). *Standard Edition.* 12:213-226. London: Hogarth Press, 1958.

——. Some reflections on schoolboy psychology (1914). *Standard Edition.* 18:241-244. London: Hogarth Press, 1955.

——. Introductory Lecture 21 (1916*a*). *Standard Edition.* 16:320-338. London: Hogarth Press, 1963.

——. Some character-types met with in psycho-analytic work (1916*b*). *Standard Edition.* 14:309-336. London: Hogarth Press, 1957.

——. From the history of an infantile neurosis (1918). *Standard Edition.* 17:3-122. London: Hogarth Press, 1955.

——. A child is being beaten: A contribution to the study of the origin of sexual perversions (1919). *Standard Edition.* 17:175-204. London: Hogarth Press, 1955.

——. Group psychology and the analysis of the ego (1921). *Standard Edition.* 18:67-144. London: Hogarth Press, 1955.

——. The ego and id (1923*a*). *Standard Edition.* 19:3-68. London: Hogarth Press, 1961.

——. Two encyclopaedic articles (1923*b*). *Standard Edition.* 18:235-262. London: Hogarth Press, 1955.

——. The infantile genital organization: An interpolation into the theory of sexuality (1923*c*). *Standard Edition.* 19:141-148. London: Hogarth Press, 1961.

——. The dissolution of the oedipus complex (1924*a*). *Standard Edition.* 19:173-182. London: Hogarth Press, 1961.

——. A short account of psycho-analysis (1924*b*). *Standard Edition.* 19:191-212. London: Hogarth Press, 1961.

——. An autobiographical study (1925). *Standard Edition.* 20:3-76. London: Hogarth Press, 1959.

——. Inhibitions, symptoms and anxiety (1926*a*). *Standard Edition* 20:77-178. London: Hogarth Press, 1959.

——. Psycho-analysis (1926*b*). *Standard Edition.* 20:259-270. London: Hogarth Press, 1959.

——. The question of lay analysis (1926*c*). *Standard Edition.* 20:179-258. London: Hogarth Press, 1959.

——. Moses and monotheism: Three essays (1939). *Standard Edition.* 23:3-140. London: Hogarth Press, 1964.

——. An outline of psycho-analysis (1940). *Standard Edition.* 23:141-208. London: Hogarth Press, 1967

Friedlander, K. Children's books and their function in latency and prepuberty. *American Imago*, 3:129-150, 1942.

——. The formation of the antisocial character. *The Psychoanalytic Study of the Child*, 1:189-204, 1945.

——. *The Psycho-Analytical Approach to Juvenile Delinquency.* New York: International Universities Press, 1947.

——. Latent delinquency and ego development. In: Eissler, K.R., ed. *Searchlights on Delinquency.* New York: International Universities Press, 1949. pp. 205-215.

Fries, M.E. Review of the literature of the latency period, with special emphasis on the so-called "normal case." In: Levitt, M., ed. *Readings in Psychoanalytic Psychology.* New York: Appleton-Century-Crofts, 1959. pp. 56-69.

Furman, E. The latency child as an active participant in the analytic work. In: Geleerd, E.R., ed. *The Child Analyst at Work.* New York: International Universities Press, 1967, pp. 142-184.

——. Treatment via the mother. In: Furman, R.A., and Katan, A., eds. *The Therapeutic Nursery School.* New York: International Universities Press, 1969. pp. 64-123.

——. On readiness for school (1976). *The North American Montessori Teachers' Association Quarterly,* 2(3)28-44, Spring 1977.

Furman, R.A. A technical problem: The child who has difficulty in controlling his behavior in analytic sessions. In: Geleerd, E.R., ed. *The Child Analyst at Work.* New York: International Universities Press, 1967. pp. 59-84.

——. Personal communication, 1976.

Furman, R.A., and Katan, A. Scheme for lines of development and mastery of tasks in latency. In: *The Therapeutic Nursery School.* New York: International Universities Press, 1969. pp. 299-305.

Goldings, H.J. Jump-rope rhymes and the rhythm of latency development in girls. *The Psychoanalytic Study of the Child,* 29:431-450, 1974.

Hall, J.W. The analysis of a case of night terror. *The Psychoanalytic Study of the Child,* 2:189-227, 1946.

Hamm, M. Some aspects of a difficult therapeutic (working) alliance. In: Geleerd, E.R., ed. *The Child Analyst at Work.* New York: International Universities Press, 1967. pp. 185-205.

Harley, M. The role of the dream in the analysis of a latency child. *Journal of the American Psychoanalytic Association,* 10:271-288, 1962.

Jacobson, E. The self and the object world: Vicissitudes of their infantile cathexes and their influence on ideational and affective development. *The Psychoanalytic Study of the Child,* 9:75-127, 1954.

Kaplan, E.B. Reflections regarding psychomotor activities during the latency period. *The Psychoanalytic Study of the Child,* 20:220-238, 1965.

Katan, A. Personal communication. 1978.

Kestenberg, J.S. The development of the young child from birth through latency, as seen through bodily movement. In: *Children and Parents—Psychoanalytic Studies in Development.* New York: Jason Aronson, 1975a. pp. 235-266.

——. The effect on parents of the child's transition into and out of latency. In: *Children and Parents—Psychoanalytic Studies in Development.* New York: Jason Aronson, 1975b. pp. 267-281.

Klein, E. The reluctance to go to school. *The Psychoanalytic Study of the Child,* 1:263-279, 1945.

——. Psychoanalytic aspects of school problems. *The Psychoanalytic Study of the Child,* 3/4:369-390, 1949.

Kolansky, H. Some psychoanalytic considerations on speech in normal development and psychopathology. *The Psychoanalytic Study of the Child,* 22:274-295, 1967.

Kramer, E. *Art as Therapy with Children.* New York: Schocken Books, 1971.

Lampl, H. The influence of biological and psychological factors upon the development of the latency period. In: Loewenstein, R.M., ed. *Drives, Affects, Behavior.* New York: International Universities Press, 1953. pp. 380-387.

Lampl-de Groot, J. On masturbation and its influence on general development. *The Psychoanalytic Study of the Child,* 5:153-174, 1950.

Latency period. Scientific proceedings—panel reports. Reporter: S. Kaplan. *Journal of the American Psychoanalytic Association,* 5:525-538, 1957.

Latency. Panel, reported by T. Becker. *Journal of the American Psychoanalytic Association,* 13:584-590, 1965.

Maenchen, A. On the technique of child analysis in relation to stages of development. *The Psychoanalytic Study of the Child,* 25:175-208, 1970.

Meers, D.R. A diagnostic profile of psychopathology in a latency child. *The Psychoanalytic Study of the Child,* 21:483-526, 1966.

Nagera, H. On arrest in development, fixation, and regression. *The Psychoanalytic Study of the Child,* 19:222-239, 1964.

——. Early childhood disturbances, the infantile neurosis, and the adulthood disturbances. Monograph series of *The Psychoanalytic Study of the Child,* No. 2. New York: International Universities Press, 1966a.

——. Sleep and its disturbances approached developmentally (Sleeping disturbances of the latency period). *The Psychoanalytic Study of the Child,* 21:393-447, 1966b.

Novick, J. The vicissitudes of the "working alliance" in the analysis of a latency girl. *The Psychoanalytic Study of the Child*, 25:231-256, 1970.

Novick, J., and Kelly, K. Projection and externalization. *The Psychoanalytic Study of the Child*, 25:69-95, 1970.

Pearson, G.H.J. A survey of learning difficulties in children. *The Psychoanalytic Study of the Child*, 7:322-386, 1952.

——. The importance of peer relationship in the latency period. *Bulletin of the Philadelphia Association for Psychoanalysis*, 16:109-121, 1966.

Peller, L.E. Libidinal phases, ego development and play. *The Psychoanalytic Study of the Child*, 9:178-198, 1954.

——. Daydreams and children's favorite books. *The Psychoanalytic Study of the Child*, 14:414-436, 1959.

Pine, F. On the concept "borderline" in children: A clinical essay. *The Psychoanalytic Study of the Child*, 29:341-368, 1974.

Rosenfeld, S. *Beyond the Infantile Neurosis*. London: Sara Rosenfeld Research Fund, Hampstead Clinic. 1977.

Sandler, J. On the concept of superego. *The Psychoanalytic Study of the Child*, 15:128-162, 1960.

Sandler, J.; Kennedy, H.; and Tyson, R.L. Discussions on transference: The treatment situation and technique in child psychoanalysis. *The Psychoanalytic Study of the Child*, 30:409-442, 1975.

Sarnoff, C. *Latency*. New York: Jason Aronson, 1976.

Scharfman, M.A. Perverse development in a young boy. *Journal of the American Psychoanalytic Association*, 24(3):499-524, 1976.

Shane, M. Encopresis in a latency boy: An arrest along a developmental line. *The Psychoanalytic Study of the Child*, 22:296-303, 1967.

Smith, R.P. *"Where did you go?" "Out." "What did you do?" "Nothing."* New York: W.W. Norton, 1957.

Sperling, M. School phobias: Classification, dynamics and treatment. *The Psychoanalytic Study of the Child*, 22:375-401, 1967.

Widzer, M.E. The comic-book superhero: A study of the family romance fantasy. *The Psychoanalytic Study of the Child*, 32:565-603, 1977.

Williams, M. Problems of technique during latency. *The Psychoanalytic Study of the Child*, 27:598-620, 1972.

The Course of Life: Psychoanalytic Contributions
Toward Understanding Personality Development.
Vol. II: Latency, Adolescence, and Youth.
S.I. Greenspan and G.H. Pollock, editors.
NIMH 1980

Some Vicissitudes of the Transition into Latency[1]

Robert A. Furman, M.D.[2]

Perhaps others may have a difficulty similar to mine in writing scientific papers. A new concept or a new way of thinking about an old concept is stimulated by a paper, by some research work with a group, or by a clinical case. An idea forces itself upon the mind until some degree of understanding and integration is possible and then seems to fade from conscious thought. Weeks, months, or years later the same concept seems to surface again to demand more thinking and more attention, after it has been unconsciously worked on, with questions and disparities better pinpointed for further mental work. When a concept finally seems fully integrated, it no longer demands the attention it does when it is not fully thought through. Many wait to write until the moment of apparent resolution and consolidation has been reached, their papers representing an end point in their thinking. For me the process can often be a bit different in that writing may help to focus unresolved problems and to stimulate the thinking of others, seeking their aid in completing the mental work or in indicating where the thinking has gone astray. Writing often seems easiest when a concept has not yet fully found its place in an integrated fashion, the irritation of the incomplete nature providing the stimulus needed for writing. This paper surely falls within this category, its thinking not fully completed but perhaps far enough along to seek the responses of others.

---

1. This chapter is a companion to the preceding chapter, "Early Latency—Normal and Pathological Aspects" by E. Furman.

2. Some of the clinical work upon which this chapter is based comes from the project, Children of Divorce, made possible by the support of the Cleveland Foundation and the Gund Foundation.

In the mid-sixties I worked in a research group that was struggling with formulating diagnostic categories for prelatency children. As described by Daunton (1969*a*), the greatest difficulty was encountered with

the children in our study whose disturbances did not appear age- or phase-appropriate, on the one hand, and did not fit into the category of neurosis or character disorder on the other. All of these children as we saw them at the nursery school showed partial arrests caused by pathological fixations. Some, in addition to these arrests, showed the beginnings of regression from phallic or oedipal stages. All had symptoms maintained by pathological defenses and, in most cases, there was secondary defensive interference with ego functioning.
    We reached the conclusion (formulated by Dr. Anny Katan) that there was an important difference between those children with the pathological formations described above, who had not yet completed the oedipal phase, and those who were already in latency or adolescence. In the former, the neurotic conflicts endangered the proper resolution of the oedipal conflict [p. 212].

The concept of disorders, particularly in the phallic phase, precluding subsequent successful mastery of oedipal conflicts in a prelatency child who does not yet have a fully crystallized neurosis, has stood the test of time for our group. Although in essence a predictive diagnosis, it has pinpointed the significance of the pathology of a number of children seen at the Hanna Perkins Therapeutic Nursery School and Kindergarten. Given a mother who is able to work in treatment via the mother as utilized at the school (E. Furman 1957), the children in this category have done extremely well, their improvement well maintained in subsequent followup studies (Daunton 1969*b*). This diagnostic concept, once evolved, was readily assimilated. In addition, however, it focused clinical attention simultaneously on the resolution of oedipal conflicts and hence the transition into latency.
    Observation over the years in our nursery school and kindergarten of the oedipal development of the children has seemed to me to reveal in many an almost diphasic sequence. In nursery school there is often a period of quite open, intense feeling for the parent of the opposite sex, a yearning that seems to ignore the existence of the parent of the same sex. In kindergarten the situation is often quite different, with the yearning less evident for the parent of the opposite sex, a clear struggle in existence, however, regarding the ambivalence conflict with the parent of the same sex.
    A nursery school girl I had in analysis many years ago may illustrate this point. At the outset of her treatment she had no difficulty in bringing into her analysis her longing for a close, affectionate, exclusive relationship with me in the transference and with her father in real life. Many efforts on my part to explore the fate such plans held for her mother or my wife fell on deaf ears. As

I persisted, she became exasperated with me, finally declaring that her mother or my wife could serve in some grandmotherly type of way. The puzzle of what to do with the parent of the same sex was a conflict avoided, to be sure, but was also something that was not of paramount concern to her at this juncture of her development. A year or so later, when she was in kindergarten, the same constellation of feelings was revived, but this time with an entirely different focus. In dreams associated with her enuresis she clearly struggled with wishes for her father, enormously guilty over the accompanying aggression toward her mother. When this conflict was made conscious, there was no assuaging her distress. I can recall telling her one day that many girls, in fact I felt all girls, at some point wanted mommy dead so that they could have father to themselves. She was adamant that I did not understand her: The other girls just wished it; she *really* wanted mommy dead!

From this and many similar examples it was impossible to avoid the thought that oedipal wishes are very different at the beginning of the phallic-oedipal period from what they are at the end of this time; they are essentially diadic early in the phallic period, triadic later in the oedipal period. The many other profound differences between the 3- and 4-year-old nursery schoolers and the 5- and 6-year-old kindergarten children led to the conclusion that the phallic-oedipal phase encompassed just too much to be considered a homogeneous whole; in fact, we deal with two phases, phallic and oedipal, not just two aspects of the same phase with oedipal relationships characterizing the latter part of the period.

Here thinking seemed to halt until the appearance of the Edgcumbe and Burgner contribution on the phallic-narcissistic phase, "a differentiation between the preoedipal and oedipal aspects of phallic development" (1975). In a carefully reasoned way they began with distinguishing levels of object relations from phases of drive development and then moved to describe the characteristics of drive derivatives and object relationships in the preoedipal phallic child.

> In the preoedipal phallic phase, exhibitionism and scoptophilia are the most pronounced drive components. In the child's object relationships, correspondingly, the real or fantasied use of the genital serves primarily exhibitionistic and narcissistic purposes, to gain the admiration of the object. In the preoedipal phallic phase, the one-to-one relationship is still dominant, since the rivalry of the triangular oedipal relationships has not yet developed [p. 162].

They discussed the historical origin of the lack of division between the two phases, to which I shall return in a moment, and then introduced the phrase "phallic-narcissistic" to describe the earlier, preoedipal part of the phallic phase, a term for which Anna Freud was given credit. Their clinical examples highlighted the diadic aspects of the phallic-narcissistic phase, a third party often just an "intruder" interfering with the child's attempt to obtain the praise of the object of his affection. Certainly in her response to my questions about her mother or my wife, the little girl I described above treated my queries as just that, intrusions. They also reported the oedipal-like advances of this earlier period as precursors of true oedipal feelings and described the anxiety of this phase as a castration anxiety born of competitive wishes for the phallus rather than of wishes to replace the parent of the same sex.

Regarding the historical origin of the failure to distinguish the two phases, phallic-narcissistic and oedipal, from one another, yet another source of confusion might well be mentioned. It will always be quite easy to confuse the two clinically unless there is an awareness of the difference between them. A little nursery school girl some years ago was most fascinated by her father, most attentive to him, eager to have a baby. Careful attention to her mood soon revealed the source of her interest, the phallus, whose absence the baby was to repair or replace. Likewise, a litle boy so attentive to his mother for her praise, resenting his father as an intruder, fearing his father's retaliation for envy of the father's larger phallus, is easy to confuse with the oedipal boy, attentive to his mother as an object of his love, resenting his father as a rival and fearing retaliation for his wishes to replace his father in the relationship with the mother.

At the end of their paper, which had so well knit together so many clinical and theoretical points, Edgcumbe and Burgner discussed the role of phallic-narcissistic fixation in disturbances of adolescence and adulthood and stated:

> Indeed, we were struck, as we examined the level of object relationships of these patients, how many of them could be described as *hysterical characters*, and we would further suggest that in the hysteric the phallic-narcissistic level rather than the oedipal one is the nodal point of the regressive behavior [p. 178].

They felt it was possible in these patients to reconstruct the "regression from a brief and imperfectly resolved oedipal level of relationships" that had taken place in early childhood.

This concluding section of the Edgcumbe-Burgner paper can only stimulate thinking to start anew. It recalls and relates to a number of clinical observations of children in transition into latency, observations which have not previously seemed capable of easy assimilation.

In describing a case of treatment by way of the mother sometime ago (1969), I reported how Sally, a kindergarten girl, told her mother of her distress that George, a classmate and object of her affection, as well as myself, seemed to love others and not her. It was for her a great and sad time. What was not reported at that time was the nature of Sally's relationship at age 5½ to George. Sally's father had left home when Sally was 2, following the onset of a character change, later to be identified as paranoia. This had presented many developmental and neurotic difficulties for Sally, which her mother had been able to help her master. Sally had an older adolescent brother named George toward whom she directed her oedipal feelings. She also brought these to school in the very fond and intense relationship to her classmate George. Her teachers and I were struck with the intensity of her feelings, her wish to please and thoughtfully do things for George, who reciprocated her affection. The feeling that emanated from their relationship was one of love and was described by the teachers as having all the components usually thought to characterize an early adolescent romance. The feelings soon succumbed to repression as Sally moved into her latency and became a most effective schoolgirl. Many years later she was able to combine a work career with marriage and finally motherhood, apparently making an excellent adult adjustment.

Another child comes to mind in this regard, a 5-year-old boy named Tom who had started at the Hanna Perkins Nursery School with great difficulties with self-control. The work via his mother had been quite successful, and at the onset of kindergarten he moved into a state of apparent good control, which was first accepted by the staff as representing a tenuous adjustment, their memories clear of his earlier troubles. But something remarkable happened to Tom when he turned his affection toward a little girl classmate, Kathy, with whose mother I was working at the time. It was as if a brief romance flourished, with Tom a thoughtful and considerate swain. I remember my surprise at watching him hold Kathy's chair for her one day at lunch, going to the kitchen to get seconds for her almost before she had indicated her wish. This was true, vigorous masculine behavior which persisted for about 2 months before Tom became a latency schoolboy, his attention more directed to the learning process.

At the opposite end of the spectrum I think of a current kindergarten boy whose alternating passivity and exhibitionistic responses to me at lunchtime betray his difficulties with his phallic adjustment. Just recently he has calmed enormously and wants to tell me at the table of his progress with his reading, of his activities of the morning in the classroom. Although I know that oedipal material has appeared in the work by way of his mother, his appeal to her has been more of a passive, dependent kind, not a vigorous masculine one. He seems now to have moved into his latency after perhaps the most brief of contacts with oedipal feelings.

Retrospectively, I was able to construct a similar transition into latency of a boy with whom an analysis was started at age 12. It seemed from his analytic material as if problems in controlling aggressive outbursts had barely been brought into order and an exhibitionistic tendency only partially controlled around 5½ before he moved into his latency. This time was marked by the transient appearance of a school phobia in kindergarten which lasted but a few days. Early latency seemed most successful for him with many scholastic, social, and athletic achievements before a parental divorce ensued, and his adjustment failed with the appearance of temper outbursts and the return of many phobic symptoms.

With Sally and Tom, the first two children described above, their transition into latency came at the end of a period of oedipal feelings which were even displaced to the school setting in what seemed to me a possible precursor of the object removal A. Katan (1951) has described as characteristic of successful adolescent development. With the two boys described above, their transition into latency seemed much more to come in the midst of phallic-narcissistic concerns, oedipal strivings much less in focus. Both boys had strong relationships with their mothers, but both were more of the diadic, exhibitionistic nature that Edgcumbe and Burgner have described.

The thought occurs from these examples that it is possible for children to move into latency from many points along a continuum from the phallic-narcissistic phase through the oedipal phase. Castration anxiety to motivate this progression is available at both ends of this continuum: at the phallic-narcissistic, emerging from the envious aggression toward the father for his phallus, prized as a possession in itself; at the oedipal, from an aggressive wish to replace the father in the relationship with the mother, the wish to acquire his phallus arising from the conviction that it is the father's phallus that gives him his preeminent status with the mother.

Describing this phenomenon in terms of a continuum may be inadequate and misleading. It is easier for me to conceptualize it in this fashion, but it might be equally well described in terms of an almost infinite variety of combinations of various aspects of the phallic-narcissistic and oedipal phases that can be operative at the time of transition into latency. For example, the two boys who seemed to move into latency from a predominantly phallic-narcissistic position were not without some true oedipal feelings and conflict. It is rather that these latter aspects had both in duration of time and quantity of feeling involved been much less dominant.

Certain factors can be identified that could be responsible for a transition into latency more from a phallic-narcissistic position. Temporary arrests of development at any preceding level could delay forward phase-by-phase progression so that quite simply not enough time would remain to deal adequately with oedipal conflicts before the curtain of repression descended. Katan has described (E. Furman 1978) the situation that may exist with a parent absent during the oedipal phase. An oedipal development did ensue in proper time sequence with the parent absent, but on the parent's return the oedipal struggles were revived and repeated with greater intensity at a later date before latency was belatedly entered. This observation, of course, makes one wonder about what happens in those single-parent families where the absent partner never returns or is present so intermittently as to preclude his full availability as an object for complete maturational development. A third possible factor would be constitutional, one hard to evaluate beyond commenting on its potential existence.

The main point to emphasize here would simply be that it is not just problems of the phallic-narcissistic phase alone that can cause a delay in development that leads to a transition into latency from this level.

Clinically and diagnostically it is difficult to distinguish between three different groups of children: those early latency children with a phase-appropriate regression to the phallic-narcissistic level (E. Furman 1978); those whose phallic-narcissistic posture represents a pathological fixation point, either as a neurotic conflict or as part of a crystallized neurosis; and those whose phallic-narcissism represents the unfortunate outcome of a normal identification with a phallic-narcissistic parent in the resolution of the oedipal conflict. A transition into latency from the earlier phallic-narcissistic position will certainly make more difficult the proper mastery and integration of phase-appropriate regression. It will provide crucial or additional potential fixation points for neurotic disturbances. Early transition would not be a factor for those with an oedipally phase-appropriate identification with a parent with a phallic-narcissistic disturbance.

The phase-appropriate regression should in the course of latency evolve toward mastery with, for example, the exhibitionistic and narcissistic gratifications becoming increasingly and progressively integrated through reality-based sublimations, even if the level of object relationship stays basically, though not rigidly, narcissistic. Progression and flexibility might be the diagnostic hallmarks here. The neurotic conflicts and a proper crystalized neurosis will be more rigidly entrenched, further regressions probable to accompany them. I do not know any way short of analytic work to select out those whose pathology represents an identification with a disturbed parent. An example of such work follows.

With the 12-year-old analysand mentioned above, his many areas of good functioning initially in his latency inclined me to think that the basic mechanism involved with the phallic-narcissistic aspects of his clinical picture was an identification with his father, who had a severe disturbance at this level. Only after intensive analytic work on this identification produced little modification in both his level of drive development and the regressed level of his ego functioning could I reluctantly conclude that his phallic-narcissistic fixation point was a primary and intrinsic one.

The question of identification leads to another aspect about a phallic-narcissistic dominance to the move into latency: the quality of the accompanying introjections. It would seem reasonable to assume that the representative of the father that is introjected by the son, for example, will be less reality based, will be more the father as seen through 4-year-old rather than 6-year-old eyes. The introjection will be motivated more by fear and aggression, with little modulation by the conflict between love and aggression toward the father, than would be the case with the truly oedipal boy. As would perhaps be true of all earlier identifications, it might be expected that the introject would be less easy to integrate, less easy to modify or correct by reality exposure, than would be the case with a developmentally more mature identification.

I have introduced these thoughts about the nature of the introjection because of certain difficulties that characterized the analysis of the 12-year-old boy to whom I have referred. His parents separated when he was 10, divorced when he was 11, and the divorce was apparently instrumental in causing the appearance of his neurotic disturbance. What was so difficult to understand and work with in his analysis concerned the nature of his identification with his father. His father was a seriously disturbed man, but not a man without some redeeming characterological aspects. His son was at first unable to identify with any discrimination, to identify selectively with any of his father's virtues. E. Furman (1978) has reported the work one family did with an early latency boy who had identified with some delinquent aspects of the father's behavior. Discussion of this by the father, expressing the wish his son would not use these attributes as a basis for identification, successfully modified the boy's behavior and personality. Granting that such a healthy attitude from the father was not available to my patient, still he was much older, an early adolescent, was in analysis, had a good therapeutic alliance, and the problem was openly available for observation and work. Modification of his identification, however, was very slow to evolve and never felt to me, despite a long analysis, to be well integrated.

Another characterisic of his analysis was an apparent intermittent availability of certain ego and superego attributes and the level and quality of his object relationships. Self-observation, reality testing, tolerance of anxiety, thoughtfulness for others, a sense of responsibility could be present in most adequate strength at one phase of the work, only to seem totally absent a short time later. It was difficult to understand these fluctuations. On one hand, I felt they represented an identification with the inconsistency that was one aspect of the father's personality. On the other hand, it became clear that this was not all that was involved, as analysis of this factor was not fully helpful. Later in the work it became clear that he was apprehensive that any alteration of his identification with the father threatened the entire fabric of his sexual identity. The more intensely he was involved with his adolescent struggles, the more inflexible he seemed to become in terms of modifying his identification with the father.

I could only understand the situation in terms of an early introject that existed in such a fashion it could not be well integrated within the rest of his personality, modifying and blending with his self-representative. As such, the introject could be dealt with at times basically only by total rejection, something done at great peril in early adolescence. Elsewhere, in discussing "Some Developmental Aspects of the Verbalization of Affects" (1978), I have described a mechanism for the acquisition of autonomous functions of the conflict-free sphere of the ego through gradual identification with the caretaking parents, a process finalized by the introjection at the time of transition into latency. The thought occurs to me that among the multiplicity of factors that could operate to produce this intermittency, perhaps my patient's ego functions never achieved autonomy through integration because the early quality of the introjection made them at times subject to a type of total rejection.

This quality of intermittency applied as well to levels of relationship and to superego functioning. This is to be distinguished from consistent but immature levels of functioning that may occur when regressions in the ego and superego accompany instinctual regressions. These two, intermittency and immaturity, may occur together in varying admixtures, to be sure, but ultimately are capable in an analysis of being distinguished one from another.

Another avenue for consideration made possible by this thinking concerns some of the developmental tasks of latency and adolescence. I am accustomed to thinking that in latency the superego slowly becomes more civilized and integrated within the personality functioning and that such ego functions as reality testing, integration, self-observation and tolerance for anxiety, and other unpleasant affects are slowly matured. I am used to thinking that in adolescence consolidation of a sexual identity, identification with the parent of the same sex as an active sexual being, and object removal occur as the basic maturational tasks. I still think in these ways but find myself adding a new dimension to this thinking. Many of these tasks may well be initiated by the time latency starts for some, may not even have begun to be approached by others, the difference dependent on the point on the continuum of phallic and oedipal development that marked the step into latency.

Those children who enter latency from a phallic-narcissistic position have much greater tasks ahead of them in both latency and adolescence. These tasks may, of course, prove to be insurmountable ones for many, and otherwise inexplicable deteriorations in functioning in response to external stress or the internal pressures of adolescence may betray a latency entered more from the phallic-narcissistic point of development. I do, however, have an impression that some children in latency and adolescence master these tasks belatedly if these periods of their lives are free from external stress. E. Furman (1978) has emphasized the significance of the maturational progression possible during a thoughtfully managed latency. My thinking has been stimulated by observations of children of divorce. One stress of divorce for boys, for example, would be that it throws them back into diadic relationships, providing regressive seductions that cannot be resisted. Simultaneously it may deprive them of their fathers as models for their sexual identity and as reality figures whose presence could allow modification and hence integration of earlier introjections. The more a child of divorce would have entered latency from an earlier phallic-narcissistic position, the more he would be at risk, and the more these factors would be operative.

In this context it seems possible that the good results so often obtained in treatment by way of the mother may in part result from the identification that parents make with the aim of the work (E. Furman 1969), enabling them to provide for their children in latency and adolescence the milieu that favors mastery and consolidation of developmental tasks the children may have come to belatedly.

In this paper I have tried to trace the evolution of the thinking that has led to the concept of latency being entered across a continuum that spans both the phallic-narcissistic and oedipal phases. This thinking started as part of a group working on diagnostic categories for prelatency children, was stimulated by the paper of Edgcumbe and Burgner, and more recently by work with children of divorce. It has continuously been fed both by analytic work and the unique opportunities for observation of the transition into latency that are possible at the Hanna Perkins Kindergarten.

I have reviewed my understanding of the distinction between the phallic-narcissistic and oedipal phases and have given examples of children in transition into latency from the different phases. Some factors possibly responsible for the variations in timing of this developmental step have been mentioned.

The concept of children making the transition into latency from many points along a continuum of the phallic-narcissistic and oedipal phases may possibly contribute to understanding two attributes of certain analytic patients: an intermittent availability of some ego functions; a difficulty in selective identification that may be particularly evident in adolescence. I have introduced the thought that the earlier, in a developmental as opposed to chronological sense, some children make the transition into latency, the more vulnerable they may be to later difficulties and the more they may require an externally stressless latency and adolescence belatedly to complete maturational tasks. The significance for these vulnerable children of a stress such as divorce has been mentioned.

Finally I want to emphasize that this thinking can only be described currently as tentative and ongoing, and to mention that after so many years of working and thinking as part of a group of analysts it is impossible any more to tell which ideas and thoughts have originated with which participant of this group.

References

Daunton, E. Diagnosis. In: Furman, R., and Katan, A., eds. *The Therapeutic Nursery School.* New York: International Universities Press, 1969a. pp. 204-214.

——. Description, evaluation and follow-up of cases treated via the mother. In: Furman, R., and Katan, A., eds. *The Therapeutic Nursery School.* New York: International Universities Press, 1969b. pp. 215-230.

Edgcumbe, R., and Burgner, M. The phallic-narcissistic phase. *The Psychoanalytic Study of the Child,* 30:161-180, 1975.

Furman, E. Early latency—normal and pathological aspects. This Volume, 1980.

——. Treatment of under-fives by way of their parents. *The Psychoanalytic Study of the Child,* 12:250-262, 1957.

——. Treatment via the mother. In: Furman, R., and Katan, A., eds. *The Therapeutic Nursery School.* New York: International Universities Press, 1969. pp. 64-123.

Furman, R. Case report. In: Furman R., and Katan, A., eds. *The Therapeutic Nursery School.* New York: International Universities Press, 1969.

———. Some developmental aspects of the verbalization of affects. *The Psychoanalytic Study of the Child,* 33:187-211, 1978.

Katan, A. The role of displacement in agoraphobia. *International Journal of Psycho-Analysis,* 32:41-50, 1951.

The Course of Life: Psychoanalytic Contributions
Toward Understanding Personality Development.
Vol. II: Latency, Adolescence, and Youth.
S.I. Greenspan and G.H. Pollock, editors.
NIMH 1980

A Developmental Approach to Systematic Personality Assessment:

Illustrated with the case of a six-year-old child

Stanley I. Greenspan, M.D., James L. Hatleberg, M.D.,
and Cecil C.H. Cullander, M.D.

While the importance of systematic personality assessment has been highlighted by a number of authors (Freud 1962, 1965, 1969; A. Freud et al. 1965; Kohut 1970; Greenspan and Cullander 1973; Greenspan, Hatleberg, and Cullander 1976), the extensive time and organization required for such an assessment have compromised their routine use. In order to facilitate a systematic approach to personality assessment, we have presented a profile structure (Greenspan and Cullander 1973; Greenspan and Cullander 1975; and Greenspan, Hatleberg, and Cullander 1976) for both the initial assessment and the course of analytic treatments for children and adults. In this paper we will present a refinement of our assessment profile for children (Greenspan, Hatleberg, and Cullander 1976). A new theoretical section for the developmentally based assessment of children or adults will be followed by a case illustration of a child. Whereas this profile resembles the Freud-Nagera profile, it is different in several respects. This profile is constructed so as to provide a structure for assessment that would draw on only a limited number of interviews. It is oriented more toward the structural elements of personality functioning, while including specific content or fantasy considerations. It is somewhat shorter, and it is hoped that it can be completed within a limited number of interviews. Most important, it provides a scale by which the interviewer can assess and rate personality functions in order to compare an individual with himself at various points in time and compare one person to others rated reliably within the same scale.

The profile assesses personality functioning sequentially, going from a broad, encompassing perspective to specific evaluation in detail. The initial categories focus on the overall intactness and flexibility of the ego, while the later categories consider specific ego functions, superego, object relations, affects, defenses, and drives.

The profile is constructed to take into account the age of the individual. Impressions are based on a comparison between the age-expected developmental accomplishments and the observed level of development. In order to arrive at these determinations, a knowledge of developmental stages in the various categories is necessary. The theoretical structure of the profile will be presented, followed by a case illustration.

Introduction to the Profile

The narrative account of evaluation interviews, and auxiliary data such as psychological testing and school reports, should be followed by a meta-psychological assessment of the person's functioning in the format presented here.

In this format the interviewer first describes the individual's functioning in each category. Following this, he is to rate his impressions from "good to inadequate." Whether or not ratings can be applied to the descriptions is an open question and should be attempted with this in mind. Ratings are indicated by a check in the appropriate box. If the area of functioning falls between two of the descriptions, e.g., fair to good, a check is placed on the line between the two relevant boxes. In addition, confidence in the accuracy of the rating is indicated on a scale of 1 to 3, with 3 indicating relative confidence and 1 indicating relative lack of confidence.

Systematic descriptions in each category have been developed to help orient the interviewer toward a systematic report of his impressions. The descriptions are not intended to be comprehensive but rather to give the flavor of those areas of functioning that are to be assessed. It should be emphasized that the style and structure of the session with the individual is to be one's own, independent of this outline. In addition, it is expected that it may not be possible to gain impressions about all of the listed areas of functioning.

For ready reference and visibility a rating sheet appears as figure 1.

Category 1. Ego intactness (vs. ego defects). Included in this category is the general basic integrity of the ego—an overall evaluation of the ego apparatuses and functions.

a. Ego apparatus—This category includes the basic organic integrity of the ego: the perceptual, visual, auditory, and motor apparatuses; apparatuses that

Figure 1
Metapsychological Assessment Profile

Categories	Good	Fair	Marginal	Inade-quate	Confidence of Rating 1-3 Scale
1. Ego Intactness					
a. Ego apparatus					
b. Basic ego functions					
2. Ego Flexibility					
a. Adaptive capacities					
(1) Relationships					
(2) Education; learning; work					
(3) Play					
b. Intrapsychic experience: Specific maladaptive tendencies					
(1) Organized disturbance					
(2) Relinquishing area of experience					
(3) Unmodified discharge					
(4) Tendency for fragmentation					
c. Overall ego flexibility					
3. Ego Functions Related to Autonomous and Conflict-free Spheres of the Ego					
4. Relationship Potential					
5. Superego Functioning					
6. Affects					
7. Defenses					
8. Drive Organization					
9. Reality Considerations					
10. Intuitive Impressions					
11. Capacities for Further Growth					
12. Recommendations					

coordinate these (perceptual-motor); and other similar apparatuses, such as memory, that have to do with the integrity of the mental apparatus.

b. Basic ego functions—This category includes only the basic overall functions of the ego (e.g., reality testing, predominance of secondary process thinking, presence of ego boundaries). Special attention should be paid to the more subtle aspects of these functions that will give the interviewer clues about well-hidden borderline organizations, for example, the predominance of magical thinking, extreme impulsiveness, and avoidance and withdrawal covering up a subtle ego defect. In evaluating this category, attention must be paid to what would be considered *age-appropriate* levels of development in ego functioning. The relative attainment of reality testing, secondary process thinking, and ego boundaries must be evaluated in the context of the expectable developmental accomplishments, as follows:

1. *Good.* The organic ego apparatuses and ego functions are basically age appropriate. Interference from neurotic formations, developmental lags, or organic dysfunctions are minimal to none.
2. *Fair.* Physical or psychological factors, e.g., neurological dysfunctions, ego defects, neurotic or characterologic constrictions moderately impair the ego's capacity for age-appropriate functioning.
3. *Marginal.* Same as above, only there is marked interference with the ego's age-appropriate capacities.
4. *Inadequate.* Either physical or psychological factors severely interfere with the ego's capacity, e.g., severe neurological dysfunction or ego defects resulting in psychotic precesses.

Category 2. Ego, flexibility (adaptive capacities of the personality). This category assesses the flexibility of the ego in its capacity to utilize a variety of finely discriminated operations in contrast to the degree to which the ego is rigid with only a few poorly discriminated operations at its disposal. Included are the age-appropriate capacities to tolerate internal or external tension and to form and tolerate conflicts and a variety of affects. This should be compared to signs of arrested ego development, severe ego constrictions, below age-appropriate externalizations of inner tensions, and altered or restricted modes of drive gratification. In addition, the individual's capacity to develop transient symptoms, affective states, or behaviors in response to internal or external stress, which do not interfere with developmentally relevant ego functioning, should be contrasted with the development of symptoms, affective states, or behaviors which compromise developmentally relevant ego functions and lead to restrictions in a capacity for further development (e.g., withdrawal).

In this category, behavior should be described and rated from two perspectives: (1) the flexibility of adaptation to development and phase-expected tasks; and (2) the flexibility of the ego in dealing with "intrapsychic" experience. Note: These capacities are only separated here for conceptual and descriptive purposes.

a. Adaptive capacities—Ability to engage in a broad range of life experiences in the major life arenas of relationships, work, or learning experiences and play.

These available experiences may be scored quantitatively by considering: variety and richness of available choices; depth of experience; and degree of differentiation and appropriateness.

1. Relationships
   a. *Good.* Has full satisfying age-appropriate relationships, e.g., has intimate continuing relationships with significant other person; has friends; feels loved.
   b. *Fair.* Restricted in close relationships; e.g., relationships repeatedly get neurotically tangled and/or yield little satisfaction.
   c. *Marginal.* Severely restricted in close relationships; limited in capacity for maintaining relationships in general or deriving satisfaction from them.
   d. *Inadequate.* Incapable of relationships.
2. Work, Career, Education, or Learning Experiences
   a. *Good.* Works and/or learns at full creative, productive potential, with satisfaction.
   b. *Fair.* Productivity or satisfaction from work and/or learning limited or distorted.
   c. *Marginal.* Severely limited in learning activities and/or work; e.g., major characterologic interferences result in frequent self-defeating behavior in home, school, or career; gets little satisfaction from above.
   d. *Inadequate.* Totally unable to maintain work or learning experience or derive satisfaction from it.
3. Play
   a. *Good.* Has capacity to relax, experience pleasure, and enjoy a variety of age-appropriate experiences.
   b. *Fair.* Mild limitations in above; conflicted about having pleasure.
   c. *Marginal.* Moderate to severe limitations in capacity for relaxation and pleasure, e.g., must always be "serious" or studying, or working and when not, is sleeping; other conflicts often interfere with pleasure.
   d. *Inadequate.* No capacity at all for play activities, due to inhibition or interference.

b. Intrapsychic experience—Capacity to form, perceive, and tolerate conflict; and to remain in touch with thoughts and feelings (no matter how unpleasant or intense) concerning the important issues confronting the individual at the time. Implied is the ability to use these thoughts and feelings to work out adaptive life solutions.

Deviations from this most desirable position may be represented by four tendencies:

1. *Tendency to formation of an age- and phase-appropriate organized disturbance* in part of the ego, which condenses, with great economy, many

other conflicts and issues and allows the remainder of the ego to function normally. This includes many neurotic symptoms, a circumscribed compulsion, and short-term, temporary affective disturbances or other states, yet leaves the person still able to involve himself in most life endeavors and to experience a wide range of thought, feeling, and/or other age-appropriate internal experiences.

2. *Tendency to relinquish age- and phase-appropriate areas of experience* by walling off or preventing access to certain types of behaviors, thoughts, or affects, e.g., limited capacity to experience anger, love, sadness, anxiety, sexual feelings and fantasies, etc. The expectable range of thoughts and affects is limited by certain of these being walled off by the ego; ego gives up flexibility through avoidance of expectable range of inner experience.

   The ego may also relinquish areas of behavior to protect itself, e.g., avoidance of intimate heterosexual relationships or intimate friendships, avoidance of accomplishment in work, avoidance of all human relationships, etc.

   In this category the ego may be dominated by an overwhelming defensive operation. This would include many character disorders, chronic affective disorders, and arrests of development.

3. *Unmodified discharge* of drives or expression of affects, e.g., impulsive, aggressive, or sexual behaviors; extreme affect states, e.g., manic states; may include sexual perversions.

4. *Tendency for fragmentation of age- and phase-expected levels* of ego organization under stress, e.g., in an older child or adult, compromise in basic ego functions such as reality testing, integration of thought and affect, cohesion of sense of self and sense of other (feelings of depersonalization, derealization), loss of attention to outer world (total withdrawal, acute psychotic phenomena). This fragmentation may be encouraged by the use of primitive defenses, such as projection or denial.

Standards for rating each style of ego flexibility
1. *Tendency to formation of an organized disturbance:*
   a. *Good.* Tendency to form organized disturbance is transient (e.g., transient phobia) when person is under stress.
   b. *Fair.* Organized disturbance is more continuous with only minor stress.
   c. *Marginal.* Organized disturbance is chronic and severe. While in part protecting the other areas of ego function, it is quite painful, e.g., severe obsessional, compulsive symptoms, hand washing, chronic doubting, etc.
   d. *Inadequate.* Organized disturbance is chronic, painful, and potentially debilitating, e.g., severe obsession about own sexuality that keeps person awake at night. Compromises work performance and makes relationships extremely painful.

2. *Tendency to relinquish areas of experience*
   a. *Good.* Tendency to relinquish areas of feeling, thought, or experience is minor and transient and related to internal or external stress, e.g., mild withdrawal after a relationship breaks up.
   b. *Fair.* Tendency to relinquish areas of feeling, thought, or experience is more continuous, though only in very limited life areas, e.g., moderate, continuous avoidance of competition.
   c. *Marginal.* Tendency to relinquish areas of feeling, thought, or experience is chronic and in major life areas, e.g., avoidance of all intimacy.
   d. *Inadequate.* Tendency to relinquish areas of feeling, thought, or experience is chronic and in so many areas of life as to be debilitating, e.g., withdrawal from all human relationships.

3. *Unmodified discharge*
   a. *Good.* Occasional—in relationship to stress
   b. *Fair.* More continuous, but relatively minor incidents, e.g., regular mild temper tantrums
   c. *Marginal.* Chronic and severe, e.g., sexual perversion
   d. *Inadequate.* Chronic and severe, and in many areas, e.g., violence and sexual perversion, potentially debilitating.

4. *Tendency for fragmentation*
   a. *Good.* Very occasional episodes of fragmentation with very extreme stress and lowered capacity for integration, e.g., occasional depersonalization, when getting to sleep, working very hard, and under extreme psychological stress.
   b. *Fair.* Occasional episodes of fragmentation in the context of moderate internal or external stress, e.g., feelings of derealization when very angry.
   c. *Marginal.* Frequent episodes of fragmentation, e.g., frequently feeling unreal, illusionary experiences, misperception of reality, e.g., paranoid fantasies, disassociation of parts of self (object and self-object splitting, etc.)
   d. *Inadequate.* Total experience of fragmentation, psychotic delusions, e.g., bodily delusions, hallucinations, persecutory delusions, total disintegration of affect regulation and/or tolerance (completely flat affect, etc.)

c. Ratings of Overall Ego Flexibility
   1. *Good.* The ego demonstrates age-appropriate flexibility in its response to internal or external stress. Developmental interferences and conflicts, neurotic conflicts, and neurotic formations only minimally interfere with this flexibility. Either no or very mild, impairment of ego's flexibility; e.g., mild, organized disturbance such as some phobic tendencies.
   2. *Fair.* The ego is somewhat rigid in terms of age-expected capacities, but along with this rigidity there is a capacity to tolerate internal or external

stress of varying degrees without marked disruptions in age-appropriate ego functioning.

May have #1 tendency to mild organized disturbance, e.g., phobia; may have some minor #2 tendency to relinquish areas, e.g., tends to deny anger at authority or avoid competition with authority; mild use of #3 unmodified discharge, e.g., mood swings under stress; very rare use of #4 fragmentation, and only under extreme stress, e.g., occasional depersonalization.

3. *Marginal.* The ego tends to be quite rigid in regard to age-expected capacities. Internal and/or external stress markedly intensifies this rigidity and/or leads to minimal breakdowns in age-appropriate ego functioning; for example, in a latency child there are occasional losses of age-appropriate reality testing, severe states of inhibition, or markedly impaired impulse regulation.

Moderate to severe use of #2 relinquishing areas, e.g., very passive individual who avoids almost all experiences of rage, expression of anger, or assertion; narcissistic individual who avoids any intimacy and cannot experience balanced empathy; moderate use of #3 unmodified discharge, e.g., severe mood swings, some perversions, impulsiveness; moderate use of #4 fragmentation, e.g., loss of reality testing under stress, depersonalization, etc.

4. *Inadequate.* The ego is severely limited in its age-appropriate capacities and has only a few poorly discriminated operations (defenses) to cover more basic earlier structural defects (as is seen in psychotic or borderline organization). Where the ego is in its early formative stages, it is severely limited in its capacity to use the objects in its environment to further its own development.

Severe use of #2 relinquishing areas, and #3 unmodified discharge and/or fragmentation, e.g., psychotic character disorder, extreme lability of affect, perversions, and psychotic phenomena.

For a more differentiated assessment, the interviewer may also rate the person's ego flexibility for each style of ego inflexibility and for overall ego flexibility in each of these life areas:

1. *Relationships*
   a. *relationship* with one or a few individuals
   b. *friendship*—relationships in general
2. *Work*
3. *Play*
4. *Intrapsychic phenomena*

Category 3. Ego functions related to autonomous and conflict free spheres of the ego. This category, which is related to ego intactness and ego flexibility, should include a description of the individual's age-appropriate precursors or capacities for: (a) self-observation; (b) regression in the service of the ego; (c) the ability to learn; (d) intelligence; (e) creativity; (f) curiosity; and (g) synthesis and integration. In addition, describe any other assets or liabilities that would facilitate or hinder adaptation and the capacity for further differentiation.

These abilities or capacities are to be looked at from two points of view: their *potential* utility and their *current* functional utility (the degree to which current stress or conflict may or will continue to interfere with their functioning).

1. Good Autonomous functions are age appropriate and are capable of being used to integrate new experiences and facilitate development.
2. *Fair.* Age-appropriate, autonomous functions are slightly restricted by internal or external stress and/or are mildly impaired due to other factors (genetic endowment, cultural background).
3. *Marginal.* Age-appropriate, autonomous functions are markedly restricted by developmental interferences, developmental or neurotic conflicts, neurosis, ego constrictions, and/or are relatively deficient due to other factors.
4. *Inadequate.* Functions usually considered autonomous are *not* autonomous. They are severely restricted, below age expectations and are used mainly in the service of developmentally early drive gratifications or to cover up early ego defects. Where the ego is still in its early formative stages, these functions are not used in the service of further ego development.

Category 4. Relationship potential (object relationships). This category should include an assessment of the individual's capacity for relationships with others. The history of early object relationships, growing relationship patterns, current patterns, and the quality of affect and relatedness in the assessment situation should be used as indicators. Predominant aspects of relationship patterns should be assessed: autistic, narcissistic, anaclitic, symbiotic, sadistic, masochistic, phallic, sharing, loving, etc. Special attention should be paid to age-expected accomplishments. For example, in a latency child, attention should be paid to the degree to which relationships are based on pregenital dyadic patterns versus the degree to which they represent an integration and resolution of triangular oedipal patterns and movement on to age-expected peer relationships. In a pre-oedipal child of 2½, where one would expect predominantly dyadic patterns based on pregenital concerns, attention should be paid to the degree of internalization occurring. The relative attainment or movement toward object constancy in the context of age expectations should especially be noted (i.e., by 3 years of age).

1. *Good.* Relationship patterns reflect age-appropriate capacities for intimacy and stability as well as age-appropriate capacities for frustration and rage. Earlier than age-expected relationship patterns are capable of being integrated with current levels of relationship. For example, in the oedipal child there is a capacity for a full range of affective ties, e.g., sharing and loving as

well as capacities for envy, jealousy, and anger. In the preadolescent there is a significant "chum" relationship.

2. *Fair.* Relationship patterns reflect age appropriate capacities but are mildly compromised by earlier unresolved issues.

3. *Marginal.* There are relationships, but they are predominantly characterized by developmentally earlier patterns. For example, in a disturbed latency child, relationships may be markedly unstable and based on pre-oedipal concerns.

4. *Inadequate.* Relationships, if they occur, are markedly below age-appropriate expectations. For example, in a severely disturbed latency child, relationships either might not occur as such or would be based on anaclitic or symbiotic patterns. In a severely disturbed 2-year-old, autistic patterns might be prominent.

Category 5. Superego functioning (rewarding, self-esteem producing vs. punitive, guilt- and depression-producing). This category should include an assessment of the degree to which the superego or its precursors have achieved and maintained an age-appropriate level of functioning: (1)Consider the degree of age-expected structuralization (e.g., in a late latency child the superego should be relatively internal and organized). (2) Consider the degree to which the age-appropriate superego processes or its precursors are smoothly integrated with the ego and id and the degree to which there is finely discriminated regulation in the context of a relatively stable esteem system and capacity for pleasure. This would include an assessment of the character and consistency of either the figures for identification or established introjections and their relationship to the developing identity, sense of self, and attitudes toward predominant types of age-appropriate drive discharge expression.

At the other extreme, this category should include an assessment of: (1) the degree to which the superego or its precursors are below age expectations and/or are experienced as separate and in conflict with the ego; (2) the degree of inconsistency in age-expected regulation (e.g., in a latency-child superego lacunae or overgeneralized strictness and punitiveness—everything is bad); (3) the degree of instability in the age-expected esteem maintenance and capacity for age-appropriate pleasures. At this extreme, consider how the character and consistency of figures for identification or established introjects may interfere with identity formation, sense of self (e.g., incomplete or negative sense of self), and/or drive discharge expression (e.g., aberrant, inhibited).

Because the superego is continually forming during childhood and adolescence (and even to some degree in adulthood) and is only relatively organized with the oedipal resolution, knowledge of age expectations is particularly important in assessing this category. The two extremes presented above have definite implications for pathology only where a relatively complete superego organization is expected. In the pre-oedipal child, for example, inconsistency is to be expected. Assessment of the superego precursors of the very young child will, by necessity, be more speculative and depend in part on assessments of aspects of his early drive and ego organization and his family.

1. *Good.* The superego or its precursors are age appropriate and in balance, provide for a reasonable amount of age-appropriate drive gratification and self-esteem while exerting age-appropriate regulation.
2. *Fair.* The superego or its precursors are relatively age appropriate, but there are mild compromises in age-appropriate drive gratification, self-esteem maintenance, and impulse regulation.
3. *Marginal.* The superego or its precursors are below age-appropriate expectations, resulting in a lack of regulation, over inhibition or vacillations between the two. Age-appropriate drive gratification and self-esteem maintenance are markedly impaired.
4. *Inadequate.* The superego, or its precursors, is significantly below age-appropriate expectations. The structures dealing with age-appropriate impulse regulation, drive gratification, and self-esteem maintenance are either defective, developing improperly, or not developing at all.

Category 6. Affects (multiple, flexible, developmentally appropriate vs. few, rigid, developmentally retarded). This category should include an assessment of:

1. The types of affects (those that predominate and those that emerge under stress).
2. Their developmental level in the context of the expected developmental level based on age and environment. For example, in a 5-year-old, predominant affects of emotional hunger, fear, rage, jealousy, and envy may represent developmentally immature affects, while some capacities for sharing and loving together with the former may represent an age-appropriate pattern. For a 2-year-old, however, the former pattern would be age appropriate.
3. Their flexibility and selectivity. For example, are there a number of expected affects potentially available, some of which can be selectively called forth in the appropriate situation (fear and rage in one situation, love and concern in another)? Or there may be only a few below age-expected affects (fear and rage or pseudo-warmth) which are used in most situations.

Special attention should be paid to the type of anxiety manifested:

1. Is it related to integrated, internal structural conflict, i.e., signal anxiety?
2. Is it related to a combination of internal-external concerns, e.g., partial projection of fears onto external world or poorly integrated internal conflicts, e.g., fear of the instincts?
3. Is it predominantly related to external concerns such as:
   - fear of castration
   - fear of punishment
   - fear of loss of love
   - fear of separation

- fear of object loss
- fear of annihilation by the subject

1. *Good.* There is an age-appropriate variety of affects which can be used selectively in response to external or internal stimuli as well as conflict. Anxiety is age appropriate. For example, in the post-oedipal child, anxiety is related to internal, integrated structural conflict (signal anxiety), whereas, in the 3-year-old, anxiety is in part related to a fear of loss of love from the mothering figure.
2. *Fair.* There is a capacity for age-appropriate affects when not under stress. Anxiety is also age appropriate, but regressions occur under stress.
3. *Marginal.* A few affects which are below age expectations predominate. For example, in a latency child there are predominantly feelings of emptiness, sadness, rage, envy, and pseudo-warmth. Anxiety is below age expectations; for example, in the oedipal child the anxiety is predominantly related to fear of the instincts and/or concerns over separation and annihilation.
4. *Inadequate.* The affect system is significantly below age expectations, to a degree that it is either inappropriately or incompletely developed. This results in either flat or highly inappropriate affect. Anxiety is related to concerns which are significantly below age expectations to such a degree that the type of anxiety significantly interferes with age-appropriate ego development and functioning, e.g., intense fear of self- or object destruction.

Category 7. Defenses (age appropriate, stable, flexible, selective and effective vs. developmentally retarded, unstable, rigid, overly generalized, and ineffective). This category should include an assessment of the general defensive styles and specific types of defenses or groups of defenses used both ordinarily and under stress. Included should be an assessment of:

- Their age-expected developmental level (e.g., in a latency child, primitive defenses such as projection denial and introjection vs. developmentally more appropriate defenses such as repression, reaction formation, sublimation, and beginning capacities for intellectualization)
- Their stability (what happens under stress)
- Their flexibility (how well do they adapt to new situations)
- Their selectivity (can the most effective defense be called forth in a given situation)
- Their effectiveness (do they protect vital, age-appropriate ego functions).

Because this is an important category which often reflects general personality functioning, a number of defenses will be listed, and the rater is asked to evaluate the relative roles of these or others: avoidance, withdrawal, denial, blocking, projection, introjection, somatization, undoing, acting out, displacement, repression, identification, isolation, excessive use of affects (affectualization and magical thinking), the turning of emotions into their opposites, reaction formation, sublimation, rationalization, intellectualization, regression.

1. *Good.* The defenses are age appropriate and organized. They tend to protect the ego without significantly hampering the age-appropriate functions. For example, in a latency child defenses only minimally interfere with memory (repressed memories), age-appropriate reality testing, or ego flexibility.
2. *Fair.* The defenses are mixtures of age-appropriate and immature defenses. The immature defenses are used mainly in response to stress. Age-appropriate ego functions are only compromised under stress.
3. *Marginal.* The defenses are below age expectation. They hamper age-appropriate ego functions markedly to moderately by constricting them (phobias), impairing their regulatory capacity (impulsive behaviors), leaving them open to severe ranges of affects (anxiety or depressive equivalents), or in cases of unusual stress allowing disruptions in age-appropriate reality testing.
4. *Inadequate.* The defenses are significantly below age expectations; for example, the predominant use of incorporation, projection, and denial in a latency child. They are unselective, and severely hamper age-appropriate ego functions (reality testing). At best they serve as only a fragile defense against psychotic processes.

Category 8. Drive organization. This category should include as complete a description as possible of the person's current level of drive organization. It should: (1) assess the degree to which the drives (libidinal and aggressive) are age-appropriately fused and have progressed to age-appropriate levels of organization (e.g., have the drives fused and progressed to a phallic-oedipal level of organization in a 5-year-old; (2) determine whether aspects of drive organization which are below age expectation tend to reflect potential regressions to fixation points or major fixations.

States intermediate between age-appropriate drive organizations and earlier levels of drive organizations should be assessed in terms of: (1) *quantity,* how much is still tied to the earlier position vs. how much has progressed to the age-appropriate position; (2) *quality,* how rigidly is it tied to earlier positions (secondary gains, severe conflicts at the next position).

1. *Good.* The drive organization is predominantly age appropriate. Regressions are temporary. If neurotic manifestations exist, they represent regressions to fixation points.
2. *Fair.* The drive organization represents a mixture of age-appropriate levels and earlier developmental levels.
3. *Marginal.* The drive organization is predominantly below age expectations. This is due to arrested development, major fixations, or marked regressions.
4. *Inadequate.* The drive organization is significantly below age expectations. The drives are primitive and disorganized to such a degree that activation of

drive derivatives, even from routine stresses, results in states of panic, fear, and ego disorganization.

Category 9. Reality considerations. This category should assess the reality circumstances of the individual and/or his family to implement and support potential recommendations. The individual's or family's stability, economic status, and capacity to understand and fully support treatment and, in the case of a child, establish a productive working relationship with a therapist if treatment is indicated, etc., should be considered. The reality situation is:

1. *Good*
2. *Fair*
3. *Marginal*
4. *Inadequate*

Category 10. Intuitive impressions. This category should include impressions of the interviewer that are not captured in the preceding categories. Special assets, liabilities of the individual, or feelings about the individual, based on the interviewer's experience, although not easily formulated in metapsychological terms, should be described. This category is also to be rated "good to inadequate," based on the implications of the intuitive impressions about the individual's capacity for current coping and further growth.

1. *Good.* Special assets or liabilities and intuitive impressions considerably strengthen the estimate of the individual's potential for further growth.
2. *Fair.* Special assets and liabilities and intuitive impressions neither strengthen nor weaken the estimate of the individual's capacity for coping or further growth.
3. *Marginal.* Special liabilities and intuitive impressions weaken the estimation of the individual's capacity for coping and further growth.
4. *Inadequate.* Special liabilities and intuitive impressions weaken considerably the estimation of the individual's capacity for coping and further growth.

Category 11. Assessment of capacities for further growth and development in an average expectable environment or in the continuation of the current environment. This category is to include a description of the capacities for further development in terms of the categories previously outlined (ego, superego functioning, drive organization, defenses, affects, etc.) and anticipated special problems. For example, does the current evaluation of the individual's ego structure forecast difficulties in schoolwork or peer relationships? Is treatment necessary or will it become necessary; if so, what kind? In this category it is especially important to present the interviewer's evaluations in narrative form so that the basis for these impressions will be clear.

1. *Good.* Capable of optimal development and should be a relatively well-integrated, happy person.

2. *Fair.* Capable of relatively healthy further development, but may encounter some difficulties of minor to moderate proportions in his development and may need some therapeutic intervention.
3. *Marginal.* Does not appear to be capable of further healthy development without some major intervention. Without intervention it is expected he will have, or continue to have, significant problems in major life areas.
4. *Inadequate.* Expected to have or continues to have significant difficulties in most major life areas. Even with major interventions, development will likely be compromised.

Category 12. Recommendations (if indicated—no rating). Justify recommendation in the context of the total assessment.

Assessment of a 6-Year-Old Boy

Sessions with Parents

Session One—First Parental Visit. Bryan, 6 years old, was presented by his parents, an attractive couple in their midthirties, as having numerous problems. Among these was his refusal, from the time he was trained, to defecate regularly, sometimes withholding for as long as 2 weeks. Occasionally he would soil himself. He was stubborn and had temper tantrums. He was unable to make a choice and be happy with it. He would cry hysterically when his mother left him at school.

Bryan's playtimes with his parents would end disastrously. With mother, the sessions would result in mutual irritation and bickering. With father this was less likely. Rather, Bryan would jump and wrestle long after father felt it was time to stop, and play would come to an unhappy end with Bryan being scolded and pushed away, whereupon Bryan would sulk. Bryan, they both implied, never knew when enough was enough. At the same time they were saying he had "an extraordinary ability to get under your skin, and he also knows how far he can go."

Mother thought Bryan's problems stemmed from the time of his brother's birth. She had been hospitalized for 10 days, and Bryan had been cared for by a "witch" of a nurse, a rigid, depriving woman who was fired immediately upon the mother's return home. Up to that time, Bryan, like his brother Robert now, was characterized as a happy-go-lucky child. As difficult as Bryan has been, he has apparently gotten on well with his younger brother, Robert, now 3. From the very beginning he wanted to see and hold the baby and was never hostile toward him. He pals with him sometimes, and although they fight occasionally, Bryan acts "maternally" toward him.

Their present housekeeper, an Italian woman of 27, gets on well with both children. Recently, when she was on vacation for 5 weeks, Bryan regressed markedly. He was temperamental, threw temper tantrums, would not move his bowels, and had a number of soiling accidents. Yet along with all this, he seemed very sad.

The parents described their family relationships as open and vocal with each other. Mother felt they might be too open about some things, such as nudity, for example. Only a month ago, Bryan and his father were still taking showers together. Also, recently, Bryan started to climb into bed with them, but she was firm about making him leave.

Mother, a bright, tense, clever woman, organized somewhat along hysterical lines, saw herself as "up-tight, and unable to express love." She did not want Bryan to grow up similarly handicapped. At least on the surface, she scape-goated herself by attributing all the negative aspects of their family interactions to herself and the positive ones to her husband. Her hidden agenda, however, seemed to be one of controlling what went on in the family while keeping her husband on the perimeter. She accomplished this through her family role of protecting her husband from family feuds.

Father seemed a likable, warm, and self-satisfied man, who conveyed an underlying sense of sadness and depression through the expression in his eyes. From him I learned that his business was a great source of pleasure, that he relished its success and gave it a great deal of his attention.

Session Two—Meeting with Mother. Bryan's mother talked about her own earlier years, as a schoolgirl, her meeting and marriage with Bryan's father when she was about 20, and her relationships with the family and Bryan.

As a youngster, she had been uninhibited, skilled in music and dancing, and a good student. When she entered high school, the increased competition intimidated her, and her self-esteem diminished considerably. A series of psychosomatic complaints that never quite incapacitated her completely eventually led her to therapy, which terminated about the time she met her future husband on a blind date.

Her father, a physician, had been in the military. For the past 10 years he has been ill and partially paralyzed from a "stroke." Bryan shows him much compassion, plays with him, and is able to touch him. Mother barely mentioned her own mother until asked and then termed her "terrific." Her mother was described as gentle, her father as intimidating.

Mother described her relationship with her husband as good, except for her "sexual hang-ups." She added that her husband would "tune himself out" when a family flare-up occurred, and this frightened her.

Session Three—Meeting with Father. Father explained that his main concerns centered around his work, that it consumed much of his time and brought him his enjoyment and fun. His own father, a dynamic trial lawyer, had died of a stroke when he was 14. He had gone to work and attempted to take his father's place at home. He was surprised and annoyed at his mother's remarriage when he was 16. Thereafter, he felt that he could depend only on himself, that he couldn't look to anyone else for comfort.

Father said that since coming to the last session, he had begun to feel concern that Bryan, when angry, would threaten to kill himself, whereas he hadn't paid attention before. This was not pursued further. Instead, he went on to issues of competition. He viewed himself as a nonaggressive person who had avoided competition as far back as he could remember, in his family of birth, in school, in sports, and in business.

From talking about himself, he turned to his family relationships. He spoke of his inability to provide emotional supports, shutting the family out instead. He mentioned that his wife would reject him sexually when she was angry. And he described Bryan's inability to set or accept limits to his physical activity when they were playing together.

The main theme that emerged was Bryan's absolute need to control; his use of passive and withdrawing mechanisms to feel in control; and his resentment at being regimented or controlled.

Session Four—Developmental History. Mother conceived easily and felt healthy throughout her pregnancy. Bryan was delivered by Cesarean section. He was a "good baby," who slept a lot, cried little, and was easily pacified. Mother nursed him for about 8 months. She spoke again of her exhaustion and need to sleep, her nervousness, acute stomach aches, and severe depression that first year ("All I could do was care for Bryan"), and her self-preoccupation she felt must have interfered with her mothering of Bryan. Yet they did play and have good times together and enjoyed a one-to-one relationship. She said, "I was thrilled; I am still thrilled with infants." Her emphasis on "with infants" was more narcissistic than a response to her son as a person. Father's role in helping with Bryan seemed to be feeding him breakfast occasionally after the first few months.

When Bryan was 6 months old, his parents distinctly recalled that he differentiated between them and others. When he was 8 months old, his mother had to leave him for 3 days. On her return, she found Bryan covered with a rash from head to foot. He was put on a soybean diet. Other than this, he seemed a happy baby that year. Speech developed early; he was walking by 11 months and appeared very coordinated. Bryan is smaller than most children his age and has frequently asked if he would be bigger when he grew up. Father said that he, too, had been a late starter in growing.

Bryan was extremely inquisitive and explorative, qualities he still retains. What he had never developed, according to his parents, was patience. He is extremely impatient, dislikes structured situations, and doesn't like to be shown how to do things.

From the time Bryan was 18 months old, father's business had him traveling 2 or 3 days at a time, and mother went with him. Frequently the parents took Bryan along; other times he was left with babysitters. All had gone well, apparently, until he was almost 2. From then on, he grew very stubborn. Between 2 and 2½, his negativism increased even further, and things really "started going downhill" after his brother's birth. Bryan was then 2 years and 3 months.

Toilet training Bryan was "not easy." He was about 2 when mother decided to try, but he wanted no part of it. Her efforts were intermittent; sometimes a week would elapse between attempts, with mother feeling extremely frustrated. Then one day he said, "Today I'll make you happy and go in the bathroom." This happened when he was 2¾ years old—just about the time he was to go to nursery school. Up to that moment, mother had been sure she would not succeed and had about given up. She had tried bribes—reading to him, comparing him to father, offering him candy; nothing worked. Comparing Bryan with his brother, Robert, at this point, mother related that the housekeeper had successfully trained Robert when he was 2, with only a few accidents occurring recently when she had been on vacation. As for Bryan, his bowel movements had been regular for the past 12 days, ever since the housekeeper's return. Prior to that, almost from the time he was trained, he would often hold back for as long as 2 weeks at a time. Bryan has always had to be reminded each day, whereupon he would complain and cry, saying he didn't like to go. During this entire recital, father appeared to be keeping himself aloof.

While Bryan has had no serious medical illness, twice, between his first and second years, his temperature had risen to 105°. There had also been a fever of unknown origin just after his brother was born. He did frequently get sick when his father was away for more than a day or two. When this happened, there was much rectal temperature taking.

When Bryan was about 2, he joined a play group of four little boys on a regular twice-a-week basis and adjusted well to the change. When Bryan's friends came to his house, he needed to be "king of the castle," whereas at other people's homes, he apparently modified his behavior. At 3, he was enrolled in nursery school. Although hesitant and shy at first, he again did very well. As the youngest in the class, the teacher treated Bryan as special, often holding him on her lap.

Bryan has a few friends on the block and tends to get along well with them, but he doesn't seem to enjoy going out to play. The only friend Bryan is attached to is a child next door who seems retarded. Bryan seeks out nobody else, although sometimes he will play with his brother. Often mother suggests other children to play with, but Bryan refuses.

Bryan seemed to withhold in other ways, too. If father suggested something they might do together, he would agree, only to change his mind and show disinterest. Neither parent ever felt effective with him and was in a perpetual power struggle with him. The parents often disagreed about Bryan, and both experienced a chronic sense of uncertainty in their dealings with him. Mother thought his problems were very serious and blamed herself, while father thought they just didn't know how to handle him. Their self-doubts and conflicting opinions prevented them from pooling the information they obviously possessed to put together a consistent picture of their son. Instead, their differing points of view distorted their personal perceptions and undermined their individual efforts to set limits.

Toward the end of the session, the parents added new information—that Bryan now insists that a light or the TV be on when he sleeps; otherwise he is frightened. His brother compares this to his own "security blanket." They agreed that Bryan's problems had magnified when he was to attend school all day and also repeated that he had improved significantly since the housekeeper's return and the inception of these sessions.

In discussing Bryan's upcoming visit, they expressed concern with how he would react to a strange adult. His mother thought he would cry, and she would have to run off. His father thought he would have to be tricked into staying.

Playroom Sessions

First Playroom Session. Bryan appeared as a very cute, small, somewhat shy and frightened 6-year-old, with big, bright eyes. He was sitting far back in the chair in the waiting room. When I motioned for him to come with me and offered him my hand in greeting, he came much more willingly than I anticipated from the parents' expectations. His walk was relaxed and coordinated. He entered the playroom readily and went first to the big bean bag and sat in it. He looked at me with his big, bright eyes, which seemed to be asking for something, then oriented himself with a series of "What's this? What's that?" questions, pointing to things from where he sat. He wanted to know who had drawn a certain picture, saying, "I could do better." He then took some paper and wrote his name.

Bryan was able to make eye contact with me almost from the first and continued to stay in warm and friendly eye and voice contact throughout. However, he did not come close physically, but seemed to keep his distance. His gross coordination appeared to be excellent, much better than his fine coordination (e.g., when he tried to write his name). His speech was distinct and easy to understand.

After writing his name, he sat back as though waiting, quite firm in his passivity. He appeared reluctant to do anything further on his own initiative— draw, play, talk, etc. Instead, he wanted me to do the drawing and also wanted to direct me. When I asked him what he wished me to draw, he told me to draw a face. Only then did he take over and begin. I felt that had I not taken the lead, he would have maintained a stubborn, negative attitude.

He began to draw a face. When prompted, he said it was a happy face. I was taking some notes, and immediately he inquired about this. I told him that I was writing down some of the things we were doing together and assured him that everything would be just between the two of us. I took this occasion to tell him about the rules of the playroom. Subsequently, he was able to walk around and explore. He took it all in, looking at all the toys and asking many questions.

In looking at a particular box, he asked why there were two holes in it and then volunteered the answer—because someone had cut them out. I was feeling relaxed and comfortable with him at this point.

Bryan questioned me about a collage of butterflies that had caught his attention in the office, and when I asked him what he thought, he was again able to figure out the answer for himself. Right after this he began jumping on a footstool which he then placed on the beanbag. He appeared to be enjoying himself, jumping around and building things with blocks. Next he wanted some paper from a pad and asked, "Can I take the paper off?" He then moved to the blocks, picking out red and blue ones. When he heard a noise outside, he went quickly to the door, apparently very concerned that anyone would be doing anything close to our playroom. He did not explain the nature of his concern, but did show some annoyance and discomfort. I had some question about just how distracted he could become by a relatively minor sound outside.

After this interruption, he returned to the blocks and began to construct a building. From here he went to a toy turtle whose neck had been stretched out of shape and tried to push it back in place. However, it ended up being stretched even further. Taking the turtle with him, he went to the play school-room and said, "Now this turtle can go to school." He toyed with the idea of the turtle blasting off. Then he took a pad and began showing me that he could add one and one, and two and two, putting in the proper signs and writing the answer. After this, he returned to the beanbag and jumped onto it. Next he showed me how he could jump off a platform onto the beanbag with "no hands."

During this time, his activity level was well modulated, even, and rhythmical. He was reasonably well coordinated; his speech patterns remained clear throughout. There were no shifts in feeling tone, neither extreme happiness, nor extreme sadness, nor anger.

About this time he asked how much longer the interview would last. I wondered aloud what he was thinking about and why he had asked this, and he quickly changed the subject, saying that there were no more blocks and wanting to know "what got lost?"

Bryan now began to look into everything—in a cabinet—What's in there? and there? and there? He went back again to the blocks to build a very high tower and wondered, "Which way will it fall?" He picked up a rubber wolf, calling it a dinosaur and commenting on its big mouth and ears. Again he returned to the tower to add more blocks until it toppled. He quickly asked what time it was and said he was hungry. Now he built a corral and again asked the time and then began to laugh, claiming he did not know what he was building. Back to the wolf again, commenting that it was "scary."

While I sensed attachment and warmth from Bryan, I did not feel that he became more involved with me as the hour passed. Instead, just after he had finished expressing these last concerns, I could feel him beginning to pull away. At the same time, he was flitting from one thing to the next rather than developing a theme within one or a few play areas.

When I asked what his understanding was of why he had come to see me, he replied, "I forgot what my mommy said." Going back yet again to the blocks, he commented that his building would be really tall. I suggested that he didn't want to talk much about his reasons for coming to see me, and he then said, "You talk to kids" and knocked down the blocks, adding that he didn't wish to talk, he would rather play. My response was that I could understand that; sometimes it is hard to talk, but I wondered if it wouldn't be helpful if we talked about a few things. I asked him if he ever had any dreams. He was able to tell me somewhat shyly that he always had dreams about monsters, that he often dreams he is standing somewhere and the monster grabs him and he gets scared. Then he said, "I want to go home." I remarked that it was "scary" to talk about such "scary" dreams and he said "Yes," and again said he wanted to go home. Each time the anxiety level rose, he said he wanted to go home. It should be emphasized that there was no sense of disorganization or panic, nor any attempt to go to the door. He was able to verbalize his feelings directly.

When Bryan picked up a little puppet and began to play with it, I tried to start a dialog around it, but he became frightened of talking and said once again, "When can I go home?" He went to the blocks and then picked up the wolf and bit it. (This was one of only two overt acts of aggression during the interview.)

As we were cleaning up together, he became more openly aggressive toward the turtle, pulling off its neck and head and talking again about its blasting off. He clearly avoided participating in straightening up the room. At the end of the interview, when I explained that I would like to see him again, he looked scared, but immediately asked if we would be doing the same kinds of things. I responded that we would have a chance to play again and to talk about some things. At this time I also told him about psychological testing in the near future.

At the very end of the interview, I asked once more if he knew why he was here to see me, and he stated *very* quietly, "To help me understand things." I said, "Yes," and there seemed to be a nod of understanding between us. When I opened the door, his mother came toward him giggling and while we were arranging for the next interview, said in front of him, "When do I find out what he did?"

A subjective feeling of caution on my part permeated the interview with Bryan. I found myself being more careful than usual about being intrusive. I was impressed with his initial negativism, his minimal-to-mild displays of aggression (a gun was left untouched by him), as well as the number of times he had said, "I want to go," in juxtaposition with his fear of talking about his dreams. Despite his fears, however, he did mention his dreams directly during this first interview.

While the play session was reasonably active, what impressed me more was

Bryan's flitting from toy to toy and theme to theme. Not only was there a lack of theme development, but a richer sense of relatedness with the interviewer never emerged. Rather, communication was superficial and scattered. Both affect and activity were restricted, yet well modulated. He did not show the characteristic rich, oedipal fantasy production, and I speculated that he had not quite moved fully into this phase of development.

Second Play Session. A week later, Bryan came in with an eager look on his face and a rash on his cheek. He looked demure and shy, very appealing, almost seductive. Once again he sat on the beanbag, making himself quite comfortable, smiled, and made eye contact with me. From where he sat he examined the room and wanted to know where the paper was. He then proceeded to make a series of drawings, placing them in a makeshift album to which he then proudly attached his full name. For the first picture he drew a head, then two lines showing the unclothed body extending directly downward into the legs, with circles for the feet. This he labeled "big man." A square that he drew he called "the swimming pool." He labeled its different parts, drawing circles for stairs and other circles for himself and his brother. Another square represented a playground, again with circles to show different areas. A wishingwell looked more like a rocket ship or a pencil; it had a cone-shaped head and rectangular bottom. "You drop something in where the pointed head is and you look for things." He pointed out that water could be put in the bottom. He wished for a dog, a German Shepherd, a watchdog to make sure nobody came when he was not ready. The need for protection was the theme that evolved.

Next he drew a picture of a house which looked more like a shoe (with pointed parts of the foot), drew two faces, one representing himself and one, Robert, with circles for the eyes and a line for the mouth. Then, in a scribble game, he drew a big man who, he said, was a nice man, again with circles for the head, lines for the body and legs, and circles for the feet. In a picture of his family, he placed himself next to his father, then his little brother, and then his mother. He and his brother were in the middle, his mother and father at each end. All of them were in a car. The only things he elaborated on in the drawings were the big men and, as he pointed out to me, that he always drew his brother, Robert. He simply commented that he was interested in "big men."

Next he asked me to draw and do some things for him and that he would direct me. First he asked me to draw his family, guiding me. I tried to comply with his instructions. He was fussier about drawing his mother than the others. When I remarked that he liked me to do things for him, he agreed. He then told me he wasn't feeling well and showed me the rash, saying that it hurt.

Immediately after, he set up the beanbag and began jumping onto it. In an athletic exhibition, he kept moving the beanbag further and further from the platform he had made to show me just how far he could jump. Next he was jumping all around the room, at times making some motions toward me, but never quite jumping on me. He did come closer to me during this interview, however. After this he built an ingenious bridge to help him between the beanbag and the platform. It was apparent that he did not wish to stop what had become more zealous activity. I commented about his saying that he felt sick and yet being so active; he paid no attention. When it came time to stop, having spent most of his time jumping around the room and playing a variety of athletic games with the beanbag, he didn't wish to. He indicated that he wanted to continue and then showed some concern about locking away the things himself and making sure no one would have access to his drawings.

During this second interview there was again no development of thematic material except in the very early stages when he was making the drawings. However, the contact with me remained; he remained emotionally even; and his inclination to explore and his natural curiosity were intact.

Psychological Tests[1]

Behavioral Observations

Bryan is a nice-looking, thin child who had a cold and was extremely nasal. He left his mother immediately and took my hand, but looked at her sidewise. His hearing was not accurate which may have been a function of both his cold and difficulties in attending. Toward the end of the three-fourths of an hour of testing, Bryan inquired, "Where's my mommy?" and "When can I go back home?" Bryan came into the room very quietly and was attracted to the toys at once. When I suggested we play later, he could not wait but immediately ran to grab the toys. I asked him to draw a picture, and he said he would draw a bag of candy, then decided he was going to trace his hand. He did so and then went on to draw a picture of a person. Everything took a very short time. He was more interested in playing with the Pick-Up Sticks, putting the sticks into little holes in the box. Then he found a hammer and started hitting it against the table, against the test cards, and against a toy gorilla that he brought to the table. He could not sit still. He was constantly up and moving about. His high level of anxiety may have been caused by what I found out later. On the way into the Center, he slipped, fell on ice, and had a big bump on his forehead which he showed me. When questioned he would constantly say, "I don't know, I don't know," without trying. If he didn't say "I don't know," he would look at me and immediately say, "Tell me what it is." He did things very quickly; for example, when counting blocks (which he could do very easily), he threw the blocks vigorously at me from about a 4-foot distance. He constantly scribbled, marked on the cards, even though he had been told not to, and paper was offered. He could not stop moving and constantly doing things. On the way out he remembered that there was a sign that we put up not to be interrupted. He asked to take it and gave it to the receptionist. As soon as he came near mother, he put his coat on and started toward the door, although

---

1. As reported by the clinical psychologist, Milton Shore, Ph.D.

mother was not yet ready to leave the room. He tried to turn the handle of the door leading outside but was unsuccessful until mother came to open the door, and he rapidly started on his way out, obviously being very eager to leave.

Test Results: Tests Implemented at 5 Years 7 Months of Age

On the Stanford Binet Form L-M, Bryan obtained a mental age of 6-0, with an IQ of 112 (high average). He passed all the items at a 6-year level and failed all the items at a 7-year level on the test. There is very little to indicate that his abilities are higher than the high average range. He demanded to do things he wanted to on the test. He would only do the things that he chose, carrying out my requests in a very resistant way. I was able, with a great deal of patience, to get him to complete the tests required for some valid evidence of his intellectual ability. He made up some vocabulary words. He also heard words like "roar" as "war." When he said he didn't know something, he would anxiously say, "Tell me what it is." He constantly wanted to draw pictures, and it was very hard for him to accept any limits. However, there was a very manipulative quality to everything he did, as if he wanted to get me involved in doing things he wanted to do, not wanting to respond to requests from me. In the completion of the man, he immediately translated it into damage, pointing out that the man had a cast on his leg before he had broken his leg. It was then that he pointed out how he had hurt his own head.

On the projective techniques, Bryan constantly denied knowing what things were. There was an intense, anxious quality to what he said. He would vary between fantasies of omnipotence and tremendous fantasies of fear and annihilation. There was a constant feeling of being eaten up, devoured, and overwhelmed. Repeatedly asking me to tell him seemed to be a way of giving him structure and order. For example, he recognized an animal, but couldn't figure out the name for it. He would keep asking for the name, making up names that he knew were quite inappropriate. Having gotten the correct word by himself, he then felt relieved. There is no evidence on the testing that Bryan has any basic reality difficulties, but there is clear evidence of the mixture of a great deal of lack of control, and aggressiveness, with some remnants of oedipal material. It appears that he has tried to reach the oedipal phase, but easily regresses and cannot control himself. His fears are very great and his demands strong. He does not accept limits well and will not meet requests that are made. Anything that can be seen as damaged or being overwhelmed by powerful forces is picked up by him so that in the Rorschach he sees huge dinosaurs.

In summary, from the psychological testing it seems that Bryan is a boy of high average intellectual ability, who has not adequately been able to deal with the oedipal situation because of many pre-oedipal, particularly anal, issues that he has not adequately resolved. There are separation fears that he regresses to very rapidly, and strong feelings of annihilation. Any demands or requests by an authority figure are resisted as he narcissistically wants to do what he wants, when he wants to, and how he wants to do it. His aggression is free floating, and he is unable to handle or control it. He becomes anxious when he does not feel that he is adequately dealing with reality, although basically, his reality testing seems adequate for his age. Because of the fear of powerful forces, he cannot accept his dependency. Denial and avoidance are two of his major mechanisms for handling situations. I think Bryan is currently dealing with issues on a 2½-to 3-year-old level. The intensity of his uncontrolled activity and demands in the test situation may have been aggravated by his having hurt himself prior to coming in. On the basis of testing, he does need therapy, probably twice a week. I do not feel, however, that he could handle more frequent sessions.

Assessment Profile

1. *Ego intactness*

a. Ego apparatus—Good (2)—The basic organic integrity of the ego (including perceptual, visual, motor, and auditory apparatuses), coordinating apparatuses (perceptual, motor), and other similar apparatuses such as memory, appeared to be intact. However, early history revealed a delayed Cesarean section and some early jaundice leading to questions of interference with optimal early maturation, although there is no present evidence of such. Fine motor coordination, as indicated in the playroom sessions, did not seem as well organized as gross motor coordination, but he demonstrated a capacity to write his name, to color, and to draw, that appeared age appropriate. The drawings were well done, indicating that while fine motor coordination is not as good as gross, it seems to be within the range of age-appropriate expectations. There were questions about his attention span. In the playroom sessions, he flitted from one topic to another. Was this due to anxiety or to a difficulty in focusing and organizing attention on one task? Given these questions, which only further work would answer completely, the general feeling was that less than optimal performance in focusing attention was due more to functional issues and their concomitant anxiety than to a compromise in the basic organic integrity of the ego apparatus. The psychological tests appear to support this by the fact that his scores on all the tests were at age-appropriate or slightly above level.

b. Basic ego functions—Fair (2)—Overall, it was felt that basic ego functions were age appropriate, but it was also felt that there was a proneness toward regression of certain ego functions in response to conflict greater than expected for an optimal 6-year-old. For example, were there occasional compromises with reality testing when he was involved in a regressive, symbiotic pattern with his mother? Did he depend on her to define reality? When she was feeling good, he would feel good; but when she was feeling bad, did the bad or angry feelings of mother so pervade his own reality that there was a compromise in his ability to perceive how things really were? The question centered on the degree of real resolution of the separation-individuation process. How vulnerable was his capacity to see the world accurately? There did not appear to be sufficient data to answer this question completely from the initial evaluation interview.

In the history, when he had his temper tantrums, particularly while the maid was away on vacation, he seemed to be completely out of control, and there, too, questions were raised about his capacity for regulation of motility. Was there a compromise in his ability to control his impulsiveness, or was this a conflict-generated, goal-directed, organized attack? There were some questions about his capacity to care for his own body. When he becomes exhibitionistic, he seems to take risks and occasionally is accident prone.

On the other hand, in his playroom sessions he showed a clear capacity to regulate his motor activity. He understood the rules of the playroom and seemed to have an internalized sense of what was expected as he played within the boundaries of the situation. There was even regulation of motoric activity and affect, and interpersonal contact was maintained. While there was not a rich thematic development, more a sense of flitting, the flitting themes seemed in themselves to put together a picture of his concerns. Thus, while he did not indicate his concerns as directly as some oedipal children would, they were communicated during the course of the interviews. In addition, he could write his name. His picture representations were at age-appropriate level. He had a clear perception of his family, knew his birth date, and so on.

Thus, in terms of certain structural properties of the ego when not under stress, he seemed to be at the age-expected level of a 6-year-old in terms of his ability to regulate wishes, impulses, affects, motoric activity, to appreciate the situation he was in, and to regulate himself in a reasonably expectable way, organize his communications, and integrate (with thought and affect) a sense of relatedness. On the other hand, as indicated from the history, under certain situations, particularly those that touched on unresolved symbiotic issues, there were questions of compromises in aspects of basic ego functions dealing with reality testing, impulse regulation, regulation of bodily function, and a firm boundary between his self-representation and the representation of significant others (i.e., his mother).

While the data in support of the last statement are obviously speculative and should be treated as such as part of the initial evaluation, historical data are suggestive. When Bryan was about 2 or 2½ (just prior to or just after the birth of his brother), his parents claim he went "downhill"—negativism and stubbornness began emerging. There were extreme temper tantrums, particularly around issues of separation; an extreme reaction to separation from the maid who was gone for 5 weeks, and his loss of certain regulatory functions, e.g., occasional soiling.

Therefore, under stress, it appears that some of the basic ego functions are compromised.

2. *Ego flexibility vs. rigidity*

a. Adaptive capacities

1. Relationships—Fair (2)
   Intimate relationships with all family members, especially mother, were as indicated markedly compromised, while relationships with friends and other adults were somewhat more age appropriate.
2. Learning experiences—Fair to Marginal (2)
   From psychological reports and parents' description of B's ability to concentrate, it appeared that learning experiences would be markedly compromised.
3. Play—Fair (2)
   From descriptions of parents and playroom interview, it appeared that play activities were only mildly interfered with by low frustration tolerance and special conflicts with mother.

b. Intrapsychic experience—specific maladaptive tendencies

1. Organized disturbance—Fair (2)
   As evidenced by transient symptom of withholding bowel movements.
2. Relinquishing areas of experience—Fair to Marginal (2)
   As evidenced by fixed character traits to be described below as part of overall ego flexibility.
3. Unmodified discharge—Fair (2)
   As evidenced by current impulsiveness.
4. Fragmentation—Good to Fair (2)
   As evidenced by occasional "out of control behavior," otherwise use of characterologic restrictions to deal with anxiety.

c. Overall ego flexibility—Fair to Marginal (2)—Ego flexibility appears to be compromised by stereotyped patterns of feeling and behaving. There appear to be constrictions in the ego's capacity for dealing with internal or external stress. For example, in the psychologicals, there was an extreme amount of negativism. Historically, the parents indicated that the negativism began around age 2 and increased dramatically after the birth of Bryan's brother. This seems to be a chronic pattern implying a fixation and therefore an early constriction in the ego's flexibility to tolerate a wide variety of internal drive derivatives, feeling states, or external stressful situations.

In addition, there appeared to be another constriction in Bryan's ego which seemed somewhat more fluid and more under the influences of present internal or external stimulation, and that had to do with his flitting and motoric activity. In the playroom interviews, he did not develop organized, rich thematic material around any issue or within the context of one or another play area, but rather, he flitted from one thing to the next, occasionally appearing to be out of control, with phallic exhibitionist activity. In these activities, he did not always demonstrate expected concern for his own body as he jumped from a platform into the beanbag, and there were times when he might have hurt himself. This would also appear to be a fixed and stereotypic pattern of responding to internal or external stress (in the context of age-appropriate, expectable patterns, as a "hypertrophy" of phallic issues and a defensive constellation to deal with implied castration anxiety from multiple sources of development).

Along with the negativism, there was a general pattern of withholding. This was supported by the symptomatic withholding of feces upon the departure of the maid and his chronic pattern of uncomfortable defecation and withholding. In this context, it is interesting to note that when confronted with the interviewers, the two diagnostic playroom interviews, and the psychological testing, the negativism increased dramatically as the interviews became more structured and demanding. For instance, there was a decided increase in negativism in the psychological testing situation, a more demanding situation in comparison to the much less structured playroom situation which allowed him more leeway in his course of action.

In addition, there seemed to be a compromise in ego flexibility in being able to tolerate and form internal conflict. At times he dealt with internal stress through unmodulated discharge of activity. Historically this occurred with his temper tantrums, for example, when he would strip his bed and, seemingly, would be out of control. This was suggested in the interview when he became hyperactive after some anxiety-laden curiosity about the "two holes" in the box. As indicated in the unstructured interviews, he flitted from one thing to another, probably under the pressure of anxiety.

There appeared to be another compromise in the general flexibility of the ego to form the age-expected, thematic expression of feelings and thoughts, the rich thematic development that might be expected in a 6-year-old.

Questions should be raised about the level of rich thematic development that a 6-year-old should be capable of optimally. Although we find this capacity well-developed in some children, it may be related more to precocious, cognitive development which serves as a considerable asset in organizing their drive derivatives and affect states, and not necessarily expected of all 6-year-olds.

On the positive side, it should be emphasized that Bryan's ego did show flexibility in being able to adhere to the basic structure of the playroom. He was able to regulate his motoric activity even under situations of stress. For example, when he was dealing with destruction around the dinosaur and the wolf, he wanted very much to leave the playroom, yet he was able to stay and return to the theme, indicating some abilities to contain and deal with uncomfortable affects. There was also a rather significant moment when he showed capacity for self-observation by acknowledging that he was "here" to get "better understanding." There also appeared to be an implied awareness of some unhappiness in his life.

It should also be added that there was some question about a compromise in his curiosity and capacity to learn, indicated by both historic material and playroom material. It was speculated that this might be due to his bathroom behaviors and the potential overstimulation of seeing both mother and father nude. This would have to be watched for more closely, if treatment were undertaken. Along the lines already suggested around anxiety about "knowing," there is some question about the type of defensive pattern he employs to handle this anxiety. He gave some indication of trying to pretend he knows everything. It was shown in the psychologicals that when he did not know an answer, he either tried to get one quickly or demanded that the psychologist give him the answer at once, indicating a general lack of tolerance for being in the nonknowing state.

In summary, then, there appeared to be considerable compromises in optimal flexibility, with fixations around stereotypic patterns; negativism; withholding; diffuse discharge of aggressive impulses; occasional regressions in reality testing (as indicated in the prior category); together with more developmentally appropriate types of increased activity around expectable stress points in the phallic-oedipal stage of development and age-appropriate capacities for dealing with painful affects and self-observation.

3. *Ego functions related to autonomous and conflict-free spheres of the ego— Fair (2).* From this evaluation, it was hard to assess Bryan's capacity for self-observation, regression in the service of ego, synthesis and integration, creativity, and curiosity and new learning. However, even in the brief material, it did seem he had some capacity for self-observation, since at the end of the first playroom he was able to say, with some prodding from the interviewer, "I've come here to try and understand." This suggests that the capacity was there, but his negativism often kept him from bringing it out. He did show some capacity to regress as he let himself go in the playroom and was able to reorganize himself at the end and leave in a contained state. He has not yet tried school, and his ability to learn really cannot be estimated at this time. His psychological tests show his intelligence to be in the high-average range. Not much can be said about his creativity. He did convey to the interviewer a sense of curiosity. A very intuitive impression is that he has a fairly good capacity for integration.

There appear to be age-appropriate, autonomous functions somewhat restricted by internal and external stress. His genetic endowment and cultural background seem sufficient to support further development of these functions.

4. *Relationship potential—Fair (2).* Bryan seems to have attained the phase of triangularity as evidenced by the definite capacity he shows to separate from

the maternal figure, both from the way he enters the playroom and engages with a new person, and his ability to go to school, play with peers, and generally to feel safe and secure when mother is away. In each case he is able to call on a relatively constant internal representation of the nurturing figure, suggesting resolution of aspects of separation-individuation, the attainment of object constancy, and implying movement into a triangular period of relationships. This is further supported by clear-cut phallic-oedipal concerns demonstrated in the playroom. He plainly manifests competitiveness when the first thing he says in the playroom is that he can draw a picture better than someone else. He also builds towers and shows off in a phallic, aggressive way. When he plays cards, he tries to beat the interviewer, and there are indications that he wishes to rob father.

At the same time that he appears to have moved into the phallic-oedipal stage in terms of object relationships, there is some interference in the earlier stages. He does not appear to have consolidated a firm sense of object constancy, that is, a firm internalized representation of himself and the significant other. This is indicated historically by the amount of separation anxiety he experienced and the symptoms he developed when the maid was away. The strong negativistic battles with mother imply regression to dyadic patterns of relatedness and anal concerns.

In his play with other children, the level of expected peer relationships is somewhat constricted. Bryan does not look forward eagerly to playing with them for the fun of it. As his parents said, he does not seem to really want to go out and play with other youngsters on the block, yet he does engage actively once involved. His capacity for empathy could be questioned at this point in terms of appreciating the rights of other children, although not a great deal is to be expected at this age level. There are some indications of empathy and concern for his brother, however.

In summary, Bryan's relationship potential reflects age-appropriate capacities that are compromised by earlier unresolved issues. He seems to have moved into triangular relationship patterns which are vulnerable to regressions, reflecting difficulties in earlier dyadic patterns. The relationships, however, are not predominantly characterized by the developmentally earlier patterns.

5. *Superego functioning—Fair (2).* The superego shows age-appropriate structuralization. For example, Bryan was able to stay within the rules of the playroom during his sessions there—not to break anything or hurt either of us. He was explorative and took it all in, yet stayed within the boundaries of the stated and implied rules. At one point, recall that he was able to ask for permission to open something, again showing an appropriate capacity for regulation. Since the interviewer was always present, the degree of internalized regulation may be questioned. Nevertheless, from history, the presence of this capacity is supported by the fact that when away from parents and with friends

and peers, in school, and out of the sight of adults, his behavior seems to be within the range of expectable limits. There are, however, the periodic temper tantrums which do show a compromise in age-expected structuralization of the superego. Under general stress, or, as related in the recent historical material, stress stemming from separation anxiety around the maid's absence, or from interaction with mother colored by an aggressive power struggle, temper tantrums are likely. It is difficult to assess whether this represents an impairment in age-appropriate structuralization or more of a regressive movement.

In summary, age-expected structuralization appears to be present. There is some internalization appropriate for an oedipal-age child, but it seems to be open to regressive movements under stress.

The superego processes and precursors to later superego organization do not appear to be smoothly integrated with ego and id so as to bring about finely discriminated regulation in the context of a stable esteem system and capacity for pleasure.

The capacity for regulation did not appear to be finely discriminated. In the playroom there seemed to be a general inhibition in the development of richly detailed themes characteristic of his developmental stage. There was a skipping from theme to theme. At home the temper tantrums, negativism, belligerence, and in the office, the defensively used, counterphobic behavior indicate that while regulation is present, it is not finely discriminated, but rather at times tenuous and compromised by internal and external stress.

There was a sad quality to Bryan which was present throughout the initial playroom session. His explorations and curiosity did not seem to bring pleasure. While esteem appeared to be stable, there was little variation and almost no internal rewarding sense of goodness, even when he performed something that he felt was a complicated feat. For example, in the second interview, when he drew pictures, there was no sense of real internal pride. He showed them to the interviewer but did not appear to be pleased with himself. Historical material also revealed that he was rarely able to give pleasure to his father in play, nor did his father feel that Bryan experienced much pleasure when they interacted together. The occasional comments he made to father—"I want to kill myself," which worried father, also manifest that the esteem system is highly vulnerable to early primitive aggressive and guilty feelings.

The character and consistency of his present figures for identification (his parents), and the already existing introjections, lead to questions regarding difficulty for his developing identity, sense of self, and attitudes toward predominant types of age-appropriate discharge expression. There seemed to be a great deal of inconsistency in the parents' view of Bryan. They could not get together on discipline—father feeling that mother was too harsh; mother, herself, vacillating between an intrusive and at times seductive, sadomasochistic relatedness to Bryan, and at other times a firm, limit-setting relatedness to him. Father, on the other hand, enjoyed playful, seductive, warm activity, but would withdraw as soon as it got too aggressive. Mother and father continually undermined each other. Father would tell mother to let Bryan be. Mother would always feel that father wanted to avoid the tough times by coming home late from work. From the degree of negativism already existing in Bryan and his concern with diffuse angry feelings, both his own and those externalized upon others, one could already see a part of the maternal introject and its projection onto the world. Father's fear of aggression, it would seem, would cause Bryan to have a hard time working out his current oedipal situation. Therefore, difficulties were expected due both to earlier dyadic sadomasochistic issues he seems involved in with mother (which have already formed part of an introjective pattern), and because of father's inability to fully engage Bryan in warm, loving, as well as competitive play.

It could be observed in Bryan's tendency to externalize interpersonal conflicts, i.e., maintaining his negative position in the sadomasochistic power struggle with mother, that some early introjects at the base of the superego may be laden with punitive, hostile affects. His tendency not to want to help clean up the mess in the playroom also shows a lack of internalized regulation in this area. It was noted, too, that when playing with other children, he often likes the parents of one of the other youngsters to be present, indicating that he wants external support and lacks trust in his own internalized system. His feelings toward his brother are not clear from the initial data. What is clear, however, is that he does find beginning identifications with more adult versions of mother and father somewhat painful, and this is making it hard for him to form a more oedipally oriented superego system which will help him resolve this phase of development. The pain seems to have to do with issues of closeness with father and hostile sadomasochistic interactions with mother.

In summary, the superego system is partially at age-appropriate levels and partially below. Unresolved sadomasochistic struggles in the maternal introject and an inability to fully engage father in a balanced relationship are compromising the development of optimal appropriate capacities.

6. *Affects—Fair (3)*. Affects appeared to be developmentally appropriate. For example, he showed a capacity for warmth with the interviewer; a capacity to exhibit warmth with friends and peers at school and to relate warmly to the teacher. He also showed an intermittent capacity for this kind of engagement at home with the maid and the family. There was some capacity indicated for compassion with an ill grandfather, although the accuracy of mother's reporting must be questioned. There was some selectivity of affects in the playroom in terms of concerns with anger on some occasions, and warm engagement of the interviewer at other times. The aggressive, phallic affects seemed developmentally appropriate, as was the increased activity that emerged around the anxiety generated by these affects.

On the other hand, developmentally immature affect states seemed to be prominent, especially his concerns and discharge of angry feelings. As was noted, when the play material reached a certain level, there was diffuse and unmodulated discharge of aggressive behavior. Within the demanding situation of the psychologicals, he threw blocks at the psychologist, despite the psychologist's attempts to structure and contain him; he insisted on leaving the psychological testing session early. Thus there seemed to be a predominance of primitive angry concerns. The extreme amount of negativism and stubbornness suggests an extraordinary amount of anger from these pre-oedipal, pre-phallic levels.

His anxiety seemed to demonstrate itself on all developmental levels. There was some capacity for signal anxiety, as shown in the playroom by his ability to switch themes when he came upon anxiety-provoking material. For example, when he was involved in elaborating the themes of destruction, talking about the dinosaur and the wolf, and then said he wanted to leave, he clearly showed a signal of internal danger. However, he did not dart for the door, but was able in a moment to switch to phallic exhibitionistic concerns in the service of defense (of these earlier, perhaps oral, destructive issues). This "counterphobic" defense did not always work for him because it brought forth a new kind of anxiety, namely developmentally appropriate castration anxiety, in that he became concerned at times with loss of bodily parts and the general theme of what was missing.

While Bryan showed concerns on the psychological tests about being devoured by his fears of the wolf and dinosaur and showed developmentally appropriate castration anxiety by his fears of physical injury, his most prominent anxiety was a theme of separation. It seems that it is here that there are some fixation points to which he regresses under stress. This was historically documented in terms of his temper tantrums when the maid left, his difficulty in separating from mother to go to school, and in other ways which will be mentioned later on.

There is some question as to whether there was some anxiety related to fears of his own instincts, particularly in terms of his wish to come close and perhaps even to reunite with the mother. This is speculative at this point. Historically, it is suggested by his vacillating interaction pattern with the mother from closeness to distance and in the interviewer's feeling that he should avoid being intrusive with this youngster. Similarly, mother's greeting to her son as the interviewer opened the door, her wanting to know what the boy had talked about, clearly showed mother's own tendency toward intrusiveness. Thus there might be some anxiety around these kinds of concerns which may be elaborated should treatment occur.

In summary, this category would be rated Fair. While Bryan demonstrates a number of developmentally appropriate affects and shows some selectivity and flexibility under internal conflictual pressure or external stimulation and often in the presence of mother, he also demonstrates developmentally immature, stereotyped affects around anger and negativism and occasionally a hypertrophied, phallic exhibitionism. Also present is a high degree of castration anxiety around the issues of separation.

7. *Defenses—Fair to marginal (2).* A mixture of both age-appropriate and developmentally immature defenses was present. Although it appeared to be relatively stable, at times there seemed to be a breakdown in defenses and in capacity for internal regulation, e.g., diffuse impulsivity and discharge of motor activity. The defensive structure appeared to be rigid in that there was not a capacity to use flexibly age-appropriate defenses to fit the situation, but rather the predominant use of certain groups of stereotyped defenses.

The major defensive constellation emerging from history and playroom behavior was a passive, negativistic stance. The stubborn negativism seemed to be Bryan's way of dealing with angry feelings. Recall that in his first play session, he entered and sat in the center of the room as if to issue orders from an omnipotent position, and then demanded that the the interviewer draw first. On the psychological testing, the negativism predominated as he refused to comply with even minimal requests from the examiner. His parents, as related in the history, complained of stubbornness and negativism as "his major problems at home." In addition to the negativism in his playroom behavior, he also used what appeared to be counterphobic defensive mechanisms. For example, during his second assessment, immediately after reporting that he did not feel well and showing the interviewer the rash on his cheek, he began exhibiting his power and strength in a daredevilish way by moving further and further away from the platform he had built. Use of identification with the aggressor seemed to be predominant also, as illustrated in the playroom when he began talking about the wolf and dinosaur, and themes of destruction emerged. Suddenly a shift occurred, and he became the aggressor, jumping around, showing off, and doing the biting himself. Bryan seemed to use increased diffuse motor activity in the service of dealing with anxiety. He also appeared to use denial in his general refusal to want to talk about things, for example, his frightening dream. Along these same lines there appeared to be some use of avoidance. While there was no direct use of projection, it was implied by how scared he became when he heard a noise from outside, and from the historical material which suggested that he saw the world as a dangerous place at times, e.g., his extreme degree of separation anxiety.

With the limited data, it was difficult to determine if a reaction formation defense was being used. If so, it would be in relation to his brother. When Bryan spoke of his brother, he showed no angry feelings, yet neither did he talk very much about him. Nor did his parents indicate any rivalrous or aggressive behaviors or feelings toward the brother.

In terms of expected, age-appropriate defenses, there seems to be some compromise in age-expected capacities for beginning sublimation. There seem to be compromises in age-expected initial use of some obsessive-compulsive defenses to contain and handle some of his anxiety. There also seem to be limitations in his capacity to identify with certain positive aspects of his parents in order to help better resolve oedipal and pre-oedipal issues.

In summary, there appears to be a mixture of some developmentally immature defenses such as negativism, denial, avoidance, and projection, along with some age-appropriate defenses such as the counterphobic defenses, identification with the aggressor, and some sublimations. However, the immature defenses seem to be used excessively and the particular defense of negativism to an extraordinary degree. While most of the defenses are stable and work to protect the ego, they are extremely rigid, not permitting the ego the experience of a wide range of thought or affect. They hamper ego functions moderately by constricting the ego, as in the case of the negativism, and by impairing its regulatory capacity in terms of the impulsive, counterphobic type of behaviors. They do not, however, leave the ego open to disruptions in age-appropriate reality testing.

8. *Drive organization—Fair (1)*. Trying to determine Bryan's level of drive organization in an initial evaluation would be highly speculative. However, the history and playroom data do suggest some facts about his drive organization. During the playroom there was one short shift in movement between phallic-oedipal concerns and oral and anal concerns. In playroom one, he began by sitting expectantly, showing a controlling, narcissistic attitude. He then shifted to a competitive stance ("I can do it better"); then to explorative concerns; he saw two holes, wondered about this, became anxious, and started jumping around. He then became extremely scared by a noise and built higher and higher buildings; became sadistic toward a turtle, concerned with blasting it off; showed the therapist school skills; became frightened and then concerned with destruction around the dinosaur and wolf with themes of "what was missing." In this session he also spoke about tall buildings, how he didn't want to talk, dreams of monsters, and how he wanted to go home. Thus, the negativistic starting position is seen; the base of security, the return to that position near the end (when he wouldn't help clean up), and in between, the movement from only a hint of curiosity about the two holes, to then what appeared to be a lot of defensive, phallic-aggressive activity around jumping, and much anxiety at the oral level and at the phallic, castration level. The other playroom situation, where he was more relaxed and drawing a great deal, was consistent with this material in terms of thematic development. In his psychologicals, there was much stronger emphasis on the negativistic or anal aspect of his drive organization, which seemed to show up in relation to the increased demands put on him in playrooms where more questions were being asked. Thus, he would seem to have advanced to the level of curiosity about holes; defensively activating the aggressive components of his phallic-oedipal drive organization in terms of exhibitionistic derivatives; and regressing further to show his concerns with basic hunger and the more intense fears of destruction at oral and anal levels. In summary, although he seems to have advanced to a phallic-oedipal level, there are strong fixation points to which he regresses, especially at the anal level, but also somewhat at the oral level.

It should be added that in the second interview Bryan exuded a very appealing, seductive quality, suggesting there may be some potential fixation points at the negative oedipal position. It may also indicate some of his unresolved, symbiotic concerns.

In summary, the drives are somewhat fused and partially at age-appropriate levels. There appear to be major fixation points at the anal level which are quite rigid. Fixation points at the oral levels and the phallic levels seem to be more mobile.

9. *Reality considerations—Good (3).* The parents showed a capacity to understand their child's situation and indicated support of treatment if it were recommended. Both parents seemed to have enough observing ego to establish a working relationship with the interviewer.

10. *Intuitive impressions—Good (3).* The sense of curiosity, interest, activity, relatedness to the interviewer, and the way in which the patient entered the playroom and seemed to make use of the time to communicate the wide range of his concerns led to an optimistic impression about his ability to use therapeutic involvement to facilitate development.

11. *Capacities for further growth and development in an average expectable environment or in continuation of the current environment—Marginal (2).* This child did not appear to be capable of optimal age-appropriate psychological development without major intervention. Without intervention, it was expected that he would encounter continued problems in major life areas. For example, it was felt that while his basic ego functions were intact, there were severe compromises in the flexibility of the ego, highlighted by his already existing constrictions around the patterns of negativism and the likelihood that there would be further constrictions with occasional impulsive and counterphobic activity. Similarly, without intervention, the superego would continue to be organized around rather punitive, unintegrated introjects. Most of the drives would remain fixated mainly at an anal level, with some at the oedipal level, and there would be little oedipal resolution, leaving the drives predominantly organized in oedipal and pre-oedipal structures. It was felt that he would continue to use a variety of developmentally appropriate, but also a number of developmentally immature, defenses and affects that would pervade his future personality organization. Without intervention, it was expected that there would be interferences in ability to learn, in peer relationships, and, later, in capacity for intimacy.

In general, it was felt that without intervention, this youngster would most likely have a rather marked character disorder, highlighted by his anal fixations and unmet earlier needs. Passive negativistic, impulsive, and counterphobic behavior would predominate. Counterphobic behavior would tend to defend against fears associated with needs from all three levels—oral, anal, and phallic—of psychosexual development. His character structure would probably appear as immature, with negativism, impulsivity, and depressive features predominating. While, during latency, he might be capable of some relationships with peers, impulsive, counterphobic, and negativistic patterns would interfere with learning, and the unresolved oedipal and pre-oedipal issues would compromise new identifications, limiting further ego and superego development. Puberty and the new demands of adolescence, it may be speculated, would tax unresolved issues sufficiently to lead to the possible primitive character structure outlined above.

12. *Recommendations.* Because of the depth and internalized nature of the difficulties, the clear strengths in terms of the attainment of age-expected capacities in ego development and drive organization, and the clear capacity to communicate, regress, and reorganize in the playrooms, psychoanalysis was recommended. Questions regarding his occasional soiling, withholding, and other characteristics which might indicate severe fixations and difficulty in using the analytic process were viewed in light of his capacity to function at age-appropriate levels when not under stress, the goal-directed quality of his maladaptive patterns, particularly as they related to conflicts with mother, and his capacities to use the initial playrooms and establish a working relationship with the interviewer.

In summary a personality profile was presented and illustrated with the case of a 6-year-old. This profile is also appropriate to adolescent and adult cases and, it is hoped, will facilitate greater attention to the systematic assessment of functioning at each stage in development.

References

Freud, A. Assessment of childhood disturbances. *The Psychoanalytic Study of the Child*, 17:149-152, 1962.

——. Normality and pathology in childhood: Assessments of development. *The Writings of Anna Freud*, 6. New York: International Universities Press, 1965.

——. Difficulties in the path of psychoanalysis: A confrontation of past with present viewpoints. *The Writings of Anna Freud*, 7:153-156. New York: International Universities Press, 1969.

Freud, A.; Nagera, H.; and Freud, W.E. Metapsychological assessment of the adult personality: The adult profile. *The Psychoanalytic Study of the Child*, 20:9-14, 1965.

Greenspan, S.I., and Cullander, C.C.H. A systematic metapsychological assessment of the personality—its application to the problem of analyzability. *Journal of the American Psychoanalytic Association*, 21:303-327, 1973.

——. A systematic metapsychological assessment of the course of an analysis. *Journal of the American Psychoanalytic Association*, 23(No. 1): 107-138, 1975.

Greenspan, S.I.; Hatleberg, J.L.; and Cullander, C.C.H. A systematic metapsychological assessment of the personality in childhood. *Journal of the American Psychoanalytic Association*, 24(4):875-903, 1976.

Kohut, H. Scientific activities of the American Psychoanalytic Association—an inquiry. *Journal of the American Psychoanalytic Association*, 18:462-484, 1970.

*The Course of Life: Psychoanalytic Contributions
Toward Understanding Personality Development.
Vol. II: Latency, Adolescence, and Youth.
S.I. Greenspan and G.H. Pollock, editors.
NIMH 1980*

The Normal Development of
the Seven- to Ten-Year-Old Child

Marshall D. Schechter, M.D., and Lee Combrinck-Graham, M.D.

Developmental propositions go far beyond the discovery and isolation of the childhood prototypes of reaction tendencies. Psychoanalysis interests itself in the nature of the problem, why it was not solved in childhood (a question that requires specification of what phase the child was in), why it was solved in a particular manner, how this solution affected later development. A complete answer to such questions requires knowledge of what problem-solving and adaptive functions were available and how the environment responded to the problem—i.e., to the nature of the experience (Weiner 1965).

In truth, of course, the infant is neither a "homunculus nor a tabula rasa," either in his psychological or biological development. The influence of the infant's biochemical and physiological characteristics, temperamental traits, and cognitive and perceptual attributes is determined by the opportunities, constraints, and demands of the family and society. Conversely and simultaneously, the influence of the family and society is shaped by the quality and degree of its consonance or dissonance with the infant's capacities in style of functioning. Furthermore, this reciprocal interaction is not a static process. It is a constantly evolving dynamic, as the child and family and society change over time (Thomas and Chess 1977).

Part I

The beginning school years have traditionally been termed by psychoanalysts as the "latency" period. Throughout Sigmund Freud's writings, he referred to this chronological phase as the quiet interlude between the conflict-prone pre-oedipal and oedipal periods and the tumultuous period of adolescence. Latency was the lull after the resolution of the oedipal conflict and the establishment of the superego. It was the period during which the intrapsychic and physical forces gathered strength for that final adult personality configuration which would take shape in the crucible of adolescence. Latency was the period when major psychiatric symptoms would not likely appear unless the oedipal conflicts were unresolved or unless some specific trauma occurred causing a regression to a conflict state between instinctual forces and the tenuously established superego. The latency period was seen to be dominated by reaction formation, identifications, and sublimations of instinctual drive forces, and curiosity about sexual matters was channeled into formal academic learning.

Sigmund Freud, in his *Three Essays on the Theory of Sexuality* (1905), spoke of the biphasic quality of the sexual instincts with one peak during the pre-oedipal period and the second during adolescence. He suggested both a physiological shift (1905) and possible cultural or social shifts as well (1923*a*). In *The Dissolution of the Oedipus Complex* (1924*a*) he wove together physiologic and cultural viewpoints. But in *An Autobiographical Study* (1924*b*) he indicated that he thought that the phasic physiological aspect of the sexual drives dominated the advent of the prelatency period and that social forces merely capitalized on the repression of the instinctual drives by introducing schooling with its pressure for the development of an internal ethic.

Psychoanalytically, S. Freud indicated the child enters the school-age period after the dissolution of the Oedipus complex. It is, he said, the threat of castration and experiencing of disappointments of nonfulfillments of his fantasies along with maturational development (e.g., genetically determined timing, going from the pre-oedipal phase to latency) that forces the child into latency. Latency (1905) referred to that period beginning at the end of the 5th year and continuing to puberty, around the 11th year, in which there is a diminished sexual activity period. It is the period which occurs after the passage of the Oedipus complex and the establishment of the superego when the infantile sexual impulses are mainly handled by suppression. The chief task, according to S. Freud (1926), was to avoid the pressures for masturbation. S. Freud (1905) indicated that the period of latency was a physiological phenomenon influenced by education. He stated (1935)[1], "It can, however, only give rise to a complete interruption of sexual life in cultural organizations which have made the suppression of infantile sexuality a part of their system." During the latency period libidinal impulses are partially repressed, partially desexualized and sublimated, and in part inhibited in aim. From these mutations and modifications of instinctual drives derive the beginnings of morality, social order, and religious attitudes (1923*b*), as well as creative writing which can represent sublimations of the repressed infantile wishes (1924*c*).

It is striking to note a paucity of literature on this period despite the fact that

1. S. Freud. Footnote on p. 37, Vol. XX of *Standard Edition.*

the greatest numbers of referrals to child psychoanalysts, child psychiatrists, and child mental health clinics are in the 7- to 11-age range. With a few notable exceptions little work from other theoretical conceptualizations about development is integrated with psychoanalytic understanding of this time frame. Only recently, for example, have some of the constructs of Piaget and his coworkers been related to psychoanalytic understanding of the school-age child (Sarnoff 1976).

In this chapter, we shall attempt to disturb the quietude of the latency period by recognizing that critical developmental issues for the child in this period do not simply rest with the intrapsychic processes of integration of the active sexualized experiences of the prelatency years; rather the school-age years are characterized by an extremely active exchange between the child's inner world and the world around his expanding, now, for the first time, beyond the bounds of his family. We will comment, too, on the complex ecological forces affecting physiological and psychological outcomes which begin well before birth and determine the way a child enters the school years, and we will describe the specific effects of these forces in the school years, demonstrating the vitality, beauty, and poignancy of our school-aged youngsters.

In our task, we will cite a number of approaches to describing development so that we can elucidate some processes with which to frame our discussion. We will characterize the process by which each approach discussed attempts to integrate environmental and organismic factors in its account of development. We will discuss how each approach characterizes the accomplishments of the youngsters entering the school years. We hope to enrich the previously described psychoanalytic view of these years by a review of biological, egopsychological, temperamental, cognitive, and cultural methods of describing development and the issues relevant to the school-age child.

We want to detail in this chapter principles of development from all of the above sources mentioned in the last paragraph. We will not specify all of the literature in support of these various propositions but will rather note only the significant and most relevant references. It is our purpose to describe contributions, psychoanalytic and nonanalytic, which can broaden the understanding of the normal in this timespan and, in this sense, to allow (a) an appraisal of the deviations which can occur and (b) the treatment potentials and approach for these deviations. After presenting some of the underlying principles and precursors of normal development leading up to ages 7 to 10, we will illustrate the features of this age in developmental terms, including psychoanalytic, paradigmatically the weaving together and utilization of all of the aforementioned principles and precursors. Specifically, we will touch on present day contributions related to Temperament (Principle I), Psychobiological Givens (Principle II), Gender Identity (Principle III), Cognitive Development (Principle IV), Cultural Influences (Principle V), Coping and Adaptive Styles (Principle VI), Physical Development (Principle VII), and Psychoanalytic Understanding (Principle VIII).

Part II

As is now understood, the healthy newborn comes into the world with not only preformed ego structures, e.g., the five senses and motility (Hartmann et al. 1946; Piaget 1951; Mittelmann 1954) but the capacity to respond, react, and initiate interactions with animate and inanimate elements within his context (Klaus et al. 1976). Many have recognized the fact that infants differ. Thomas and Chess (1977), who have described characteristics of these different temperamental styles (Principle I), have observed the interaction of these styles with the child's environment and have been able to trace the continuity of some of these characteristics over time. These authors selected the following nine categories to characterize temperamental style: activity level, rhythmicity, approach or withdrawal, adaptability, threshold of responsiveness, intensity of reaction, quality of mood, distractibility, and attention span and persistence. It is in reference to the first item that parents will speak of the child who is either hypo- or hyperactive *in utero* and whose activity level persists similarly after birth. This activity level can be interpreted idiosyncratically by whomever does the observing.

> Kathy was 2½ years of age when referred because of hyperactivity. The referring pediatrician said that he had tried medication and behavior modi-fication to no avail. On history, the mother related that Kathy was hyperactive before she was born, came out running, and had been running ever since. Yet when seen in the five diagnostic interviews, Kathy seemed only slightly above normal in her activity level (with no driven quality). But her parents, who were present throughout the sessions, once they assumed a seated position—never moved any part of their body except their heads for the entire hour.

A child's normal behavioral patterns can be identified as pathological if for any reason there isn't a match or good fit between the child's and parent's behavioral styles. Conversely, if a pattern of behavior might be outside of the norm, but the child fits into a familial style (e.g., a hyperactive child in a hyperactive family) or if the parents learn early to accommodate and not label these behaviors as pathological, they can be fitted into a normal conflict-free sphere of development. As Thomas and Chess state (1977, p. 11), "Goodness of fit results when the properties of the environment and its expectations and demands are in accord with the organism's own capacities, characteristics, and style of behaving. When the 'consonance' between organism and environment is present, optimal development in a positive direction is possible. Conversely, poorness of fit involves discrepancies and 'dissonances' between environmen-tal opportunities and demands in the capacities and characteristics of the organism, so that distorted development and maladaptive functioning occurs." These authors group youngsters into three constellations: the easy child, the difficult child, and the slow-to-warm-up child, based on the following factors. The easy child is characterized by his regularity in sleeping and eating schedules, positive responses to new stimuli, mild or moderately intense moods which are mainly positive, and a high adaptability to changes. The difficult child is characterized by negative withdrawal in response to stimuli, irregularity in biological functioning, intense mood responses which are mainly negative, and wide swings in moods so that frustrations usually produce tantrum behaviors. The slow-to-warm-up child has mild mood reactions and slow adaptability to new stimuli, mild to moderate irregularities in biological functions, but with repeated exposures to new situations; these children tend to quietly and positively respond with interest and involvement. Thus we have one principle of development which looks at the fit between the individual's particular attributes and response of the environment.

A vast number of biological processes govern the evolution of the individual. If we look at a few—physiological growth, endocrine systems, and neuroanatomic developments (Principle II), we can see an unfolding process occurring as if a time schedule were built into man's genetic system. Yet each area of development is highly sensitive to the environment. A dramatic example of this is in the work of Powell et al. (1967 a, 1967 b) on the condition of failure-to-thrive due to maternal deprivation. The infants fitting this description were found not to be gaining height or weight, and on close study, were found to have growth-hormone deficiency. In a hospital where attention was focused on adequate nutrition and affective bonding, without any injection of growth hormone, the children began to grow and to produce increased levels of growth hormone. However, when having attained nearly normal height and weight the children were returned home, they again stopped growing, and growth-hormone levels dropped. A return to the hospital environment with its affectional warmth and individual stimulation resulted in a return of normal pattern of growth and of growth hormone. This experiment in nature, akin to a demonstration of Koch's postulates, gives evidence of the intimate relationship between the child and environment affecting the most delicate neurochemical mechanisms. It shows that even with normally available and functioning anatomical structures, the child still needs the right kind of external stimuli to trigger the production of biological substrates necessary for development.

Studies by Green (1974), Stoller (1968), and Money (1968) bear upon the important interaction between biological and environmental influences in the formation of gender identity and sexual expression (Principle III). Gender identity refers to the sense of being male or female and the behaviors corresponding to this internal self-percept. Children become aware of genital differences often as early as 18 months and their own self-concept within a male or female sex role is quite well established by age 5. There are suggestions that having male and female adult figures to relate to enhances and insures normal gender identifications. Within the first few hours of life—even when there may be genital ambiguity—the child is usually related to by parents with their own expectations of gender-appropriate behavior. In this fashion, boys are often handled more roughly (e.g., the father buying a football and helmet within the first year of life), and girls are talked to more than male babies are. The increased roughness in handling the boys may encourage greater aggressiveness in males later, while greater verbal interaction between girls and mothers may stimulate earlier verbalizations in females. Although there is some question about prenatal hormonal influences determining gender identity, it is clear that the environment plays an enormous part in solidifying this aspect of personality development. The wish to be a mother or father remains stable from earliest verbal productions on, and while the vocational role assumed at any given phase of development may change, it too has the cast of a sex-role function as the child fantasizes himself as acting as an adult. The games of playing house, playing doctor, cops and robbers, etc. are all preparatory activities for gender-related adult functions. Even the toys that adults give to children unconsciously tend to funnel children into specific sex role-related functions (i.e., giving girls dolls and boys cars and guns). Anthropologists Whiting and Edwards (1973) note: "All of the behaviors which are characteristic of males and females seem remarkably malleable under the impact of socialization pressures which seem to be remarkably consistent from one society to another."

The father's role in a family has become the focus of a number of studies. Lynn (1974, p. 255) states: "The unfavorable consequences of father-absence may manifest themselves at an earlier age in boys than in girls. Father-absence may cause problems in the young boy's masculine identification; the girl, having to execute no shift in sex-role identification, may not manifest problems until later, when she lacks an adult male with whom to relate as she matures. Her problems in relating to males might be expected to surface during adolescence when her interest in the opposite sex heightens."

The work of Piaget (1952, 1954) in Europe and Werner (1948) in the United States yields another important developmental principle. Looking at cognitive development (Principle IV), Piaget described a process by which the individual, building first on inherent abilities, and later on acquired ones, assimilates new experiences and accommodates to his environment in a stepwise process that leads to the development of mature cognitive processes. The processes described in this model demonstrate that the individual's rate and kind of development depend upon the abilities already achieved and the opportunities in the individual's environment—again, an exquisite relationship between constitution and environment as the important factor in development—this time, cognitive development.

S. Freud, himself, as observed before, was cognizant of the relationship between the social and cultural issues (Principle V) affecting development, but the specific nature of these effects is more clearly investigated by the work of anthropologists in cross-cultural studies on the one hand and the more recent contributors to the psychoanalytic movement, including A. Freud (1946, 1951, 1965), and Mahler et al. (1975).

Assuming that individuals do have relatively similar fundamental schedules of development, cross-cultural studies help to delineate which developmental principles are invariable in an average expectable environment and which are highly subject to the issues of a particular culture. For example, Thomas and Chess (1977) compare their temperament scores from the New York Longitudinal Study (NYLS) with an African sample from the Kikuyu, Digo, and Maasi tribes to find that threshold was the only category where there was congruence. They state: "In every other category there were significant differences between the African and American sample, as well as among the three tribes. The cross-cultural data indicate that temperament must be interpreted within a cultural context." These authors also note that in comparing their NYLS sample with a sample from a Puerto Rican Working Class parent group (PRWC), sleep problems did not occur frequently in the ages 5 to 9 NYLS sample because the parents did not tolerate irregular sleeping patterns early on in life. Contrarywise, the ages 5 to 9 PRWC sample had frequent sleep problems emanating from a laxness in parental insistence on regular sleep habits in the preschool child. This occasioned, then, problems referrable to getting off to sleep and then awakening in time, once regular school began.

The neo-Freudians (including Erikson 1968; Horney 1939; Sullivan 1953) focus particularly on the nature of the interaction of the environment and the individual's intrapsychic development. A model for this is presented by Murphy and Moriarity (1976) detailing children's coping mechanisms (Principle VI). The authors indicate that styles of coping need to be seen in relationship to the situation as experienced by the child and that coping styles and techniques shift and modify over time. This idea is similar to A. Freud's (1946) in describing defense mechanisms. So another principle of development is conceptualized which relates the individual's particular experience in his context with intrapsychic mechanisms of adaptation, coping, and defense. Murphy and Moriarity (1976) indicate that styles of coping need to be seen in relationship to the situation as experienced by the child and that the coping styles and techniques shift and modify over time. During the preschool period, vulnerabilities were noted with disorganization, deterioration, and/or inhibition of affection, cognitive, motor, or integrative functioning. Coping styles to stress included gating excessive stimulation and restructuring the environment, acceptance of people, and clearly having an ability to differentiate reality from fantasy. The authors noted that the mother's respect for the natural pace and rhythms and the acceptance of the child's autonomy she displayed consistently supported in a positive fashion the child's vegetative, integrative functioning, increasing coping capabilities decidedly. Murphy suggests (p. 339) that: "The mother's adjustment may be facilitated by the compatibility, but the mother's adjustment has little relation to the infant's activity level and sensory re-activity: the latter seems to be determined by constitutional dispositions. However, there is a reciprocal relationship between the infant's drive level and mother's responses through speech and facial expressions. The evocative, responsive baby draws responses from the mother that in turn stimulate that baby."

Murphy has noted that the capacity for self-regulation of sensations varies for different infants and varies within each individual according to a number of variables. These self-regulatory mechanisms include the utilization of rest and active behaviors in regard to the intensity of stimulus and the tempo of mastery and integration achieved by each individual. If helped to overcome successfully the stresses to which they are exposed, infants can develop a resilience to overwhelming stress in the future. They state (p. 343): "It is not surprising, then, that we found continuity in some motor and cognitive zones of the personality consistent with plasticity in the child's overall adaptational pattern: a stable core permits flexibility of response to change in pressures. But also variability, imbalances, moderate early instabilities and difficulties are balanced by coping efforts leading to creative integrations, reflectiveness and insight. *Mild vulnerabilities stimulate coping efforts*" [italics added].

Exemplifying the above is the physical development (Principle VII) of the child as he enters the 7-10-age era. After a rapid growth period up to age 2, there is a slower increase in total body size until the growth spurt before puberty. The volume of the brain at birth is 10 percent that of the adult volume and climbs to 90 percent adult volume by 5 years of age. The remaining 10 percent of brain growth occurs gradually over the next 9 years. So by age 7, the youngster has acquired over 90 percent of his brain volume.

Normal physical development takes the child from complete dependency for physical and emotional care at birth to at age 7: (1) an ability in the gross motor area (to walk, run, jump, skip, ride a bike, balance, hop, catch, throw, somersault, etc.); (2) an ability in the fine motor as well as visual-auditory motor areas (to use pincer's grasp, imitate geometric figures, draw a six-part person, develop printing and even elementary cursive writing skills, follow visual and auditory cues, etc.); (3) an ability in the language sphere (to track auditory stimuli, imitate speech, define words, identify bodily parts, express ideas, differentiate between make-believe and reality with an ability to convey these differences verbally [primary process vs. secondary process], count, differentiate colors, begin punning and enjoy verbally expressed humor besides scatological physical clowning behavior, etc.); (4) an ability in the personal-social spheres (to separate from parents for considerable periods, dress self, including tying shoes, relate with peers, express needs and desires verbally, be participant in some group activities, e.g., "Simon Says," "Put Your Little Foot," follow direction, e.g., "Follow the Leader").

As anatomical development of the central nervous system proceeds—perhaps measured and judged by myelinization—the cellular structures become more refined for specific functions (cf. language development and the difference between childhood and adult aphasias with the latter's reliance on the function of Broca's area), and simultaneously these same tissues become less sensitive to infection and toxins. This is seen, as one example, in the effect of phenylalanine in children deficient in phenylalanine hydroxylase which, in this inborn error of metabolism, inhibits the breakdown of phenylalanine to its normal amino acid byproduct, tyrosine. In these cases, phenylalanine becomes toxic to the brain, and unless there is a limitation in intake very soon after birth, the child can become severely mentally retarded. However, if phenylketonuria (PKU) is detected early and a low phenylalanine diet is instituted, the chances are that normal intellect will be preserved as long as the diet can be maintained through age 6. The suggestion from this research is that concommitantly with the shift in Piagetian stages of development to the phase of concrete operation and to the Freudian construct of the resolution of the Oedipus complex, we see also an increase in the alpha activity in the electroencephalogram from 8 cycles per second to about 11 cycles per second, probably representing a greater definity of and specificity in utilization and localization of central nervous system function. Is it possible that the infantile amnesia may truly be a combination of psychological events being played out against the background of normal central nervous system maturational processes?

The normal 7-year-old has developed adequate visual motor and auditory motor control which help him to stop reversing letters, numbers, or words, making reading, spelling, and mathematics within the realm of his efforts. There is some evidence that just about this time there is a major growth in the frontal areas of the brain, those areas most associated with socialization. The 7-year-old, therefore, is well prepared physically for the tasks which psychoanalytic theory has described and which society designates for him (as Erikson puts it, to learn the trade of the society).

The contributions of the psychoanalytic movement (Principle VIII) have offered major ideas about the interaction between the individual and his environment to help better characterize how development occurs. Mahler, Pine, and Bergman (1975) have made a most significant contribution in observing the nature of the infant's interaction with his mother, for example, demonstrating on the one hand the invariant stages of development—autistic, symbiotic, and separation/individuation, and on the other, that the outcome of these stages is entirely dependent on the nature of the infant-mother interaction, which is, in turn, dependent on the particular attributes of both infant and mother. In her highly focused work on infants and young children and their mothers, Mahler has specified the processes alluded to theoretically in the work of Hartmann et al. (1946) who discuss the unfolding and development of ego functions as the environment provides opportunities.

Just prior to the school-age period, psychoanalytic theory describes the phase in which there is a primacy of interest in the genital area that simultaneously relates to attachment to the parent of the opposite sex which then gives rise to the Oedipus complex. The increased libidinal tie to the opposite sex parent, and concurrently the increased aggressive-destructive drive toward the parent of the same sex, creates an intolerable psychic bind. As a result of the negative thoughts and feelings toward the same-sex parent who needs to be destroyed if the positive libidinal attachments to the opposite-sex parent are to be fulfilled, the child becomes fearful of retaliation by the same-sex parent, who, being bigger and stronger, must be more damaging to the child than the child can be to the parent. Out of this conflict a solution is evolved born from the concept, "if you can't lick 'em, join 'em." Three outcomes help the child unravel the oedipal dilemma and move on into "latency." The first is that of identification (with the perceived aggressor) which has clear implications for how the child fits into the social world (of parents, peers, teachers, and other relevant persons) and also how the child perceives himself functioning at that time and into the future. (From these identifications the ego ideal is drawn.)

The second outcome is that of superego formation which goes beyond merely the capacity to judge right from wrong and includes the development of ethics, morality, guilt, anxiety, depression, altruism, social conscience, and the ability to put oneself in another's place.

The third outcome is the loosening of bonds to the family—in effect getting out of the combat zone—with the resulting opportunity to experience values and judgments of others outside the family. Psychoanalytic theory of development, then, places our ideal 7-year-old with an emerging sense of who he is and who he wants to be, a conscience by which he can manage himself in the larger world, and enough comfort about his relationship with his parents that he can begin to form significant relationships with others outside his family.

A. Freud (1965), in describing the steps toward independence, as detailed in the concept of developmental lines regarding object relationships states (p. 66): "The latency period, i.e., the post-Oedipal lessening of drive-urgency and the transfer of libido from the parental figures to contemporaries, community groups, teachers, leaders, impersonal ideals and aim-inhibited, sublimated interests, with fantasy manifestations giving evidence of disillusionment with and denigration of the parents ('family romance,' twin fantasies, etc.)." In the same volume she notes the following developmental lines from play to work which are so cogent to the school-age child (p. 82): "Ability to play changes into ability to work when a number of additional faculties are acquired, such as the following:

a. to control, inhibit, or modify the impulses to use given materials aggressively and destructively (not to throw, to take apart, to mess, to hoard), and to use them positively and constructively instead (to build, to plan, to learn, and—in communal life—to share)
b. to carry out preconceived plans with a minimum regard for the lack of pleasure yield, intervening frustrations, etc., and the maximum regard for the pleasure in the ultimate outcome
c. to achieve thereby not only the transitions from primitive, instinctual to

sublimated pleasure, together with a high grade of neutralization of the energy employed, but equally the transition from the pleasure principle to the reality principle, a development which is essential for success in work during latency, adolescence, and in maturity.

Part III

What happens during this period from ages 7 to 10—the "middle years of childhood"? What developmental tasks are to be tackled during this period, and what issues will be addressed during this time? And when the child has finished his 10th year, what will he have accomplished in order to move on to the next phase of development?

As we have noted before, classical psychoanalytic theory describes the beginning of this period as occurring when the Oedipus complex is resolved, thus setting the youngster free to move outside the family into a larger society of peers and other adults. In the process of resolution of the Oedipus complex, the superego is formed, and this enables the child to deal with his newly expanded society with an accommodation which allows him to function more effectively without the protection of his family. Though in actuality both the resolution of the Oedipus complex and the formation of the superego are gradual processes and extend well into the middle years of childhood, there does seem to be an almost discrete jump at around age 7.

Shapiro and Perry (1976) examine latency in its classical and psychobiological connotations and make a number of important observations. They note the importance of the age 7 as a turning point in child development historically. In the Middle Ages children began the formal training for adulthood as apprentices or pages at court; modern children in England are often sent to boarding school at this age; children in our own society (USA) begin grammar school at just around this age; in the Roman Catholic Church, age 7 is considered the "age of reason," and at this time a child begins to study for the First Communion. Erikson (1963) observes the importance of this age in a number of societies. Because of the frequency with which societies identify this age as a *turning point*, we must consider the possibility that something is built into the psychological template of the individual so that he is able to make these shifts at this age.

What are the shifts that must occur to adapt to the situation of new social demands? The child must be ready to move from an egocentric view to one in which he perceives himself as a part of the complex ecological system and can function competently within it. An historical analogy is a shift of perspective like the shift from the geocentric view of Ptolemaic astronomy to the heliocentric view of Copernicus, the latter recognizing that the earth is only one of several planets orbiting the sun. At a greater level of complexity is the recognition that this solar system is only a minute part of an enormous universe.

Using this analogy, then, if all the tasks of the middle years of childhood could be summarized into one important one, it would be the child's realization of himself in larger contexts. If successful, the child would also have a perception of how he needed to function in these varied contexts and some of the rules that would govern his participation—just as the Copernicans understood elliptical orbits and the forces which held the planets in their orbits.

The child in the middle years has developed a personal competence in language, motor, and ego functioning which allows him to present himself to society like a butterfly emerging at first from the chrysalis, sticky, shaky, unpracticed, but equipped to try himself in a larger world—to be introduced, as Erikson put it, to the "technology of this society." The timing of this introduction appears to be related to the development of the brain at this time (refinement of motor skills, inhibitory feedback systems allowing for longer attention span, and frontal lobe development which seems to be related to socialization). It also seems to be related to a stability regarding the parental introjects, the formation of superego and an ability to repress, suppress, and/or sublimate instinctual drives with a subsequent increase in capacity to concentrate, to order thoughts and consequent increase in fantasy. We realize that in our own society in the United States there are children in the middle years of childhood for whom environmental emphases differ from the mode, and the outcome differs because the societal expectations are different. These children at the extreme ends of the population distribution—inner city and rural—may need to utilize psychic energies to properly adapt to their environment and may emphasize some areas of ego function at the expense of others. For example, the farm child will need to master a different technology—animal husbandry, driving a tractor, etc., and his social contacts with peers may be more limited, even though attendance at school is mandatory. On the other side, the inner city child from a chaotic neighborhood may have important concerns with survival which take priority over the concerns for formal learning. Clearly there are common denominators between these children, but the differences relate more to the pressure of parents, teachers, and social mores rather than to the presence of intrapsychic conflict states.

Sullivan (1953) characterizes this time period and its vicissitudes thus (p. 227): "This is the first developmental stage in which the limitations and peculiarities of the home as a socializing influence begin to be open to remedy. The juvenile era has to remedy a good many of the cultural idiosyncrasies, eccentricities of value, etc., that have been picked up in the childhood socialization; if it does not, they are apt to survive and color, or warp, the course of development through subsequent periods." According to Sullivan, the child in this era, the "juvenile era," now entering into a broader interpersonal context, becomes subject to a variety of new experiences which he must learn to handle. Primarily these are related to the exposure to a group of peers who are not his siblings and therefore bring with them customs different from his family, and a group of adults who will evaluate him, and through him, his family. In order to adapt to the requirements of these new situations, the child must learn certain things which Sullivan characterizes as follows. First there is "social subordination" through which the child recognizes a more general and impersonal adult authority, for example, the authority of policemen and crossing guards. And through the recognition of their authority over himself and his peers, he also learns a way of evaluating his peers—in effect by how they are treated by these adults. In so doing, of course, he learns at first to evaluate his own behavior. "Social Accommodation" refers to the process of grasping how many differences of living there are. The child arrives into this era with little sensitivity to others' feelings of worth, and for this reason, juvenile society tends to be rigid and cruel, and the participation of the individual in it is at first compliant. As the child moves further into the period he begins to "differentiate authority figures," and this allows him for the first time to reflect critically about his own parents and to begin to evaluate them. The pressure of society then forces the child to give up many of the egocentric ideas of the childhood era and to focus more on the reality of his existence in society, and this is called "control of focal awareness." These social pressures are internalized in the individual in "sublimatory reformulations," orientation of focal awareness according to group-approved behavior, and the development of "supervisory patterns," reflecting an awareness of one's own effect on others or in groups. The "supervisory patterns" become monitors or critics which help the individual plan and evaluate the effect of his behavior, not only during and after, but in advance. In this way, Sullivan takes the view that the pressure of the social experience forces the development of self-evaluation skills, social awareness, and conformity which are so critical to the individual's survival in a civilization. That the child in this era does, in fact, develop these skills is confirmed by a number of psychological studies, even though the forces of this development may be perceived differently from those Sullivan has presented.

As far as observational material on the theories of development in the "juvenile" era, two areas of psychological studies seem relevant. One concerns the child's perception of others and his self-awareness, and the other concerns the child's sense of responsibility in society—his sense of morality. Both of these areas are central issues of development for the child between 7 and 10 years of age.

In her excellent review, *The Middle Years of Childhood*, Minuchin (1977) describes many studies that illustrate the movement of social and personal awareness in the child during this era. In the area of personal awareness, for example, children are described as moving from an egocentric view of themselves to a more differentiated, more objective position of self-description. By 9 or 10 years of age children are able to put themselves in another's shoes and view experiences from another's perspective. As we shall see later, this ability is intimately connected with the development of the ability to perform logical operations. The perception from another's position, then, clearly will reflect on how the youngster sees himself from another's view.

Similarly, one sees an increase in objectivity during this era in a child's description of others. A number of studies cited by Minuchin (1977) present the shift of the child's descriptions of others and the social situation from an egocentric one expressing the child's own situation. This ability to objectively evaluate others and one's self as seen by others undergoes major development in the middle years, but, as with the evaluation of the self, critical evaluation of others becomes a major issue in adolescence.

These abilities of self, other, and social evaluation are intimately connected with the child's moral development during these years. Both Piaget (1932) and Kohlberg (1967) describe the growth of morality in a gradual way—as the process of maturation combines with social experience. Piaget's classic study of boys playing at marbles demonstrates his observations about how children of different ages deal with rules. Children at ages 7 and 8 have very rigid respect for the rules, though they may argue vehemently about what the rules are. Toward the end of the middle years, children begin to understand the "spirit" rather than the "letter" of the rules, and the actual negotiations about the rules often hold more interest than the game itself. In one of Piaget's experiments (1932), a child's understanding of intention and transgression is tested. Piaget presented two stories to the children, one in which a youngster breaks a cup in trying to get a cookie which he has been told not to get, the other in which the youngster breaks 15 cups while running to get something for his mother. Each child is then asked which child should be punished more, and why. By 9, most children can differentiate the issue of wrong by intention, according to Piaget.

Kohlberg's work is now commonly studied in relation to moral development. His three stages—preconventional, conventional, and postconventional—are each subdivided into two substages. Although Kohlberg, like Piaget, is loath to associate specific chronological ages with stages of development, the years between 7 and 10 are usually times in which children pass through the conventional stage of moral development. Kohlberg's view is that each stage builds on the prior one and occurs in invariant sequence. They depend on maturation and experience to develop. He has, however, maintained that people do not inevitably go through all the stages, and that depending on cultural norms and expectations as well as other factors, individuals may not reach the postconventional stage at all, but still be well-functioning members of society.

The conventional stage of moral development, as one can imagine, is the first stage in which the individual registers the effect of his relationship with a society in his moral reasoning. In the first substage, the individual is concerned with others' approval and defines his behavior as good or bad in those terms. One earns approval by being a "nice" person. In the second stage, the individual responds to the "law and order" of the society, has a fixed interpretation of the rules, and is interested in maintaining the social order for its own sake. As concrete as the second of these substages is, one can see what an immense change there is from the morality of the preschool child who measures good and bad in terms of the punishment he will receive.

Another major contribution to modern psychoanalytic theory is that of Erikson (1963) who characterizes the middle years of childhood as the stage in which the child deals with the issues of "industry verus inferiority." In discussing the psychosocial issues of this period, Erikson refers to it as the "time to go to school." The child, in leaving the family for the wider society for the first time really, leaves it in order to learn the industry of his society, in order to become an adult. He focuses on the issue of personal competence in the activities of the adult society. Erikson states (1959, p. 83): "Children at this age *do* like to be mildly but firmly coerced into the adventure of finding out that one can learn to accomplish things which one would never have thought of by oneself, things which owe their attractiveness to the very fact that they are *not* of reality, practicality, and logic; things which thus provide a token sense of participation in the real world of adults." In this sentence, Erikson characterizes what he perceives to be the important transitional nature of the middle-years period, with one foot in childhood and the play activities of childhood which have allowed the child to master conflicts, the other foot in the work of adulthood, mixing seriousness and play.

In chapter 6 of *Childhood and Society* (1963) Erikson reacquaints us with a chum of Tom Sawyer's, Ben Rogers, who is described as he appears just before Tom bamboozles him into whitewashing Aunt Polly's fence. Of Ben, Erikson says:

My clinical impression of Ben Rogers is a most favorable one, and this on all three counts: organism, ego, and society. For he takes care of the body by munching an apple; he simultaneously enjoys imaginary control over a number of highly conflicting items (being a steamboat and parts thereof, as well as being the captain of said steamboat, and the crew obeying said captain); while he loses not a moment in sizing up a social reality when, on navigating a corner, he sees Tom at work. By no means reacting as a steamboat would, he knew immediately how to pretend sympathy though he undoubtedly finds his own freedom enhanced by Tom's predicament.

In this way, Mark Twain and Erik Erikson have characterized the child in the middle years—a child who is actively developing mastery and independence in his own relationship with himself and with the social world around.

To a large extent the success of this psychosocial stage depends on the youngster's sense of competence and mastery of the learning tasks which are placed before him. The child's thrust in learning is backed by his sense of competence (White 1960). For Erikson, the success of the child's accomplishments in this period depends often on how successfully the Oedipus complex has been resolved, for if the child is still wrapped up in issues of the family he is not free to learn how to read, for example. Current observations of the

struggles of youngsters in this period add two other factors which determine
how the child succeeds at these tasks—temperament and physiological development. The tasks themselves, for this society, involve first learning to read,
spell, calculate, and later learning simple facts—about history, for example—
which can be recombined by the child into his own understanding in a rather
concrete way. Let us examine some deviations about temperament and physiological development first and later examine the cognitive approaches that
develop in this period.

In their book on temperament Thomas and Chess (1977) present evidence
from several studies that is strongly suggestive that despite level of intelligence,
temperament has a strong influence on the middle-age child's achievement,
both academically and socially. In one study cited, there was a significant
correlation between low academic-achievement scores and the temperamental
characteristics of nonadaptability and withdrawal—characteristics of the slow-
to-warm-up child. In a teacher prediction of children's IQs, teachers tended
most often to underestimate the intelligence of the children with the slow-to-
warm-up characteristics. Qualitatively, the authors comment on the difficulties
presented by the child with temperamental characteristics of low persistence.
Children with this characteristic have difficulty establishing appropriate
amounts of attention for mastering academic tasks or for moving from one task
to the next.

When a child cannot master the fundamentals of reading, writing, spelling,
and mathematics because of a specific learning disability, or cannot be a part of
the peer group because of awkwardness in coordination and confused lateral-
ity such as in minimal cerebral dysfunction, he will develop a sense of inferiority and low self-esteem. Organic central nervous system dysfunctions can disrupt academic performance and peer interrelations—two of the major tasks of
this phase of development.

These areas of dysfunction are first discovered and highlighted by exposure
to the beginning school years and the academic tasks, plus the interpersonal
interactions this forces onto the child.

The cognitive tasks of the child between 7 and 10 years of age are some of
the most exciting of this era, since they do provide the tools for the adjustments we have already described in socialization and academic mastery. Piaget
(1954) and his followers have described the major movement in cognitive
development from the preoperational, associative, egocentric "rules" of "logic"
to the concrete operational stage, with its logic bound to object and situations,
but nevertheless, transferable from one situation to another. Though some
children develop more sophisticated concepts earlier than others, there is no
doubt that most of the development of concrete operations occurs in the ages
between 7 and 10.

The two major cognitive accomplishments of concrete operations are classification and conservation. Very simply, classification represents the ability to
form categories, and conservation represents the ability to conceive sameness

in the face of some apparent differences. Realizing that the child starts with an idiosyncratic associative form of thinking, one can see that the process of development of each of these cognitive skills is a gradual process. In conservation, for example, the child starts from a position of "concentration," the ability to focus on only one property at a time. So that if the child looks at density of a group of objects, he cannot also take into consideration the length of the space occupied by them. In a transitional period, the child may alternately consider density and length but be unable to put the two together simultaneously. Only when he has achieved conservation of the particular property in question can he simultaneously consider two factors and see that changes in one may be compensated for by changes in the other.

It is worth considering for a moment how essential these abilities are to the academic tasks of the middle years. Consider the practice in first grade reading of classifying words by a particular sound (e.g., "cat, mat, pat, rat, sat," etc.). The preoperational child is quite likely to become interested in "patting the cat" or having the "cat chase the rat." In fact, it is often helpful to the beginning reader to connect like-sounding words (categories) into stories as the Dr. Seuss books do. But the later school-age child is expected to learn how to connect things, using dimensions other than the story connecting them. In first and second grade, the student learns to subtract, and this, while at first often being done by memorization, later requires a familiarity with reversibility. How much easier it is, having learned that 6 (no matter what they are) and 7 (no matter what they are) always equals a total of 13 (combining), to know that if you reverse the operation you get two groups—one of 6 and one of 7—rather than having to memorize that 13 minus 6 equals 7. It is possible to teach a child to spell words and to read a particular book as well as to add, subtract, even learn multiplication tables. But for the child to be able to use these skills and apply them in different situations from which he has learned them, he must know *how* to do these things, and knowing how in this period requires the operations we have described. Thus the child's success in school in the latter part of this era particularly requires the appropriate cognitive development. By 10 years of age, many children are ready to begin formal operations—building operations on operations (instead of on objects). An early example cited in Minuchin's book (1977) is the capacity to consider alternatives, even to consider that several solutions might be equally valid.

We alluded earlier to the intimate connection of cognitive development in these years to socialization and the ability to participate thoughtfully and responsibly in the interpersonal context. We have therefore come full circle to illustrate that in all areas of development the middle years of childhood normally have the task of becoming competent in one's society, separate from one's family, and to test out intimate relationships with others. In this period, though children do travel in groups, the achievement for the child is especially an individual accomplishment, developing the basis for self-esteem and competence. He measures himself against others, competes for himself. It is for the next state of development that children form teams and can be truly gratified by the achievement of an important other in adolescent group formation.

Cultural factors always impinge on and influence the middle-age child, since the educational system carries with it the structure and mores of the society it serves. It is the school which promotes the language of the elders, permitting through the teaching of social studies the transmission of the myths of the peoples of the area. It is the specific culture which dictates the spoken and written language, its idioms, and its accents. It is expected that the child after a few years of schooling will reflect the attitude and the idiosyncratic emphases of the culture and the individual's family. The educational system—formal and informal—is what accounts for the different languages in the world, the differences in religion, philosophies, and character inherent in each community or subsection of community. The normal child in the first few years of schooling is exposed to the pressure of emotionally charged music carrying the message of the culture. Sayings and customs are transmitted from class to class, e.g., "step on a crack, break your mother's back," which fit well with the obsessive compulsive defenses erected during this period. The inculcation and indoctrination of children into their society are the expected tasks to be accomplished during the middle-age child's beginning time in school.

Generally by age 7, sexual identity has been adequately established in boys and girls. The determination of identification with the same-sex parent has been built up by innumerable societal attitudes and overt and covert messages from family, adults, and older siblings. Tasks without specific categorization are given gender assignment so that girls are assigned washing dishes and house cleaning and boys are allotted garbage removal and mowing the lawn. Girls are permitted babysitting jobs and boys delivering papers. Up until recently boys were encouraged to engage in physical contact sports, while girls were discouraged from physical contacts, playing games like jump rope, hopscotch, and jacks. Cleanliness, neatness, and interest in clothing are facilitated in females, while the typical middle-age boy is characterized by being dirty with tousled hair and smudged clothes.

Fathers who have a significant position in the home offer models for identification for the male and aid the female child in asserting a feminine role. Typically in families where the dynamics lead to feminine boys, the boys are presented for consultation around the age of 7 (cf. Green 1974, p. 241).

Around age 7, in females there may be a beginning increase in estrogenization which gradually reaches adult levels later during adolescence (Kestenberg 1967 a, 1967 b, 1968). The increase in female hormone secretion results by age 9 in the flaring of the alae of the hips and budding of the nipples. In similar fashion, starting a year later in males, androgens increase giving increases in testicular size around age 10.

These physical changes usually drive the developing self-image toward a much more defined gender concept. The sexual identifications are made more secure by the interaction of peer groups and the support systems which the social system provides, e.g., Little League, Scouts, Blue Birds, ballet, etc.

During ages 7 to 10 the normally utilized defense mechanisms—obsessive-compulsive, reaction formation, sublimations, repressions, and fantasy—are developed and strengthened. These can best be observed in the unconscious derivatives seen in fantasies, dreams, and play. The superego is most often represented by monsters who in dreams early on in this period are pictured chasing the dreamer until the dreamer reaches a place of safety. As the dreamer shuts the door to the protected area, the monster has its hand (paw) on the knob with the dreamer awakening in a state of anxiety, as the question is posed in the dream as to whether the monster (or monstrous human) can open the door before the dreamer throws the bolt. This symbolic representation of superego formation indicates the severity and brutality of the internal representatives which are erected to punish the child for unacceptable wishes derived from libidinal and aggressive drives. The child at this time of life is preoccupied during play with violent sadomasochistic activities as well as concerns about their ultimate vocational and procreative goals. Movies and television programs often serve as the stimulus for the manifest dream contents and play.

In a most erudite and valuable theoretical and clinical study incorporating this age period, Sarnoff (1976, p. 92) notes: "Psychoanalytic symbol formation constitutes a primary pathway for drive discharge in the state of latency, allowing for indirect drive discharge if the internalized demands of society block the direct discharge of drives." He goes on to note that fantasies leading to masturbation, which are generally more inhibited during the earlier phases of this period due to fears of parental reaction and the internalized affects of shame and guilt, tend to relax in the later stages of this timespan. Interest in their own and others' bodily differences and changes is seen in the sublimated doctor play and in the more overt expressions of looking at pictures of nudes, looking up salacious words in the dictionary, and more direct voyeuristic peeking at members of the opposite sex. The conflict between consciously and unconsciously derived ideas of parental ethics and the developing knowledge of peer group ethics is joined with the ego of the child forced to make a series of compromises. These compromises are the resultant of a series of forces pushed by the maturation of the child, increased cognitive and verbal abilities, the awareness of their surrounding environment, and modifying attachments to parents, peers, and other adults.

Regarding superego contributions to this conflict Sarnoff (1976, p. 131) says: "Cognitive maturation, psychosexual development, and social expectations contribute to superego changes throughout this period. The popular concept of the superego—that the superego forms only at age 6 with the internalization of parental imagos that accompanies the passing of the Oedipus complex and is enforced through the negative of the affect of guilt—*is far too limited.* We present the view here that the superego is a product of a *multitude of influences*" [italics added].

Fantasies are often fragmented early in this time frame so that only parts of drive, control, and defense can be seen. Later on these fragments, displaced on to symbolic representations, are elaborated and synthesized into a series of connected conscious visual and verbal images incorporating real people and real circumstances. Sarnoff (1976, p. 31) explains this function thus: "These fantasies discharge the drives and protect the mental equilibrium of the latency state." It is through the fantasy life that we can see how conflicts may be dealt with first in thought rather than in reality leading later to specific goal-directed activities as the result of more reality-oriented fantasies during adolescence.

During the age period under discussion, aggressive drives are observable not only in the fantasies and play of these children but also in their curiosity in learning (in the broadest of meanings), their competitiveness, and in some regressive phenomena such as self-injury, nail biting, self-blame, and self-doubts. These later expressions of the turning of the aggression inward can be evidenced by depressions, projection mechanisms giving an almost paranoid quality to some children, as well as phobic reactions to the expected responses from the environment for destructive impulses.

Masturbatory activity occurs in both sexes with often psychologically similar accompanying fantasies. Sensitive genital areas are identified early in life in males and females. Spontaneous erections in males are observable from birth on during wake and sleep periods. Similar clitoral responses can be assumed with the stimulation of cleansing. In general, in either sex, compulsive masturbation during years 7 to 10 most likely reflects disturbed mother-child relationships. Orgastic potential during this period seems debatable, but retrospectively in adult analyses a number of females and males have described orgasms before puberty (cf. Sarnoff 1977, p. 49). Whereas S. Freud (1905) originally considered the reported early life events in females as actual seduction, he later felt that they all were part of oedipal fantasies. There is increasing evidence that many of the females' early memories are not merely fantasies deriving from the oedipal, but in actuality they represent incestuous relationships with adult members of their family. (cf. Schechter and Roberge 1976). This suggests the possibility that females can have an awareness of their genitalia from childhood experiences which color and modify subsequent masturbatory thoughts and actions. Many female children during the 7- to 10-age period may have difficulty in fully appreciating the geography of the vaginal area and its uterine connections which remain cognitively amorphous with a future promise of adult configuration and function. Kestenberg (1967a, 1967b, 1968) points to the beginning estrogenic increase starting at around age 7 as described before indicating the stimulation provoked by these hormonal changes can lead to what Sarnoff describes as "masked masturbation."

The fact of the exposed nature of the penis and scrotum in males, the occurrence of erections associated with urinary urgency, friction, and in Rapid Eye Movement sleep, and the visual and manual availability of the genitals permits boys of this age to be very specific in their localization of erotic sensations. Although ejaculation does not occur until adolescence, orgastic responses do occur frequently with boys during this time (cf. Sarnoff 1976, p. 54). In the later stages of development of this age boy, masturbation becomes less indirect, and many of these children enter adolescence with an already well-established pattern of genital stimulation which leads eventually to ejaculation during puberty.

In both sexes the primary love object in their masturbatory fantasies involves disguised parental figures. It is with little pressure that the camouflage is uncovered in these children who, like the song says, "want a girl just like the girl who married dear old Dad."

Uncertainties about identifications frequently will occur in the child between the ages 7 to 10 with a recrudescence of bisexual conflicts. Males will envy the adult female role as will females envy the adult male role with cross dressing and cross play frequently occurring. The occurrence of the menarche and ejaculations ultimately serves an organizing influence toward biologically defined sex-role identifications, with the objects of the masturbatory fantasies shifting from preoedipal and oedipal to more current reality-based contacts. The severe castration fears so evident at the beginning of this time period gradually diminish with a greater capacity to identify with a same-sex parent in their relationship with the opposite sex. At the end of this epoch, usually by age 10, the children, whether male or female, can distance themselves from their primitive superego, permitting them to see movies, TV programs, and to read literature without these serving as a stimulus for the manifest contents of the dreams—especially anxiety dreams.

Part IV

What follows are brief paradigms which demonstrate the intertwining of the described developmental principles. Awareness of the various contributory forces, significance to and understanding by the child of these phases, are crucial in determining normality or pathology and the needed, most effective intervention for deviations from the norm.

As noted in the beginning of this presentation, differences between the activity level of the child and the parents can effectively create symptoms from what are normal temperamental and constitutional givens. Any lack of congruence between parents and child can enforce the underlying feeling in the child of being the bad person who causes difficulties for his family, others, and of course himself. This attitude is especially reinforced during ages 7 to 10, when guilt is so likely to be stimulated due to the primitive aspects of the internalized parental imagos. This is also true if the child is one of the difficult children whose rhythms, avoidance behaviors, intensity of reactions, quality of mood, and lack of adaptability are antagonistic to the familial styles of reacting. These children have problems with academic learning and peer relationships which affect their cognitive abilities and their coping mechanisms. Their object relationships are constantly exerting internal pressures which result in chaotic behaviors. Interventive modes which do not include an involvement with the family, psychoanalytic psychotherapy, the possible use of medications, and consultations with the schools are bound to end in treatment failure.

Retardation in growth in the physical and mental spheres can be the resultant of insufficient nutrition—emotional and/or food. This effect can occur at any phase of development; obviously the earlier in a child's life it takes place, the more devastating the effects can be. When it happens during the child's middle years, one can see a stunting in the growth pattern, low self-esteem, a fragility in object relationships, depressions, poor impulse control, and possibly self-destructive behavior. The children of this age group may have normal or above normal intellect but do badly in school; their daydreams and night dreams reveal a preponderance of oral regressive features with the contents most often of a lack of fulfillment. Again, involvement with the family is required plus intensive psychoanalytic work to get at the aggression which is present but turned against the self.

Those children who demonstrate a confusion in gender identity between ages 7 to 10 are similar to borderline adults with poor ego boundaries and sexual confusion. When these symptoms are combined with fire-setting, enuresis, and injury to living animals (poorly established empathic capacities), there may be in *statu nacendi* the development of what can be called the Lee Harvey Oswald Syndrome. Some of these children are impulse ridden and represent a realistic threat of outburst of violence especially during and after puberty. For those males who have a confused gender identity, there is a great increase in passivity creating a resistance of significance. There is often found a passive or absent father, a powerful dominant mother, both of whom support the crossover gender confusion in the child. In the female with sexual identity conflicts there may be a similar familial setting or one that is just the reverse. Although there are truly no absolute formulae regarding the familial dynamics in these cases it is generally apparent that some of these dynamics—some conscious, many unconscious—play a considerable role in the evolution and perpetuation of this symptom. Since the parental compliance in this picture is generally so evident, it presents a therapeutic situation in which the parents' motivations for treatment are minimal indeed. At times, it is the child who asks for help because of peer pressure at this time of life for clear-cut, unambiguous sex role performance. When presented for treatment between the ages 7 to 10, even with the overt conscious agreement of the parents, the symptoms may be so relatively fixed that major change may be difficult to effect. Undertaking psychoanalysis at this time along with family therapy should be considered. Treatment in these cases needs to continue well into adolescence to engage the powerful physiological spurt as a positive drive element for psychological awareness and change. In the boys with sexual confusion and the added features of the Lee Harvey Oswald Syndrome, there needs to be a thorough neurological study with, ultimately, the possible use of anticonvulsive or psychotropic medication.

Deficits in cognitive development can involve relatively discreet areas of functioning or can be diffuse and generalized in effect. Neuropsychological and emotional factors are of particular importance in this age child, since it is during these years that the fundamentals of all subsequent academic learning are acquired. With minimal cerebral dysfunction, there can be an object inconstancy as it relates to the printed letters or numbers (so that a "p" is always a "p" and not a "q," "d," or "b"), but also there is an object inconstancy regarding the introjecting of stable parental imagos. This, and other symptoms, makes this type of child difficult to live with and one who has very realistic difficulties in impulse control due to superego lacunae. These are the children of whom it is said that they are "like the girl with the curl in the middle of her forehead, when she was good, she was very, very good, but when she was bad, she was horrid." With difficulty in auditory and visual sequencing and problems with attention and concentration, interpretations given in psychoanalysis—even though timed and dosed correctly—are forgotten and/or distorted. Problems with passage from one Piagetian phase to another have the effect of restricting development, interfering with peer relationships, disrupting scholastic progress, effectively diminishing self-esteem, and limiting the child's capacity to feel productive at a period where productivity is the key word for this age. Ego functions can also be limited so that memory and judgment are affected, interfering even more with the verbal exchanges which are part and parcel of the psychotherapeutic process. Transference reactions are as unstable as are the relationships to the parents. Treatment approaches need to deal continuously with the fragmented levels of psychosexual development and the tenuous object ties so characteristic of this condition. The family in toto and the school (including tutors) must be included in the treatment process. Since delayed maturational factors are a significant portion of this deficit and since there is no guarantee that development will permit this child to attain age appropriate behaviors and reactions, the psychoanalyst needs to utilize the positive transference developed to get the child to use his intellect to solve problems.

A lack of knowledge of the social mores of the family of origin and of the culture within which children live is antithetical to proper treatment. Various cultures can emphasize different aspects of psychosocial and psychosexual development, and the meaning of the idiom and metaphor must be understood as originating from that cultural base. If a child is chronically hungry, if violence or sexual exploitation is an integral part of familial interactions, if there is little help for the child in focusing in on the differences between figure and background, or if the parents have abdicated their authority, various symptom patterns can develop which require specific interventions by the psychoanalysts. These societal influences can disaffect physical growth, coping mechanisms, cognitive development, and object ties.

Interferences in the psychoanalytic lines of development can represent themselves as fixation points or as regressions. In the former there are not only areas of delayed development in ego functions and psychosexual stages, but the magnetic pull of these fixations attracts to their nuclear core all aspects of emotional, cognitive, and behavioral disabilities. The possibility of some of these fixations representing some organic and/or constitutional anlage is present and tends to determine parameters of psychoanalytic treatment. In the case of regressions, treatment can be focused much more toward the traumatic incidents which have occasioned the developmental interruptions and subsequent slipback. Clearly, since the regressive pull takes the child aged 7 to 10 to earlier stages of relationships and accomplishments, normal attainments leading to feelings of esteem because of the productivity of this period are not possible. Even with successful psychoanalytic treatment of the child with regressive phenomena and symptom removal, the child often still requires tutorial help and family therapy to reintegrate him back into the family with new, more age-appropriate behavior and feelings.

Part V

We have attempted to demonstrate how knowledge of specific principles of normal development is needed to understand the children ages 7-10 sent to psychoanalysts, child psychiatrists, mental health workers, and psychiatric clinics. An awareness of the developmental precursors leading up to this age and of the accomplishments during this age bears out the more current psychoanalytic thought that this age child is not at all within a latent phase.

What is clear is that this period is one of exciting growth in self-esteem, a capacity to separate from family and interact with peers and other adults, a shift from primary-process to secondary-process thinking, an ability to undertake formal schooling, a greater joy in bodily control, a development of sexual identity, a control of primitive impulses leading to sublimated pleasures and a gratification in learning, a sense of humor, and a sense of mastery and competence which permits the child of this age for the first time to really conceive of himself/herself as a functioning adult. As psychobiological development and as competence in his/her body and mind occur, there is an increasing feeling of an internalized locus of control within the individual. Aggressive and sexual feelings and fantasies begin to separate from earlier primitive and preoedipal objects and start attaching to people outside of the family.

The mutual interaction and interplay between inherent constitutional forces, developmental principles, and family/society/culture go on continuously, tending to positive, progressive reality-oriented changes. Interruptions in the normal progressions can occur with various psychological/physical traumata and/or the time bomb effect of some constitutional defect. Familial influences are major at the beginning of this time epoch and grow to lesser importance as this period ends.

The child from ages 7-10 is growing in a physical and mental sense, emphasizing the continuous active exchange between the child's inner world and the world around him. The psychoanalytic understanding of this age child is enriched by describing developmental concepts from the biological, egopsychological, temperamental, cognitive, and cultural points of view. All of these facets of development add to understanding and are necessary to properly evaluate and treat the child who may show deviations from the norm.

References

Erikson, E. *Identity and the Life Cycle*, Psychological Issues, Monograph #1, New York, 1959.
——. *Childhood and Society.* New York: Norton, 1963.
——. *Identity, Youth and Crisis.* New York: Norton, 1968.
Freud, A. *Ego and Mechanisms of Defense.* New York: International Universities Press, 1946.
——. Observations on child development. *The Psychoanalytic Study of the Child*, 6:18-30, 1951.
——. Psychoanalysis and education. *The Psychoanalytic Study of the Child*, 9:9-15, 1954.
——. *Normality and Pathology in Childhood.* New York: International Universities Press, 1965.
Freud, S. Three essays on the theory of sexuality (1905). In: *Standard Edition*, 7:125-245. London: Hogarth Press, 1953.
——. Two Encyclopedia Articles (1923a). *Standard Edition*, 18:235-259. London: Hogarth Press, 1955.
——. The ego and the id (1923b). *Standard Edition*, 19:3-63. London: Hogarth Press, 1961.
——. The dissolution of the Oedipus complex (1924a). *Standard Edition*, 19:173-179. London: Hogarth Press, 1961.
——. An autobiographical study (1924b). *Standard Edition*, 20:7-74. London: Hogarth Press, 1959.
——. A short account of psychoanalysis (1924c). *Standard Edition*, 19:191-209. London: Hogarth Press, 1961.
——. Inhibitions, symptoms and anxiety (1926). *Standard Edition*, 20:77-175. London: Hogarth Press, 1959.
Green, R. *Sexual Identity Conflict in Children and Adults.* New York: Basic Books, 1974.
Hartmann, H.; Kris, E.; and Loewenstein, R. Comments on the formation of psychic structure. *The Psychoanalytic Study of the Child*, 2:11-38, 1946.
Horney, K. *New Ways in Psychoanalysis.* New York: Norton, 1939.
Kestenberg, J. Phases of adolescence: With suggestions for correlation of psychic and hormonal organization. Part I. Antecedents of adolescent organization in childhood. *Journal of the American Academy of Child Psychiatry*, 6:426-463, 1967a.
——. Phases of adolescence: With suggestions for a correlation of psychic and hormonal organization. Part II. Pre-puberty diffusion and reintegration. *Journal of the American Academy of Child Psychiatry*, 6:577-614, 1967b.
——. Phases of adolescence: With suggestions for a correlation of psychic and hormonal organization. Part III. Puberty, growth, differentiation and consolidation. *Journal of the American Academy of Child Psychiatry*, 7:108-151, 1968.
Klaus, M.; Hand, J.; and Kennel, C. *Maternal-Infant Bonding.* St. Louis: C.V. Mosby, 1976.
Kohlberg, L. Moral education, religious education and the public schools: A developmental view. In: Sizen, T., ed. *Religion and Public Education.* Boston: Houghton-Mifflin, 1967.
Lynn, D. *The Father: His Role in Child Development.* Monterey, Calif.: Brooks/Cole, 1974.
Mahler, M.; Pine, F.; and Bergman, A. *The Psychological Birth of the Human Infant.* New York: Basic Books, 1975.
Minuchin, P. *The Middle Years of Childhood.* Palo Alto, Calif.: Brooks/Cole, 1977.
Mittelmann, B. Motility in infants, children and adults: Patterning and psychodynamics. *The Psychoanalytic Study of the Child*, 9:142-177, 1954.
Money, J. *Sex Errors of the Body.* Baltimore: Johns Hopkins Press, 1968.

Murphy, L., and Moriarity, A. *Vulnerability, Coping and Growth.* New Haven: Yale University Press, 1976.

Piaget, J. *The Moral Judgment of the Child.* New York: Free Press, 1932.

——. *The Child's Conception of Physical Causality.* London: Routledge and Kegan Paul, 1951.

——. *The Origins of Intelligence in Children.* New York: International Universities Press, 1952.

——. *The Construction of Reality in the Child.* New York: Basic Books, 1954.

Powell, G.; Brasel, J.; and Blizzard, R. Emotional deprivation and growth retardation simulating idiopathic hypopituitarism. *New England Journal of Medicine,* 276:1271-1278, 1967 *a.*

Powell, G.; Brasel, J.; Raiti, S.; and Blizzard, R. Emotional deprivation and growth retardation simulating idiopathic hypopituritarism. *New England Journal of Medicine,* 276:1279-1283, 1967 *b.*

Sarnoff, C. *Latency.* New York: Jason Aronson, 1976.

Schechter, M., and Roberge, L. Sexual exploitation. In: Helfer, R., and Kempe, C., eds. *Child Abuse and Neglect.* Cambridge, Mass.: Ballinger, 1976.

Shapiro, T., and Perry, R. Latency revisited. The age of 7 plus or minus 1. *Psychoanalytic Study of the Child,* 31:79-105, 1976.

Stoller, R. *Sex and Gender: On the Development of Masculinity and Femininity.* New York: Science House, 1968.

Sullivan, N. *The Interpersonal Theory of Psychiatry.* New York: Norton, 1953.

Thomas, A., and Chess, S. *Temperament and Development.* New York: Brunner-Mazel, 1977.

Weiner, H. Psychoanalysis as a biological science. In: Greenfield, N., and Lewis, W., eds. *Psychoanalysis and Current Biological Thought.* Madison, Wisconsin: University of Wisconsin Press, 1965.

Werner, H. *Comparative Psychology of Mental Development.* New York: International Universities Press, 1948.

White, R. Competence and the psychosocial stages of development. In: Cole, J., ed. *Nebraska Symposium on Motivation.* Omaha: University of Nebraska Press, 1960.

Whiting B., and Edwards, C. A cross cultural analysis of sex differences in the behavior of children age three to eleven. *Journal of Social Psychology,* 91:171-188, 1973.

The Course of Life: Psychoanalytic Contributions
Toward Understanding Personality Development.
Vol. II: Latency, Adolescence, and Youth.
S.I. Greenspan and G.H. Pollock, editors.
NIMH 1980

The Latency Stage

Selma Kramer, M.D., and Joseph Rudolph, M.D.

Part I. Normal Latency

Latency is that phase of the human life cycle during which the organizational process, the ego, produces a transcendental structure, the self. In normal development it is this primary structure which serves as the bedrock, the unshakeable foundation, during the disequilibrium of the adolescent phase. The late adolescent's concept of self is built upon the earlier foundation established during latency. Freud (1905) first gave latency its name; authors who followed Freud contributed to concepts of the psychodynamics of latency. They include such notables as Anna Freud (1965), Bornstein (1951), and Blos (1962), all of whom recognized the importance of latency and the effect of structures and functions developed during this period upon the resolution of adolescent tasks and conflicts.

A powerful repression at the end of the oedipal phase and the establishment of the superego through introjection of parental authority lead to latency. Latency itself is not uniform, but may be divided into at least two major phases (Bornstein 1951): one from 5½ to 8 years of age, and the other from 8 to 10 years of age. During the first phase, the superego is usually strict and harsh. This condition is not only dependent upon the way the parents are in actuality, but also upon the way the child perceives the parents, plus the projection of his hostility onto them. In the early phase of latency, the ego finds itself under pressure from the drives on one hand, the superego on the other. Regression is employed to defend against genital impulses, because pregenital impulses seem less threatening. Soon the ego realizes that this maneuver is equally dangerous, and other defenses, such as reaction formation, denial, and identi-

---

fication with the aggressor, are mustered. Identification with the aggressor serves a dual purpose, that of allying the child's with the parent's superego, and also keeping the impulses under control.

In the second half of latency, the superego is less strict, and the impulses are less demanding in seeking expression. The ego becomes more involved in coping with reality, so that sublimation of the impulses takes place in play and games and through the learning process. Thus play and school add another important impetus to development: They aid and abet separation from the parents. The function of the peer group also becomes increasingly important; in fact, the inability to use the peer group by middle or late latency must be considered pathological. The peer group adds its own structure to the latency child's ego and superego by introducing nonfamilial competition, learning and mastery within the context of "fairness," and appropriate rules and regulations. Aggression may be expressed in very active games (especially in boys); at the same time, every nuance of this expression is controlled by strict rules. Younger children play "Red Light" and "Giant Steps" in which permission to move must be given by the leader. Older boys engage in contact sports, partly in imitation of their older male friends and siblings, and partly as an expression of their own controlled aggression and need for body contact.

Latency boys and girls play quite separately and differently. Girls' active games are rhythmic, often involving jumping, skipping, and hopping, with rules which control the limits of their physical aggression, but which permit verbal aggression. This latter is particularly aimed toward their mothers, e.g., "walk on crack, break your mother's back." The girls' games also include not too deeply hidden sexual allusions.

Both sexes become interested in organizing clubs. These serve to increase the distance from the family and also function as an auxiliary superego. Often a club is organized, rules established, officers chosen, and then the club disbands. The process will repeat itself. Formal organizations, such as the Cub Scouts and the Brownies, offer greater stability and longevity in latency.

Just as peer friendships serve the purpose of separation from primary love objects, so does the growing importance of other-than-family adults. As children begin to relate to and become attached to teachers, relatives, parents of friends, and club leaders, they are able to take the first steps in comparing and contrasting their parents with other adults and to arrive at the realization that their parents are imperfect. Although this realization will be worked through with greater intensity in adolescence, younger children of school age begin to challenge their parents' authority with, "My teacher says...." This contributes to the decrease in rigidity and harshness of the superego.

Concurrent with the above realization, there appears the "family romance": The child has fantasies of having come from much nobler, superior parents (royalty at the least) and is being raised by ordinary people who are not his biological parents.

In both periods of latency, the children struggle against the breakthrough of incestuous fantasies and the temptation to masturbate. In neither period do they completely succeed, nor would it be advantageous to completely stop masturbating. Total suppression of masturbation blocks the discharge of libido and aggressive energy which then flow back onto ego functions and interfere with the child's relationship with the environment (A. Freud 1948).

Latency may also be viewed as the period of relative sexual quiescence between two peaks of sexual activity, i.e., between the oedipal and the adolescent psychosexual stages of development or between the resolution of the Oedipus complex and the onset of puberty. It should be noted here that the question as to whether or not the latency period is biologically determined is a moot point, for a decrease in sexual activity is not universal. In some primitive cultures, overt sexual activity continues unabated through the years 6 through 10. In more advanced cultures, however, direct expression of the drives is curbed and modified, and the energy of the drives is used to augment the energy available to the ego for further development, particularly the cognitive sphere. Whereas the oedipal child felt buffeted by the urgency of the impulses which were in conflict with parental prohibitions (as well as aspects of child's psyche), in latency, the impulses are muted and directed into other channels for gratification as a result of more sophisticated ego defenses and the help of the superego. As a consequence, we see changes in the child's relationships with other members of his family, an increased interest in peers and their values, and a sublimation of sexual curiosity into intellectual curiosity and learning. The latency child becomes "calm, pliable and educable" (Sarnoff 1976).

This shift in mode of expression of the drives is a result of the increased complexity and efficiency of the ego in its adaptive and organizing functions. The organizing function is at first relatively weak, but with the abandonment of splitting and its replacement by repression and their high level defenses, it gains in strength. As the organizing process progresses, a more harmonious relationship results among the three mental structures, the id, the ego, and the superego, as well as with the environment. This is the essence of normal development.

Variations in the process of integration and organization are dependent upon both constitutional and experiential factors. Those children who constitutionally have increased aggression, increased lack of frustration tolerance, and decreased threshold for anxiety, have a greater than average probability of failing to reach the state of latency, and thus the highest level of organization, the real self. The chances of failure would also be increased for those children whose life experiences have been so traumatic, so devoid of the tempering influence of love, that their destructive aggression toward others and themselves has been abnormally increased. When aggression has not been modulated by libido, there is interference with the development of the state of latency (Sarnoff 1976).

The major task of the latency-age child is to learn and master those skills which increase the child's chances of becoming a happy, loving, creative, and productive member of society. The basic skill required in our society is literacy, to be able to use written language to acquire and dispense information. Failure to achieve this basic skill is caused by one or more factors: organic, emotional, or cultural. The following are examples of such failures: gross or subtle cognitive impairments caused by damage to the brain; emotional privations, defects, or conflicts in early phases of development which prevent the child from entering the state of latency; regressions after entering the state of latency as a result of emotional turmoil; or, the use of language appropriate only to a minority culture, resulting in the failure to attain the necessary abstract concepts and nuances of the primary language.

Mastery of the basic skills produces in the child a sense of accomplishment which is confirmed by the attitude of the important people in the environment. This mastery produces a greater independence from the drives and the objects, resulting in a constancy of behavior and elevated self-esteem. Failure to master the needed skills results in lowered self-esteem and behavioral difficulties. Or, as Erikson (1964) stated, success produces the ego quality of industry, whereas failure produces the ego quality of inferiority.

During normal latency, certain physical, cognitive, and emotional changes occur. Physically the latency child grows at a rather even pace; there is none of the rapid increments in height and weight of the previous 6 years. Familial physical characteristics become more evident during this period. The child becomes more adept in fine as well as gross muscle coordination. Each child is an individual, and it is not only difficult but unfair to make comparisons with other children of the same age. Comparisons should only be made with the earlier records of the physical growth and development of the child. Girls as a rule are more mature than boys at each chronological age.

Parents and children need to be aware that the parts of the body grow at different rates and patterns. The brain grows very rapidly at first, especially during infancy, as would be expected by the rapidity of the development of cognitive, sensory, and motor skills. By age 6, the growth of the brain slows and is almost completed by 12. The lymphatic system is very pronounced during latency but gradually decreases thereafter. The genital organs grow very little during latency but begin to increase more rapidly toward the end of latency.

Sexual development during latency will be discussed separately for the boy and the girl. In the latter, the genitalia are less accessible both visually and tactilely. As a consequence, except for the clitoris and labia, the genitalia generally remain a mystery to the latency-age girl. Masturbation in latency usually does not involve the use of foreign objects in the vagina. There is a continuum of activities used to discharge the drives. At one end of the spectrum is a combination of symbolic functioning and whole body rhythm movements such as jumping rope, gymnastics, dodge ball, and dancing. At the other end is the more direct stimulation of the clitoris such as sliding down bannisters, rubbing against desks or tables, riding bicycles or horses, and, less often, manual stimulation of the clitoris.

Several factors occur to produce cessation of masturbation in girls. For some, the intensity of the orgastic experience with transient loss of ego boundaries is so frightening that inhibition of masturbation follows. In others, especially in those who think of the genitalia as a cloaca, the affect of disgust produces inhibition of masturbation through reaction-formation. In addition, the girl is influenced by parental attitudes regarding such activities; she fears loss of approval and love. Guilt, associated with sadomasochistic masturbation fantasies, also causes the child to limit or avoid masturbation. Total inhibition is pathogenic, leading to pathology, whether it occurs in the girl or boy.

In contrast to girls, boys have a greater possibility of meeting with stimuli which increase masturbatory activity, for example, the visual and tactile availability of the penis with its attendant erections. There is also the same spectrum of masturbatory activity as in girls, from symbolic fantasy and whole body movement to masturbation, accompanied by sadomasochistic fantasies. As a result of recent findings, the supposition that boys indulge more frequently in genital masturbation than girls has been challenged. Boys may also be disturbed by the intensity of their response to masturbation and/or by the accompanying sadomasochistic fantasies; this may therefore inhibit the activity. Castration anxiety, aggravated by direct threats or more subtle ones from adults, seems to result in a decrease in masturbation. Alternative pathways of drive discharge are similar for boys and girls: regression to orality with overeating or thumbsucking, discharge through whole body rhythmic movements, and other activities mentioned above.

In cognitive development, a distinct shift occurs during latency. Piaget's studies of cognitive development (1936) reveal that at about 7 years of age preoperational processes are gradually replaced by concrete operational processes. In the preoperational mode of mental functioning, the youngster (2 to 7 years) tends to focus on a limited view or single dimension of a given situation. This Piaget calls "centration." The concrete operational child (7 to 11 years) decentrates; that is, he takes into account several factors or dimensions of a problem before arriving at his conclusion. The preoperational child concentrates on the static state of a situation, rather than on the dynamic transformation. The concrete operational child can form images of the changes in matter. The preoperational child's thinking lacks reversibility, whereas the concrete operational child can reverse processes in his mind.

Piaget conceived of three aspects of thought as characteristic of the preoperational and concrete operational child, respectively: centration-decentration, static-dynamic, irreversibility-reversibility. All three of these are interdependent. Piaget thought that cognitive growth was the result of two processes, development and learning. Of the two, he felt development was the more important. Development depends on maturation, experience, social transmission, and equilibration (the child's self-regulatory processes). As a result of equilibration, the child acquires a new structure of mental operations, a form of learning which is stable and lasting. Piaget thought that learning in the narrow sense (responses restricted to a specific situation) did not appreciably enhance development, that such learning was too unstable, impermanent, and unlikely to lead to generalization.

Piaget also studied the derivation of moral judgment and moral behavior in children. From 4 to 7 years of age, children do not follow or know rules, but they claim they do. This stage is the egocentric stage. The stage that follows, that of incipient cooperation, is concurrent with latency (7 to 10 years). In this phase, basic rules of a game are mastered and attempts made to learn the rest. The child cooperates with his playmates. During latency, rules are immutable. Rules are treated with absolute respect because they derive from a significant or important person, either an adult or older child. As the child goes off to school and is exposed to the influence of his peers, the adults appear less knowledgeable and formidable, and the child adopts a position of mutual respect rather than unilateral respect for his elders. It is only then that rules can be changed.

In studying the development of judgment with respect to explicit moral situations, Piaget discovered that children, until the age of 10, judged moral situations in two ways. One way was based on intent which Piaget called the "subjective" concept of responsibility. The second type of judgment, less mature, is based on a quantitative factor, that is, on the amount of damage created by a misdeed. The greater the damage, the greater the guilt and punishment for the deed.

Psychoanalysts can agree with much that Piaget has written in this area, but more needs to be considered, namely, the presence and influence of the superego. The introjection of parental values, inhibitions, and prohibitions is the essence of the superego. It would seem that the crystalization of superego into a psychic structure would affect the moral judgment of the latency-age child through the use of guilt.

Sarnoff (1976) divided the cognitive development of latency into an early, middle, and late stage. He felt that the state of latency, which is characterized by calmness, pliability, and educability, occurs when the demands and prohibitions of society are internalized through identification (introjection) with the parents. The first stage of cognitive development extends from 6 to 7½ years of age. To reach this level of functioning, the child must have the capacity to symbolize, to repress, to have a highly developed verbal conceptual memory organization, and to have achieved behavioral constancy.

Sarnoff's next cognitive organizing period is from 7½ to almost 8½ years of age. It is during this period that there occurs the shift from preoperational to concrete operational thinking and the development of abstract conceptual memory organization. Fantasy thought contents shift from fantasy objects to real objects. The organization of superego contents changes from those based on parental introjects to those more closely related to reality. This is a result of the child's increased exposure to his peers and newer experiences outside the home.

The last of Sarnoff's cognitive organizing periods is from 8½ to 10 years and is characterized by an increase in the conflict with the parents; peers are now used as criteria for behavior. There is an increase in masturbation during this period. Night fears change from fear of fantasy objects to fear of reality objects. In some youngsters there is an increase in compulsive symptoms, such as rituals; in others, an increase in phobias may occur, both probably related to conflicts associated with forbidden wishes. This period is then replaced by the struggles and changes which occur in preadolescence.

Part II. Precursors of Pathology in Latency

Many authors have emphasized the concept of multiple determinants in psychic development. The ego, the organ of adaptation, has the task of integrating and organizing the disparate elements. These include a multiplicity of constitutional and experiential aspects and stress traumata, as well as developmental and maturational rates and their interactions. The task is not simple because of the great number of factors which affect development. If these factors are "average" and do not overwhelm the ego's capacity to adapt, development proceeds normally; if some are pathogenic, development may proceed abnormally or atypically. Even in the best of circumstances, development does not proceed in a straight line becuase of the variety of influences. It can best be described as a series of phases, marked predominantly by progression, but also by some regression.

The root causes for failure to attain normal latency are divided between heredito constitutional and experiential factors. Examples of former factors are as follows: inborn drives which may be too weak or too strong, or out of kilter with each other or with intellectual development; inherited neurologic syndromes affecting the neuromuscular or the sensory systems (including hyper- or hypo-reactivity); mental retardation; damage to the infant caused by poor prenatal care, poor nutrition, or an adolescent mother; and inborn errors of metabolism. Examples of experiential factors would include an abnormal infant-parent relationship, creating either emotional deprivation or its opposite, smothering; absence of either parent for any cause; excessive stimulation or excessive frustration; or, lack of stimulation. Other experiential factors are socioeconomic which (when accompanied by cultural deprivation) may result in the child's inability to cope effectively in the greater society.

Descriptively, the latency child can manifest any of the following categories of disturbance (International Classification of Diseases 8):

1. Reactive disorders
2. Specific developmental disorders
3. Neurotic disorders
4. Personality character disorders
5. Psychotic disorders
6. Somatic disorders
7. Disorders directly due to acute or chronic brain condition
8. Mental retardation
9. Antisocial behavior not classifiable elsewhere
10. Disorders not classifiable under 0-9.

Too often, however, the manifest, the symptoms, do not tell us what was and is operating beneath the surface. For a better understanding of the latency-age child, it is important to know what took place with the infant and toddler. It would also be helpful to learn the psychoanalytic concepts of child development. Such notables as A. Freud (1949), Erikson (1964), Mahler (1975), Spitz (1965), and Winnicott (1965) have contributed a wealth of knowledge to our comprehension of child development. These researchers have shown that early precursors of pathology may be caused by deviations in the development of instinctual drives, object relations, and/or the ego. Such deviations produce abnormalities in the cognitive, emotional, and social spheres, or a combination of these. This knowledge could be used for early remediation or prevention.

Following is a brief review of normal development prior to latency and the deviations occurring in these early phases which might produce pathology in latency:

In the first phase of life, the oral phase, if the match is a good one between the baby and his drives, on the one side, and the mother and her needs (conscious and unconscious), on the other side, a sound symbiosis (Mahler 1975) occurs. Ego and object development proceed normally, and the infant develops a sense of basic trust—trust in himself as well as in the people about him.

If the next phase of life, the anal (or from Mahler's viewpoint, separation-individuation) proceeds normally; the child emerges with a sense of autonomy.

The last phase before latency, the oedipal, is characterized by intense feelings about the important objects in the child's life, the parents. If these feelings are adequately resolved, the child retains a sense of initiative.

If the infant experiences an excess of frustration during the first or oral phase, he will develop a sense of mistrust and will feel that neither others nor himself can be trusted. Even at this early stage of life, deviations in ego development can be noted, e.g., delay in the development of anticipation which is manifested by poor frustration tolerance. Derivatives of this may be seen in latency when poor impulse control is exhibited. More than average intensity of separation anxiety may be a forerunner of school phobia in latency. Too great or too little stranger reaction (that is an inability to accept strangers or parent substitutes or, conversely, a too great readiness to accept parent substitutes) may appear in latency as excessive suspiciousness of strangers, an indifference to people, or lack of closeness in human relations. These are the youngsters who do not readily accept what the school or the teacher offer, thus creating learning and/or behavior problems.

If during the anal phase (corresponding to Mahler's rapprochement subphase of separation-individuation) the mother is libidinally unavailable, difficulties may be created in several intrapsychic processes. There may be an increase in ambivalence, an increase in the love-hate conflict, which can persist throughout the life cycle of the individual. The libidinal unavailability of the mother or an excessive intrusiveness of the mother during this phase negatively affects the process of separation and the development of a sense of separateness. As a result of such an adverse environment, the toddler will react by either excessive shadowing of, or darting away from, the mother. In latency, this may manifest itself as a school phobia or another neurotic entity with a borderline base. During the anal phase, repeated experiences of rejection and abandonment and feelings of helplessness will produce a too rapid deflation in the child's sense of omnipotence, leading to a tendency to develop depressions throughout life. Frequently, such depressions go unrecognized in latency, because they appear as school and/or behavior problems.

The anal phase is also a period in which symbolic representation and language development rapidly increase. As a result, there is enhancement of secondary process functioning, and thus the reality principle gradually replaces the pleasure principle as the regulatory principle of mental functioning. Inadequate language development due to constitutional and/or environmental factors at this stage will impair the school child's language skills and ill prepare him for life. He will exhibit immature behavior and have learning difficulties.

Modulation of affect also occurs during the anal phase. It is produced by the fusion of libido and aggression. This serves to decrease the destructiveness and hostility of the child and results in better object relations. The child becomes willing to wait for gratification and to do for others because he wants their love and approval. Failure of this process of fusion, wholly or in part, along with inadequate symbolic representation produces a child who seems totally or partially out of control, at the mercy of his impulses. In latency, such a child is difficult to reach. He frequently develops learning and behavior problems; truancy and delinquency are not uncommon.

In the oedipal phase, the child has to come to grips with triadic object relationships and his conflictual impulses, fantasies, wishes, and feelings with respect to those objects. He resorts to various defenses to protect against unpleasant affects resulting from the oedipal desires and conflicts. The dominant anxiety in this phase is castration anxiety, a fear of bodily injury. The male especially fears injury to his highly prized sexual organ. Defenses of repression, identification, reaction formation, and sublimation are used to resolve the dilemma. Incomplete resolution of the Oedipus complex leaves the child vulnerable to the development of neurotic difficulties during latency.

The oedipal conflicts are complicated for the little girl because she needs to shift from her first love object, mother, to her father, and she has no such highly cathected sexual organ, the penis. Nevertheless, she too fears bodily injury and defends against unpleasant affects in the same ways as the boy, with equal success and failure.

The heir to the Oedipus complex is the superego. In latency, pre-oedipal and oedipal superego precursors are integrated and organized into a psychic structure, the superego. The health of the superego depends upon all that went before.

Certain signs in the phases prior to latency should alert us to the presence of psychic distress. These are:

1. In the normal autistic phase (Mahler 1975):
   a. gastrointestinal: colic, vomiting, refusal to suck, coeliac syndrome, chronic diarrhea, and constipation
   b. irregular sleep patterns, excessive wakefulness
   c. allergic manifestations: skin disorders, eczema, asthma
   d. excessive irritability, restlessness, crying
   e. excessive quietness, persistence of autistic pattern (failure of the development of symbiosis), and excessive autoerotic behavior
2. In the normal symbiotic phase (Mahler 1975) which overlaps differentiation, the first subphase of separation individuation:
   a. failure of appearance of nonspecific smiling response (failure to perceive the "mothering principle")
   b. the inability to distinguish the libidinal object out of those available to the child. In lesser instances, objects are too easily substituted one for another without evidence of stranger responses or separation anxiety
   c. indiscriminate clinging to such easily substituted persons
   d. an inability to separate (actively and psychologically) from the symbiotic partner without manifest separation panic
   e. excessive stranger anxiety or panic
3. In the separation-individuation phase (Mahler 1975):
   a. differentiation subphase (see symbiosis above)
   b. practicing subphase:
      (1) failure to develop and improve upright locomotion
      (2) excessive imperviousness to falls and frustrations
      (3) excessive low-keyedness
   c. rapprochement subphase:
      (1) excessive separation anxiety
      (2) excessive or insufficient shadowing of mother
      (3) "darting away"
      (4) excessive sleep disturbances
   d. subphase on the way to object constancy:
      (1) continual clinging to mother
      (2) lack of a transitional object

(3) sleep disturbances, phobias, nightmares

(4) inability to use personal pronouns

(5) lack of beginning sex differentiation

(6) temper tantrums

4. Oedipal phase (Freud 1905):

  a. neurotic symptom formation

  b. regression to an earlier developmental stage

Another factor (frequently overlooked) which may contribute to difficulties in latency is the physical or emotional absence of the father. The mother who faces pregnancy, delivery, and childcare without the support of the father, is easily frustrated, angered, and depleted of libidinal supplies; she may become depressed. The presence of the father during the early months of the baby's life acts to provide the mother with the libidinal supplies she needs, as well as to channel the mother's anger toward him and away from the infant. At the toddler stage of development, a good relationship with his father aids the child to resolve his ambivalent ties with mother, thus leading to autonomy. The father's active intervention helps the child separate from a too close relationship with his mother.

At later levels of development, the father becomes someone to fear as well as to admire, someone with whom to identify. The identifications are of both the ego and superego variety. These enable the child to cope more effectively with the pressures from the id and reality. Failure in this area creates varying degrees of pathology in latency.

It is evident from the above that normal development proceeds as a result of a good endowment, good parenting (mother and father), and experiences at each stage within the coping range of the ego. Fortunate is the child who receives all three. Knowledge of the dangers to the normal processes of development should help prevent serious pathology.

References

Blos, P. *On Adolescence: A Psychoanalytic Interpretation.* New York: Free Press, 1962.

Bornstein, B. On latency. *The Psychoanalytic Study of the Child,* 6:279–285, 1951.

Erikson, E. *Childhood and Society.* 2nd Edition, New York: Norton, 1964.

Freud, A. Certain types and stages of social maladjustment (1948). In: *Searchlights on Delinquency.* New York: International Universities Press, 1949. pp. 193-204.

——. *Normality and Pathology in Childhood: Assessments of Development.* New York: International Universities Press, 1965.

Freud, S. Three essays on the theory of sexuality (1905). *Standard Edition,* 7:125-245, 1953.

Mahler, M.S. *The Psychological Birth of the Human Infant.* New York: Basic Books, 1975.

Piaget, J. *The Origins of Intelligence in Children* (1936). New York: International Universities Press, 1952.

Sarnoff, C. *Latency.* New York: Jason Aronson, 1976.

Spitz, R. *First Year of Life.* New York: International Universities Press, 1965.

Vaughn, V.C., and McKay, R.J. *Nelson Textbook of Pediatrics.* Philadelphia, Pa.: W.B. Saunders, 1975.

Winnicott, D.W. *Maturational Processes and the Facilitating Environment.* New York: International Universities Press, 1965. Chapter 7.

The Course of Life: Psychoanalytic Contributions
Toward Understanding Personality Development.
Vol. II: Latency, Adolescence, and Youth.
S.I. Greenspan and G.H. Pollock, editors.
NIMH 1980

Between the Oedipus Complex and Adolescence: The "Quiet" Time

Edith Buxbaum, Ph.D.

Freud's Concept of Latency

The period between the seventh and tenth years covers approximately what Freud called the period of sexual latency, a term which he "once again" borrowed from his friend Wilhelm Fliess (1905, p. 178). In the *Three Essays* Freud discussed for the first time the existence and importance of infantile sexuality and "the period of sexual latency in childhood and its interruptions," that is, the manifestations of sexuality in a supposedly asexual period, and how only in adolescence sexuality continues uninterrupted into adulthood.

In 1920 (1905, p. 177) Freud writes in an addendum: "Those authorities who regard the interstitial portion of the sex gland as the organ that determines sex have on their side been led by anatomical researches to speak of infantile sexuality and a period of sexual latency." This was important confirmation for Freud, who always strove to find a physiological basis for his ideas. But he added cautiously: "Since a period of latency in the psychological sense does not occur in animals, it would be very interesting to know whether the anatomical findings which have led these writers to assume the occurrence of two peaks in sexual developments are also demonstrable in the higher animals." He describes how during the period of latency feelings of disgust and shame, aesthetic and moral ideals are developed which seem to be a product of

121

education, yet in reality are fixed by heredity. The period of latency "appears to be one of the necessary conditions of the aptitude of men for developing a higher civilization" (1905, p. 234). "It would seem that the origin of this peculiarity of man must be looked for in the prehistory of the human species." Following Ferenczi's ideas (1913), he ventures to say (1923, p. 35), "According to one psychoanalytic hypothesis the . . . diphasic onset of man's sexual life . . . is a heritage of the cultural development necessitated by the glacial epoch." Ferenczi in a paper, "Developmental Phases of the Sense of Reality" (1913), says, "May it be permitted to be so daring as to suggest that the geological changes of the surface of the earth with their catastrophic consequences forced the predecessors of mankind to the repression of their fondest habits and forced them to 'development.' " He continued: "Let us not shy away from the last analogy to connect the great phase of repression of the individual, the latency period, with the greatest catastrophe that struck our forebears, i.e., with the misery of the glacial periods, which we still repeat in our individual lives." Freud liked this idea which fit with his biological concepts, that ontogeny is a repetition of phylogeny, that certain characteristics and habits of the individual are precipitates of the experiences of the species in the past, according to Darwin. However tentatively Freud and Ferenczi proposed these ideas, their idea of the importance of latency as a period of hominization in the past, as acculturation and civilization in the present, still stands. Education itself, which was somewhat deemphasized by Freud, keeps its place in this scheme, facilitating adaptation to culture and thereby taking the place of necessity "that forced our predecessors to give up and change their ways of life."

Educators found by experience that the age of 6 years plus or minus 1 is in fact the time when children can be taught because their abilities to concentrate, to think abstractly, and to reason have greatly increased in comparison to the preceding years. Anna Freud quotes S. Freud's explanation of this development as the "biologically determined lessening of drive activity" (Anna Freud, *Normality and Pathology in Childhood*). He says *(Three Essays)* "Insofar as educators pay any attention at all to infantile sexuality, they behave exactly as though they shared our views as to the construction of the moral defensive forces at the cost of sexuality as though they knew that sexual activity makes a child ineducable; for they stigmatize every sexual manifestation by children as a vice!"

Maturation and Ego Development

In their paper, "Latency Revisited," Shapiro and Perry (1976) bring together research in the areas of brain development, behavior, and maturation, which seem to converge around the age of 7 years. Rapid integrative growth of auditory-visual functioning coincides with maturing temporo-spatial orientation around the same age. Cognitive development is found to be involved in the development of moral thinking and socialization. Shapiro and Perry argue "that processes within the central nervous system and cognitive strategies derived from maturation may provide latency with its biological clock. . . . The greater stability and invariance of mental process and the new cognitive structure at seven also permit the inhibition and control of drives and the postponement of action. . . . These confluences in development are not fortuitous but are part of the design feature of the human organism and this design feature permits higher level organization and, therefore, latency." This paper supplies the physiological basis for the development of ego functions in the latency period, whereas Freud looked upon the same period from the point of view of drive development. Hartmann says: "[The] consideration of maturational processes also on the side of ego development seems natural enough if we keep in mind that the ego aspect of development is no less biological than its id aspect" (1952, p. 19). He adds the remark that "it is particularly the study of the ego-functions which might facilitate a meeting between psychoanalytic and the physiological, especially the brain-physiological approach. . . . As to the physiological aspect of the problem, Freud always maintained that in some future time physiological data and concepts would be substituted for the psychological ones, referring to all mental functions and not only to those of the id." Shapiro and Perry make us aware that the future time is now by compiling the physiological and brain-physiological data for the development of ego functions. The symposium on the Mutual Influences in Development of Ego and Id (1952) pointed out that factors in the nonconflictual sphere codetermine the ways of conflict solution and are in turn influenced by the latter. In the case of the decline of the Oedipus complex the consolidated ego functions may facilitate the inhibition and control of drives, whereas the biologically diminished drive may allow the consolidation of ego functions. It is not a question of priority, but a question of mutual influences.

The Decline of the Oedipus Complex

It is the consensus of educators, researchers in the natural sciences, and psychoanalysts that the period between 6±1 and 10±1 years is of great importance for the development of the child into a member of his society. We might say that the period before this time ideally allows the child to develop his body and his functions to the point of independence from the mother. His libidinal drives as well as his aggression are still dependent on the guidance by another person. He needs somebody to be his supplementary superego; somebody has to tell him what is right and wrong, or he may forget it when that person is not around.

The mother satisfies all the needs of the young child and is his first love object. He wants her all to himself. The mother is for a long time not seen as a separate person from himself; he learns to recognize their separateness only gradually. The world interferes in this unity, while it also reveals itself to him at the same time. He turns his affection to other people in addition to the mother. In the schematic model we see the dyad between mother and child disturbed but also enlarged into a triad which includes the father. The child cannot have his mother all to himself any more but ideally has gained another love object. This first restriction of the baby's all-consuming desires forces his first important adaptation to the world at large, because it demands of him the recognition of a person outside of his unity with the mother. His sexual feelings are directed toward her as all his other needs are. But while she has satisfied all his previous demands to a great extent, his genital needs are not accepted and not gratified. He is excluded from sleeping with her, while the third person in the triangle can do so. This frustration heightens his desire for her and arouses his aggression against the rival. He would want to eliminate him if he would not risk losing him this way.

The Role of Narcissism and Object-Loss

His aggression against the father, wanting to kill him and to take his penis away, flounders at his fear of retaliation—really his fear of talion—i.e., he fears what he wants to do to the other one will be done to him; and since the other is stronger, he capitulates. This conflict between his love and hate for the father but also his instinct for self-preservation is the bulwark which forces him to relinquish his wishes for the mother; he solves his rivalry with the father by identifying with him. This is one model for the decline of the Oedipal complex.

It is different for the girl child. Things are essentially the same for her as for the boy, until she becomes aware of her father. She too wants the mother all to herself, wants to sleep with her, and sees the father as her rival. Her aggressive wishes against him are not as strong as those of the boy because her loving feelings are stronger, fortified by the sexual attraction she feels toward the father. Her jealousy turns her against the mother. However, her dependency and love for her curb her aggression. Her feelings toward both parents are ambivalent but less threatening than those of the boy. Under normal circumstances her feelings toward both parents continue; she has no penis to lose but is concerned to lose their love. The decline of the female counterpart of the Oedipus complex, the Electra complex, is not as violent as that of the boy. Despite the decline, the mother remains the prime love object for the boy and the girl; the girl's love for the father remains intact, while the boy identifies with his rival. The passions are calmed down. The decline of the Oedipus complex is crucial for the development of drive control.

Sexual Feeling

Yet sexual feelings continue; the children masturbate but are more discreet about it. They do not express their sexual wishes as blatantly as before; they keep them to themselves in their fantasies. Sexual play between children is to some extent exploratory and experimental; their attempts at intercourse are unsatisfactory because of their immaturity. They usually do not spend an excessive amount of interest and time with these activities. If they do to the exclusion of other play and interests, it is usually the reaction to being exposed to a great deal of sexual stimulation either by witnessing nudity and sexual relations between adults or having been seduced by a person who is older and sexually mature. Such experiences are traumatic to the child, who feels overwhelmed by the other person as well as by his own feelings. The children may react by repeating the traumatic experience to which they were passively exposed in an active way, either with other children or by themselves in excessive masturbatory activities. Or the children may also react by total repression of all sexual feelings. Fraiberg (1972) has discussed this outcome and connects it in girls with the frigidity in adult women.

Aggression

Aggression in the latency period comes from different sources as it does in other phases of development. In every phase of development the child uses its phase-specific tools in libidinal, functional, and aggressive ways. The baby, who learns to put something in his mouth and develops this important function, practices the function, enjoys it, and uses it aggressively; the modes of the activity will be determined to a high degree by the handling and reaction of the caretaking person to the child. An observation comes to mind: A boy baby of about 12 to 13 months, sitting on his mother's lap next to a curtained window, pulled the curtain because it was there to be pulled; the mother disagreed and said "no." The child did it again; the mother slapped his hand. He persisted, and so did she. The interaction became a battle of wills which the child lost with crying and tears. Pulling the curtain, which had started as a joyful activity, became an aggressive one in response to the mother's aggression. Part of the aggressive feelings in the latency period are displaced sexual feelings. The children's fantasies are full of aggressions; they fantasy that they are stronger and smarter than anybody, that they will conquer the world. They have changed their aggression to some extent from the oedipal rival to other objects. They act out these rivalries in their more or less serious fighting with other children, in their competitive strivings in learning situations, and to a high degree in organized games. In learning and organization, in making rules and regulations for themselves, both libido and aggression are sublimated. Running, jumping, and climbing are necessary activities for healthy children. When they are restrained for a while, as happens in varying degrees, e.g., in the schools, they practically burst out in recess or when school is out. They run, yell, throw balls, jackets, or stones, and roughhouse with each other. While the children at a younger age are acting out these needs more or less at random, after age 6 or 7 the children have a tendency to organize in groups and play games.

Kaplan, in a paper read at a Panel on Female Sexuality, pointed out that girls have a proclivity for rhythmic movement which she sees biologically and hormonally determined. Girls' liking for horseback riding is partly related to this; besides, they are satisfying their tomboyish and masturbatory needs. Rhythmic games like jumprope and jacks, with accompanying jingles and songs, are played by girls in all countries. These rhythms and verses give the aggression form and organization; the organized games of boys from Indian and cowboys, war games, to baseball and football serve the same purpose. Aggression is expressed but organized and restricted by rules and regulations.

Superego Development

The ability to formulate rules and to follow them, even if they should result in one's own defeat in a game, is not easy to come by. The children go through different phases: They make the rules, but they also change them and break them, while they do not allow others to do so. Sometimes they are quite strict with others in observing rules in games or behavior, but not with themselves. Tattletaling is one of the side effects of this struggle, because it is a struggle with themselves about obeying rules, only at the time being it is projected on to others. Eventually they accept the rules for themselves as well, except when they cheat. There is a difference between breaking rules and cheating. The one who breaks the rule feels in his right and does it openly—like certain delinquents or psychopaths who act as if they had the right to make their own rules. When the child cheats, he does so secretly, knowing that he does something wrong. By accepting rules for himself, the child shows that he has arrived at certain concepts of right and wrong, that he is in control of his aggression, and that he has developed a superego. "Play is to the child what thinking, planning and blueprinting are to the adult, a trial universe in which conditions are simplified and methods exploratory, so that past failures can be thought through, expectations tested" (Erikson 1973).

Sarnoff (1976, p. 115) names the cognitive skills which mature and develop during the years 7½ to 8½ that produce the shift to late latency:

1. Concrete operational thinking: This is a term used by Piaget to describe cognitive improvement in reality testing.
2. Abstract conceptual memory organization: This is a skill which relates to the ability to recall on an abstract rather than a rote level.
3. Reorganization of superego contents in the direction of the child's own motives and away from motivational contents derived from parental demands: The latency child who renounces his openly sexual demands and his open aggression toward his parents is more reality oriented. He has lost his belief in his omnipotence.

The Decline of the Oedipus Complex as an Organizing Agent

Children who grow up with a single parent and whose sexual drives remain relatively unrestricted may be retarded in their development of morality and socialization; their ability to sublimate and to concentrate may be poor. The case of a girl of 9 years may illustrate. Mary grew up with her mother without a permanent man in the house. She stole, had no friends, and was a bed-wetter. Frequently she went to bed with her mother, wetted, and then returned to her own bed. She fantasied when urinating, that she was her mother's lover who ejaculated, but also that she was her mother's baby. She was intelligent but behind in her schoolwork because she didn't pay attention and didn't do her homework. At some point in her treatment she decided that she wanted to become a good student, that she wanted to do her homework, but that she needed her mother's help. She practically forced her mother to help, keeping her and herself up at all hours of the night and incidentally out of bed. She achieved what she wanted in school, stopped stealing, and stopped wetting. In chronological order her ego functions developed before she achieved instinct control. She structured it so that her mother helped her to accomplish age-appropriate tasks; she had to help her to replace instinctual-regressive satisfactions with age-appropriate achievements.

An experience to the contrary happened in a classroom of 6-year-old children. These children had a great time playing in their dollhouse where they acted out all their fantasies including mutual explorations. The teacher complained that they were not learning the three Rs because they were not interested. When the time for playing was restricted and their attention and work demanded before they were allowed to play, the result was immediate. They learned, and the intensity of their dollhouse play diminished. After a short time they were not even interested in it any more. Too much drive discharge and gratification prevented or made it unnecessary to sublimate, although the children had the ability to do so and had matured to that point.

Reality-Oriented Fantasies

The reduction of instinctual demands and the maturing of ego functions seem to happen nearly at the same time. The child finds abilities in himself which give him satisfactions in reality and make it easier to renounce the incomplete satisfactions of his immature sexuality. The id forces, diverted from the sexual struggle, supply the ego functions with energy, while the superego, expressed in moral thinking and socialization, regulates the id discharges and the aggression. The decline of the Oedipus complex acts as an organizing agent around which a number of changes occur. The integrative growth in auditory-visual functioning enhances memory and conceptualization. The heard and remembered word becomes internalized as part of the inner voice, that is, the voice of the superego; the superego however is the precipitate of the Oedipus complex. The child changes from acting out his oedipal wishes to fantasizing. His increased ability to think logically make his fantasies less magic and more reality oriented. Instead of fighting monsters, he fights burglars in his fantasies; instead of moving his magic wand, he fantasies flying an airplane. Then again, it might be interesting to build an airplane instead of only imagining one in fantasy, and fantasy is being changed into activity. Concrete operational think-ing is at his disposal. The fantasies may become continued daydreams which are changed many times, yet less fleeting and more complex than the short ones of earlier times. Sometimes they are written up or drawn in pictures. The sublimation which was already present in the first change from acting to fantasizing becomes more strongly developed and requires the learning of certain skills. The ability of the child to recognize spatial relations enables him to construct, build, and draw. A similar development takes place in girls. Their doll play and playing house provide many opportunities to implement their fantasied, dramatic role play with making things, from making dolls and their dresses, to cleaning, cooking, making furniture, and building houses. Their mothers, who may or may not work outside the house or may be homemakers and breadwinners, influence the roles which they take in their play and eventually in their planning for the future. For fantasies may become day-dreams of the future and the beginning of planning. The ability to think and distinguish past, present, and future is due to the child's newly developed sense of time, his remembering, conceptualizing, and distinguishing past experiences from fantasy.

The Sense of Self- and Object Constancy

The continuity of his fantasies is parallel with his sense of self; he is today what he was yesterday and what he will be tomorrow. He is not as much under the sway of his changing identifications; when he gets into a different environ-ment, he is not as confused as he used to be: He can more or less maintain his ego functions—he can speak, eat, sleep, and use the toilet in most environ-ments. He can tolerate separations from his parents more easily than before. Partly because he can function by himself, he remembers longer, feels less insecure in the absence of the parent, less angry at being left, less anxious because his death wishes against the parent are weakened and so he feels less vulnerable. However, his security and self-assuredness do not last indefinitely. There comes a time when he cannot stand the strain of being alone, on his own without his parents.

Two Novels

There are two novels where the main figures are latency children; through some accident they become separated from their parents without knowing when, or if ever, they would be reunited with them. One is *High Wind in Jamaica* by R. Hughes; the other is *Lord of the Flies* by W. Golding. In both novels the authors sensitively describe the anxiety of the children, who feel unprotected against the unpredictable and possibly dangerous external situation and the precariously civilized self within themselves, and how they defend against it with denial and bravado. In the course of these struggles they regress to their more primitive selves and their superego dissolves; they become the murderers they had been afraid of and fantasied about. As unexpectedly as they were removed from their civilization in these novels, they are returned to it, and with it they return to their civilized selves. The memory of the time they experienced in that other world fades into a dream. However, they are left vulnerable for the future: Some of the children are afraid that it could happen again, and others remain susceptible to breaking the law should the occasion present itself. Both authors caught the essence of the latency child, who stands on the brink of becoming a responsible member of his society or falling back partly or entirely into the lawless self-indulgence of the prelatency child. In both books the catastrophes of the outside world could be interpreted as symbolic representations of the inner storms of the children. However, we are reminded of the effects of wars and revolutions, which are manmade catastrophes, upon adults and children. The horrors of My-Lai were perpetrated by people whose conscience had been put out of function by legalized acts of destruction ordered by their superiors. A. Freud and Burlingham (1943) described how the children in London enjoyed using the bomb craters of the Blitz in their games, adding their own destruction and making it their own.

The cataclysms in these stories are real and symbolic and act as catalysts to unleash the only tenuously tamed jungle instincts of the children. Being children of latency age, they have only just started to have a conscience of their own, independent of their parents; it is still not well enough established, is as weak as they are themselves in the face of threats and bribes; they are still in need of the presence of their ideals in order to identify with them. The plight of the children in these novels is similar to children who are left on their own through any circumstances—death, illness of a parent, marital discord, psychiatric illness, or natural catastrophes like floods and airplane crashes. Delinquent behavior, stealing, breaking into houses, destructiveness, and overt sexual behavior happen frequently in the wake of these happenings, indicative of the breakdown of the only recently established superego. The children's anger and disappointment in their parents play an important part. They blame them for having left them, regardless of the reason. The parents failed them by not being omnipotent; or if they are omnipotent, the children blame them for wanting to destroy them. They see their parents as evil and become so themselves. They need the image of the ideal parent to follow his example; if that image is destroyed, the ego ideal and the superego may become destroyed with it.

Splitting and Projecting

In the two novels, during the separation from their parents, the children are exposed to evil authority figures, while the parents are left as the representatives of all that is good. The parental images are then split into good and bad. This is a device to which children often resort. It helps them to distance themselves from their parents in order to achieve the independence and autonomy which they need; by splitting the parental image and projecting one part onto another person, they preserve the ideal parent whom they need in order to form themselves in his image. The ideal which they choose to identify with is not necessarily the socially desirable one. Their choice will again depend on the outcome of the oedipal solution and on the superego of the parents. There are parents who are part of a criminal society. Their relations to their children may be nurturing and protective and at the same time so threatening that the children have no choice but to adapt to them for self-preservation. They may see the persecutors of their parents in the people outside their immediate family, become identified with the criminal parents, and become their defenders.

Regressions and Reaction Formations

Bornstein (1951) divides the latency period into two phases. In the first one, which she sets from 5½ to 8, the child's superego is not yet sufficiently consolidated, and the child frequently regresses; his ability to sublimate is easily disturbed. The regressions which take place in this period consist of giving up reaction formations. Cleanliness, orderliness, modesty are reaction formations to the younger child's lack of concern for dirt, disorder, and exhibitionism. In the course of learning how to take care of himself, he identifies with the caretakers' demands and frequently overdoes them in order to fight his own desires to do the contrary. When he gets tired at the end of the day or when he is under stress, he gives up the fight and regresses to being a dirty, disorderly little kid. Usually he recovers again after such letdowns; when he is under too much stress, the regression may become permanent and is then a sign of pathology.

Guilt Feelings and Projections

The second period from 8 to 10 Bornstein characterizes as one when guilt feelings appear but are defended against with projections. The splitting of the parent image into a good and a bad part allows for projection of the child's own forbidden impulses onto the bad parent and spares him feeling guilty. Frequently the child projects his forbidden impulses upon a playmate or a sibling. It is the well-known syndrome of saying he or she did it, not I. Sometimes this is a blatant lie, but at other times the child honestly thinks it is the truth. He attributes his forbidden wishes to the other child and feels himself free of guilt. Sometimes two or three children plan to do something, like stealing or running away. One of them might come to a parent or teacher and tell about the other's plans in order to prevent them and himself from carrying them out. Not only does he split his wishes from himself and project them onto the other child, but he also calls upon the help of the adult to become his supplementary superego because his own superego is not strong enough. He is oscillating between good and bad, between identifying with those representing his id and those representing his superego.

Identification and Its Uses

Identification is an important mechanism that goes on through much of the child's life and serves different functions. By making the parents' demands his own, he identifies with the parents in his superego. By acting like his parents, he identifies with them in his ego. In the oedipal triangle, the child acts like the father in order to be loved by the mother; he acts like the mother in order to be liked by the father. But the child also identifies with those characteristics of the parents of which he is afraid. He tells himself to brush his teeth like father does and told him to do, but he also hits little brother like father hit him. To identify with a parent is also a way to become independent of his presence; if he is like his father himself, he can do without him. The identification allows the child to feel safe when he is away from home, because being identified with the caretaking parent, he can take care of himself. Having achieved control of his body and his body functions, his ties to his parents are loosened, and he is free to some degree to enter into new relationships. The child is ready to learn, due to his matured skills.

Acculturation and Self-Esteem

Most cultures offer their children instructions in the skills which they consider important at this age, i.e., beginning at 6 ± 1. They are initiated into their society. In some cultures there are schools; in others the boys are taken from their mothers and live with the men and learn their ways, while the girls help their mothers and take care of the younger children. But for all the children it is a time to learn the ways of adults, to take on duties and responsibilities. Failing to do so, they feel inferior to their peers and compensate with antisocial acting out or withdrawal. The child defines himself in doing things; he is what he does and what he can do. He "shows and tells" what he has achieved, his picture, his story, the stones he has collected, or how high he can jump. He needs the parents' and teachers' approval and disapproval, but peer judgment becomes increasingly more important. Both are necessary for him to be proud of what he can do and what he has achieved. His self-esteem which has suffered in the defeat of the oedipal crisis needs to be restored. The child who did not go through this crisis, who did not give up his incestuous strivings, to some extent does not accept anybody's judgment for what he does, but his own judgment of his achievements is unrealistic. He thinks he can do anything; he thinks of himself as omnipotent. He does not learn because in his fantasy he already knows and can do, even if in reality he fails. His fantasies of being an adult are sometimes reinforced by the parent who participates in them, while in reality he does not learn what is necessary for him to become an adult.

A 6-year-old boy who was of normal intelligence did not learn in school. He talked and acted like an adult; he pretended to know more than the other children, but they found out that he didn't and made fun of him. His father had been a pilot and was killed in the war. The mother said in an interview that, when the father died, she told her boy, who was 5 years old, that he would have to take the father's place and be the man of the house. She let him sit at the head of the table and push her chair in when she was sitting down. He was her companion when she went out to restaurants or shows. But she also complained that he misbehaved and was not like a gentleman when she had a man visitor or when she went out with a man. Obviously, the little boy was confused by her demands to behave like a man in some situations and in others to behave like the child he was. However, to be his age deprived him of his privileged position and his mother; he was then left without either parent. He could not admit his helplessness. In school he had to pretend to know and to be able to do, as he had to pretend to be adult with his mother. To learn to read and write like the other children meant to admit that he didn't know, that he was not an adult, that he could not in reality take the father's place with the mother. Normally children at this age develop friendships and enter peer groups; these children do not. They remain outsiders and feel excluded.

The ability to learn and to do things for himself leads to self-esteem and to increased autonomy. If a child achieved autonomy in his body functions in early childhood, he is now learning to use his brain, his hands, and body for doing things. Visual-motoral and auditory-visual integration and temporal-spatial orientation have matured around the age of 7 (Shapiro and Perry 1976). He can concentrate and be attentive for longer periods. He can plan to do things which will not be finished the same day. He can set a timetable for himself so he will know what he will do first and what next. He wants to decide on his own what he will do, when, and how. The 6- or 7-year-old may be able to plan two or three things to do in sequence. When it gets to be more, he will get confused and forget. As he gets older, he is able to plan for longer periods, but characteristically he wants to do things on his own and wants to decide on his own. He resents parents' and teachers' helpful interference. He wants to make his own mistakes and correct them, wants to decide for himself. As his superego gets stronger, he becomes more reliable; he can perform certain tasks and take on obligations. He is pleased with himself that he can do so, but he is also sensitive and angry when he is interfered with. When he plans to take out the garbage and the parent reminds him to take it out, he becomes angry and may not do it. This is comparable to a young child who wants to do it himself and gets angry at mother who helps him when he wants to do it alone. In both cases, the parent interferes in a developing ego function. The prelatency child is in the process of mastering a function. The parent interferes in his blossoming autonomy, holding him back in dependence when he struggles for independence. He reacts with anger because his development in being able to live separately from the parent is threatened. The latency child is in the process of becoming his own master, to internalize certain demands, to develop an autonomous superego. He feels interfered with in this learning process by the parents' reminders. It is a difficult task for the educator to steer a course between allowing too much autonomy where the child does not have the tools to do something and letting him make his decisions and plans when he is able to do so. Robert Hall Smith caught the flavor of the stubborn 6-year-old perfectly in the title of his book: *"Where Did You Go?"—"Out."—"What Did You Do?"—"Nothing"* (1958). It is part of this striving for autonomy to have and keep secrets; of course, at times it is to avoid confrontation and punishment, but to have secrets by oneself or with peers, to form secret clubs, is part of growing up.

The Group

The peer group becomes increasingly more important for the child. He feels alone and unhappy if he doesn't have friends. The group serves a number of functions for the latency child. The school group which is the choice of the parents and licensed, i.e., sanctioned by the State, is supposed to introduce the child into the knowledge and mores of his society. The knowledge which he is taught is censored, i.e., it is selected by the educators who decide what he should or should not learn. The child is being indoctrinated. That word is usually reserved for those regimes who are teaching the children an ideology which may or may not be in agreement with that of the parents. If it is different from that of the parents, it may bring the children into conflict with teachers or parents. Yet teaching with the system or against the system has in common that in either case it is an authority figure who superimposes his ideas upon the child. However, the child uses the group in ways which do not serve that purpose alone. By joining or making a children's group within the school group or outside of it, he gets into a group which has a life of its own, unsupervised or directed by adults. In such a subgroup he may recreate the world as he sees it: play house, or school, or church—but also form a gang, roam the streets, break into houses, and terrorize younger children. In either case, the children devise their own rules and organizations, decide what is or is not permissible within their group. It is the subgroup which allows the child to think differently from his parents; the subgroup's judgment may supercede the parents' judgment and strengthen his own. Depending on his own strength or weakness, he may go from being dependent on his parents to being dependent on the group or making himself independent from both if he feels secure enough to do so. The authority-directed group will help the child to move away from the parents by accepting other than the parents' authority; the subgroup may help in the transition from dependency to independence. Through the group the children may learn from others what the parents cannot teach them—and eventually surpass them. The latency child is exquisitely malleable, and it is to a certain degree in the power of the educator to adapt him to society in one way or the other. Bernfeld, making Macchiavelli his spokesman, calls the educator the servant of society (Bernfeld 1925). The Russians call their dissidents mentally disturbed and force them to undergo psychiatric treatment. When Sarnoff (1976) says, "The healthier the structure of latency the more closely does the content (of fantasies) hew to the patterns of culture," he agrees with the Russians by calling the well-adapted child healthy and, by inference, the child who is less adapted, sick. In this way the psychiatrist joins the educator who considers it his task to adapt the child to the society as it is. The latency child has a wealth of fantasy and is creative with all kinds of material in arts, crafts, writings, and dramatic play. Most frequently these creative abilities disappear in the latter part of the latency period or in early adolescence. Logical thinking and verbal communication take their place.

The Outsider

However, there are some talented children who continue to be creative later on as well. They may not be as well adjusted as the others and have difficulties with both peers and teachers. Yet they produce something which may eventually bring them recognition. Such a child was a boy who lived in a world of his own in fantasies which he continued and represented in innumerable drawings. He fantasied how he would free his mother who was locked up in a dungeon. It was true that she was hospitalized off and on. He also fantasied and drew complicated machines, played and worked with electronics. His relationships with children were nonexistent. He only waited to visit his mother when she was well enough to see him either in the hospital or at home. He was attached to his therapist who helped him to disentangle himself from the frightening identification with his mother. The father was a mad scientist who had committed suicide when the boy was 2½ years old. The boy was drawn to identify with the father but afraid that he might go mad and kill himself, too. The therapist helped him to follow the father in what was viable and to stay away from his self-destructiveness. Identification with the therapist was one of the ways to achieve this. He eventually went to college to study physics and mathematics. The child had therapy and was able to use it. He never really adjusted to the children's group in which he grew up, but he gained their respect with his skill in electronics by which he could make things work. He was able to continue to be creative because he had a talent; but he also learned to accept his position of being an outsider without becoming paranoid like his mother or suicidal like his father. He developed the ego strength to live in society as an outsider.

The child may become well adapted to society but at the cost of his creativity. Maybe this is one of the reasons for so many interesting, creative children and so few interesting, creative adults. Also we may be aware that people who remain creative as adults are rarely well-adjusted people. Margaret Mead (1970) talks about the allowance for the occurrence of genius that is necessary for new cultural forms to be created "by a vision—or a dream." The outsider may have a talent, even if he is short of being a genius. Nonconformity is not necessarily maladaptive or sick. Psychoanalytic psychology is developmental psychology. The people who are working within this theory feel committed to allow and promote the child to develop his faculties and to allow him to establish his way of dealing with himself and the world and with himself in the world. This will be his character which will determine his development in adolescence, which in turn will determine his adult person. However, we have to recognize that our theory is shot through with value judgments which are the values of our society by which we decide what faculties we promote and which ones we suppress. By calling somebody healthy, unhealthy, normal, or abnormal, we are giving good and evil other names.

Summary

The latency period is a time of great importance in the child's life. It is a period of relative quietude between the anxiety-ridden, early childhood and the stormy adolescence. When the task of being physically independent from a caretaking person is sufficiently accomplished, when separateness is comfortably established and maturation has occurred as far as it will go, the child is ready to acquire what he can of the knowledge of his society and to adapt to its mores. He is being less forced into the mold than he was at an earlier age when he was entirely dependent on the parent and when he had to submit passively to what was being done to him. Although still dependent in many ways, he has more choice of action. He adapts to the demands made upon him by making compromises between his inner and outer world. But the balance between the two will be relative to their respective strength: A child with strong drives will deal differently with outside demands than a child with weak drives; object relations and identifications will help or disturb in establishing the balance. The more self-assured and self-sufficient he is, the better established his superego, the better he will be able to deal with the assault of adolescent drive increase; the more he can do, the better he will be able to deal with reality and to use fantasy in the service of the ego. His ability to learn, to fantasize, and to play is the foundation on which his ability to work creatively as an adult is based. His relations to others determine his future ability to love others and himself.

References

Bernfeld, S. Sisyphos, oder Die Grenzen der Erziehung [Sisyphos, or the limits of education]. Leipzig: *Internationale Psychoanalytische Verlag,* 1925.

Bornstein, B. On latency. *The Psychoanalytic Study of the Child,* 6:279-285, 1951.

Buxbaum, E. *Troubled Children in a Troubled World.* New York: International Universities Press, 1970.

Erikson, E.H. Dimensions as a new identity. In: *The 1973 Jefferson Lectures in the Humanities.* New York: W.W. Norton, 1973.

Ferenczi, S. Developmental phases of the sense of reality (1913). Leipzig: *Internationale Psychoanalytische Verlag,* 1927.

Fraiberg, S. Genital arousal in girls. *The Psychoanalytic Study of the Child,* 27:439-475, 1972.

Freud, A. *Normality and Pathology in Childhood.* New York: International Universities Press, 1965.

Freud, A., and Burlingham, D. *War and Children.* London: Medical War Books, 1943.

Freud, S. Three essays on the theory of sexuality (1905). *Standard Edition.* 7:135-145. London: Hogarth Press, 1953.

——. The ego and the id (1923). *Standard Edition.* 19:12–66. London: Hogarth Press, 1961.

Golding, W. *Lord of the Flies.* New York: Putnam, 1959.

Hartmann, H. The mutual influences in development of ego and id. *The Psychoanalytic Study of the Child,* 7:9-68, 1952.

Hughes, R. *High Wind in Jamaica.* New York: Harper, 1957.

Kaplan, E. Manifestations of aggression in latency and pre-adolescent girls. *The Psychoanalytic Study of the Child,* 31:63-78, 1976.

Mead, M. Culture and commitment. *The American Museum of Natural History, Special Members' Edition,* 1970.

Sarnoff, C. *Latency.* New York: Jason Aronson, 1976.

Shapiro, T., and Perry, R. Latency revisited: The age 7 plus or minus 1. *The Psychoanalytic Study of the Child,* 31:39-106, 1976.

Smith, R.H. *"Where Did You Go?"—"Out."—"What Did You Do?"—"Nothing."* New York: Norton, 1958.

The Course of Life: Psychoanalytic Contributions
Toward Understanding Personality Development.
Vol. II: Latency, Adolescence, and Youth.
S.I. Greenspan and G.H. Pollock, editors.
NIMH 1980

The Eye of the Hurricane:
From Seven to Ten

Ronald M. Benson, M.D., and Saul I. Harrison, M.D.

Idealized or stereotypic images of the golden age of childhood often focus on the typical grade school child who is the subject of this chapter. Notwithstanding inevitable changes over time within this age range, children from 7 to 10 are characterized by their stable educability, pliability, and adaptability to external demands, and by relative calmness (Sarnoff 1976). Although a modification of psychological organization from action in favor of ideation characterizes all child development, this shift is particularly evident in the latency phase of development.

As a discrete developmental phase, latency is well demarcated from the developmental phase that precedes it as well as from the phase which follows it. Descriptively, these children are differentiated from the preschooler in several ways. For example, the latency-aged child's needs and desires seem much less preemptive and undisguised. While the preschooler appears to change physically and psychologically at a rapid pace, the grade school child changes and grows emotionally, cognitively, and physically in a seemingly more slow and steady fashion. Dramatic spurts are rarely obvious in this phase of development.

Similarly, these school-age children are in marked contrast to preadolescents and adolescents. Latency-age children's interests seem much more directed toward mastery of external challenges, and their attention is focused more on acquiring new skills than on their inner lives or on rapidly changing body images in a swiftly altering "self." Characteristically, latency-age children seem relatively uninterested and untroubled by their "inner life." This maturational turn away from internal feelings and undisguised concern with impulses make

137

it easier for learning to be a highly valued activity. Children's knowledge of the world around them increases notably during this time, as attested to by the vast educational, psychological, and anthropological literature devoted to the cognitive development of the child in this phase of life.

During the years 7 to 10, the locus of children's activity shifts from the home as the almost exclusive center of life to the official "dual headquarters" of home and school. In addition, other community-based loci assume expanding importance, e.g., the playing field, church or synagogue, the locale of special activities such as music lessons, the swimming pool or gym, or the place where Cub Scouts, Brownies, or self-generated clubs meet.

By the same token, the important people in the child's life become more diverse. Although parents remain uppermost in importance, it is evident that teachers and friends play an ever increasing role in the child's life and thoughts.

During this period, both boys and girls become "joiners" and begin to belong to organizations such as Cub Scouts, Brownies, Camp Fire Girls, Little League, and so forth. The trend is that each sex seems to avoid and depreciate the other. Sometimes, less formal clubs and cliques are formed. Again, these are generally unisexual. Elaborate rules are quite frequent, especially in 7- or 8-year-olds.

Boys seem to retain friendships more constantly during these years than girls, who seem to form very intense, but relatively short-lasting relationships that appear more fickle.

In school, girls seem to do better than boys as a group during this period, although both sexes may enjoy and like school. Girls probably are more open in their fondness for school and teachers, most of whom are female. The enforced quiet and lack of motor discharge and the "feminine" characteristics of school seem to impose a greater burden on boys than on girls. In addition, girls are superior in language skills.

Some parents welcome these years in their children. Fathers finally can play a sport with their sons. Mothers often characterize this phase as a relief from the unceasing demands of earlier years. Parents who have experienced their children's adolescence often speak longingly of the latency years as a breathing spell for parents in the course of their children's development.

On the other hand, there are parents who regret their children's decreased dependence on them as school and friends become more important. The end of the exclusivity of the parent-child pair may pose a threat for some parents. Particularly those mothers without an outside career may find a troubling void in their lives, requiring a new adaptive response.

Metapsychology

To this eye in the hurricane of development, Freud gave the name "latency" (1905), referring to the seeming quiescence of the libidinal drives following the resolution of the oedipal complex and extending to prepuberty. Freud (1923) pointed out that it is the massive repression and subsequent amnesia for infantile sexuality and the withdrawal of object cathexis from the primary objects and identification with them, as well as internalization of their prohibitions, which begin the latency period. Since this process begins over time, so does the onset of latency occur gradually.

In many ways, the designation "latency" has proved to be an unfortunate choice because it is so often misunderstood and misapplied. To many, it implied that sexual interest come to an abrupt halt, both consciously and, by implication, unconsciously. As a matter of fact, sexual interests persist during latency. Too often manifestations of sexual interest and occasional breakthroughs of direct sexual activity such as masturbation have been inappropriately assessed as pathological. Indications that sexual interest and activity may be in evidence during nonpathological latency does not alter the fact that impulse life is certainly much less directly expressed during latency than in the earlier infantile phases of development preceding it.

Reviewing Freud's views on latency, Sarnoff (1976) notes that at times Freud attributed latency to a primary diminution of the drives, while at other times he supported the theory that latency resulted from an initial increase in defenses damming up the drives secondarily. Controversy regarding these two perspectives has continued in the literature that followed Freud. Both viewpoints have found eloquent adherents as some writers assert that there is a biological change associated with a biphasic sexual drive resulting in diminished drive pressure accounting for the principal manifest features of the latency period. Other observers maintain that it is the maturation and development of ego functioning and coping mechanisms that facilitate a more sophisticated range of adaptations permitting less direct expression of the drives which nevertheless are basically undiminished in strength.

Notable among those pointing to a decrease of drive pressure in the postoedipal period as primary have been Bornstein (1951) and Anna Freud (1965). Drawing upon data from disciplines outside psychoanalysis, Shapiro and Perry (1976) assert that there is indeed a significant discontinuity in development occurring in the vicinity of the seventh year of life. They assume that since this is demonstrably cross-cultural, it must be biologically determined. But they argue that it is not the libidinal drive demonstrating the long-assumed classical sequence of pre-oedipal growth, succeeded by dimunition of the drive, to be followed by a new upsurge in adolescence, that is "the significant substratum" on which latency is based. Instead, they cite exhaustive neurobiological and cognitive data pointing to "processes within the CNS and cognitive strategies derived from maturation . . . provide latency with its biological clock." In other words, expressed metapsychologically, they attribute latency to maturation and development of the ego with increasing structuralization.

Sarnoff (1976) also takes issue with the primary drive reduction as the core concept of latency. Employing rich clinical observations, he demonstrates convincingly that drive pressure continues unabated during the middle-grade school years.

Regardless of whether it is attributed primarily to drive reduction or increased coping mechanisms as most fundamental in latency, there is unanimity that the relative balance between id and ego is shifted to the latter during latency.

In a comprehensive review of the psychoanalytic literature on latency, Fries (1958) noted that in addition to Freud's focus on repression, other authors pointed to additional defenses common in latency, e.g., temporary regressions to pregenitality, reaction formation, and sublimation. Sarnoff (1976, p. 31) schematically summarized the characteristic mechanisms of defense that contribute to the maintenance of latency. As forbidden genital impulses threaten to become conscious and manifest, the child regresses to an anal, sadistic drive organization. Repression is increased, and a turn toward reality and away from inner life takes place. To then deal with the anality to which he has regressed, the defenses of sublimation, doing and undoing, reaction formation and repression tend to be used. Once the latency state has been achieved, breakthroughs of anal, genital, and oedipal conflicts tend to be dealt with via repression, fragmentation, displacement, symbol formation, synthesis, and secondary elaboration in fantasy formation. Sarnoff refers to this third group of defenses and maneuvers as the structure of latency.

Thus, while the preschool child prefers to gratify impulses directly with primary objects, and adolescents by preference are moving toward heterosexual and nonincestuous objects to satisfy their sexual and competitive needs with actual objects in the real world, neither of these solutions is open to the latency child. These unavailabilities stem from both internal and cultural prohibitions as well as the child's immaturity. Yet, the most compelling evidence suggests persistence of considerable drive pressure demanding adaptive management from the latency child. In latency, the preferred and normative means of discharge, albeit partial, is through fantasy.

Two phases of latency generally are recognized (Alpert 1941; Bornstein 1951; Sarnoff 1976), with 8 years old considered to be the prototypical line between them. Early latency is characterized by the child being preoccupied with himself. The superego is very strict. Fantasies, often of amorphous monsters, serve simultaneously as both the means of defense and partial discharge of both genital and pregenital aims. Ambivalence is marked. In later latency, real objects and sublimations are more available and permitted. The early latency child represents the archetypical model whose sexuality is manifestly less visible. As latency continues, however, sexual curiosity becomes more directed. Objects and activities in the external world play a more significant role. As the maturing latency child returns toward objects and away from fantasy as the preferred route of drive discharge, the latency phase is approaching its end, and preadolescence assumes greater importance. Presumably, this stems from a combination of the maturation of ego functions and the biologically derived increase of drive pressure associated with puberty.

The ego during normal latency is developing, establishing strong defenses, increasing the strength of secondary processes, acting more and more in accord with the reality principle, and establishing positive object relations (Fries 1958).

In most areas of functioning, the self-representation of a latency child is quite well demarcated from the object representation. An age-appropriate exception to this involves those developmental lines in which the latency child still experiences the parents' capacities as his own and vice versa. For example, latency children usually act as if they had little responsibility for their own health maintenance and hygiene, fully expecting this area of their lives to be properly managed by their parents. Anna Freud (1965, p. 77) points to this as a residue of the original symbiosis between mother and child.

In contrast to the situation prevailing in the preschooler, self–esteem regulation and self–regard in the latency child are based to a far greater degree on real accomplishments in relation to internalized standards and goals (Benson 1974). Doing well in school, at games, and in other social situations enhances self-esteem. The fact that the standard accomplishment is becoming less dependent on external authorities and more on the child's own internalized standards and values represents, in structural terms, the child's self-esteem regulation depending increasingly on his performance being consonant with his ego ideal and superego.

The typical latency-age child has progressed a long way in relinquishing infantile omnipotence and grandiosity. Nevertheless, on occasion, he will boastfully overestimate his own capabilities. Often, this has a much more defensive quality than was formerly the case. Now, the youngster remains relatively aware that he is small, limited in capacity, and in need of help from parents and teachers.

The infantile idealization of parents diminishes manifestly during latency, although the infantile parental images remain the unconscious objects of the drives. Latency children will idealize their teachers, sports heroes, and TV stars. From the point of view of self-esteem maintenance, identification with these representatives serves as attempts to regain some of the infantile omnipotence that has been otherwise relinquished. In addition, these objects of idealization are more distant than the parents; that absence of physical availability makes them more suitable and less threatening for partial discharge of libidinal and aggressive drives in disguised derivative form.

Typically, the latency child develops a particular kind of fantasy to aid in this process of continuing separation from the early narcissistic involvement with the primary parental objects. Simultaneously, these fantasies deal with conflicts and guilt stemming from the fact that the parents continue to serve unconsciously as objects of the drives—particularly oedipal wishes. This fantasy, which has been designated the family romance, is characterized by two central themes (Moore and Fine 1968). In the first theme the child typically imagines himself as not really the biological offspring of his parents but as adopted by them. He fantasies that he is descended, instead, from exalted, often noble parentage. The second theme entails the child imagining himself as accomplishing a dramatic rescue of someone important. Both the narcissistic aggrandizement and relief from unacceptable oedipal wishes are quite transparent in such fantasies. The specific variations on these themes elaborated by a particular child are revealing clues to the details of that child's state of development and conflict. Therefore, these fantasies are not only useful developmentally for the child, but have much potential diagnostic significance for a clinician's understanding and can be helpful in psychotherapeutic work with a child as well.

Despite the use of fantasy and all the channels for sublimation and other defensive maneuvers noted above, direct breakthroughs of impulse do occur, even in latency children with adequate ego development and who are sufficiently gratified by a good enough environment. Usually, this takes the form of direct or masked masturbation or temper outbursts. Though typical, such behavior tends to be quite guilt provoking for latency aged children and often leads to punishment-seeking activity. This conflict over the direct emergence of impulse in relatively undisguised forms such as masturbation has been termed the central conflict of this phase of development.

As noted above, the characteristic manifestations of the latency phase depend on an optimal balance between drive pressure and ego development. Further, the typical resolution of the pregenital and oedipal phases should have occurred, entailing identifications and introjections contributing to consolidation and structuralization of superego functioning. But in addition to these vital developmental strides derived from the vicissitudes of the drives, the resolution of conflict, and from object relations, the maturation of autonomous ego functions is a necessary precondition for the characteristic state of latency to develop. In Piaget's formulation (Piaget and Inhelder 1969), the child must pass from preoperational (prelogical) thought to the kind of cognitive processes characterized as concrete operational thought. The attainment of a certain degree of rationality and conceptual constancy is integral to latency. The child's knowledge, perception, and memory all increase dramatically to usher in this phase of development and to maintain it, and they continue to expand throughout this period. The world of objects (in the Piagetian sense) around the child becomes stable and orderly. Physical quantities, such as volume and weight, become constant, despite changes in size or shape. The capacity for symbol formation and the attendant advances in development of language function are also important. Failure in the appropriate development of these cognitive capacities will handicap the child's efforts to deal with impulses in ways other than direct gratification with the primary objects.

If ego development has not proceeded adequately up to the latency period of development and/or does not continue to progress in the latency period itself, the typical pathological result is a habit or impulse disorder. However, the psychopathology par excellence of latency is the learning difficulty in which the capacity of the child to sublimate is interfered with, either secondarily through conflict, or primarily through the failure of the development of the requisite ego functions. The latter can stem from either endowment, internalized conflict, or environmental interference.

Treatment of the latency child depends, as it does with all other age groups, on determining the appropriate interventions based upon a diagnostic understanding of the youngster and his difficulty. Therefore, in some cases, ego-building skills must be taught through an educative approach. In others, intervening in the child's environment with special programs or parental guidance might be most helpful. Although the numbers of children for whom medication is indicated are controversial, there is general agreement that for some children psychotropic medications, such as stimulants and occasionally tranquilizers, aid in the organizing of the child's mental functioning, e.g., his capacity to focus attention or the reduction of anxiety. For a large group of children, intervening in a form designed to reduce internal conflicts based on an inadequate resolution of oedipal and earlier neurotic solutions impresses psychoanalytic observers as most helpful. This might be accomplished in individual psychotherapy accompanied by parental guidance, in systems-oriented family therapy, or in group therapy. Child psychoanalysis might be the treatment of choice for well-entrenched, neurotic processes already firmly established by the latency age.

Many of the deviations occurring at this phase of development often are quite pliable to appropriate intervention; however, impairments of development at this age may lead to severe consequences in later life. For example, obsessional neuroses and childhood schizophrenia may become manifest at this phase of development. In addition, any set of circumstances interfering with the attainment of the state of latency very likely will result, if untreated, in the reduction of subliminatory channels throughout life, resulting in an adult who lacks certain capacities and skills, e.g., intellectual functioning could be interfered with on a permanent basis.

It has long been assumed on the basis of uncontrolled clinical observations that failure in the establishment of the state of latency would render it impossible for preadolescence and adolescence to take their typical form (Blos 1962). This might, in consequence, lead to significant problems in object relations, sexuality, and independent functioning.

References

Alpert, A. The latency period. *American Journal of Orthopsychiatry,* 11:126-144, 1941.

Benson, R. The psychoanalytic assessment. In: Novello, J., ed. *A Practical Handbook of Psychiatry.* Springfield, Ill.: Charles C. Thomas, 1974. pp. 71-86.

Blos, P. *On Adolescence.* New York: Macmillan, 1962.

Bornstein, B. On latency. *The Psychoanalytic Study of the Child,* 6:279-285, 1951.

Freud, A. *Normality and Pathology in Childhood: Assessment of Development.* New York: International Universities Press, 1965.

Freud, S. Three essays on the theory of sexuality (1905). *Standard Edition,* 7:123-234. London: Hogarth Press, 1953.

———. The ego and the id. *Standard Edition,* 19:3–68. London: Hogarth Press, 1961.

Fries, M. Review of the literature on the latency period. *Journal of the Hillside Hospital,* 7:3–16. New York: International Universities Press, 1958.

Moore, B., and Fine, B., eds. *A Glossary of Psychoanalytic Terms and Concepts.* Second Edition. New York: American Psychoanalytic Association, 1968.

Piaget, J., and Inhelder, B. *The Psychology of the Child.* New York: Basic Books, 1969.

Sarnoff, C. *Latency.* New York: Jason Aronson, 1976.

Shapiro, T., and Perry, R. Latency revisited: The age 7 plus or minus 1. *The Psychoanalytic Study of the Child.* 31:79-105, 1976.

The Course of Life: Psychoanalytic Contributions
Toward Understanding Personality Development.
Vol. II: Latency, Adolescence, and Youth.
S.I. Greenspan and G.H. Pollock, editors.
NIMH 1980

The Child Analyst and the Prediction of Psychopathology Based on the Study of Behavior in Young Children

Serge Lebovici, M.D.
(translated by Frances N. Dropkin)

There are many works which define mental disorder as a continual process whose diverse manifestations depend on the social and cultural milieu, the circumstances, and especially the age of the patient. Such is the tendency still expressed by traditional psychiatry.

Nonetheless, since Freud took infantile neurosis as his model to define the transference neurosis, and also to reconstitute it within the psychoanalytic cure of adults (S. Freud 1918, p. 13), we have been able to study the pathological value and the evolutive potential of neurotic symptoms in children. With the Little Hans case, Freud showed that neurotic symptoms could disappear spontaneously, but that it was impossible to know what scars they would leave on vanishing (S. Freud 1909, p. 12).

Since the psychopathological manifestations or the behavior disturbances of the child are of an aleatory nature, we consider that some of them belong to normal developmental relations (A. Freud 1965, p. 8; Lebovici 1968, p. 26) and that still others constitute the precursors of ulterior mental disorders.

As an example, it would be of interest to show briefly that we can venture imagining an ulterior pathology, not yet expressed, based on the study of another child in the same family (in this case a brother). An 8-year-old boy presents sleep and eating disorders. He is perturbed by an intrusive phobic system; among other things he is in the habit of keeping his food in his mouth a very long time. He is part of a family of Portuguese immigrants who live in Paris. His mother complains of being tired by the constant presence of her small daughter, who is with her all the time.

During the session, the boy draws an automobile which falls into a pool. For diverse reasons which are unnecessary to enumerate here, this shows the meaning of his ruminating and that of his phobic inhibition.

When invited to talk with the consultant, the mother has great difficulty in separating herself from her daughter who is constipated because she is afraid of "falling into the hole of the W.C." She evokes her past, her childhood in Portugal, the surveillance which her mother kept over her, the depression she went through when she arrived in Paris (in order to join her future husband) because of "the air pollution." When the mother is told that she does not want to be separated from her daughter, just as her mother had not wanted to be separated from her in order to protect her against sexual impulses, and that her daughter keeps her inside of herself by being constipated, and her son, by keeping his food in his mouth, she accepts leaving her daughter.

She is surprised that her daughter accepts this separation, but she fears an accident. She might fall down the stairs, which is what happened to her son who was pushed by a cousin and fell. She adds that her father brought her up without accidents and that she wants to do as much for her children. Of course, she is evoking here a moral education which preserved her from "falls," that is moral offenses. Finally she refuses all psychotherapeutic approaches and explains her son's difficulties by the existence of mental disorders in two of her father's brothers. The therapeutic space which is proposed to her is thus peopled with seductive men who provoke a fall, like that which menaces her daughter.

It must be mentioned that the hostess in charge of watching what happens in the waiting room had to intervene in order to prevent this little girl from rushing down the emergency stairs, whose use can only be learned from the sign which indicates its existence, in spite of a door which cuts off the exit. In short, the hole—space peopled with a dangerous sexuality—becomes both provocation and danger, both organized by the mother's fantasies. The boy uses holes for fighting against his aggressive sexuality and manifests obviously phobic behavior concerning swallowing. The little girl might fall into the hole. One might imagine that later this hole/space will be represented by the road which separates home from the school and that we are in the presence of a case which might lead to a school phobia.

This example, of metaphoric value, would show that the constipation of a little girl expresses the maternal fantasies. It can also allow us to imagine the organization of a constraining symptom which took another form in her older brother. In this work, I particularly intend to study the conditions for such prediction based on the study of the child's development and one's knowledge of the parents' fantasies. To begin with, it is probably necessary to review the way in which the child psychoanalyst sees the impact of development on the child's mental functioning and its normal and pathological variations.

Psychoanalytic Considerations on the Relationship between Child Development and Psychopathology in Children

We have already mentioned the difficulty encountered in evaluating the appearance and disappearance of neurotic symptoms in children. The presence of phobic symptoms in the nonconsulting population of children in the latency period presents the problem of the utility of the concept of normality (Lebovici and Diatkine 1974, p. 27). We know that these neurotic symptoms do not tend to persist into adulthood. They are of a composite form, and they may be linked to various behavior disorders (Lebovici and Braunschweig 1967, p. 25). Neurotic disorders in adults organize themselves on the basis of ego-syntonic symptoms which often appear in a brutal manner at least on the surface. Through anamnestic study of the childhoods of these subjects, we recognize diverse disturbances: Often we learn that these were turbulent children in which diverse manifestations of anxiety were hidden under the agitation. The specificity of the infantile neurosis can be reconstituted through the psychoanalytic treatment of the adult, without, however, being able to attain, through this work, a precise dating of the event or situation, which had been a potential organizer. The reconstruction or the constructions in psychoanalysis (S. Freud 1937, p. 17) have a very different meaning from recollection and rememorization, as shown by M. Kris (1956, p. 19).

Inversely, certain serious character neuroses of adults seem to constitute the latest phase in childhood disorders which were difficult to classify, but which seem to be part of a psychotic potential. It is for this reason that certain child analysts, belonging to what one may call the Parisian school, have proposed the notion of *pre-psychosis* (Lebovici 1963, p. 23; Chiland and Lebovici 1977, p. 5). It is a question of dysharmonic evolution which is translated by diverse clinical particularities on the behavioral and language level, but in which one does not find neurotic symptoms. Such children express their fantasies in a raw state; and organization of reaction formations and defensive systems is very fragmentary. Their mental functioning remains largely impregnated with primary mechanisms.

We have briefly recalled these considerations (which are frequent for child psychoanalysts who have the occasion to deal with the problem of continuity in the disorders they observe, and especially to question what are the relationships between infantile psychopathology and that of adults) in order to study the limits of the field of neurotic symptoms and the different modes of organization of infantile psychosis with respect to the child's development. Several theoretical trends come into conflict precisely over this matter.

The genetic point of view is amply represented in the Anna Freud school as well as in numerous psychoanalytic schools in the United States. All of Anna Freud's work aims at introducing the child and its environment, his dependency on his family throughout the vicissitudes of his development, into psychoanalytic thought. We read about this particularly in *Normality and Pathology in Childhood* (A. Freud 1965, p. 8). "The real child," who can be observed directly, must be taken into consideration in order to understand his development and his pathology (*The Concept of Developmental Lines,* 1963, p. 7).

Given this point of view, Nagera (1966, p. 33) is justified in differentiating neurotic conflicts and neurotic symptoms described as such only after the post-oedipal period when the psychic agencies, differentiated according to the tripartite structure defined by Freud, are in function. As we know, he distinguishes between reactions and intrusion, defined in other terms as internalization, neurotic conflicts, and actual neurotic symptoms. They suppose the reinvasion of reaction formations by more or less displaced instincts or their substitutes.

Such a description implies a knowledge of the child's development, that is, the interaction between what is linked to his maturation and the environmental intervention. The longitudinal study carried out at Yale first by E. Kris (1950) and then continued after his death by his followers (in particular, M. Kris 1957) showed the utility of understanding those errors in prediction which are particularly linked to the reciprocal interaction between mother and child.

This interaction defines, according to many authors, the developmental lines, thus assuming that a certain number of conditions are fulfilled which constitute, as it were, the prerequisites. For example, Spitz (1965, p. 35) underlines that this development cannot be assured unless:

1. There exists an adequate progression of libidinal cathexes.
2. The maturation of the child's perceptual-motor apparatus allows him to take interest in his environment.
3. His mother invests her libido in him sufficiently for him to obtain reassurance and satisfaction.

One could cite many other authors who have concerned themselves with these basic prerequisites. We will mention only two of them here to show that these prerequisites have been described in different forms by different authors. Mahler, in her numerous works, has studied the separation-individuation process and has shown that the differentiation between object representation and self-representation necessitates a sufficient motility maturation, certain epistemophilic ego functions, and a basic confidence which allows for object constancy. In order to ensure this, the mother must, on her side, find pleasure in the child's autonomy (Mahler 1968, p. 32). Winnicott, for his part, described certain varieties of what he called maternal holding which is indescribable in words, but whose accidents can provoke "catastrophes which never happened." They must be reconstructed or even "predicted" in adulthood, because of their influence on development (Winnicott 1971, p. 38).

These authors' works show that any modern genetic study of the development of the young child and the prediction of consequences pass through the knowledge of the interactions between a mother and her child. This is a fundamental point of view which we will come back to. Nevertheless, the reference to maturation, a concept which implies that the program of development, in particular of nervous system functions, can be taken into consideration independently of the interaction with the environment, is sometimes used.

It seems to me that it can be done when it is a question of studying the consequences of aptitudes and inaptitudes. A. Freud (1977, p. 9) shows, for instance, that in blind children the attachment to the object world is retarded and often expresses itself in a primitive way. In an extensive way S. Freud (1913, p. 14) has shown that the predisposition to obsessional neurosis rests in particular on the hypermaturation of the ego, with respect to the libidinal development, which observers of children confirm in connection with the premonitory signs of this pathology. For instance, in the manifestation of tics, forced toilet training is often too intense and too precocious. The maturity of language which one often observes in so-called prepsychotic discordancies, leads to hypercontrol of an obsessional character type, that is, a neurotic mode of resolution of hypermaturation. I have also observed this mode of evolution in boys either precociously preoccupied with their sexual identity or who refuse their sex (Lebovici and Kreisler 1965, p. 24).

On the other hand, in a study devoted to hysteria in young children, I thought it could be a relevant hypothesis that the libidinal maturity is too precocious with respect to the ego development in such cases (Lebovici 1974, p. 27). This idea would lead to the answer that the expression of symptoms would depend on the evolutive stages of the ego. That is, hysteria would correspond to the first manifestations of anxiety and would be followed by phobias and obsessions. This is a classical theory which has been valorized by Rivto's study of a patient seen during his childhood by Bornstein (Rivto 1966, p. 34). This phobic child became obsessional as an adult.

But this perspective is not the only one which has led me to propose the idea of libidinal prematurity in infantile hysteria. I saw in it the possibility of defining a particular predisposition at the origin of these disorders. Also, considering the range of early pathology as characterized by an opposition between externalized cases and internalized cases, I esteemed hysteria to be situated on the side of those expressed in behavior. The future may lead to the organization of phobo-obsessional symptoms; hysterical character traits, with or without the formation of conversion symptoms; and prepsychotic discordance, etc.

Thus, rather than considering only the effects of maturation, I propose to study the potential of morbid "prestructures" and their eventual sequences.

The point of view of the Kleinians: Apparently, psychoanalysts who consider themselves to be followers of M. Klein separate themselves completely from those who take maturation and development into account. In fact, they consider that the object relations are organized from the beginning, since the instinct implies an object that is cathected by it. The well-known aphorism formulated as follows: The oral instinct supposes a breast to be sucked or devoured.

The sequence which leads from needs to desires, which will be considered later on and which is fundamental in the metapsychological study of the genesis of object relations, is absolutely neglected by Klein. However, a genetic perspective is not foreign to this author, whose ideas on the central psychotic position organized on the basis of a splitting into good and bad objects are familiar enough. Thus it will suffice to say that according to her, neurotic symptoms are an elaboration of the central depressive position which she places in the second half of the first year of life after the necessary repairing of the object, perceived as a whole. From this point of view, we will now see that it is not impossible to find the importance of the depressive position within a coherent metapsychological study of development.

On the Necessity for a Metapsychological Point of View on the Precocious Development of Object Relations

S. Freud did not neglect direct observation in order to propose his theory of infantile sexual development (S. Freud, *Three Essays on the Theory of Sexuality*, 1905, p. 11). He made use of it as well in studying his grandson's game with the spool in a theoretical essay entitled *Beyond the Pleasure Principle* (1920, p. 15).

Genetic studies of the object relation are numerous, Spitz (1965, p. 35), and Lebovici (1960, p. 22; 1977, p. 29) in particular, have shown that on the road which leads from an undifferentiated stage to a differentiation and constancy of the object one must take into account the initial cathexes of the object before it is perceived. Taking this point of view, I described—probably more systematically than others—the narcissistic stage, and the pre-object stage previous to the organization of the object relationship.

Nonetheless, I have remained faithful to the fundamental hypothesis of Freudian metapsychology in explaining the origin of desires by their being rooted in the hallucination of pleasure. This hypothesis has been formulated by S. Freud in diverse ways of which the most categorical is read in chapter 7 of *The Interpretation of Dreams* (1900, p. 10). I present it here in a voluntarily schematic manner. The memory traces of pleasurable experience are reactivated and hallucinated in a state of need which provokes an interoceptive excitation. For example, pleasure accompanying ingestion and deglutition of milk leads to the hallucination of this satisfaction. Soon the sucking becomes independent of the need and its satisfaction. The hallucination of the pleasure through these activities which are independent of the feeding rhythm leads to a first fantasy, the hallucination of the breast. It is therefore the autoerogenous buccal zone which creates the internal object, the breast (S. Freud, *Three Essays on the Theory of Sexuality,* 1905, p. 11).

Confrontation between metapsychology and direct observation is doubtless a necessity, but semantic and/or conceptual difficulties intervene here and render the debate unclear. The problem is to describe the evolution of the object relationship, by means of, on the one hand taking into account the evolution of the relationships with the external reality, on the other hand, describing the process of creation of the internal object—internalization which implies incorporation, introjection, identification; these three terms are meant to designate the different effects of the same work.

From the undifferentiated stage to the stage of a permanent and differentiated object, it is sufficient to remember that the newborn, who is protected from intero- and exteroceptive excitations, lives in a state in which he cannot distinguish between himself and the environment. To a certain extent this is what we would call narcissism. However, one can note that on the level of the most primitive automatism, the influence from what goes on outside is undeniable. For instance, the archaic bucco-lingual orientation reflex is reinforced when mealtime is far off and tends to fade once the infant is satiated (Ajuriaguerra and Diakine 1956, p. 1). As we have observed, everything shows that the child has cathected the object before perceiving it. Evolution toward the preobject relationship is made because fortunately the child, whose life rhythms become more precise, learns to distinguish the external from the internal. According to the Freudian hypothesis of the initial unity of the infant and the mother's care, he escapes from mental death through the constant satisfaction of his needs which he obtains through his dependency on his mother's care and which he does not distinguish from himself.

Spitz (1965, p. 35) has shown how the first smile specific to the approach of the mother's face from the front constitutes a first organizing element in the preobject mental life constructed on the basis of peribuccal reflex movements. After a phase of several months during which the relationship between mother and child is reciprocally organized on the basis of situations which set positive and negative affects, the phobia of a stranger's face sets in around 6 months of age and testifies to the differentiation of a permanent object. To a certain extent, it is an actual phobia since the mother's absence is equivalent in that moment to danger, new experiences, and strangers, which awaken all the negative affects. It is also this period which inaugurates fantasy life in the usual sense of the word, a time when one is sure that the infant disposes of a mother image with which he can identify inside himself.

I will go no further into the description which shows how the recognition of the object leads to the permanence of its image, that is, to the object relation which also assumes representation of the self. The genesis of object relations depends largely on the specific particularities which define the interaction between the infant and mother. Various events can have cataclysmic influences on it. Such is obviously the case when a child is separated from his mother, once he recognizes her, particularly during the second half of the first year of life. But even the simplest events can intervene in this dual and direct relationship and have unforeseen effects. This was the perspective which allowed Spitz (1965, p. 35) to link a range of functional disorders of newborns to their relationships with their mothers.

This description of the origin of object relations is based on the dependency in which the newborn finds himself; it is genetic and tends to integrate all knowledge of the child's development, be it neurobiological or even cultural. This would not be as true of another description, which would in fact be closer to Freudian metapsychology and would aim at a definition of the process of organizing an internal object.

The metapsychological status of the internal object. The emergence of desires on the basis of the experience of need satisfaction, according to the Freudian hypothesis of which I have already spoken, is understood as belonging to the hallucination of pleasure.

The erogenous zones, precociously differentiated, such as the buccal zone, define orality by means of their very functioning, organize the hallucination of the object of pleasure, and thus create the object which is thereby incorporated. The initial undifferentiated state leads, in this description of autoerotism, to both narcissism and the creation of the object, in an interplay of successive and reciprocal investments.

This description is genetic in the sense that it implies that the pleasure experiences and their memory traces lead first to the hallucination of the pleasure and then to the object. But it is ahistoric, since finally the creation of the object, the first fantasy, does not depend on its specific particularities.

The reading of countless works on the origin of object relations and the particularities of the first phantasmic organizations, permits—through the opposition between the two approaches which I have just defined schematically—an evaluation of the excesses of certain theses.

Numerous works tend to specify the embryology of the newborn's behavior. From animal ethology we have gone on to that of babies. One describes very early behavior of the infant which bears witness to a surprising interaction with certain kinds of maternal behavior, dialog with the eyes, for example, and vocal dialog; certain experiments going on at present have shown that the infant from the fourth week on reacts specifically to the voice of its mother hidden behind a screen. Other works show that from the very first days after birth, mothers have differentiated reactions toward boys and girls in their ways of feeding them (Lezine et al. 1975, p. 31).

Two kinds of consequences are tied to this tendency: The first aims at specifying the precocious aspects of development, but at the same time at limiting the theoretical hypotheses as to the mother's role, reducing it to a presence whose particularities intervene but little in the programs of behavior development. The second, essentially represented by Bowlby (1969, p. 2), defines the nature of mother-child relations on the basis of a series of mechanisms, such as have been described by ethologists. Harlow's experiments in the United States (1965, p. 18) justify beyond doubt the importance of this point of view, as well as other ethological studies on imprinting mechanisms. But the description of attachment behavior and its vicissitudes eliminates the understanding of mental fantasy life, taking away from it all description of psychoanalytic economic aspects. To take just one example which has practical consequences, one would no longer speak of the consequences of separation of mother and child. Anaclitic depression, such as Spitz described it (1965, p. 35), would become a rupture of attachment ties.

Thus, one would tend less to protect children from these separations and educate mothers to avoid them than to create replacement institutions which furnish rich experiments for the purpose of furthering progress in programed behavior. This theory results in emptying psychoanalytic theory of the study of the specificity of ties between mothers and children and would claim to emphasize the creation of social institutions for warding off difficulties and filling lacks in mother-child care.

This approach has the same practical consequences as that which leads to ahistorical perspectives. We have seen why we can class the Kleinian analysts in this category, at least to a certain extent. According to them, the fantasies express, in effect, the contradiction between life and death instincts; thus the internal object exists from birth and is at once split into good and bad objects.

Other psychoanalytic works—perhaps more specifically French—tend to deny the importance of the genetic and historic point of view in psychoanalysis. They refute the diachronic studies and connect themselves more or less clearly with structuralist theories.[1] Viderman (1970), for example, considers the historically marked conflicts as belonging to a sphere which is not really that of psychoanalytic investigation. Unconscious fantasies lie dormant—repressed— elsewhere in the primary and come to light via the creation of the psychoanalyst who actually invents them to give them life and meaning. This primary repressed material is independent of all actual experience and constitutes the "structure" of the unconscious.

From this perspective, a patient's personal history must be constructed and created by the psychoanalyst in order to take on its full meaning. The unfolding of time is not a history of events. In the final consideration, the knowledge of mother-child relations—and in particular that which is gathered through direct observation—is of no interest to the psychoanalyst, whose role is to decode or give life to the primary repressed material.

I have compared these two theoretical approaches, the one directed toward ethological studies, the other ignoring direct observation. In spite of their

---

1. These theories have quite a different connotation than that which is evoked by the Anglo-Saxon psychoanalysts when they speak of a structuralist point of view when referring to the Freudian tripartite agencies of the psychic apparatus.

absolutely different points of view, they end up with the same result, which is to say, to prevent us from deriving benefit from the utilization of our knowledge of child development for diagnostic and prognostic purposes. Therefore I would like to take into consideration some theoretical and clinical data which will give consistency to our knowledge of the infant's mental life.

From the Behavior of the Infant and His Parents to the Prediction of His Mental Disorders

The preceding discussion has been focused on the study of the genetic theories of the object relationship and on the necessity of a recourse to a Freudian metapsychology for the understanding of this organization.

The very young infant's evolution can, in fact, be reconstructed from the psychoanalytic treatments of adults and children. Nevertheless, one must be on guard against making naive judgments on the regressive positions observed in them. Their depth does not allow for a judgment on the precociousness of their organization. The predominance of raw fantasies which express themselves through pregenital fixations, both oral and anal, does not allow us to conclude the existence of simple sequences, first pre-oedipal, then oedipal. Primitive mechanisms can persist within the organization and vicissitudes of oedipal conflicts. Avoidance of the latter can obviously reactivate them as well.

In any event, it is a matter here of judging the evolutive potential of the behavior observed in infants and which mental mechanisms can lead to the understanding of conflicts. This is only possible by taking into account interpersonal and intrafamilial interaction, knowledge referring to the mother's mental life and also the derivatives of her unconscious.

We have seen schematically how this interaction organizes itself through a development which leads to the differentiation of a whole object and also to the recreation of the object of which the imago is the fruit of its internalization. In the course of this progress, completely adequate, almost perfect maternal care, according to Winnicott's expression, must be combined with other preoccupations. The child's capacity to hallucinate pleasure which he has procured organizes not only the object, but also the continuity of lived experience, the self.

The mother functions in the first place as an excitation shield and protects the budding psyche of the child by her own narcissism. Her weaknesses on this level lead her to exaggerate the pressure of her care and lead the child to the development of a false self. To the mother-nurse corresponds the baby who uses his energy to repair the mother (Winnicott 1958, p. 37) and who will become narcissistically fragile, which shows that the study of early behavior does not only lead to a prediction concerning modes of organization of unconscious conflicts, but also flaws in narcissism.

During the course of such evolution, the mother's worry for the child tends to diminish; her relation to the husband, the father of her child, and her own fantasy life with her parents increases. Braunschweig and Fain (1971) have shown how the "shattering" reality of the mother is mediated by the fact that she puts the child to sleep, both because she is able to calm his excitation and because she would think of her "lover." Such mediation plays a fundamental role in the evolution of neurotic conflicts. According to the expression of Castoriadis-Aulagnier, (1975, p. 4), the mother is the "spokeswoman" of the father, which allows the child to interpret reality and not have to face parents as reproductions of their imagos, as is the case, we shall see, in psychosis. These considerations show that predictions concerning observed behavior cannot be validated unless one includes the parental fantasies.

The child, on his side, even full and satisfied, lives through moments of angry excitation which, according to Winnicott (1958, p. 37), can only worry him. His concern for repairing makes him go through depressive phases which must be rich in incorporative and introjective work, in regard to which the external reality is without framework. Here we must look again at the Kleinian theories in a larger sense and consider that the mourning for the object is the source of identification and introjective processes, the primary origin of external reality on a mental level, as Freud in fact repeatedly observed.

All during this process, the mother gives meaning only to that which is observable. According to a very eloquent and often used expression in France, *her anticipations are creative.* It is obvious in the first smile of her baby and also in his cries, since this manifestation, which is purely an expression of excitation and discomfort, is understood by the mother as a call. It becomes in fact a summons, because the mother considers it as such; when it occurs, she takes care of her baby, either by comforting him or by reprimanding him.

Nonetheless, it would be advisable for a mother to leave a certain margin of nonexplained mystery in her baby's behavior. Complete understanding would take away from the infant all exploratory value and all possibility for action in the outer world.

These few introductory remarks on interaction between mother and child indicate the direction of the road which leads from observable behavior to the interpretation of behavior through the study of neurotic conflicts and their elaboration. I will give two examples in order to propose some hypotheses in this work which aim beyond the mere confrontation between the developmental point of view and the exploration of fantasy life.

On the interaction between a baby and his mother and the prediction concerning previous sleep disorders. Here is a baby whom I have seen at 6 months of age because of an insomnia described as almost total. Suffice it to say that it was a little boy, only child of a young couple of a good economic and cultural level, adamantly in favor of modern education. In keeping with these principles, the mother, who worked during the day and took care of him in the evenings, undressed for these tasks in order to favor "skin to skin" contact, she said. After a long interview, about which I will say more later, calm returned to the baby who, for the first time, fell asleep in his mother's arms. First of all her behavior had been rectified; in fact she took her little boy on her forearm and rocked him against her, sitting in this position. In this way, he had his head above her shoulder, and, though rocked, he could see only the wall behind her. Second, this mother was told that her baby could see in her eyes the effect he had on her as her baby, that is, conferred upon her the status of mother. It is a fact that the sleeping disorders stopped that very day during this interview.

Three months after this first contact, the mother and child were seen again. One might describe his behavior as both agitated and rather advanced, in particular on the level of overall and specific motor functioning. However, his exploratory tendencies were constantly frustrated by the mother who anticipated them. For example, when the baby looked for a hidden object, she constantly gave it to him. While viewing the magnetoscopic recording of this examination, she was able to accept the idea that no desire could emerge in her child, since she tried to satisfy the desire, even before it was expressed.

This young woman refused on several different accounts diverse forms of help which were proposed to her, that is, psychotherapy based on observation of her relations with the child, participation in groups of young mothers, etc. She made a short attempt at psychoanalytic psychotherapy, quickly interrupted on the pretext of her professional occupations.

Two years after the first interview, the mother asked for psychiatric help once again. Her son was almost 3 years old; he was dangerously agitated and almost mute, and banged his head incessantly. Briefly, it was a clinical picture more or less close to that of an autistic child.

The scope of this article does not allow me to go into great detail about the mother's mental life. I will merely indicate that she married in order to collaborate in the rather important business of her future husband. When they had nearly died in the Sahara as a result of some imprudence, they recounted that they were then prepared to die, happy with what they had experienced. The couple decided to have a child several years later. Shortly after his birth, the child was moved out of the mother's bedroom so that she could continue to have intimate relations with her husband; at the same time, as we remember, she undressed when giving her infant maternal care. She also knew that her husband could very well feel jealous of his son.

In short, this little clinical vignette shows the genesis of a psychosis. Without any doubt, one might say that the early insomnia was the first of the symptoms. It was expressed:

1. In the situation in which the child found himself, the impossibility to confer upon his mother a maternal status. Here, observation of behavior shows the inconsistencies in the support given to the baby, but it also testifies to the lack of eye-to-eye dialog which prevented this baby from seeing his mother looking at him. In other words, it is not simply a matter of noticing educational errors, but also of giving them meaning, by taking into account *both*

our knowledge of child development *and* our observations of the influence that the baby exercised on his mother.

2. The mother's fantasies made her unable to divide herself between her status as mother and her status as a woman and, above all, to be the "therapist" of her baby for whom she wanted to facilitate the realization of any exploratory project.

One could also invoke the sociocultural conditions which favor maternal activism and the interpersonal relationship of the couple, in which a very dependent husband exhibits his search for a second mother in his wife.

I shall simply underline that what one might have considered as elements of hypermaturation and rapid development, ended up—in the circumstances I have described which obviously can only be considered as an etiologically closed constellation—with difficulties which invoke the possibility of psychosis.

In such cases, it is the understanding of the child's behavior through the interaction which he manifests with his mother, understood both by way of her behavior and her fantasy life, which allows for the prediction of eventual future mental disorders, such as those which finally surfaced.

On the choice of first names as an expression of phantasmic familial interrelations over several generations. This is a case of a 4-year-old child, a little girl who was adopted rather late—at 9 months of age. She is an autistic child. This case is interesting if only because of the present, focused studies on psychoses of adopted children, as compared to psychotic evolution in those who have psychotic parents themselves.

I shall study only a few aspects of the adopting family: The wife declares right off that the adoption is due to her husband's sterility; she soon forgets this declaration and explains that her ovarian tubes were blocked, but that her husband was depressed because he couldn't have children (with his wife).

The adoption came late. The little girl was living with a foster family and was called Christiane. The mother changed her name and gave her the first name, Helene, a name to which the child became "accustomed" within 2 weeks. The choice of this first name is interesting. According to the mother, it is linked to the circumstances of her own life. In effect, she was the daughter of an unwed mother, a piano teacher. Her father, who was married, was himself a musician. He took her in after her mother's death, when she was about 10 years old. The choice of "Helene" is linked to the fact that it is the name of the saint of music, and then it signifies that her parents *"are united in heaven."*

Helene played with a doll from which she never wanted to be separated. From her language fragments, one learned that this doll was called Marie, a name chosen by the mother, because "the virgin Mary didn't need a man in order to have the baby Jesus."

These notes illustrate a most particular aspect of the relationship of the mother to her husband and her underlying fantasies, which refer to a denial of the primal scene. Her parents are united in heaven. Her husband is sterile. The parthenogenetic line which denies the sexual role of men thus begins with the maternal grandmother, continues through the adopting mother, and ends with Helene and her doll, daughter of Helene, and also husbandless mother of a child without a father.

The weight of the maternal fantasies might be expressed in numerous ways. But I have often had the impression that the choice of the children's first names, which is obviously linked to many factors—often to traditions or to passing fashions, is a significant factor in the intrafamilial organization of psychotic or (as in this case) prepsychotic children.

These two observations, whose very reduced presentation has been oriented with a demonstrative aim, concern two cases of this type. It is not surprising that the prediction based on observation of the behavior of young children and their parents, along with the study of the mental life of the latter, allows above all for the understanding of the risk of ulterior psychosis.

Among other factors, psychosis expresses a nonmediated relationship between the child and his parents. The mental elaboration does not express the adaptive functions of the ego. The fantasies are raw, charged with fragmented meanings testifying to the failures of the introjective process, which, as we have seen, contributes to the mental foundation of external reality in its continuity. In other words, the external reality conforms to the child's fantasies which it has helped to organize under the weight of the mother's fantasies, which generate the psychosis. To be schematic, I would use the following formula: The child's imagos are strengthened by the weight of the external object's reality. In children in whom neurotic elaboration can be expected, however, the imagos are constructed on the basis of a deformation of reality in the course of the incorporative and introjective work, within identificatory, and therefore conflictual perspectives.

The prediction which I have tried to describe here constitutes, for the clinician, a kind of work which aims at foretelling the healthy potential of development, the neurotic elaboration, that is, at a moment when observation only allows the following:

1. to observe types of behavior
2. to hear about functional disorders
3. to try to understand interactions between mother and child, perhaps with the introduction of the father, especially if the observation takes place in the family
4. to explore the mother's fantasy life
5. to explore also the intrafamilial interaction

The practice of long-term observations which tend to develop with the creation of community psychiatric services obviously gives meaning to these attempts at prediction and to the work of prevention which they justify. I myself have followed up some cases of infantile psychosis for over 25 years. The outcome of child psychosis is far from being clearly known: One does not find traditional schizophrenia in previously psychotic children who have been followed up and treated, once they become adults (Lebovici and Kestemberg 1978, p. 30).

But as far as this chapter is concerned, I wish simply to indicate that at the latency period there is an absence of solid defences and flexible neurotic mechanisms. In the best of evolutions, the behavior is hypercontrolled by tight pseudo-obsessional systems, which would develop into character neurosis.

During the years preceding the latency period, an examination can include children's games which facilitate exploration of his fantasy life to some extent, providing, however, that certain methodological precautions are respected. They are of two sorts, since, on the one hand, to play in an adult's presence contains a reactional aspect tied to this very situation, and on the other, to the contrary, the play gives place to a penetration in depth of the themes evoked.

In any case, what I wish to indicate in this respect is that between the period when one is reduced, as I have already shown, to predicting mental functioning on the basis of behavior observation and the period when one can study mental functioning directly, there is a lapse of several years during which behavior remains the essential means of approach for the psychiatrist. As development continues, a study of the internalization process constitutes the essential approach. Starting with the moment at which the elaboration of detailed neurotic mechanisms allows for the clarification among those cases which risk entering the psychotic register, multiple potentialities must be called to mind. Obviously, they depend on diverse factors which imply difficulties or facilities in the development of the various nervous system functions, which express themselves in variations in learning capacity. But clinical judgment may also take into account the retroactive value of what one has learned about the mother-child interaction. For example, the lack of fear at the appearance of a stranger's face would seem to announce the direct utilization of the body for the expression of conflicts (Kreisler et al. 1974, p. 21). The organization of neurotic conflicts during the period which precedes latency often grows out of a very ordinary hysteria (Lebovici 1974, p. 28). In retrospect, one may also judge the narcissistic deficiencies of the mother and the difficulties encountered in the organization of the self and the ego ideal, which are two closely linked operational concepts. The deficiencies observed lead to a narcissistic pathology involved the ego ideal, introducing, besides, the notion of depression in the young child. The instability of behavior and the states of excitation are sometimes a manic-type reaction to difficulty in object introjection and also to the failure in the evolution of the depressive phase necessary for repairing the object. From this point of view, there are, it seems to me, some connection between these states of excitement and those which might be called prepsychopathic states.

These considerations, in spite of their brevity, also introduce group values, which Freud referred to as the ego ideal (S. Freud 1921, p. 16). The familial interrelations define a group in which the social and cultural values have been expressed as well. It is, indeed, necessary to contrast that which expresses *intrapersonal* relations—the parent's fantasy life—and the *interpersonal* relations. In the latter, fantasies are again expressed, but the sociocultural environment intervenes. As we have seen in studies of communication within the family, the importance of verbal exchange, its richness and coherence, simultaneously admits to the elaboration of conflicts.

The contemporary family is, without a doubt, going through a crisis which leads to incertitude as to the values transmitted and the challenging of the ego ideal. This is particularly evident and important in certain so-called multiple-problem families. Help, if offered them, may be given in a somewhat disjointed fashion and may include access to the services of a psychiatrist who may, similarly, be inept at appreciating their type of life and also the value of the behavior observed in it. The lifestyle of these families is not ours, and the ideal values most prevalent are not, conversely, theirs. The conflicts are constantly acted out and therefore not elaborated mentally. The therapeutic or preventative policy decided upon in such cases should not be based on the psychotherapeutic relationship in which verbalization of conflicts and affects allows for interpretive activity. One can do nothing else but use a study of behavior and its rectification. It seems to me that psychoanalysts, if they accept the full use of their knowledge about the origins of behavior, must accept acting directly on the behavior of young children and their parents because of the important risk which threaten such families. We have to decide between two approaches: one, that of the behaviorists, which aims at the simple rectification of behavior; the other tries to give a meaning to the behavior which could be perceptible to the parents, not only through a dialog in which one often tries to engage—though often in vain—but also in the gestures which they can learn and by which they can express themselves. For example, such parents might grasp the value of an eye-to-eye dialog between mother and child or perhaps, for example, the connection existing between the cries and the colics of a baby whose abdomen is run through by waves of intestinal peristalsis.

In other terms, the extension of a psychoanalytic understanding to sociocultural levels of society generally unconcerned leads inevitably to a study increasingly centered on the behavior of young children and their parents, aiming at the prevention of mental health risks, provided that among these risks, the evolution toward psychopathy and oligophrenia should be included.

Conclusions and Summary

The study of behavior in young children has generally been considered by psychoanalysts as a means to minimize the dangers of extrapolation of the constructions which psychoanalytic treatment of adults and children has allowed.

The importance of the maturation potential tends to favor a contrast between the reconstructed child and the so-called real child. On the other hand, there is some difficulty in admitting that there could be as developed a fantasy life as that which has been described by the Kleinian authors. In addition, the neurobiological data and metapsychology have to be taken into account, and genetic studies of the object relationship are to be confronted with the mental creation of the object, based on the fundamental hypothesis of the unity between the child and maternal care. Conversely, through behavioral studies which resemble those of animal ethology, one highlights very refined programs which testify to the precociousness of the mother-child interaction.

Our experience tends to show that the above-cited works must be recognized by psychoanalysts, who must not merely content themselves with the comparison of the real child and the reconstructed child. In other words, the observed child is in addition the product of maternal fantasies. Such phenomena must be included when one wants to predict inherent mental health risks on the basis of the study of behavior, which is the only material available when it is a question of very young children.

I wanted to indicate in a concrete way how one might evaluate the risk of psychosis or prepsychosis during this period, in the sense accepted at present in France.

The continuous studies of children followed over long periods of time demonstrate the importance of these findings, which can then be reintegrated into the study of children before the latency period, at a time when the neurotic conflicts do not yet have the value of neurotic symptoms.

The maternal fantasies also play a role in the care and education given to children. They involve both the relationships with their husbands and their oedipal fantasies. The mother's behavior plays a role, therefore, in the introjective process which establishes external reality and allows the child to perceive a differentiated and "whole" mother, thereby overcoming what might be called the depressive position and thus achieving the first neurotic mechanism, that is, the fear of a stranger's face, which implies projection and displacement.

The direct study of behavior and mother-child interaction in the very young child allows us, therefore, to specify the psychotic potential. Later, taking this into account authorizes the study of pathological preorganizations which are necessarily composite and fluid. The importance of the maternal narcissistic deficiencies must not be forgotten while attempting to understand the weight of the young child's depression, and antidepressive struggle, which manifests itself in manifold states of excitation and their immediate consequences, that is, learning difficulties and ulterior risks even at that crossroads of acting out against the body—the psychosomatic realm, and against the family—the psychopathic risk.

I have tried to show how the family approach necessarily implies the study of parental fantasies and their consequences. But this approach must be enlarged so as to include both the specific and nonspecific difficulties of communication in our present-day society and in the social levels of cultural deprivation.

It may be that psychoanalysts from now on will be led to accept the study of behavior of those who have not yet learned how to, or cannot yet verbally express themselves, *not* in order to modify anything through the pressure of reconditioning, but to understand in effect, and to allow those, who do not know how to speak or elaborate, to feel the meaning and the weight of their acts. This might be a relevant means to develop a truly preventative action against the considerable dangers which many children face, that of perpetual acting out or of mental impoverishment.

References

Ajuriaguerra, de J., and Diatkine, R. Pschanalyse et neurobiologie. (Psychoanalysis and neuro-biology). In: Nacht, S., ed. *La Psychoanalyse d'Aujourd'hui* 2 vols. Paris: Presses Universitaires de France, 1956.

Bowlby, J. *The Attachment and Loss,* Vol. 1. Attachment. New York: Basic Books, 1969.

———. *The Attachment and Loss,* Vol. 2. Separation, Anxiety. London: Hogarth Press, 1973.

Braunschweig, D., and Fain, M. *Eros et Anteros* (Eros and Anteros). Paris: Payot, 1971.

Castoriadis-Aulagnier, P. *La violence et l'interpretation.* (The violence of interpretation). Paris: Presses Universitaires de France, 1975.

Chiland, C., and Lebovici, S. Borderline or prepsychotic condition in childhood—A French point of view. In: Hartcollis, P., ed. *Borderline Personality Disorders.* New York: International Universities Press, 1977.

Coleman, R.W.; Kris, E.; and Provence, S. The study of variations of early parental attitudes. *The Psychoanalytic Study of the Child,* 8:20-47, 1953.

Freud, A. The concept of developmental lines. *The Psychoanalytic Study of the Child,* 18:262-265, 1963.

———. *Normality and Pathology in Childhood.* New York: International Universities Press, 1965.

———. From normal development to psychopathology. *Revue Francaise de Psychoanalyse,* 16:(3) 429–438, 1977.

Freud, S. The interpretation of dreams (1900). *Standard Edition,* Vols. 4 and 5. London: Hogarth Press, 1953.

———. Three essays on the theory of sexuality (1905). *Standard Edition,* Vol. 7. London: Hogarth Press, 1953.

———. Analysis of a phobia in a five-year-old boy (1909). *Standard Edition,* Vol. 10. London: Hogarth Press, 1955.

———. The disposition to obsessional neurosis (1913). *Standard Edition,* Vol. 12. London: Hogarth Press, 1958.

———. An infantile neurosis (1918). *Standard Edition,* Vol. 17. London: Hogarth Press, 1955.

———. Beyond the pleasure principle (1920). *Standard Edition,* Vol. 18. London: Hogarth Press, 1955.

———. Group psychology and analysis of the ego (1921). *Standard Edition,* Vol. 18. London: Hogarth Press, 1955.

———. Constructions in analysis (1937). *Standard Edition,* Vol. 23. London: Hogarth Press, 1964.

Harlow, H.F., and Harlow, M.K. The affectional systems. In: Schrier, A.M.; Harlow, H.F.; and Stolinitz, F. *Behavior of Non-human Primates.* 2 Vols. New York: Academic Press, 1965.

Kreisler, L.; Fain, M.; and Soule, M. *L'Enfant et Son Corps.* (The Child and His Body) Paris: Presses Universitaires de France, 1974.

Kris, E. Notes on the development and on some current problems of psychoanalytic child psy-chology. *The Psychoanalytic Study of the Child,* 5:24-46, 1950.

Kris, M. The recovery of childhood memories in psycho-analysis: Problems of genetic interpretations. *The Psychoanalytic Study of the Child,* 11:65-78, 1956.

——. The use of prediction in a longitudinal study. *The Psychoanalytic Study of the Child,* 12:175–189, 1957.

Lebovici, S. La relation objectale chez l'enfant. (The object relationship in children.) *La Psychiatrie De L'Enfant,* 8:(1)147–226, 1960.

——. La notion de prepsychose chez l'enfant. (The notion of infantile prepsychosis.) *Bulletin de Psychologie,* 17:(1)224, 1963.

——. A propos de l'hysterie chez l'enfant. (On hysteria in children.) *La Psychiatrie De L'Enfant,* 17:(1)5–52, 1974.

Lebovici, S., and Braunschweig, D. A propos de la nevrose infantile. (About infantile neurosis.) *La Psychiatrie De L'Enfant,* 10:(1)43-142, 1967.

Lebovici, S., and Diatkine, R. Normality as a concept of limited usefulness in the assessment of psychiatric risk. In: Anthony, E., and Koupernik, C., eds. *The Child in his Family: Children at Psychiatric Risk.* Vol. 3. New York: John Wiley and Sons, 1974.

Lebovici, S., and Kestemberg, E. Le Devenir de la Psychose de l'Enfant. (The Future of Childhood Psychosis.) Paris: Presses Universitaires de France, forthcoming.

Lebovici, S., and Kreisler, L. L'homosexualité chez l'enfant. (Homosexuality in children and adolescents.) *La Psychiatrie De L'Enfant,* 8:(1)57-134, 1965.

Lebovici, S., and Sadoun, R. L'enregistrement du diagnostic au Centre Alfred Binet. (Recording of diagnosis at the Alfred Binet Center.) *La Psychiatrie De L'Enfant,* 11:(2)533-550, 1968.

Lebovici, S., and Soule, M. *La Connaissance de l'Enfant par la Psychanalyse.* (Knowing the Child through Psychoanalysis.) 3rd ed. Paris: Presses Universitaires de France, 1977.

Lezine, L.; Robin, M.; and Cortial, C. Observation sur le couple mère-enfant durant les premieres experiences d'alimentation. (Observation of the mother-child couple during the first feeding experience.) *La Psychiatrie De L'Enfant,* 18:(1)75-146, 1975.

Mahler, M. *On Human Symbiosis and the Vicissitudes of Individuation.* Vol. 1: *Infantile Psychosis.* New York: International Universities Press, 1968.

Nagera. H. *Early Childhood Disturbance: The Infantile Neurosis and Adult Disturbances.* New York: International Universities Press, 1966.

Ritvo, S. Correlation of a childhood and adult neurosis. *International Journal of Psychoanalysis,* 47:2-3, 130-132, 1966.

Spitz, R. *The First Year of Life.* New York: International Universities Press, 1965.

Viderman, S. *La Construction de l'Espace Analytique.* (The Construction of the Psychoanalytic Space.) Paris: Denoel, 1970.

Winnicott, D.W. *Through Pediatrics to Psychoanalysis.* New York: Basic Books, 1958.

——. *Playing and Reality.* London: Tavistock, 1971.

*The Course of Life: Psychoanalytic Contributions
Toward Understanding Personality Development.
Vol. II: Latency, Adolescence, and Youth.
S.I. Greenspan and G.H. Pollock, editors.
NIMH 1980*

On Phase-Characteristic Pathology of the School-Age Child: Disturbances of Personality Development and Organization (Borderline Conditions) of Learning, and of Behavior

Fred Pine, Ph.D.

In this chapter, I shall describe some of the characteristic psychopathology of school-age children, in particular borderline disturbances, behavior disturbances, and disturbances of learning. The period that I have in mind is the one that Bornstein (1951) called the second period of latency, roughly the years from 7 or 8 to 10 or 11, following the early latency period wherein the child is still very much involved in residual oedipal issues. By way of introduction, I shall describe the age period in overview and give a rationale for the selection of the three specific areas of psychopathology.

What is that age period like? Let me contrast it to the surrounding developmental periods and, additionally, look at some of its internal features. By age 7 or 8, the child is normally solidly involved in the world of school and peer relations. The contrast to the preschool years is striking (though, of course, not absolute). At home, in early childhood, the preschooler is ordinarily in close proximity to the mother and other family members for much of his day; the sights, sounds, smells, feel of family members are at all times the background, and often the foreground, of life and contribute percepts and memories to the thought processes from which fantasy and wish are formed. The learning that takes place is in considerable measure learning on and about the own body and the bodies of others. From early self-other bodily differentiation (Mahler et al. 1975), through the learning of self-feeding, bowel/bladder control, self-toileting, and self-dressing, critical learnings have an intimate relation to body and mother. Additionally, family members in general have no peer in their significance as external others in the life of the child.

But the entry into school brings major changes. While family members remain central figures in the psychic life of the child, teachers and peers begin to assume importance as representatives of a wider world, affectively a bit more neutral, less intimate, providing new avenues of identification and attachment. Learning, too, changes. While motor skills continue to develop, learning linked to the body itself is less intimate and less central. And nonbodily learning assumes enormous importance—reading, writing, arithmetic, social studies (the world of school), and chants, games, tricks, rules (the world of child-hood) (Stone and Church 1973). The learning process is itself less tied to the parents; not only are they not always the teachers, but things may be learned (formally, from the teacher; informally, by observations of others) that the parents do not even know or do not do. And, importantly, the child's physical proximity to mother is less, as he spends time in school and has the afterschool skills and inner achievements to go out of the house without mother to play with peers.

The contrast to the subsequent adolescent period is equally sharp, but I need only go over it in a surface way. In adolescence, once again, intimate bodily learning (the new sexuality) becomes central; the old family relation-ships and infantile fantasy are reactivated and achieve renewed force (Freud 1905; Spiegel 1951; Blos 1962); and the child's task of defining his position vis-a-vis learning and same-sex peers, ordinarily reasonably well-accomplished (for good or ill) in the school years, gradually becomes secondary to the task of defining his position vis-a-vis sexual development, heterosexual relationships, and the anticipation of full independence from the parents and physical sepa-ration from their home. For the child whom we will be discussing, all of this still lies in the future.

The contrast of the school-age years to the preschool and adolescent periods helps bring out the internal features of that age period as well. It is a time of the child's entry into the wider, nonfamilial world—typified by peer relations and school. The formation of new relationships (with the opportunities they pro-vide for displacement and reworking of old familial relationships) and the achievement of new learnings are major psychological tasks of the period. Character formation (the establishment of a reliable personal style of thought, relatedness, impulse expression, and defense), while inevitably beginning ear-lier, continues in this period; and its *external* accompaniment—socialization

to the nonfamilial world—is of increased importance. While many of the indicators of such socialization are quite visible (play, relationships, school behavior and attitude), the more subtle ones (modes of thinking, feeling, and doing)
are also being shaped. Certain kinds of disturbances in this age period—
including the ones I shall be discussing—can be viewed against this age
backdrop, descriptively, as failures successfully to accomplish the tasks of the
age. From a more interior/clinical view, they will also be looked at in terms of
their intrapsychic specificity and their developmental implications.

To repeat, the three areas of psychopathology that I shall discuss are borderline disturbances, behavior disturbances, and disturbances of learning. The
three are not really parallel with one another; nor is any one of them a unified
entity. But I select them because they are common, because they can be
viewed as failures in the adaptational tasks of the school-age years, and because
light can be shed upon them by taking a depth-oriented, interior view.

These three forms of disturbance do not first *begin* in the school-age period,
but they are often first identified as problematic in that age period. Working
clinically, one is deluged with complaints regarding learning or behavior and
with diagnoses of "borderline" in this age group. And this is the first immediate
clinical reason why, when asked to write about phase-specific disorders of the
school-age period, my thoughts immediately went to them. It should be noted,
however, that this paper is entitled "phase-characteristic" (not "phase-specific")
disorders. The difference is by no means trivial for a developmentally oriented
approach. For, though these three disturbances are common in, and thus
characteristic of, the school-age period, they are by no means *specific* to
it—having roots earlier (even being full-blown earlier), and certainly also
continuing or even first clearly emerging later on. But at the age we are talking
about, they often are first identified or at least first begin to clash with social
expectations regarding the child; hence they come to the clinician's attention.

We might suspect that any referral complaint that we hear about with very
great frequency is being overused, in overextended or vague ways. And such is
indeed the case, I believe, with the three areas to be discussed. A depth-
oriented psychoanalytic view can lead to some clarification, however. The
approach taken here will be consistent with the one Anna Freud (1970)
espoused in her paper on the symptomatology of childhood—that is, to specify
common genetic and structural features that underlie divergent surface pathologies and (more to the point for this paper) to specify *varying* genetic and
structural features that underlying superficially *similar* presenting pictures.

Besides their commonality in current clinical work, their relation to the age
period at hand, and my belief that an analytic approach will shed light on them,
there is one other reason—an exclusionary one this time—for my choosing to
discuss these three areas of disturbance. That is, at least two other areas—
psychoneuroses and psychoses—are probably best discussed in terms of ages
other than the ones I am focusing upon here. The psychoses are best discussed
in terms of very early formative (and genetic) conditions in relation to the

infantile psychoses and in terms of both infantile and postchildhood periods for those psychotic conditions ordinarily first becoming apparent in adolescence or later. And what can be said about the classical psychoneuroses in the school-age period is not distinctively different from what can be said about them (in terms of dynamics, psychic structure, and symptom formation) at other ages.

I have already indicated that the three areas that will be discussed are not parallel. Disturbances of behavior or of learning, as varied as each area may be regarding appearance or cause, have in common at least a more-or-less "point-at-able" surface sign: A child is not learning, or a child presents a behavior problem. The same cannot be said of borderline children. At best, the common surface sign is that these children are "peculiar" in some way—hardly an adequate clinical formulation. And, at that, it may at times be that they are only peculiar to those who have sufficient familiarity with the quality, the "feel," of normal children of this age.

And the three areas are also not strictly parallel in their relatedness to failures in the adaptive tasks of the school-age years, and again the borderline disturbance is the conceptual oddball. The identification of behavior problems and learning problems is clearly connected to school entry and the requirements of school performance, and many a child is first referred at the initiative of the school for one or another (or both) of these complaints. Behavior problems are additionally linked to issues of the age because of their impact on peer relations and because of the increasing strength and opportunities for independent action in children of this age—making problems in the behavior domain much more worrisome or dangerous. But borderline pathology is not linked to anything as explicit in its age-linkage as school entry and school requirements. Yet I think there are important ways in which it is age-linked, specifically reasons why the "peculiarities" (to be specified more, later, when I turn to this area in detail) are identified at this age. This is reflected in the title I selected for this chapter, specifically its reference to "disturbances of personality development and organization (borderline conditions)." That phrase has to do with the greater degree of character stability, of socialization, and of peer and/or teacher relatedness that is normally expectable at this age; the "peculiarities" of these children are often violations of these age-linked, normally fulfilled expectations. When the major relationships are solely within the family, peculiarities of object relation or of ego function may go unnoticed by equally peculiar family members or may be compensated for by them in the mix of habitual family interrelatedness. Teachers and peers may not be so generous.

So the three areas of disturbance are not truly parallel. Indeed, I have not elected to discuss them because they are parallel, but because they are common in clinical practice, characteristic of the age, and vague and therefore requiring specification. They do, in addition, profit from being looked at in terms of the adaptational expectations of the school-age child (already described) and, from an interior-developmental perspective, in terms of the child's progress along a number of developmental lines. I shall discuss these in detail, below, as I get into each of the three specific areas.

In what follows, then, I shall discuss borderline disturbances, disturbances of learning, and behavior disturbances (in that order), attempting, in each case, to specify the nature(s) of the disturbance(s) by taking an indepth interior view of the developmental, dynamic, and structural contexts in which they are set. Each will be approached somewhat differently, in ways tailored to the issues in each area; but each will include a discussion of (a) distinctions within the general area of disturbance, (b) treatment implications following from these distinctions, and (c) the achievements and failures on normal developmental lines that underlie problems in each of these areas.

The Borderline Disturbances

In recent clinical practice, the flow of children who are given the diagnosis "borderline" has reached flood proportions. Whence the flood? I believe that one source is the decreasing frequency with which the classical symptom-psychoneuroses are seen, in childhood as in adulthood, causing clinicians to be alerted instead to issues of character pathology, a form of pathology which can be essentially neurotic in structure but which shades into more serious conditions at its more disturbed extreme. Additionally, the post World War II growth of the child guidance movement, as well as of research utilizing direct child observation, has brought to clinicians an acute awareness of the flagrant "psychopathology of everyday childhood" in the lives of young people growing up. Third, the rapid extension of clinical services to poverty and ghetto populations, following upon the sting to professional and governmental conscience of the civil rights battles of the 1960s and represented in the spread of community mental health centers, brought us in greater contact with children whose lives are blighted by social pathology (crime, addiction, prostitution, violence, hunger, abandonment, etc.) as well as psychopathology, and whose overall functioning shows the toll taken by such massive pathological intrusions upon development. And fourth, the writings of a number of individuals (to be noted below) who have tried to isolate and define key intrapsychic mechanisms and/or failures in what they called borderline children (or related entities) gave a sophisticated clinical-intellectual context for formulations in this area.

Whether these be all or any of the sources of the flood, the phenomenon is clear: a high frequency of the labeling of children "borderline" with an associated looseness in the key meanings intended to be attached to the term. A multitude of phenomena—including isolation from others or indiscriminate relationships, nonavailability of stable defenses or rigid reliance on pathological defenses, panic states or affectlessness, hollow pseudomaturity or infantile behavior, and an assortment of peculiarities of social behavior, thought and language, or motor style—are used to produce the umbrella diagnosis: borderline. Is there something real here that so many clinicians are grasping at? Can the morass be sorted out? Earlier (Pine 1974*a*), I took a stab at answering these questions, as did a number of other writers on child psychopathology (Ekstein and Wallerstein 1954; A. Freud 1956; Rosenfeld and Sprince 1963, 1965; Weil 1953, 1956). I should like to review some of that work here, additionally attempting to formulate some of the broad developmental lines that have gone awry in borderline patients, to draw distinctions within the broad borderline domain, and to specify at least some implications of these distinctions for the treatment process.

Some years ago, a group of colleagues and I agreed to meet regularly in a small clinical study group to discuss issues in child psychopathology. Our ready consensus, for reasons apparent in what I have already said, was to begin with a look at the borderline child. Influenced by the writers whom we studied, when we looked at children who had been (or could easily be) diagnosed borderline, we kept concepts in mind such as the absence of phase dominance and regression to primary identification (Rosenfeld and Sprince 1963), the tendency toward panic anxiety (Weil 1953), fluidity of psychic organization (Ekstein and Wallerstein 1954), heavy reliance on splitting mechanisms (Kernberg 1967, 1968), and, from the point of view of Mahler's concept of the separation-individuation process (Mahler et al. 1975), early failures in that process (Masterson 1972). While our group creative imagination could press clinical and metapsychological constructs into forms that would subsume most of the cases we examined, my own sense was that in so doing we were engaging in a rather forced exercise.

In contrast, shortly thereafter, an enormous freeing of thought took place with our abandonment of the word "the" in the phrase "the borderline child" and its replacement by the term "borderline children." That is, we gave up the self-imposed demand to find a single unifying mechanism and considered instead that we were dealing with an array of phenomena, having some larger developmental and pathological commonalities perhaps, but also having specific variant forms. In this it would be parallel to psychoneurosis, with its commonalities and variant forms. In back of this change also was the idea, still very clear to me, that the term borderline is a *concept*—one that *we* can *decide* how to use—and that our job was to specify the phenomena to which we would apply it. This rephrasing of our key term ("borderline child*ren*") also set another aspect of our task: to identify the larger developmental and pathological commonalities that make this a reasonable, even if not tight, conceptual grouping, and then to describe its specific variant forms.

Put another way, children described as borderline are first defined by a dual negation: They are not (merely) neurotic, and they are not (clearly) psychotic. What they *are* remains to be stated. Or, put yet another way, while we could manage to subsume many children who are called borderline under one or another clinical construct (e.g., fluidity), we came to see this not as a *gain* in clinical generalization, but as a *loss* in clinical specificity. In short, we felt we could do better with the joint conceptual tools of (1) *broadly-defined commonalities* plus (2) *specific variants* in these children than we could do with any single concept, mechanism, or process alone. Let me propose that as a way of thinking here, as well.

What is the *general commonality?* I believe that all of the children who come to be considered borderline show failures in one or another of the developmental lines associated with the development of major ego functions or central aspects of object relationship; the failures may be in the form of developmental arrest, aberrant development, or both. Normally, by the ages of 7 or 8 to 10 or 11 that we are considering here, ego development has proceeded to the point where secondary process thinking and reality testing are well established and where some capacity for delay and at least some reliable and well-structured defenses have been attained. In addition, object relations have developed more or less normally through the early autistic (objectless) and symbiotic (undifferentiated) stages (Mahler 1968); some degree of libidinal object constancy (Hartmann 1952; Pine 1974*b*) and of specificity of object attachment have been achieved; and object relations have been subjected to the shaping influences of the drives at each of the psychosexual stages of development. Furthermore, the triadic relations of the oedipal period have been experienced and dealt with in some manner. Superego development, additionally, has proceeded to the point of at least some degree of internalization of standards— that is, with some experience of guilt for transgression and with some internally powered efforts at control and delay of impulses.

By contrast, the group of children who are generally considered borderline or severely disturbed do not show this context of normal development of ego function and of object relationship. In particular, ego malfunction in them may include disturbances in the sense of reality and at times in reality testing, as well as a failure in the development of signal anxiety so that unpleasant affect readily escalates to panic instead of triggering reliably available defenses. Object relations may be characterized by their shifting levels, by too great a dependence of ego structure upon the object contact (Ekstein 1966), and by regression to primary identification (Rosenfeld and Sprince 1963). While superego forerunners are also likely to impaired, these are not in fact readily separable in their impact from failures of judgment and affectional attachment that are already implied by pointing to failures in ego function and object relationship. Final superego formation is likely to be secondarily interfered with by prior developmental failures. The precise developmental failures, and their breadth and severity, may vary from one child to another.

These basic failures in the normal developmental progression of ego functioning and object relationship are what differentiates borderline children from neurotic children. For, though we may define the classical *psychoneuroses* as involving an unsuccessfully resolved conflict between drive and opposing forces (superego and defense), unsuccessfully resolved in that it culminates in anxiety and/or formation of compromise symptoms and/or neurotic character traits, we also assume that these features exist in the context of *more-or-less normal* ego function and object relationship, at least outside of the area of focal conflict. That is why, though they involve personal suffering and, at times, impairment of functioning, we generally consider the neuroses to be relatively "healthy" conditions.

In passing, I should say a bit also regarding the distinction of borderline from psychotic conditions. I have discussed this more fully elsewhere (Pine 1974*a*), and shall do no more here than to assert what was discussed there, in the interest of saving space and avoiding repetition. In brief then: I believe that there are some psychotic conditions of childhood—notably infantile autism (Kanner 1942, 1949), symbiotic psychosis (Mahler 1952, 1968), some organic conditions, and (though rarely) adult-like schizophrenias involving apparently adequate functioning followed by regressive disorganization—which can be fairly clearly differentiated from borderline conditions. But, for the rest, I do not believe a sharp line divides borderline and psychotic conditions, each of the borderline conditions that I shall describe below shading into what can be called psychosis at the more severe end of its particular spectrum.

What are some of the specific developmental failures in borderline children? One that is frequently mentioned (Weil 1953; Rosenfeld and Sprince 1963) is the failure to achieve the signal function of anxiety (S. Freud 1933). That is, even rather early on in development, the normal child begins to anticipate when an anxiety-inducing situation is imminent (based on memory of previous experience). Such anticipation is accompanied by mild anxiety which sets defensive operations into motion, be these flight, a turn to mother, or (later) intrapsychic defense. But the capacity for this (both to anticipate and to have modes of defense available) is a developmental achievement of great moment. For the infant cannot do this and is instead helpless in the face of anxiety (unless mother intervenes), and the intensity of this anxiety can rise to traumatic proportions, i.e., well beyond the organism's capacity to master or discharge. For certain children, the failure to develop the capacity to use the anxiety signal to set a reliable array of defenses into operation is both an indicator of past developmental failure and is a source of continuing inability to develop mastery. For, if anxiety rapidly escalates to panic, the kinds of new learning, new trials at mastery, that can come at moments of delay in the face of danger, will not be able to take place.

Early failures in the process of separation and individuation (Mahler et al. 1975) also have consequences for the later stability of ego boundaries and of object attachment under stress. Rosenfeld and Sprince (1963), acknowledging their debt to Anna Freud, find a regression to primary identification to be a characteristic phenomenon in their severely disturbed children. That is, quite the reverse of those later identifications which are basic to the growth of individuality and are a prime form of "adding something" to ourselves, some severely ill children begin to lose their sense of self as they merge into an undifferentiated self-other duo. Masterson's (1972) work on borderline adolescents also draws heavily on concepts of failure in the process of separation and individuation.

Ekstein and Wallerstein (1954; see also Ekstein 1966) describe the unstable, fluid ego organization characteristic of some severely disturbed children. These are children in whom the developmental achievement of stable personality organization has not taken place but where, instead, personality organization varies with (has not achieved autonomy from) changes in affect level and object attachment. Weil (1953, 1956) describes their pervasive unevenness of development and the equally pervasive oddness that follows from it. And Kernberg (1967, 1968), working mostly with adult patients, focuses on the pathological consequences of excessive reliance on certain primitive defenses, most notably "splitting," i.e., the developmental failure of, or the regressive interference with, the integration of representations of the good and bad (both self and other) into more realistic whole images. As I have noted elsewhere (Pine 1974b), such integration can be conceptualized as fostering a toning down of idealization (via the effect of the "bad" on the "good" images) and a tempering of rage (via the effect of the "good" on the "bad").

All of these mechanisms, and others, are found in borderline children—that is, in children who show the broad defining attributes of developmental failure or aberration in major aspects of ego function and object relationship. In many ways, the persons whose work most closely links to my own views are Knight (1953a, 1953b), writing on borderline adults, and Redl (1951) writing on ego disturbances in children. For Knight emphasizes not single mechanisms but a general tendency to ego regression in borderline adults; in any particular instance, the specific nature of the regression would still have to be identified. With a shift in emphasis from regression to primary developmental failure, that approach is essentially my own as well. And an argument for the value of specificity of identification of pathology within any broad domain is given by Redl in his paper on ego disturbances. There he indicates that generalized "support" for an ill-defined "weak ego" leaves us high and dry when it comes to choices regarding technique. Rather, careful specification of particular areas of ego pathology permits tailoring of technical interventions to those weaknesses. That clinical philosophy underlies my approach to the specification of particular psychopathological phenomena in the borderline domain as well (Pine 1976).

Let me turn, now, to some of the observable clinical entities, the *variant forms*, with which child clinicians are familiar. These entities can be viewed as subtypes within the borderline domain, in part defined by the ways in which the mechanisms already described, among others, appear in them. Since I have given case examples of these subtypes elsewhere (Pine 1974a), I shall, in the interest of avoiding repetition, not give them here. What I shall describe may alternatively be considered to be variations in the *phenomena* (rather than *subtypes*); by this I mean to suggest that more than one kind of "borderline phenomenon" can be found in any particular "borderline child."

1. Some children show remarkable variation in the degree of pathology of their overall mode of functioning; I shall try to capture this phenomenon in certain particular children by the term *shifting levels of ego organization*. At one moment sensitively, often painfully, in touch with their thoughts and feelings, expressed in the context of a stable alliance with a trusted therapist, or, alternatively, simply playing-thinking-behaving in age-appropriate ways in the context of that same alliance and sense of therapeutic presence, these children may at another moment, often suddenly within a single session, become peculiar, voice odd ideas, lose the more mature relatedness to the therapist, and instead speak illogically, uncommunicatively, and affectively withdraw. But, in the instances to which I refer, there is no apparent panic; rather, there is a sense of familiarity, of ego syntonicity in the child's move into peculiar functioning.

Ekstein and Wallerstein (1954; Ekstein 1966) have written on such children, emphasizing how critical are the loss of contact and return to contact with the therapist in setting off or terminating such states. The absence of panic in the "peculiar" state is, I believe, an important key to understanding what is going on. Such children have not simply "broken down"; rather, they have regressively moved to a more primitive level of ego organization (and object relation). In the face of some disturbing (inner or outer) stimulus, anxiety arises and culminates not in the triggering of a set of more or less adaptive defenses but in the onset of this single, massive, regressive, maladaptive defense. But maladaptive how? Only to the outside; only for social adaptation. For internally it is highly adaptive; that is, it terminates the anxiety; it truly "works" for the child (hence I refer to it as an ego organization), though it works at a substantial price.

My understanding is that such children have achieved two quite different levels of ego organization. But both are *organizations;* they include means of thinking, relating, and handling anxiety. The "higher" level is vulnerable, however, and too easily slips away. In terms of mechanisms described by other writers (and reviewed earlier), these children show marked fluidity of functioning and a pervasive oddness when in their more primitive mode of functioning; though they do not demonstrate panic anxiety, they avoid it at a major adaptive price by a massive ego regression.

In terms of treatment, it is my impression that it is critical to recognize the anxiety-binding functions of the more primitive ego organization. Hence, while work with such children (and all severely disturbed children) must include a very real sense of the benign qualities of the therapist conveyed gently and nonobtrusively to the child, a good deal of exploratory, interpretive work is also required. The work is not simply a matter of educatively making up for deficits, of supportively seeing the child through panic, or developmentally fostering delayed growth. While, as any therapist knows, these may all come into play at times, work with these children includes exploration and insight into the source of the anxiety, the function of the regression, the secondary gains in it, and the historical basis for its use.

2. In contrast in many ways to those children just described are those who evidence *internal disorganization in response to external disorganizers.* These are children whose lower-level functioning is not *their* achievement—it is not an "achievement" at all; it does not "work" for them but instead reflects a true incursion upon their functioning, the result of an invasion that disrupted it. Hence the descriptive name: *internal disorganization in response to external disorganizers.*

It is my impression that such children are most commonly the product of rearing environments where a high level of social pathology (addiction, criminality, prostitution, violence, etc.) are part and parcel of everyday family life. In a children's psychiatric ward of a big-city municipal hospital where I have seen them, they are often from ghetto/poverty areas as well, though I see no reason to believe that the same (disorganizing) result cannot be brought about in other settings of intense psychological barrage upon the child's functioning. In any event, observation of such children through our ward setting teaches something about the "clinical course" of the illness and in turn permits inferences about its structure. These children arrive in the emergency room, sometimes with reported hallucinations or delusions, often with confusion in speech and relatedness, and frequently with reports of recent suicidal or homicidal behavior. On the ward they rapidly pull together and indeed often come to be seen as more or less normal children. What are we to make of this?

I believe that the rapid recovery in the benign setting of the ward (shielded from their disorganizing environment) suggests that the basic developmental tools of ego function (here reality testing, reliable intrapsychic defense, secondary process thinking) and for nondestructive trusting object relationship had indeed been formed, but that they were fragile, unable to withstand the disintegrating effect of chaotic life circumstances. In a benign setting integration can take place. From a purely descriptive point of view, these children can also be seen as fluid, i.e., functioning at different levels at different times; but the "fluidity" is very different here, captured better, I believe, by words like breakdown or collapse than by a phrase like "shift to a different level of functional ego organization."

From the point of view of treatment, there are important things to be said. I believe the key first line of treatment is rescue. The first-line rescue is not a fantasy of the therapist, in this instance, but a need of the child. It is essentially the benign setting, including a caring adult, without need for exploration or insight, that fosters integration and use of capacities that are present in seed form. But it would indeed be a rescue fantasy if we were to believe that work is done at that point. First and most obvious, of course, is the issue of return to the offending environment; and either extensive family work (often impossible to accomplish), or placement, or long-term help for the child in withstanding the barrage is required. But second, and more subtly, the child's tendency to repeat actively what he has experienced passively, both as a form of mastery and as an expression of his continuing love/hate attachment to his parents, can only be forestalled through long-term treatment that both supports and interprets, as needed and as possible for the particular patient. Obviously such long-term treatment is often more an ideal than a possibility, and so the generational repetition remains with us.

3. The group of children who show what I call *chronic ego deviance* are not really a group at all, since there is no unifying underlying structural or developmental feature by which all can be characterized. So this is a loose array, perhaps waiting for distinctions within it to be described as our clinical knowledge advances. Described by Weil (1953, 1956) some time ago, these are children who show any one or more of an assortment of aberrations of logical thought, reality testing, defense or object relation. Panic anxiety, failure to achieve phase dominance in the course of psychosexual development, unreliability of object attachment, of self/object differentiation, of stable defense may, in any one child, be characteristic. I emphasize the word *chronic* in describing their ego deviance to emphasize that the impairment is part of the child, not reactive as in the group who respond to disorganizing environments, and also to emphasize that the instability of their functioning can be expected to continue to show up; their instability is stably present.

In my own experience, I have discovered one phenomenon in treatment that differentiates these children sharply from the preceding group. Those children (the group disorganized in response to external disorganizers) tend to *heal* rapidly in the setting of a benign environment and a trusting relationship to the therapist; soon, from the point of view of basic ego intactness at least, they appear more or less normal. But some of the chronically ego-deviant children show a quite opposite phenomenon. That is, as the trusting relationship to the therapist develops, they permit themselves to *reveal*, perhaps for the first time, isolated bits of bizarre thought or behavior that they have concealed until that time.

Treatment for these children must vary with the nature of the specific failure or aberration of ego development (set, of course, in the context of the patient's whole life). It was Redl (1951) who first argued compellingly that indiscriminate support for a vaguely defined, weak ego would get us nowhere; instead we have to specify the area of deficit and tailor intervention techniques to this. In an earlier paper (Pine 1976), I tried to demonstrate some instances of such work in the context of the implicit parenting function served by the therapist for the ego-deviant patient. Indeed, this (present) whole chapter, on specific variants among borderline children (and among learning-disturbed and behavior-problem children), has that same intent: to specify pathological conditions more precisely so as to enable us to adapt an essentially psychoanalytically informed treatment approach to the particular patient.

4. Of the borderline children whom I have thus far described, two of the groups (shifting levels of ego organization and chronic ego deviance) carry their pathology within, the former as a pathological defense organization and the latter as the result of developmental failure of various sorts; the current *reactive* component in the pathology is relatively small. In contrast the reactive component is more substantial in those children whose internal disorganization is responsive to external disorganizers. A group of children in whom we see *incomplete internalization of psychosis* also shows an important reactive component. In this group, however, the reactive component does not simply reflect a destructive intrusion upon the child's functioning but is a core part of the child's attachment to the primary love object, usually the mother (see Anthony 1971).

I am referring to children, generally children of a psychotic mother, who assimilate parts of the mother's psychosis as a way of being close to mother and of having her within. It involves more than conscious mimicry; hence, it is pathological. But the internalization of the mother's psychosis is still incomplete; hence I call these children borderline rather than psychotic. The incompleteness of the internalization is made clear by the relative speed with which some of the more obvious indicator-behaviors drop away when the children are separated from their mothers and other love objects become available (again see Anthony 1971). Descriptively, fluidity of functioning is again apparent; formulatively, since the child moves toward merging with the mother, failures in the separation-individuation process (Mahler et al. 1975) can be inferred, as can the child's reliance on regression to primitive forms of incorporation for defense. There is no question but that treatment is a long and complex process, notwithstanding the gains the child may make if separated from the mother (e.g., by the hospitalization of either one of them). For like the other reactive group of borderline children (internal disorganization in response to external disorganizers), a large residue remains even when the obvious "reaction" terminates. In these children, extended work is required to relive (in the transference), to understand (through exploration), and to work through the relation with the primary love object. Within the essentially analytic/exploratory content of the sessions, the benign presence of the therapist—a differentiated other, who allows individuality and who does not require sharing of pathology as a condition for relatedness—will (whatever his theoretical orientation) inevitably provide corrective emotional experience (Alexander 1956).

5. There are other children who, though they vary in the precise area and quality of their pathology of ego function and object relationship, show enough similarity in the developmental route to that pathology to warrant grouping them for purposes of conceptualization and discussion of treatment. I call

them children with *ego limitation.* That term could be used to refer to inhibited children, dull children, culturally deprived children, or whatever. But let me describe the children for whom I intend to use it.

Sometimes, for inner and familial reasons, a child "happens upon" an early adaptive-defensive mode that markedly curtails large areas of subsequent development. If this happens, and if at the same time the defense is "successful" (in inner terms, i.e., lessening anxiety, allowing gratification, fitting with the family), it may be retained for a long time with ever-growing damage to the developmental process. Thus, a pseudo-imbecilic child (Mahler 1942; Pine 1974a), whose inner psychological requirements are not to learn, will show effects of that learning stoppage in formal school learning, peer relations, social sense, and everywhere else. Or, to take another example, Youngerman (1979) reports on a child, electively mute fairly continuously since age 3, the development of whose entire thought process was impaired as a consequence of the refusal to speak. Speech externalizes inner fantasies and permits their correction against the response of others; by verbalizing certain ideas and seeing that wishes do not always produce effects, the child learns to abandon ideas of the omnipotence of thought; and of course speech is the instrumentality of relationships at a distance— permitting distal connection and not requiring highly charged body contact and affect and gesture as the continuing modes of communication.

It is my experience that children showing this early and severe ego limitation bring a wide range of serious failings in ego function and object relation into their later treatment. It is also my impression, however, that a defensive-adaptive style of such long duration and (though pathological) such great "success" (intrapsychically) is not readily renounced. Not only does work with such children require sustained and sophisticated interpretive work to penetrate their heavily relied-upon defense organizations but, and this is critical, once it is penetrated we are still left with a child with substantial deficits. That is, the years of nonlearning have taken their toll. Interpretation (of, for example, the basis for the pseudo imbecility or the mutism) may lead to lesser reliance on the defense but does not create what has been missed in development. For this, an extensive educative process is required, along with continuing therapeutic work. But two cautions are in order: First, the educative process cannot be undertaken until the defense barrier is more or less abandoned, until the child understands it and is trying to give it up, or else the "education" will be greeted with that very same defense style and be cast away; second, optimism about making up for the lost development of years, even after the defense is penetrated and educational supplementation is begun (either within or outside of the therapy), is hardly warranted in such cases where, in my experience at least, the child remains with considerable deficit.

6. *Schizoid personality* in childhood, exactly parallel to its adult form, seems to me to warrant inclusion in the broader group of borderline children. Such

personalities, characterized by a sharply constricted and undeveloped affective life with emotional distance in human relationships and preoccupation with their own (often rich but peculiar) fantasy life, can be seen quite clearly already in childhood. The peculiarities of thought and severe limitations of object relationship reflect the developmental aberrations or failures of the general borderline domain.

Like the children with shifting levels of ego organization whose shift to a more primitive organization successfully wards off anxiety (even at the price of often severe disturbance of function), the preoccupation with fantasy in the schizoid children also will often work well to avoid anxiety (or indeed any affect). Treatment is therefore difficult. Since fantasizing works well for the children, it will not easily be given up; relationships to others are quite cut off, and so the therapist cannot easily become important to the child. And, since the child does not shift between in-touch and fantasizing states, but rather stays safely shielded from others by affective distance and fantasy preoccupation, the therapist does not see the variability that allows for even periodic contact or interpretive inroads. Once again a long sustained treatment seems necessary, with all of the patience, restraint, and interpretive skill that is part and parcel of any full treatment, and all of which can lead to the slow growth of a therapeutic alliance.

7. I should like to describe one more subgroup of borderline children that I had not been able to describe at the time of my earlier paper (Pine 1974*a*). Alerted by Kernberg's (1967, 1968) writings on adult borderline patients, I became attuned to certain children who show an omnipresent splitting of good and bad images of self and other. Such children, often "sweet" or "good" on the surface, will, in treatment, reveal an absorbing inner preoccupation with hate and violence, often with homicidal or world-destruction fantasies, equally often with scant and precarious control over them. The splitting is evidenced in the lack of connection between the "good" and the "bad" self and other. Hate, unmodified by affectionate images, becomes icy or fiery, devouring of the self or the other (in mental life), and frightening— to the patient and to the therapist who learns about it.

I first became aware of this as a phenomenon in childhood from an adult patient, suffering from her irreconcilable love-hate images toward her adoptive parents, who was able to recall the phenomenon vividly from her childhood. The "teachers pet" in school, the good girl, she nonetheless recalls sitting in class absorbed with violent and destructive fantasy. Hearing it, I was reminded of the recurrent newspaper stories of mass murderers who, as the history unfolds, were "good" children, generally quiet and not too well known to anyone, but well behaved, disciplined. And then I was reminded of the comment heard among educators, that troublesome (noisy, school-failing) children come to the attention of the school, but that quiet children who may also be in trouble may not be noticed. Might not these quiet children not only be "in trouble" as nonlearners but also as instances of the kind of child of which I am now speaking. Not all of them by any means! But here and there.

Such were my thoughts at the time, listening to my adult patient speak. Since then, more alert to the issue, I have come across the phenomenon three or four times in a few years through supervision of the work of others or through direct consultation or treatment myself. There is no question but that the phenomenon exists in childhood. Its attendant disturbances in thought processes and object relations warrant its being considered another form of the borderline disturbance. Just beginning to work in the area, I do not yet feel comfortable commenting on any repeated issues in the treatment of such children; my impression is, however, that the work is exceedingly difficult, that the "split" modifies only slowly if at all, and that the primitive rage and violence are constantly in danger of either erupting or succumbing to repression rather than undergoing modification.

In summary of this first section: I have advanced the idea that a loose, but defensible, conceptual category of "borderline children" can be defined in terms of central developmental failures or aberrations in ego development and object relationship. These disturbances are identifiable in the school-age period because, by that age, one ordinarily expects to see some degree of stability of character and of socialization in the child; the "peculiarities" of the borderline child generally violate that expectation. Within the broad borderline domain, there is a distinct clinical gain from seeking not a single unifying mechanism that is shared by all such patients but individualized descriptions of subtypes of borderline phenomena—subtypes which *do* have essential commonalities and whose commonalities of etiology and/or structure can lead us to individualized implications for treatment.

About treatment, I have made a number of specific comments regarding each subgroup along the way. But I would like, in concluding this section, to make one final point. Once recently, when I was discussing an earlier version of the ideas presented here with a rather unsophisticated group of beginning therapists, the discussion began to turn around the question: Should we or should we not make interpretations to borderline patients? Referring to Knight (1953b) in excessively simplistic form, one person concluded that we were not supposed to make interpretations. And another, referring to Kernberg (1968), equally simplistically concluded that indeed we were supposed to interpret. What, they asked, did I think they were "supposed" to do?

I assume by now my answer to that question is clear. With fuller understanding of the range of pathology subsumed under the concept "borderline," one cannot avoid the responsibility of creating an answer tailored not only to the events of the moment (as in all dynamic psychotherapy) but also to the specific form of the pathology. Sometimes we do one thing, and sometimes another. I can only say: It all depends. On what? That is what I have tried to spell out, at least in part, herein.

Disturbances of Learning

A second characteristic area of disturbance in the school-age period is the broad one of learning. It is an area where concerns of parents, educators, child clinicians, and the children themselves can often come together.

It is not surprising that this should be so. As discussed earlier, one of the basic tasks of the age is the establishment of the learning process as a sufficiently neutralized and automatic one such that new learnings can be accumulated. Such learnings, especially in school, are ordinarily different from the earlier, preschool learnings in that they are less intimately tied to the body (that is, they are unlike learning about dressing, toileting, eating) and are received from relatively more impersonal sources (teacher, not parents). Peer group learning is also prominent (games, rules, rhymes, tricks), but it is principally the disturbances of school learning that lead parents to seek help for their children, and it is this on which I shall concentrate here. While it has often been said that failures in love and work are central in adults' seeking of treatment, we can also readily recognize how central learning is to the "work" of the school-age child. Love, in this case especially "self-love" (self-esteem), is also centrally involved with success or failure in learning, as is one's esteem in the eyes of peers, teachers, and parents. Problems of learning are not only important because of the disturbances they reflect and the suffering that may accompany them, but because they obviously have real consequences for the paths open to a child as he grows into later life.

In my discussion of the borderline disturbances, I tried to show the clinical value of recognizing the similarities and differences among borderline children. I suggested that core failures in the development of ego functions and object relations conceptually unite the group, but that the specific nature of the failures vary. I further suggested that, while ordinarily showing one or another form of oddness in their functioning and thus again similar (even if only vaguely so), they can be importantly differentiated from one another in terms of organizational and etiological features of their pathology—the subtypes that I described. Related considerations apply to the disturbances of learning. There is no question but that a wide array of routes to learning disturbances exists and that this variation speaks to a nonunified set of pathological entities in the area of learning failure. But in various secondary, though still highly important ways, these conditions have much in common. Descriptively, the presenting symptoms are of course learning difficulties; functionally, they all have major implications for school success; and as a consequence of their presence, they often have an impact on self-esteem. Additionally, they all reflect failures in (what I will formulate as) one or more of three broad developmental lines on which the child must have progressed in order for learning to take place. Before turning to description of specific forms of learning disturbance, let me describe the three developmental lines. These are, of course, abstractions from the developmental process. I shall give them a form that is helpful in highlighting the disturbances that I shall later describe.

To begin, then, for learning to take place, the basic tools for the process must be biologically and psychologically intact and must have developed in age-appropriate ways. First and foremost, it is obvious that learning capacity will vary with general intelligence; indeed one definition of general intelligence is precisely in terms of the capacity to learn. Beyond that, specific tools are needed for one or another kind of learning, tools such as capacity for intake of information through visual, auditory, and tactile channels (and output through all channels as well), perceptual discrimination, visual organization, visual and auditory short- and long-term memory, sequencing of concepts, sustained attention, and the like. The last-listed, sustained attention, should alert us especially to the psychological-developmental achievements underlying some of these basic tools. The capacity to attend and, even more, the emotional investment in learning (i.e., so that learning matters and/or gives pleasure) are achievements forged in the developmental mix of object relatedness, drive-defense arrangements, and inborn capacities, and are core tools (capacities) for the learning process.

Additionally, for school learning to take place, the child must have developed to the point where there is a reasonable inner harnessing of those affect states and behavioral expressions which, when present in unharnessed form, would readily upset the delicate balance of receptivity, sustained attention, and interest outside oneself that is necessary for optimal learning. If the child is still subject to affect storms (for example, of panic anxiety, of needy longing) and developmental-defensive modulation of these has not taken place, learning will ordinarily suffer. Similarly, if impulses and affects readily spill over into gross motor activity, the state of receptivity for learning will have suffered. I recognize, of course, that much learning is enhanced by affective involvement and even motor behavior. This is no contradiction. The "harnessing" of affect and motor behavior in development does not refer to their elimination but rather to their coordination with other aims of the individual.

And third, for learning to take place, the learning process must have a reasonable degree of autonomy (Hartmann 1939; Rapaport 1967) from a person's major urges and the fantasies connected with them. There are changing currents in the relation of fantasy to function in the course of development. Very early on, for example, eating (sucking) is clearly a biological, life-sustaining process. That it remains so goes without saying, but the presence in childhood of food fads, of disgust reactions, of food avoidances reflect the intrusion of fantasy (anal, cannibalistic, etc.) into the biologically based process. Still later, with the attainment of "rational eating" (A. Freud 1965), these fantasies have been more or less tamed in relation to the act of eating. Again this does not mean that they are eliminated. The relativity of autonomy from drives implies two things: (a) An ego function or a process (such as learning) is relatively autonomous from drives in that it can always be reinvaded, reinterfered with; it is not impervious; the autonomy is not absolute. And especially relevant right now, (b) it is relatively autonomous in the sense not that drive components are totally eliminated but that they are united with the function or process in nonconflictual ways; thus learning can be enhanced by the fantasy of becoming "just like mommy or daddy" and not only interfered with by such an idea.

So then, from the point of view of development, learning requires (a) the availability of basic tools; (b) the harnessing of potential interferences with the learning process, such as too intense affect or too impulsive behavior, that can disrupt attention and intake; and (c) (akin to, but differentiable from the second) the achievement and maintenance of a secondary autonomy from drives and their attendant fantasies. In addition, with reference to developmental lines, and though it is not as widespread in its relation to the normal range of the psychopathology of learning, I shall have to introduce issues in the development of self-other differentiation, object constancy, and object relations in order to clarify one particular area of learning disturbance.

Let us turn now to an examination of some clinical material to see how differentiations among the disturbances of learning can be made with these developmental lines as background. I shall include instances with problems of a built-in nature and of a psychogenic nature, as well as various distinctions within and mixes between the two. I shall organize the illustrations under eight headings: problems of general intelligence, specific-cognitive deficits, interrelation of cognitive deficits and broader psychological functioning, learning problems secondary to other psychological conditions, learning failure as a specific symptom, learning failure as part of a general character trait, learning failure as a reflection of disturbance in object relations, and family-based disinterest in learning. "Learning" is of course not a unity in itself; I shall be drawing upon interferences with various aspects of that process and with various areas of information intake that may be disturbed.

Problems of general intelligence. I start simplistically and briefly to state the obvious: Sometimes a child's reported "problem" of learning is based on a lower level of general intelligence than those on the outside are aware characterizes him. I mention this here not only for the sake of completeness but because it comes up as a problem in clinical work. It may become a problem for the child, but it starts as a problem for the parents or educators in their role of goal-setters.

Some children, because their eyes are bright and facial expression winning, or because their social grace is captivating, or because they are very verbal (though not necessarily complexly so), or because their parents are quite successful, or for none of these reasons but because of parental hopes, are taken to be brighter than they are. This can be at any level: children whose work is fair rather than excellent or poor rather than adequate. Were the clinician to accept the problem as defined by the parent, even find rationale in the perennial intelligence test conclusion that "this score does not represent his true optimal level of functioning" (an often accurate but often misused phrase), or find no need to make an adequate intellectual assessment at all and work with the child around his so-called "learning failure," then the problem becomes compounded.

No need to beat a dead horse. Such problems exist. I have more than once encountered the resistance to the conclusion "low intelligence" in clinic or private work. The diagnostic task is adequate assessment; the therapeutic one, work with parents and school toward a realistic view of the child to avoid creating secondary problems for the child. Easily said, but not easily done. We well know that, especially in some families and in most schools, intelligence is intensely, often irrationally, valued. To help parents to develop a realistic view, without the consequence of the child's being viewed as debased, without provoking irrational feelings of guilt or failure in the parents, is a consultative (sometimes extended therapeutic) task of no small delicacy and magnitude.

Problems of specific-cognitive disability. In this book around the theme of psychoanalytic contributions to an understanding of development and psychopathology, one may wonder why specific cognitive disabilities (and also problems of general intelligence) are included. They are included because there *has* been a psychoanalytic (or at least psychodynamic) contribution in this area, albeit a negative one. That is, it has been all too easy to find psychodynamic "reasons" for any learning failure, especially since fantasies are bound to get attached to any significant failure and the clinical method provides the clinician with no good basis for distinguishing fantasy as "cause" from fantasy as secondary consequence. Additionally, I list cognitive disabilities here (a) for completeness, (b) because the working clinician should have knowledge of his full range of options, and (c) because (as I shall turn to in my next grouping) these disabilities exist in people who "have psychodynamics" so to speak, and almost inevitably they become interlaced with the individual's defense system, wishes, self-esteem, and object relations.

Two brief illustrations of the phenomenon of specific disabilities: Some years ago, I consulted with a father and his young girl about her problems in learning to read. Tutoring had not helped; the school regularly threatened failure and urged therapy. The girl herself seemed (by and large) rather well functioning, related, adequately expressive, adequately controlled. Numerous test findings suggested a deficit in the capacity for organization of the visual field; though the negative case cannot be proven, nothing in the test or consultation findings suggested a specific psychological "meaning" of this failing. The problem slowed her enormously in her comprehension of that complex visual field that is the printed page. Interestingly, just at the time of this consultation, this preadolescent girl had gotten fascinated with photography as a hobby. That fact fit. My impression was that she inarticulately sensed her disability and that photography was a kind of mastery, a turning of passive to active—it organized the visual field for her. I had followup many years later.

She never had therapy; her reading never did more than inch along; and she became a professional photographer.

A second child, presenting with pervasive and crippling pseudo-imbecility (Pine 1974a), gradually (and only partially) gave that up during a long period of intensive psychotherapy. His intelligence blossomed in social perceptivity and language use. Many gaps remained in school learning, though some areas slowly gained over time. But arithmetic skills remained abysmal. While again the negative case cannot be proven, my impression was (and I knew this child well) that the arithmetic failure reflected specific disabilities in various aspects of number concepts and could not gain with the general freeing of intelligence. Thus, what we had after therapy had begun to have its impact was a residual specific cognitive deficit. A depressed paraplegic who recovers from his depression will show livelier facial movement but still will not walk. So, too, work on psychological aspects of learning will not automatically aid certain specific disabilities.

The growing attention to minimal cerebral dysfunction calls attention to problems such as those just described but also obscures and overstates for the uninformed. For what I am describing here is not a single syndrome, not necessarily a syndrome (a connected set of signs) at all, not necessarily including hyperactivity or poor attention span for example (and neither of these two children showed hyperactivity or poor attention span), but specific failings in special areas. As people vary in height and eye color, and as they vary in visual acuity and general intelligence, so too can they vary (presumably on neurological grounds) in specific cognitive capacities. Benjamin (1968, 1969, 1971) has done considerable work in the assessment and tailor-made remediation of such specific disabilities. These children show a deficit of the basic tools for at least certain specific kinds of learning. While work with them might at times involve major dynamic therapeutic issues (see below), and may involve sensitive work with parents (as discussed above), much of the work is also remedial and supportive in relation to their real difficulties in the educational environment.

Interrelations of specific cognitive deficits and the broader psychological functioning of the child. Though the distinction is necessarily arbitrary, I discuss these phenomena separately from the ones just described (specific cognitive deficits) for the sake of clarity of exposition. I am still focusing on specific deficits, presumably with a neurological basis, that affect learning; but here I shall focus on their secondary effects in interplay with the child's intrapsychic life. I want to describe two phenomena: reactions to the deficit and the deficit as a nodal point for further symptom formation.

A child was brought to me for psychological assessment. The symptom picture (failures in writing and drawing among other things) and a previous assessment were highly suggestive of specific problems in visual-motor coordination; he could also spell well orally, but not in writing. The father's instruction to me was, however, "don't tell me he's brain-damaged, I've already been told that." Indeed, the data again suggested visual-motor coordination problems. One especially revealing moment was the boy's attempt to draw a rocket. He could not get his hand to turn the pencil to make the angles go in the direction he wished; yet his eye could easily see that his final drawing was grossly distorted in its angles. The capacity for visual-motor coordination was flawed, but the negative visual feedback was received. The boy, pervasively anxious and embarrassed with regard to his deficit, wishing to please his father who refused to acknowledge the deficit, and (not-too-far-from-consciousness) trying to turn the passive (failure) into active (success), announced to me with feigned enthusiasm that he was going to be a blueprint designer when he grew up. To my response (after our work was nearly completed) that he had real skills, that those were not among them, that I thought he knew that from his rocket drawing, and that he was intelligent and could however do many other things successfully, he responded with enormous relief and the touching exclamation: "This has been the best day of my life!" I believe the failure (of which he was aware but which he could not understand), plus the paternal denial, pushed the boy into a brittle denial of the reality that he experienced everyday (his failures) and left him preoccupied, on the edge of humiliation, and vulnerable (in self-esteem and in reality testing) to each new failure.

Such secondary reactions to deficit are not rare. Though "secondary" in a causal sense, they can be of major impact for the child's functioning. (I think here, also, of children with depressed mood and low self-esteem secondary to reading problems or to problems in acquisition of other skills, also on a neurological basis.) The therapeutic problem here is not minor. These children, and their parents, have to be helped to understand the reality of the deficit, including understanding of its specificity, i.e., that the child is not totally "damaged." But such information itself can (after a frequent response of "seeing the light," as many facts of the child's life fit into place) produce further depression or denial. My own experience is that when these secondary reactions are reasonably well established, only a period of intensive psychotherapy will break into them, this quite to the side of the patient's specific remedial needs.

A different phenomenon in this domain: Like the views of "somatic compliance" in psychosomatic illness which held that biologically weak organs would be the ones to show malfunction related to psychological conflict, or as body deformities or even special names can "attract" fantasies to themselves and become focal points for the development of symptoms (or, more constructively, interests), so too can specific cognitive disabilities become nodal points for symptom formation. By way of example, let me mention a child with a dyslexic syndrome who experienced inordinate confusion in her struggle with the printed page. Subsequently, when strong aggressive or sexual impulses were aroused, they culminated in parallel states of confusion. An anlage for experience had been laid down. The two came together especially in school where impulse arousal led to "confusion" and thus further learning failure (in nondeficit areas). The latter learning failure (math, history) gave way with interpretation of intrapsychic conflict; not so the dyslexia. Incidentally, it should be clear that we are unlikely to be able even to be aware of such subtle interconnections of functioning without psychotherapy, let alone to work toward resolving them.

I have just discussed psychological problems secondary to learning problems. Now let me do the reverse.

Learning problems secondary to other psychological conditions. In discussing the positions on various developmental lines that a child must have attained for learning to take place, I suggested that a child must be able to hold in abeyance those powerful affect states or behavioral impulses that, when present, can disrupt the attentiveness and receptivity requisite for learning. The absence of affect- or impulse-control reflects problems which, while not focal to learning, nonetheless affect learning. Or, put otherwise, some children who show failure to learn need help, not primarily in the area of learning, but in other areas that have a secondary impact on the learning process.

Examples are, unfortunately, not hard to find; so let me be specific. Janey, an abused and neglected child, was "not doing any work at all" in school, and this, combined with her severe behavior problems and absenteeism, led to her clinic referral. Extremely needy, preoccupied with wishes for, fears of, and in general thoughts about her mother, this child showed near average intelligence and no specific cognitive disabilities upon close assessment. Put simply, emotions were her problem; nonlearning was a secondary effect, one of many areas affected by her extraordinarily painful home situation. Preoccupied with her mother and anxieties linked to that relationship, she was unable to focus on learning. Apart from the sad and frustrating attempts to do something for the home life of such children, I would like to comment on her remediation experience. Put in contact with a tutor, the child began to learn. No specialized (deficit-linked) remediation techniques were needed. Rather, the one-to-one relationship itself toned down her neediness and permitted attention to learning; even more, the learning became the vehicle for the relationship to the tutor and was fostered (by the child herself) as a mode of contact.

Other disruptive states operate similarly. An 8-year-old boy would get depressed at the (recurrent) intervals when a favorite pet was given away; learning would cease at these times. (While nonlearning had the secondary gain of an attack on his family who gave the pets away, the depression was primary and affected many areas beyond learning.) A school-refusing boy, with fragile ego structure, was preoccupied with wishes for and fears of the destruction of his mother and therefore could not learn even when he was in school (and stayed home with the fantasy of safeguarding her). Similarly, chronic thought disorder or pervasive behavior problems (with constant fighting and running in the classroom) will obviously have effects on learning as well as everywhere else.

Each of these children shows a specific area of difficulty (learning) that can only be understood (and worked with therapeutically) by taking into account the broader pathology of which it is probably a relatively minor part. This is by no means the case with all psychogenic learning problems. Let me turn now to some quite different clinical pictures where the learning failure is far more central.

Learning failure as specific symptom. I have described learning failures resultant from deficiencies in the tools of learning (general intelligence or specific deficits) and from the learning process being swamped by other disorders of affect, thought, or behavior. But the process of learning *in itself* can be invested with psychological meaning that leads to interferences. Here we come to more classical neurotic pictures with bound symptoms that eventuate from conflict between impulse and defense. We see interferences with the secondary autonomy of the learning process, an invasion of the *process* itself or of specific *content* areas by conflictual fantasies.

Thus, learning can come to be equated with knowing about sexual events or family secrets and, in either case, can succumb to an inhibition (in school) that parallels the repression of ideas connected with sex and/or secrets. Allen (1967) has described voyeuristic and exhibitionistic conflicts intefering with seeing/knowing or "showing" what one knows. And the group working out of the Judge Baker Child Guidance Center in the 1950s and early 1960s described other essentially neurotic interferences with learning, for example, where success stimulates castration anxiety (Sperry et al. 1958; Grunebaum et al. 1962). In these instances, learning (as a process) and knowledge (as potentially taboo content) are the central targets of the pathological formation, not secondary to anything else. Just how it becomes that way, i.e., the problem of symptom choice, is a question we know little about at the level of general clinical theory but which we learn much about in the indepth study of each individual when intensive treatment is undertaken.

Sometimes the interference can be much more specific. For example, a child referred because his school grades were falling sharply turned out to have a specific interference with the writing process. He had begun to write so slowly, with such a burden of inhibition, that he never finished his tests and would therefore get low grades. The fantasy that writing was an aggressive act, more specifically that writing involved "signing a death warrant," turned out to be central and had taken shape after the death of a relative. In other children, neurotic interference with specific content areas also occurs: difficulty learning about wars in history class in a child struggling with aggressive impulses; failure in English composition in a boy, anxious about whether body parts were "long enough," who would feel compelled to make his sentences longer, extending and overextending them until they became "run-on" sentences that were grammatically incorrect and unintelligible. In each of these instances, the specific school failure has an intrapsychic "meaning"; something about learning process or content has become involved in intrapsychic fantasy and conflict, has lost its affective neutrality in the process, and has become subject to defensive avoidance or other interference.

Learning failure as a part of a general character trait. I have just described psychological disturbances that have specific impact on particular aspects of learning process or content. I would like now to turn to interference somewhat less precisely directed at learning per se, but yet far more closely tied to learning failure than those conditions (thought disorder, impulse disorder, affect flooding) that interfere with learning in an almost incidental way. I am referring now to maladaptive character traits which subsume aspects of the learning process. That learning is interfered with is no accidental secondary effect; neither is learning itself the focal or original "target" of the psychopathological process. Instead, broad characteristic features of a child such as a generalized inhibition (linked to unconscious active impulses) or avoidance of success or achievement (having roots in oedipal fantasies) will affect modes of play, of movement, of relatedness—and of learning as well. The issues will be structurally similar regarding those other impairments and learning, even though learning itself is not the central focus of the difficulty.

Let me give one example. An 11-year-old girl was referred by her pediatrician who could find no organic basis for her constant fatigue. Home reports were that she was "lazy," often "lethargic." A picture gradually emerged of a very ambitious-aggressive young girl, caught in an (oedipal) rivalry with a bright and successful stepsister, who defended against her active wishes by a turn to passivity. But the "lethargy" affected her schoolwork as well. Learning became impaired; work output slowed; grades went down. Success, activity, ambition in general were renounced; learning, one more form of activity and success, was drawn into the inhibition.

Learning failure as a reflection of disturbance in object relations. While the disturbances of learning that I am now going to describe are of psychogenic origin and can be said to have a "meaning" to the person, I distinguish them from those just described (specific symptom and character trait) because of what I believe to be in general a greater severity of the diagnostic picture. Based on disturbances in earliest object relations, they show, as do other sequelae of such early disturbances, the profound developmentally distorting impact of failures and aberrations in the mother-child dyad. I shall give illustration of two different kinds of interference with learning.

In recent years, two female patients, one a middle-aged adult and one a college student, told me about school difficulties in similar terms. Each could not do well because she could not study or do homework. And each could not study because the process, the sustained engagement with inanimate words and books, produced profound and painful feelings of aloneness. The result: flight into sociability, talk, no work, poor grades. Though both patients were well beyond childhood, both dated the problem back to that time as well. These were both sensitive and articulate patients; I think perhaps it would be quite difficult for a child to verbalize this material. There was an important

difference in the early childhood experiences of these two patients, a difference that was reflected in the further subtleties of the painful feeling of aloneness. One had had early, repeated experiences of object loss; the love object
(mother) was experienced as a differentiated other but was periodically lost.
While studying, her experience was one of isolation and the need for contact.
The other patient had early experiences that interfered with self-other differentiation; her life showed cycles of panic over merging (loss of differentiation)
and moments of a heightened sense of individuality (differentiation) which
were accompanied by pained feelings of loss of connectedness to her family.
Studying produced that feeling of individuality and was accompanied by feelings, not only of isolation, but of fear of merging as well. The wish underlying
the fear, the wish to terminate the isolation through merging, ultimately
became clear. Neither patient had developed that "capacity to be alone" (Winnicott 1958), here alone with work, that comes from carrying the sense of the
mother's presence inside.

A related report, this time of work with young children, shows early disturbances of learning that are linked to pathological mother-child narcissism
(Newman et al. 1973). The children, all bright and precociously verbal, were
their mother's pride, shown off by her—such that their intellectual functioning
(especially the precocious speech) came to be experienced as an extension of
the mother's narcissism. When these children reached school, they did poorly.
(Admission to this research project was by way of being a "gifted undera-
chiever.") What had happened, broadly, was that intellect had become part of
the connectedness to mother, not a tool for learning about the nonmother
world; and further, the narcissistic investment in intellectual precocity made it
such that failure could not be risked by making the effort to learn; self-esteem
vulnerability was too great.

Family-based disinterest in learning. Before stopping, I do want to mention, at
least in passing, another phenomenon of sociocultural and educational significance, though it rarely comes to us as a clinical problem in its own right. It has
to do with those children, often the ghetto poor, for whom there are no family
models for the value of learning, little or no family support for their learning,
and little in the economic-cultural surround holding promise for those who
learn. Many (by no means all) of these children learn poorly. But to say there is
"learning failure" is to presume they share our goals and have failed to meet
them. It is not at all clear that this is the case, and I would think here instead of
motivational, identificatory, and, especially, socioeconomic problems in work
in this area.

To sum up regarding disturbances of learning: I have suggested that learning
requires the child's adequate movement along developmental lines associated
with the growth of the basic cognitive tools of the learning process; the maintenance of the relative autonomy of the learning process such that it does not
suffer repression, inhibition, or other malfunction because it has been invested
with conflict-ridden symbolic meaning; the harnessing of affective and behav-

ioral flooding that would swamp the attentional-receptive processes requisite for learning to take place; and the development of adequate self-other differentiation, object constancy, and early object relations so that peremptory needs for object contact do not make work-in-isolation impossible. Along the way, I have attempted to be specific regarding both the particular aspect of the learning process or content that is impaired (i.e., the presenting problem and its variations) and the psychological or neuropsychological route to that impairment (i.e., the underlying genetic and structural sources of the problem and their variations). From a clinical-therapeutic point of view I have called attention to issues requiring (1) careful assessment of cognitive skills and capacities; (2) guidance and education for parent or child; (3) sensitive handling of the affective accompaniments to information regarding deficits; (4) work with children around their secondary reactions to deficits of which they have an inarticulate awareness; (5) recognition of the need at times for remediation, at times for therapy, and at times for both; (6) recognition also that some disturbances of learning are secondary consequences of major affect, thought, behavioral, or even sociocultural disturbances which require primary attention in their own right; and (7) the need for intensive treatment of some learning disturbances that reflect the development of bound and focal symptoms, of pathological character traits, or the end result of early disturbances in object relations.

Behavior Disturbances

Behavior is obviously omnipresent in human functioning. Broadly defined, to include "verbal behavior" and "thinking behavior" as well as motor behavior, it becomes practically coterminous with the totality of human psychological functioning. Even with a narrower definition of behavior (as action involving large movements of the voluntary musculature), we are still dealing with phenomena which, like affect, thought, and impulse, are omnipresent; we accept and expect them as part of life.

Though we accept and expect behavior as part of life, we certainly cannot view behavior *disorder* with like equanimity. That is obviously so because pathology involving the behavioral sphere is of great significance for clinical management. At its worst destructive of self or others, even the milder forms of behavioral disturbance have impacts upon others. They affect the interpersonal sphere and not only the intrapsychic one. As such, they are highly visible and are often red-flag warnings evoking the concern of parents, teachers, the courts, and others in contact with the child.

In spite of their importance, and perhaps because of their omnipresence, disturbances of behavior do not have any very specific diagnostic significance. They spring from many developmental sources and are found in varying personality contexts. In this section of the paper I shall, once again, try to describe and clarify some of the internal features of the broad landscape of behavior disturbances. Before turning to that, however, I shall first narrow the range just a bit and then show the special significance of behavior disturbances for the school-age child.

First, the narrowing: Let us imagine a child who engages in compulsive rituals which involve his walking around his room at bedtime to arrange its contents in particular ways, or a child with tics that involve flailing motions of the arms or posturing of the whole body, or a child who is a sleepwalker, wandering in his home at night. In each of these instances, motor behavior (large movements of the voluntary musculature) is enmeshed in some inner psychopathological system, but in none of these instances is the term "behavior disturbance" likely to be applied by working clinicians. Clinical custom reserves the term for those disturbed behaviors that have an antisocial or at least interpersonally disruptive component. They are troublesome or dangerous in some way. It is that set of disturbances—in the motor sphere and troublesome to others—that I shall focus upon here. I shall refer to them simply as actions that are antisocial or interpersonally disruptive. These are often called "behavior disorders," a term which remains imprecise diagnostically (i.e., it fails to indicate what may be going on under the descriptive behavioral surface) but a term which I shall try to specify further as we go along.

Behavior disorders are another characteristic form of pathology in the school-age child. Like the borderline disturbances and the learning disturbances, a clinician working with children comes across that term constantly, though often imprecisely and in ways that clarify little. There are at least three reasons why behavior should be a characteristic area of disturbance in the school-age child, all having to do with his/her position in the developmental ladder. First, school makes a great demand for motor restraint. With the exception of a very few, quite atypical, school programs that allow a great deal of free movement, the child is seated at a desk for several hours each day. Not only does this place a great demand upon his capacity for motor restraint, but violations of that restraint come to be perceived as socially disturbing acts reflecting individual disturbance. The traditional shouting and running of young children as the end-of-day schoolbell rings attest to the coiled-spring quality of the motor apparatus as that spring tightens through the long school day. Second, if we see development (as I believe we can) as a more or less steady movement toward decreased need for motor activity, or an increased capacity for sedentary activity as cognitive potentials expand, it becomes clear that the school-age child is still at the very early end of that continuum. Starting form the seemingly unending and exuberant capacity for movement in the younger toddler, just learning to crawl and then walk, and culminating in the sedentary lives of the aged a lifetime later, movement plays a declining (though always significant) role in human life. Mittelmann (1954) speaks of an early motor phase in the second year, and Mahler (1972) discusses roughly the same time in terms of a normal motor "practicing" period of great activity. Motility serves expressive, adaptive, and defensive functions. It gives pleasure, releases tension, serves as communication, and is a basis for peer relationships through play. That the motor apparatus should be involved in disturbed behavior as well comes as no surprise in this context. And the third developmentally linked reason why motor behavior is an expectable area for disturbance in the school-age child, and this is in contrast to the toddler, is that the school-age child is not only very active but has motor capacities for strength and independent action that make his behavior a potential source of concern for others when it goes awry. He can hurt himself or others; he can run away; he can steal; and he can disrupt a classroom. So we have, in the school-age years, the setting for multiple disturbances in the motor domain: a child naturally motoric, with the capacity for motor behavior of wide injurious as well as constructive range, and often (in school) in a setting where motor restraint is emphasized and motor action is disruptive. (I do *not,* however, mean to imply that these problems would go away if only schools would allow more activity. Would that problems were so simply resolved! Occasionally, yes. But, as I shall discuss, the routes to behavior disturbance are multiple, and I am here only trying to describe the setting for the child's vulnerabilities.)

There is considerable diagnostic confusion in the area of behavior disorders. In 1966, a working committee of the Group for the Advancement of Psychiatry proposed a classification of childhood psychopathology (GAP 1966) in which they listed (though they did not endorse!) no less than 11 terms frequently used diagnostically. Their overall definition is compatible with the one I am using here: "Children in this category exhibit chronic behavioral patterns of emotional expression of aggressive and sexual impulses which conflict with society's norms" (p. 254). Among the 11 listed terms are a number which can be used to highlight some of the sources of confusion in this area. Thus, "antisocial personality" or "sociopathic personality" or "dyssocial personality" are all purely descriptive terms; such a "personality" could behave in nonsocialized ways out of allegiance to a deviant subculture, out of neurotic self-defeating urges, or out of defective development of conscience, among other things. However, other terms in the list (such as "psychopathic personality" or "impulsive character") purport to have specific diagnostic significance (the former in relation to conscience development and the latter in relation to characteristic features of action/delay or drive/defense relationships). Even in the latter instances, however, there is far from complete agreement on the meaning of the terms. In any event, their applicability in any particular case requires a depth-oriented, interior view of the person and not simply a symptom-descriptive approach. Still other terms in the list of 11, terms such as "affectionless character" and "acting-out personality," have little agreed-upon meaning at all.

The GAP report's very real contribution to clarification is embodied in their delineation of two subtypes. They are: (1) impulse ridden personality (characterized by poor impulse control and little anxiety, guilt, or attachment to others); and (2) neurotic personality disorders whose "behavior often assumes a repetitive character, with unconscious significance to their acts, rather than the predominance of discharge phenomena" (p. 249). A revealing contradiction in their formulation comes in their grouping these two under the overall term "tension discharge disorders" even though the second is said not to have a "predominance of discharge phenomena." What the contradiction is revealing of is the loss of clarity that comes when disorders are grouped as instances of broader entities in ways that fail to retain sufficient respect for their differences. In any event, let me continue to draw distinctions within the behavior disorders, as the GAP manual does, and as I have done for borderline disturbances and disturbances of learning. Since, in fact, behavior is omnipresent in human functioning, I should like to begin with a look at the various ways it appears inevitably in all development and then at the ways in which it can become implicated in one or another of an unending array of intrapsychic disturbances.

Behavior, then, is inherent in childhood, as indeed it is at every point in the life cycle. Such behavior includes at least exploratory behavior in new situations (Berlyne 1960; White 1963), "Functionlust" (Hendrick 1942) or pleasure in and exercise of capacities for functioning such as the grasp or eye-hand coordination early on, and hopping, jumping, racing in the school years, fight/flight reactions in the face of danger (Bowlby 1969), and what we on the outside would designate as "appropriate" behavioral expression in the service of need satisfaction or tension reduction (e.g., in eating, going to mother). All of these reflect evolutionary continuity; they are sources of the impetus to action that are characteristic of all of the higher animal species at least. And there is another normal form of behavior that is characteristic of human beings, whether or not of any other animal species. Freud refers to it in his writing on the repetition compulsion (1920); it involves the general tendency to repeat actively what we experience passively; thus, a child is frightened of an operation, and then plays doctor, or is similarly frightened of too fast a car ride, and then zooms his own cars around his room. All of these (exploration, exercise of capacities, fight/flight, gratification seeking or pain avoiding, and active repetition of things experienced passively) are expressed in the motor domain (among others), yet no one of them is reflective of behavior disorder. If anything their absence, their inhibition, may reflect disorder of another kind. Nonetheless, *any one* of them may shade over into pathology in ways that may or may not be clear from the outside. Let me give two examples. They are intended as arguments for the need for an inner view of any behavior in order to understand its specifics and to know how to approach it therapeutically. Such an inner view represents the specification I have in mind within the "behavior disorders."

In talking with a mother regarding her 12-year-old son whom she had brought for help, I learned about his earlier life as well. She said that "he always ran away." I immediately wondered (silently, to myself) about the solidity of his delay/defense capacities and about the stability of his attachment to his mother. But when I learned, to my question about his running away, that this began at about age 15 to 18 months when he "would always run down the street and I would have to dash after him to get him," my inner formulation shifted rapidly. Here seemed to be a mother not only with no understanding of the normal mode of motor activity of the toddler, but one, perhaps, who imposed her fantasy-explanations on those behaviors when they occurred. When I next heard that he also ran away (this time more seriously, to various places in the neighborhood, but for short times only) several times at about age 9 or 10, I had to entertain various explanatory notions in the light of the history. Was this a "behavior disorder"? What would that mean? Was he impulsive? Insufficiently aware of the consequences of his acts? Insufficiently attached to mother? Or was this (as the case turned out) the form of his attachment to mother? He acted upon her expectations of his "badness" (and in ways specific to her fantasies, such as the running away) and was then punished in the setting of a sadomasochistic mother-child bond. Misbehavior and punishment were essential to their relationship; as he later (age 13) said to me: "How would I know she loved me if she didn't punish me?" Interestingly, in his midteens a new symptomatic act emerged transiently, that of wandering through the streets to fixed locations in a semifugue-like, obligatory state. Our work revealed this to be a repetition of a forgotten traveling incident with his father who had disappeared from his life many years before; so "wandering" (a form of running away) had yet another object-related connection in his life: now to his father as well as to his mother. What we see here is neurotic character pathology—structuralized, ego-syntonic, object-related, and characteristic—that expresses itself in seemingly unsocialized behavior as well as in other areas.

Let us look at a second instance, or rather set of instances, where normal behavior (as in the first child's "running away" at 15 months) shades into disturbed behavior: A young child came dangerously close to being hit by a passing truck as he crossed a street with an adult, the adult quickly picking him up out of harm's way as the truck raced past; in his home afterward, he went to play with his trucks, controlling their movements in his play. The passive experience is turned to an active one as a means to mastery. Constructive; hardly pathological. But take another child for whom the passive experience is one of being beaten and who then goes to school and beats up others. The inner situation is similar to that of the first child—mastery of a passive experience through active repetition—but the second child would present as a "behavior disorder." To proceed hypothetically for a moment, if the first child continued at his truck play for days on end, the play becoming more compulsive, repetitious, less pleasurable, we would begin to consider that a mini-pathological process was at work, that the movement toward mastery had gone awry. But, though the reflection of the disturbance is in motor play, we certainly would not call it a "behavior disorder," since it does not break social rules. Yet, to switch back now to another actual situation, parallel phenomena (from an intrapsychic viewpoint) would be considered indices of behavior disorder if they did violate social rules. Thus, a particular child who chronically felt weak and unmanly would regularly, in a driven way, climb to high places, race up and down stairs, and in general take risks, as a means of compensatory reversal of those feelings. Such behavior at home or at school leads to the complaint that he is "hyperactive." I adduce these two examples to show how normal behavior shades into disturbed behavior. But I also want to emphasize how much of our labeling of behavior disorders comes from external, social criteria, even though we know very little about the "disordered behavior" without an understanding of its interior features. With this in mind, I should like, now, to describe a number of phenomena that satisfy the external defini-tion (antisocial or interpersonally disruptive action) in order to show differen-tiations in the interior circumstances underlying them. Which of these should "properly" be called "behavior disorders" is essentially an optional matter, though one requiring definition by consensus based on a reasonable rationale. While I shall make a proposal regarding this later on, my major aim is to describe at least a sample of the array of interior circumstances associated with disruptive action because an understanding of that array is critical to both the diagnostic and the therapeutic processes.

1. We often speak of "tension discharge" through the motor apparatus. Pre-cisely what is meant by either term—tension or discharge—is generally not clear; but "tension discharge" is a phenomenological language, on the model of a corked bottle where pressure builds up and the cork pops. And yet, corks and pressure interact in different ways. A well-corked bottle may indeed build up great pressure and pop the cork; but a cork may incom-pletely seal the bottle, having a slight air leak, and then pressure will be released through it in a slow leak as the pressure mounts; or, finally, the cork may be on so loosely as not to require any real pressure buildup before it comes off. I should like to describe psychological parallels to each of these three situations.

    In its most vivid presentation, "tension discharge," the "popped cork," is an "outburst." A child (or adult for that matter), ordinarily reasonably self-controlled, "reaches his limit" or "blows his top." In recognition of the atypicality of this response we say that "he wasn't himself." The specific picture may be of a child, reasonably controlled or even inhibited, who is deprived/frustrated, insulted/humiliated, or provoked/injured to the point where he lashes out—hitting, perhaps crying, perhaps cursing, perhaps all of these. There need not be external provocation; the outburst may come, once or regularly, as the outcome of inner experiences, conflicts, anger, longings. The point that I wish to emphasize, however, is that very real and substantial controls over behavioral expression exist in such instances, even though, episodically, they give way, allowing socially disruptive behavior to emerge. In partial contrast, though also with important parallels regarding the presence of inner controls, are those finger-tapping, knee-bouncing children whose motor restlessness is often evident, but whose "contained" restlessness, a kind of overflow phenomenon, is also indicative of the presence and maintenance of great control. Like the infant who sucks or rocks, and in contrast to the infant who screams and thrashes around or the toddler who races everywhere, there is a limited motor outlet here that permits a great deal of control to be retained. The parallel is to the cork that holds pressure, but has an air leak. There is a kind of slow release valve in situations where major motor restraint is required (e.g., in school). While the motor overflow may have nuisance qualities, it is rarely viewed as a "behavior disorder," having no antisocial, interpersonally disruptive aspect.

2. And then there is another situation that looks superficially like "tension discharge" but where, in actuality, little tension is either built up or "discharged." The cork is not really on tight at all, and it takes no pressure to release it. I refer to children where an impulse (to hit, to steal, to grab food, to run out of the classroom) has ready access to action, to motor pathways, with little or no delay, little or no cognitive or defensive working over of the impulse as a mediating process. In Shapiro's (1965) work on impulse disorders he attributes this phenomenon to a defect in planning, a defect in the capacity to envision consequences of action, and he reserves the term impulse disorder for just this phenomenon. While I believe that the planning/anticipatory defect may be only a part of the picture (albeit a substantial part), I would also propose, following Shapiro, that the term behavior disorder is best reserved for this constellation—a constellation of minimal control, of minimal cognitive mediation of impulse, of ready access of impulse to motor pathways. This, in an internal diagnostic sense (rather than simply an external-social sense) gives the term behavior disorder some specificity and diagnostic significance; but more on that after I have presented the other constellations. For now let me just note that, although this phenomenon is seen clearly in adolescents and adults, it can already be identified in early and middle childhood when the normal developmental achievement of delay over automatic motor expression of impulse should have been attained.

3. Turning to quite different internal phenomena that may, however, still be described as behavior disorders from an exterior view, I should like to describe neurotic character disorders or neurotic symptom disorders that culminate in disturbances in the behavioral realm. Freud first discussed such a phenomenon (in adults) in his paper on some character-types met with in psychoanalytic work (1916), specifically criminals from a sense of guilt. There he describes a person whose criminality has the unconscious aim of justifying a preexisting sense of guilt; it creates a cause for an already present affect. By extension, the point I wish to make is that these behavioral disturbances have unconscious meanings in a context of impulse derivatives in

fantasy, of guilt, and of compromise formation, just as do other neurotic symptoms. The boy I described earlier (running away, "wandering around") presents such a picture; his running away reflects neither a defect in delay nor a gap in superego, but rather the expression in action of unconscious memories and the form of his attachment both to his mother and his father. In short, the action expresses a fantasy in compromise (disguised) form.

The phenomenon is not rare. Children whose constant fighting and provocation are attempts to reverse feelings of weakness, damage, and passivity illustrate it. Similarly the phenomenon is seen in a child whose stealing reflects not the needy longing for food of a deprived child whose longing is not subject to control and delay, but whose stealing instead acts out (dramatizes) an oedipal-level fantasy—say, of possessing the mother (taking her "valuables") or of reversing the loss (in fantasy) of a penis by the theft of a water pistol. In each of these instances, the disturbed behavior serves some unconscious aim. As such, the behavior is the end product of a complex cognitive process, reflecting delay, defense formation, and disguise, and is hardly a simple failure of control.

4. In his paper on Ego Disturbances, Redl (1951) emphasizes how critical it is for us to have a refined conception of the particular area of ego disturbance in individual instances. Relevant to our present concern, he refers to a psychotic child who attacks a childcare worker under the delusional idea that he (the worker) is the child's (hated) father. He differentiates this from other forms of attack by a child, though each culminates in disturbed behavior that may look the same in exterior view. Thus, hypothetically in his paper, one child has no delay capacity in the face of some frustration of need and attacks the frustrating person. Another, with considerable delay capacity, expresses all that pent-up (delayed) rage against the father, but does that under the sway of the delusional idea and perceptual distortion that a nonfather is the father. If we consider, in addition, that it may be precisely such a distortion that permits the expression of rage, we see here again that considerable cognitive work has gone on between impulse and expression in this psychotic child.

5. Yet another phenomenon often subsumed under the term behavior disorder involves those expressions of "antisocial" behavior which themselves reflect socialized behavior within a particular deviant subculture. In the case of adolescent marijuana usage today, we can no longer even refer to a "deviant" subculture. Marijuana smoking is part and parcel of identification with a group, acceptance of its values, and connectedness in reliable patterns of relationship to others within it. Within *this* group, some—whose drug use is excessive or otherwise eccentric—may themselves be viewed as outsiders, or at least no longer governed by the shared guiding values of the group. Some instances of childhood theft, of childhood gang fighting, similarly reflect socialized behavior within a particular family or group subculture. This does not imply that clinicians need not be concerned with such behavior, nor that it might not simultaneously reflect failures in delay, reac-

tions against depression, or the acting out of an unconscious fantasy in a particular individual. Quite the reverse, it may reflect any of these, or others, which is precisely why the externally identifiable antisocial behavior has so little specific diagnostic value.

In the preceding material, I have taken the term behavior disorder loosely to refer to actions that have an asocial or interpersonally disruptive aspect. But then I have tried to demonstrate that a number of quite different interior circumstances may underly such action. Diagnosis, which I see precisely as the process of understanding external signs through understanding of their inner structure and genetic roots, and which then speaks to issues of treatment technique, is obviously enhanced by taking such an interior view. Since behavior is omnipresent in human functioning and is certainly a central aspect of the active lives of young children, its disturbances can appear in any pathological context; what I have given here can only be regarded as a sample of the range.

My aim has been to detail some of the wide array of phenomena subsumable under the term "behavior disorder." But my personal preference, as already noted, is to reserve that term for those children characterized by a failure of delay between impulse and action. I have emphasized failure of delay. The delay of automatic motor or affectomotor expression as need or affect mounts is a major achievement of development in the infancy to early childhood period, and its failure has important consequences. In giving my examples above, I have tried to show that some of the examples reflect such failures of delay, while others reflect a considerable amount of what I have called, for want of a better term, "cognitive working over." In these latter instances, delay, control, and disguise have taken place, and the disordered behavior is embedded in memories, fantasies, cognitive/perceptual distortions, bound symptoms, and/or character traits.

Just *how* the failure of delay develops, or rather, just why delay does not develop is another issue. I believe that delay normally develops from a number of interlocking circumstances. (1) The infant has sufficient experience of gratification and relief following upon need that he begins to trust that relief will come again, and so he can sustain tension states next time round in anticipation of relief; this is already delay. (2) As part of this, the child who is thus developing a "basic trust" in his caretakers can scan his environment expectantly and learn about its features (since he will not be in a desperate, panicky, tearful state), thus learning where need satisfaction/tension relief will come from. (3) Though considerably later, a marked additional force is added to the tendency toward control and delay through the internalization of parental standards, the formation of the superego, with its accompanying affect of guilt that tends to accentuate control processes. Following this reasoning, the failure to develop the capacity (or tendency) to delay impulse expression may be seen as the inverse of these normal developments. Paralleling the three points above, respectively, I would suggest that: (1) Insufficient attachment to, or empathy for, others—reflecting failures in early trusting object relations—can lead a child to express his impulse as he wills it without regard to others; (2) insufficient cognitive elaboration of possibility, of alternatives, of plans (cf. Shapiro 1965) may follow upon the infant's absorption in his (unsatisfied) inner state, when the surround insufficiently brought relief and he has not learned to explore it expectantly for relief; and (3) failures in conscience development, the absence of guilt, will further permit a ready access to impulse expression when those earlier tendencies are already present.

Above, I suggested reserving the term behavior disorder for instances "characterized by failure of delay." I have discussed the failure of delay, but would now like to say a word also on the phrase "characterized by." I have in mind here the point Fenichel (1945) makes in his distinction between the "neurosis" and the "neurotic conflict." In brief, the latter is a focal conflict between "the drives, that is the id, and the ego" (p. 129); we only speak of a neurosis, however, when that focal conflict has developed further, influencing a larger sphere of behavior, be this symptom or character trait. Similarly, I would suggest that the term behavior disorder might usefully be reserved for those instances of failure of delay between impulse and action, those absences of cognitive working over, which are characteristic of a particular child, are repeated, predictable modes of reaction to an array of impulses and an array of settings.

Concluding Remarks

In this chapter, I have tried to do several things. First, I have tried to describe some of the characteristic descriptive features and developmental issues of the age 7-10 period, the later period of latency (Bornstein 1951) wherein the child is normally solidly involved in the world of school and peer relations. Second, I have selected some of the characteristic areas of pathology of that age group (borderline disturbances, learning disturbances, and behavior disturbances) and tried to show their relationships to the developmental issues of the age. Emphasizing that those disturbances are characteristic of but not specific to this age period (i.e., they are also seen earlier and later), I tried to show that they are characteristic (frequent) precisely because of their tie to the developmental issues of the age. And finally, and in the bulk of the chapter, I have attempted to give a highly differentiated picture of the variations within each of the three domains of pathology, attempting to demonstrate that an interior view adds considerably to our appreciation of the specificity and complexity of particular presenting pictures (cf. A. Freud 1970).

At times I have discussed treatment issues in some detail, at times less so, and at times hardly at all. But I have attempted to discuss, in considerable detail (1) the developmental failures underlying each pathological presentation (and the normal developmental pathways that these children have been unable to follow), and (2) the many genetic and structural distinctions in varying presenting pictures within each area. A particular view of the therapeutic process underlies these choices—the choice of detailed discussion of development and of diagnostic specificity and lesser discussion of treatment technique per se. In that view the two detailed aspects of the discussion are in fact central to the issue of therapeutic technique.

Knowledge of development can be invaluable to the therapeutic enterprise. Elsewhere (Pine 1976) I have tried to show that therapy (even psychoanalytic therapy as it is traditionally carried out) can be viewed in part as a process of facilitation of normal development in addition to the more customary view of it as a process of correction of interruptions and aberrations of development. Certainly in childhood, with developmental change still proceeding rapidly, this view is useful. An understanding of the current developmental tasks of a child can help us to understand the continuing pathogenic consequences of particular presenting problems (e.g., learning failure and its implications for self-esteem regulation; or school refusal and its confirmation of attachment to home and mother, making displacement to school, peers, and learning, impossible). An understanding of how relevant normal developments that did not take place should have taken place (e.g., delay of impulse expression, neutralization of the learning process, development of signal anxiety and reliable internal structure) can give us clues to the historical loci of the sources of the presenting pathology. And, though developmental failures can by no means always be reversed by a later reexperiencing of the relevant developmental opportunities, an awareness of those normal modes of development can provide cues for technical interventions in individual instances (Pine 1976).

And finally, knowledge of specificity of pathological mechanisms is also invaluable to the therapeutic enterprise and underlies my having detailed these disorders with such specificity here. When Freud (1912) spoke of the analyst's "evenly suspended attention" to the associative material of the patient, he did not mean that the analyst's mind was blank, unaware of all that he had learned previously. What is intended is that the analyst not be precommitted to any single idea in that session, thus permitting new and surprising (or perhaps old and familiar) themes to achieve centrality. Our general theory of human functioning, our past knowledge of all our patients, and knowledge of all that has transpired and is now transpiring with the particular patient in our office are all parts of what the therapist's mind should be "evenly suspended" over; similarly, for diagnostic specificity. Only when we have the full array in mind, in short, only when we have learned from the accumulation of clinical knowledge, can our evenly hovering (uncommitted) clinical minds light upon and recognize the central phenomena in any particular patient or in any particular session. The technical attitude of the therapist has to be one of exploration and discovery; but he has to be a prepared explorer who will recognize relevant variations in the terrain when he sees them. Only then will he understand, and only then will he be able to speak to the patient in descriptive or interpretive words that will help the patient understand the pathological processes at work. Precision in interpretation ultimately follows from precision in understanding. Hence, an informed view of development and of specific pathological mechanisms makes possible a refined therapeutic technique.

References

Alexander, F. *Psychoanalysis and Psychotherapy.* New York: Norton, 1956.

Allen, D.W. Exhibitionistic and voyeuristic conflicts in learning and functioning. *Psychoanalytic Quarterly,* 36:546-570, 1967.

Anthony, E.J. Folie à deux. In: McDevitt, J.B., and Settlage, C.F., eds. *Separation-Individuation.* New York: International Universities Press, 1971. pp. 253-273.

Benjamin, L. "Learning Disorders in Children." Report to the Fleischman Commission, New York State, 1971.

Benjamin, L., and Finkel, W. "Time Disorientation in Mildly Retarded Children with Sequencing Disorder: Diagnosis and Treatment." Paper read at American Orthopsychiatric Association Meetings, April 1969.

Benjamin, L., and Green, B.E. Differential diagnosis and treatment of childhood aphasic disorder: A case study. In: Hellmuth, J., ed. *Learning Disorders.* Seattle: Special Child Publications, Vol. 3, 1968. pp. 225-247.

Berlyne, D.E. *Conflict, Arousal, and Curiosity.* New York: McGraw-Hill, 1960.

Blos, P. *On Adolescence.* Glencoe, Ill.: Free Press, 1962.

Bornstein, B. On latency. *The Psychoanalytic Study of the Child,* 6:279-285, 1951.

Bowlby, J. *Attachment and Loss. Vol. I. Attachment.* New York: Basic Books, 1969.

Ekstein, R. *Children of Time and Space, of Action and Impulse.* New York: Appleton-Century-Crofts, 1966.

Ekstein, R., and Wallerstein, J. Observations on the psychology of borderline and psychotic children. *The Psychoanalytic Study of the Child,* 9:344-369, 1954.

Fenichel, O. *The Psychoanalytic Theory of Neurosis.* New York: Norton, 1945.

Freud, A. The assessment of borderline cases (1956). *The Writings of Anna Freud,* 5:301-314. New York: International Universities Press, 1969.

—— *Normality and Pathology in Childhood.* New York: International Universities Press, 1965.

——. The symptomatology of childhood. *The Psychoanalytic Study of the Child,* 25:19-41, 1970.

Freud, S. Three essays on the theory of sexuality (1905). *Standard Edition,* 7:135-243. London: Hogarth, 1953.

——. Recommendations to physicians practicing psychoanalysis (1912). *Standard Edition,* 12:111-120. London: Hogarth, 1958.

——. Some character types met with in psychoanalytic work (1916). *Standard Edition,* 14:311-333. London: Horgarth, 1957.

——. Beyond the pleasure principle (1920). *Standard Edition,* 18:7-64. London: Hogarth, 1955.

——. New introductory lectures on psychoanalysis (1933). *Standard Edition,* 22:7-182. London: Hogarth, 1964.

Grunebaum, M.G.; Hurwitz, I.; Prentice, N.M.; and Sperry, B.M. Fathers of sons with primary neurotic learning inhibitions. *American Journal of Orthopsychiatry,* 32:462-472, 1962.

Group for the Advancement of Psychiatry. *Psychopathological Disorders in Childhood.* New York: G.A.P. Publications, 1966.

Hartmann, H. *Ego Psychology and the Problem of Adaptation* (1939). New York: International Universities Press, 1958.

——. The mutual influences in the development of ego and id. *The Psychoanalytic Study of the Child,* 7:9-30, 1952.

Hendrick, I. Instinct and the ego during infancy. *Psychoanalytic Quarterly,* 11:33-58, 1942.

Kanner, L. Autistic disturbances of affective contact. *Nervous Child,* 2:217-250, 1942.

——. Problems of nosology and psychodynamics of early infantile autism. *American Journal of Orthopsychiatry,* 19:416-426, 1949.

Kernberg, O. Borderline personality organization. *Journal of the American Psychoanalytic Association,* 15:641-685, 1967.

——. The treatment of patients with borderline personality organization. *International Journal of Psychoanalysis,* 49:600-619, 1968.

Knight, R. Borderline states. *Bulletin of the Menninger Clinic,* 17:1-12, 1953*a.*

——. Management and psychotherapy of the borderline schizophrenic patient. *Bulletin of the Menninger Clinic,* 17:139-150, 1953*b.*

Mahler, M.S. Pseudoimbecility. *Psychoanalytic Quarterly,* 11:149-164, 1942.

——. On child psychosis and schizophrenia. *The Psychoanalytic Study of the Child,* 7:286-305, 1952.

——. *On Human Symbiosis and the Vicissitudes of Individuation. Vol. I, Infantile Psychosis.* New York: International Universities Press, 1968.

——. On the first three subphases of the separation-individuation process. *International Journal of Psychoanalysis,* 53:333-338, 1972.

Mahler, M.; Pine, F.; and Bergman, A. *The Psychological Birth of the Human Infant.* New York: Basic Books, 1975.

Masterson, J.F. *Treatment of the Borderline Adolescent: A Developmental Approach.* New York: Wiley, 1972.

Mittelman, B. Motility in infants, children, and adults: Patterning and psychodynamics. *The Psychoanalytic Study of the Child,* 9:142-177, 1954.

Newman, C.J.; Dember, C.F.; and Krug, O. "He can but he won't": A psychodynamic study of so-called "gifted underachievers." *The Psychoanalytic Study of the Child,* 28:83-130, 1973.

Pine, F. On the concept "borderline" in children: A clinical essay. *The Psychoanalytic Study of the Child,* 29:341-368, 1974*a.*

——. Libidinal object constancy: A theoretical note. *Psychoanalysis and Contemporary Science,* 3:307-313, 1974*b.*

——. On therapeutic change: Perspectives from a parent-child model. *Psychoanalysis and Contemporary Science,* 5:537-569, 1976.

Rapaport, D. The theory of ego autonomy. In: Gill, M.M., ed. *Collected Papers of David Rapaport.* New York: Basic Books, 1967. pp. 722-744.

Redl, F. Ego disturbances. In: Harrison, S.I., and McDermott, J.F., eds. *Childhood Psychopathology.* New York: International Universities Press, 1972 (1951). pp. 532-539.

Rosenfeld, S.K., and Sprince, M.P. An attempt to formulate the meaning of the concept "borderline." *The Psychoanalytic Study of the Child,* 18:603-635, 1963.

——. Some thoughts on the technical handling of borderline children. *The Psychoanalytic Study of the Child,* 20:495-517, 1965.

Shapiro, D. *Neurotic Styles.* New York: Basic Books, 1965.

Sperry, B.M.; Ulrich, D.N.; and Staver, N. The relation of motility to boys' learning problems. *American Journal of Orthopsychiatry,* 28:640-646, 1958.

Spiegel, L.A. A review of contributions to a psychoanalytic theory of adolescence: Individual aspects. *The Psychoanalytic Study of the Child,* 6:375-393, 1951.

Stone, J., and Church, J. *Childhood and Adolescence.* New York: Random House, 1973.

Weil, A.P. Certain severe disturbances of ego development in childhood. *The Psychoanalytic Study of the Child,* 8:271-287, 1953.

——. Certain evidences of deviational development in infancy and early childhood. *The Psychoanalytic Study of the Child,* 11:292-299, 1956.

White, R.W. *Ego and Reality in Psychoanalytic Theory. Psychological Issues,* #11. New York: International Universities Press, 1963.

Winnicott, D.W. The capacity to be alone (1958). In: Winnicott, D.W., ed. *The Maturational Processes and the Facilitating Environment.* New York: International Universities Press, 1965. pp. 29-36.

Youngerman, J. The syntax of silence. *International Review of Psychoanalysis,* 6:283-295, 1979.

The Course of Life: Psychoanalytic Contributions
Toward Understanding Personality Development.
Vol. II: Latency, Adolescence, and Youth.
S.I. Greenspan and G.H. Pollock, editors.
NIMH 1980

Concerning the Psychology and the Psychotherapeutic Treatment of Borderline and Psychotic Conditions of Childhood

Rudolf Ekstein, Ph.D.

Historic Overview

While descriptions of borderline and psychotic conditions can already be found in the ancient literature, only with the onset of modern psychiatry in the midnineteenth century were systematic attempts made to understand and treat these conditions. Within 2 years, three great men were born who changed the picture of psychiatry: Freud and Kraepelin, born in 1856, and Bleuler, born in 1857. Kraepelin's (1900) primary contribution was in the area of *diagnosis and classification* of symptomatology, although he also studied the progress and the process of diseases and did not hold a static point of view. He was pessimistic, feeling that the prognosis for severe mental illness was hopeless. Bleuler's (1911) concern was with *thought and affect disorders* in schizophrenia, and he basically held a similarly pessimistic view concerning outcome. Freud's (1924) major contribution in this area can be traced to his article, "The Loss of Reality in Neurosis and Psychosis," in which he emphasized the structural aspects of psychosis, specifically the *loss of reality testing* and the *loss of the capacity for* normal *object relations.* While these different views seem to be concerned primarily with etiological issues concerning *the cause of the illness,* we suggest that, beyond their manifest subject, they contain latent views concerning *the cause of the cure.* One might say that they stated a disguised commitment to a specific treatment philosophy and technique.

Kraepelin, who assumed that mental patients were hopelessly ill and needed chronic hospitalization, provided them with a hospital order based on different diagnostic pictures. Bleuler was so pessimistic about the treatment that in his classic, "Dementia Praecox," he devoted only one chapter to treatment and stated it would be "unjust if we try to prevent hopeless schizophrenics from suicide." Freud's emphasis on reality testing and object relations is, we feel, an expression of his commitment to a psychoanalytic technique based upon a therapeutic relationship, making use of transference and resistance, etc.

Freud (1915–1917) once spoke about three narcissistic blows that science delivered to mankind. The first was the change from the Ptolemaic view of the universe, an egocentric one, comparable to the infant's omnipotent fantasies, to the Copernican explanation of a heliocentric universe. The second Freud ascribed to Darwin, whose genetic theory of evolution opposed religious beliefs about the creation and origin of man as the unique, rational homo sapiens, different from the other unreasoning animals. Freud saw himself as the deliverer of the third narcissistic blow with the discovery of the unconscious, thus ending the idea of man's rational uniqueness, and his assertion that man, like the other animals, is driven by nonrational forces.

Could one speak about a fourth narcissistic blow to mankind, implicit in Freud's third blow, and suggest that there is no basic difference between the psychotic and the neurotic, between ordinary conditions and those that are described as borderline and psychotic? With such a view, psychosis and borderline conditions can be considered treatable, thereby allowing more optimism in the prognosis of such patients.

The survey of the literature on serious childhood disorders reveals that during the last 40 years we have moved away from mere etiological considerations, from diagnostic pessimism, to a new kind of optimism concerning psychotherapy. Often exaggerated, perhaps this optimism is based on creative and enthusiastic pioneer effort which will increase the probability of recovery, provided society as a whole supports the therapeutic efforts and research in this area.

The complex area of serious childhood disorders has a roster of distinguished pioneers. Bender (1953) emphasized constitutional factors, the neurological lag and deficit, and medical treatment, surgical techniques, and retraining programs. Kanner (1944) was concerned with childhood autism, and he, too, put his emphasis on re-education techniques of treatment. Among the psychoanalytic workers in this field were Szurek, a student of Sullivan, and his collaborators who saw psychiatry as the science of interpersonal relations (1973). Rank (1949), most of whose critical work was done with very young children, contributed the concept of ego fragmentation. While her work was guided by psychoanalytic thinking, her techniques were more akin to educational work in nursery schools. Perhaps the most powerful contribution was made by Mahler, who together with her co-workers (1975) contributed to an understanding of symbiotic and autistic phases, the problem of individuation, and the birth of the psychological self. Ekstein's (1966) work, together with that of his co-workers, is associated with fluctuating ego states, visible in schizophrenics as well as in borderline conditions of childhood. His contributions are mainly concerned with psychotherapeutic techniques and the causes of recovery. Bettelheim's (1974) work is concerned with the total psychotherapeutic treatment program, including the use of the environment, practiced by him and his colleagues at the Orthogenic School.

A variety of articles summarizing and synthesizing the literature are cited in the reference listings.

The Diagnostic Process

Deliberately, we do not speak about the diagnosis but rather about the *process,* the interaction between doctor and patient. We speak about the process as a movement which leads from the family's first awareness that something is wrong to the final decision of commitment to a treatment program. We have in mind a "social diagnosis," a phrase borrowed from social casework, which examines not only the psychological world of the sick child but also the social forces contributing to illness and to recovery. The diagnostic categorization is not an accusation or a threat by virtue of naming the illness but rather serves as a decision, a program toward a curative process. The diagnostician does not merely look through a microscope, as one may do in a laboratory examination. He is involved with the patient and the family in solving a task which moves from the emergency of an emerging process toward the resolution of the conflict or the restoration or rebuilding of lost capacities.

One might well say that the diagnostic process is a kind of trial treatment, a way of seeing whether one can get child and family to participate in the process. An illustration of diagnostic interaction leading to the beginning of psychotherapy with a severely disturbed 10-year-old boy may clarify what is meant by the diagnostic process. The first contact was when the father telephoned the therapist concerning his boy whom the father considered to be suffering from psychotic illness. He spoke about the child as being split into two persons, and later—during the first session before the child was seen—gave more details. The father is a professional man in the engineering field. There are three other children in the family, the patient the second older boy. Mother and father gave somewhat different versions of the child's difficulties. The mother obviously identified with the role of defender of the child and had more patience with him. The father constantly stressed the seriousness of the illness and betrayed more anxiety. One could feel the underlying competition for the therapist's ear and the wish on the part of each parent to have the therapist support his specific view.

They had just interrupted the treatment of the child by a child psychiatrist. They thought the treatment was useless, that the child was not improving, rather was getting sicker. The child psychiatrist had demanded that they, too, be treated by him, in addition to the treatment hours the child had. Their overt opposition was concerned with the question of fees, but what seemed uppermost in their minds was that the child psychiatrist suggested that they were really the cause of the difficulty. Allegedly, he had said to the child during one of the treatment sessions that the parents had a bad marriage. The child quoted him and set off a flood of ambivalence and the search for a new therapist. When the therapist suggested that he ought to talk with their son's psychiatrist, the parents objected: They had lost all confidence in him. They had gotten the therapist's name through an analyst far up north and obviously were frantically searching for someone whom they could trust at a period in their lives when they did not trust themselves, the child, nor the various sources they had consulted about him previously.

The parents described nights of terror. The boy could not go to sleep, would keep them awake, was riddled by panic and deepening anxiety attacks, saw himself persecuted by all kinds of monsters, and would "freak out." This description was used by the parents as well as the boy who identified with the parents' way of describing him. The first impression was that these "freaking out" experiences might be descriptions of fluctuating states of consciousness. The parents had followed the psychiatrist's and the pediatrician's suggestion and were giving the boy heavy doses of chlorpromazine hydrochloride (Thorazine) and other drugs. He often seemed in a stuporous state and could not be maintained in any school program. This state of affairs had been going on for a number of months. The parents were quite ready to have the therapist see the child, perhaps use psychological testing, have him confer with the pediatrician, but did not want to allow him to make contact with the psychiatrist.

The therapist tried to suggest, first, that they not interrupt the treatment; that he would want merely to act as a consultant; that they must understand that treatment techniques today require immense patience and take a very long time, so that the psychiatrist could not be expected to be helpful in as short a time as they had anticipated. While he tried to maintain the role of the consultant, the parents soon and insistently cast him as the psychotherapist. The interplay between his wish for cautious evaluation and their wish for commitment went on throughout the first two sessions while he was seeing the parents alone. They did not give up, and, in the long run, they prevailed.

The child came, accompanied by the father, who could not really allow the psychotherapist to be alone, either with him or with the child, nor could he keep from explaining the child's difficulties in front of the child. He brought along a number of the child's drawings and told the child to take these up with the psychotherapist. The father also gave the psychotherapist a tape that he had made the night before while talking to the boy that would illustrate to the therapist the child's psychotic maladjustment.

The tape was most interesting inasmuch as it documented that the father was an overly intrusive parent who did not permit the boy to have his own inner life and tried to force explanations out of him. The father acted more or less like the caricature of a psychiatrist who wanted to get to the bottom of the fantasies that kept the boy from sleeping. The boy indeed gave the impression of a youngster flooded by psychotic delusional material, perhaps from drug-induced states, and suffering endless pain.

The father had also directed the boy to make a drawing which would tell the therapist about the problem. This drawing was made on the reverse side of computer paper. With that paper, the therapist felt as if he had both sides of the family coin. The engineering mind of the father, wanting everything orderly and exact, was presented on one side of the paper that he provided the boy, who then made a psychotic-like drawing on the other side. Obsessional exactness struggled with the primary process on a single sheet of paper.

The drawing depicted a little boy lying in his bed, full of fear, saying to the father who is standing nearby at the bedroom door: "Don't always scream at me. I am just asking for you to come because I am scared." In response, the father yells at the boy: "What you think about does not exist. There are no such things." During the next few sessions the boy brought the therapist other drawings, all of them representing different terrible monsters. They seemed to be archaic animals from the past, vicious creatures from science fiction, evil monsters engaged in brutal war to wipe each other out. They represented a psychotic version of oedipal material, a struggle between father and son, interlocked in an endless war desperately waged for the victory of pursuing what each wanted. One could not help but feel the invisible presence of the mother who tried to build the bridge between the boy's panic and the father's rage.

The child requested the use of the tape recorder so that he and the therapist could enact a radio broadcast. The child would be introduced by the psychotherapist to the imaginary radio audience as the one who had to tell exciting stories about the struggle of the monsters, their fears, their hopes, and their solutions to problems. The boy freely interacted with the psychotherapist, and the material that came out now was immensely different from the tape the father had provided. On the father's tape one had the impression of a delusional boy, overcome by private monsters and unable to return to reality. Now he appeared to be deliberately telling and inventing stories: a master teller of science fiction rather than a devoured victim of his own fantasy creations.

Shall we believe the material that the boy provided for the psychotherapist or the material on the earlier tape? In the first instance, we would be dealing with a boy in neurotic conflict, whose use of science fiction and fantasy indicated that reality testing was not lost and whose anxiety was nowhere near psychotic panic. If we were to believe the father's account and the earlier taped material taken during the night, we would have much evidence for thinking of him as a psychotic child. Moreover, we have a third alternative, we could think of him as borderline, as someone who fluctuates between psychotic and neurotic states with no control over the fluctuation; that is, as if he were compelled from time to time to experience the world like a dream and, unable to step out of the dream to cope with reality, distorted reality into a psychotic nightmare. The issue then becomes one of differential diagnosis.

Enough has been said about the parents, particularly the father, to make us wonder whether his anxiety and the child's panic states do not bring about a kind of symbiotic folie-à-deux. Could the father avoid his intrusive behavior? Could he stop trying to get into the child's inner world, taking it so seriously that he himself got overwhelmed by his overidentification with it and his son? Could he simply be reassuring and direct the situation in such a way that the child would bring the illness to the therapist rather than have to face a father who tries to scream his mental anguish out of him? The father promised that he would try not to intrude any longer. Every hour he asked for advice on what he ought to do. Although he experienced the therapist as reassuring and tried to follow suggestions, at one critical moment his wife, having become more aware of her husband's difficulty, telephoned. During this introductory period in the diagnostic process, the therapist tried to be reassuring and did not require that the parents get help for themselves as well, although he realized the problems this course of action entailed.

In the meantime, the work with the child went on. He brought a few more drawings and dwelt on his monsters but, after a while, lost interest in them. More and more his behavior became that of his age group. The fantasies very rarely took on psychotic-like dimensions, and he looked forward to his hours. All this took place at the beginning of the school year, and now a new problem had to be considered. The parents wondered what school to use. Did it have to be a private school, or could he go to public school? Would he have to go to a special class? What did the therapist recommend? They were utterly convinced that the boy could not be placed in the public school system. They wanted to protect him from that. At the same time, however, they also wanted to protect him from being in a school system that maintained only very regressed children. The public school was called in, and the boy was given some special testing. A special program was worked out with the school psychologist, according to which he would first be given some tutoring and would then start on a limited program with youngsters of his own age in a "regular" class. The psychotherapist endorsed that procedure. The limited testing done by the school psychologist did not really permit one to get the picture that a complete, projective testing program would have afforded. As a matter of fact, the test provided revealed more about the parents' anxiety than the boy's pathology. The psychotherapist did not want to add additional tests, however, feeling that the boy was already under too much pressure.

The child himself was asked by the therapist if he meant to cooperate with that program. He was now being dosed with Thorazine and experiencing less "freaking out." But there was enough disturbance, enough upsetting nights, so that the parents, at the time of this writing, did not want to allow him to go beyond the tutoring. The child would sometimes do excellently with the tutor, and sometimes he would utterly fail. The parents' response was one of trying to delay any attempt of adjustment in school.

This short summary illustrates the strengths and shortcomings of these diagnostic processes. We are not ready to give the boy a diagnostic label, but we know enough to be able to proceed with the treatment. We would say that he should indeed continue to be seen by the psychotherapist, presently twice a week. Also, the parents should be permitted to move slowly around the issue of school attendance, even though the therapist, if he were to be responsible for the decision, would allow him to start some schooling right now. There is enough strength in this boy. His drawings and stories show talent. He is an endurance swimmer who sometimes swims miles to strengthen himself. He is sometimes overwhelmed by anxiety and cannot quite describe what he means by "freaking out," although he is aware of increased anxiety and of the desperate wish that his parents not scream at him. Sometimes he begs his mother not to scream at him, even though she does not and has no intention of doing so. It is as if he constantly thinks his parents might develop into monsters and hurt him. Feeling completely dependent on them, he sometimes sees them as his only reliable protectors and at other times as dangerous enemies. The ambivalence occasionally takes psychotic proportions.

One must have sympathy for the parents, who—regardless of how often they do not respond well to the child and bring on their own discomfort—are under endless pressure from him. At times his behavior almost suggests that he has a diabolical knowledge of how to keep them in check and how to tyrannize them, so that he seems to become the monster trying to prevail against them.

At moments of deepest distress he seems to be as ill as the artist whom Freud (1922) described in his work on a devil neurosis in the seventeenth century. This artist painted himself into a psychotic depression, a position of isolation and of confrontation with the devils in himself, archaic monster figures which at times represented the psychotic process within him, his own monster identity, and at times represented the images of the father and the mother. But these productions went hand in hand with normal behavior and with sufficient reappearing ego strength that could be tapped.

It is interesting that the pediatrician who prescribed the Thorazine based his decision on the parents' description of the boy's behavior. He himself never saw the boy in the kind of psychotic state that the parents described. Neither did the therapist, although he saw moments that indirectly verified the parents' observations.

Once the boy stood before the huge glass window of the therapist's consulting room, which is on the seventh floor of a high-rise building. From there he could see the whole city, with huge buildings in the background. He wondered how it would be if the glass broke and he could freely step out into the air and fly, reach these other buildings, and control the city like a powerful, monstrous bird.

The therapist thought of Plato's definition of play. He saw the inception of play, children's or animals', as a big leap into the air. This desire to leap, to fly, to be independent, to have total autonomy, to be free of gravity, Plato suggests, is typical for the young. But the higher they jump and the abler they are, the more they are concerned about coming safely back to the ground. He only jumps rightly who can safely fall back on his feet on the safe ground. The myth about Daedalus and Icarus tells how they built wings so they could fly. As they came nearer to the sun, the wax they used in constructing their wings melted, and their short autonomy in the air ended in destruction on the ground instead of a return to safety. Mother Sun destroys and Mother Earth gives strength.

The boy patient, full of the wish to leap, to play with fantasies in which he has superhuman strength or creates enemies of superhuman strength, describes a leap that constitutes dangerous play. The therapist thought for a moment that such a boy might jump through an open window in order to reach the sun or the high rises and could fall to his doom. There are people who give the impression that they may leap without having a place on which to fall back safely.

Like many such people, the boy could be suffering from a borderline condition, where at times his leaps are based on a realistic assessment of how high he can jump without hurting himself. At other times though, his leaps go beyond the capacity to test reality, beyond the capacity to recognize his fantasies as such.

We may assume that the parents are torn by their own anxiety that the boy may really leap into space without some means of landing safely. The therapist's task is to help this child restore the connection between leaping into autonomy, into freedom, with the capacity to fall back on safe ground. The diagnosis is not a final one. The ongoing diagnostic work shows the existence of deep pathology that could be increasing, thereby bringing into dominance the underlying psychotic structures, which permit leaping without considerations of safety. The diagnosis also suggests that all such behavior could be kept in check and that psychotherapeutic treatment could restore or build these security systems of the self, thereby adding to the fantasies the strength of reasoning and reality testing.

In one of his recent works, "Toys and Reasons" (1977), Erikson spoke about William Blake, a poet of the 18th century, who suggested that: "The Child's Toys and the Old Man's Reasons are the Fruits of the Two Seasons." Our patient's fantasies, his toys, are sometimes stronger than his reasoning power. The parents' reasons are sometimes stronger than their capacity to deal with the child's fantasies. In the interactions so far, we have a process that allows for a beginning but not yet for a clear prognosis, nor a simple classification, nor a completed plan for treatment.

Anna Freud suggested in a personal communication (1959) that a true diagnosis can only be made after treatment, when one knows, so to speak, all the facts. But when does one ever know all the facts? We should not, therefore, expect more of the diagnostic process than that it permits us a fairly clear beginning. In this child's life we can see autistic isolation, sometimes symbiotic yearnings, touches of a thought disorder, oedipal anxieties, pre-oedipal panics, strong islands of ego strengths, and a capacity to take hold of the therapeutic situation, to transfer to the therapist expectations of trust, worries lest he fail him, a will to struggle with his outer and inner monsters. Can the therapist's knowledge and enthusiasm, the parents' willingness to participate, to collaborate, overcome the child's emotional and mental difficulties? There is hope but no certainty.

Concerning Psychotherapeutic Treatment Techniques

An old English proverb suggests that "Speech is the picture of the mind." Today, the word "speech" would have to be substituted for "language"; and language has to be understood not only in terms of verbal speech, but all the other forms of communication of which the human being is capable. If the therapist is capable of developing a system of communication between himself and the patient, he will open the door to the mind of the patient, to his interpersonal and intrapsychic life. He will gain a picture of the mind, analogous perhaps to the picture that the X-ray specialist can gain of the body. One difference in the analogy comes from the fact that the X-ray is a "still picture," not a movie. But the things that our patient tells us, as we develop them in psychotherapeutic dialog, are more like a movie, a process. Perhaps one needs to say that language can be used in order to learn about the processes of the mind, not simply about the mind's static picture.

Nevertheless, we often try to suggest a still picture of the mind. In that case, we refer to the structure of the mind, to the personality order or disorder. (Personality disorder has its own order, the order of the pathological process.)

Unlike Pallas Athene, who is said to have sprung from the head of Zeus fully armed and educated, the human being develops slowly, as do his language capacities and, often, language pathologies. The speech used by the patient, the language system developed, and the capacity for communication tell us something about the phases of normal and/or abnormal development. When there is no normal speech, as for example in the autistic child, we search for other forms of communication. These forms can be withdrawal, escape, autistic speech, echolalia, echopraxia, and other forms of speech pathology, such as stuttering, stammering, psychotic speech, delusional speech, etc. A study of the development of speech helps one to know more about its meaning, its function, in terms of interpersonal situations and intrapsychic conditions.

The first language of the child is *appeal language,* the screaming and yelling of the small baby. This is the signal the infant gives to the mother who "understands" it as a request for food or comfort, and she usually responds by an act such as feeding. Much of the language of very disturbed children is appeal

language, signal language. Even advanced speech, advanced communications—as the psychotherapist listens to the psychotherapeutic communication—are frequently dominated by mere appeal. Patients often start out with
complaints, expressions of suffering; they wish to prove the validity of their
need for help. We are to stop the pain, to reassure, to promise, or to gratify in
one way or another.

Psychotic children often do not respond to *interpretive language*. Such language can only be acquired and understood by the child if he has moved
forward to symbolic communication, the hallmark of mature human speech.
Psychotic children, in beginning therapy, therefore, do not respond to the
ordinary interpretive language of the psychotherapist. The system of communication between a therapist and such a child has to take other forms.

The first appeal of the hungry baby leads not to communication, but to
communion. The baby is once more, in some form, united with the mother.
The mouth finds the nipple of the breast, and that is the goal of the first
communication. Can the psychotherapist allow himself to respond to appeal
language, to understand the patient on his own level? How often will he have
to make the kind of overture which aims at the restoration of communion
rather than at the establishment of communication?

We have no difficulty in responding to an infant's baby talk and are willing
periodically to regress with him without fearing the consequences. We know
that he will grow up and identify with our higher modes of speech; we know
that our identifying with him, using baby talk, will help him to respond and
learn our language.

While we have no difficulty in accepting the needs of the infant, we find it
difficult to respond similarly to psychotic and borderline children who take
away from us our achievement of symbolic, interpretive, explanatory systems
of communication.

With psychotic and borderline children we have a situation where we must
be "bilingual." Only he who understands baby talk can help the baby to wish
to learn our language. The developmental schemata tell us that there is a long
way from appeal language to representational and symbolic language. The
sending of a message might be appeal, expression without appeal character,
symbolic communication, or all at the same time. No symbolic communication
is free of the other forms of communication, and therefore, we frequently find
behind the manifest content of a communication its deeper meaning. That is,
much of what is suggested in concrete terms has hidden meaning, unconscious meaning, unconscious symbolism, or carries much multidetermined
metaphoric meaning.

Freud (1900) characterized the dream as the royal road to the unconscious
of the patient; Erikson (1950) saw the play of the child as the royal road to the
unconscious of the child. Both stressed what they considered the best therapeutic communications available. In the treatment of psychotic and borderline
conditions of childhood, the psychotherapeutic dialog is best characterized by

the use of metaphor, analogy, simile, or illusion. A kind of twilight language is used, which is neither the language of reality in pure daylight, nor the language of the dream during the night, but a language based on fusion and confusion of the poetic and the commonplace.

When the young patient described earlier speaks about monsters, he speaks about his internal world of panic, an almost dreamlike, often hypnogogic preoccupation with himself and the adult figures in his life. This language becomes threatening to the father who, needing to express his rage, his own unconscious fantasies, withdraws into the world of computer exactness, itself a kind of metaphoric communication concerning the way his mind feels safest. While at times the child tends to return to an autistic position, not quite successfully, and never gives up the search for the maternal matrix, the father, who wants him to be realistic, reasonable, logical, tries to impose on him a different language. Different styles of existence are in combat with each other.

The language of metaphor creates a bridge between these two worlds. It becomes a language which means something to both, even though each attaches slightly different meanings to what the other person intended. The demand for absolute clarity gives way to a language which is vague and allows for different interpretations. It is the bridge between two different minds, using different systems of communication, searching to communicate with the other, and, at the same time, trying desperately to keep their inner world hidden from each other.

What are scientific models or models of the mind but metaphors! Robert Frost (1949) suggested that "All thinking is metaphorical," and C.S. Lewis (1939) wrote that "All our truths, or all but a few fragments, are won by metaphor." Certainly, all psychological truth, insight into self or into interpersonal relationships, is won by metaphoric means of communication.

The earliest systems of communication, such as the contact between mother and baby, can also be considered as metaphors—action metaphors. The screaming of the baby is to tell the mother that he needs her, that he loves her in his particular way; her act of feeding him is a way of telling him that she protects and loves him. But the telling is not yet the customary language of speech. It is a telling through the act.

The neglected baby, such as the children Spitz (1946) describes as suffering from anaclitic depression, moves from human contact, turns to the wall, and gives up the search for the mother—gives up the appeal function—and regresses in despair. He assumes an autistic position that is also language, an attempt to be independent in his way, to have autistic autonomy, and indirectly, to accuse the mother. Thus, autistic withdrawal is also a communication system, a warning that ordinary communication is being given up and that a protective wall is being built. Therefore, we see autistic children who have acquired some language, using this language, not as a basis for direct communication, but as a way of withdrawing, as a way of having merely intrapsychic communication. Such autistic children talk, but to themselves. The psychotherapist, or the wise educator, teacher, nurse, or the re-educated parent, anyone trying to make contact with such a child, tries to break through the autistic barrier. The withdrawal from interpersonal contact, the apparent giving up of the love object, is the child's desperate struggle to maintain himself against objects that are experienced as dangerous, as devouring—often the projection of his own wishes to devour the object—and against being overrun by the other. The struggle of the boy described earlier is one against the intruding parent, against the "yelling" mother, and at the same time, an appeal for a safe object. Projection and identification are interchanged, often fused, at war with each other, before there is clear differentiation between them.

The way the child "speaks" helps the psychotherapist decide on a possible bridge of communication. A good many of these bridges, as with those in the real world damaged by accident, have to be thought of as auxiliary bridges, at least until the more permanent ones can be restored, or—if they have never existed—built for the first time.

It should be clear by now that certain revisions of psychoanalytic methods in the treatment of psychotic and borderline children are aided by a study of language. We are not speaking about sheer linguistics but rather about the considerations which permit us to deduce, from the special use that a sick child makes of communication, how to establish a bridge to him. It is a special bridge, sometimes unsafe, sometimes one that immediately breaks again, sometimes one that lasts; the attempt to bridge differences, lack of understanding, and lack of communication must be made over and over by ever-changing methods. Making this contact may sometimes be based on communion, a kind of feeding of the patient, sometimes by action and action metaphor, sometimes by primitive language, and sometimes by metaphoric communication which appeals to affect, builds a bridge to the preconscious or unconscious mind, and opens a way for mutual identification, such as incorporation. The way of speaking, of communicating, may be preverbal or verbal. It may not only serve to establish a diagnosis, but also indirectly to describe the kind of object relationships of which the child is capable, respectively, the kind of avoidance of object relationships and the kinds of precursors of object relationships. It provides a measure of the individual's ability to distinguish between self and nonself.

During the different phases of the establishment of speech we find that sick children have particular difficulties in going beyond imitation, such as is the case in echolalic speech and in echopraxia, or in moving further from imitation to identification. We find children whose overidentification is so firmly established that they remain on a symbiotic level where self and nonself are not differentiated.

The development of the self, individuation, is a slow process. Our work with psychotherapeutic tasks has given us much insight into the relationships between the development of language and the development of the self as differentiated from the nonself. One is impressed by how much these early studies of children, especially severely sick children, have also helped us in our psychotherapeutic methods with adults. A rich literature, initiated by Kohut (1971), concerning the development of the self and the overcoming of primitive narcissism, has been influenced, we believe, by these studies.

Differentiation, however, may go so far that it drives the patient into autistic positions, into distance from the object. It does not always express itself in a lack of speech. For such a patient has problems concerning not only symbolic communication but also the experience of normal emotional response. Many an autistic child may "communicate" with us but may be far away, without the capacity for emotional response. There is the logic of speech, the secondary process of thinking, and there is also the question concerning appropriate affect. Many a mother cannot establish emotional contact with such a child. The child uses the mother as an anaclitic object, literally uses her for gratification without moving on to more advanced forms of emotional contact, that is, without the capacity for the experience of love and hate, of turning toward and away from the object. We are referring to primitive fixations and regressions frequently characteristic of our child patients. In earlier days of psychoanalytic theory, all these phenomena were understood merely in terms of psychosexual and psychoaggressive development. Our concern with systems of communication has moved us beyond the consideration of basic conflicts, of positions of sexuality and aggression, and toward the consideration of ego psychology, the different steps of self-development and the different forms of object relationships.

We have touched on methods of approach, of keeping appropriate distance, of optimum systems of communication, and we have advanced notions concerning the use of language. Presymbolic language, symbolic language, communication based on action metaphor or metaphor, each can provide a system of language which allows the patient either to move toward contact and object relationships in a way that is appropriate for him, or to keep him equidistant from external objects and the not fully integrated or accepted inner world.

At times the therapist cannot use symbolic language with the psychotic child. He is tempted himself to use only signal language, almost an an imitative echolalic language which at least satisfies the child's yearnings for contact and allays some of the fantastic anxiety attendant on the failure to achieve such contact. However, if the child gets back only an echo, he can never learn that there is both a self and an object, a Me and a You. Therefore the therapist gradually pushes the process in such a way that he does not merely act as an echo. He needs to open an avenue for two-way communication, at first a kind of mirroring, an indication for imitation. His contact development must eventually lead to symbolic communication based on mutual identification. Thus, echoing and mirroring are followed by the slow development of symbolic communication, accompanied by the capacity to observe and to communicate about the inner world and the interpersonal world.

For years, one such patient had only allowed contact on a metaphoric basis, a basis which does not touch the issue of clear differentiation between self and nonself. Then she began to challenge the therapist and wondered why they always talked indirectly about a topic rather than speaking more directly. By so doing, she demonstrated that she had achieved the capacity for symbolic language and no longer needed the distance device of metaphoric communication. Her capacity for a relationship had developed in the transference struggle with the therapist.

When we speak about "transference of psychotic children," we must keep in mind that the concept here has to be understood within a special theoretical context. Ordinarily, transference describes relating to the psychotherapist in a way that recalls earlier experiences with significant adults. Repressed early attitudes, feelings, recollections, etc., vis-a-vis parent figures are reexperienced with the therapist in the transference. But for many psychotic children these early relationships were not usual object relationships. They dealt with part objects, often with fusion states, often with no clear differentiation between parent and self. These early fusion states are now transferred to the psychotherapist who becomes the heir of very primitive early complexes.

An example illustrates such primitive processes. The child wondered how he could be sure that the therapist really existed. Perhaps the psychotherapist was no more than a picture, a dream picture or a television-screen picture, and his words were not really communication with the patient, but prewritten stage scripts in a television show. As he developed these fantasies, his anxiety mounted, and he became panicky. How could he restore reality testing? How could he be sure that the psychotherapist truly existed and that he, the patient, was not alone in his nightmare world of panic? The therapist suggested that perhaps their present give-and-take conversation could establish that both he and the child were "real." But the panic mounted, and as he lost contact with the object, decathected the object, the boy slowly described and experienced depersonalization. This open psychotic experience of depersonalization existed for a little while, until the patient came toward the therapist and touched him. As soon as he touched him, the anxiety evaporated, and contact was restored.

During this interlude, symbolic speech, the discussion together, had no convincing value whatsoever as evidence of reality. But the touch did, as if this patient suddenly returned to an early system of communication which actually consists of direct physical contact. We are reminded of a panic-stricken child who comes running to the mother, crying. She lifts him up and holds him close to her. His tears disappear as the union with the mother is restored. Under such circumstances this is the only convincing "language"; it is action language, evidence based on touch, on being held, on feeling the body. Its power is evident in the case of our youngster who from time to time was overwhelmed by psychotic episodes with loss of contact, the experience of the internal object, the internal parent who makes it truly possible for him to transfer trust to another person. As soon as he lost the intrapsychic object, he could not experience the therapist as being alive in spite of reassuring verbal communication. He regressed to a level of primitive object relationships, a level of primitive communication, where touch and communion are dominant and where later functions of communication, never firmly established, have lost their strength as if drained away.

How quickly can a psychotherapist become an integral part of the ever-changing communication systems of his severely disturbed patients? How capable is he of learning linguistic systems of communication which, once part of his own life, he has forgotten, given up, repressed, and now finds anxiety provoking as he copes with countertransference experiences? Yet the therapist can only work with such patients if he feels himself in their world and their system of communication. Hence he sometimes may feel overwhelmed by the burdens of his task.

Another patient, experiencing herself as first identifying with Christ, as being driven later to experience merging with Him, accused the therapist of having blasphemous thoughts. The therapist, feeling anxiety, understood his anxiety as being accused by the patient of thinking of himself as omnipotent, as being a deity himself. Further, he felt a kind of guilt, as if he were thinking of himself as more powerful than the deity and struggling with the patient over whether she was going to work with him or whether she was going to rely entirely on religious experience. As soon as he understood himself, the therapist was able to communicate again. He was able to help the patient see that he was not attacking her religious beliefs, but rather wanted her to know he understood her difficulty in identifying with an ideal. She felt in danger when her experience of self was invaded by symbiotic experience, a merging of self and nonself. She could not allow herself this experience since she could not move beyond it toward self-realization.

Such psychotherapeutic techniques require immense support by parents, other relatives, school and church, cooperating agencies; they are very rarely useful without therapeutic alliances beyond the patient-doctor alliance. Bettelheim (1974) speaks about the therapeutic environment. Others speak about forms of behavior modification, reeducation, and the necessity to bring the parents into the treatment process. Certain parents, however, as Bettelheim suggests, should be kept out of the treatment process, and this usually requires hospitalizing the child or providing some other therapeutic environment. Other authors, such as Bowen (1975), suggest that the parents be included in the hospital setting, that the whole family be treated. And finally, those of us who work in clinics and in private practice develop ways of working with parents, either seeing the parents in psychotherapeutic treatment or involving them in casework treatment. The most difficult aspect of work with severely disturbed children, based on our experience during the last few decades, is the length of treatment. Occasionally, there are cases of the very ill who respond favorably in a very short time. But most cases demand endless patience, time, experimentation, and cooperation with the parents. Treatment processes may last from a few years to much more than a decade. In some cases treatment seems to be interminable.

Freud's (1900) early work with psychoanalytic patients was often clarified by his use of Greek mythology, psychological insights based on metaphor. One of the powerful themes that he used was the one concerning *Oedipus Rex.* The story of the rejected child, who left his surrogate parents, killed his father, and married his mother, is a beautiful representation of the unconscious conflict over patricide and incest which the child must overcome in order to gain the capacity for mature object relationships.

To describe the difficulties of those who work with borderline or psychotic children, we call attention to another Greek myth. One of the heroes of the Trojan War, Achilles, was considered by all to be invulnerable. Thetis, a sea goddess, and mother of Achilles, wished him to become a great hero, but she was also anxious to protect him from all physical harm. So that he could become the hero she wished for without risk to his life, she took him as an infant to the river Styx, knowing that immersion in its waters would render him forever invulnerable. To prevent the baby from drowning, however, she held him by his heel, and in so doing, established the legendary Achilles' heel, the unprotected area. Achilles did indeed become a hero, but died in battle from a wound to this single vulnerable spot. It is interesting at this point to remember that Oedipus presumably had a deformed foot as implied by his name, that his mother sent her infant away, and that his father feared his son's potential rivalry. The fatal flaw, the basic weakness that everyone possesses, is different for the two heroes. That of Oedipus centers about the Triad, the triangle which is father, mother, and son. That of Achilles is in the pre-oedipal, one-to-one relationship with the mother, the kind of relationship that is established between mother and son. The ambition of Thetis was a premature attempt to determine the goal, the future identity of the baby.

One could take the story of Thetis and Achilles, the holding on in the wrong way, as an allusion to the problem of psychotic children. They are caught in the separation and individuation phase and cannot get out of it. Their struggle is between the wish for eternal attachment and counterphobic separation. In modern terms attachment and separation (Bowlby 1969) are a struggle between the autistic and the symbiotic position (Mahler and Furer 1968), maternal deprivation (Spitz 1965), a failure of early environment (Szurek and Berlin 1973), or a biological deficit, a maturational lag (Bender 1953).

Etiological controversy seems to be but a disguised description of the technical interventions by means of which these pathological states can be cured, improved, or at least temporarily changed.

At times one has the impression that the synthetic and the integrating function of self, of ego, cannot be fully restored. There are children who are in permanent need of help. Such children forever need a protective environment, a kind of halfway house between the first home, which they must leave, and the adult community which they can never fully reach.

The Work with Parents

Parental collaboration is always necessary in child psychotherapy, but it is particularly difficult to achieve in dealing with severely ill children. The parents frequently experience themselves as the cause of the illness. They feel guilty, self-accusatory, alarmed, and desperate. They waver back and forth between hate and deep guilt toward the child and a wish to find help and the proper resources, even if doing so means sacrificing everything. Most of us who treat such children find that the parents have made many previous efforts before they come to the last resource; have lost confidence in, or have magic expectations of us; hope that we can do the impossible; love and hate us at same time; are completely dependent on us and challenge us constantly with their doubts and their displaced or open hostility.

For years they may have denied any awareness of pathology and only slowly may have admitted that something is wrong. We spoke about our own difficulties in dealing with such parents. The overidentification with the child leads us to believe, if not consciously, in the parents' incompetence, and we often believe it would be desirable to move the parents away from the situation, permitting ourselves to have complete control over the child. Feeling the need for complete control over the child leads us to a variety of assumptions which can hardly be proved. Each sick child faces a different social situation with a different set of parents, and our plans can never be based on omnipotent prescription giving, demanding this or that kind of sacrifice, but must be based on diagnostic awareness which includes the total situation.

It may be true that the parents contributed to the pathology. Or as Goldfarb (1961) suggested, they may have been so overwhelmed by the illness that they could not cope with it, even though they otherwise proved to be fairly competent adults, having done quite well with other children in the family. Therefore, a static view as to what one should do with parents, or what they ought to do in order to help us, is contraindicated, especially since the very same parents who contributed to the illness are also the ones who will contribute to recovery. But they must be helped to help us achieve that.

The nature of that help depends on the kind of help they need. Frequently we think of them as auxiliary personnel who ought to do whatever we demand in terms of the child's needs, thus overlooking their own needs. They could be parents who are not able to maintain the child because of their own physical or emotional illness or because of a precarious balance in the marriage or the presence of other children who should not be growing up with a very sick sibling. Or they may be parents who are capable of sacrifice and insight into the child's difficulty and able to provide—if guided correctly—immense help in the upbringing of the child.

The child not only needs treatment. He needs living space, a home, and education. While often we cannot precisely differentiate between the tasks of education and the tasks of psychotherapy, between rearing a child and resolving inner conflicts, we must believe that in most cases the parents have a place in the treatment program. Even when the child has to be removed or when the parents, overanxious and distraught, must be freed of a burden they cannot carry, we deal with a process to be developed rather than a prescription to be given or demands to be made.

It may be a long process before the parents are capable of facing the fact that they have to give up the illusion of a healthy child. At first they may deny the pathology; then they may deny their wish to get rid of the child. They have to work through their own conflict and have to learn to accept the degree of pathology and the need for separation.

Whenever we think of a child going to the hospital, we think of the child's trauma, but separation is as traumatic for the parents as it is for the child. It is difficult for us to think through this trauma of the parents who must let go. The letting go is not only the child's problem, but also the parents' problem. Yet, how can a mother let go if she is attached to the child in a symbiotic way? And the parents that let go of the child and apply to a treatment center have to go through a process of helplessness, of mourning, and of deep disappointment, as they experience the narcissistic blow of having parented a severely sick child.

Therefore we usually assume that a parallel process of helping is necessary. Just as the child needs help, so do the parents. It is hard to make clear how children of the type we describe produce and revive immense anxiety and rage in the parent. Only he who has treated such children and has experienced the hate in the countertransference so well described by Winnicott (1949), as well as the helplessness in the countertransference, can sympathize and identify with the parent.

The task of the psychotherapist is to remain equidistant from the needs of the parents and the needs of the child so that he may keep the child in treatment and help the parents to permit him to continue with the child. Often he is not able to meet the task alone. He needs collaborators who work with the parents.

These forms of collaboration are endlessly difficult since every worker, concentrated as he is with either the parent or the child, tends to overidentify with his own tasks in such a way that he does not see the task of the other. He may thus create in the total situation a kind of fragmentation which will be neither more nor less than the replica of the internal, fragmented world of the sick child. Such treatment programs, carried out in institutions, in social agencies, and in hospitals, are in constant danger. Sometimes the whole staff is caught up in the countertransference and organized hate, forcing the end of treatment for such a child. The attempts by the staff, the parents, and the psychotherapist of the individual child to meet these endless provocations explains why therapeutic programs frequently include group psychotherapy, group meetings with parents, and endless staff meetings and consultations.

In the end, the parents may see improvement in the child but may have to accept that they have lost years of valuable contact with the child; that with him it will never be the same even when he returns to the family; that they may have to give him up prematurely. Sometimes a child, kept for years in a therapeutic environment, grows up, goes through school into college, and never returns to his childhood home, except as an adult. He has become a stranger to the family, having more life contacts with the institution, the foster home, the therapist, and the social worker, who have become the real, albeit second world, of his childhood.

The letting-go process always is a painful one. The most complex act of true parental love is the one that permits the child to move away toward his own life. This act of letting go is an act of love. Frequently we think of love in terms of "forever, until death do us part." Parental love, however, suggests that if we are to love forever, love must include letting go, separation, and giving up. That act is even more painful when the children are seriously ill.

Parents need children just as children need parents. In the case of these children, however, the needs of the parents are frequently of a pathological order, and therefore we must work with them as well as with the children in order to help them to turn pathological needs or anxiety reactions into appropriate responses contributing to the autonomy of the child. Unlike adult psychotherapy, the work with this category of children is a kind of tie-in sale. We must take the parents with the child, even though we often feel we only want to work with the child. Today the work with parents is perhaps the weakest link in our technical armamentarium; yet we must remember that we need them as much as they need us. They are a significant part of a new triad: the therapeutic forces, the parental forces, and the growing adaptive forces of the child patient in constant collaboration or, sometimes, in deadly conflict, in an endless process of working toward the goal of recovery which is uncertain.

Most of the people who have worked for a long time with such children have reported in the literature occasional successes. Some of our psychotic or borderline child patients have made immense achievements in the world. But there are also total failures. The same holds true of our work with parents. Are they the failures? Is our lack of technical skill or theoretical understanding the cause for the interruption of work? We should be careful, not dogmatic, with our answers when our experiences so far represent just initial efforts in the work of solving extremely complex problems.

Training and Research

Jones (1951) suggested that every psychotherapist unconsciously feels that he is God. He dreams and fantasizes about omnipotence. His curative abilities can do what nobody else can. Those of us who dedicate much of our time to psychotic or borderline children know that our sense of omnipotence is frequently accompanied by a experience of helplessness. We vacillate, not unlike our patients, between a sense of omnipotence and a sense of omni-impotence.

We are usually alone and fight the battle of pioneers in treating this group of patients so as to live in a world in which there is still considerable lack of knowledge, an enormous lack of resources, limited facilities, and little support by community or government agencies.

Because of our special interests, we do not always get along well with our colleagues. Much of what we do arouses in us or in others enormous conflict. We are hardly easier to live with than the children with whom we work. We have to learn to work in institutions with other colleagues, and we deal with a body of knowledge which gravitates back and forth between the feeling that we are the possessors of absolute truth—which makes us dogmatic—and the feeling that we are in a jungle of dangerous uncertainty.

We must also cope with students who are interested in this field and bring us similar fantasies of rescue and omnipotence as well as helplessness. They are always willing to believe in miracle cures, to turn to schools of thought which are the newest, the most revolutionary, and give promise for immediate answers. They are, therefore, reluctant to learn, unwilling to participate in slow training programs which frequently seem dull or prosaic, and they often insist on fast prescriptions rather than slow insight. Surrounded by emergencies, they are not quite ready to permit themselves to have ideas of treatment techniques emerge slowly.

One would wish that those who choose to engage in psychoanalytic work with children undergo a thorough personal analysis, but that indeed is not enough. Besides the need to know oneself, there is also the need to understand the patient, brought about by methods of supervision, a tedious process of developing insights into the psychotherapeutic process.

As pointed out earlier, the treatment of the psychotic child or the borderline condition in childhood is a kind of intertwining of patient and therapist. The lines of the interpretive process and the associative process of the patient—psychotic acting out, psychotic plays, dreams, and fantasies—all frequently merge. Often, the words of the patient and the therapist merge: The psychotherapeutic notes of therapists who do such work are frequently unclear as to what was said by the patient and what they themselves have said. Their memory becomes unreliable. These constant fusion experiences are in part necessary in order to understand the patient, but they also make the recording of data unreliable and simultaneously create an intense, yet vague situation with the supervisor. The demands that are made on the supervisor are a kind of parallel process, showing in reverse what takes place between patient and psychotherapist. The transferences and the countertransferences blur and merge. Frequently we have the impression that the process of communication regresses to symbiotic communion. It is difficult for the supervisor to distinguish between interpretive interventions and the patient's material. The records of such treatment often seem to picture and recreate the mother/child symbiosis, or autistic conditions, rather than to communicate about these processes.

The supervisor frequently experiences himself so immersed in the process that he wants to relinquish his supervisory task and take over the treatment. Wanting to take the patient away from the treating therapist is a kind of counter-identification with the parents who occasionally lose trust in the work of the therapist. In short, the blurring between the task of the supervisor and the psychotherapist resembles the blurring of the object relationship.

The drain on the psychotherapist is enormous and never ends. The frustrations and the lack of visible success create a special problem. It seems that the only vital counteractivity which helps to sustain the psychotherapist, as he faces difficulties that invite pessimism, is involvement in research. The best supervisor, the best seminar leader in the training of such psychotherapists, is not one who insists on certain answers, but rather one who experiences his work with the one supervised as joint discovery. It is necessary for both somehow not to differentiate sharply between teacher and student, but to accept each other as scientific collaborators. Both are searching. Neither knows completely. Master teachers in this field are usually surrounded by a number of devoted students who soon become their collaborators, partly because the few enterprises in consistent work with such children are small and dedicated. They tend to form into cult-like groups where the leaders are surrounded by devotees—not merely students seeking credit—who identify with the task of the primary investigators.

This form of training has many advantages and brings forth productive and creative students. At the same time, these small circles suffer certain limitations. The hold on each other is powerful. Group cohesion around such a leader is deep and strong. They frequently develop their own language, their own conceptualization, their own system of communication, and thus they become a kind of advanced replica of their patients. They create autistic islands which are an exaggerated version of what exists between different psychotherapeutic schools. Whenever something new is found, new concepts arise which are not completely free of ideological overtones. Only slowly is it possible to build bridges between the schools and to learn from each other.

We have also found that in working with such children another issue arises, that of worthwhileness. One must only think of how difficult it is to refer such a patient to a proper source to realize the significance of this issue. Usually we try to "sell" such a patient to someone else, speak about the worthwhileness of the child or the parent, as if one expects such great hostility to arise in the treatment of such a child that one needs to fortify the therapist beforehand against the anticipated negative experience. To treat such children it is essential that the therapist himself feel worthwhile and able to commit himself, without time limitations or other conditions, to situations where there is no end in sight and where it is difficult to be optimistic. Those who need the patient to be worthwhile are most likely searching for the worthwhileness in themselves. Only if they experience themselves as worthwhile can they make such a commitment.

Erikson (1964) suggested that frequently such children, as well as the parents, lack "sending" power. They do not "turn each other on," nor do they turn us on. We who work with children and try to treat them also lack sending power and, therefore, need to create in ourselves sustaining power. Only those of us who have such a sense of personal worthwhileness can live without the guarantees of positive outcome, good financial income, precise and simple techniques, predictable success.

Only clinical research makes it possible to sustain such treatment situations. Formal research is oriented toward the establishment of truth. Here, however, we advocate the kind of research that helps to free these patients and helps them overcome their illness and move toward some form of autonomy. Therefore we need to build into our treatment models, unclear and unfinished as they often are, clinical research directed toward the development of techniques for the facilitation of treatment—research which is not objective but is tied to an attitude about the work itself, which must, in part, be based upon faith, an identification with humanism. This faith needs to be based on one's own worthwhileness as a therapist so that one can develop a capacity to make no demands upon the patient to be worthwhile. He cannot be the evidence for our own worthwhileness. We must not be like Thetis who plunged her infant son into the river to protect him from all harm, while at the same time she planned for him to be a great warrior. We must not set goals for the child, but must do what is needed to help him set his own goals.

How can one teach such an attitude? How can such attitudes become part of our training program? Some of our students, seeking identity models, as all students do, may be able to identify with us. They use us for professional self-realization. Those who cannot, leave such training. We do with them what we do with our patients: initiate a process—the treatment process there, the educational process here. Our potent strength as teachers, as well as therapists, depends on developing the capacity to participate in these therapeutic and educational processes without the illusion of omnipotence and to accept the limits and uncertainties as well as the challenges of a new dimension in treatment.

References

Bender, L. Childhood schizophrenia. *Psychiatric Quarterly,* 27:663, 1953.

Bettelheim, B. *A Home for the Heart.* New York: Alfred A. Knopf, 1974.

Bleuler, E. *Dementia Praecox, or the Group of Schizophrenias* (1911). Translated by J. Zinken. New York: International Universities Press, 1950.

Bowlby, J. *Attachment and Loss.* New York: Basic Books, 1969.

——. *Attachment and Loss: Separation, Anxiety and Anger.* Vol. 2. New York: Basic Books, 1973.

Bowen, M. Family therapy after 20 years. In: Arieti, S., ed. *American Handbook of Psychiatry.* Vol. 5. New York: Basic Books, 1975. pp. 367–392.

Ekstein, R. *Children of Time and Space, of Action and Impulse.* New York: Appleton-Century-Crofts, 1966.

Erikson, E. *Childhood and Society* (1950). New York: W.W. Norton, 1964.

——. *Toys and Reasons—Stages in the Ritualization of Experience.* New York: W.W. Norton, 1977.

Freud, S. The interpretation of dreams (1900). *Standard Edition.* Vols. 4/5. London: Hogarth Press, 1953.

——. Introductory lectures on psychoanalysis (1915–1917). *Standard Edition.* Vols. 15/16. London: Hogarth Press, 1961.

——. A seventeenth century demonological neurosis (1922). *Standard Edition.* 19:69–105. London: Hogarth Press, 1961.

——. The loss of reality in neurosis and psychosis (1924). *Standard Edition.* 19:183–190. London: Hogarth Press, 1961.

Frost, R. Education by metaphor. In: Latham, E., and Lot, H., eds. *Selected Prose of Robert Frost.* New York: Holt, Rinehart & Winston, 1949.

Goldfarb, W. The mutual impact of mother and child in childhood schizophrenia. *American Journal of Orthopsychiatry,* 31:738, 1961.

Jones, E. The god complex (1913). In: Jones, E., ed. *Essays in Applied Psychoanalysis.* Vol. 2. London: The Forsythe Press and The Institute of Psychoanalysis, 1951.

Kanner, L. Early infantile autism. *Journal of Pediatrics,* 25:211, 1944.

Kohut, H. *The Analysis of the Self.* New York: International Universities Press, 1971.

Kraepelin, E. *Einführung in die Psychiatrische Klinik.* [Introduction into the Psychiatric Clinic] (1900). 3 Auflage. Leipzig: Verlag von Johann Ambrosius Barth, 1916.

Lewis, C.S. *"Bluspels and Flalansferes." Rehabilitations and Other Essays.* New York: Oxford University Press, 1939. pp. 135–158.

Mahler, M., and Furer, M. *On Human Symbiosis and the Vicissitudes of Individuation.* New York: International Universities Press, 1968.

Mahler, M.; Pine, F.; and Bergman, A. *The Psychological Birth of the Human Infant.* New York: Basic Books, 1975.

Rank, B. Adaption of the psychoanalytic technique for the treatment of young children with atypical development. *American Journal of Orthopsychiatry,* 19:130–139, 1949.

Spitz, R. Anaclitic depression. *The Psychoanalytic Study of the Child,* 2:313–342, 1946.

——. *The First Year of Life: A Psychoanalytic Study of Normal and Deviant Development of Object Relations.* New York: International Universities Press, 1965.

Szurek, S., and Berlin, I. *Clinical Studies in Childhood Psychoses.* New York: Brunner/Mazel, 1973.

Winnicott, D. Hate in the countertransference. *International Journal of Psycho-Analysis,* 30:69, 1949.

The Course of Life: Psychoanalytic Contributions
Toward Understanding Personality Development.
Vol. II: Latency, Adolescence, and Youth.
S.I. Greenspan and G.H. Pollock, editors.
NIMH 1980

Eleven, Twelve, Thirteen: Years of Transition From the Barrenness of Childhood to the Fertility of Adolescence

Judith S. Kestenberg, M.D.[1]

The ages of 11 to 14, like all periods of transition, are difficult to characterize and label. They mark an era of growth and change in internal and external sex organs. As years of impending fertility, they are most illustrative of the psychoanalytic tenet of the relationships between biological characteristics and psychological experience (Freud 1905). From this perspective, we can view the principal developmental task of this phase as an integration of reproductive inner genitality with external and internal manifestations of sex-specific sexuality.

In this presentation, I shall refer to the ages of 11 to 14 as *prepuberty*, and I shall try to define and elaborate on its dynamic, somatic, cognitive, and social aspects, placing a special emphasis on the progressive changes in organization which proceed from diffusion to reintegration (Kestenberg 1967a, 1968a).

Copyright 1980 by Judith Kestenberg.

1. Peter Blos, Aaron Esman, Kurt Eissler, Melvin Grumbach, Roger Short, and James Tanner supplied supplemental data. Mark Sossin added bibliographical data and conducted an informal survey about the onset of ejaculations.

Some Problems in Nomenclature

Diverse terms and age-ascriptions cloud both the psychological and endo-crinological literature concerning adolescence. Some of the differences are basically semantic, while others stem from the difficulty in pinpointing the time when fertility is established.

The word "Adolescenz" is rarely used in German. In all his writings, Freud referred to puberty as the time when genital primacy was established. Since Hall's (1916) famous book, *Adolescence*, this term has been firmly established in American literature. Anna Freud (1936) and H. Deutsch (1944) looked upon prepuberty as the time in which latency organization is dissolved, but changes in primary and secondary sex characteristics have not yet become a challenge to the ego. In the English translation A. Freud (1949), Erikson (1951), Blos (1958), Harley (1970), and others referred to this phase as preadolescence.

For researchers in somatic development, puberty generally means the attain-ment of fertility, but many authors use this very term to indicate that sexual maturation is progressing toward this attainment. Some authors call this pre-paratory or transitional period "pubescence" and the time after fertility ensues "postpubescence" (e.g., Schonfeld 1943). In the most general sense, prepu-berty connotes all years of childhood prior to the substantial release of steroids effecting the growth of primary and secondary sex characteristics. In a narrow sense of the word, prepuberty is a synonym for pubescence, and it is in this sense the term will be used throughout this paper. The term "adolescence" will connote the growth that occurs between childhood and adulthood which can be divided into the subphases of prepuberty and early and later puberty (Kestenberg 1967a, 1968a, b).

Ages and Stages

The difficulty in assigning developmental phases to specific ages is com-pounded by the wide range in individual rates of maturation, by the changes that occur from decade to decade, as well as by differences due to ecological, socioeconomic, and family-size variations. Well-nourished children are now taller than they were a few decades ago. The mean age of menarche dropped from 13½ in 1965 (Wilkins 1965) to under 13 in 1975 (Cone 1976). According to Hamill (1974), the difference in maturation between boys and girls has diminished from 2 or more years to 1½ years or less. At the same time, the span between menarche and fertility has shortened. From research on childbearing in adolescence, it has become evident that, at times, menarche is followed immediately by an ovulatory cycle (Fineman and Smith 1977; Hansen 1978). Kinsey et al. (1948) put the mean age of the first ejaculation as 13.88. Tanner (1962, 1970) reports that the first ejaculation occurs a year after the onset of accelerated penis growth at the mean age of 12.85. Sperm has been detected in the urine of boys as young as 12, with the mean age of first spermaturia placed at 13.3 or less (Richardson and Short, 1978), but neither spermaturia nor ejaculation is an indicator of fertility.

All researchers agree that phases and ages need not coincide. In order to study phase development within the context of 3-year periods, one has to rely on averages rather than individual differences. The ages between 11 and 14 are considered average in identifying landmarks of prepuberty progression (see table 1).

Suggested Correlations Between Stages of Physical and Psychological Development

Very little headway has been made since Freud's first attempts to correlate soma and psyche, but new discoveries in endocrinology tend to confirm many of Freud's basic hypotheses.

Freud's theory of biological bisexuality has received confirmation from the discovery that gonads produce not only sex-specific hormones but also hormones of the opposite sex (Freud 1905). The immature reproductive organs are sensitive to hormones, and both estrogens and androgens are secreted in small quantities in childhood (see table 1). This may well be the physiological base of infantile sexuality. Puberty is no longer looked upon as the result of a "sudden activation of a previously dormant system but gradually increasing function of a system that has been continuously active from the in utero stage of development" (Root 1973, p. 14; table 1). The psychoanalytic theory about the intrinsic continuity between childhood, adolescence, and adulthood (Jones 1922) receives corroboration from modern endocrinology.

In childhood, there exists a high sensitivity of the hypothalamus to the secretion of small amounts of hormones. Thus, when gonadotropins rise slightly, they effect a fall in the quantity of gonadal hormones. Conversely, a small rise in the latter effects a fall in the former. In prepuberty, there is a significant decrease in hypothalamic sensitivity which continues until the final attainment of a new set point of the hypothalamic gonadostat. Through the mediation of gonadotropine-releasing factors in the hypothalamus, large quantities of steroids can be secreted before the feedback is set in operation through which a pituitary secretion of gonadotropins effects a lowering of gonadal hormone output. In prepuberty, the irregular production of hormones seems to indicate that the hypothalamic gonadostat has lost its childhood sensitivity but has not attained a new equilibrium as yet. The change in sensitivity ". . . seems to correlate with the attainment of a critical level of the CNS and general somatic maturation that correlates with skeletal age" (Grumbach et al. 1974, p. 127). There appears to be a comparable change in the regulation of the "affect-ostat" of the psyche. Drives and affects rise and fall episodically in transition from the equilibrium of latency to the creation of a new equilibrium before adulthood is attained.

The change in sensitivity in prepuberty is reflected in an alteration of day and night periodicity. The growth hormone (GH) and the luteinizing hormone (LH) are secreted in several pulses during the night, with the mean average of quantities considerably lower during sleeping than during waking. In latency as well as in adulthood, the average quantity of secretion is constant during sleep and waking (Boyar et al. 1972; Finkelstein et al. 1972). We are confronted here with changes in periodicity which begin in the prepuberty of both sexes and can be understood only within the framework of the beginning transformation of rhythms altogether (e.g. food intake, body temperature, heart rate and blood pressure, responses to light and darkness). A new periodicity of drives and a changed reactivity of the psyche reflect the new somatic rhythms. These are balanced by the maturing cortically controlled cognitive structures (Kestenberg and Robbins 1975, p. 416). Psychoanalysts look upon latency as steady and upon prepuberty as unpredictable. Endocrinologists contrast the steady (tonic) level of hormone secretion in childhood with the episodic and cyclic modes of secretion in the beginning of adolescence.

The growth of reproductive organs precedes the appearance of secondary sex characteristics in prepuberty. The increase in mass and volume of the uterus and ovaries and the prostate and testicles creates the internal somatic base for the acceptance of inner genitality in preparation for a new sexual and reproductive functioning in puberty. The rising need for a representation of the inner genital in prepuberty led me to designate it as the "prepuberty inner-genital phase" (Kestenberg 1967a, 1968b, 1975). Most of the external changes, other than the estrogen-dependent breast development, are influenced by the increase in androgenic substances (e.g. pubic, axillary, and body hair). Testosterone, rising much more in the boy than in the girl, also enhances body growth and the increase in size and quantity of muscle cells. It is more than likely that androgens, especially testosterone, have a bearing on the considerable increase in aggression in prepuberty (Freud, A. 1936). The imbalance between the internal and external changes effects episodic shifts of libidinal and aggressive cathexes from the inside to the outside and vice versa. Moreover, prepuberty diffusion is not limited to drives. Ego and superego structures break down, not only under pressure of irregularly increasing drives, but also because of a decrease in hypothalamic sensitivity and perhaps because of a decrease in cortical inhibition.

In prepuberty, the disruption of the body image is counteracted by each successive step in the acceptance of new landmarks in the body, internal and external. In all likelihood, the task of prepuberty to reintegrate inside and outside is correlated with a reintegration of hormone secretion on the basis of a new timeclock in the hypothalamus. A related change in the CNS seems to influence the progression toward a new organization via the newly acquired cognitive structures (Inhelder and Piaget 1958).

The following tables of stages of sexual maturation serve as a reference for the correlation of psychic and hormonal changes. The inclusion of anatomical

Table 1. Stages of Sex Maturation

AGES	BOYS	GIRLS
Fetus	FSH and chorionic LH are detectable at 68 days of gestation.	
	From 84-150 days FSH rises, falling in late months of gestation. LH decreases in newborn (see table 2 for abbreviations and definitions).	
	Secretion of androgens by the fetal immature Leydig cells	Higher concentration of FSH and LH than in boys
Infancy		
First 3 days	Initially rapid, then slower decreases in estrogen Testicular activity present	
1-12 mos.	Higher levels of FSH and LH than in childhood	
	Gradual increase of testosterone, at 3 mos. gradual decrease until 7th month	
	At 3-6 mos. LH elevated, decreasing to low levels until the age of 6 yrs.	
Up to 2 yrs.		Bursts of FSH secretion may be characteristic of female infancy. The disappearance of episodic secretion of FSH after the age of 2 yrs. may be the result of increasing ovarian function (Winter and Faiman 1972).
2-4 yrs.	Testosterone drops.	
3 yrs.	Small amounts of estrogen and 17-ketosteroids in urine, the former higher in girls and the latter higher in boys	
4 yrs.	Testosterone rises. Androsterone and androstenedione in urine	
3-9 yrs.		Ovaries similar to adult's, but smaller and have no corpora lutea. Uterus growth
Latency		
5-10 yrs.	Urinary FSH and LH increase, the latter by intermittent spurts	
7 yrs.	Gradual increase in ketosteroids and estrogen excretion	
9-10 yrs.	Increase in serum FSH and LH is followed by *testicular growth*.	Initiation of adolescent growth spurt
10-11 yrs.	Dehydroepiandrosterone, an adrenal androgen, increases. Rise in 17-ketosteroids excretion, more so in boys	

Table 1-continued

AGES	BOYS	GIRLS
	Most rapid increase in muscle cells which continues more gradually until end of third decade. *Prostate and testicular growth.* Incomplete spermatogenesis	Considerable, rapid rise in estrogens. Maximum size of muscle cells. With an abrupt rise of FSH, *ovaries* reach 20% of adult weight (60% at the age of 16)

Prepuberty

| 11-12 yrs. | Considerable increase in FSH and LH, gradual in the former and abrupt in the latter. 20-fold rise of testosterone. (Circulating LH and testosterone continue to rise until 17 or later, while FSH reaches a plateau earlier). Initiation of adolescent height and weight spurt. *Growth of penis, of seminal vesicles and the bulbourethral glands. More rapid testicular enlargement. Thinning of scrotum.* | Large FSH increase heralds onset of female sexual maturation. Plasma estradiol and estrones augment. The relative scatter of estradiol may indicate *episodic ovarian function before menarche.* Urinary excretion of testosterone and epitestosterone increases. *Accelerated growth of external and internal genitalia.* Remolding of the bony pelvis and accumulation of fat. *Vaginal secretion,* Ph changes, cornification and glycogenization. Increased proliferation of vaginal epithelium and irregular cell sizes. Some of these changes are cyclic. *Pubic hair over mons* and labia pigmented. *Breast budding.* |

| 12-13 yrs. | *Episodic secretion of GH and LH, with mean levels higher during sleep* | |
| | Further increase in testosterone. Decrease and stabilization of estrogen excretion. *Pubic hair,* sparse, long, downy, somewhat pigmented. Accelerated growth of penis, continued enlargement of scrotum | Continued enlargement of *breast* and areola. Pigmented *nipples. Pubic hair dark, coarse and curly.* Peak *height and weight velocity* precedes menarche (highly correlated with bone age). *Menarche* appears ½–1½ years before ejaculation in boys. Acceleration of fat deposits reaches maximum at 13. |

| 13-14 yrs. | Progressive rise in testosterone. *Rapid testicular,* penal and scrotal enlargement. Pubic hair darker, coarser, | Rise and stabilization of androgenic substances. Adult type hair on mons. Axillary hair and perspiration odor. |

Table 1–continued

AGES	BOYS	GIRLS
	still sparse. *Active spermatogonia,* Leydig cells may be present, but they are of puberal rather than adult type (Wilkins 1965). Increased pigmentation of scrotum. Subareolar node on nipples (not in all cases). Spermaturia (Richardson and Short, 1978). *Ejaculation* (Kinsey et al. 1948).	Voice changes. Thyroid hormones rise after previous decline. Postmenarcheal serum LH increases. Progesterone rises and is becoming cyclic. *Earliest pregnancies* (still earlier impregnation unusual)

Puberty

14-15 yrs.   Serum LH mean quantity still higher during sleep but waking LH concentration on the increase (adult LH levels are constant)

	Great rise of testicular androgens. Voice changes noticeably. Peak height velocity. Size of muscle cells reaches maximum. Auxillary hair. Odor of perspiration. Further growth of testicles and penis, rapid growth of prostate. Down on upper lip. Pubic hair resembles adult type but no spread to thighs.	FSH and LH, estradiol and testosterone reach normal adult ranges, but no comparable progesterone level in the luteal phase of the menstrual cycle. Ovaries grow more quickly. Pubic hair spreads to thighs.
15-16 yrs.	Thyroid hormone rise. Marked rise of testosterone. Considerable increase of FSH and LH reaching adult levels. Beginning of facial and body hair. Acne. Adult type genitals. *Mature spermatozoa* (Wilkins 1965).	High cyclic progesterone levels. Ovulatory cycles frequent, as progesterone rises to adult levels in appropriate phase of cycle. Mature breasts. Voice deepens. Acne.
16-17 yrs. plus	Testosterone levels continue to rise well into the third and fourth decades. Bone maturation completed. Period of rapid growth almost completed. Muscle cells still enlarge and increase in number, much more than in females.	Arrest of skeletal growth. Ovulatory cycles stabilize. Size and weight of reproductive organs still on the increase, reaching adult levels at 18-20.

Source: Compiled from Botstein and McArthur 1976; Boyar et al. 1972; Jenner et al. 1972; Kestenberg 1967*a*, 1968*a* and the bibliography contained there; Kulin et al. 1973; Lamberg et al. 1973; Marshall and Tanner 1969; Reiter and Root 1975; Richardson and Short 1978; Root 1973; Sonek 1967; Tanner 1962, 1970; Wilkins 1965; Winer and Faiman 1972, 1973, from "Gonadotropins," ed. by Saxena et al. 1972; and from "The Control of the Onset of Puberty," ed. by Grumbach et al. 1974. Additional references specified.

Table 2. Abbreviations and Definitions

FSH—Follicle-stimulating hormone; in appropriate quantities it promotes the growth of ovarian follicles or testicular tubules.

LH—Luteinizing hormone; in appropriate quantities it induces ovulation or stimulates Leydig cells in the testicle to produce testosterone.

These hormones act synergistically to stimulate estrogen production. They are controlled by the hypothalamic-releasing factors. First signs of pubescence are said to appear when there is a negative feedback between FSH and LH and gonadal steroids. The change in feedback sensitivity begins prior to the onset of puberty, and the process continues through the early pubertal years. The ability to release LH following estrogen stimulation may be attained only in mid-puberty (Kulin and Reiter 1973).

Chorionic LH is secreted by the placenta.

GH—Growth hormone.

Leydig cells are said to secrete testosterone.

Androsterones and androstenediones are precursors of testosterone.

Dehydroepiandrosterone is an adrenal androgen. It is said to be responsible for the growth of hair in adolescence, especially in the girl.

Estrones and estradioles are estrogenic hormones, the latter being most responsible for the growth of female target organs. It becomes cyclic in prepuberty and increases until it has an effect on the endometrium to produce bleeding.

Progesterone is a corpus luteum hormone. It is responsible for the maintenance of the corpus luteum. Cyclic production of estrogens and progesterones in appropriate quantities is responsible for ovulatory cycles.

Testosterones affect the growth and differentiation of male target organs. They promote growth of body and hair. The feedback mechanism between the hypothalamus, the pituitary gonadotropins, and testosterone is not yet clarified. The secretion of male hormones is said to be tonic rather than cyclic.

and endocrinological data before prepuberty and after should be looked upon as a framework for the appraisal of *prepuberty as a psychobiological phase* .

Transition Into and Out of Prepuberty

There is a continuity in the development from latency into prepuberty and from this phase into puberty, differences becoming apparent when progressive changes in organization become the subject of scrutiny.

Changes in the Organization as Seen in Masturbation Fantasies

A successive change in masturbation fantasies of a boy at 10, 12, and 13 years of age, as reported by Wermer and Lewin (1967), elucidates the transition from early to later coping with internal genitality.

At the age of 10 Johnny dreamt about a house with all kinds of electronic equipment and a central switchboard, like the family's hi-fi system which he was forbidden to touch. The house was owned by a queen who was everybody's boss. In the basement was a bomb factory and next to it a vault in which the queen's money was kept. The queen let the boy play with the controls of the bomb factory; when he pressed a button the periscope went up. However, he was careful and did not let any bombs fall out; he stopped playing with the buttons when the "lady" told him to.

At 12, Johnny had pubic hair but did not like it. At this time, he had the analyst participate in his fantasy rather than the queen-mother. Driving together they backed into a cliff, overlooking the ocean.

"When they try to leave, they find that their rear wheels are stuck in the sand and begin to spin, causing sand and rock to be cast off in the ocean . . . ." The ocean engulfs the territory where the cliff used to be, inundating more land and killing a multitude of people.

After Johnny (at 13) had experienced ejaculations, he experimented with syringes and tubes he emptied and squeezed out. He began to think for hours about the shoes and boots in his mother's closet. Feeling an erection, he had the wish to rub his penis inside the shoe.

When he got older, Johnny replaced the fetishistic fantasy with a fantasy about sex play with his sister and later with a daydream about girls he knew.

At 10 Johnny had forebodings of what a 12½-year-old patient of E. Furman (1973) referred to as explosions and clandestine night activities. He represented his rectum as the money-storing vault which adjoined the bomb factory (the prostate?). The construction of his inside as an electronic device belonging to his mother and his obedient touching of the button with permission only, as well as his caution not to let the bombs explode, reflect his orderly and stable latency organization. By the time he was 12, he no longer sought his mother's permission, but used the analyst as his alter-ego—an object of mirroring. Stuck together and spinning together, they caused an erosion, an avalanche, and a mass killing through engulfment. The breakdown of latency organization is depicted in the fantasy, as are the overwhelming sadistic excitement and the fear of losing a substantial part of his body. It is understandable that he did not welcome the external symbol of his new sexuality, the pubic hair. However, the experience of ejaculation had a mitigating effect upon his fears. He began to concentrate on the mechanics of ejaculation, and he hoped to achieve control over the ejaculatory reflex. His fetishistic fantasy expressed the wish to contain on the outside what was exploding from the containers in his inside. Throughout the fantasies, we can see the influence of anal-sadistic upon genital drives, but their organization (through continuity and order in latency; through the escape from genitality into thoughts of the toilet in prepuberty; and through a seeking of an external container for his new discharge in late prepuberty) proceeds from latency stability through prepuberty diffusion and regression to prepuberty reintegration between the inside and the outside. Concomitant is the progress from latency dependence on the mother to the seeking of sameness in prepuberty and the shift toward the oedipal mother before puberty begins.

It is interesting to speculate that 10-year-old Johnny's representation of an inner electronic system reflected the growth of his testicles and his prostate which adjoins the rectum (see table 1, ages 9-10 and 10-11). The flood and avalanche fantasied by a 12-year-old correlate with the 20-fold increase of testosterone at that time. The reorganization following ejaculation may correspond to the more uniform increase of testosterones at this stage. Only when he reached puberty—the age of fertility—could he develop an affective commitment to an object which evolved from growth of excitement and deep feelings, based perhaps on the new organization of sex-specific hormone production (of LH secretion becoming equal in sleep and waking time; see table 1, age 14-15).

Sequential Changes in Attitudes As Seen Through the Rorschach Test

Statistical studies such as those by Gesell et al. (1956) and his followers (Ames et al. 1971) provide means reflecting changes in attitude from year to year, without consideration for the process of transformation, stressed by psychoanalysis. No doubt, both methods complement each other.

On the basis of many Rorschach tests administered to children and adolescents, Ames et al. (1971) described *the ten-year-old* as concrete and seeking order, using isolation of parts to make sense out of shapes, but becoming diffuse when his defenses break down (p. 129). I believe that his interest in anatomy and maps reflects his latent attempts to cope with what is going on in his body.

Described by their parents as belligerent and argumentative, *the eleven-year-olds* lose their 10-year-old calm. Girls more than boys become diffuse and repetitious, their verbalizations approaching a stream of consciousness: . . .

On the other side of the mountain, away from the dinosaurs, looks like a couple of—sort of cow—with a cow's head and a kangaroo's body, big long horns—and they are running down between the mountains, about to land on top of the dinosaurs. . . . [excerpt from an 11-year-old boy's response to card X, pp. 147-48].

The twelve-year-old according to Ames et al., appears to be in an equilibrium, but his emotions are unmodulated and shapeless. He tends to conform to a peer group, showing few individual differences. However, his tendency to put "all parts into a whole" to counteract disintegration is so strong that it surpasses his ability to make combinations. Contaminations and confabulations make images flow into one another, and displacement wins over coherence. He abounds in responses about cutoff or split-open parts of the body and frequently sees fires and explosions.

At the age of *thirteen* , there seems to be a greater mobilization of force to pull things together and to think about things (Ames et al. 1971, p. 180). At the same time, 13-year-olds display many body responses such as grimaces, frowns, sighs, and tongue-play. Things appear queer, weird, jagged, bloody, and wild. Despite the high number of explosion-responses and a sometimes "diffuse and vague sense of self" (p. 186), there is a gradual approach to adult forms of thinking and relating. Prepuberty reorganization prepares the adolescent to withstand the onslaught of "boundless exuberance and energy" (p. 201) he will experience as a *fourteen-year-old* .

Rorschach responses confirm conclusions drawn from analyses. Prepuberty is a period of diffusion and reintegration of psychic structures. Late latency forebodings about the feelings inside the body are superceded in prepuberty by regressive responses to the irregular increases in sexuality and aggression. Inner-genital drives and interests help to reintegrate regressive infantile drive components under the aegis of the new adolescent genitality, and the newly developing cognitive structures become the foremost tools for the reorganization of the ego and superego.

The Development of Abstract Operations in Prepuberty

At the same time as childhood inhibitions are removed and the first line of defense against the new sexuality is a massive regression, a novel way of thinking comes to the rescue of the young adolescent (Piaget and Inhelder 1969).

The 10-year-old conceives reality via the use of concrete operations; the 11- to 14-year-old grasps and assimilates reality in terms of imagined and deduced events. The new structures are part of a developmental continuum; the early sensorimotor structures are followed by internalization of actions through symbol formation and then by a grouping of internalized actions into coherent reversible systems, such as joining and separating. Built upon these achievements is the 11- to 14-year-old's ability to test hypotheses. He takes many factors into consideration all at once. He begins to use abstract propositions such as implication (if-then), disjunction (either-or, or both), exclusions (either-or), and incompatibility (either-or, neither-neither). Schemes become operative which take into account proportions, the double system of references, understanding of hydrostatic equilibrium, and certain forms of probability. The newly won ability to manipulate propositions via combinations and transformations calls for precision in the use of language, a precision which counteracts prepuberty diffusion of thought. Piaget and Inhelder (1958, 1969) indicate that the older adolescent becomes progressively more proficient in the use of symbolic logic and acquires the capacity for the creation of his own hypotheses, which lead to new ideas and new value systems.

The emerging cognitive structures play a decisive role in the rebuilding of the body image in prepuberty, based as it is on combining of representations of the inside with those of the outside of the body. All previous fantasies about the inside of the body were based on concrete images of bodily products and on externalized impulses to touch and nurture (Kestenberg 1975). Rejected as unreal and repressed, in the past, they are revived now and reorganized through transformations and combinations as well as through deductions, based on observations of one's own functioning and that of others.

Metapsychological Assessment of Prepuberty Through the Interpretation of Movement Profiles[2]

The solid and dependable latency child looks proportionate and symmetric. His trunk seems to be hewn from one piece and is isolated from the mobile limbs. In prepuberty the waist becomes loose and flexible and the limbs shoot out every which way. The girl becomes clumsy (Benson 1937), and the boy seems in continuous danger of losing his balance and breaking things. These derailments are counteracted by an inhibition of flow in the pelvis where the center of gravity is located (Kestenberg and Robbins 1975). Experimentation with shifts in weight (toward a restoration of balance) becomes the vehicle for the release and containment of shifting pelvic sensations.

---

2. It is not possible to give here the data from movement studies which warrant the conclusions presented above. Movement notations are of the same order as the immunoassays from which the hierarchic changes in hormone production are derived, as the raw data of the Rorschach Test, administered by Ames et al., and as Piaget's experiments on which their respective formulations are based. Movement notations of a subject are scored and the results are used for the construction of a movement profile (MP) devised to correlate with Anna Freud's developmental assessment (1965). Recommended readings of movement studies on which profiles are based include Laban 1960; Lamb and Turner 1969; Kestenberg 1965, 1967b, 1975, 1980a; Kestenberg and Buelte 1977; Kestenberg and Marcus 1979; Ramsden 1973.

Rhythms of Drive Discharge

Rhythmic changes in tension from free to bound flow and vice versa characterize the motor patterns for drive discharge. Whereas in latency there is an
even distribution among well differentiated pregenital and early genital drive
components, prepuberty brings on a disorganization, with various drive-dis-
charge forms vying for dominance, interrupting and derailing one another. In
addition to oral play, anal type twisting, and straining and urethral restlessness,
prepuberty brings on a preponderance of inner-genital modes of languid
stretching and an admixture of phallic-type leaping and dropping. The inner-
genital drive expressions assume leadership over others, as they are capable of
absorbing them without the loss of their own distinctive quality. Toward the
end of prepuberty and with beginning puberty, we see an increase in combinations between inner-genital and phallic modes of discharge which very likely
constitute adult genital modes (Marcus 1966, personal communication).

Regression to earlier forms of drive discharge is accompanied by rapid shifts
of narcissistic cathexis, from one body part to another and from the body to
objects. Rapidly changing moods are reflected in exaggerated facial expressions, such as frowning, grinning, pouting, and scowling. Reactivity to stimuli is
either too high or too low. Every little touch can produce pain, but at the same
time there may be a conspicuous lack of response to a punch or a slap. A rapid
sequence of grimaces and odd gestures may herald the emergence of a hebe-
phrenic disorder, but more frequently, responding to stimuli in an inappropriate manner and rapid shifts in positioning, gesturing, and grimacing are
transitory phenomena of prepuberty. Through them, the youngster becomes
acquainted with all body parts in such a way that a relocation and reevaluation
of libidinal and aggressive cathexes can take place. From such practices there
evolves the image of the whole body which becomes the core of the body-ego
in puberty.

Movement observation reveals the sources of a complaint by parents and
teachers that their children are lazy or in a daze. When kids are sprawling,
unable to mobilize themselves, and wanting to be left alone, their bodies seem
to lose in elasticity and plasticity, and they appear to be in abnormal states of
consciousness. These states must not be confused with passivity which invites
actions by others (Kestenberg and Marcus 1979). They are probably responsible
for what adolescents in this phase call "feeling like nothing" or "feeling dead."
They can develop into states of depersonalization or alienation. Various means
are used to recover alertness. One of them is restless, moving about to remobil-
ize oneself; another is taking drugs in order to experience vivid feelings instead
of feeling empty and depressed. Hypercathecting body parts which were "lost"
during the inert states can be a prelude to hypochondria. Young adolescents
who suffer from learning disabilities seem to have more frequent states of
inertia than the average 11- to 14-year-olds. However, they are never as all-
pervasive and long lasting as in catatonic episodes. In the normal youngster of

this age, they come and go, perhaps in conjunction with drops and rises of hormone secretion.

More conspicuous than the passing states of inertia are the variety of conflicts which are acted out in movement. Conflicts between activity and passivity, between aggression and libido, and more specifically between pregenital, inner-genital, and phallic-drive components, run rampant. Particularly significant is the integrative influence of inner-genital drives which bring harmony into disorder. Integration is reinforced by the renewal of identifications with the pre-oedipal mother. Maternal attributes, derived from sublimation of inner-genital drives (Kestenberg 1975), are instrumental in the many ways the young adolescent mothers himself and, thus, can become independent of his mother. Young adolescents cater to their bodily needs and tend to soothe their frequent "hurts" by staying in bed and/or eating. Underneath their rough exterior there hides a gentleness which reveals itself in the way they cuddle pets and soft animals or care for their machines—their radios and guitars—which are both their transitional objects and their babies (Kestenberg 1968b, 1971). Underneath a hateful grimace there may hover an unexpressed feeling of lowered self-esteem. Clashes between withdrawal and approach are many; shrinking away from someone on whom one has a crush is a commonplace occurrence. Gradually, these clashes become mitigated by identifications with idolized heroes and heroines—substitutes for the idealized pre-oedipal mother.

Compounding the intrasystemic conflicts in the id are the intrasystemic conflicts in the ego and the superego (Hartmann 1939). There is an almost continuous conflict between externalization and internalization. Defenses serving the taming of drives clash with those directed against external dangers. A breakdown in the superego expresses itself in conflicts between its punitive and permissive aspects, and between the ego-ideal and archaic intolerant attributes of the superego. Family and peer loyalties are pitched against one another, but acting out by trying new solutions is the vehicle via which the ego and the superego are rebuilt. In this process, becoming like one of the in-groups and being popular fill the void created not only by the loss of the pre-oedipal parent, but also by the loss of the former self.

Nowhere is it more noticeable than in prepuberty movement studies that regressions and disintegrations, due to too many conflicts, are followed rather quickly by a reorganization to a higher level of functioning. Each regression becomes a challenge for refitting and rebuilding the old into new attitudes and functions (Geleerd 1964; Eissler 1958; Kestenberg 1967a, 1975). Prepuberty has at its disposal two principal organizers of ego and superego functions:

1. *New ways of problem solving, not only by the use of multiple combinations and transformations, but also by a phrasing of actions and thoughts which matures at this time.* Trial actions are followed by a total commitment to a given attitude, and these are followed by a limitation of the commitment to a realistic degree. In terms of thought (modeled after movement) we can

speak of phrases in which one thinks something over, then becomes totally engaged in the theme, ending the process by finding the appropriate degree of acceptance for the given attitude. Conflicts between the ego and the super-ego are expressed by adopting attitudes contrary to those suggested in the trial action or in the ending of a total commitment by an acceptance of the opposite. Through many variations of such conflicting sequences, the 11- to 14-year-old finds a solution which brings him peace.

2. *A capacity to adopt structures from external models. A successful conflict-free performance is more likely to occur if and when a formal demonstration is provided by a parent, a teacher, or an admired idol.* The clumsy, conflicted 11- and 12-year-old girl becomes graceful during a dance lesson where she can model herself after the harmoniously integrated adult teacher. The boy of this age who horses around with his peers may perform superbly when engaged in sports under the guidance of a coach or in emulation of an admired sports hero. Similar types of unexpected solutions of problems are encountered in intellectual functioning.

The process of adaptation through problem solving in prepuberty can be progressive, but, more often, it is interrupted by resurgences of regressions. Under optimal circumstances, the 14-year-old has integrated drives, ego, and superego functions in such a way that the past becomes an important component of the present without an undue pull toward infantilism and dependence. He leaves his prepuberty, prepared for the onslaught by the enormous upsurge in drives and the equally enormous societal challenge that requires him to give up old objects while seeking new ones.

The Nature of Prepuberty Regression and Reintegration: Its Genetic Roots

Despite changes in growth patterns and social organization through the ages, prepuberty remains much the same. Aptly called "Flegeljahre" (fledgling years) in German, it has been defined in 1955, as it is today, as years of indiscretion, insolent, clownish, and impertinent (Cassel's German/English Dictionary, Breule, K., ed., 1955).

Psychoanalysts agree that prepuberty revives pre-oedipal problems (Deutsch 1944; Blos 1962), but oedipal strivings are revived as well, sometimes in a crude undisguised form (Freud, A. 1949; Harley 1970). There is further consensus that prepuberty is initiated by a pregenital regression, more striking in boys than in girls (Blos 1962). There is no doubt that there is a quantitative increase in drives (Freud, A. 1936, 1949), but the more important characteristic of prepuberty is the drive-diffusion and drive-dedifferentiation which become the springboards for the progressive reintegration of pregenital and genital drives.

I look upon the period between 11 and 14 as an inner-genital phase whose developmental process can be subsumed under the heading *"From Diffusion to Reintegration ."* It is that subphase of adolescence which initiates and carries through a major portion of the reorganization that is necessary to achieve adulthood (Eissler 1958). This reorganization, achieved via a regression to all prelatency phases (Jones 1922), is given a special direction by the recognition of inner-genital sensations and representations. Its immature prototype is the "inner-genital" phase in childhood which follows the pregenital and precedes the phallic phases (Kestenberg 1967 *a*, 1968 *b*, 1975, 1980 *b*).

The Early Inner-Genital Phase

In transition from pregenital to early genital phases, pregenital representations come into the service of making an illusory baby out of the insides of the child and the mother. The externalization of inner-genital impulses and their transformation into maternal forms of sublimation go hand in hand with an all-encompassing identification with the pre-oedipal mother. The formation of images of the inside and the creation of sexual theories (Freud 1923) are aided by the new ability to symbolize and verbalize. The mother and her accessory, the father (Kestenberg 1971), act as external organizers who provide explanatory models for what the child is trying to understand and teach the child words and phrases with which to communicate. Inner-genital drives act as internal organizers, with sensations and wishes contributing to the rebuilding of the body image.

When drives rise too high and sublimations fail, the 3- to 4-year-old child responds to the nagging "funny feelings" inside by nagging, arguing, or otherwise passing excitement to the mother (Kestenberg 1973). The girl thinks that her baby was "deadened" when she feels depleted of inner-genital excitement. Disappointed and disillusioned with baby substitutes, such as dolls and teddies, both sexes now turn to the external genital for solace. The boy generally does this much earlier than the girl. Phallic impulses increase in intensity and frequency, achieving dominance in the phallic phase.

The Phallic Phase and Latency

Denial of the internal and overcathexis of the external genital marks the beginning of the phallic phase. When oedipal wishes to be penetrated threaten the undoing of the denial, repression sets in. At the end of the phallic phase and in latency the repression of inner-genital wishes is fortified by a projection of these wishes upon the opposite sex. When awareness of the introitus persists into latency (Fraiberg 1972), the impact of the re-awakening of inner-genital sensations in prepuberty is weakened. Consequently there is a lesser need to regress.

Prepuberty Regression

With the end of latency and beginning of prepuberty comes the re-awakening of long forgotten "funny feelings," which radiate from inside outward. Baffled by these cryptic sensations, the child tries to connect them to external organs. The nipples and the growing clitoris act as stimulators, transmitters, and resonators of the girl's internal genital sensations (Kestenberg 1968b). Only some boys experience similar sensations in the nipples. Most boys have an inkling of something mysterious going on inside which they interpret in pregenital or phallic terms. Sublimations of inner-genital drives via externalization exist side by side with explorations and manipulations of the changing sex organs. Playing with the pubic hair and on the mons and rubbing of breasts produce sensations which overflow inside the body. Producing erections, shifting the penis, pushing it inward, hiding it between the legs, and pulling on the scrotum stimulate a variety of sensations—from ano-prostatic and scrotal inner-genital waves to urethral tingling and phallic onrushes of genital tension.

At first new sensations and new secretions are experienced in terms of pregenital ideation. Trying to cope with the strange happenings in the pelvic genital area, youngsters hold back or drip urine, retain feces, or let out gas in public. All inferior things are referred to as "crap," and words with sexual connotation are used as dirty. The breakdown of defenses against the regressive ano-urethral genitality leads to an abhorrence of washing. The odor of perspiration merges with genital smells. The discovery of new secretions and playing with them may revive the old habit of eating nasal and genital mucus. All these and similar activities are new editions of the genital-pregenital confusion of the 2- to 3-year-old. Old fears of touching reappear; they may lead to symptoms, such as compulsive washing, or to transitory exaggerations of reaction formations. Overeating and food fads may be followed by an attack of anorexia nervosa or by less rigorous dieting, such as the avoidance of meat as a defense against coprophagic and genitophagic wishes.

Considerable quantities of object-libido are withdrawn from parents and invested in the body, in the self, and in peers. Mutual explorations culminate in transient homosexual episodes. The accumulated aggression is directed outward, with parents as the principal recipients. Nagging, arguing, and passing on of excitement, revived from the early inner-genital phase, mix with anal-sadistic provocations. Oral-sadistic, sarcastic descriptions of parental shortcomings alternate with confusing tirades (flowing like urine or tears). Oratories mixing logical and diffuse thinking confuse parents. They may become incensed by the manifestations of regressive mixtures of phallic intrusiveness and signs of individuation-separation. In the quest for independence, the 11- to 14-year-old practices and explores; at the same time he is offended when his mother is not available for refueling. Like a toddler in the rapprochement phase, he shadows his parents (Kestenberg 1971; Mahler et al. 1975). He spies on them to find evidence of their wrongdoings; e.g., that they are greedy, possessive, unfaithful, liars and cheats, criminals, or prostitutes. The more he repudiates his own sexuality, the more he finds fault with his parents for their lack of restraint.

The Regressive and Progressive Aspects of Ejaculations, Menstruations, and Masturbation

Cottle (1972) described vividly how, at the age of 12, he and his friends had forebodings of ejaculations—forebodings which they interpreted as pregenital and yet elevated to a superior phallic position. They pondered upon the problem of whether it was normal for the heart "to kind of flutter or beat unevenly" during urination. The heart, which symbolizes sexuality and love, became an internal measure of excitement through its externally monitored beat. Its connection to the "stomach" and to pelvic-genital sensations was revealed in the following observation of Cottle (1972):

> Some of the boys agreed the fluttering happened . . . how foolish they looked pulling up their shirt to examine their stomachs. . . . But most importantly the thought had been born, namely, that on the inside of the body, extraordinary connections, some rather delicious, but most rather terrifying were becoming evident (p. 295).

Forebodings of ejaculation and menstruation, and even more so the actuality of experiencing them, have a double effect. Expecting them as signs of maturation makes the adolescent exuberant when they finally come, but there is nevertheless the feeling that something is wrong. Thirteen-year-old Tony anticipated his wet dreams; faced with his ejaculation, he associated it with an illness—the stomachaches that had plagued him for some time (Blume 1971). Thirteen-year-old Kitty Foyle knew that menstruation was a sign of growing up, but she thought of it at first as a tubercular hemorrhage, more serious because "it has gone the wrong way" (Morley 1939, p. 37).

When a youngster experiences ejaculation for the first time in an awake state and without masturbation and fantasies, he is struck by the "delicious feeling" which overrides all other considerations (Steffens 1931). It is rare that girls speak of their menarche as a sexual experience, even though there is engorgement of the vulva and vagina. Boys masturbate deliberately, sometimes for a long time, to achieve an ejaculation. Girls frequently use menstrual pads as masturbatory props, but they may not even know that they are masturbating. Sometimes good sensations are openly associated with menarche. For example, Anne Frank (1947) noted: "I have the feeling that in spite of all the pain, the unpleasantness and the nastiness, I have a sweet secret" (p. 115).

Blood and pain become symbols of female sexuality, constituting a preparation for defloration and delivery. At approximately the same time, boys become initiated to pain experienced in the testicles, either due to "a kick in the balls" or prolonged erections. However, shame underlies efforts to hide evidence of erections and ejaculations. Unlike girls, who are usually carefully prepared with regard to personal hygiene during menstruation, boys have to invent their own ways of disposing of their "come."

Menarche revives and intensifies feminine fears of losing one's insides. However, these fears may become submerged by the ambition to excel as the peer group puts a premium on "getting it first." Popular cliches such as "you have now become a woman" also obscure the girl's real emotions. Feeling sticky from blood, she may not look forward to that kind of womanhood (Kennedy 1953). She may feel disappointed by the appearance of blood instead of a baby. Each girl in this phase has to resolve the conflict between wanting a baby and postponing motherhood until she does become a woman. Some feel driven to be impregnated as soon as possible, hoping to get love from the baby, to revive their own babyhood (i.e., to be mothered), and to feel full rather than lonely and empty (Fineman and Smith 1977, in answer to Kestenberg's discussion).

First anovulatory periods are often painless. In addition, there is currently a great deal of social pressure to disregard the pain and tiredness accompanying the menses and the irritability of the premenstrual period (Delaney et al. 1976). If accepted, prepuberty cyclicity, effecting changes in sensations and moods, becomes a rehearsal for puberty. After ovulatory menses bring on cramps and blood clots, and a new feeling of receptivity emerges in the luteal phase of the cycle (Benedek 1952), the full meaning of feminine periodicity can begin to be understood. Menarche and subsequent menstruations mark the introitus as the opening from which blood emerges. As a result, denial of the introitus can no longer be maintained, and the repression of inner-genital wishes is lifted. A massive regression revives the confusion between the inner genitals and the adjoining bladder and rectum. Experimentation with retaining stool and urine is often used to differentiate between nongenital and genital sensations and to effect a separation—individuation of genital organs. When the inner genitalia begin to assume a central role in the formation of sexual identity, both sexes, but girls more than boys, give up pregenital habits and, through externalization from inside to the outside of the body, become excessively interested in their appearance. Under normal conditions, the affirmation of the uterus and vagina as organs of containment and passage counteracts fears and paves the way for feminine identification (Erikson 1951, 1959, 1964). The tension in the ligaments of the Fallopian tubes and ovaries helps to make these organs real and acceptable. During prepuberty girls learn to anticipate the changes in sensations, tensions, and moods which are subject to feminine cyclicity. There develops a feeling of organ constancy that persists despite the waxing and waning of inner excitement.

In our culture, adults rarely prepare boys for the advent of ejaculation (Kestenberg 1968b). Advance information that makes a youngster look forward to his first wet dream is often supplied by a sibling or friends. At first he looks at his ejaculate as an excrement and a proof of incontinence revived. Once he understands it, the emergence of the seminal product frees the boy to acknowledge his previously denied and repressed inner genitality and to try to cope with the involuntary nature of the act of emission. In analysis, boys hardly ever describe the experience in terms of consistency and volume of the ejaculate, and it is only a rare analyst who discovers the connection between a youngster's drawings and his attempt to construct the image of his inside. A notable exception is R. Furman's (1973) account of Frank, a 13½-year-old boy who, during his analysis, abruptly began to draw helicopters. For a month, he focused on more and more details and elaborations of weapon systems and living quarters on board, without ever being satisfied with the result. When he stopped drawing, he confessed that he "thought" he had had ejaculations. With the help of his analyst he understood that his drawings were attempts to deal with feelings he had inside on the outside. He could not describe what he felt, and the drawings did not fully represent it. Some months after, Frank told the analyst that he had finally achieved ejaculation by masturbating. He could now describe his first ejaculations as coming upon him without warning and leaving small amounts of a sticky substance at odd times, for instance, when he was reading. His self-induced ejaculations were voluminous, but more importantly he could now "feel it coming," whereas before he was not aware of inner-genital sensations.

Adults tend to forget the degree of explosivity and frequency of contractions of their first ejaculations. Some recall worrying about the velocity and distance of the seminal trajectory. Both sexes, but boys more so than girls, tend to distort inner-genital sensations by attempts to immobilize and visualize them as static. They unconsciously depict their unseen inner genitals as a stage or a scene they can view, and both sexes allot space in their inside to their mother. In the rare instances when the first wet dream is remembered, its manifest content appears to be a representation of the internal and external genital complex. A colleague reported his first wet dream as follows:

> I was looking at something. There was a long lamp on one side and a woman holding it. On the other side was a small dog, a Scotty, holding it also.

He did not remember any contractions, but had a feeling of something "pulsatile," while at the same time he agreed that the dream was like a stage. The woman in his dream most likely represented the internal keeper of the penis (Kestenberg 1968b), and the Scotty may have been a symbol of a child, probably condensed with the pubic hair in which the penis seems "rooted." Being held and contained within the stillness of the picture has the reassuring quality of boundaries preserved and kept in place, a reassurance needed to counteract the fear of the penis flying away during orgasm.

At first boys look upon their seminal fluid as an excrement, a cross between urine and fecal mucus. In the midst of wondering where it came from and how it was ejected, they become keenly preoccupied with the method of its disposal. The unconscious wish to eat it (equating semen and milk) is sometimes realized. Smell and consistency as well as taste are distinguishing characteristics which help the boy separate the ejaculate from other excretions. As he transforms his pregenital into genital wishes, he practices ways and means of containing it, e.g., in the cupped hand, in a handkerchief, in the toilet. His preoccupation with hiding his new sexual activity from his mother is pregenitally tinged but does betray his wish to show and give it to her. Differentiating his inner-genital apparatus from the bladder and the rectum, he looks upon his genitals as a weapons system, and he measures how "loaded" he is by applying principles of ballistics to his genital machinery. Fears of being robbed of his hidden arsenal, of becoming depleted, of misfiring and hurting himself and others alternate or condense with fears of anal penetration or entry through a wound (by castration). The immature, impatient urethral or phallic impetuosity which calls for a rapid discharge, with little concern for the receiver of the product, is at the core of juvenile ejaculatio praecox. The cathexis of the male inner genitalia as a precious, life-giving, living organ-system is requisite for the transformation of pregenital representations into the image of the semen as a valued gift. The concomitant transformation of homosexual (oral and anal or urethral) into heterosexual (genital) fantasies in prepuberty prepares the boy for his future role as a generous provider and depositor of good things in the girl's vagina.

Both sexes gain mastery over their genitals by hidden or overt homosexual play and masturbation. Girls do not masturbate less than boys, but their methods are hidden and often unconscious. Tensing thighs, "squeezing," and closing off all sphincters are associated with contractions of vaginal and pelvic muscles. Holding excitement for a long time is a female control mechanism which leads to feeling full (being pregnant or having an inner penis). Lubrication, secretions, and the "disappearance" of the clitoris during orgasm, gradually change their pregenital and phallic connotations to become models for the anticipated heterosexual experience of receiving the penis and keeping the ejaculate.

Masturbation as a regressive phenomenon is maintained by genital practices and fantasies, with sadism prevailing in boys and masochism in girls. By fostering the dominance of genital libido, masturbation exerts an integrative effect upon drives (Kestenberg 1967a; Laufer 1968; Sarnoff 1976). Genital masturbation fantasies bring harmony into the precarious balance between narcissistic (masochistic) and object-related libido and aggression. They form the base of secondary masturbation fantasies in individual and shared daydreams. Daydreams, usually disclosed to the analyst, are precursors of sublimations and creativity. Girls repetitiously spin yarns about preparations for dates and locales of encounters; boys depict their exceptional achievements (as athletes, inventors, generals, scientists) in the hope of inducing feminine admiration. Both sexes dream of being performers, popular and thus desirable. Daydreams effect a transformation of homosexual into heterosexual interests, and first heterosexual group experiences become the next step in the transition of narcissistic seeking of sameness to the appreciation of complementing differences between sexes.

Prepuberty Reintegration

Prepuberty regression gives the growing adolescent another chance to work out unresolved problems and to use new solutions as a bedrock for the reformation of psychic structure (Geleerd 1964; Blos 1967; Kestenberg 1967a, 1971; Furman, E. 1973). By reintegrating his drives under the aegis of adolescent genitality by forming new combinations of defenses and transforming old ways of coping with reality into new ones, the 11- to 14-year-old fortifies his id-ego. Only some of his defenses have a temporary value. Shallowing of affect, deanimation, and their opposites (e.g., giggling, horsing around, and mirroring gestures and postures) serve the restoration of equilibrium from day-to-day and hour-to-hour.

The breakdown of stable relationships effects an increase of secondary narcissism which, in turn, combats self-destructive tendencies. But there is more to narcissism in prepuberty than this. The libidinization of the whole body is important for the formation and persistence of a positive body image and sense of self. The narcissistic investment in new organs and functions is comparable to the primary narcissism of the young infant. Cottle (1972) described the experiential aspect of a primary erotization and valuation of the new body as follows: "As we saw it, the organism which was of course our simple self was extraordinarily complex, and lovably, thankfully incomprehensible to anyone but ourselves" (p. 229). Like a young infant, the young adolescent does not discriminate between himself and others. From this basic matrix, self- and object-representations (Jacobson 1964) are built anew, but at this time there is a decisive shift from primary objects to their new editions in peers.

In prepuberty, the lack of stability in body contours, size, and configuration brings on fear-inducing shifts in outer and inner boundaries. However, the new capacity to combine variations in shape and in space-, weight-, and time-orientation into mobile and cohesive units, and the ability to grasp and foresee reversibility of positions are all aspects of an arising cognitive mode which counteracts fears of loss or distortion of body parts.

Boys are afraid that their testicles will be stuck in the groin or will increase their asymmetry. They personify the movements they feel inside into skeletons and monsters or robots. They attempt to identify with the internal aggressors and to gain mastery over them by thinking of themselves as dangerous and by gaining control over "outer-space creatures" in fantasy. Girls are particularly afraid of losing excitement. They try to perpetuate it as a sign of the intactness of inner organs. Fantasies of phallic substructure in boys (such as electronic equipment or tree roots) and an inner phallus in girls are usually unconscious. However, pregnancy fantasies are played out in a jocular way, with boys hiding their penis and sticking out their pelvis and girls putting pillows under their dresses (Deutsch, H. 1944). Boys are keenly aware of the growth of their phallus which they compare with that of others, and girls speak openly of how "we must increase our bust" (Blume 1974, p. 72). Both sexes worry about the penis being too big or too small for the vagina. Each of the many prepuberty worries becomes the basis for a new conceptualization. Paramount in this process is the externalization of inner-genital impulses and a thorough investigation of objects to be used as models for a schema of the body. Externalizations of the inner and outer genitals lead to daydreams about machines and inventions, about constructions and animations of the inanimate. They stimulate interests in maps and mazes. Clothing like sweaters and shirts is used to give an outer shape to internal organs. Machines are of greater interest to boys, clothing to girls. Boys have fantasies of touching girls (brushing against them or holding them), and girls dream of being touched. Pushing, shoving, tripping are not only a fantasied but also a real pastime. Whether in fantasy or in reality, these contacts give a liveliness to the outstanding landmarks of the sexual body. What is going on in the body is understood by a matching of internal and external experiences and by a linking of past, present, and future (Kestenberg 1968*b*).

Constructions related to erections and ejaculations are many, in support of symbol formations and as an incentive to hypothesizing and feeling "brainy." Boys at that time are beginning to exceed girls in school work. The interest in internal movements combines with the investment in the growing muscular system to provide an outlet for aggression. Watching and listening are the passive counterparts of real activity.

Boys are primarily interested in the reproduction of the movement mechanism they feel; girls are much more touch and shape oriented. Girls are more interested in enclosed structures, while boys use space to build things up and out (Erikson 1951). A girl's interest in dolls and large, soft toy animals frequently persists way into adulthood. However, real pets are the most sought after recipients of maternality in both sexes, with girls nowadays being more interested in horses than boys (Freud, A. 1965; Kestenberg 1975). Despite the spreading of feminism, girls usually use sports with boys as a platform for reaching them. However, a fixation in the negative phallic-oedipal phase may motivate girls to want to be stronger and better than boys in every endeavor.

External Organizers in Prepuberty

The regression in prepuberty is not only a source of annoyance and dismay to parents. It also gives them another chance to deal with such basic problems as training for cleanliness, developing of good eating habits, and nurturing a tolerant (not seductive) attitude toward sex.

Intimidated by their children and their public advocates, harassed by their own problems, parents often miss the opportunity to reminisce with their youngsters and help them connect today's disappointments with yesterday's hurts and tomorrow's challenges. A beautiful example of a mother who knew what to say to her daughter, but could not say it, is Mollie (Kennedy 1953). When, upon her menarche, her daughter Valerie had been told the usual cliches, she ignored them and said: "It's an awfully sticky feeling." Mollie wanted to say that:

> . . . when a man makes love to you sometimes that's a sticky feeling too. So was eating candy when you were a baby, or sweating when you gave birth to one. Sticky wasn't bad. Being immaculate . . . isn't the key to a clean and happy life. Sticky with living can be something good (1953, p. 287).

What Mollie eventually could say was: "It will make you even prettier and allow you to feel wonderful things you never felt before." Even this encouraging and truthful statement is an invention of a male author. Men, fathers, brothers, and "boys who like me" can all help the girl feel desirable, and vice versa; women, mothers, sisters, and "the girls who like me" make a growing boy feel good about himself.

Where relationships with primary objects were too tenuous, the breakdown in prepuberty may be lasting, without any prospect of resolution of an unsuccessful individuation-separation or a traumatic inner-genital phase. The road is open then to a deepening of an anaclitic depression or to delinquency as a mode of life.

Under average expectable conditions (Hartmann 1939), parents now reinforce socially acquired taboos but are capable of giving praise and recognition to developmental advances. A parent who cannot say, "You hurt my feelings" will respond with depreciation that lowers the youngster's self-esteem. Fortunately, through relationships with young adults and peers, in groups and in pairs, the overwhelming libidinal and aggressive wishes toward parents become diluted. Disappointment in friends and feeling unpopular plague adolescents in prepuberty. They revive the mourning of the loss of the mother (later the father) and the loss of the self—both gone and past—that characterize the passing of each developmental phase. The current mother is frequently called upon to sympathize with the rejected daughter or son, and, in this manner, she has a chance to repudiate the hurts she had imposed upon her child in earlier times, especially in prelatency. Quite often, older siblings become a source of solace and encouragement, especially as parents often turn out to be "brutes," since they themselves strive for the achievement of "letting go" that eventually makes them into "childless parents" (Kestenberg 1970).

Teachers, older siblings, and friends, and parents also, can be of great help in encouraging those "tertiary masturbation fantasies" in which intricate problems are solved in science or feelings are expressed in poems. Acceptance of the youngster's contribution is not enough. Help in organizing his creative thoughts is crucial at this time. Youth leaders and teachers may have a lasting, unforgettable influence upon an individual's development in prepuberty.

With the experience of menses and ejaculations, there begins a renewal of identification with parents which superimposes itself upon childhood identifications. Maternal moods, parental relationships, and their concerns begin to be better understood. The current reality of a gentle father who can be affectionate without being overbearing and of a mother who truly admires the father without being subservient are far removed from prepuberty fantasies of sadism and masochism as a base of adult relationships. There follows a need to see parents united and loving one another and an ensuing desire to form a similar relationship with a peer. The ego-ideal of courtship and love contributes to the mitigation of narcissistic types of relationships and fosters true friendships.

The breakdown and the rebuilding of the superego proceed through fluctuations of relationships, competition and generosity, envy and altruism. A community of interests fosters identifications as a model for new solutions of conflicts and for internalization of new values, now less family- and more community-oriented. The sense of social justice which had begun to be incorporated in the superego during latency (Kestenberg 1975, chapter 10) goes far beyond the confines of fairness in treating siblings and friends. Parents are reinvestigated from the viewpoint of their behavior toward others, their friends, and associates. Building triangles at home and in school and within larger groups of friends, deserting some in favor of others, or provoking desertion goes hand in hand with weighing issues and changing viewpoints. These prepuberty experimentations transpose oedipal configurations into a larger social context. The new social framework prepares the ground for the development of true friendships and of intimacy. Persistent feelings of isolation and alienation in later adolescence and in adulthood are based on a failure to lay a proper foundation for a structured social role in prepuberty.

Therapy in Prepuberty

I have highlighted the development of pathology in prepuberty in terms of exaggeration of normal tendencies. A failure in reintegration in prepuberty lays the ground for future disturbances. In the brief discussion of therapy in prepuberty that follows, I shall focus not on specific pathologies but rather on special problems of therapy during prepuberty. In doing so, I shall rely more on the concluding case presentation than on theoretical considerations.

The problem of analyzing adolescents has been a subject of attention for many years (Freud, A. 1936, 1958; Katan 1935; Deutsch 1944; Spiegel 1951; Eissler 1958; and others). Fraiberg (1955), in a comprehensive study of psychoanalysis during prepuberty, focused on problems involving early resistance, the establishment of positive transference, on questions regarding how to interpret, how deeply to analyze, and on the dangers of acting out.

The 11- to 14-year-old, suspicious of adults, fears that the analyst may be in cahoots with his parents (Katan 1935). Being made to come for analysis evokes masochistic fantasies; shame over the developing affection for the analyst leads to silences and crude behavior in sessions. Playing the role of a chum (Deutsch 1944) may work with some children, but it can also lead to accusations of insincerity and putting on airs, incompatible with one's age. Perhaps a grand-parently attitude is least innocuous of all approaches at this time (Deutsch 1967). It puts the therapist above parents and promises greater success for the child's expectation of getting parents to change their behavior toward him/her.

If treatment has begun during latency, the previously developed trust carries over into prepuberty, but beginning analysis at this time is not an easy under-taking. The choice of the same sex analyst for the 11- to 14-year-old usually makes the course of analysis smoother (Katan 1951). A good friend who has been in treatment will induce some young adolescents to seek therapy, even when parents approve only reluctantly. The resistance of parents to have their children analyzed at this age is considerable. In many cases it is necessary to prepare them for the treatment of their 11- to 14-year-old children. Either their own behavior has been so extreme that the child's problems have become obscured, or they find it doubly difficult to share their children with the analyst at a time when they are being excluded from his confidence.

The most difficult problem during the analysis of this age group is the patient's fear of his own regression, his shame, and his reluctance to talk about it, lest it will make him even more babyish. Recollections of childhood events may be shunned as if there were a danger of shrinking into an infant when one thinks about having been one.

Perhaps the most important guidelines for the analysis of prepuberty patients are:

1. Follow the child's interests in whatever direction they take without probing and without losing patience.
2. Introduce confrontations and interpretations at the time when reorganiza-tion is being sought, in a form which most befits the ongoing process of reintegration.

At first, the analyst may be baffled by the frequency and unpredictability of regression from day to day and from one part of the session to another. Careful attention to the patient's typical changes in periodicity makes it possible to keep in tune with his moods, fears, and pleas for help in solving problems. Playing games rather than speaking or talking incessantly about trivia is less boring to the analyst when he can study the modes with which affects rise and fall and resistance follows a brief period of receptivity. Perhaps treating this age group demands the greatest amount of versatility in the analyst. It presents a special challenge to the psychoanalyst's ego to regress in the service of therapy without losing sight of the therapeutic goals.

The salient points made in this paper may best be illustrated in the presentation of a brief account of the psychoanalysis of a girl from the ages of 9 to 13.

Margie and her brother, 2½ years her junior, were both adopted. A trauma at 9 affected Margie so that she began to demonstrate prepuberty behavior relatively early. At this point she reported a frankly incestuous dream, as might be expected of an 11-year-old. Against the backdrop of the dream's fairy-tale setting, however, was content more characteristic of latency.

She and her brother were kidnaped by a king who kept them "until I would say that I'd be his princess. So I was his princess and my brother was his prince and we got married and lived happily ever after. After a few weeks we got a baby, half-boy and half-girl. We did not like the baby, so we decided that we will divorce and get married to someone else." The dream reflected Margie's fantasies about adoptions by kidnaping, divorce, or abandonment stemming from parental disapproval of the baby's sex.

Veering from concerns about her mother's illness to fears of robbers who would take her away, Margie would jump rope ceaselessly, not letting me talk because I had to count her jumps. When her pre-oedipal type of attachment to her mother (and in transference, to me) threatened to break through, Margie shifted to negative oedipal fantasies, still within the framework of fairy tales. She was writing her own version of *Sleeping Beauty*. When I commented that Sleeping Beauty wanted her mother to love her, she added, "Her mother loved her so much that she hated the king and got married to Sleeping Beauty."

Margie's latency defenses were breaking down quickly, and she regressed to the time when her brother had been adopted. In a long, confused, forever-shifting story, she told me first that she had a baby sister and a baby brother, and that she had no brother, just a sister who was her baby, Mary, who was 2 or 3 years old (the age of Margie when her brother came into her life). Margie restored herself as a toddler and played the role of both mother and older sister to a female baby. Her regression to the inner-genital phase was in full swing. However, the influence of premature prepuberty led Margie to invent another Mary-sister-daughter, 2 years older than Margie was at this time.

Soon, Margie's body attitude changed, and she looked like an "S," sticking out her belly and wobbling her pelvis. In addition to talking about her two sister/children, she became preoccupied with mazes. I suggested that she wanted to know what was inside of her and how a baby fit in; she drew a maze, placing little Mary at the entrance. The end of the maze carried the inscription: "Help little Mary find her way to Dr. Kestenberg's house." Not until several years later was it possible to show Margie that she wanted to be my child.

There followed a period of resistance in which Margie yawned, went to sleep on the couch, and complained of headaches, stomachaches, and dizziness. She was grateful when the doctor to whom I sent her found her free of physical illness. She told me that I must like kids better than parents. This promising rapprochement was followed by endless play with paper and Barbie dolls, getting dressed and ready for dates. When I asked her once what they were all doing, she replied: "Nothing. They are talking privately, nobody can know. I don't even know." Margie's boring repetitiousness and shallowness of affect served as a defense against the exciting secret of sexuality. About the same time, she began to defend herself against any good feelings she had toward me and especially her mother. She was undergoing a transformation from a silent and resistive child to a rude, irritable "Flegel" who threw things around to annoy me. She opened each session with the persistent demand: "I am hungry," and she ended by leaving me with a mess. Her personal appearance deteriorated. She refused to wash, clean, comb her hair, and do her homework. She fought relentlessly with her mother and impressed both parents as stupid. Occasionally she would give me glimpses of her secret life with little Mary and with big Mary, but their conversations became repetitious and diffuse, difficult to listen to.

In a way, I was glad that she turned to playing games. She began to cheat and invent new rules. At home she got into arguments with girl friends by refusing to obey the rules of games they played. However, while she was abrasive and crude, her paintings began to reveal that something much subtler was unfolding within her. Flowers were opening up, displaying languidly spreading reddish colors. A small child emerged from the flowers.

By the time Margie was 10½-years-old, she went through a brief renewal of latency. She drew houses and roads, coloring them in various shades. After a while she would interrupt this routine with outbursts of anger, or she would lapse into inertia. She did not want me to talk about anything that was not trivial; she matched each question or confrontation with a shrug of the shoulder and a stereotypic phrase, "I don't know." At home she was provocative, and she annoyed her father with clumsy, annoying advances. No one seemed to like her now. When she tried to be physical with me, interpretations were of no avail, but I could control her by a decisive "no" which was respected, resented, and yearned for at the same time.

At 11, her physical development proceeded by leaps and bounds. Her breasts and pubic hair were a source of shy pride, but also a burden. She got into people's way, fought with her brother, and seemed to want to get feelings from mechanical stimulation during acts of aggression or awkwardness. Sometimes she would get easily offended by her friends during play outside, upon which she would trod home. Her mother could not stand looking at her sour, depressed face, so she would aggressively send her back outside. Margie felt rejected by her mother and found less solace from her little sister/baby Mary. Talk about chasing boys became almost her only source of exhilarated pleasure.

At 11½, Margie had numerous fantasies about associating with groups of children who had no interest in her. Both little and big Mary grew older by a year and became part of the group. She controlled her imaginary friends, making up for her helplessness in relations with children who would not listen to her. Her mother became once more the prime recipient of her nagging discontent. Margie tried to master in the present the traumata her mother had inflicted on her when she was a child under 4. At that time, her mother used to ignore her and talk to her women friends. Margie then maneuvered to alienate her mother from some of her friends by starting quarrels with their daughters.

There began a long phase in analysis in which Margie veered from acting out her mother's past to mirroring current idiosyncrasies of both parents. She became silent because her father was moody; soon afterward, she began to look out of the window while I talked to her. During a conference with her parents, I discovered that her mother behaved identically. Upon inquiry, I heard that this had been mother's characteristic when Margie was young, and the current alienation was only a small revival of the past. I was able to describe to Margie how she felt when her mother turned away from her because I had experienced it myself when Margie treated me that way. She looked at me when I told her how much she yearned for contact with her mother, now and in the past.

Margie began to cooperate with me in our common endeavor to improve her writing. Studying her movements and consulting photographs, we discovered that Margie's cramped position during writing was a carbon copy of her mother's position when she held Margie as a baby. This opened up a scrutiny of Margie's infancy and toddlerhood and led us back to her third and fourth years in which she had failed to integrate her baby-past with her big girl-self. She began to present me with material indicating thoughts about babies. Some were connected with her growing awareness of breast sensations ("bosom babies flying out") while others were anal ("the baby got into me like doodie"). Penis envy, apparent for some time, receded, but babies condensed with primal scene fantasies and theories of adoption (e.g., babies flying out of their houses and fighting at night or being kidnapped).

Margie began to draw houses with girls looking out windows and with various objects inside visible to the outside. I suggested that she might want to find out about what was inside of her. Reluctantly, out of the corner of her eyes, she looked at drawings and books about the body and, at last, admitted her interest in the route of delivery. In the midst of this unearthing, she began to renounce her imaginary sisters, projecting them upon her parents. This solution gave bizarre results which caused me a great deal of concern. Margie began to hear voices at night—voices of her parents' "real children" who came out at night but were hidden during the day. Talking about the scary noises and voices which frightened her, Margie began to draw concentric circles as if she needed to conceptualize several layers from the outside to the inside. When we clarified that the night children represented the hidden genitals of her parents whose noises and voices she heard, nights became more peaceful. Now she revealed in a dream that her sexual feelings were so strong that they threatened to consume her and many others unless she was rescued by a boy before her father had a chance to help her.

The new sexuality was soon followed by renewed or intensified bouts of regression. Margie was trying to seduce me with odors in the double meaning of pregenital and genital smells. I had to tell her that she could not come to my office literally stinking. My interdiction had an organizing effect on the whole regressed family. Margie's pregenital type of aggression had become contagious to her mother, and both seemed to respond to an inner excitement by nagging each other and arguing who should clean the house. Now things became cleaner, clearer, and less seductive. Margie's attention turned from her parents to her peer group, both girls and boys.

Preoccupied with kissing games and finding out who smoked tobacco and who "pot," Margie secretly yearned to belong to the group of "smoking girls" who had boy friends. When at 12 years and 3 months she had her first period, without pain and without fuss, she once more denied all previously admitted sexual knowledge. It seemed impossible at this time to approach any subject directly. A whole group of girls and boys became engaged in a matchmaking fever, carrying messages about a youngster's interest in going out with a friend of the messenger. In this manner, Margie acquired a boy friend, 1 year younger than herself.

Margie had proven by this time that she was capable of strong feelings. She was worried when I took sick, and she helped her mother to organize things at home. However, when she got close to being loved by a boy, she regressed and humiliated him in front of her assembled girl friends. Her desire to be admired by the girls overrode her feelings for the boy. She seemed as callous as she had previously been to her mother and brother. After the loss of the boy friend, Margie fell back into a degraded position in which no one liked her and girls humiliated her publicly. Soon, she began to drown her sorrow over the lost boy friend in a sea of names which grew in number as she entered junior high school. She reverted to bring uncooperative at home, and her disappointed parents wanted to discontinue her treatment.

For some time Margie complained that her mother forced her to come to see me. Faced with the choice of coming for treatment or not, with her parents offering her another chance without insisting on it, Margie somewhat shame-facedly admitted that she wanted to continue. She embarked on a period of months in which she participated wholeheartedly in the analytic work. Her school work improved, and her perennial "I don't know" was transformed into its opposite. Her body attitude had changed after menarche, and now she began to look like a young, almost fully grown woman. She wore clothes well and took care of herself. At the same time she was convinced that boys would like her if she could outwrestle them and beat them up. This did not mean she wanted to be a boy ("If I was a boy I could not have a boy friend"). In the daydreams and plays she wrote she returned to the kidnap theme, but this time she yearned to be forced to associate with groups of her similarly imprisoned peers.

The theme of wanting to improve her relationships with the mother of her infancy and toddlerhood was repeatedly worked through, but the need to show her mother how deserted she was seemed to continue. I suggested to her that she should not let her mother know how she felt, as that type of restraint might help us to understand her problems with peers. At once she became friendly, even gleeful. Her new behavior really brought her closer to her mother who now enjoyed being with her. Soon 'she began to complain that her mother had been intruding into her social life and into her innermost feelings. True enough, her mother called me repeatedly giving me accounts of how she questioned her daughter about her girl friends and did not allow her to conceal her rejections. I helped her to understand the value of restraint and reported this to Margie. It became clear that Margie yielded to mother's encouragement and would produce scenes of a rejected child in need of mother's help. Margie began to describe her parent's squabbles with a benign condescension and tolerance and did her best to organize the family, giving them directions and helping them to find adult-type solutions.

As Margie's 13th birthday was approaching, she came closer to acknowledging her sexual desires and her fears of involvement with one boy. She daydreamed about becoming a popular singer, loved by all, and rejecting all but two. She could not commit herself to one, but now she was not marrying the king and her brother as she dreamed at the age of 9. Now she chose two contemporaries to escort her. She avoided older and more forward boys who smoked and got into trouble.

All along, Margie felt no cramps during periods and had not seen any blood clots. However, 2 weeks before her 13th birthday, she reported a long dream which became a source of a continuous daydream. In one of the sequences, she and a group of boys and girls went up in the air in an airplane. There was a window in the bottom of it and on top. Boys threw a ball up and broke the lower window. Margie was afraid of falling out and fainted. Somehow, through closed doors, she came close to the opening and was rescued in time by the boy she currently liked. She pointed out that another boy who was closer to her would not help her. When I asked Margie whether she had her period, she immediately understood that the dream related to having gotten it the night before. She looked away from me when I remarked that she was worrying about the blood coming out of her hole and connected it with her feelings about boys. In the next session, the location of her sexual excitement became the topic, and she drew question marks on a drawing of female sexual organs. She did not want to have a period and did not want to be a boy, but she would rather keep her period because she wanted babies. I had the impression that something had changed about Margie's period, that she now felt that her "hole" existed and looked upon menses as a result of penetration. The boy who did not rescue her in the dream signified her father who had refused her advances. Margie was now close to puberty, if not in it. The removal from her oedipal father had proceeded from a fear of sexual excitement (in the previous rescue dream) to a disappointment in his reliability as a reliever of genital needs. She was becoming ready to face her mounting excitement and her fears of injury, death, and rejection.

This excerpt from a long analysis illustrates the numerous regressions and progressions of prepuberty. It begins with the transition from latency into prepuberty and ends with the transition from prepuberty into puberty. It highlights the changing vicissitudes of the young patient's preoccupations with her inside and her ways of coordinating her maternal wishes with her new genitality.

Summary

The period between 11 and 14 years of age was ascribed to prepuberty, a phase in which the influx of hormones brings on a new kind of rhythmicity in preparation for physical and psychic aspects of the onset of fertility in puberty. Reviews of new endocrinological findings were correlated with psychoanalytic insights and with findings of developmental psychologists, specialists in cognition, and students of movements patterns.

Proceeding from diffusion and regression to reintegration of psychic functions, prepuberty affects a reorganization of the id, ego, and superego. The central theme in these processes is the revival of childhood inner-genital feelings and representations. It culminates in the erection of a new body image, built on a solid foundation of accepting the reproductive core of both sexes and reconciling it with heterosexual interests that make intimacy and love possible after puberty.

References

Ames, L.; Metraux, R.W.; and Walker, R.N. *Adolescent Rorschach Responses.* New York: Brunner/Mazel, 1971.

Benedek, T. *Psychosexual Functions in Women.* New York: Ronald Press, 1952.

Benson, S. *Junior Miss.* New York: Doubleday, 1937.

Blos, P. Preadolescent drive organization. *Journal of the American Psychoanalytic Association,* 6:47–56, 1958.

——. *On Adolescence.* New York: The Free Press, 1962.

——. The second individuation process of adolescence. *The Psychoanalytic Study of the Child,* 22:162–186, 1967.

Blume, J. *Then Again Maybe I Won't.* New York: Dell, 1971.

——. *Are You There, God? It Is Me, Margaret.* New York: Bradluns Press, 1974.

Botstein, P., and McArthur, J.W. Physiology of the normal female. In: Gallagher, J.R.; Heald, F.P.; and Garell, D.C., eds. *Medical Care of the Adolescent.* New York: Appleton-Century-Crofts, 1976. pp. 519-528.

Boyar, R.; Roffwarg, H.; Kapen, S.; Weitzman, E.; and Hellman, I. Synchronization of augmented luteinizing hormone secretion with sleep during puberty. *New England Journal of Medicine,* 287(12):582–586, 1972.

Breul, K. *Cassell's German/English Dictionary,* revised and enlarged by Lepper, J.H., and Kottenhohn, R., 12th edition. London: Cassell, 1955.

Cone, T.E. Secular acceleration of height and biologic maturation. In: Gallagher, J.R.; Heald, F.P.; and Garell, D.C., eds. *Medical Care of the Adolescent.* New York: Appleton-Century-Crofts, 1976. pp. 87–92.

Cottle, T.J. The connection of adolescence. In: Kagan, J., and Coles, R., eds. *12 To 16—Early Adolescence.* New York: W.W. Norton, 1972. pp. 294–336.

Delaney, J.; Lupton, M.J.; and Toth, E., eds. *The Curse.* New York: E.P. Dutton, 1976.

Deutsch, H. *The Psychology of Women,* Vol. 1. New York: Grune and Stratton, 1944.

——. *Selected Problems of Adolescence with Special Emphasis on Group Formation.* New York: International Universities Press, 1967.

Eissler, K. Notes on the problems of technique in the psychoanalytic treatment of adolescents: With some remarks on perversions. *The Psychoanalytic Study of the Child,* 13:223–254, 1958.

Erikson, E.H. Sex differences in the play configurations of preadolescents. *American Journal of Orthopsychiatry,* 21:667–692, 1951.

——. *Identity and the Life Cycle.* New York: International Universities Press, 1959.

Erikson, E.H. Reflections on womanhood. *Daedalus,* 2:582–606, 1964.

Fineman, J.B., and Smith, M.A. "Some Effects of Lost Adolescence: The Child Mothers and Their Babies." Unpublished paper, 1977.

Finkelstein, J.W.; Roffwarg, H.P.; Boyar, R.M.; Kream, J.; and Hellman, L. Age-related change in the 24-hour spontaneous secretion of growth hormone. *Journal of Clinical Endocrinology and Metabolism,* 35:665, 1972.

Fraiberg, S. Some considerations in the introduction to therapy in puberty. *The Psychoanalytic Study of the Child,* 10:264–286, 1955.

——. Some characteristics of genital arousal and discharge in latency girls. *The Psychoanalytic Study of the Child,* 27:439–475, 1972.

Frank, A. *The Diary of a Young Girl* (1947). New York: Doubleday, 1952.

Freud, A. *The Ego and the Mechanisms of Defense* (1936). London: Hogarth Press and the Institute of Psychoanalysis, 1937.

——. On certain difficulties in the preadolescent's relation to his parents (1949). *The Writings of Anna Freud,* 4:95–106. New York: International Universities Press, 1968.

——. Adolescence. *The Psychoanalytic Study of the Child,* 13:255–278, 1958.

——. *Normality and Pathology in Childhood: Assessment of Development.* New York: International Universities Press, 1965.

Freud, S. Three essays on the theory of sexuality (1905). *Standard Edition,* 7:125–245. London: Hogarth Press, 1953.

——. The infantile genital organization: An interpolation into the theory of sexuality (1923). *Standard Edition,* 19:141–145. London: Hogarth Press, 1961.

Furman, E. A contribution in assessing the role of infantile separation-individuation in adolescent development. *The Psychoanalytic Study of the Child,* 28:193–207, 1973.

Furman, R. Excerpt from the analysis of a prepuberty boy. Presented at the Baltimore/D.C./Columbus/Cleveland/Philadelphia Psychoanalytic Congress, June 1972. Abstracted in the *Bulletin of the Philadelphia Association for Psychoanalysis,* 23:259, 1973.

Geleerd, E.R. Adolescence and adaptive regression. *Bulletin of the Meninger Clinic,* 28:302–308, 1964.

Gesell, A.; Ilg, F.L.; and Ames, L.B. *Youth: The Years from Ten to Sixteen.* New York: Harper, 1956.

Grumbach, M.M.; Roth, J.C.; Kaplan, S.L.; and Kelch, R.P. Hypothalamic-pituitary regulation of puberty in man: Evidence and concepts derived from clinical research. In: Grumbach, M.M.; Grove, G.D.; and Mayer, F.E., eds. *Control of the Onset of Puberty.* New York: Wiley and Sons, 1974. pp. 115–166.

Hall, G.S. *Adolescence* (2 vols.). New York: Appleton, 1916.

Hamill, P. Discussion: Somatic changes in puberty. In: Brumbach, M.M.; Grove, G.D.; and Mayer, F.E., eds. *The Control of the Onset of Puberty.* New York: Wiley and Sons, 1974. pp. 471–472.

Hansen, K. Sex: How to explain it to the kids. *Daily News,* January 31, 1978.

Harley, M. On some problems of technique in the analysis of early adolescence. *The Psychoanalytic Study of the Child,* 25:99–121, 1970.

Hartmann, H. *Ego Psychology and the Problem of Adaptation* (1939). New York: International Universities Press, 1958.

Inhelder, B., and Piaget, J. *The Growth of Logical Thinking from Childhood to Adolescence.* New York: Basic Books, 1958.

Jacobson, E. *The Self and the Object World.* New York: International Universities Press, 1964.

Jenner, M.R.; Kelch, R.P.; Kaplan, S.L.; and Grumbach, M.M. Hormonal changes in puberty: IV. *Journal of Clinical Endocrinology and Metabolism,* 34:521–530, 1972.

Jones, E. Some problems of adolescence (1922). *Papers on Psychoanalysis.* 5th Edition. London: Baillier, Tindall and Cox, 1948.

Katan (Angel), A. From the analysis of a bedwetter. *Psychoanalytic Quarterly,* 4:120–134, 1935.

——. The role of displacement in agoraphobia (1937). *International Journal of Psycho-Analysis,* 32:41–50, 1951.

Kennedy, J.R. *Prince Bart.* New York: Farrar, Straus and Young, 1953.

Kestenberg, J.S. The role of movement patterns in development, I and II. *Psychoanalytic Quarterly,* 34:1–36 and 517–563, 1965.

——. Phases of adolescence, I and II. *Journal of the American Academy of Child Psychiatry,* 6:426–463 and 577–614, 1967a.

——. The role of movement patterns in development, III. *Psychoanalytic Quarterly,* 36:356–409, 1967b.

——. Phases of adolescence, III. *Journal of the American Academy of Child Psychiatry,* 7:108–151, 1968a.

——. Outside and inside, male and female. *Journal of the American Psychoanalytic Association,* 16:457–520, 1968b.

——. The effect on parents of the child's transition into and out of latency. In: Anthony, E.J., and Benedek, T., eds. *Parenthood—Its Psychology and Psychopathology.* Boston: Little, Brown, 1970. pp. 289–306.

Kestenberg, J.S. From organ-object imagery to self and object representations. In: McDevitt, J.B., and Settlage, C.F., eds. *Separation-Individuation.* New York: International Universities Press, 1971. pp. 75–99.

——. Nagging, spreading excitement, arguing. *International Journal of Psychoanalytic Psychotherapy,* 2:265–297, 1973.

——. *Children and Parents—Psychoanalytic Studies in Development.* New York: Jason Aronson, 1975.

——. Ego organization in obsessive-compulsive development in the Rat-Man. In: Kanzer, M., ed. Vol. II. *Volume Commemorating the 25th Anniversary of the Psychoanalytic Division.* Down State University, N.Y. 1980a.

——. The three faces of femininity. *The Psychoanalytic Review,* 1980b.

Kestenberg, J.S., and Buelte, A. Prevention and infant therapy, and the treatment of adults. I. Towards understanding mutuality: II. Mutual holding and holding oneself-up. *International Journal of Psychoanalytic Psychotherapy,* 6:339–396, 1977.

Kestenberg, J.S., and Marcus, H. Hypothetical monosex and bisexuality—A psychoanalytic interpretation of sex differences as they reveal themselves in movement patterns of men and women. *Self-In-Process Series.* New York: Behavioral Publications, 1979.

Kestenberg, J.S., and Robbins, E. Rhythmicity in adolescence. In: *Children and Parents—Psychoanalytic Studies in Development.* New York: Jason Aronson, 1975. pp. 411–460.

Kinsey, A.C.; Pomeroy, W.B.; and Martin, C.E. *Sexual Behavior in the Human Male.* Philadelphia: W.B. Saunders, 1948.

Kulin, H.E., and Reiter, E.O. Gonadotropins during childhood and adolescence: A review. *Pediatrics,* 51:260–271, 1973.

Laban, R. *The Mastery of Movements,* 2nd edition, revised by L. Ullman. London: MacDonald and Evans, 1960.

Lamb, W., and Turner, D. *Management Behavior.* New York: International Universities Press, 1969.

Lamberg, B.A.; Kantero, R.L.; Saarinen, P.; and Widholm, O. Changes in serum-thyrotropin, thyroxine and thyroxine-binding proteins before and after menarche in healthy girls. *Acta Endocrinologica (kbh) supplement,* 177:302, 1973.

Laufer, M. The body image, the function of masturbation, and adolescence: Problems of the ownership of the body. *The Psychoanalytic Study of the Child,* 23:114–137, 1968.

Mahler, M.; Pine, F.; and Bergman, A. *The Psychological Birth of the Human Infant. Symbiosis and Individuation.* New York: Basic Books, 1975.

Marcus, H. *Personal communication,* 1966.

Marshall, W.A., and Tanner, J.M. Variations in patterns of pubertal changes in girls. *Archives of Diseases of Children,* 44:291, 1969.

Morley, C. *Kitty Foyle.* New York: Grosset and Dunlap, 1939.

Piaget, J., and Inhelder, B. *The Psychology of the Child.* New York: Basic Books, 1969.

Ramsden, P. *Top Team Planning. A Study of the Power of Individual Motivation in Management.* New York: John Wiley, 1973.

Reiter, E.O., and Root, A.W. Hormonal changes of adolescence. *Medical Clinics of North America.* 59(6):1289–1304, 1975.

Richardson, D.W., and Short, R.V. The time of onset of sperm production in boys. *Journal of Biosocial Science,* 10(Supp. 5):15-25, 1978.

Root, A.W. Endocrinology of puberty. *Journal of Pediatrics,* 83(1):1–9, 1973.

Sarnoff, C. *Latency.* New York: Jason Aronson, 1976.

Saxena, B.B.; Malva, R.; Leyendecker, G.; and Gandy. H.M. Further characterization of the radioimmunoassay of human pituitary FSH. In: Saxena. B.B.; Beling, C.G.; and Gandy, H.M., eds. *Gonadotropins.* New York: Wiley Interscience, 1972. pp. 399–416.

Schonfeld, W.A. Primary and Secondary sexual characteristics: Study of their development in males from birth through maturity. *American Journal of Disturbed Children,* 65:535–549, 1943.

Sonek, M. Vaginal cytology during puberty. *Acta Cytologica,* 11(1):41–44, 1967.

Spiegel, L.A. A review of contributions to a psychoanalytic theory of adolescence: Individual aspects. *The Psychoanalytic Study of the Child,* 6:375–393, 1951.

Steffens, L. *The Autobiography of Lincoln Steffens.* New York: Harcourt, Brace and World, 1931.

Tanner, J.M. *Growth at Adolescence.* Oxford: Blackwell Scientific Publication, 1962.

——. Physical Growth. In: Mussen, P.H., ed. *Carmichael's Manual of Child Psychology,* Vol. 1 (3rd edition). New York: Wiley and Sons, 1970, pp. 77–155.

Wermer, H., and Lewin, S. Masturbation fantasies: Their changes with growth and development. *The Psychoanalytic Study of the Child,* 22:315–328, 1967.

Wilkins, L. *The Diagnosis and Treatment of Endocrine Disorders in Childhood and Adolescence.* Springfield, Ill.: Charles C. Thomas, 1965.

Winter, J.S., and Faiman, C. Pituitary-gonadal relations in male children and adolescents. *Pediatric Research,* 6:126–135, 1972.

——. Pituitary-gonadal relations in female children and adolescents. *Pediatric Research,* 7:948–953, 1973.

The Course of Life: Psychoanalytic Contributions
Toward Understanding Personality Development.
Vol. II: Latency, Adolescence, and Youth.
S.I. Greenspan and G.H. Pollock, editors.
NIMH 1980

The Pubescent Years:
Eleven to Fourteen

Morris A. Sklansky, M.D.

Introduction

Adolescence may be said to begin with pubescence. In no other phase of development is the direct correlation of the physiological with the psychological as obvious as it is in pubescence (Kestenberg 1967). Pubescence (puberty) is a critical physical maturational process which profoundly affects personality development and initiates adolescence itself. The hormonal secretions produce physical changes and psychological reactions which, although universal, are novel and remarkable to the growing child himself. The reactions to pubescence within the individual and of others to the pubescent are crucial and determinative of the subsequent course of his personality development and life.

The physiological process which constitutes pubescence encompasses approximately the first 2 to 4 years of the second decade of life, varying within the range of 9 to 14 years of age. It begins with the secretion of the hormones which specifically differentiate the genders. Maturationally timed, the hypothalamus secretes gonadotrophin-releasing hormones. These act on the pituitary to produce secretion of gonadotrophins. In turn the gonads are activated to produce testosterone in males and estrogens in females. There is evidence that testosterone, in much smaller proportion, is also produced in girls. The pituitary also releases the growth hormone whose effect is to produce the well-known "growth spurt" of pubescence (Karp 1977, p. 25).

Although we first present the pubescent physical changes and some specific psychological reactions to them, we should keep in mind that these specific reactions are best understood in the context of the total psychological development that takes place at this time. Reactions to body parts are meaningful only in the framework of the early adolescent's self-image which includes his body image.

The same may be said of the other important aspects of early adolescent development. Pubescence produces profound changes in the nature of object relations, in drive intensities, and in the narcissistic equilibrium in the self. These modifications lead the early adolescent into a process of deidealization of parental imagos which instigates an increasing shift to extrafamilial objects, including peers, and the beginning of heterosexual object relating. Throughout pubescence, the young adolescent begins to experience an intensified drive for autonomy which is essential for maturation but may lead him into maladaptive forms of behavior.

The Physical Changes and the Psychological Reaction to Them

The first sign of pubescence in girls is the beginning of tumescence ("budding") of the breasts, and in boys it is testicular enlargement.

The characteristic physical changes are traditionally categorized into primary and secondary sex characteristics. The primary characteristics are those directly involved in coitus and reproduction: the internal reproductive organs and the external genitalia. The secondary sex characteristics are not exclusively differentiating between the sexes, and, varying between them only statistically, they may at the extremes be shared by both genders. Thus, enlarged breasts may occasionally occur in boys, and facial hair may grow thickly for some girls. But normally the differences between the sexes in both primary and secondary sex characteristics are great enough to be universally acknowledged and to arouse psychological reactions to them in all adolescents.

In describing these pubescent changes and the psychological reactions to them, one recognizes that the hormonal increment exerts a disequilibrating effect upon the relatively cohesive personality integration of latency. The latency structure is loosened, and there are frequent breakthroughs into consciousness of the previously repressed impulses and fantasies: the "return of the repressed" (Freud, S. 1939). The new experiences, being so bodily in content, are experienced with primary process quality, and regressed, pregenital phase associations accompany them.

When the menarche occurs, adolescent girls commonly react with dystonic affects. The first menses may be discovered as a surprise and embarrassingly, e.g., exposed on clothing. The embarrassment is as if the girl had now revealed a previously prohibited function or behavior. Commonly what is thought to be revealed is the arrival of mature femaleness with all of its sexual implications.

The adolescent girl feels that through her menarche she exposes that she is now capable of sexual acts and childbearing, oedipally prohibited wishes. An infantile castration fantasy underlies the anxious thought that she may be wounded in some unknown way. The primitive maternal superego resurgence is evident additionally in thoughts of suffering a disease or of now being afflicted with "the curse." The common usage of this phrase to describe the menses, while often acknowledged as only a figure of speech, nevertheless indicates the long history in mankind of anxiety, awe, and prejudice related to this primary female function. Cloacal fantasies re-evoked from the anal phase arouse reactions of revulsion and disgust to menstrual flow. Not infrequently young adolescent girls at first hide the evidence of their menses. Occasionally there may be unconscious denial of the existence of the menses. For a smaller number of adolescent girls, the menarche may be greeted with a sense of achievement and fulfillment (Kirstein 1977). Clinical experience in psychoanalysis and psychotherapy would indicate, however, that such a positive reaction is still rare, and even then one remains curious about the possibility of a counterphobic defensive orientation. It may be that a favorable change in the cultural attitude toward women, girls, and girl babies will ultimately be seen in a more positive attitude in girls toward their menses.

The first ejaculation in the pubescent male is reacted to similarly. It, too, may occur as a surprise (e.g., in exercise), as a noctural emission, or a spontaneous emission in masturbatory acts. While most boys have already learned (usually from their peers) of the nature of ejaculation, the sudden sequence of spasms in the genito-urinary system, the wetness, and the viscosity of the ejaculate are all subjectively unfamiliar, and previously repressed fantasies of bleeding or damage (castration) and disgust reactions to the "excretum" (anal phase association) occur. For each adolescent the particular pregenital associations depend on his unique history, though we emphasize here the commonality of such fantasies revealed in clinical experience. (When the adolescent is unenlightened by accurate information, whether from parent, school, or peers, then fantasies of pregenital origin are the only information he has, usually accompanied by anxiety. Misconceptions about the nature of semen, menses, conception, pregnancy abound among early adolescents, reactivated in this phase, and may exist side by side with facts gleaned from sex education courses.) Yet for some boys, this proof of adult masculinity is a phallic narcissistic gratification.

Of the primary external sex characteristics, we note that the early adolescent girl is less aware of the changes that take place than is the boy. The comparatively more difficult visualization of the external genitalia and the almost complete lack of correct anatomical information foster the continuation of infantile and childhood misconceptions and imagery. Education for little girls about their anatomy is minimal. Few girls are aware of the changes in the labia, the enlargement of the introitus, and the changes in the character of the mucous membrane of the vulva and the vagina. Nevertheless, in early adolescence, girls respond with "wetness" to excitatory fantasies and contacts. Orgasmic spasms may occur. At first, such responses are anxiety-producing. Not uncommonly, as for the first menses, the girl wonders if she has had a urinary loss of control or a discharge from some disease. But the early adolescent girl soon becomes fully aware of the pleasurable sensations in the genital area. Conflict over sexual excitation will of course result in shame over the presence of the evidence for her wishes. Preoedipal and oedipal phase fantasies about the nature of their genitals are common—the universal cloacal fantasy: the common outlet for urine, feces, and babies; castration fantasies, a lost penis, a damaged little penis (clitoris), a penis torn from its roots, etc.

Few adolescent girls admire their genitals, as do boys. For many, penis envy is literal and specific (Ritvo 1976). Commonly, adolescent girls react to the thought or the sight of their genitals with degrees of disgust varying from dislike to revulsion. These affectively laden attitudes derive from the disgust of the anal phase. These attitudes may exist concomitantly with the pleasurable excitations felt in the genital area. They become clinically significant when they lead to frigidity or when they are part of a more general debasement of the self as woman.

The pubescent boy, on the other hand, is fully aware of the changes that take place in his genitals. He can readily visualize the changes, directly and in the mirror. The penis becomes elongated and widened. The scrotum becomes looser and longer, and the testes larger. While most pubescent boys take pride in this development, it may be accompanied by embarrassment if the unconscious (or conscious) implications of potential for masturbatory and coital pleasure are conflicted. The penis is now highly sensitive to stimuli, both intrapsychic and external. Ejaculations, both spontaneous and masturbatory, are now frequent.

Young adolescent males are much preoccupied with the size of the penis, and comparisons are made regularly, whenever exposure and examination are possible. For most adolescent boys these may be conscious, though unspoken. But many adolescents are raucous and teasing about this highly cathected subject. Those whose penises are small may be subject to ridicule, as may those whose penises are too large, the latter implying excessive masturbation. The unconscious concept that the large paternal penis is more satisfying to the woman lingers on into adolescence from the oedipal phase and its competitive strivings. The knowledge of the accommodative capacity of the vagina and of the more complex relationship interests of the female is not achieved until later in adolescence and, in any case, does little to dispel this phallic narcissistic concern even among adult males.

For most young adolescent boys the phallic narcissism involved is maintained, if necessary, by isolation of the distressing affects or by compensatory mechanisms in the development of alternative phallic skills—athletics, intellectual interests, etc. The young adolescent does not yet compensate for the sense of masculine inadequacy when he feels his penis is too small by an exaggerated heterosexuality, but is more likely to avoid sexual encounters and exposures for fear of rejection and ridicule.

Concern about penile adequacy becomes of clinical significance when it causes the young adolescent to isolate himself from peers, to avoid gymnasium, swimming, and other possible exposures. As the young adolescent begins to develop heterosexual interest and encounters, an anxious preoccupation may be sufficiently intense to prevent this next developmental step. Frequently the preoccupation is simply a focal point within the area of a broader narcissistic vulnerability, indicating a low self-esteem, and a defective sense of self. Upward displacement to the nose of the unconscious fantasy of the small (castrated) penis may lead a young adolescent boy to request rhinoplasty even when no objective evidence of a misshapen nose exists. Such requests should be carefully investigated for the possibility of psychopathology. The small penis complaint may be part of a persisting unresolved oepidal conflict or one in which a passive oedipal resolution is maintained.

Pubescence is usually followed by an onset or increase in genital masturbation (Sklansky 1958, 1965). It is now acknowledged that girls masturbate in latency as well as in adolescence (Clower 1976). Nevertheless, adolescent girls, like latency girls, masturbate less frequently than do males. Manual clitoral stimulation and the use of phallic-shaped items for insertion are common methods. Adolescent boys masturbate frequently, usually manually. Once a source of the greatest anxiety, promulgated by church, medicine, other helping professions, parents, and peers (Hall 1904, p. 432), more adolescent boys find it possible to masturbate with greater equanimity. Shame and guilt reactions are still common because the fantasies accompanying masturbation are unconsciously oedipal.

Specific reactions to masturbation depend on individual psychosexual development. Girls may masturbate to resolve penis envy (Ritvo 1976), overcome castration fantasies, indulge masochistic fantasies, or discharge less specific tensions associated with narcissistic personality problems. Similarly, boys usually masturbate with heterosexual fantasies in mind. But compulsive masturbation may occur in both cases, out of a sense of narcissistic defect, castration anxiety, gender confusion, etc. The autoerotic excitation provides some reassurance against fragmentation (in seriously disturbed adolescents) and personality disintegration (schizophrenia, psychosis). Masturbation in all instances is the individual's attempt to provide a maximum erotic sensation experience, to provide pleasure, and to discharge tensions of varying origin.

The secondary sex characteristics, readily available to public inspection and commentary, are the basis of common interest, attention, and concern to the pubescent child. Peer approbation has already been important from the latency years, and now the narcissistic mirroring (Kohut 1971a) or reflective-appraisal (Sullivan 1953) previously provided by the parents is sought from the peers. Being accepted by them, being one of them, and being "popular" with them are conscious wishes of great significance. Consequently, peer opinion about the secondary sex characteristics is the basis for the adolescent reaction to them. In early adolescence, the interest in being desirable to the heterosexual object is present, albeit with conflict, and the quality of the secondary sex characteristics as part of the ideal (sexually desirable) body and self-image carries grave import. Thus the intensified sexual impulses provide the underlying motivating force which engenders the concerns about the secondary sex characteristics. However, the rapidity of the physical change is also disequilibrating to the previously formed body image and creates experiences of anxious unfamiliarity or even fragmentation in vulnerable adolescents. Tensions, adequately contained by prior body and self-image formations, are reactivated.

Although these secondary sex characteristics differentiate between the sexes, they are, as indicated above, not absolutely differentiating, but rather only statistically so. Hence, in many instances they may be common to both sexes. This observation is important in alleviating the anxieties that some adolescents may have about characteristics which they are convinced are signs of the sex opposite from their own.

The earliest change in these secondary sex characteristics is in the breast. Usually, of course, the greater breast changes take place in girls. There is local enlargement of the glandular tissue, the accumulation of fat, and change in the elevation of the areola surrounding the enlarged nipple. In some males, too, in early pubescence, there is some change in the breast—usually slight tumescence—due to the precipitous hormonal imbalance. Because unresolved gender identity may continue into adolescence in some children, these boys are often made anxious by the change, thinking they might "turn into a girl." There is, however, a rapid realignment in hormonal proportions, so that no further enlargement takes place. Boys tending toward obesity may have the appearance of female breast formation. In older adolescent males, there may be development of gynecomastia (female breast formation) from the extensive use of marijuana. But only a true physiological hermaphroditic male would have breasts with glandular tissue capable of lactation.

Adolescent girls suffer from having breasts whose size is opposite to that of the acceptable style of any particular period. These styles may change cyclically from voluptuous to flat to voluptuous, etc. In recent years, there has been some stylistic pressure to do without brassieres. (In part, this may be an outcome of the women's liberation movement). Early maturing girls may have enlarged breasts prior to their age mates, and boys in early adolescence or preadolescence react with embarrassment and tension to these girls. Short girls with large breasts are unhappy about this feminine attribute. But later in middle and late adolescence, the girls who are flat-chested are the ones who feel retarded. Of course, it is not their nurturant significance but, rather, the breast as sexual symbol in our culture which underlies the distress. Some girls in pubescence deny the development of breasts, when they are obvious to all, refusing to wear bras. Others wear extra sweaters or tight shirts, hoping to hide them. But there are also the eager adolescent girls who long for adult status and may already be pleading for bras and wearing them when they still have insufficient cause.

Hair is another outcropping from the skin that carries gender significance for adolescents. Before the recent generation of adolescents, hairstyle clearly distinguished male from female. But it is not uncommon nowadays to make a serious error in judgment in limiting one's observation to the head hair alone. Adolescent males may have hair as long, as blond, and as waved as any girl. Short hairdoes for girls, formerly called "boyish bobs," have not returned to popularity at the time of this writing, so the confusion is rare for short hairstyles. A decade ago, there was tremendous hostility engendered in short-haired fathers toward long-haired sons, because of the implied femininity. Hirsutism, hairiness on parts of the body other than the head or pubes, is sometimes distressing to girls who feel they have too much of it. Not only does it interfere with being attractive, but it may arouse bisexual anxieties. A parallel problem exists for adolescent boys who don't get enough beard where their peers are bearded. The style among late adolescents is now to be bearded if at all possible, and those whose facial hair is sparse may feel themselves lacking in masculinity. Some adolescent boys, fearing growth into adult sexuality, avoid shaving. Occasionally, adolescent girls too may deny the presence of facial hair or feel it to be giving in to male chauvinist pig sexist views of females were they to remove such hair cosmetically. These girls may let their facial, arm, and leg hair go unheeded or at least unshaved.

The pubic hair appears simultaneously with the first bodily changes. Although not insignificant as a psychological sign of maturation and sexuality, it is mentioned infrequently in analysis and therapy. The shape of the "escutcheon" is different in males from females, but seldom discussed.

Another skin change has to do with the "scent" and sweat glands. Both genders share these changes almost equally. The scent glands (apocrine) develop to function more profusely in the genital area in pubescence and are occasionally problematic. However, the sebaceous glands concern many adolescents. For when these glands enlarge and their pores remain small, the accumulated secretion is subject to infection and darkening at the surface. "Blackheads" and "pimples"—acne vulgaris—may be the result. Adolescents, concerned as they are about sexual attractiveness, go to great lengths to cure this condition. For some, acne carries the connotation of excessive masturbation, "unclean" sexual thoughts and feelings, now revealed for the world to see.

The voice changes in both sexes, but the enlargement of the larynx and the lengthening of the vocal cords are greater in males, so that the pitch of their voices is much lower. In any case, even high-pitched male voices differ in quality from most female voices. There are many jokes among adolescent boys about high-pitched voice, castration, emasculation, and femininity—all to be feared.

A sudden increase in height takes place early in pubescence. This "growth spurt" is due to the effect of the increased secretion of pituitary growth hormone. In girls it usually occurs somewhere between 11 and 12; in boys, a little later, about 14 to 15 years of age. The rapidity of the growth spurt is in itself disturbing to the body image and may explain the physical awkwardness of some adolescents. However, height has phallic-narcissistic significance for both sexes. In Western culture, especially the United States, a premium is placed on height, and studies have shown that tall men are statistically more successful in achieving executive and leadership positions, as well as being considered more attractive sexually to females. Consequently, short adolescent boys suffer feelings of inferiority on this account alone. Girls prefer to be shorter than their male companions. However, each generation of girls tends to be taller than the previous, and being a very short girl may be as much a source of narcissistic vulnerability as being too tall. Generally, the oedipal configuration of little girl and big daddy is preferred.

With growth comes increased strength as well as change in muscle and bone structure. Although it is now postulated "that the female has the same potential for strength development as the male of comparable size" (Douglas 1977), after puberty there is still a widening disparity between males and females in athletic ability and strength. It is not altogether settled whether this disparity is strictly on a physiological basis or on the basis of the stereotypic image of femininity engendered in little girls. Although the women's liberation movement has created some change, many girls at puberty are still prone to give up athletic interests, while boys continue and even increase their interest in these male-image activities. It will be of interest to note the effect of the ongoing cultural press toward equalization of the sexes.

Adolescent males, with few exceptions, value their muscular prowess. Their preoccupation with their muscular development and with athletics is often as constant as it is with sex. We can see in weight lifting, an activity rarely of interest beyond the adolescent years, a concomitance of two interests—prowess and body shape. The interest in all this muscle power and appearance is often an upward displacement from concern with the potency and size of the penis. Certainly the adolescent male is interested in his sexual attractiveness, and his female compeers are naturally attracted to the shape, size, and tautness of his muscles. Small adolescent boys suffer painfully if they are lacking in this area, and frequently they compensate by developing their muscles excessively. If this is not possible, they then compensate in nonphysical areas of achievement. Adolescent boys who are fearful of appearing feminine because of shape and size or who are reactive to latent homosexual tendencies may defend themselves by exaggerated development of their muscles. Girls, on the other hand, are by and large not so much interested in the long muscles on their own bodies, and when a girl is physically structured muscularly like a boy, she may be concerned about her inadequate femininity. She may worry about her gender. Homosexual girls may be happier with such a physique or attracted to girls who have one. Often such girls with male-like physiques are latently or overtly homosexual, but not always. Differences in body shape due to the size of the muscles, fat distribution, and widening of the pelvis all go to define the genderic aspect of body image, and if the difference is insufficient or extreme, one may expect untoward psychological reactions in the adolescent, sometimes of clinical significance.

The anxiety of insufficient gender difference in the young adolescent is based on the unsettling of the specific gender identity established in latency and the pubertal stirring of the bisexuality of prelatency development. The definition of self-image includes gender definition, and a narcissistic investment in the specific gender contributes to cohesion of the self. Unconsciously, intrapsychic bisexuality continues from infancy throughout development. In most children the specific gender definition is maintained with concomitant anti-cathexis or defense against opposite-sex aspects of this pregenital bisexuality. Latency, preadolescent, and early adolescent boys taunt girls, even avoid their company, and fear being labeled "sissy." Girls who pride themselves on their achieved femininity and who have repressed their penis envy act similarly to protect their gender identity prior to development of heterosexual longings. When body changes do not fit the essential gender body images, as described, the anxiety of insufficient gender difference is aroused in pubescence.

The implications may be far-reaching. Regression to bisexuality and other gender positions may evoke a regressive passive relationship to the same-sex parent, temporarily for most adolescents, and a regressive fixation for some, with pathological consequences. Passivity longings may include infantile regression of a pre-oedipal nature with even more maladaptive quality. Fortunately for most adolescents, there are sufficient defensive and adaptive mechanisms to foster maintenance of cohesion and maturation.

In early adolescence, the stress of puberty undermines the security of previously established gender identity. But defenses set in quickly to prevent disintegration into bisexual components and homosexual resolution. Commonly boys engage in nonserious homosexual play. There is also some homosexual activity among girls. Neither is necessarily an indication of a homosexual outcome. Concern about being too much like a member of the opposite sex does intrude into consciousness. Girls may exaggerate behavior into a pseudofemininity; boys, a machismo, both defensively correcting such concerns. In camp experience, early adolescents may engage in homosexual liaisons, usually of a temporary nature. Periodically, those destined to have a homosexual outcome in character development may find the partner and the experience which introduce them to it and thus serve to satisfy essential personality and relationship needs.

While these specific psychological reactions to the pubescent changes are in themselves highly significant in adolescent development, they are to be understood more fully in the context of the image that the adolescent has of himself. The adolescent's awkwardness and discomfort with his "new body" in its various aspects are an outcome of the incongruity between his previously developed image of himself as a latency child, including the modified infantile and early childhood self-images and this new image. The image of the body and its parts comes to be part of the total self-image, both as to gender and ideal self. It is that aspect of the total self-image which is presented to the world to see. For the adolescent that image may represent adequately or inadequately his gender, his worth, his sexual and social self, and his ambitions for himself in his world and in his relationship to others. We shall discuss these further below.

Object Relations and Drive Increment in the Young Adolescent

The pubescent physiological changes are comparatively sudden and upset the relative hormonal homeostasis of latency and preadolescence. The relative drive quiescence of latency (Sarnoff 1976) and the characterological equilibrium in the personality are affected by this hormonal increment. Included among these effects is the nature of object relations. The latency equilibrium is brought about by the repression of the oedipal complex (Freud, S. 1905, p. 178). That complex involved the parent of the opposite sex as the object of sexual strivings, and ambivalent feelings for the rivalrous parent of the same sex. Sexual interest in the same sex parent was active, though transient. Identification with the latter parent and the superego attitudes of that parent became part of the defensive and characterological outcome in the latency personality formation.

The intensification of drive in pubescence acts upon the latency personality structure to loosen it and to cause once again a surge of intensified libidinal investment in the repressed oedipal objects. Young adolescents may experience transitory conscious erotic fantasies and feelings about the oedipal parent (Werman 1977). Often these incest fantasies appear in dreams. When they are quite conscious and explicit, they arouse reactive anxiety, shame, or guilt, and are almost immediately defended against by denial, rationalization, humor, etc. and are quickly repressed again. Sometimes they appear in masturbation fantasies and are similarly defended against. Adolescent behavior is evidence for this reactivation of the oedipal conflict. Girls begin to find it quite uncomfortable to sit on daddy's lap or even to be touched in a friendly fashion by their fathers. Aware of their fathers now as male sexual beings, they are uncomfortable about his sexual expressions with them or with others, including their own mothers. They prefer that the parents keep their sexual lives private, suppressing their own great curiosity.

There are some adolescent girls who, by use of defensive mechanisms, can permit rather close physical contact with their fathers. We imagine that such defensive safeguards permit the pubescent to get through this sensitive reincarnation of the oedipus and that many girls go on to further maturation and "normal" development. If such girls come to analysis, then they reveal that the defensive stand was not perfect, and the rediscovery of the intimate feelings and fantasies is accompanied by reactive distressing affects.

The situation is similar for boys. They may "kid" with their mothers, make innuendoes, and suggestive remarks, always denying (to those who ask as well as to themselves) that they have any sexual interests in their mothers. Defensively, they find their mothers "old fashioned," dressing "funny," etc. They may also, like the girls, react with easy irritability to any interactions which suggest too much involvement with the parent as oedipal object.

Nevertheless, boys are more comfortable with their mothers than they are with their fathers during this phase of adolescence, reflecting a sensitivity to paternal superego and castration anxiety. Some adolescents in this early phase fear their mothers (Blos 1970). The image of the mother is split into the mother as pregenital object and the mother as sexual object. The pubescent boy, like the oedipal boy, sees his father as a potential rival and castrator.

Pubescent girls relate ambivalently to their mothers. The mother is reacted to as rival and depriver of autonomy, and intruder on developing adult femininity. The constant bickering and quarreling with the mother in many pubescent girls are a derivative of the reawakened image of the oedipal mother as a superego image.

Erotic excitation is always on the edge of awareness yet dealt with tentatively and defensively by young adolescents in contrast to older adolescents. Young adolescent males become suddenly conscious of the turn of a woman's ankle, her explicitly sexual configuration, and her physical attractiveness as sexual object. They are aroused by sexual imagery, and they burn with longing for sexual contact. But these feelings and thoughts are commonly kept secret. To others, including peers, they may contain the intensities by common peer group defensive modes, teasing, joking, bragging, etc. The young adolescent is not yet comfortable with members of the opposite sex, although there is not usually total avoidance. There is much interaction at a distance. Heterosexual contacts which are approved of socially, by peers or adults, may be engaged in ambivalently.

In most of the subcultures that we come to know in our society, there is a more suppressed sexual interest among young adolescent girls. They, like the boys, subjectively take note of the boys—their faces, their muscularity, their hips, and their genital area. They are curious about the nature of sexual experience. But there is less talk about sex among girls than among adolescent boys, and in early adolescence there is still a major sublimatory press in girls, who are consequently more involved in scholastic and creative interests than are their male age mates.

However, girls more readily indulge in romantic fantasies about heterosexual objects and begin to elaborate fantasies of fulfillment in the future. For some adolescent girls, object-involvement takes priority over scholastic and vocational interest, and for these girls a decreasing interest and success in school become evident. Exceptions are always found among those for whom sublimations were already active or in the process of development prior to adolescence. Freud (1929) thought of women as having little sublimation capacity. But it may be that the cultural relegation of girls to "küche, kinder, and kirche" of the Victorian period was the basis for his observation and conclusion. How much the recent change in cultural attitude (toward an expectation that girls may achieve intellectually, academically, and vocationally, etc. as much as boys) will indeed bring about psychological change in girls remains to be seen.

However, for both sexes in this phase of adolescence, the object shift from familial to extrafamilial persons is evident though still tentative, while the detachment from the parents as oedipal objects is a phase-specific issue.

The Narcissistic Equilibrium in Early Adolescence

Young adolescents begin to suffer the narcissistic vulnerability characteristic of the entire adolescent phase (Spiegel 1951). Again we may attribute the onset of this disruption in the cohesion of the latency structure to the hormonal increment of pubescence. The altered physiological state intensifies drive tensions. Tension-regulating mechanisms achieved previously are no longer adequate to the task of maintaining the integration and cohesion of the personality. The narcissistic equilibrium is therefore upset concomitantly. Young adolescents have yet to experience an adequate assessment of their own talents and capacities and rely on the opinions and evaluations of their elders at home and at school. Few of them have specific educational and vocational goals to reify ego-ideal and identity. Consequently, they are subject to the variations in mood which result from unstable self-definition. Compensatory grandiosity in fantasy and behavior alternates with periods of low self-esteem and a sense of fragility. Irritability, argumentativeness, and withdrawal from offending objects are common. Those adolescents who are fortunate enough to have a consuming talent, a definite goal, or a preadolescent history of constant positive narcissistic internalizations will be less vulnerable than the others. But few adolescents are so cohesive in their integration and so stable in their narcissistic gratifications that they are without some degree of vulnerability in their sense of self (Kohut 1971b).

Deidealization and Related Effects on Personality Structure

In this early phase of adolescence, deidealization of the previously idealized parent comes to the fore. During latency the infantile grandiosity attributed to the parent (idealization) had found its denouement, along with the resolution of the oedipal conflict, in its transmutation by identification with the same-sex object, superego internalization, and ego-ideal formation. The latency child maintains his actual parent in the necessary position of being the object for externalization of these internal imagos. Yet the actual parents are related to with an optimal degree of neutrality, so that the conduct of the routines of latency life at home, school, etc. is relatively stable.

But in early adolescence, cognitive maturation increase of experience with other adults and the internal repellent force against the infantile and oedipal objects combine to make it possible for the adolescent to react to the limitations and faults of the parents with annoyed disappointment. The reaction is to the incongruity between the real parent and the internal idealized parent imago. For most adolescents this deidealization is in the service of ego development and autonomy. For some the reaction may be one of depression, loss of self-esteem, or even diffusion in the sense of identity. That the deidealization serves an intrapsychic growth process, rather than being simply an accurate assessment of the reality of the parent, is evident from the frequent exaggeration of their faults and the amount of affect that accompanies the faultfinding. Of course, parents naturally do not react amiably to this process of deidealization, especially if they are unaware of its significance as part of the adolescent growth process.

The deidealization of the parent in the early adolescent phase often makes for familial disharmony. But it makes it possible for the adolescent to reevaluate and restructure the latency superego, to modify the ego-ideal, to include a larger variety of new, extrafamilial values and, on the basis of these, to develop, in late adolescence, a more adaptive character synthesis (Gitelson 1948).

The deidealization leaves the adolescent character structure temporarily in a state of disequilibrium. The latency superego and ego-ideal had served for ego control and goal setting, gross and unsophisticated as they may have been. The positive narcissistic affects aroused in their successful function provided the necessary motivation.

Now with these structures deidealized, the controls and direction are temporarily nonfunctional, and the adolescent character integration is in some jeopardy. A solid sense of cohesion and narcissistic fulfillment is absent. The state of disequilibrium is highly dystonic and can be endured for only short periods. Consequently, a variety of ego mechanisms are quickly activated to prevent its continuation and potential further disintegration or fragmentation. These ego defensive mechanisms may be regressive and maladaptive. Yet it must be recognized that they may be ultimately in the service of individuation and autonomy (see below).

The adolescent in this early phase has a nonspecifically defined sense of self. Having momentarily put aside the specific latency attributes of superego and ego-ideal, he has little settled content as to the values and goals which are his own. Periodic indulgence in infantile grandiose fantasy alternates with compliance to parental and other adult-imposed values and rationales for compliance.

The identity (Erikson 1959) of the young adolescent is still very much defined by the same specific familial and cultural factors that had contributed to the child in his latency years. His values are those of his parents. His ego-ideal and superego encompass the internalization of representations from his relationship to them throughout the first decade of life. The immediate surround of the community provides the definition for social identity. And yet the seams of character structure, integrated sense of self, and the inner defini- tion of identity are being pulled at by the stress of the burgeoning instinctual increment of pubescence. The effect of pubescence and the psychological effort to maintain the personality structure in the face of it account for the psychology of the early phase of adolescence.

The regression to grandiose fantasy may be in the service of maturation in some adolescents by motivating them to engage in pursuits that will ultimately have beneficial characterological value. These adolescents may become crea- tive, scientific, studious, athletic, political, etc. But when the grandiose fantasy is resorted to without attempts at fulfillment in activity, or when they are so far out of the realm of the realizable, pathological disorders may be the outcome, even psychosis.

The Significance of the Peer Group

The deidealization of superego in conjunction with the peer group influ- ences may lead to instinct gratification of a maladaptive nature, as in group delinquency, so common in this early adolescent phase.

The peer group values are highly influential, filling the gap left by the abrogation of previous parental values. Sometimes, under fortunate circum- stances provided by the social environment of the adolescent, such peer group influence may be socially desirable—athletic teams, music groups, religious activities, and membership in various scouting, hiking, artistic, and other groupings. But the peer group, even among very well-brought-up adolescents may sometimes influence the individual to engage in socially abhorrent activi- ties—mischief, destructive acts, drug abuse, etc. Peer-prescribed activities, however, tend to provide a system of values and modes of behavior for a large number of young adolescents. Indeed, Bronfenbrenner (1977) asserts that a large proportion of our adolescents are more influenced by the peer culture than by the adults in their lives. While he attributes this phenomenon to an insufficient participation of adults in the life of the young adolescent, it should also be recognized that the intrapsychic restructuring which takes place during this period presses the adolescent to choose his peers over the adults in his life.

Without the previously formed ego-ideal to direct and motivate his activities, the young adolescent may find himself disinterested in those activities which the adult world has established to prepare the young person for his adult life, especially education. That vacuum may also be invaded by peer group influ- ences. However, the young adolescent may turn to others as well. Various adults in reality or in fantasy and fiction may become alternative ego-ideals— teachers, scout and church leaders, therapists, and heroes in literature, on television, and in the movies may become idealized, usually for several years during the adolescent period.

Both superego and ego ideal are revised during later adolescence and find a more adaptive and reality-determined form in later adolescence.

While the infant, oedipal, and latency child depended largely on parental empathy, approval, and admiration for the narcissistic gratification of the self, the young adolescent begins to displace to extrafamilial objects this function too. He is still susceptible to the effect that his parents may have on him, but he turns now more to other adults and, of course, his peers.

To be popular among his peers is a major goal for the young adolescent. Not being accepted by an idealized peer group can be excruciatingly painful and a blow to the adolescent's narcissism. It is therefore obvious that the group now serves the function of providing an admirable sense of self and self-esteem. Rejection by the peer group may be a sufficient trauma to lead to depression and isolation. During these years, the empathic, admiring responses of the real parents may be helpful but insufficient, for the displacement of the self-admiring function onto the peers has taken priority. Age and sex equality make for easier identification and mutual empathy among peers. The peer-group phenomena in early adolescence serve compensatory, defensive, and often adaptive purposes.

Adolescent Love

The extrafamilial object shift which now becomes more intensified ultimately leads to adolescent love. While love during the course of adolescent development is among the most passionate experiences of life, in actuality it undergoes several modifications during the adolescent phase before crystallization into young adult heterosexual love. In analysis love is revealed to be a highly complex affect state which imbricates narcissistic, sexual, and aggressive drives. The object of these drives may be a composite of object imagos from all or several phases of development or one chosen from an intrapsychically preferred object imago from a specific phase.

In early adolescence it is possible to observe love in its still unamalgamated drive and object components. Early adolescents are often aware of a desire to be in love, the object not yet chosen. They may also be more specific and feel intense erotic desire, with the character of the object nonspecific. Following the effects of deidealization of the parent imagos, we observe that the need for continued idealization of an object can be fulfilled in the love experience.

Idealization may thus be displaced now onto extrafamilial loved objects. In early adolescence, secret and unspoken love affairs may include an idealization of the loved one which may be more intensely felt than the erotic longing for the object. For boys of this age, this can rarely be admitted to peers, and the boys act toward girls in the teasing and avoiding manner described above. Girls, too, avoid the loved one but are more able to sustain thoughts and fantasies of a love relationship and to describe them to friends, diaries, and therapists. While the object is idealized, sexual desire may be suppressed as inappropriate to feel for the exalted person, reminiscent of the repression of sexual impulse in the oedipal phase. These relationships may be very intense and preoccupying, yet the sexuality is not conscious. Witness the idealization of rock stars in the present era and of the heroes of story, stage, and screen in the past.

Nevertheless, the libidinal component in the love affairs and infatuations, repressed though it may be, lends an affective intensity to the idealization, so that one finds it difficult to separate the affects of exaltation from those of erotic involvement in these young adolescents. Neither unmitigated sexual desire for the object nor the acceptance of sexuality as a necessary component of a heterosexual relationship is fully acknowledged in this early phase of adolescence (Sklansky 1977).

Within the past decade, there has been an increase in sexual behavior among adolescents generally. While adolescents in the early phase of this period have also been subjected to the cultural "permissiveness," their increased sexual behavior is more in conformity with peer group expectation and challenge than it is with a true inner longing for heterosexual involvement. Consequently, the increased sexual activity in early adolescence can be understood as a narcissistic issue rather than an object-instinctual drive necessity. The young adolescent wants to be accepted and admired by his peers and engages in the sex act to fulfill that need.

In vulnerable adolescents the need for the maintenance of a sense of worth and self-cohesion may force them into sexual activities in which they may experience compensatory contact, warmth, and admiration from the sexual partner (Sklansky op. cit.).

Autonomy

In early adolescence, intrapsychic separation from the parental objects of infancy and the assertion of autonomy begin a process of individuation which will not be complete until late adolescence or young adulthood. For this reason among others, Blos (1967), adopting Mahler's apt description of a developmental process of early childhood (1963), has called adolescence "the second individuation phase."

The assertion of autonomy is manifested in a variety of independency behaviors in inappropriate and bizarre forms. It also continues to alternate with recurrent infantile forms of behavior in these young persons. Autonomy as a conscious subjective experience for the adolescent is the feeling of being self-determined in action. The conative ego function of willing one's own behavior is narcissistically prized, highly ego-syntonic, and exciting of transmuted grandiose affects of self-satisfaction, pride, and self-esteem. The adolescent experiences the longing for autonomy intensely and equates it with becoming adult—being *his own man* or *her own woman*. (In our culture, it is felt as being only fair and right that an individual be allowed to be himself—a feeling of entitlement, a constitutionally guaranteed right to equality with the adult.)

The longing for the sense of autonomy is so strong that it may motivate the adolescent into disobedience, rebellion, and sometimes delinquent and pathological behavior. Commonly the disruption of familial peace and harmony over trivial matters is expression of the assertion of autonomy: the bad manners, messy room, disobedience, rising late, forgetting chores, not doing one's homework, dallying at play or the TV set when asked to do something, etc.—all of these are evidence that the young adolescent is no longer willing to be the good, loving, compliant child and wants to assert his independence.

However, in the early phase of adolescence, the young person cannot afford a total disruption in the relationship with the actual parents. The real parents are themselves still necessary for material gratification and primary need satisfaction (food, shelter, clothing, protection). All the structures to be formed from interaction with these objects are not yet internalized. Specific intrapsychic structures remain incomplete—definitive superego controls, ego-ideal definition, educational, vocational, and social identity. While the sexual impulses may no longer be ego-syntonically directed toward the parental object, the shift to extrafamilial objects is still incomplete. The young adolescent still depends on the parents themselves for structure formation. The assertion of autonomy entails a risk of loss of the object for the young adolescent. Consequently, there is an irregular alternation between the assertion of autonomy and childlike behavior in relation to the object. Nevertheless, the wish to be autonomous will become increasingly stronger and its modes of assertion more constant with adolescent maturation.

The sense of autonomy is a subjective preconscious and conscious experience. Structurally and developmentally, no *actual* autonomy can exist psychologically, for structure implies the internalization of object-related need gratifications and frustrations from earliest self-object merger to post-oedipal superego formation for identification. The parental objects have served from earliest infantile psychic development for the internalization of evolving structure and continue to do so in adolescence. Inexorably, it is the specific quality of this structure which determines the specific quality of the sense of autonomy that the adolescent will experience. Those adolescents who as infants and young children had developed no adequate positive sense of self (Bernstein 1963) will probably not have been able to undertake the infantile separation-individuation and will therefore suffer in adolescence a continued need to depend on parental objects to fill the persistent defect in autonomy, remaining excessively compliant to their parents or developing similar infantile attachments to parental substitutes. No true sense of autonomy is experienced by them.

Young adolescents who in their earlier development were forced into a passive compliant relationship to the object out of a defective sense of self, from a difficult anal phase training, or punitive superego development, may develop in early adolescence a fear of autonomous striving accompanied by unconscious hostility toward the parental object. This is then manifested by passive-aggressive behavior at home and at required tasks at school, often resulting in school underachievement and failure. Rather than experiencing the ego-syntonic sense of autonomy, these young adolescents are distressed over the continual helpless failing that takes place. These adolescent cases are difficult to treat and require a thorough psychoanalytic approach.

Even more extreme and pathological forms of adolescent behavior may contain this striving for autonomy. In the adolescent's search for self-fulfillment or self-actualization, he may be induced by peer influence and what is contemporaneously available in the environment to join groups and engage in behaviors totally abhorrent to the parental value system. While becoming obviously dependent on the leaders and members of exotic theologies, philosophies, and ideologies, the adolescent feels he has made his own decision, asserted his own will, and chosen his own way of life. Clinical observation, however, reveals the continued need for objects that fulfill infantile need, as well as the striving for autonomy.

The adolescent sense of autonomy begins its evolution in the positive experiences of self-function in the nuclear self-object matrix of earliest infantile experience. From these arise a confident sense of self in tension regulation, body mastery, and adaptation to the childhood milieu. Adequate infantile separation-individuation leads to further integration, cohesion, and confidence in self in relation to objects. In pubescence, then, striving for even further autonomy in separation from the actual parents and in functioning as a self-determined individual becomes a dominant behavior, characteristic for the phase.

Adolescent Aggression

What happens to aggression during early adolescence? Theoretically one may assume that an increase in aggression takes place on a hormonal basis, as does sexual drive. But what hormones are involved in aggression? Testosterone increases in both sexes during pubescence, but proportionately the increase is many times greater in boys (Conger 1973, p. 119). It has also been observed that early adolescent boys are more aggressive than girls. One observes that adolescent boys act out their hostility more, more frequently engaging in delinquent acts and physical combat than do girls (Henderson et al. 1977). How the intensified aggressive impulse is managed will depend then on ego mechanisms used to handle aggression from prior phases of development, the pressure of peer and other influences in the environment, and the specific superego attitudes, faltering though they may be during this phase of development. Of course, aggression may be discharged in sublimations and near sublimations like athletics. Increase in muscular strength makes it more possible for adolescents to discharge aggression via this route and causes a considerable modification in the relationship between the adolescent and his parents. The increase in aggressive drive may be seen in neutralized and sublimated forms in the playful jousting and boisterousness of young adolescents, in the vigor of self-assertion and demand for autonomy, and even in the energetic involvement in intellectual endeavor. Often vigorous activities within a peer group are mistaken for vandalism and delinquency, but much of the available hostile aggression may be expressed in antisocial destructive and rebellious behavior which is the actual delinquency frequently encountered in this age group.

Character Structure and Pathology in Early Adolescence

The cohesiveness of the early adolescent character structure is maintained largely through characterological dynamisms formed in the prepubescent years, especially during the latency phase. Technically these dynamisms must be looked upon as regressive when reasserted under stress, or as fixations if continued from the earlier phases. Often it is difficult to differentiate them without close observation. Because they are used so readily, quickly, and repeatedly, the character of the early adolescent does not seem as fragile as the impression from psychoanalytic study and description gives. But the sensitivity, hyperreactivity, easy irritability, restlessness, frequent "obstreperousness," and surprisingly unpredictable behaviors are all evidence that the solidity of the integration is not as constant as it appears to be. However, there are individuals who in the years when most young persons are undergoing the "adolescing" process maintain a rigid preadolescent character structure. They may be labeled generally as preadolescent characters of the preadolescent developmental phases—latency, phallic, anal, oral, etc. For them, the adolescent process is foreclosed. In the analysis of adults who have had such preadolescent character formations, it is remarkable how much the qualities of anal character formation have continued into the character structure—the stubbornness, obsessive-compulsive syndrome, the perfectionism, efficiency, etc. These young persons may not suffer "the turmoil" of adolescence, but they also miss its maturational benefit and the enrichment that may accrue from it.

Interestingly from a clinical point of view, such adolescents will not be sent for treatment, for, if they are highly adaptive to the adult-defined value system, no parent or teacher would find fault. Such adolescents do well at school and are quite compliant with their parents' wishes. They may even be successful achievers, in school, in acceptable groups, etc. Their peers may find them a bit stuffy and superior, but they are not sources of referrals to psychoanalysts. From a psychoanalytic point of view they are immature and therefore abnormal.

Such preadolescent characterological styles which persist into adolescence may indeed protect the early adolescent ego from the intensified drives and the disturbing intrapsychic regressions. But by midadolescence the character structure of the latency and preadolescent years may be adaptively insufficient, and the adolescent process is then engaged.

The young adolescent ego capacity to contain the intensified drives and withstand alternation between regressive pull and maturational push which characterizes this phase will determine the clinical picture. Alternation of defensive and adaptive mechanisms, when extreme, is distressing subjectively and maladaptive in the parental and school environment, while alternation of the ego defenses and adaptations which is less in amplitude can be tolerated and is recognized as typical teenage behavior. It is evident that it is a quantitative or comparative basis that is used for the determination of pathology.

Persisting regression and persisting "pseudo maturity" are both characterological defensive positions which may bring the young adolescent to clinical attention. Let us consider regressive positions first. Young adolescents who suffer from severe anxiety over separation from the maternal object, as in school phobia, are unable to engage the adolescent object-shift or adapt to the several necessary achievements in school and among peers for that age group. It is a common observation that the beginning of the first high school year is a precipitant for early adolescent psychopathology (Sklansky et al. 1969, p. 24). The implications of this new environment are highly laden with anxiety. Some adolescents regard the high school life as meaning sexual freedom or at least the opportunity for such freedom. Others react to the achievement requirements as being an impossible goal for self-esteem maintenance. For still others, the change from a familiar grade school or junior high school, with well-known teachers and peers, is a disturbing intrusion on their intrapsychic integrative boundaries, with a consequent sense of anxious fragmentation.

The regression to the infantile bad mother (breast) image results in the adolescent's inability to get along with his present mother and female teachers, on whom this image is displaced. The clinical presentation then is that of home quarreling, recalcitrance, disobedience, refusal to do homework, and misbehavior at school, including truanting. A variant of a regression to anal phase ego mechanisms is seen clinically in adolescents who are remarkably compulsive in activities which are not parent or school approved, combined with passive-aggressive defenses to those that are. For example, a young adolescent girl was an avid collector of a variety of dolls, doll clothes, doll houses, furnishings, etc. She was meticulous and detailed in the way she set them up in her room and spent most of her playtime with this "hobby," but she could not find time for her school work, was failing at her subjects, and was involved in constant angry bickering with her parents about chores, etc. Such anal-compulsive, regressive integrations seem, however, to be more common among boys.

In those early adolescents who use anal compliance and compulsive behavior to establish a "pseudo-maturity," we observe that their adaptation to adults, their successful application to school and home requirements, goes on parallel with a tendency toward social isolation, avoidance of peers, and especially heterosexual relationships. They get no pleasure from the play activities appropriate to the age group, except in institutionally prescribed activities, where they are sometimes favored by the adults in charge. They suffer from emotional constriction and, often, arrogance.

Although we have yet to discover the definitive etiology and therapy for anorexia nervosa, it seems evident that pubescence and its psychological significance is a precipitant for the disorder (Bruch 1975). The female sexuality of adolescent maturation, its pregenital and oedipal implications, its alterations of the body image, and its threats to the infantile maternal object relationship are all observed from a psychoanalytic orientation. The condition is one of the most life-threatening disorders that come under the clinician's purview for this age group.

We cannot, in this review, encompass the numerous disorders that come to our attention. Suffice it to say that, clinically, adolescents from this early phase develop pathology when the ego mechanisms for managing the real and imagined stresses of the phase result in behaviors that are maladaptive. Inability to cope with the pubescent stress may lead to loss of interest in schooling which, except in a few subcultures, is considered a sign of maladaptation by parents and teachers alike. Disobedience and passive-aggressive noncompliance at home, a source of constant and common difficulty, may eventually result in psychiatric and psychoanalytic referral. In "good" families, delinquency and sexual activity of a precocious nature will bring young adolescents to clinical attention. Depression and psychotic reaction are seen less frequently in early adolescence than they are in mid- and late-adolescence. It may be that the permission to continue functioning as a child protects against the inevitable pressures from within and without to undertake the role of adult, with all the anxiety-producing implications of that role in the youngster's mind.

Psychoanalytic Treatment of the Young Adolescent

Analytic treatment in early adolescence requires not only conflict resolution, but the abatement of mechanisms which interfere with the ongoing adolescent process. The young adolescent patient transfers phase-specific, need-fulfilling objects onto the analyst, which cannot go unfulfilled. The analyst must undertake the parameters which make this maturational evolution possible. Any therapy must take into account the specific dynamics of the early adolescent phase of development—namely, that the stress of puberty requires ego mechanisms for integration of the instinctual drives; that conflict is an outcome of the individual adolescent's attempt to integrate those drives; that adolescence means the development of mechanisms for becoming autonomous as an individual; that there is a necessary distancing from infantile and childhood (oedipal) objects; that adult character formation requires substructures like self-image, identity, ego ideal, and superego, *still incomplete in development* in early adolescence. Therapy of adolescents, then, cannot be only undoing and analytic, but must also facilitate the development of the essential character substructures. Usually the latter means the modification of the preadolescent structures, rather than the creation of these structures *de nouveau*. This requirement applies to analysis as well as psychotherapy for this phase of development. The nature of the adolescent personality structure will determine the process, not the imposition of the therapist's technical preference.

Transference in adolescence includes transference of those object and superego imagos that are included in the conflict which the adolescent child may have. But there is also transferred onto the therapist—analyst or other— those essential structures in development for which the parental object is used developmentally: the self-object for mirroring and idealization, the object of dependency gratifications, the modified superego and ego ideal of adolescence. Consequently therapy cannot be only analysis of the conflict but provides, whether the therapist is aware of it or not, these substructures of personality that make for growth and development. The adolescent developmental need forces the adolescent to put the therapist into *loco parentis*, and he projects upon the therapist the transference images mentioned above. This process goes on throughout the therapy with an adolescent, along with whatever insights, direction, reassurance, etc., may be necessary. Indeed if the adolescent does not transfer upon the analyst or therapist a sufficient idealization, the therapist's words will fall upon psychologically deaf ears. Furthermore, to divest these personality developing transferences of their emotional significance by a premature "analysis" of them empties the therapeutic relationship of its effectiveness. It would be like giving a hungry man the chemical formula of the components of bread.

It is a rare adolescent in this age group who can participate in a prototypical analysis. A true therapeutic alliance, directed primarily toward insight accumulation, rarely develops. The young adolescent is amused by the clever insights of the analyst. Only occasionally does he make them himself. The introspective capacity, for most adolescents, is only now beginning to develop. Therapy and analysis are not given the necessary priority in the adolescent's life. The therapist finds himself more active with adolescents than with adults generally, but especially with early adolescents. Prolonged silence without intervention is definitely contraindicated in therapy of adolescents. They often mistake it for disinterest, hostility, or peculiarity on the analyst's part.

Alleviation of conflict makes it possible for the adolescent process to proceed unimpeded. But only theoretically can one say that no crises will arise later. How the adolescent will react to later critical events, what their meaning will be to him in advanced phases of development and life is unpredictable. Whether a stress is a crisis will depend on the maturation that has taken place in the total personality and the specific meanings of the stress at the time to that personality (Sklansky 1971).

Determination of Pathology in Early Adolescence

The determination of pathology in adolescence is sometimes complicated by the mix of phase-specific mature and regressive behaviors manifested during adolescence. Consequently, behavior even in "normal" adolescents may appear highly deviant, though it may be only transitory. Such deviant behaviors, when they are investigated analytically in neurotic adolescents, may have as their basis dynamics similar to those deviant behaviors which are part of the structure of highly disturbed ones. For example, the resistance to doing homework in an "ordinary" adolescent or in a delinquent may both be the manifestation of the expression of the drive for autonomy. Manifest behaviors in "normal" populations do not reveal the dynamics of neurotic adolescents seen clinically (Offer and Offer 1975, p. 163).

Of course, no adequate clinical evaluation is based on the observation of single symptoms and behavioral manifestations. It is the total developmental history and clinical picture which will differentiate pathological from normal. Pathogenicity from earlier phases of development usually exists in the serious disturbances of early adolescence. The earlier the onset of the pathogenic factors, the greater the likelihood of pathology in adolescence. A history which indicates inadequate ego mechanisms for conflict resolution and adaptation prior to adolescence will suggest a greater degree of pathology when pubescence takes place. Developmental difficulties in infancy and early childhood inadequately resolved prior to pubescence prognosticate pathology during adolescence.

In the manifest clinical picture itself, the *persistence* of maladaptive behavior and symptoms over an extended period of time—let us say several months—is an indication of pathology, for it indicates inflexibility in the ego or the inability of the ego to utilize more adaptive and defensive mechanisms. The *intensity* of a symptom—difficult as it may be to ascertain, except comparatively—is also a measure of pathology. For example, an anxiety severe enough to prevent an adolescent from taking a school examination should be considered more pathological than anxiety prior to an examination which does not inhibit taking it. *Recurrence* and *frequency* of maladaptive symptoms and behavior are additional measures of pathology. Behavior which is self-destructive or destructive of others requires investigation for protection of the individual and others, though it may turn out that the overall picture of pathology may not be as grave as the behavior itself suggests. Regression in libido and forms of object relating are less pathological than are regression in ego processes and in cohesion of self. Actual loss of ego boundary, hallucinatory experience, and distortion of reality perceptions are indicative of potential psychosis.

Parents are loathe to think of their children as psychiatrically disturbed. They hope the adolescent child will "grow out of it." In many cases, spontaneous remission and integration with maturation do occur, but it is better to assess the situation during adolescence rather than wait until a resolution of a more maladaptive nature develops. The later integrations are not as readily modified as they might be during adolescence. A characterological integration in late adolescence or young adulthood may remain rigidly cohesive for several reasons. Maladaptive though a cohesion may be from the point of view of others, subjectively it serves to allay both structural conflict and fragmentation anxiety. Selected and preferred object choices as part of the intrapsychic resolution come to be absolutely essential in later adolescence. They are adhered to in some cases with a feeling of such necessity as to make alternate choices impossible, even when reality would dictate otherwise. Finally, ego mechanisms, defenses, and adaptations, which serve these specific purposes in the context of characterological integration, are held with a force that yields only with the greatest difficulty, if at all. The older adolescent manifests the inner process with the conscious conviction of dogmatic belief. These later possible character crystalizations suggest that assessment and therapy in early adolescence would be of great benefit in their prevention.

However, there are early adolescents who are themselves fearful and resistant not only to treatment, but even to psychiatric interviewing, and it may be necessary to wait until introspective capacities, self-observation, and personal suffering motivate the young person to seek help. Often while a young adolescent may be fearful of seeing a psychiatrist, it may be possible for him to accept consultation with a school social worker, counselor, or psychologist.

The Parents of the Early Adolescent

While we have emphasized the psychology of the young adolescent in this section, several points must be made briefly about the parents.

There is a developmental lag in the psychology of the parents compared to the accelerated psychological changes that take place in the pubescent child. The parents tend to continue to regard the 12-year-old child as they had their 10-year-old child. Consequently, they find it disruptive to their own psyches to observe the previously cheerful and compliant or cooperative child now behaving in the moody, unpredictable, and rebellious manner described above. Few parents modify their expectations in accord with the psychological changes in the pubescent child.

Another important consideration is the effect of the pubescent changes on the psychological equilibrium of the parent. The parent has, after all, mastered his own adolescence more or less successfully. Whatever distress he may have had during adolescence, he has found ego mechanisms for relative resolution in the late adolescent or young adult character formation (Sklansky and Richmond). He has himself undergone the complex process described for adolescence at least two decades previously. Observing now the adolescent process repeated in his own child, with whom he is in all likelihood identified and about whom he has elaborated a variety of expectations, there is aroused in him anxiety about the process he himself experienced. Once again there is a reaction to the return of the repressed—the unacceptable impulses, the struggle with superego, and the questioning of the values in the ego ideal. All of this creates anxiety in the involved parent, an anxiety which the empathic clinician will take into consideration. From the point of view of the parent, psychological developmental lag and reactivation of his own adolescent process account for much of the "generation gap."

In benign relationships and happier circumstances, parents may not only enjoy their adolescents' development, but even profit from it psychologically. Because of the identification with the adolescent child and empathy with his psychological struggles, the parent may appreciate and enjoy the narcissistic pleasures of admiration and pride in his child's mastery over conflict and disturbing affects, and in his child's maturational achievements and successes. Thereby, the parent himself may add to his own maturation during the adolescence of his child.

Summary

We commonly search for phase-specific issues in development. Blos (1970, p. 140) describes in detail the major task of prepubescence as the ego's successful management of regressive tendencies: in the girl, the regressive pull toward the pre-oedipal mother and pregenital drive gratification; in the boy, both the regressive pull toward the archaic malevolent mother and the passive relationship to the oedipal father.

Early adolescence (Blos 1962, p. 72) is characterized as a period of repeated attempts at separation from the primary objects, while during adolescence proper there is a decisive turn toward heterosexuality and the final and irreversible renunciation of the incestuous object.

We must emphasize, in agreement with Blos, that in development we actually observe overlapping regressive and progressive phenomena. "The demarcation of phases is an artifact, construed for the convenience of establishing milestones along the path of development" (1970, p. 212). However, careful study makes possible the observation of significant differences in direction and psychological dynamisms as development moves forward in time.

In early adolescence, then, it is the maximal effect of pubescence upon the adolescent personality that is broadly phase specific. The hormonal physiological change brings about both profound alterations in the body and in instinctual function. The adolescent ego reacts to these changes with alternating regressive and progressive adaptive mechanisms. Differing in degree and direction from the prepubescent child, the early adolescent becomes more familiar with his bodily changes and is directed toward separation from the pre-oedipal and oedipal objects. While regressive defensive maneuvers alternate with the continued evidence of a press toward maturity, interest in extra-familial objects is definitely and increasingly taking place.

The narcissistic equilibrium of the latency character structure is also upset by the hormonal increment, and cohesion of the personality is maintained with some degree of difficulty. A well-defined identity is not yet established and varies between continued childhood formation and that suggested by the peer group. Self-esteem is similarly affected. Deidealization of childhood parent imagos begins to take place, and the continued need for idealization leads to idealization of extrafamilial objects, especially peers, heroic figures, and others. Idealization is also part of the love experience which now begins to develop and, in conjunction with sexuality, leads to heterosexual relationships. The disequilibrium in the previous character structure begins a considerable reassessment in superego, ego-ideal, and social value systems.

The experience of autonomous functioning becomes an increasingly strong motivation in early adolescence. Ordinarily it is adaptive and maturational. But the drive for autonomy may also contribute to family educational and social maladjustment. Sometimes it takes pathological forms.

Pathology in early adolescence is not always evident from the manifest behavior, which may even be adaptive. Latency character formations may appear to be "normal," though they are not appropriate to the age. Extremes in regressive and progressive behavior are maladaptive. Pubescence may precipitate early separation anxiety, as in school phobia, inability to function academically in the high school environment, and failure in age-appropriate social activities. Regression to anal-phase ego mechanisms makes for pseudo maturity and functioning acceptable to adults more than to peers. Pubescence may be the precipitating factor for anorexia nervosa. Pathology develops in this early phase of adolescence when ego mechanisms for managing its phase-specific stresses, real and imagined, result in maladaptive behavior and internal distress.

Psychoanalytic therapy takes into consideration the phase-specific needs for character formation, and the analyst becomes a figure for the transference of the object still to be used for character formation and structure building as well as for conflict resolution. While the mixture of phase-specific and regressive behaviors manifested during adolescence makes assessment difficult sometimes, persistence of regressions, intensity of disturbing affects and reactions, recurrence and frequency of maladaptive symptoms and behavior indicate pathology. Assessment of pathology in adolescence is important to prevent later characterological resolutions in which rigid cohesion of character structure, adhesion to infantile objects, and conviction of the reality of attitudinal stands make modification difficult.

Parents of adolescents react to them with disharmony because of their own psychological developmental lag and the reactivation of adolescent anxieties within themselves. In more positive relationships parents may enjoy and profit from their adolescents' developmental experience by identification and empathy with their struggles and successes.

References

Bernstein, H. "The Reality of the Sense of the Self and Identity." Paper presented at the Chicago Psychoanalytic Society, 1963.

Blos, P. *On Adolescence. A Psychoanalytic Interpretation.* Glencoe, Ill.: The Free Press of Glencoe, Inc., 1962.

———. The second individuation process of adolescence. *The Psychoanalytic Study of the Child,* 22: 162–186, 1967.

———. *The Young Adolescent. Clinical Studies.* New York: The Free Press, 1970.

Bronfenbrenner, Y. Quoted in: Byrne, N.S. Nobody home: The erosion of the American family. *Psychology Today,* May 1977.

Bruch, H. Anorexia nervosa. *American Handbook of Psychiatry,* 4(1):787–809, 1975.

Clower, V. Theoretical implications in current views of masturbation in latency girls. *Journal of the American Psychoanalytic Association,* 24(5):109, 1976.

Conger, J. *Adolescence and Youth: Psychological Development in a Changing World.* New York: Harper & Row, 1973.

Douglas, J., and Miller, J. Record breaking women. *Science News,* 12:172–174, September 10, 1977.

Erikson, E. The problem of ego identity. *Journal of the American Psychoanalytic Association,* 4: 56–121, 1956.

———. Identity and the life cycle. *Psychological Issues,* 1(1), 1959.

Freud, A. The ego and the id at puberty. *The Ego and the Mechanisms of Defense.* New York: International Universities Press, 1946.

Freud, S. Three essays on the theory of sexuality (1905). *Standard Edition,* Vol. 7. London: Hogarth Press, 1953.

———. Civilization and its discontents (1929). *Standard Edition,* 21:59–145. London: Hogarth Press, 1961.

———. Moses and monotheism (1939). *Standard Edition,* 23:3–137. London: Hogarth Press, 1964.

Gitelson, M. Character synthesis: The psychotherapeutic problem of adolescence. *American Journal of Orthopsychiatry,* 18:422–431, 1948.

Hall, G. *Adolescence,* Vol. 1. New York: Appleton, 1904.

Henderson, S.; Davidson, J.A.; Lewis, D.C.; Gillard, H.N.; and Barkie, A.G. An assessment of hostility in a population of adolescents. *Archives of General Psychiatry,* 34(6):706–711, 1977.

Inhelder, B., and Piaget, J. *Adolescent Thinking in the Growth of Logical Thinking from Childhood to Adolescence.* New York: Basic Books, 1958.

Karp, M. Diagnosis and treatment of delayed puberty. *Drug Therapy,* June 1977.

Kestenberg, J. Phases of adolescence; With suggestions for a correlation of psychic and hormonal organization. *Journal of the American Academy of Child Psychiatry,* 6:426–463, 577–614, 1967.

Kirstein, L.S. "Age, Menses and Adolescent Development." Paper presented at the VI World Congress of Psychiatry, Honolulu, Sept. 1977.

Kohut, H. *Analysis of the Self: A Systematic Approach to the Psychoanalytic Treatment of Narcissistic Personality Disorders.* New York: International Universities Press, 1971a, p. 116.

———. *Analysis of the Self: A Systematic Approach to the Psychoanalytic Treatment of Narcissistic Personality Disorders.* New York: International Universities Press, 1971b, p. 55.

Mahler, M. Thoughts about development and individuation. *Psychoanalytic Study of the Child,* 8:307–327, 1963.

Offer, D., and Offer, J. *From Teen-age to Young Manhood. A Psychological Study.* New York: Basic Books, 1975.

Ritvo, S. Adolescent to woman. *Journal of the American Psychoanalytic Association,* 24(5):127–138, 1976.

Sarnoff, C. Sexual development during the latency age. In: *Latency.* New York: Jason Aronson, 1976. pp. 37–146.

Sklansky, M. The management of puberty and sex in adolescence. In: Lieberman, S., ed. *Emotional Problems of Childhood.* New York: Lippincott, 1958.

———. Impulse experience and control in adolescence. *Journal of the American Academy of Child Psychiatry,* 4, 1965.

———. (reporter). Indications and contraindications, in The analysis of adolescents. A Panel Report. *Journal of the American Psychoanalytic Association,* 21:134–144, 1971.

———. The alchemy of love: Transmutation of the elements in adolescents and young adults. *The Annual of Psychoanalysis,* 5, 1977.

Sklansky, M., and Richmond, B. *The Second Chance. A Study of the Interactions between Adolescents and the Parents.* Forthcoming 1981.

Sklansky, M.; Silverman, S.; and Rabichow, H. *The High-School Adolescent.* New York: Association Press, 1969.

Spiegel, L. A review of contributions to a psychoanalytic theory of adolescence: Individual aspects. *The Psychoanalytic Study of the Child,* 6:382–395, 1951.

Sullivan, H. *The Interpersonal Theory of Psychiatry.* New York: W. W. Norton, 1953. pp. 263–296.

Werman, D. On the occurrence of incest fantasies. *Psychoanalytic Quarterly,* 46(2):245–255, 1977.

The Course of Life: Psychoanalytic Contributions
Toward Understanding Personality Development.
Vol. II: Latency, Adolescence, and Youth.
S.I. Greenspan and G.H. Pollock, editors.
NIMH 1980

Ages Eleven to Fourteen

Helen R. Beiser, M.D.

Introduction

Children, ages 11-14, compared to younger children, are not as uniform as a group, either physically or psychologically. There are not only marked differences in the age of onset and rate of development of prepubertal changes in boys and girls, but also considerable differences among girls, and also boys. In other words, although girls generally mature 2 years before boys, there are early and late developers in both, and some early-developing boys overlap late-developing girls.

The psychological changes usually, but not necessarily, parallel the physical. Consequently, some children still act like those in the latency phase, and in the literature, papers relating to this phase may be found under headings of "late childhood" or the last phase of latency. Other authors consider this age as an introduction to adolescence, calling the phase "preadolescence." A further division may be made, indicating that the ages from 10 until 12 may be considered preadolescence and the ages 13-15, early adolescence, usually including puberty. If the physical changes leading up to puberty are emphasized, this phase may be called "prepuberty." By age 14, most girls have achieved their menarche, or first menstrual period, which should close the preadolescent phase both physically and psychologically, but many boys have not yet had their first ejaculation, considered the point of puberty for males. I would like to concentrate on the psychological changes that take place in preparation for adolescence proper, usually marked by the physical onset of puberty, as this event has a considerable psychological impact on the young person.

293

Literature

Although there are considerable psychoanalytic and other writings on adolescence, the specific consideration of the preadolescent period is a later development. Freud (1905) does not mention it at all, moving directly from latency to adolescence. Although previously published in German in the 1930s, the English literature does not deal with preadolescence until the 1940s. Redl (1943) describes those preadolescents who border on the delinquent with great clarity *and* complexity in his deceptively "adolescent" jargon. In a chapter on puberty, Anna Freud (1946) briefly alludes to the indiscriminate increase of libido at this period. The first chapter of Deutsch's (1944) well-known book *The Psychology of Women* is entitled "Prepuberty." She, as well as Josselyn (1952), saw this age period as the last phase of latency stressing the drive toward reality, ego development, and ease of handling by adults compared to adolescents.

There were important contributions in the 1950s, first with Erikson's (1951) classical study of the differences in play patterns of boys and girls of this age. Blos (1958) published his concept of the drive organization of preadolescents, later included in his book (1962), *On Adolescence.* Sullivan (1953) included a chapter on preadolescence in his book on *The Interpersonal Theory of Psychiatry.* In the nonanalytic literature, Gesell et al. (1956) published a detailed cross-sectional descriptive study of each year, boys and girls, in *Youth: The Years from 10 to 16.* Inhelder and Piaget (1958) added to our understanding of the cognitive development in *The Growth of Logical Thinking.* Galenson (1964), in reporting a panel report on "Puberty and Child Analysis" summarized psychoanalytic thinking up to that point.

Since then, some interesting details and expansions have been added. In the biological area, studies of Connor and McGeorge (1965) and Money and Alexander (1969) of children with early puberty give food for thought and question the correlation between hormonal and psychological changes. Kestenberg (1967), on the other hand, develops a very careful and detailed relationship between physical and psychological changes at this time. Gardner and Moriarty (1968) studied the cognitive development of middle-class, nonurban children, confirming that, at least in this population, cognitive development approaches that of adults. Wolff (1977) has studied the cognitive differences between early and late developers, which may explain some of the differences between boys and girls.

Harley (1971) and Kaplan (1976) have added to our understanding of the psychology of the preadolescent girl and question whether Blos' original formulations were not based on his experience with passive boys and with girls who do not express their aggressive and anal preoccupations with a male therapist, but do with a woman. It is interesting that Sarnoff (1976) includes preadolescence and even puberty and early adolescence in his book, *Latency.*

Physical and Cognitive Development

Physical changes can be classified into internal changes, which include hormonal and internal sex organs, secondary sex characteristics, and general bodily changes such as height, weight, and facial features. There is a definite sequence for boys and girls, girls usually starting at age 9 or 10, and boys 2 years later. Details are available in the works of Gesell and Kestenberg. Although the sequence is the same, there can be considerable variability in the age of onset. This means that any group of 11-year-olds will contain children who have shown no evidence of prepubertal changes, up to children who are fully pubertal, but that, on the whole, girls will appear more mature than boys, at least in this culture. Wolff quotes some evidence that Chinese and Japanese children do not have the time discrepancy in the sexes observed in other races.

It may be that increased hormones are responsible for an observed restlessness in both sexes, but it is harder to explain the impression of awkwardness and incoordination on this basis, as formal tests actually show an increase in strength and skill during this age period. It may well be that the psychological changes have an effect on body movements. In other words, the child's awareness of body changes, especially sudden changes in height, make him unsure of his physical boundaries, especially when not focused on a specific goal.

Cognitively, interesting changes take place. Although Piaget states age 11 is the age at which concrete thinking shifts to formal modes, this is not sudden and probably takes several years. I have observed, however, that children in treatment are now able to conceptualize formal perspective in drawing and accept the innate properties of substances. Simple tests, for example, will prove that clay in oil will melt in heat, and clay in water will harden. They will also experiment with new ways of playing games. This awareness, as well as the development of some skills, seems to precede the ability to express such ideas in words, so that many children in this age group are unable to carry on an abstract conversation for very long, although they have some idea of what an adult conversation is like. There is a self-consciousness, but without the ability to report introspectively.

Gross Personality Characteristics

General

Children of this age have been described long before any psychoanalytic explanations were available. The restlessness and awkwardness have already been mentioned, as well as the difficulty in verbal expression. Even those whose physical development may be slow give a message to the adult world that they are no longer to be treated as children. Nevertheless, they cannot act in an adult or even an adolescent way. An education professor of mine explained the difficulties of teaching students of junior high school age as, "They are too big to respect adults, but not big enough to have attained self-respect." Often, they have poor body hygiene, and clothes are determined more by peer fads than by parents or teachers. Groups form, even gangs, which cannot be penetrated by even concerned and friendly adults. Although there is not quite a war on adults, they tend to exclude them, except when using them to improve various physical and intellectual skills. This can be particularly frustrating to adults, parents or teachers, who have previously had a pleasant relationship with a friendly, respectful, latency child. Instead, the child may voice an idealization of a rock star, an actor of questionable morals, or older children or peers with different values than those of the child's family.

However, there is great variation, depending on the population under consideration. In a tightly controlled, homogeneous culture, children this age may still act like children, even though their physical and cognitive development may proceed on schedule. In a disorganized culture with high crime rates, the resistance to authority may actually become delinquent. In a psychoanalytic patient population, there is a different group, probably one in which the child has had trouble becoming a part of a peer group and may actually be overly friendly with authority. Nevertheless, as they improve, this patient group has given us important insights into the psychology of this age group. There may also be important changes over time. Social changes, including the prolongation of adolescence by compulsory education, have produced important changes in attitudes of both children and adults. Even the utilization of psychoanalytic knowledge has changed the behavior and some of the psychology of children. Children are given far more information about expected sexual changes than in previous generations and given far more freedom in many ways.

Boys

Aside from the general characteristics, there are some specific differences between boys and girls. Although not noticeably developed, boys show different behavior, even at the beginning of this age period. They tend to be dirty personally, sloppy with their possessions, and still may spend hours on a hobby such as collecting stamps or less valuable items. They prefer groups of boys with similar interests and are not interested in girls until late in this period. They tend to tell dirty jokes and use anal language among themselves, with the jokes having a sexual tone at the older age. They are interested in the workings of things, machines, models, science, as well as sports. They may have a special friend, or group of friends who are almost identical, although there may be experimentation with friends who seem markedly different. If such friendships become intense, which is more likely in less active and group-oriented boys, there may be overt homosexual behavior as well as feelings. Sullivan (1953) feels that this is the first real "love" relationship. According to Money and Alexander (1969), boys with precocious puberty do not show homosexual interests, even though they receive offers from the older boys with whom they have been associating. Although a period of homosexuality has been considered normal for preadolescent boys, the social situation of pressure to accept homosexuals as "normal but different" may produce a different attitude toward this phase by both the boys and by parents and teachers.

Girls

There may be considerable variation in the observed personality of girls of this age. Some seem to be like little women, actively involved in learning household arts and preparing for marriage and motherhood. Even in these "old-fashioned" girls, however, their mothers may be questioned as ideals, and they may use neighbors or models from books or magazines to learn from. A variation of the feminine type is the girl who is mostly involved in enhancing her appearance, experimenting with the latest fashions in clothes, hair, or makeup. The effect may be somewhat less seductive than the girl expects, due to the immaturity of her body, the directness and aggressiveness of her exhibitionism, and a tendency to an incoordination of her attempts. I recall a flat-chested girl of 12 who arrived for her treatment hour in a plunging neckline, spike-heeled shoes, dangling earrings, and a floppy hat—in *her* eyes, the ultimate in adult sophistication. Others girls may be active in other ways, such as athletics, or be especially fond of horses. Some want to perform with animals, others to take care of them. It is these girls who may be more like the boys, with poor personal hygiene, and interest in dirty jokes.

All girls of this age, however, tend to share secrets of a sexual nature with friends, and giggle. Girls tend to have strong friendships, which, if intense, may have homosexual aspects. There are more likely small groups which tend to break up and re-form as those who cannot keep up with the more knowledgeable are excluded. Progress in physical development is compared, as well as ability to attract older boys. Blos has called the 12- and 13-year-old girl "Diana on the hunt." I have observed even tomboyish 13-year-old girls to be markedly aggressive sexually, both throwing themselves at men and putting down the less mature boys of their own age. Battles with mother may start over care of clothing, care of their room, and limitation of social activities.

It should be mentioned that the behavior of girls of this age has shown considerable change over the years. At the beginning of this century, it was not unusual for girls to play with dolls. Deutsch (1944) mentions girls playing at being pregnant by putting pillows under their dresses. Early in my practice, it was more usual for girls to imitate adult women in their clothing and makeup. Now it is unusual to see a girl in a dress, and pants are no longer the sign of a tomboy. Girls now seem to want the privileges of adolescents, choosing their own styles, friends, and coming and going as they please. In the same time-span, the ideal of the preadolescent girl has shifted from teachers to movie stars to popular singers.

Internal Psychological Changes

Etiology

Although the psychological changes of preadolescence usually take place along with the hormonal and physical changes of prepuberty, there is not a complete correlation. Certainly the increase of sexual hormones may directly relate to the indiscriminate increase in activity noted at this time. However, in children with precocious puberty, although cognitive development seems to be stimulated, and these children are both bigger and smarter than same-age peers, they still act like children until age 11. Under certain circumstances, latency attitudes persist beyond puberty, in spite of the expected hormonal and physical maturation. In fact, I have treated adults who still act like latency children although married and with children.

Therefore, the *fact* of preadolescence seems to be a psychological prepara-tion for adolescence, *usually* occurring in the prepubertal period. The *form* depends on many factors. First, there is a difference between boys and girls. Second, there is a variation depending on previous personality development. There is an expectable sequence in children who have solved pre-oedipal and oedipal conflicts adequately and utilized their latency years to develop depen-dable coping and defense mechanisms. If these are too rigid, preadolescent loosening may be delayed or inadequate. If these have never been adequately developed, or if major conflicts have not been resolved, the loosening may bring pathology to light. Of course, this previous personality development has been influenced by parental attitudes which may also influence the process of preadolescence as well. Harder to evaluate, although certainly influential, are society and its changing mores. I have already mentioned the increased availa-bility of sex information, including contraception. Of considerable importance are the various Civil Rights movements for women, blacks, and homosexuals, which have increased the range of adult roles available. One could look on technological advances in the same light. Another influence is the prolonga-tion and glorification of adolescence, so that *it* becomes a goal rather than adulthood. But with all these changes, one that has not changed is the psycho-logical impact of the peer group itself. Does the individual see himself or herself as one of the early developers and therefore superior? Or does late development lead to a sense of inferiority or bitterness with fantasies of revenge? How does the early development of girls as compared to boys influ-ence heterosexual object relations at different ages?

General Tasks of Preadolescence

Before one can become an adult, one must stop being a child. This negative step seems to precede each forward step in development. If one superimposes Mahler's (1975) observations of the pre-oedipal child to the post-oedipal period, one could say that the latency period, with its good adaptation of the child and his environment, is like the symbiotic period of infancy. Preadolescence, then, is like the first subphase of separation-individuation, that of differentiation. I doubt if *all* subphases are recapitulated, but certainly the negative precedes the positive, or, separation precedes individuation, which is the task of adolescence. This requires that the child change his internalized concepts of his parents, as well as of himself. He does not seem to say, "I am not a child anymore"; in fact, he may resent any adult commenting on how much he has grown. Instead, he criticizes the adults or avoids them. In either case, he is saying that they do not understand him, or they are old-fashioned or repressive. In other words, he projects the tensions onto them, blaming them for his own change in attitude. Similarly, he does not introspect on his need for a new identity now that he is not a child, but searches for this in the mirror of his or her peers. This explains the often intense, but possibly changing, relations to peers of the same sex. The true friendship or object relatedness of the preadolescent peer attachments is doubtful, although it may develop into such friendship after the search for the self in the mirror of the other is complete. In cases where the peer relationships seem quite different from the individual child, there is probably an extension of the need to separate himself from the values of the parent. On the other hand, the child may have to search for different aspects of himself, both good and bad. As this criticism of parents may leave the child feeling without support, he tends also to experiment with finding ideal adults, again experimenting with those quite different from parents, who at least give him fantasy support. Often the parents of friends seem much better, and there may be a fantasy ideal family. Such substitutions are an indication of the difficulty the child has in giving up the close, dependent relationship to parents, especially mother. In case of illness, the dependency is reestablished, and the real increase of dependency in chronic illness may interfere with the preadolescent process.

The other task of preadolescence is to anticipate the future. This could be compared to Mahler's (1975) "practicing" subphase. It is the variations in this that give such a wide range of individual behaviors. The practicing has an awkward or uncoordinated feel to it, as in the clothing worn by my patient. Although these attempts are more realistic than the oedipal-age child who parades around in the parent's clothes, or wants to be a fireman, there is still a fantasy character about it. For example, when I asked my patient what her idea of adulthood was, she replied that you could smoke, drink, and go to the race track. It seems to be the pleasure aspects of adulthood that are desired most, and much more actual learning and testing are necessary before a realistic work identity can be internalized. It is for this reason that the real anticipation of the preadolescent is for the body changes of puberty and for the social life of the adolescent. Here there are considerable differences in boys and girls.

Boys

Blos (1958) states that the drive organization of preadolescent boys regresses to an anal, or at least pre-oedipal, one. This seems to be the preferred method of loosening the tie to the mother or declaring independence from childhood, by becoming like a much younger child. It is using an old mechanism to be negative. Blos also emphasizes that the boy must deal with the castration threat from the phallic mother. I think that to free himself from dependency and childhood, the boy must not risk the erotic feelings that were possible in the oedipal period, as this would pull him back into dependency, felt at this time as castration. At this age, he usually refuses physical affection from his mother *and* father as childish, but his sloppiness may actually require a lot of care from mother, which can be tolerated because it is seen as an unnecessary imposition.

Although it is most important for the boy to see himself as not dependent on his mother, he may not have a good relationship to his father either, even though it would seem desirable to learn from him about the changes going on in his body, as well as his approaching puberty. This, too, seems dependent, and he prefers to learn from older boys, as well as peers. Many boys go through a stage where they are chubby and undergo some breast changes. Such physical changes, along with cutting off dependency on reliable adults, allow boys to play with ideas of femininity and express their dependency through a homosexual desire to an older or stronger boy. Others may develop a strong attraction to an older woman, usually a teacher.

The boy's strong interest in how things work, as well as his own body, gives him sublimated interests in sports, mechanics, and science. These are ego supportive and also give him relationships to a variety of teachers.

As the parental dependency ties are loosened, the superego values are also questioned. New values are experimented with, sometimes in a dangerous way. Gangs provide a group superego, often at variance with the culture and parents. If boys have had inadequate dependency, the peer group will give it, and an individual child will take on the superego values of the gang in order to get the support he wants. In less dangerous ways, boys will temporarily overthrow the parental or cultural values in pairs or small groups which aid in loosening the childish superego.

Although most writers talk about the ease with which boys accept their sexuality, how clear and external their genitalia are, this ease seems doubtful when one comes to know the concerns of the preadolescent. Although he has no true object-related heterosexuality, in fact, will avoid or dislike girls, he has to deal with erections that occur without his control; and when puberty and the first ejaculation finally arrive, he has another function which may occur without control, and at embarrassing times. In many ways, the preadolescent boy seems even less sure of his ability to deal with the future than the girl of the same age.

Girls

There is some question as to whether girls regress to a pregenital drive organization like boys. Blos (1962) sees them as rather pressing on to early sexual drives. On the other hand, women analysts, like Harley (1971), feel that girls reveal this side of themselves to women therapists, and men therapists stimulate their sexual feelings. It is possible that when motherhood was the only acceptable goal of females, the anticipation of this was predominant in preadolescence and served as a sufficient mode for the girl's separating from a dependent relationship to her own mother. With the wider range of adult roles open to females, there may be more of the male mode of changing from the child's dependence on parents. Rather than purely anal defiance, however, there may be more shifts in the oral level and also a greater tendency to bisexual experimentation than in the boy.

Whereas oral greediness may serve the boy in a regressive way, it also can serve as fantasy that he will grow faster. The girl, who is already growing rapidly, may experience her increased oral drives in a more conflictual way. If she sees orality as continuing her dependence on the mother, she may fight this by dieting. If this reaches pathological proportions, it may even foster a fantasy that she can control her development and *not* grow up. Before puberty, she can still fantasy that a penis will yet grow, or at least can be substituted for by riding a horse, or owning a large and powerful animal. This path does foster the separation from the mother and combat the temptation to remain in a childish dependence but may interfere with a comfortable femininity. What should be seen as the last gasp of "normal" penis envy may also be seen in the aggressive put-down of the immature boys of the same age.

Although girls tend to have best friends to mirror their interest in themselves and their own development, these do not seem to have as much of the homosexual component as in boys. This may be because girls develop early and are able to direct their heterosexual feelings to older boys. Groups of girls, rather than forming semidelinquent gangs, tend to share sexual interests and brag about their usually fantasied conquests of older boys or men. They also anticipate their menarche, compare notes on development, and the slow developers may feel there is something wrong with them. It is now more usual to look forward to the first menstrual period, although the more compulsive girls may still suffer from feelings of dirtiness and loss of control relating to the menstrual flow. Certainly this is one area where education and the technologic development of more esthetic modes of handling menses have allowed girls to welcome the event as a positive evidence of maturation and not as a "monthly sickness" or "the curse."

Ego development in the girl of this age is similar to the boy's, although she may have different areas of interest. Rather than machinery and science, she enjoys dramatics, music, and art. I have seen the wish to perform that Erikson describes but not the interest in closed spaces. Except for the anticipated menarche, girls seem more interested in enhancing their outward attractiveness in preparation for heterosexual relations. Also, the superego of the girl may not undergo the same testing as does the boy's. If experimentation does take place, it is less in the area of violence and more in the area of sexual contact and running away, or a combination of both.

Implications

Phase-Specific Pathology

In general, children who cause concern at this age fall into two main groups: those who move into adulthood too quickly and those who are fearful or reluctant to face growing up. These children have shown disturbance earlier, or they are those whose disturbance first appears with the specific problem of approaching adolescence. Some of the suffering is not really pathology, but occurs in both the children and parents and other adults because of the phase-specific changes in personality.

First, adults, mother in particular, must deal with the child's wish for greater independence which is often demonstrated by disobedience, sloppiness, and a refusal to accept affection, enjoy family outings, or even be given sex education. Particularly disheartening can be the child's idealization of adults representing a totally different value system than the parents'. Even well-informed parents may feel this change as a narcissistic blow and can use some professional support to tolerate the negativism, as well as suggestions as to when to place firm limits on the experimentation.

There is also a certain amount of expectable pain for children in this age period. The loosening of ties to parents without yet having adult object relations leaves the young person feeling isolated and unsure of himself. Although activity and peer relations handle this to a large extent, the restlessness and instability of interests and friends indicate that the process is painful. Another area of distress is in comparing oneself to others. The very early developers may feel like monstrosities, but this is rare. It is the late developers who more commonly feel the pain of being left behind or wondering if they will ever develop. This is particularly true of boys, where even the normal delay in the growth spurt causes feelings of inferiority and anxiety. Those who experiment with adult dress or skills find that their wishes exceed their abilities, and they may feel depressed by failures or find themselves teased by older and bigger young people, or even adults.

Professional judgment as to what constitutes a real problem requiring treatment is often taxed, as not all parental concern or unhappiness in the child can be dismissed as "just a phase." Valid concerns that may first come to light at this age, although having roots in the past, relate to children who want to grow up too fast. This shows up by delinquent behavior in boys and excessive early sex interests in girls. Often these are children of busy parents who have provided a great deal of material things, but inadequate relationships. Such children do not want treatment, but freedom, and it is necessary to provide control and supervision first. The girl who is delayed in her sexual interests usually does not cause concern at this age, but the immature boy does. He is usually passive and may be a bit fat. He prefers younger children, and, rather than belonging to a peer group, he is often the butt of teasing by that group. He has usually been too close to his mother and, if bright, may have been a favorite of women teachers. Treatment can be a valuable experience for mother and son, the treatment process itself loosening the bond, often by encouraging him to come to sessions himself, interesting him in competitive games, and helping him to deal with his sadistic fantasies in a constructive manner.

More serious problems in the precocious developers cannot be treated in ordinary psychotherapy. Parents are rarely cooperative, and it usually takes a well-coordinated community team or a supervised, controlled institution to protect the child *and* the community. It should be mentioned that such delinquency is easier to control at the preadolescent stage than later in adolescence. At present, drug abuse is probably the most frequent problem in this area.

Problems relating to fear of adolescence or adulthood are more commonly dealt with in psychotherapy. Anorexia nervosa, or school phobia, represents severe conflicts with the mother, or dependency problems. Obesity is the opposite side of the anorexia coin. A more common problem, and less serious, is poor school work. This is not a "learning problem," which usually has been present throughout the school years, but an inability to work toward a goal or set even a direction for the future. This is sometimes accompanied by disobedience, but in the more compulsive child, there may be compliance with assignments, but a failure to set personal goals. Another common problem, usually voiced primarily by the child, is lack of friends. Here again, the problem is longstanding, as the attachment to the parents prevented the usual latency peer relationships, but at preadolescence with its strong peer attachments it becomes more apparent and painful.

Many authors describe an increase in somatic symptoms at this age. These may take various forms, such as tics, relating to increased motor restlessness. Awareness of bodily changes promotes expression of anxiety through hypochondriasis. Those with the constitutional predisposition may also develop psychosomatic symptoms such as asthma, ulcers, or migraine for the first time.

The Preadolescent in Treatment

I would like to describe briefly the problems for psychotherapy specific to the preadolescent personality. Early in the period the treatment process is much like that of the latency child. Especially an immature preadolescent enjoys being the sole focus of attention of an interested adult. Boys especially still enjoy a wide range of play activities, board games, models, drawing, etc. They may bring their collections to the hour for demonstration and talk about sports heroes or the latest feat of their favorite athletic team. Direct interpretation of symbolic material is met with disavowal and even fleeing from treatment, but they will utilize alternate solutions couched in the language of the metaphor. Play is sometimes used for expression and exploration, and sometimes for symbolic representation of conflicts. One very small 12-year-old boy confided in me that he had found a way to make money by cutting paper currency in half and turning in each half for a new bill. It was his way of trying to make something valuable out of what he saw as a defect. I informed him that it was necessary to have five-eighths of a bill to get a replacement, but we discussed other ways of making money. Some other boys will experiment with new techniques for playing checkers, being willing to risk losing while testing them out. At this age this represents exploration, not masochism.

Girls this age are, in many ways, harder to treat than boys. It is probably not an accident that there are fewer play materials available for girls of this age than there are for boys. They are more likely to refuse play activities at an earlier age than boys, although some may draw and play games, but then they are left with the problem of verbal communication at an age when introspection and abstract thinking are not sufficiently developed. With women therapists, the girl also has the problem of her conflicted relationship with her mother, especially at the time of puberty. I have sat many times with a silent, hostile 13-year-old girl, totally unable to communicate. I have come to the conclusion that such girls do better with a nonseductive male therapist. The closer relationship of problem boys to their mothers may be an advantage in starting therapy with a woman.

With both sexes, therefore, it is best to start when they are a little immature, so that the positive relationship can carry the process at least partially through the preadolescent and early adolescent phases. Even this cannot be accomplished without strong support from parents and usually also from the school. After age 12, the more motivation from the child himself, the better. Because a disturbed child has a strong need to assert independence from adult authorities, it is difficult to discriminate resistance from improvement, and termination as evidence that an immature child is ready to deal with separation. Again, in the area of content of the therapy hours, it is best if some play material could be accepted early, and flexibility of play and conversation established. Play may aid the physical restlessness of the preadolescent, and he may be able to talk *while* playing, rather than use play as a vehicle of communication.

I have already mentioned the problems involved in the content of preadolescent conversation. In an analyst's office, the subject of the couch also comes up. Highly sophisticated children, who intellectualize, come from homes where parents have been in analysis, or who have read about it, may lie down on the couch. This more often leads to sleep than to free association. These same children may be able to talk about dreams and fantasies like adult patients but, strangely enough, do not seem to change. Their pseudo-adult talk is a symptom and is split off from an infantile part which resists integrated maturation. Actually, children in the preadolescent phase do not act like *good* patients, either of the childhood type or the adult type. With patience and persistence, however, therapists *can* treat at least some preadolescents and have the satisfaction of watching the change from playing children to intro-spective early adolescents. If one wants them to behave like adults, one is asking for pathology.

Implications for Future Pathology

It is interesting to speculate on the influence of the preadolescent period on adult personality. I have long thought that it is the basis for many problems between the sexes. The early development of girls, with their search for older boys as the objects of their first heterosexual strivings, seems to carry on in the custom of women being younger than their husbands. It might also make men uncomfortable with women of their own age. It may be that this preadolescent phenomenon may be more influential than an unresolved oedipal conflict, which has been the usual explanation for this happening. Of course, it is not universal and probably depends on how much of a problem was actually encountered. Girls who have socialized very early and who then find them-selves without a source of older boys, such as in the senior year of high school, may become depressed as their age mates are being actively sought by the younger girls. Very late developers may maintain their sense of inferiority into adulthood, and it is certainly something to keep in mind in the treatment of adults.

Some of the problems that arise in preadolescence may not be resolved during the course of adolescence and persist into adulthood. Drug abuse and delinquency may seriously affect the individual's adult life if not successfully treated. Similarly, if the defense mechanisms against delinquency, such as tics or hypochondriasis, are not handled, they too may persist as adult problems.

Those problems indicating a fear of growing up, if not resolved, may inter-fere with the adult's achieving his full potential, and such adults appear as neurotic or having character disorders. I worked with one boy throughout his preadolescence until we finally uncovered his fear, based on the early deaths of a number of male relatives, that he would die or become sick if he passed the age of 13. He had no learning disability, but read only to feed omnipotent fantasies and not to attain a life goal.

A more interesting speculation relates to the idea of fixation in latency or preadolescence as a way of dealing with the fear of growing up. Fixation in latency would avoid the risks of preadolescence and adolescence as well. I believe this used to be a fairly common occurrence in girls, and the compliant little-girl personality was often mistaken for ideal femininity. It usually was very successful in attracting a husband, but such immature women had a hard time dealing with the problems of marriage and motherhood when compliance did not solve all problems.

I have felt that the "hippie" generation was fixated in preadolescence. Rather than remaining as compliant children, they rebelled from childhood, but could not set realistic adult goals. Instead, they criticized the available adult models, regressed anally to poor personal hygiene, and had poorly defined sexual identities. The emphasis was on sensuality rather than object relations.

Implications for Home and School

In an individualistic, democratic culture or society, adolescence is considered a desirable and necessary phase of development to produce the most autonomous adult. Preadolescence is then a necessary prologue. The adolescent opportunity to question the values and relationships of childhood and construct a new personality means that the representatives of society must bear the brunt of the questioning.

Schools have reacted to the increased activity patterns by providing a different class structure allowing movement between classes and different teachers. This makes it easier for the students to keep a distance and for the teachers to avoid too much attack by the same students. It also prepares for the more specialized learning during adolescence. Perhaps what has not been taken into consideration is the faster preparation for adulthood by those who do not wish for a prolonged educational experience. This is complicated by compulsory school laws and the democratic ideal of equality. Compulsory school attendance during the teen years is not a true adolescence, and those students who do not use it to increase their knowledge tend to behave like preadolescents, resenting being treated like children, but unable to move toward valid adult goals.

On the other hand, those young people who are likely to have a long educational experience in which they are really preparing for a complex, adult-work identity tend to be flooded with vocational information and advice at earlier and earlier levels. It is possible that this frightens the bright students, and they feel that they cannot really learn or aspire to something so difficult. This situation may influence young people to a fixation in preadolescence or adolescence.

The home has perhaps been less able to prepare for the immediate accommodation of the preadolescent. It is strange how many parents think that *they* were really misunderstood by their parents at that age and that their different methods of childrearing will prevent rebelliousness or withdrawal in *their* children. Most finally make the adjustment, but there might be a fight which keeps the child in the latency period for a time. On the other hand, some parents give up and actually do not fight with the child for the control needed for his basic protection. A battle won so easily is not worth the victory, as it may be dangerous.

Other parents push for maturation. Some do this by early and excessive sexual information, some by inordinate and specific demands for adult goals. It is not easy to keep lines of communication open without demanding confidences or to dose information to that which is immediately pertinent and looks just enough to the future to give a general direction. Those parents who had to struggle against family attitudes and financial troubles to get their own education are frustrated that their children refuse the same goals made easy for them. Luckily, the activity drive of the preadolescent is so strong that it cannot be easily turned off by the need to demonstrate independence from parents and society. Perhaps the biggest problem to this generation is that there are too many alternatives, too many roles available to them, and it is hard to give up any of them in the process of making a choice.

Summary

The age period of 11 until 14 years is one in which most children experience both the physical and psychological changes leading up to puberty, the first menstrual period in girls, which occurs on the average of 2 years before the first ejaculation in boys. Girls show a growth spurt during this time, but boys usually do not. The psychological changes of the preadolescent period are primarily those of loosening the childhood character structure which had been developed up to that time. This produces the characteristics of negativism toward adults, which sometimes mask the more positive developmental occurrences of increased physical strength, more abstract cognitive thinking, and the beginnings of meaningful relationships to peers of the same sex. Bodily changes stimulate a change in the perception of the self, with an increased interest in the functioning of the body, especially the sex organs, but libido is more generally increased rather than focused on a person of the opposite sex. The temporary homosexual interest is seen as a projection of the interest in one's own functioning.

Observed behavioral characteristics vary with the previous personality structure of the child, the reaction of his parents to this new developmental phase, and the social environment. That aspect of preadolescence which anticipates adult roles depends on the expectable length of the adolescent period and the perceived adult roles available for the individual with his particular capabilities and expectations of himself.

References

Blos, P. Preadolescent drive organization. *Journal of the American Psychoanalytic Association*, 6:47-56, 1958.

——. Preadolescence. *On Adolescence.* Glencoe, Ill.: Free Press of Glencoe, 1962. pp. 57-71.

Connor, D.B., and McGeorge, M. Psychological aspects of accelerated pubertal development. *Journal of Child Psychology and Psychiatry,* 6:1161-177, 1965.

Deutsch, H. Prepuberty. *The Psychology of Women.* Vol. I. New York: Grune and Stratton, 1944. pp. 1-23.

Erikson, E. Sex differences in the play configuration of preadolescents. *American Journal of Orthopsychiatry,* 21:667-692, 1951.

Freud, A. The ego and id at puberty. *The Ego and the Mechanisms of Defense.* New York: International Universities Press, 1946. p. 154.

Freud, S. Three essays on the theory of sexuality (1905). *Standard Edition,* 7:173-231. London: Hogarth Press, 1953.

Galenson, E. Prepuberty and child analysis: A panel report. *Journal of the American Psychoanalytic Association,* 12:600-609, 1964.

Gardner, R., and Moriarty, A. *Personality Development at Preadolescence: Explorations of Structure Formation.* Seattle: University of Washington Press, 1968. p. 344.

Gesell, A.; Ilg, F.; and Ames, L.B. *Youth: The Years from Ten to Sixteen.* New York: Harper, 1956. p. 542.

Harley, M. Some reflections on identity problems in prepuberty. In: McDevitt, J.B., and Settlage, C.F., eds. *Separation-Individuation.* New York: International Universities Press, 1971. pp. 385-403.

Inhelder, B., and Piaget, J. Adolescent thinking. *The Growth of Logical Thinking from Childhood to Adolescence.* New York: Basic Books, 1958. pp. 334-350.

Josselyn, I. Psychological growth patterns. In: *The Adolescent and His World.* New York: Family Service Association of America, 1952. pp. 9-25.

Kaplan, E. Manifestations of aggression in latency and preadolescent girls. *The Psychoanalytic Study of the Child,* 31:63-78, 1976.

Kestenberg, J. Phases of adolescence: With suggestions for a correlation of psychic and hormonal organization. *Journal of the American Academy of Child Psychiatry,* 6:426-463 (Part I), 6:577-614 (Part II), 1967.

Mahler, M.; Pine, F.; and Bergman, A. On human symbiosis and the subphases of the separation-individuation process. *The Psychological Birth of the Human Infant.* New York: Basic Books, 1975. pp. 41-122.

Money, J., and Alexander, D. Psychosexual development and absence of homosexuality in males with precocious puberty. *Journal of Nervous and Mental Diseases,* 148:111-123, 1969.

Redl, F. Preadolescents—What makes them tick? *Child Study,* 1943. pp. 44-48.

Sarnoff, C. Sexual development during the latency age. Cognitive development. *Latency.* New York: Jason Aronson, 1976. pp. 37-146.

Sullivan, H.S. Preadolescence. *The Interpersonal Theory of Psychiatry.* New York: W.W. Norton, 1953. pp. 245-263.

Wolff, P. "Development of Behavioral Sex Differences." Unpublished presentation, Chicago Institute for Psychoanalysis, 1977.

The Course of Life: Psychoanalytic Contributions
Toward Understanding Personality Development.
Vol. II: Latency, Adolescence, and Youth.
S.I. Greenspan and G.H. Pollock, editors.
NIMH 1980

Disturbances in Early Adolescent Development

Joseph D. Noshpitz, M.D.

Introduction

One of the difficulties in evaluating the clinical status of a troubled adolescent is distinguishing between the more dramatic vagaries of normality and the warping impact of true psychopathology. The fluid, changing state of character during rapid growth and transition makes evaluation uncertain and prediction a trap for the unwary. Even a delineation of some of the clinical conditions likely to be found among any population of adolescents poses difficulties.

To deal with these, the material in this communication is organized along hierarchical lines. At the outset there is a brief account of the events associated with normal puberty, followed by the minor adjustment reactions of the time, then by the more serious syndromes, and finally by those with the gravest prognosis. Specifically, the initial section deals first with biological, cognitive, and affective dynamic aspects of normal development (including pre-genital, phallic-oedipal, superego, and identity dimensions), and then with some of the varieties and dynamics of unusual talents and abilities.

The problems of the normal adolescent are reviewed under such headings as turmoil, rebellion, and the phenomena associated with socialization outward. These include young love, hedonism, romanticism, moodiness, boredom, shyness and inhibition, and asceticism. In addition, the encounter with the new physique is discussed under the rubrics of appearance, deviations in height, problems in breast development, squeaky voice, acne, and unusual physique.

This completes the review of "normal" developmental problems, and the focus moves to a few of the milder disturbances in development. The areas selected are classified as gender-identity problems along with precocious and delayed puberty. Problems of intermediate levels of severity are then described. These include accidents, adolescent depression, psychophysiologic reactions, the minor alienation syndrome, group delinquency, and minimal brain dysfunction (MBD).

Some of the more serious conditions are touched on: anorexia nervosa, the true neuroses, and the depersonalization syndrome. The material closes with a discussion of delinquency and psychosis in adolescence.

At each level, comprehensiveness has been sacrificed for an illustrative sampling of some of the conditions that beset young people. The afflictions are numerous and, in some instances, unclassified. Thus the psychological implications of dental braces, the meaning of premature baldness, the simple realization of having an unattractive fact or an unpleasing figure—or for that matter of beauty and voluptuousness—are topics that have been little studied. The sexual identity issues of adolescence, the variety of antisocial patterns (in spite of all the study, much remains to be learned about this realm), the work inhibitions, the pathologic religiosity, in short, a great many fairly serious dimensions of adjustment also remain in a sort of professional limbo. There are indeed practitioners who know a lot about them, but the field as such has only partially assimilated them, and there is no recognized, generally held therapeutic approach for their management.

Since there is much here that is ambiguous, one cannot communicate about these areas with apodictic certainty. The emphasis here is on a brief, rapid account of a few of the typical problems of early adolescence. The need is for far more extensive study.

Highlights of Pubertal Development

Biological Factors

There is no precise point at which puberty begins, nor is it certain why it begins. Somewhere in the brain, and particularly in the hypothalamus, a biologic clock reaches its appointed hour, and a series of neuroendocrine changes ensue. The pituitary is alerted. Its many tropic hormones begin to pour into the bloodstream; the adrenarche follows with the secretions of the adrenal cortex adding themselves to the pituitary liquors; and at last the sex hormones as such begin to pour out of testes and ovaries and add their moiety to the heady endocrine soup that is now bathing all the body tissues. Growth follows according to the templates laid down in the basic genetic code, and, given adequate nutrition, a host of body changes come into view. As these become visible, the youngster is said to have entered puberty.

In any sizable population of youngsters, the onset of this phase will be evident in girls about 1½ to 2 years before it is manifest in boys (Tanner 1962). Both the age at which changes begin and the rate at which they proceed are highly variable. Certain youngsters, not all, show a prepubertal fat stage—they become plump or chubby as they approach puberty. For the majority of girls, the first tufts of pubic hair and the earliest areolar changes and breast budding occur about 10 or 11. Menarche follows in 1½ to 2 years. Increase in the length of the long bones, widening of the pelvis, and rotation of the neck of the femur come in their turn along with redistribution of the subcutaneous fat and altering of facial contours.

Presently the flat, latency girl body is transformed into the shapely form of a young woman, while the maturation of the ovaries and uterus initiate the menstrual cycle and prepare the way for fertility. The boy undergoes parallel changes, although they usually do not appear until age 13 or 14. The first hints of puberty are again the appearance of pubic and axillary hair, increase in the size of the genitalia, and presently, a considerable lengthening of the long bones. The boy begins to have frequent erections, becomes very alive to sexual stimuli, and experiences his first nocturnal emissions. In short order, he elaborates viable sperm in adequate number, and he too is physically ready to reproduce. Collectively these changes are known as the appearance of the secondary sexual characteristics (the primary characteristics, present prenatally, define the child's gender). They continue over a period of 5 or 6 years, although some of the changes, e.g., deepening of the boy's voice and growth of the beard, may not begin till later in the process.

Cognitive Factors

Piaget (Inhelder and Piaget 1958) places the initial appearance of the stage of formal operations in thought at about age 11. Increasingly, there is a capacity to think abstractly, to draw ever finer distinctions, to see essential consistencies despite superficial differences, to hold a chain of cause-and-effect sequences firmly in mind, and to use concepts as manipulable entities. The youngster begins to think in abstract formal propositional terms; no longer is he bound to the concrete occasion. He reasons more effectively in academic pursuits and argues ever more trenchantly in his altercations with parents, teachers, and other authorities. Presently he can invest himself in such abstruse concepts as religion, ethics, truth, etc.

Affective-Dynamic Factors

Pre-genital arousal. Along with the new maturational capacities, there is a major disruption of the relatively quiescent instinctual life of latency. There is a vigorous reawakening of the pre-genital and phallic-oedipal phases. The early drives are swept up with the pubertal advances and begin to make themselves felt in a variety of forms. Behavioral changes commonly ensue: The youngster begins to gorge or grows finicky, changes his or her food interests, and eats

only natural foods or only junk. Some young people go through minor anorexic periods and are said to be "off their feed" for a while. Orderly children
may become careless and defiantly sloppy; there are major hassles about maintaining one's room. Others become protective, secretive, and lock their doors,
or at best, protest vehemently if anyone enters their area. Occasionally the
pendulum swings toward their becoming excessively, obsessively neat and
orderly. Temper outbursts are common. Language characteristically changes to
reflect both the recrudescence of anal interests and the cognitive advances.
Sometimes street terms which were formerly confined to peer interactions now
burst forth within teacher/student and parent/child contexts. There is often a
far greater interest in money—making it, saving it, hoarding it, and spending
it—than previously.

Phallic-oedipal instinct pressures. The phallic-oedipal drives are soon much in
evidence with many dirty jokes, questions about sex, bumptious inquiries into
the intimate practices of surrounding adults (including often enough the parents), grandiose assertions of one's own sexual mastery ("I know all about
that"), and flaunting of sexually related materials such as underclothes, sanitary
napkins, jock straps, *Playboy* magazine, or bits of erotic "art." For many a boy
and girl, active sexual behavior begins at this point. Their newly mature bodies
become objects of considerable interest to sexually experienced individuals in
their immediate environment, leading to all manner of seduction and sexual
abuse; and their own interactions with one another may all too easily spill over
into various forms of sexual expression. Boys become much involved with
looking and girls with showing. There is commonly some experimenting with
body manipulations; coitus is by no means uncommon. As a rule, the more
direct experiences of sexual response to the bodies of the parents are quickly
warded off. They are suppressed and repressed. A pattern of distancing reactions may follow; the parents may come to be regarded defensively as old,
disgusting, and altogether unattractive. There follows a determined plunge into
peer group interests. Even at home, moody withdrawal or hours spent on the
phone with friends may speak volumes for the need to fend off oedipal impulses; and patterns of willful and unreasonable opposition to parental values
and stances may well ensue.

The final chapter of the work deals with the phase of separation individuation (Blos 1967). The youngster must accomplish the task of achieving true
autonomy, no longer the partial way station of yore, but the beginning march
toward the end of the adolescent process, adult independence. The particular
task at puberty is the detachment of the affective bonds, both erotic and
aggressive, from the persons of the parents, and their reworking, displacement
outward, and reattachment to the variety of nonincestuous objects available in
the larger world; in particular, their investment in age-appropriate peers and
near peers.

There are many ports of call on this voyage. Initially, as the youngster encounters his/her own body transformations, much passionate interest and intense sensuous excitement are aroused by considering oneself. The new muscles, the new height, the new bosom, the new genital size, the new contours, the new face, the new possibilities offered by clothes, make-up, hairdos, gestures, modes of speaking, facial expressions, and all manners of posturing are explored in detail. The body is felt, studied, tested. Not infrequently there are grandiose thoughts about one's attractiveness, sexual prowess, strength, beauty, handsomeness, intelligence, talent, and the like. Masturbation figures in the life of almost all boys and probably a majority of girls. Fantasy is rife, and masturbatory fantasy in particular plays a profound role in the psychic life of these youngsters. The cumulative experience of the formative oedipal and pre-genital interactions now crystallizes in the form of powerful interests and dispositions which thrust themselves into the awareness of the boy or girl, and with which each must cope. Perhaps the fantasy life involves whipping or beating. Sometimes overt images of sexual interaction with a family member may appear; even the encounter with relatively "normal" well-defended images (such as a boy seeing an unknown woman taking off her clothes as he masturbates) can all cause reactions of considerable dismay.

Superego changes. The instinctual stirrings of puberty arouse the superego to excited activity. It was precisely to deal with such oedipal issues that this agency of the mind was created, and with these newly energized wishes now hammering at the gates of consciousness, it is radically alerted. Guilt feelings, moodiness, a sudden distaste for parents, an inability to speak to them (despite excellent relationships in earlier years), and indeed, a readiness to accept everyone's opinion but theirs tell something of the effects of the superego alarm system. The injunction is: Thou shalt not think of oral clinging, of anal sensuousness, and especially not of genital incest. The ego must find ways to carry out this injunction. At the same time, the youngster's newly acquired sense of intellectual competence leads him to look at the superego in a new way. Perhaps for the first time he begins to study its proscriptions, to question its values, to evaluate its stances, and presently to challenge something of what he finds. He is suddenly finding fault with his parents—with their ethics, their politics, their religion, their prejudices, and their "weltanschauung." This fault goes all the way from demanding proof that there is something wrong with staying out till 1 a.m. to criticizing the fact that the parent chuckles over a racist joke.

Identity. One of the major issues the youngster faces is the nature of his identity (Erikson 1959). He can no longer think of himself as a child or accept the social role of child. At the same time, clearly, he is not yet a man. But he begins to question why not and how come he isn't and what's the difference anyway. The organization of self as latency child is fragmented; into the breach leap all manner of posturings and fantasies. There are grandiose moments when he feels himself infinitely more on top of things than his fuddy-duddy parents. And yet, there are moments when the comforts of being in the relatively safe state of knowing who one is, of being someone's child, dependent and taken care of, are remembered. From time to time, one can regress and be the compliant "good" child of yore, but at best, this regression can only be a temporary state, perhaps a response to stress, and the resurgent yearnings of puberty rise up again, and once more the great uncertainty looms ahead.

The usual solution found by most youngsters is to create a new persona in fantasy, to try on identity roles, and thus, through experiment, to discover who one is and what one does best. Identity must be worked at, and many, many such experiments must be carried out. Indeed, it usually takes several years before a stable sense of self becomes set (GAP 1968). The first truly major step into adulthood involves the establishment of a reasonably stable and consistent organization of this sort. The nature of the organization may be infantile; indeed, it may be a state of protracted adolescence. But once the experiments are over, once it is clearly set, the outcome is adulthood.

Unusual Talents and Abilities

There are several varieties of giftedness—in the realm of the intellectual, esthetic, creative, mathematical/scientific, mechanical, body action (sports, gymnastics, ballet), etc.

In many instances (these can involve everything from high IQ to gymnastic ability), the presence of some unusual capacity was evident in early latency; in a few rare instances it is obvious from the very beginnings of personality development. But it is quite common for talents to blossom with puberty. Indeed, this period of life makes many an average person feel talented. New intellectual worlds are opening. Suddenly the youngster understands all manner of things heretofore hidden and obscure; without warning he feels emotions whose sweetness and intensity seem like radically new discoveries, something no one could have felt before. It is a time of life when many a youth will write poetry because he must, and perhaps the only time in his life he ever does. It is not surprising that a latent capacity for some form of creative expression, be it singing, boxing, or abstract mathematics, now comes to fruition and finds concrete expression. One rather special development that might not necessarily be designated a talent functions in a somewhat similar way. This is the appearance of unusual beauty or handsomeness. Psychologically it plays an analogous role.

A genuine talent is a remarkable phenomenon. It has the quality about it of changing reality. Money, status, recognition, adulation, sexual favors, bids for friendship, opportunities for travel and for training, and many other awards come the way of the gifted, and many doors open for them in a manner calculated to affect the self-concept and the sense of social orientation of anyone. It is no exaggeration to say that it takes rather a fortunate personality organization and an unusual degree of maturity to cope with talent. All too often, brilliant and talented young people arc across the sky of their social surround and burn out like meteors so that by the time they reach adulthood they are lost and no longer able to achieve. In some instances, the unusual factor was precocity rather than talent, i.e., the youngster performed in an amazingly competent fashion at a much earlier age than his peers; when they finally caught up, he was no longer outstanding. In many instances, however, quite a different combination of events ensues.

Dynamics

The resolution of narcissistic issues can be radically interfered with by such factors (Kohut 1971). The original grandiose residues of symbiotic fusion must gradually resorb during the separation individuation phases so that by the time of oedipal resolution, the last flareup of grandiosity is seen in the structure of the oedipal fantasy itself. It is after all a very considerable presumption on the part of the child to dream of sexual rights with one parent or the other and to contemplate the destruction of the rival. As this total wish-fantasy construct is gradually given up, the superego forms with its multiple principles and prohibitions. The grandiose idealization of both self and parent slowly converts into a part of the superego, the ego ideal which then continues to evolve and develop into an ever more mature presence in the mind, a part of the self that holds up a model for striving and self-realization.

Such a complex sequence of developmental events is clearly vulnerable to the many vicissitudes of growing up. In particular, inadequate resolution of the work with the grandiose elements of childhood thinking leaves a youngster with a distorted self-concept and an uneven and hazardous quality in his estimation of significant others. All these factors undergo an explosive recrudescence at puberty. As the pre-genital and phallic-oedipal concerns are once again aroused, the associated grandiose narcissistic elements are rekindled, resonating with the normal increase in self-directed interest, the searching attention to and fantasies about one's changing body and mind, and an outburst of considerable narcissistic preoccupation can ensue.

Evidently a state of unusual talent will set up many reverberations within this grandiose system. Or, more precisely, the normal tendency toward overestimation of the self will not be reinforced by the adulatory regard of the surrounding human environment; the consequence is a tremendous enhancement of this aspect of self-concept. One sees oneself as larger than life; all sorts of advantages belong to one by right. No criticism of one's work can be tolerated without a tremendous flare of resentment and suspicion of personal attack. Self-centeredness becomes exaggerated to the point of distorting the appraisal of reality; and there ensues a state of heightened expectation of the self and vulnerability to any breath of criticism that inevitably pave the way toward failure. For such people, competition is excruciating (How can they compare themselves to me?), and failure to be first, best, the chosen one, is catastrophic. Under such circumstances, peer problems can be considerable, and the prodigy often thinks of himself as having no need for those clods or, worse still, he may develop an entourage of followers who are sufficiently awed by his talents as to abandon the usual peer interactive practices which do much to help the individual recognize the implications of his actions and the nature of social reality. As the youngster gets more and more isolated, he relies evermore on his talent to carry him through—often it is not enough. He doesn't understand what is going wrong and becomes angry and depressed. In due course there comes the burnout that blights the careers of many promising and talented adolescents. They fall into states of confusion, depression, work-block, and failed productivity that leave them wounded and able to work at only a fraction of their actual potential.

There is no technical name for this condition; names such as worker's block and work inhibition fall far short of conveying the personal tragedy and the serious loss to the culture of such a chain of events. Narcissistic dysrealization of talent may say in capsule form what has occurred here. On the other hand, when the combination of genetic endowment and wise environmental management has avoided fostering such narcissistic fixations, such youngsters can have a remarkable adolescence, full of rich and challenging experience, replete with many gratifications, and thoroughly preparatory for a magnificent adulthood.

Problems of the Normal Adolescent

Turmoil

When D. Offer (Offer and Offer 1975) and his associates sought a group of normal average adolescents to study, they found that the youngsters fell into three categories. There was a relatively conflict-free cohort who did not get into difficulties with their families, who performed well at their studies, who appeared to enjoy many activities and social relationships, and who seemed stable and happy. There was another group who seemed by contrast, to be relatively anxious, depressed, at odds with their world, and plagued by numerous behavioral problems. And there was an inbetween group who felt troubled but who did not ordinarily allow the emotional upset to invade their behavioral adjustment. In brief, Offer indicated that the majority of adolescents do not actually demonstrate overt behavioral or emotional disturbance, but that of those who do, there are many who still fall within the pale of the norm. It seems safe to assert that all adolescents are probably shaken by emotional storms and troublesome floods of impulse (Freud, A. 1958); for many, these experiences are transient and readily mastered, whereas for a minority, the same issues lead to far more serious reactions.

Anna Freud's observation about the normalcy of adolescent turmoil is prob-ably as accurate a statement as one can make. The erupting instincts and the fragmenting latency identity noted earlier create conditions of disequilibrium. In effect, the adolescent ego is under considerable developmental stress. The capacity of this ego to cope with these pressures is a function of its genetic endowment, the strengths and weaknesses that have emerged during personal-ity formation in the early years of life, the kinds of traumata to which the youngster may have been exposed as he grew up, the identifications he has made, and the character and firmness of the superego formations that are his lot. The strength of the drives is another unknown that defies measurement but which thrusts itself into every discussion of this time of life. And finally, the family constellation wherein puberty takes place, the attitudes of the parents toward the changes in the boy or girl and toward the drives themselves are factors of central importance in the way this developmental stage unfolds.

In any event, the predictable state of affairs for any given youngster is a condition of episodic turmoil, sometimes ensuing because of guilt over for-bidden fantasies, sometimes because of frustrated yearnings for ever greater degrees of autonomy and independence, sometimes because of confusion and uncertainty about who one is and who one is expected to be, sometimes because a momentary imbalance between impulsive and controlling forces has led to some impulsive, explosive act whose consequences have to be adjusted to, sometimes because the shifting of defense structures and identity patterns has given rise to feelings of confusion and depersonalization that are as fright-ening as they are unexplainable. In short, there are myriad sources of that sense of profound disturbance which is usually designated as adolescent turmoil.

The one virtue of this state of affairs is that the actual experience of turmoil is usually shortlived; in one way or another, most of the time the youth copes with the imbalance and adjusts. The adjustment may be short-lived, but it does occur, and the basic stability of life is preserved. In less fortunate situations, the turmoil is not so much episodic as chronic, and the youngster may enter a state of depression, agitation, and excessive reactivity that can have serious implica-tions. Occasionally such stressful sequences can lead to runaways or to suicidal gestures as the youngster attempts to free himself from an unendurable and continuing sense of crisis. On the other hand, most adolescent turmoil is probably never visible; the young person copes by talking things over with a friend or a respected teacher or other adult. Or, by use of abreaction and identification, he finds a way to resolve the issue without overt dramatics.

Rebellion

Of all the phenomena associated with this time of life, rebellion is probably the most often described and discussed. The pressures toward separation-individuation, toward giving up the lifelong dependency on the parents, toward the achievement of ever greater degrees of personal autonomy, toward seeking and finding new objects for social and sexual interest, and toward becoming a self-determining individual with the ability to make one's own decisions often set a youth on an inevitable collision course with his adult environment. The intensity of the drives toward independence can be great, and the resultant challenges to, and differences with, parents, teachers, coaches, and policemen can be of like proportions. To make matters worse, the immaturity of the pubertal youth frequently leads him to take stands and make assertions that are at best illogical and which to the adult ear may sound downright ridiculous. The resultant critical interactions may well serve to help define the youth's separate identity, but they are emotionally costly to every-one. Many a young person resorts to attitudes of pitiless defiance and even of arrogance in insisting on some valued position. Its value may rest chiefly in its ability to evoke parental reactivity.

For the more troubled youngsters, this need to achieve autonomy by defying the various authority figures in one's life represents an early form of seeking self-definition. It is the logically simplest means of separating from a source of dependency. One has been attached all of one's life; now the quest is on for full individuation. The first and easiest way to get there seems obvious: to take each point of parental value and deny it or challenge it. By differing with the parents, one has asserted a kind of independence of them.

In particular, the rebellion of the time is a reflection of the renewed encoun-ter with the superego. The need to challenge, to rebut, to explore, to test out the dictator that heretofore has reigned unquestioned within the youngster's personality comes into a kind of resonance with the search for autonomy. The outcome is a sense of rebellion which can take many forms. There can be a series of fantasied denunciations and devastating attacks on parents and teachers that are never verbalized by a youngster who is outwardly accepting and compliant. There can be alternating episodes of stubborn opposition and cheerful acceptance of rules. There can be a chronic nasty, negative attitude with sullenness and surliness within an overall context of basic good behavior. And there can also be overt hostile refusal to comply with the most elementary requirements of age-appropriate adjustment coupled with destructive out-bursts, school failure, runaways, and all manner of personal challenges to authority figures.

The nature of the early adolescent process is to experience the world and to react to it in forms that tend to be extreme. The youngster is head over heels in love, suffused with rage, covered with confusion, drowned in embarrassment, filled with maudlin sentimentality, or overwhelmed with concern—the only common factor among these being the totality of the emotion. Nuances will come later as adolescence advances; now the state is close to all or none. This emotional style gives rather a specific coloring to the interactions of the period, a mixture of intensity and childishness that speaks for the transitional character of the time. It also makes the moments of rebellion particularly difficult to bear.

Reaching Outward: The Great Displacement

Generally speaking, the types of adjustment seen as part of this time of life are not given diagnoses. They are considered as part of the fair wear and tear of growing up, the phenomenology of puberty, but it is important to note some of the more common varieties in greater detail.

Young love. In the interpersonal sphere, there are unaccountable loves and hates. The emotions are callow to be sure, but not the less intense for their immaturity. Affection, newly displaced from idealized parents, is likely to be reattached to overvalued distant figures such as pop stars, TV idols, movie actors, great athletes, racing car drivers, and the like. When a figure closer to home fills the form needed by this youngster, a crush can ensue, taking the form of an inordinately intense attachment to a teacher, a neighbor, a coach, or some other older person. It is as though the vivid idealization formerly reserved for the parent has become tinctured more and more by defensive devaluations and the need for distancing. The positive feelings are then transferred wholesale to some other parental person of either sex, and for a while the youngster feels drawn toward this individual, hangs on his every word and gesture, feels thrilled by his look or touch, and literally adores him. Only after some time does this emotional bondage release. Often enough this happens abruptly, so that the object of this attachment is sometimes bewildered by why he was so pursued and why he is now so abandoned. In the normal course of events, sooner or later, the affections turn away from the idealized adult and attach instead to a boy or girl in class or to one who lives next door. Again, the initial emotions are typically intense and overwhelming; the youngsters moon over one another, dream of one another, feel thrilled to the very core when they catch each others' eyes, and often treasure some trivial object handled by the other. This is called puppy love and has a peculiar poignancy; it is often remembered with special wistfulness for a lifetime.

Hedonism. In some instances the new capacities for pleasure, both in masturbation and in other forms of sensuous experience, cause a child to give himself up to a surge of sensation seeking. The latency defenses have crumbled, and there has not been time for the erection of a new organization. The young ego falls prey to the pressure of the instincts, and a pattern of instinctual abandonment follows. Dancing, smoking, sex play with others, masturbation, attempts at drinking, experimenting with drugs, joy riding, gorging at meals and stuffing junk food between meals, all manner of body pleasures temporarily dominate the life of a young person. Inevitably such a pattern exposes the youth to the many dangers associated with ungoverned expression of instinct. Accidents occur, the police are often involved, pregnancy is a potential complication, and tempestuous parent-child relations are predictable sequelae. Usually there is some history of overstimulation in the background of such young people, and the reencounter with the previous memories and fantasies of flooding emotional experiences throws the youngster into a state where he wants to make it all happen again but this time with himself as initiator rather than as passive victim. If no truly catastrophic event ensues, in many instances the sensation hunger does not persist, the old trauma is mastered, the youth settles down, and development proceeds.

Romanticism. At times, the hedonic tendency is more dilute and more idealized. Even at the beginning of puberty, the boy or girl may be forever falling in love, forever swooning over some matinee idol, or peer, or both. The newly aroused erotic capabilities create a state of emotional disequilibrium, but the ego strength is greater than that of the hedonic youth. He moons, writes poetry, loses himself in loud music, lives in a state of impassioned fantasy, takes many people into his confidence swearing them each to secrecy, and never quite touches earth. School work may go on as usual, but often enough this is bowled over as the youth's cognitive processes are temporarily derailed by the invasive romantic fantasy. There is usually little acting out of the yearnings and dreams; things stay on the level of wish and compromise. Again, the state is time limited and gradually gives way to a more realistic and balanced appraisal of self and other. The ego is basically competent, and no very dramatic behavior occurs. Occasionally, wish-fulfillment yearnings are sufficiently powerful to cause a youngster almost to believe a fantasy and to tell tall tales of an encounter with some famous, longed for "star."

Moodiness. Where the affective charge is powerful, but the superego strictures are more powerful still, many a youth becomes moody, irritable, and mildly depressed. The depression is complex; it is compounded by the feelings of loss associated with the decathexis of the parents plus the sense of guilt associated with the powerful aggressive and erotic yearnings that the superego condemns so roundly. The loss experience can be intense; after all, the parents have been the major figures in the child's life from the outset. To give them up at one fell swoop is no minor matter; one has abandoned the closest and most supportive attachment one has ever known. But they must be given up nonetheless, and a sadness without source steals over the youth's life. People about him note that he is down and peevish and morose "for no reason." Occasionally such youngsters will have flashes of anger and lash out bitterly and inexplicably—at some family member. Occasionally they will be glowering and depressed until a phone call comes from a good friend and they brighten up and become different people. This fluid and fickle emotionality is typical of the time of life; the moody adolescent is no rare variety.

Boredom. One major defensive position many youngsters adopt is to repress the incestuous longings and rages, and, to make sure that the repression holds, they partially withdraw cathexis from the world of objects. They become disinterested rather than deeply involved; life offers them choices and opportunities and pleasures—and none of it looks good. It's not what they want. (What they want is forbidden and hidden, even from themselves.) They experience a sense of boredom; there is a quality of strain in their lives, of a restless yearning for something, but they don't know what it is. All they know is that, for all the things they do have, nothing is very interesting or attractive, nothing seems to carry with it any promise of gratification. A sense of grayness or drabness falls over their world (the result of the withdrawal), life seems dull and cheerless, and they drag along for a while feeling unfulfilled, dissatisfied, and going through the motions of living like mechanical automata.

Shyness and inhibition. A rather common sequence comes about as the result of a compromise of forces. Many youngsters arrive at puberty with overly developed superego inhibitions. With the surge of instinct, there is an attempt on the one hand to attach their love interest to the outside world. At the same time, there is a tendency on the other to view such frank libidinous wishes as expressive of a sense of wickedness. The inner voice is clear and firm. Sex is wrong, lust is forbidden, pleasure is sinful, and action is absolutely precluded. In particular, it is the inhibition of action which some youngsters find most distressing. They may tell themselves that the way they feel is wrong, that they want romance. But in the presence of the opposite sex they become shy. They can't think of a word to say. They don't know what to do with their hands. Their heads are filled with alarm bells going off because of the terrible impression they feel they are making. But they can do nothing about it. Their verbal capacities are paralyzed; they stammer, utter banalities, and are covered with confusion. There is a state of literal ego inhibition brought about by their superego pressures.

This painful condition is not confined to the erotic life. It may appear in authority-related situations or under competitive circumstances where aggressive impulses come into play. The characteristic quality of inhibition, shyness, embarrassment, and inability to function has many roots in early experience. Often it involves the reliving of some traumatic situation when the aggressive or erotic impulse was seen by the small child as contributing to something painful (perhaps a family breakup or the injury of a sibling). The superego is at once attempting to protect the ego from a recurrence of the painful event and to punish it for what had happened. The pressures of the new puberty yearnings bring this conflict to the fore, and for a while it may be paralyzing. Again, however, as adolescence progresses, ego strength and mastery capacities grow and mature so that presently the inhibition and the shyness exist more in memory than in day-to-day living.

Asceticism. A more extreme formal compromise between resurgent id impulses and the sense of wrongness that comes from superego reaction is a movement into asceticism. It is important to distinguish this from anhedonia. The latter is a state of inability to experience pleasure; the ascetic is capable of pleasure but eschews it. Ultimately his pleasure comes from the renunciation of pleasure or from the mastery of his own yearnings for pleasure. This is not a trivial distinction. The individual who obtains gratification from the sense of worthiness that derives from giving up the pleasures of the flesh is on the high road toward moral masochism. This is the studious youngster who looks down on the dirty words, dirty jokes, sexual teasing, and accounts of sexual achievement of his peers. His gratification comes from his sense of righteousness and worthiness; he gives up on the frightening possibilities hinted at or, in fantasy, frankly offered by his resurgent pubertal id in favor of the warm glow of goodness and approval tendered him by his newly alerted, frowning superego. There are occasional falls from grace in the face of temptation, which send him into paroxysms of guilt, annealing a resolve never to do that again. A certain melancholy intellectualism hovers over such youngsters, and they often drown themselves in a sea of work and activities in order to shore up the sense of doing the right thing and to keep themselves distracted from the nagging inner voices of the id.

This type of asceticism (Freud, A. 1966) differs in basic ways from the youngster who glories in his mastery over his appetites. Here is the larval anorexic, the proud virgin who boasts that he has never masturbated, the youngster who often enough covers up a terror of loss of control by becoming a supreme master of control. As a rule, there is also a second tier of defense. Merely keeping impulse at bay is not enough; one needs to do more. Such youngsters may become expert in some discipline involving the body— anything from running, tennis, or gymnastics through ballet dancing, or horseback riding. The sense of mastery of the body, of disciplining the self so that the body obeys utterly and totally the dictates of the mind, of forcing the recalcitrant flesh to submit and obey, is the high point of pleasure for such youths. It confirms and reinforces their supremacy over the terrifying threats of id eruption and may become the single dominant focus of their lives. There are a multitude of "syndromes of normality" which may characterize early adolescence. These varieties shade over into more clearly diagnosable conditions, although at best, many complex constellations of troubled adolescent adapatation defy any conventional categorization.

The Encounter with a New Physique

Appearance

One of the most obvious shifts in behavior between latency and adolescence is the increase in the interest each young person experiences in his own body. Boys tend to study their musculature; girls their faces and figures. They may spend hours in front of the mirror, or they may avoid mirrors or look at the mirror out of the corner of their eyes, telling themselves that they don't really care about the changes and how they look—but they are all vitally concerned.

Deviations in Height

The short youth has often looked forward eagerly to springing up in height with all sorts of associated fantasies of strength, command, domination, superiority, sexual attractiveness, and prowess. When the movement into puberty fails to bring about the longed for advance, a considerable element of stress is often added to the work of development, and a sense of real mourning ensues for the person one hoped to be. The youngster may have to cope with many angry jealous feelings; a considerable measure of narcissistic injury is inflicted on him. The fact that life is unfair may reverberate in his thoughts for many days, and a tendency toward overcompensation may emerge. He may become quarrelsome, loud, or provocative; he may start to strut, or to clown. He may seek to develop some special capacity like good school work or playing an instrument well; or he may seek to ally himself with bigger, stronger youngsters, even to the point of becoming delinquent (with them and, in a sense, for them). Girls are less vulnerable than boys in this respect, but unusually short girls may also feel marked by this factor.

The sense of shortness is often experienced as a form of castration (indeed the joke is to call such a youngster "sawed off") (Rotnem et al. 1977). The nicknames and teasing that may fall to his lot confirm the sense of lack, of injury. Sometimes the readiness for people to view him as younger than his age is reacted to vigorously; behavior may become precociously mature in an effort to deal with the threat. Occasionally a boy or girl may prefer to take advantage of his childlike appearance and the uses of infantility, helping him ward off the sense of incompetence engendered by the advances of puberty. A common sequence is for the teenager to keep hoping that growth may come later; this hope becomes particularly poignant when thinking ahead to dating and socializing.

The unusually tall youth, on the other hand, has quite a different problem. The girl will often bemoan her height and feel gawky and undesirable. All the childhood sense of injury that comes with the discovery of sexual differences may be rekindled. She may feel cheated, unfairly treated, and lacking the comely form that others possess. Anxiety may pervade the formation of her sense of an attractive self, which, at this stage of development, is a formation of critical and sensitive proportions. The narcissistic injury of not feeling lovable reverberates in mutually augmenting fashion with the earlier anal-phallic theme of feeling castrated. The sense of personal deformity, of lacking congruence with an idealized image of femininity can "dog" the awareness of many an impressionable young pubertal girl. The growth itself feels like the body is out of control, and a certain helplessness is sometimes injected into the youngster's emotional state. Some girls attempt to adapt by stooping or somehow contracting their posture to deemphasize their height. Others, of course, make realistic adjustments and keep an eye out for tall boys with whom they will feel comfortable and who won't feel uncomfortable with them.

The tall boy has a different problem. Throughout childhood, the unusually large boy is always at risk. Again and again he is warned that he must not be aggressive, that he is bigger and therefore should not attack others or even hit back if attacked. The entire development of the aggressive component of personality can be skewed by such a rearing. Inhibition, anxiety, fear of loss of control, chronic resentment at being picked on and always in the wrong, tinged with an uneasy sense of guilt, are likely to characterize the unfolding of such a boy. Where the strictures are less and the child does use his strength at will, tendencies to preserve a grandiose self-concept cannot be adequately resolved, and serious deformations of peer relationships may ensue. He can all too easily become an aggressive bully who achieves a form of self-realization through terrorizing other children by his sadism and who harbors megalomanic fantasies of power.

Such large children are constantly assumed to be older than their peers, and various social expectations are directed toward them prematurely. For the child with a more competent ego, such expectations can serve as a spur to growth. For some youngsters, however, it means a crushing sense of inferiority since they are forever asked to accomplish at a level beyond their capacities; for others it acts to augment their inclination toward grandiosity. The large child, like the small one, can be genuinely vulnerable.

Problems in Breast Development

For girls, the earliest evidence of puberty and a primary expression of their femininity comes with the growth of their breasts. These are attributes which are culturally vested with enormous powers to arouse the passions of males and are hence central to the entire mystique, the magical aspect of femininity. The breasts are therefore regarded by the growing girl with intense interest and not a little concern. Their shapeliness is an important issue, but far more important is the simple element of quantity. Breast development, like height, can go awry, either through too little or too much. Somewhat similar dynamics are at work, with the special quality of being closely tied to the sense of gender identity. It is not unusual for the girl to seek to compensate for too small breasts by padding her clothes or to reduce the too large bosom by surgery. The presence of some imperfection in this aspect of her body can wound her sense of competent femininity to a serious degree. The resulting injury to her feeling of personal attractiveness can be considerable. The invidious comparisons to other family members may heighten oedipal tensions; the teasing of peers can find a ready target in generating feelings of inadequacy, even of ugliness. To some extent, the breasts have compensated for the former encounter with castration concerns. The body phallus equation to which so many girls turn after their initial sense of disappointment and the feeling that all of the body is beautiful, sexual, exciting, and very much worth displaying become resurgent with puberty. The development of the body contours is watched anxiously to be sure they retain and increase their allure. Anything which detracts from this therefore figures largely in the girl's sense of competence as a lovable sexual being in general, and as a female in particular. The flat-chested girl can feel castrated, deprived, masculinized, and lacking something essential. The heavy-breasted girl may feel sloppy, freakish, a slob, even ugly and deformed. Occasionally such body problems feed into other difficulties a girl may harbor and lead to attempts to overcompensate by sexual willingness. Sometimes such girls become "boy crazy," "throw themselves at boys," and recount that no one will like them if they are not sexually available. Given a somewhat different basic personality organization, a profound shyness and self-consciousness may ensue with some feeling that everyone is noticing and looking at their "problem."

Squeaky Voice

An analogous although by no means identical problem for the boy is the matter of change of voice. Unlike breast development which ushers puberty in, voice change tends to come at the close of pubertal transformation. Again, unlike breast development, it is subject to some measure of voluntary control. For example, a youth with excessive attachment to his mother did not lose the squeaky high-pitched quality of his vocalization until he left home and went off to college where quite literally overnight he spoke in a deeper and more masculine voice. The child voice clings at once to the image of self as child and to the sense of self as effeminate. One need face neither the rigors of independence nor the responsibilities of masculinity. Nor has one separated from mother; one has her voice and thus her presence with one constantly. The voice is the father's phallus; it is potency; it is an instrument of penetration, of self-assertion, of aggression. The failure to achieve depth and an adequate measure of loudness means castration, effeteness, and infantility.

Acne

Perhaps no other physical problem of adolescence is as ubiquitous as a distressing skin condition. For many youngsters it is experienced as a mark of shame, a signal of badness. It has at times been held to betoken masturbation, the hidden inner secret that suddenly blossoms forth for everyone to see. More often it is experienced as something that mars, defaces, and makes ugly, something that injures one's sense of narcissism. There is a quality of a botched self, a who-ness that no one would really care for, that permeates the youngster's sense of social experience. For the vulnerable youth, either the compensatory or the withdrawal reaction noted above may follow.

Unusual Physique

Physical differences may play a very considerable role in the ease and comfort of pubertal adjustment. In particular, large buttocks may become a focus of intense concern and enormous preoccupation. A boy may experience them as suggesting homosexuality or effeminacy; he watches anxiously to note whether anyone's eyes fix on this part of his body; he fantasies what he might look like from behind, or, perhaps worse still, from the side. It is as though all the growth fears of pubertal change become concentrated in this one area. A strong regressive element is present, the phallic phase issues of the time are too much, and the interests of the boy take an anal form. At some level he feels like a youngster whose pants are full after an anal accident and who fears discovery; this kind of fear is actually a compromise with the greater fear of oedipal challenge and retaliation. Guilt gives way to shame; one is less concerned with castration and more worried about the humiliation of being looked at and laughed at. Paradoxically, a certain number of young people who go through such as experience seek surgical relief. They invoke a cutting off of the feminine parts to protect the masculine self, a sort of castration in the service of preservation, or giving up the feminine part of the self in order to maintain the masculine core.

In general, any blemish, any deficiency, any aspect of the body that is deemed unattractive or that challenges the sense of gender identity evokes a host of reactions which will take their character from important early fixation points.

If oral phase, symbiotic stress has been a significant factor in development, the sense of narcissistic injury may be paramount. The flawed symbiotic unity leaves a trace in a sense of unresolved grandiosity coupled with excessive fragility. The perfection of the self is a constant issue that alternately puffs up to unreal proportions or radically collapses into a sense of painfully deflated worthlessness.

The cognitive intellectual functions may or may not be caught up in this process. If they are affected, a stubborn type of pseudo-mental retardation may emerge along with major difficulties in relationships. If they are spared, the picture is one of an intelligent child who is too vulnerable, self-centered, and grandiose to have any sort of adequate peer relations. Puberty is likely to be a particularly hard time for such a youngster since he can tolerate no criticism, needs desperately to believe in his own perfection and superiority, and yet is confronted constantly by the discrepancies between what he would like to believe and the way reality in fact presents itself to him. If puberty brings with it any of the conditions noted here, he is likely to be in a chronic panic state over the huge deficit, the tremendous destructiveness this invasion of his perfection implies.

The anal-phase child going through the rapprochement stage of object relations is particularly vulnerable. He can be profoundly affected by stressful experiences, and any sufficiently traumatic event results in fixation at this level. It is a time for consolidating a sense of autonomy, of making the first tentative explorations into what independence is all about, of constructing a first shadowy body image, of the beginning establishment of a sense of self as actor and doer; but all these processes are new and fragile and may be radically compromised. The result may be an inclination toward passivity, a sense of futility, and a chronic need for clinging attachment which easily becomes hostile dependency.

Disturbances of Development

Gender Identity Problems

The pubertal period is a critical moment for the consolidation of gender identity. For some children, the initial assumption of a sense of gender is probably accomplished by 12 months; for all children it is certainly achieved by 24 months. Gender differences are clearly recognized and responded to by 18 months. In many instances, patterns of disturbed sexual identity are recalled or can be recognized by 3 or 4 years of age. Even before they come close to adolescence, many children are known as tomboys, sissies, or otherwise somewhat atypical in their expressions of sexual identity. Puberty itself, with its major addition of phallic interest, can sometimes provide a paradoxical masculinity or femininity to a child who is basically confused in his orientation. With the injection of reinforced phallic drive, the passive sissy becomes more like a regular boy or the tomboy more conventionally feminine—for a while. As young adulthood is reached, however, the extra input tapers off, and the basic equilibrium is likely to be reestablished.

On the other hand, many sexual and gender problems surface in puberty for the first time. Incest may be triggered by the developing sexuality of the boy or girl. Impulsive acts of public masturbation, exhibitionism, or voyeurism may be functions of the new-found sexual pressures encountering an undeveloped ego. Precocious sexual experience and pregnancy are the result of a variety of individual, social, and cultural factors; the sexual exploitation of younger children by the teenager is likely to first manifest itself at this time, and in some cases, prostitution is now initiated. Some children have engaged in frankly homosexual practices since relatively early childhood, but many a boy or girl who has formerly had no hint of such interests now begins to notice sexual responsiveness to the bodies of same-sex peers (in locker rooms, showers, swimming, etc.) for the first time. If mild in degree, this can be a very common complication of normal development (stemming from earlier negative oedipal experience). But in many cases the youth is not prepared and when it happens, it may have enormous meaning to him, often begetting morbid concerns about being homosexual.

Along with these instances are the cases in which homosexuality as a primary source of gratification now become manifest. Sometimes a latent pattern is triggered by a homosexual seduction; sometimes heterosexual experiments turn out to be strangely disappointing, and a "chance" encounter reveals the predominant pattern. There are instances where powerful homosexual fantasies are pushed aside for long time, and a determined effort is made to be as heterosexual as possible, to assert one's gender by vigorous action. The youngster becomes sexually hyperactive "macho," or "boy crazy." Such excesses may have their own complications, and complex patterns of adjustment can ensue.

Precocious and Delayed Puberty

Of particular interest are the circumstances attending precocious and delayed puberty. The girl who shows breast development at 8 and begins to menstruate at 9 is radically out of synchrony with her friends and classmates. She is often painfully self-conscious, confused, and embarrassed by what is happening to her. She doesn't understand it, nor, even after it is spelled out to her, can she readily explain it to others. The factor of parental support and guidance, of help by school teachers, and of explanations, education, and reassurance by family physicians can be of incalculable value. On the other hand, an anxious peer who expresses his tension through sadistic teasing can be a source of pain in her life. Her peer group often needs some help if she is not to be excluded or in some way exploited. Paradoxically, the full gamut of pubertal emotions does not coincide with biological transformations. Strong sexual interests and the moodiness or tempestuous quality of the time may not come until a few years later. Without considerable support, such children can have radical misconceptions about what is happening to them. They may feel sick, wounded, different. They fear they may bleed to death. The sense of things being out of control is pervasive, and the latency ego is shaken; sometimes such children become anxious or depressed. They fancy what is happening is a punishment or the result of something they did wrong. The increased vulnerability of such children to exploitation is always a factor; if a seduction does occur, the guilt and confusion are surely heightened.

Given adequate management, this kind of precocity need not be a significant disturber of development; lacking that, it can cast a cloud over the sense of self that will take many years to dispel.

In boys, precocity has its own problems. Here the sexual issues are perhaps less prominent than the aggressive ones. The big boy, as noted, is always marked as a potentially destructive fellow in the rough and tumble of latency peer interaction and, to the extent that he internalizes the warnings, experiences himself as dangerous, threatening, a sort of monster. He can deal with this by identification with this image and become a bully; or he can try to undo it and become inhibited and paralyzed. Again, appropriate parental support and competent management at school can avoid these problems and allow development to proceed normally.

Delayed puberty, on the other hand, carries quite a different weight of emotional stress. Feelings of inadequacy tend to prevail, a sense of unfairness—one lacks what everyone else has, one is left out, left behind. The boy worries about the size of his genitals; he is patently smaller than his peers, and castration anxiety begins to mount. In some instances, the youngster has had many conflicts about growing up; under such circumstances the delay may bring with it a measure of relief. But the partial peer exclusion that prevails, along with the constant experience of being treated as though one were younger, is a strong goad to make development an object of great concern. For the girl the situation is different but not much better. It is baffling and frustrating to the adolescent to feel that she is lacking in this essential dimension that so preoccupies her peers, and she often feels alarmed and woebegone. More than that, the childhood castration complex which would presumably have been laid to rest long ago is now reawakened, and a tremendous envy is felt toward those who are "ahead."

Dynamically, the sense of punishment is often present. The oedipal pressures cause the youth to experience what is happening as the outome of his wrongdoing or as his victimization at the hands of antagonistic and vengeful parents. In particular, the loss of the ticket of admission to the sexual/social framework of adolescent relationships means a dismaying sense of exclusion from the critically important peer experience.

Accidents

Accidents are one of the major causes of death in adolescence. They are less of an issue during puberty than in mid and late adolescence, but the groundwork is laid down at this time.

There is no single etiologic sequence that makes for this class of events. Instead, a concatenation of developmental factors works synergistically to create a state of accident proneness.

To begin with, the acquisition of a mature body is a heady thing, a seductive evocative experience that leads one to want to use that body, to do things with it. The reflexes are fast at this time of life, and there is pleasure in exercising them.

The newly augmented sensuous capacities of the time (for the first time in the life cycle the capability of orgasm is present) lead to a kind of sensation hunger; the youth is possessed by an urgent need to feel. Excitement, thrills, novelty—every kind of stimulating experience beckons invitingly, and the avid youngster responds. He seeks opportunities for such stimuli-rich encounters, inevitably thrusting himself into situations that have high accident potential.

In effect, he is unlimbering a whole new range of ego functions which he seeks to exercise and to master. And the pleasure of such mastery is intense.

The superego is calling out warnings, commands, prohibitions, and inhibitions; the youngster is bridling in the face of these and beginning to study an inner presence which implies a certain tendency to challenge warnings and test out forbiddens. Why shouldn't one do what one feels like doing anyway?

The superego is also sending out castration messages—the punishment for rivalrous self-assertion is exactly that. The youngster must deal with this beacon of anxiety, and he may do so by a series of counter-phobic maneuvers. He turns toward the anxiety signal and says in effect, "I do not fear you; I will not let myself be panicked. No, on the contrary, I like you; you give me a thrill. I will seek you out; I will beard you, just to show you you don't scare me; just to show everyone how I like to play with you." The youngster provokes the forbidden, races past the policeman, dives into the quarry pool, climbs the dangerous mountain—to prove something.

In boys this is often associated with the sense of ordeal, with proving one's manliness. What the exhibitionist seeks to establish crudely and directly, most young people need to demonstrate in more sublimated and socially appropriate fashion. But it does involve doing manly things, and the fear of teasing if one avoids such acts is one of the powerful shapers of childhood and youth. Manliness is thus an important source of danger-seeking behavior present in everything from a bar mitzvah ceremony to a hazing. The ordeal is to perform a feat before a large audience or before a group of one's peers. A test of one's manhood is present throughout.

Finally, the general increase in emotionality during this period leads to a greater tendency to act out impulses, an action proclivity which is one of the distinguishing features of this time of life. The amount of personal tension adolescents experience, the anxiety, guilt, sensation hunger, and general pressure of instinct combine to sweep them toward various forms of tension discharge. Action obviously is a most efficient channel for such expression and is part of the normal economics of the epoch.

There may, in addition, be more direct factors in the neurological and hormonal rearrangements of this time of life that might lead to such a phenomenon.

It becomes a complex matter to distinguish the "specific" cause of accidents or even the potentially accident-prone youth from the "safe" one. Statistically, insurance companies have found that they had better raise rates when an adolescent is added to the family's roster of drivers; but that those adolescents who are doing well in school tend to have fewer accidents and hence need pay lower premiums.

Those youngsters whose basic orientation is toward externalization rather than internalization are the more likely to be caught in patterns of adaptation which make for such impacts with the surrounding reality. A variety of diagnostic categories fall into the column of the accident prone.

Adolescent Depression

Categories of depression appear at this time of life. Some are indigenous; they reflect the adolescent process and are specific to it. Others are carryovers of earlier depressive constellations, with the specific forms of their current expression now shaped by the dynamic configuration of puberty. Still others begin at this time of life and continue on into adulthood.

Exogenous Types

Identity structures and characterologic defense patterns which have stood the test of time and served the child well for years now shatter, fragment, and lose both form and function. These include: the identity of self-as-child which is the hallmark of latency; the body-image pattern which forms part of that identity but which contains outlines and definition of its own; the sense of connectedness to one's past so that the continuity of growth seems interrupted and one feels estranged from the uses of the immediately preceding life one has lived. The integrity of the bonds to the parents, the distancing devices that fend off oedipal incestuous and destructive wishes are hard at work protecting the still immature ego from the lashings out of the newly aroused superego; and the larger relationship to one's world shifts radically as development progresses. The latter is aided by the culture's decision in many instances to transfer youngsters from grade school to junior high and then to high school on the basis of age or academics rather than in response to attained level of developmental achievement.

In addition to the disruptions are the many new and threatening areas of exploration that open up. The shift from a homosexual to a heterosexual orientation toward peers is exciting, inviting, and frightening. The ability to understand and grasp the abstract and the conceptual usually brings enrichment, but it can also mean discomfort. Suddenly one understands what has been going on all these years, and it is shocking. This can be experienced in connection with politics, religion, racial issues, father's role at work, or family relationships. In brief, there is a loss of something, innocence if you will, a loss of continuity and the safe structure of things as they have always been.

And this loss begets pain. The pain is expressed as sadness, moodiness, a kaleidoscopic shifting of emotions back and forth. The youngster passes through dark spells and displays all the evidences of an ego under stress. He manifests irritability and touchiness; he is restless and full of vague inexpressible longings for he knows not what. He may become listless, bored, and apathetic; his school work may suffer, and he is hard to talk to. Or the shift may take a more explosive turn and he becomes quarrelsome, cantankerous, and easily upset. Apathy and gloom may settle down for a time. Avoidance can be a particularly serious complication.

Where the depressive mood is truly developmental in origin there is usually a cardinal sign present—the youngster's unhappiness is immediately relieved by peer interaction. No matter how much of a blue funk he is in, if a friend comes calling or even phones, he brightens immediately. If he is unable to go to school that day, he can still get to the game that night. It is a syndrome soluble in peer group interaction.

Psychophysiological Reactions

As is true of every epoch in the life cycle, many youngsters going through puberty experience their distress in part at least in terms of body sensations and malfunctions. Two of the commonest forms of such difficulty are headache and vague abdominal pains. In the more vulnerable youngsters, the sheer stress of growth and change seems by itself to be cause enough for such reactions. Add to that the many individual encumbrances which converge on that moment in life, and there is no lack of challenge posed to the adaptive mechanisms of the ego. The internalizing adolescents will often experience psychophysiologic symptoms under the same circumstances which drive the externalizers toward confrontation with their environments. In either instance, the person encounters a set of circumstances which prove too much for him. The feelings of helplessness, of being out of one's depth and unable to cope, of being hurt or shamed or embarrassed or humiliated, and no way to relieve the intense discomfort, all these collectively generate enormous internal pressure. A series of disturbing affects—rage, anxiety, depression—flood the ego and are collectively experienced as intolerable. An overflow phenomenon then occurs, a siphoning off of these tensions into the autonomic nervous system. The biological genetic constitution determines what happens next; in the vulnerable individual there is a *locus resistantia minoris*, a readiest pathway for discharge. This may result in a variety of physical complaints at which point the factors of conditioning and social supports for symptoms become powerful discriminating forces. One way to construe these events is in terms of limbic system imbalance. A series of positive feedback loops in the emotion-associated limbic pathways lead to a flow of neural pulses of progressively increasing intensity. Presently these can no longer be contained within the existing pathways and shoot out into adjacent structures. In the internalizers, the constitutional tendency is such that they pour downward into the hypothalamus. This part of the brain is capable of both secretion and neural discharge. It may therefore impinge upon the pituitary and thus the endocrine system, or it may seek preferentially to pour energy into the autonomic nervous system directly. Or both. At each juncture, the anatomical and physiological history of the individual determines which pathway is facilitated, which organ targeted. There may also be special vulnerabilities present in respect to some aspect of body image which influence the choice of path of discharge. Thus a history of early nurturant problems may precede vague abdominal pains at a later period. Problems with superego formation can pave the way for later headaches, or the overall dimension of ungovernable stress may cause nonspecific symptoms that are more or less chronically present and unrelated in time or circumstance to identifiable precipitating causes. In any case, the resulting pain or dysfunction may set up eddy currents in the ego, foci of preoccupation, cathexis, and body-image disturbance that alter the total economics of the psychic apparatus. These in turn act as additional hindrances to adjustment and complicate the youngster's problems. Or, they may generate secondary adaptations and be employed as excuses to avoid stressful situations such as school or dates. All sorts of subtle cueing within families may facilitate the choice of one symptom pathway rather than another. With sufficient reward and reinforcement of given problems (e.g., mother has herself experienced severe dysmenorrhea and becomes specially concerned about daughter's recurrent stomach aches even though these are not related to her menses), special sensitivities may ensue which increase the likelihood that one particular form of discomfort will be complained of, especially when there is a test at school, or when grandmother comes to visit.

Often these events are part of adaptation syndromes where the youngster lacks good coping methods. There is a sense of social incompetence, of intellectual inability, of defeat in trying to make one's mark in the family or in the world—and the body becomes the bearer of the message: I hurt. This sequence needs to be differentiated from conversion reaction where a symbolic compromise solution to an intense unconscious conflict causes a certain dramatization of a fantasy to be lived out in connection with body image configuration. The conversion reaction is usually found along with other neurotic symptoms in association with a hysterical personality structure. The distribution of the disability defies any known neurological, anatomical, or physiological pathway. The psychophysiological reaction on the other hand may occur with almost any type of personality organization (including the hysterical). Commonly there are specific target structures involved that show demonstrable changes: flushing, blanching, swelling, etc.; in many cases, however, these cannot be demonstrated. Treatment of the conversion reaction may require careful working out of the underlying neurotic conflict. For the psychophysiological disorder, treatment must be addressed at the overall adaptive stresses which the youngster is going through. Supportive measures can often be of considerable benefit.

The Minor Alienation Syndrome

There is a substantial group of youngsters who seek for solutions to their familial and personal problems by action within the larger social framework. They find and join some form of cultural entity that is radically at odds with the matrix within which they have been reared. Although very diverse developmental sequences can give rise to this form of behavior, certain elements of commonality seem impressionistically to be present. Usually there is a background of troubled family affiliations. Perhaps one parent has died, and the other has had a hard time coping; often marital discord, separation, and divorce have marked the parental relationship, sometimes complicated by the insistence of one parent or the other on a particular form of group adherence, be it ethnic, religious, or national. The youngster's efforts to deal with the oedipal issues of puberty are compounded by the marital disruption; it seems all too real to him that he is responsible, his forbidden incestuous and murderous fantasies have influenced the lives of his parents; he is at fault. He cannot use the available cultural structures to expiate his sin; they are part and parcel of the parental realities. If the parents would have him go to the priest or rabbi, he turns to some form of atheism or to some other faith entirely; if his parents encourage psychotherapy, he seeks out any of several convenient religions that specialize in beckoning to the disenchanted. A great many group-oriented religious structures have emerged: Scientology, Reverend Moon's disciples, the Hare Krishna movement, the "Jesus believers," and many smaller communal groups which offer haven and some sort of alternative to family life for such needy young people. In a sense, a peer group is created with adult leadership that promises a chance for a new affiliation in a guilt-free environment. A strong selling point for all such groups is that by the very act of joining, one has shed the burdens of the past and found a way to proceed in one's life with a sense of belongingness, acceptance, and a maintained sense of distance from the past. Of crucial importance in all this is the new ideology. One is no longer the guilty begettor of divorce, one is instead a part of a larger loving entity which understands all, forgives all, and shows how best one should go ahead.

Dynamically, the issues here are largely superego oriented. The peculiar vicissitudes of pubertal superego development lie at the center of this problem. Blos (1958) has indicated how in prepuberty the presence of the pregenital mother dominates the inner life of the child through both the yearning for infantile satisfactions and the fear of the oral, devouring punisher. As puberty proceeds, this presence subsides and is eclipsed by the mounting pressure of the castrating father, at once punitive and ethical. At the outset, such formations are at best undeveloped and primitive, and the youngsters must explore them and rework them with the passage of the months and the years. Gradually, with additional identifications, ever more value-oriented and mature structures emerge which are closer to consciousness and allow for greater freedom to choose ethical stances and appropriate courses of action. In the course of these developments, considerable use is made of experimental value structures often worked out within the context of peer-group interactions. Group attitudes have about them a certain moral force; they are closely akin to the basic psychological nature of superego structure. Normally, these do not altogether replace the internalized familial figures as guides and limits to behavior; they merely allow for richer experience. There is an ongoing testing out and the measuring of one's own superego elements against those of other youngsters with similar dispositions. When growth proceeds in a healthy way, the group values are used to the extent that they enrich and enhance the existing super-ego positions. The youngsters seek to give their moral, ethical, and value stances ever more precise definition, to apply them to all sorts of new situations in order to see how they work, to compare them to the views and values of others, and perhaps to add additional dimensions of structure as they are discovered.

Where the superego formation has been deformed by the nature of the experience with parents, the youngsters may feel as though they harbor an internal enemy. There is a terrible pressure that emanates from this inner presence. The messages that come in from this quarter say: shame! evil! wicked! pay! suffer! The devouring mother has not been put to rest; instead this presence joins the castrative destroyer to create a sense of intolerable threat. The youngster fends these off as best he can, but clearly it is an impossible position. Either he gets depressed, perhaps even kills himself, or he externalizes the entire sequence and strives to live it out in some way. He may try to flee from it into group affiliations that will take over and help him blanket these inner experiences—hence the all-too-ready affiliation with superego-oriented social structures that seem to have so much appeal to so many youngsters.

There are rage, frustration, and hurt connected with such a syndrome. The child is intensely troubled by the serious conflicts within and the pain engendered by this inimical inner presence. He blames the parent(s) for his distress and feels deeply wounded by their failure to protect him from this dismaying experience. It is his fault that things went wrong, but somehow it is their fault too. He wants to disaffiliate himself from these pain engenderers, to distance himself from what they stand for, and he wants to get even with them. The consequences of this alienation are often of catastrophic proportions. The parents have been having enough difficulty; suddenly their problems are compounded. There is a peculiar pleasure in the act of parenting that comes from seeing one's values transmitted. Each parent offers his child the beliefs, attitudes, and traditions that he himself holds most dear. And each child must make a decision to accept or to reject. When things go well, the acceptance seems automatic, inevitable. The youngsters certainly see other models which seem curious, eccentric. They can't really imagine behaving other than as their parents and their culture would have it; it is the only way that makes sense. Here the superego is well integrated, without the quality of hostile and critical assertiveness that is the case with the more troubled youth.

Often enough, however, as adolescence gets under way, the youngster begins to question the old ways and to explore alternative values. The parents observe this process with concern. There are always occasional notes of anxiety as the youth questions some tenet of faith, or experiments with alternative ways of life. And then there is the intense gratification when this experiment ends with a return to the basic value position the parents set forth. This transmittal of values, if successful, is one of the most positive reward aspects of parenting and is associated with moments of intense conscious pleasure.

When the transfer of values does not work well, the distress that accrues to parents is intense. There is a mixture of feelings stirred up by such an event: a profound narcissistic injury that the self, offered here in its most ideal form, has been judged and found wanting. There is a deep sense of guilt that one's responsibilities as a parent have not been carried out—one has failed in a major way to pass on one's traditions. Some sense of the extent of parental reaction can be arrived at by noting the frequency with which oral themes are reported by such parents. In his new guise their child sickens them; they are disgusted by his appearance or attitudes. Aside from what it does to the quality of parent-child interaction, the combination is often appalling in its effects on parental self-concept and self-value. In generating these feelings, the alienated youth takes his revenge. Occasionally parents respond by totally disaffiliating themselves from the youth; they disown or disinherit him. But the dry ashes of that "victory" are small solace in the face of the object loss, the narcissistic injury, and superego pain they experience.

Group Delinquency

A somewhat different form of alienation occurs when the youngster's super-ego pathology does not lead him so much toward cultural disaffiliation as toward aggression. He does not turn away from the value set, to embrace another, he turns toward it and attacks. He enters the complex and difficult world of antisocial behavior about which more is written and less understood than almost any other aspect of adolescent maladjustment.

There are an enormous number of categories of acting out. But one variety is discussed here: the youngster who does not seem individually to commit depredations, but who takes part in activities initiated by a group of peers. He seems weak and is easily led; he seems to seek companionship and peer acceptance rather than revenge or an outlet for his rage. It would appear that he wants to keep up, to avoid being shamed or teased or left out, and he joins in gang activities for that reason. When caught, he seems fearful and guilty and promises never to do it again, but often enough is back with the gang immediately and continues as before.

In such cases the dynamic element is typically a combination of ego and superego pathology. Among other things, there are present a basically low sense of self-esteem and a chronic low-grade rage that remains masked and seldom surfaces as such. Phenomenologically it is far more likely to appear as passivity and/or sullenness. The feelings of attachment to parents are weak; somehow the youngster has emerged from his developmental sequence with no great feeling of being loved or valued, and with a considerable sense of having been cheated. Much of this is quiet; he doesn't say a great deal or think about them in quite these terms. Instead, he seeks out and finds other angry youths and groups who will speak for him. His operating superego is without clear values. The values lack the introjected quality of authority of which Sandler (1960) speaks; they are indistinct and ambiguous. However, they are also threatening and inimical, and the youth feels oppressed and pushed from within. The chance to obtain relief by joining a group and letting the group mores take over the superego function is heaven-sent; it brings a measure of real relief. No longer must one knuckle under; as part of the group one has joined a functioning superego-like entity, and doing what everybody does "somehow" makes it OK. The group catalyzes the expression of the otherwise suppressed impulses and is sought out for precisely that reason. All these youngsters have the opportunity to join other groups of nondelinquent charac- ter which they cannot use because they don't feel as good with other, less angry children. Their sense of self is one of having little to offer, something no one would want very much. They anticipate rejection and failure and can conceive of success and acceptance only because they will join in the acting out. Predators may not be loved, but they are always respected. By letting it be known that they have shared in such exploits, they will be valued, and only then will they find relief for what hurts inside.

As a result, treatment of the group delinquent is not necessarily much easier than of the individual delinquent; the problems are really not superficial. But a greater element of control is present. There is a measure of compromise reached; expression of the antisocial behavior is made contingent on the external factor of the group rather than taking form as a simple, direct expres- sion of the antisocial impulses. On the whole, there is more to work with.

The Adolescent with Minimal Brain Dysfunction

This syndrome is usually diagnosed in latency in connection with school difficulties. The youngsters display characteristic patterns of hyperactivity, dis- tractibility, poor attention span, difficulties in certain patterns of movement, and, in many cases, specific learning deficits. They seem to have egos which are constitutionally incapable of mastering the drives. Even when well social- ized, the youngsters show a good deal of difficulty in "putting on the brakes," especially when they are excited. Their restlessness and awkwardness evoke teasing and many negative social pressures; when their attention and learning deficits lead to poor school achievement, they are regarded or regard them- selves as "dumb." They incorporate a picture of themselves as peculiar, weird, spastic, stupid, or, at best, different in some unfortunate way.

On the basis of EEG, neurological, and laboratory studies, several varieties have been defined. There is a group who displays minor physical anomalies (Waldrop and Halverson 1971; Rapaport et al. 1974); a group who gives evi- dence of low arousal on EEG (Satterfield 1973); a group with soft neurological signs (Werry et al. 1972); a group with reduced levels of monoamines in urine or platelets (Rapaport et al. 1970; Wender 1969; Coleman 1971). Family studies suggest at least some evidence of a genetic factor, as in reports of similar findings in parents and siblings (Satterfield et al. 1974; Millichap 1973).

As these youngsters move into adolescence, the hyperactivity seems to diminish, but the awkwardness may persist and single out the appearance of the youth's activity. More than that, the "attention deficit disorder" remains and continues to plague the youths' attempts to cope with school. A pattern of failure or, at best, of academic inadequacy has been in the picture throughout; now, in adolescence, the demands are greater than ever and the pressures more painful. Who wants to date someone like that? Who wants him at a party? As a result, the accumulated feelings of low self-esteem bear heavily on the youngster's life. These teenagers become depressed, morose, and often irritable and resentful. Their constitutionally weak impulse control apparatus sometimes results in serious eruptions. It has been estimated that many such youngsters (perhaps a quarter) drift into delinquency, and about 10 percent have police records. Longer range followups have suggested that some MBD youngsters become seriously emotionally ill (Wood et al. 1976; Menkes et al. 1967).

The ego pathology is central to this disorder. Many ego functions are affected: Perception is distorted; short-term memory is often weakened; the integration of perceptual and expressive patterns is deficient; the regulation of attention and concentration is seriously awry; the ability to screen out extraneous stimuli and to keep figure distinct from ground is abnormal; the management of emotions is poorly accomplished; and the inhibition of impulse is faulty. Motor patterns may be affected. A dysregulation of motor integration is often present with the youngster appearing jerky, awkward, and twitchy. In many such cases the saving grace seems to be that superego organization is not necessarily defective, and many of these boys and girls do reasonably well. Perhaps the largest cohort becomes part of that broad group of youngsters who do not shine at school but who struggle by one way or another, who are regarded more or less as "oddballs," yet who are not so deviant that they fail all social inclusion, and who presently get lost in the general population.

Anorexia Nervosa

This condition is found characteristically as part of puberty. It may occur earlier—it has been reported as early as age 4 (Sylvester 1945)—or later, but the large majority of cases are diagnosed at this time. It occurs far more often in girls than boys (in a ratio of 20:1) and can be most serious. Indeed in various series it has been reported to have a mortality rate between 7 and 25 percent. By and large, it is a condition of the middle class, the relatively affluent, and it appears to be increasing in frequency.

It has been studied and reported on most intensively by Bruch (1972), who divides the condition into primary and secondary varieties. In the secondary forms, the nature of the primary condition may be hysterical, phobic, border-line, depressive, psychotic, or due to some other personality aberration; in such instances the failure to eat is merely the surface symptom. Thus, a hysterical youngster who vomits on the basis of a conversion reaction, a psychotic child with fantasies of devouring and being devoured, or a phobic compulsive youngster afraid of germs—all may avoid eating.

The primary form of the condition, on the other hand, has a unique dynamic configuration and typical symptom picture. The child generally has a history of good behavior, compliance, neatness, and adequate school performance. Somewhere around the beginning of puberty the youngster becomes inter-ested in issues of overweight and diet. Occasionally this comes after an illness, sometimes there is an account of being teased about being fat, perhaps a coach or hygiene teacher has made some remark about weight. In any case, the child decides to go on a diet. Shortly the dieting takes over the youngster's life and a condition of near starvation ensues. There are occasional gluttonous food binges, followed by even more intensive efforts to lose weight. Mean-while, the youngster's activity patterns also change. There is an increasing effort to exercise (this may take the form of calisthenics, running, ballet, or gymnas-tics) which before long assumes a driven character since it is alleged to help with the weight problem. Coupled with the marked aversion to eating is a great deal of interest in what others eat. Some anorexic youngsters love to prepare elaborate meals for their friends and families. There is also an almost panicky reaction to the notion of gaining weight, which is watched with sedulous care.

In its more severe and life-threatening forms, this condition will go on until the patient is physiologically overwhelmed by the combination of overexertion and lack of nourishment, at which point any one of several forms of physiolog-ical failure can follow. As the biological imbalance gets underway, a classical finding is cessation of menses. The blood pressure falls, the body temperature drops, the pulse and respiration slow, and some cases show a light downy hair over the extremities. Emaciation is striking and stands in sharp contrast to the patient's continuing protest about overweight.

Bruch (1972) has described three characteristics which define the anorexic. First, there must be a profound disturbance in body image and concept; the cathexic patient, down literally to skin and bones, speaks worriedly of being too fat. Second, there is a distortion in the way the patient perceives stimuli from within the body. Hunger is not felt, or the patient eats almost nothing and feels full, although in the earlier stages, the patient was much concerned with hunger (Bruch 1978). And third, the patient feels as though she were a passive, ineffectual puppet in the hands of some all-powerful master. A pervasive sense of helplessness permeates the patients' lives, and it is to help cope with this profoundly distressing feeling that they develop anorexia. If they can master nothing else, they can at least control their own bodies and urges. The excesses to which this striving leads them comprise the anorexia syndrome.

Sours (1969) sees three clinical courses as typical of the illness. The first group are girls who develop their symptoms early in puberty. In effect, they are at war with their own pubescence. They seek to stifle sexual form and sexual feeling, to hold back development. To further this, they regress to a mixture of oral and oedipal levels, and the anorexia serves in part to protect them against fantasies of oral impregnation. However, the regression exposes them to a reencounter with the engulfing images of early experience, and by not eating, they seek to master these as well.

The symptoms of the second group tend to appear in middle and late adolescence. These are girls who most closely meet Bruch's criteria for primary anorexia. Primitive defenses such as splitting, projecting, denying, and acting-out predominate. The body-image distortions and the disturbances in inner perception are marked. In particular, the sense of personal ineffectiveness is the hallmark of their adjustment.

The third category are the anorexic boys. They are prepuberty children or young adolescents, usually rather chubby, who fear their newly burgeoning oedipal yearnings. They strive for masculinity by overcoming maternal dependency feelings, or tendencies to merge, and they do so by stopping the intake of nourishment.

There are many secondary characteristics associated with all these young patients, regardless of the subgroup to which they belong. They are often manipulative and deceptive, finding many ways to put off eating or to convince their caretakers that they have indeed eaten (when they have hidden the food or flushed it down the toilet). They argue, bargain, accuse, complain, and are by no means easy to deal with. Careful, precise pediatric management, coupled with close observation and a stringent routine, is basic to their initial biological recovery. Psychotherapeutic intervention is essential, and family involvement is a critical factor for the longer range psychological healing. Behavioral therapy has been tried and is currently felt to be undesirable (short-term improvements are readily achieved at the expense of long-term recurrence), but there is no guaranteed or "standard" means of cure. Recovery comes rapidly in some cases, but many others drag on as chronic problems, regardless of the specific approach.

True Neuroses

The neuroses are usually assumed to take form in latency. Prior to that, the immature ego can develop neurotic symptoms as it strives to cope with some of its conflicts, but it does not have the necessary organization to construct a true neurosis. The presence of the superego supplies the component heretofore lacking; it allows for the full structure of a neurosis to be elaborated.

In particular, this condition speaks for a failed ego operation. It begins with an id impulse contained within an ego defense. But the protective measures of the ego are insufficient, and the resulting configuration partially conceals and partially reveals the forbidden impulse. There is always a measure of success achieved by the efforts to keep the impulse at bay; this is evidenced by the fact that the awareness of the impulse is successfully curtailed (the factor of unconsciousness is here paramount). The element of failure lies in the fact that the patient is not functioning well in some area: He has symptoms which are troublesome and inconvenient. He may have had to become "paralyzed," to lose his voice, to lose his memory, to be obsessed by some troublesome thought, to feel compelled to do some symbolic action, to feel anxious "for no good reason," or to feel depressed "for no good reason." In brief, he develops some thought, feeling, or behavior which is limited in scope, which is felt to be unpleasant and foreign to the smooth functioning of the self, and which spares the rest of the ego.

Hysterical symptoms, anxiety attacks, and neurotic depressive reactions are particularly likely during early adolescence; they represent the initial struggles to keep a cap on the newly emergent erotic and aggressive impulses. Occasionally, these organize into full-blown neurotic conditions that are stable over time.

The Depersonalization Syndrome

Among the common phenomena that characterize pubertal experience is the state of transient depersonalization. Many pubertal youngsters pass through such states for a few seconds or a few minutes at a time. As a rule, these episodes are fleeting in character; when the boy or girl comes out of it, he can scarcely say what has happened, where he has been. Nor is it easy to describe. Occasionally, however, the transformation is not momentary; the youngster gets "stuck" in such a frame of mind and cannot "come back." This disturbing experience gives rise to intense feelings of dismay. It is immensely distressing, sometimes to the point of engendering suicidal ideas. Resolution of the condition is usually spontaneous, but in many instances psychotherapy is necessary to carry the youngster past the sense of despair and to help relieve the symptoms.

The actual experience involves several dimensions. To begin with, the sensory world is altered. Vision seems strange, sometimes all perception is hazy, and the images seem far away. When the youngster stretches out his arm, it appears to be elongated; his hand seems much more distant than the actual length of the arm. Sound, too, is altered; there is a harsh, or brassy, or tinny quality when people speak. Sometimes it is described as though they were talking through some barrier, and always it seems to come from a distance. The distantiation is characteristic of the syndrome.

The feelings about one's body are also very different. It is as though the body belonged to someone else; it has a wooden or a dead feeling. There is a distinct sense of estrangement here, a quality of occupying a body that is in some vital way not one's own. The relationship to thoughts has also undergone a transformation. One's thoughts have a kind of independence; they march across the field of awareness as though they were generated outside the self, as though one were a hapless spectator, while thoughts and actions proceeded on their own. Finally, the feelings are fundamentally changed. They seem muted or absent. One feels unrelated to one's emotions or altogether distant from them. Sometimes they are described as leaden or gone. The whole sense of self is transformed; identity is split. One is a person living his usual life, and one is also a small helpless figure who stands at the side and observes himself react, who reaches vainly for contact with others and with himself, who feels himself barred from access to his world, and who can do nothing to get back. The condition seems to be a form of hysterical dissociation, one that operates defensively at a time of major identity fragmentation and reconstruction. The more transient and commonplace moments of depersonalization seem to emerge from the ego's efforts to integrate all the new elements of ego function and character formation. In a sense, the fleeting experiences of estrangement reflect the occasional slips that occur on the way to assembling this complex array in a balanced and symmetrical fashion.

Occasionally, however, there is a more major disruption in the assemblage of parts of the self. The ego's integrative functions cannot quite make elements match—some affective valence is too intense; some forbidden unconscious conflict too invasive. Things have to be kept apart for a while until the defensive structures can knit a firmer webbing and reconstruct a tighter seam. Instead of uniting the various fragments and functions, they need to be kept isolated for a while, and the syndrome follows.

The major problem is to distinguish between this temporary neurotic solution and the beginnings of a far more serious and persistent psychotic process. Certain schizophrenic syndromes also begin with a state of depersonalization, but in these instances the degree of disturbance is usually far more severe and tends to be progressive. Bizarre notes creep in. Delusions are almost always present. Hallucinations are common; and the quality of the affective state is far more empty as a rule than is true for this syndrome. Occasionally, a period of observation is necessary in order to be certain about the diagnosis.

Problems in Adolescent Sexuality: Pregnancy, Promiscuity, and Incest

The process of transforming the self into a young man or woman is seldom simple. Gender role is assigned by the nurturing environment, gender identity achieved by the work of separation-individuation. As one leaves the initial unity of self and mother, and the later involvement between self and oedipal

couple, a certain element of each is retained. The child incorporates the messages and the models of the circumambience within which he grows and
develops. Where these are discordant and cacophonous, the identity that is
presently forged, including the sexual identity, will be in like proportion
askew. The youth may find himself prey to conflicting models or impulses and
ideals that are radically at variance one with another. The inner signposts which
guide behavior and relationship point simultaneously in different, and
opposed, directions. There is no inner compass that points the way, that tells
one who to be and how to act.

The needs for nurturance and for the elementary protections against primary
loneliness may never have been met. The deepest yearnings of a young devel-
oper's life may center on just such issues; compared to these needs, all other
drives are of secondary force. Thus, one basis for adolescent pregnancy is
formulated again and again by teenage girls who speak of the baby as the
answer to all the pain of early privation. In fantasy, the infant becomes someone all their own, to whom they can show all the love and care that they seek
so urgently for themselves, someone who will need them, love them, and will
not leave them. It is a possession treasured beyond all other treasures, something so uniquely one's own that it is a part of the self. Impregnation and
gestation may become the primary goals of such a life. The girl child may
dislike the act of copulation, fear it, have frightening fantasies about it, about
pregnancy, and especially about childbirth. In spite of all these, she will be
driven by an aching inner emptiness to seek to fill herself with life and thus
relieve the profound depressive void bequeathed by her impoverished childhood. Neither reasoning nor education offer her much protection; the hunger
is too great.

Another force at work in many pregnant teenage girls is the unrelieved stress
of the unresolved castration and oedipal complexes. Thus, a girl may have
been the one female of four siblings; she is bracketed by older and younger
brothers, and her mother fails to understand her plight and help her with her
burgeoning femininity. The girl may grow up always feeling the outsider,
deficient and incomplete. With her entry into puberty, however, her position
changes. Suddenly she is regarded differently; she can command the eyes of
male peers. She has something to offer. She has the power to excite, to make
conquests. She can find worth in the previously despised femininity itself. Her
own uncertain gender identity, her wish to be a boy like the others, her fantasy
at times of really being a boy except for not having a penis, all give way to the
need to assert herself as a girl, to prove that she is fully female. There is no
more certain way to achieve that state than being pregnant. In contrast to the
first group, such girls often can benefit from sex education courses, from rap
sessions, from counseling, or from work with the family.

Under certain conditions, powerful cultural and familial vectors can come to
bear on the pubertal girl and move her toward pregnancy. A mother may send
many covert messages to the budding young woman that she is grown up now,

that mother has lost her baby. Mother recollects with a sigh how when she was 13 she had her own first baby and never loved anybody like she loved that baby. As a matter of fact, mother remarks, she had been grandmother's baby when grandmother was in her teens. Thus, in this, or in some analogous way, the family and the culture it represents impinge on the pubertal youngster and head her in this direction.

Like most conditions, early pregnancy has its primary and secondary forms. Some youngsters do not seek pregnancy as such. They may wish to trick a boy into marrying them or seek an excuse to get out of their homes. They may desire principally to spite a parent, compete with a rival, or demonstrate that nobody can tell them how to behave. The pregnancy, then, is only one of many ways they may invoke to achieve that end. Some youngsters are overwhelmed by the encounter with the sensuous. They seek the sexual experience as such and have no wish to be pregnant; carrying the gestation to term may come about because they are so busy denying and concealing what they are doing that their condition is recognized only when it is too late for safe abortion. The large majority of such secondary syndromes are far more susceptible to preventive or early intervention than are the various examples of primary pregnancy.

The role of the boys who impregnate is beginning to receive a certain attention. Much of their behavior is a result of the sensation hunger of adolescence, the exploratory interest in gratifying body yearnings. They have little or no interest in impregnation. There is a definite subgroup, however, whose emotional situation involves a profound concern about masculinity. There is a pressing need to prove their manliness to themselves and their world. In line with this, they seek to get as many girls pregnant as they can and take pride in the achievements. This often helps shore up a fragile sense of maleness forever tottering on the brink of effeminacy or infantilism—they need this overt, visible demonstration of the fact of their manliness to undo their hidden inner weakness.

Similar dynamics are at work in certain forms of promiscuity. Both boys and girls are likely to discover that their sexual apparatus is a means of bringing people close; it is like a beacon, drawing interest, attention, attempts at conversation, and acts of friendliness. On the part of one partner, these may all be means to an end; but for the deprived, depressed, relationship-starved youth, the bargain is a good one. Instead of a void, there is a presence; instead of emptiness, there is sensation; instead of loneliness, sex play. Words of love are bandied back and forth and gestures of affection exchanged. Perhaps it is all a trick to obtain sexual advantage, but for the moment, at least, it offers the illusion of caring that serves as an anodyne to the pain.

The later forms of promiscuity are often connected to phallic oedipal issues. There is a constant striving to undo castration, to prove one's sexual capacity, to reaffirm the intactness of one's own body, or to overcome the gnawing sense of its defect. This necessity drives many a boy and girl to extremes of sexual hyperactivity that make for very disturbing patterns. The need to overcome the hurt and fear of oedipal encounter can act as a continuing goad and spur protracted attempts to recoup. But each reassurance, each bit of "success," lasts only briefly. The nagging need reappears; the unmastered tension mounts once more and must again be striven with. One young girl with a history of extensive sexual activity described an affinity for married men. During intercourse she would think to herself: What would his wife say if she knew he was doing this? Thus, the youngster's oedipal hunger would be slaked by a momentary "victory" whose effect was as evanescent as the act itself, and she then would need another "victory," and yet another. The permutations and combinations of such needs often lead to intricate patterns of love-hate relationships that enmesh young lives in complex transactions that are even more destructive than they are involved.

Perhaps the most potentially dangerous pattern of this kind is that associated with the direct acting out of oedipal impulses in the form of incest. This is a behavioral sequence that typically embraces a number of elements. Its most common form includes a newly pubertal daughter, an unconsciously compliant mother, and an unstable father. The father is sexually drawn to the daughter's budding sexuality; he begins to explore her body and presently involves her in intercourse. The mother manages to remain oblivious to this or even to foster it, and the pattern, once established, may persist for years. Numerous studies have indicated that both mother and daughter may lend themselves to the maintenance of the arrangement. The child herself is often caught in the midst of conflicting yearnings. On the one hand are the sexuality of puberty and the realization of the oedipal wish. On the other, the full weight of the superego presses on her with a nagging insistent sense of doing something shameful, wrong, forbidden. Often the situation is not revealed until the child begins to tell school friends or neighbors. Sometimes her attempts to report it to her mother lead only to disbelief and punishment. For that matter, this can happen with community people as well.

The long-range outcome was long held to be dismal, but in recent years, studies indicate that a wide spectrum of developmental consequences may occur. Thus, there are instances where a history of incest is reported by apparently well-adjusted adult women or where the subsequent effects appear to be mild. But in the light of the many severe reactions that do occur, it is well to regard it as a serious stress for the child's work of development, one that carries with it the possibility of catastrophic personality disturbance.

Delinquency

One of the most common forms of emotional disturbance in adolescence takes the character of antisocial acting out. Although the subject of intense research over many decades (Martin and Fitzpatrick 1964), it continues to defy easy formulation; an enormous literature has developed. Here only a limited number of different aspects are presented.

Etiology. Antisocial behavior has been variously ascribed to, for example:

1. a given set of social conditions that would affect any population that was subjected to these conditions (Burgess, Lohman and Shaw 1937)
2. an array of personal and behavioral traits characteristic of lower working class populations (Miller 1958)
3. the limited peer group models available which require a child growing up in such a neighborhood to mingle with and, ultimately, to emulate the tough kids (Sutherland 1947)
4. the frustrations attendant on lower class youths who are tempted by, yet lack, any means by which to achieve middle class advantages (Cohen 1955)
5. the rage engendered by the lack of opportunities for upward mobility in a society which demands such progress (Cloward and Ohlin 1960)
6. a lack of affection during early developmental periods (Bowlby 1944)
7. transmission of covert instructions to act out because of familial superego lacunae (Johnson 1949)

There is a clear socioeconomic dimension here; statistically, delinquency is characteristically associated with poverty. Many factors are present at once, such as emotional exhaustion of single parents, lack of adequate care and nutrition during pregnancy and the postnatal period, alcoholism and drug abuse among caretakers, adolescent parenthood, households characterized by the coming and going of many people where interpersonal relationships are attenuated and primitive, emotional instability among significant adults, unpredictable eruptions of violence and brutality, child abuse and sexual exploitation of children, wildly inconsistent management of children, much passing of care responsibilities among caretakers, an absence of stable and wholesome identification models, frequent moves, and chronic lack of adequate funds to ensure a sense of safety and stability in the home. In varying combinations these lead to a childhood characterized by a lack of trust; a paucity of opportunities for forming stable identifications; a ground-in sense of being small, weak, and inadequate in the face of an overwhelming unpredictable world; defensively maintained status of infantile grandiosity; chronic rage at the frequent frustration of the need for care and attention; recurrent depressive reactions because of shifts from home to home and caretaker to caretaker; periodic episodes of flooding overstimulation as a result of sadistic abuse and sexual exploitation during the infantile period, along with lack of adequate stimulation of cognitive functions; patterns of spotty health care that might fail to deal with early lead intoxication; the effects of undiagnosed and untreated petit mal, temporal lobe, or even grand mal epilepsy; and undetected disturbances of vision and hearing, along with a variety of other physical disorders.

The result is a suspicious, distrustful child who experiences a sense of basic unfairness in the very fabric of things. The youngster cannot develop good impulse controls and faces life in a state of chronic rage. Again and again, he must deal with the consequences of loss of control. Later on he cannot concentrate or learn in school. If he has the ego strength, the street teaches him to become wily, manipulative, and an excellent dissimulator. He learns to be devious and opportunistic; and he never learns to be other than totally self-centered. Social and sexual relationships are exploitative and exhibitionistic. He is early attracted to the "rackets" and gets used to lots of money. And a sizable fraction of his youth will be spent in various lockups and industrial schools.

The less gifted youth is likely to lack the ego capacities to become an adequate manipulator; his fate is therefore to be read in the annals of the violent and the vandalistic. He is filled with anger, bitterness, and self-hate and can be merciless and vicious in his depredations. In the course of an interview, he is likely to be silent and monosyllabic, often sullen and negative, and usually lacking in the ability to express fantasy. Fixations are at a level where anal sadism and power struggles dominate his horizon.

The more sensitive or more vulnerable youth is likely to add the dimension of drug abuse or alcoholism to his lifestyle. This becomes a major begetter of delinquent behavior in its own right, as well as a source of numerous destructive medical complications.

Often the attempts such youngsters make to help themselves are aborted by their organic difficulties. The residue of lead poisoning and the malnourished brain, the chronic interference of undiagnosed seizure potential (petit mal or psychomotor temporal lobe discharges), the disruptive effects of MBD or some low-grade chronic brain syndromes, the stress of trying to adapt with subnormal vision or hearing, or the vitiating effects of other chronic diseases which are not properly cared for, may singly or in combination pose insuperable hurdles for even the well-motivated child to overcome. The acting-out pattern appears during the early years at school and continues throughout childhood and youth. By the time puberty arrives, the youngster is wise in the ways of the street and firmly locked into his characterologic set. In brief, certain forms of socioeconomic stress seem to be prime breeders and maintainers of a state of antisocial adjustment.

It is all too evident that many other forms of delinquency exist. Dynamically, the approach to etiology is couched in somewhat different terms. In order to give some sense of the way these syndromes are constructed, three etiologic factors are described along with some of the prime ego mechanisms that are typically present.

The etiology of these conditions seems primarily environmental. Various genetic theories have been advanced, but none has really fulfilled its promise. The environmental factors that seem especially important include: emotional deprivation—the lack of adequate emotional nurturance in the first year of life leaves the individual with a seriously diminished capacity to empathize or even to identify with others (Bowlby 1944). As a result, adequate superego formation does not take place, the impulse control mechanisms develop awry, and the potential exists for the formation of an "affectionless character." In a sense, the youngsters who come out of it that way are the lucky ones. The rest become cases of failure to thrive, mental retardation, schizoid character, or frank psychosis. There are, of course, numerous variants in terms both of constitutional differences and of environmental management. Thus, one youngster can flourish on even minimal emotional nurturance, whereas another remains frustrated and unfulfilled with even a solid and adequate maternal input. Similarly, one environment is characterized by minimal care for baby at the hands of a 9-year-old sister; another by passing the baby back and forth among a host of transient caretakers (some of whom give more, some less); and a third by a disturbed mother who punctuates extended periods of neglect by transient moments of excessive holding and loving. In each case, it is the individual equation of what shaping factors were present, when, and for how long, that lend the resulting personality its unique coloring.

Overstimulation

The essence of traumatic experience is the flooding of the ego and the overwhelming of its defenses by emotional arousal of excessive intensity maintained for too long a time. For certain children, the erotic and sadistic attentions thrust upon them make their early lives one chronic prolonged trauma. Some react by withdrawal, in effect, puckering up their sensory world to shut out this torrent of input and making themselves into dulled, constricted, empty people in the process. Others, however, adapt to this "aggressor" by identifying with it. They become sensation-hungry, chronically excited, hyperalert, and hyperactive. They are forever into things, as invasive of others as they have themselves experienced invasion, and constantly probing and manipulating their environment. Inevitably they are reacted to as destructive pests. They are repeatedly being yelled at, chased away, or punished, and intense negative self-feelings ensue. This adds to the accumulation of trauma, and the youngster reacts with even more activity and hostility. As a rule, it is the encounter with school that brings these problems to a head. Labeling occurs early—these are bad children. Presently they have an image, and they feel pressured to live up to it. As a result, these youngsters often learn deftness, and during latency they become expert thieves, liars, and vandals.

At puberty, the shifts in drive and affect tend to intensify the entire constellation; this phase magnifies the difficulties. It also lends these young people a host of physical and intellectual strengths, new resources that become harnessed to their now highly developed antisocial proclivities. Shoplifting and purse snatching may give way to more organized housebreaking and the more serious kinds of street crime. Such youngsters can become dangerous people.

Lack of Limits and Overgratification

This is the spoiled child syndrome. It characterizes the youngster who is denied nothing by his parents, who asks for and gets the moon if he wails long and loud enough. As a result, he is simply unprepared to deal with the vicissitudes of normal give and take among peers, with the predictable moments of frustration that come into the average life. The end result begins to be visible in the latency years but truly comes to a head in puberty. The aroused oedipal yearnings of this time of life cannot be satisfied in any direct way, and in these low-tolerance individuals, the experience is galling. They become filled with rage and feel intense vengeful resentment toward their parents, sometimes splitting off part of their lives and living out all sorts of antisocial patterns sub rosa. In other cases, the child becomes a sort of mortal enemy of the parents, overflowing with vindictive spleen, heaping endless accusations of deprivation and unfairness on the mother or father, and seeming to work night and day to punish them even if he has to destroy himself in the process. Underneath all this there is often a veritable sea of guilt on which the entire syndrome floats and into which the youngster cannot peer.

To have gotten one's own way and been given more than one's fair share is gratifying—but it heaps burdens on personality organization. In particular, it begets conscience problems, disturbing feelings of something wrong. To avoid encounter with the tormenting superego, the entire problem is externalized; along with the parent, the teacher is seen as the enemy, as is the policeman, the employer, or anyone with the aura of authority. The youngster takes up cudgels against them all; they are all unfair, all frustraters, depriving him of his entitlements. He feels justified in employing the most egregious measures to redress the balance. The more guilty he feels, the more violent he becomes. It is a situation rife with paradox.

There are mental mechanisms basic to these syndromes. Although relatively few in number, in their many permutations and combinations they form the core of much of what passes for adolescent delinquency. The four most prominent mechanisms are: converting passive into active, the counterphobic defense, identification with the aggressor, and externalization. As with most defenses, they imply that an attempt at repression has failed; the conflicting forces will not stay in the unconscious. The nature of what is repressed varies, however. Converting the passive into active implies a state of earlier trauma which has left an ineradicable residue within the personality. There is a haunting feeling of painful helplessness that will not be identified and cannot be forgotten. The pain can be relieved, however, by doing to someone else that to which one has been subjected—for a little while at least, one can be doer and not victim. But it is only for a little while, for, the need for relief is endless. The sexually exploited child becomes a seductress or prostitute. The victim of child abuse becomes, in his turn, an abusing parent. The tough, rapacious street-wise youth was once a terrified youngest child cruelly dominated by a whole hierarchy of destructive, envious older siblings. The child subjected to early object loss and later castration threats becomes a shoplifter, a thief. Each in his turn has tried to swallow a bolus of trauma that has lodged in his throat, and all his adaptive resources are marshaled to dislodge it. His delinquency is an endless reliving of the original state of helplessness in reverse. Now it is he who renders the other helpless, dominated, humiliated, castrated, deprived of his precious possession, and crushed physically and spiritually. Some very vicious behavioral patterns indeed are fueled by this mechanism.

Identification with the aggressor is somewhat similar in function and in effect. The source of the trauma in this instance can usually be specifically identified, and one is reliving and reworking a particular relationship with a known person. The conflict here is perhaps somewhat closer to consciousness. It tends to occur in more mature individuals whose traumatic experience has not been as massive or as early; the mechanism itself is less diffuse. It is a more specific response to interaction with particular individuals, an explosive, narcissistic mother, an alcoholic, battering father, or some other figure with like force in one's life.

Externalization has several forms. In its simplest version, it involves the turning of some neurotic fantasy onto the environment. The child gives to teacher the value of some early version of mother or father. The principal at school is another in the archaic pantheon. The peers are perceived as the primordial siblings. Loves, hates, suspicions, dependency attachments, fearfulness, revenge impulses, all are distributed in keeping with the unconscious assignment of roles. The behavior then follows this scenario: There is an unexplainable and inordinate reactivity toward one person or another, with violent flareups, baiting, provocation, and all manner of causeless behavioral disturbance. The nature of the provocations is calculated to evoke the proper responses from the significant others; presently the child recreates about him the entire constellation of the early traumatic experience and continues to relive and replay it endlessly.

Another, somewhat more specialized, version of this adaptive style is the sequence which S. Freud (1916) designated "criminal from a sense of guilt" (pp. 332-333). In this pattern the chief conflict is between an attacking primitive cruel superego and a defending ego which is unable to cope effectively with this onslaught. The ego tries to repress, to sequester the superego, but that is not so easily done. The inner voice is too harsh and powerful. A compromise formation is then arrived at: The superego is repressed, and that portion which will not stay unconscious is externalized. The various environmental figures, especially the authority figures, are invested with the quality of hostile, unrelenting, inhumanly vicious predators. They are all versions of the implacable, unloving conscience. One must take up arms against them and seek by every possible artifice to evade, outwit, and defy them. Since they are seen as knowledgeable and dangerous, one must be even more wily and more destructive to stay ahead. In the end, one's efforts are doomed to failure; sooner or later they will win.

When some given depredation succeeds, the transient sense of elation is considerable. There is a pervasive quality of guilt associated with all this; these individuals are in a real sense trying to ward off a depression by their antisocial acts. The compromise therefore serves them well. The superego is omniscient; it knows everything one thinks, all of one's evil intentions, every twist and turn one might make to evade the assault. The outside world is much less dangerous; one has a chance. One can hide, dissimulate, get a lawyer—there are many possibilities.

Ultimately, these youngsters tend to get themselves caught or punished. The nature of the psychopathology demands this; they are committed to punishment of the self whether at their own hands or at the behest of society. Again, the degree of destructiveness with which they are involved can be quite serious.

The counterphobic defense is the fourth major mental mechanism: The presence that demands warding off is the imminence of being flooded by anxiety. From early in the lives of these youngsters they have had to cope with separation fears. Later, when gender identity issues come to the fore, they are ill prepared to master castration anxiety; after all, life had already taught them that important presences do come and go, that one can be left bereft. Now it is the wholeness of their bodies that can come and go. Vital organs like the genitals are here and not there, on this child's body and not on that one's. The terrifying possibilities of losing that which is vital, be it narcissistic support, object relatedness, or body part, are excruciating and omnipresent. Again, the child with a potential for acting out seeks an action-oriented means for relieving the pain, for coping with the anxiety. The way that is repeatedly found is to seek out the phobic area and to thrust oneself into it or more than that, to eroticize the anxiety itself, to make the dangerous pleasurable. Then one can get one's "kicks" in that way—by being daring, bold, adventuresome, thrill seeking in just those realms that have heretofore been the scariest and the most stressful. The child fearful of being left becomes the chronic runaway; the child most concerned about loss of dependency gratification drops out of school early and is most resistant to parental authority; the child terrified of castration becomes sexually promiscuous and is constantly thrusting at life with his or her genitals, or picks fights or exposes himself to accidents, or is much involved with weapons. Whatever was once traumatically frightening is now sought out for repeated reliving; one must demonstrate to oneself and to one's world that one is not afraid, not worried, not cowardly, that, on the contrary, one loves this kind of thing and will seek it anywhere, anytime.

In their various ways, the complex interplay of individual endowments, familial vectors, group pressures, socioeconomic factors, and a host of health, educational, and chance events produce the pattern for the delinquent personality. The individual may come from any socioeconomic level and may represent the expression of a highly varied and uniquely individual set of etiologic tendencies. The term "delinquency" is at best nonspecific; it speaks more for the bitter taste the activities of these youngsters leave in the mouths of those who encounter them than it does for any unitary syndrome. Interventional modes, as various as prolonged protective incarceration and psychoanalysis, have been employed with highly unpredictable degrees of success and failure. This is a prime area for future research.

Psychotic Reactions

Of the conditions which can produce psychotic reactions at puberty, the most common today is an acute drug intoxication. Methedrine (or other amphetamines) in large quantities are the most frequently encountered psychotogens, but lysergic acid diethylamide (LSD), phencyclidine (angel dust), and other hallucinogens can be all too effective. (In a number of rare instances, marijuana has been implicated.) Glue sniffing subjects the brain to the dubious consequence of certain volatile organic solvents that can have a powerful toxic impact on a vulnerable subject.

The second most frequent variety of psychotic reaction is the acute confusional state of adolescence. This stormy syndrome generally comes on abruptly with a host of frightening behaviors that resemble major psychosis. The youngster is terrified, confused, depersonalized, and feels totally lost. He may transiently fail to recognize familiar people, assert that he no longer knows who he is, break up furniture, and act drunk without being drunk. Moments of perfect lucidity alternate with this wild, confused behavior. However, there is no real thought disorder, nor are true delusions or hallucinations present, and the reaction may clear up as abruptly as it appeared. Albeit frightening, such a reaction does not ordinarily lead to prolonged illness. Major tranquilizers are said to be contraindicated since they interfere with the coping mechanism necessary for recovery. In general, the syndrome responds well to various supportive measures.

Etiology is not specific. It seems to come on as a consequence of massive developmental stresses; in effect, it represents a transient overwhelming of the defenses by the tide of impulse that comes with puberty. The existing ego structures simply cannot support the load, and for a while the whole apparatus is shaken. But the ego does not fragment, it recoups, control is reestablished, and, as a rule, the youngster seems to come out of it well, frightened, but not otherwise damaged. The panicky agitation that accompanies the syndrome represents the fear of loss of control over the forbidden impulses as well as the threat to the ego's basic integrity.

Schizophrenic Psychosis

This condition usually tends to appear in later adolescence. Current thinking sees it as the response of an inherently predisposed ego to normal developmental stress. The usual picture is for developmental factors to combine with external demands so that the vulnerable ego begins to fail to cope, leading to behavioral maladjustment which begets negative social responses and hence more stress. A downward spiral ends with the appearance of psychosis.

There are varying modes of onset, the most common of which is the acute outbreak of symptoms. There is also a type of gradual onset with a slow, progressive slipping away from reality into a more and more withdrawn life-style. Not infrequently, the onset appears as a turning toward aggressive acting out, and the patient is considered to be, and all too often managed as, a delinquent. In any case, there is a loss of boundaries, a cloudiness about the body outlines, a loosening of the ego's perimeter, and a sense of withdrawal from people and external reality. Things slide and slip; thoughts and day-dreams become as real or more real than external perceptual elements. The distinction between the two is lost, and the patient responds to his mind's creations and to the distortions he has himself introduced into his perceptual world. The fragile ego boundaries are experienced as open and vulnerable; sights, sounds, meanings intrude on the youth with enormous force; sounds reverberate strangely with hints of inner dread; visual images are too sharp; the boundaries are less a defensive perimeter than a ravaged no man's land.

Initially, there is some awareness that the real world is slipping away. The youngster seeks to cope by sharpening his sensibilities; he hears more clearly, sees more brightly, feels all keyed up. His affects come in gusts. There are intense rushes of emotion; sexual fantasies dance before his eyes; he feels curiously alive. At the same time, there is a diminished capacity for sleep; a sense of dread or imminence hovers over him; something is about to happen. Then his thoughts begin to gain ever greater automony; they march alone and in unusual forms. Strange phenomena (ideas of reference) begin to be noted. People are signaling or laughing about him; they are trying to influence him. He becomes frightened because he is being menaced, insulted, threatened, hounded. All sorts of restitutive attempts are made to overcome this loss. One kind of youth begins to flail out at the environment and becomes the delin-quent mentioned above. In other cases, the thinking may take a mystical, philosophical, or religious turn; there is a sense of moving into another plane. Great forces are at work in the world, and evidence for this begins to be sought and found.

As the youngster senses the crumbling of the basic structure of the ego and the loss of its boundaries, he attempts to construct an alternative arrangement, a logical explanation for what is happening based on delusional formations. Now it all makes sense; he understands. He regains a measure of coherence and some lessening of the overwhelming anxiety by the pseudo-logic of magi-cal thinking. In effect, he has regrouped at an infantile level of ego develop-ment and object relations where self and others flow into one another, and the distinction between what is inside the self and what is outside is in large measure lost. Distancing devices come into play, as he is far from his own affective life. Now as the integrity of the ego is lost, islands of function, isolated identifications, voices from the superego, memories, fantasies may each become tangible; they speak to him or appear visually. It is hard to put thoughts together because things are blocked or running too fast and without control.

In the face of this enormous influx of threat the youngster falls silent or becomes incoherent. With more intellectual youths, where the level of ego fragmentation is less, there is a constant pressure to reorganize a sense of self and self-in-the-world. The adolescent may turn to vast generalizations about religion, philosophy, or political ideology and seek to make sense out of what is happening by addressing the forces implicit in the particular system. He is one with God; he is possessed by the devil; he is persecuted by communists or losing himself in the great proletariat movement; he is partner to the third world mystique, involved in mystical union with unearthly forces, or lost in some other high order form of abstraction. The combinations and permutations are endless, but the loss of a coherent distinction between inner and outer experience and between magical and rational thinking is universal.

The acute state may resolve rapidly. Feinstein and Miller (1979) consider this more transient condition to be a separate entity, an acute psychotic reaction of adolescence and not properly a schizophrenic syndrome. The characteristic chronic reaction may initially look like a borderline state, an acute adjustment reaction, or a deteriorating character disorder (Masterson 1967). Ultimately, it involves thought disorder, anhedonia, intense dependency, impaired competency, and an injured sense of self (Holzman and Grinker 1977).

The duration of the condition is highly variable, but after the initial surge of symptoms, there is usually a gradual reintegration so that the florid psychotic manifestations presently disappear. Feinstein and Miller speak of a postpsychotic phase characterized by progressive lessening of the vestiges of the illness, heightened vulnerability to stress, and particular fragility in the face of separation. Those residual disabilities may make it difficult for the youngster to work in school. Thus, after the overt psychosis clears, there is a slow process of consolidation which may take as long as a year. It is a time for continued active treatment, often for continuing hospitalization, and it needs the most careful attention in order to allow for adequate emergence from the previous pathological state.

Much work has been done on the family structure of such patients, and concepts such as double bind, pseudomutuality, and mystification have been invoked to describe the childrearing styles and the inner patterns of communication that typify their operation.

An almost passionate quest has been conducted to learn the character of the biological events that accompany these conditions. Endocrine research, genetic explorations, neurotransmitter studies, and the creation of experimental psychoses by means of various psychoactive agents have all been pursued in depth. Thus far the results are powerfully suggestive but not finally conclusive. It does appear however, that extensive twin studies have demonstrated beyond reasonable doubt that a genetic factor is present.

References

Blos, P. Pregenital drive organization. *Journal of the American Psychoanalytic Association,* 6:47-56, 1958.

——. The second individuation process of adolescence. *The Psychoanalytic Study of the Child,* 22:162-186, 1967.

Bowlby, J. Forty-four juvenile thieves: Their characters and home life. *International Journal of Psycho-Analysis,* Volume 25, 1944.

Bruch, H. *Eating Disorders: Obesity, Anorexia, and the Person Within.* New York: Basic Books, 1972.

——. *The Golden Cage: The Enigma of Anorexia Nervosa.* Cambridge: Harvard University Press, 1978.

Burgess, E.W.; Lohman, J.D.; and Shaw, C.R. The Chicago Area Project. *Coping With Crime: The Yearbook of the National Probation Association.* New York National Probation Association, 1937. pp. 8-28.

Cloward, R., and Ohlin, L. *Delinquency and Opportunity.* New York: The Free Press, 1960.

Cohen, A.K. *Delinquent Boys: The Culture of the Gang.* Glencoe, Ill.: Free Press of Glencoe, 1955.

Coleman, M. Serotonin concentrations in whole blood of hyperactive children. *Journal of Pediatrics,* 78:985, 1971.

Erikson, E. *Identity and the Life Cycle.* Monograph, Psychological Issues, Vol. 1, No. 1. New York: International Universities Press, 1959.

Feinstein, S.C., and Miller, D. Psychoses of adolescence. In: Noshpitz, J., ed. *Basic Handbook of Child Psychiatry,* Vol. 2, *Disturbances in Development.* New York: Basic Books, 1979.

Freud, A. Adolescence. *The Psychoanalytic Study of the Child,* 13:279-295, 1958.

——. *The Ego and the Mechanisms of Defense.* 2nd Ed. New York: International Universities Press, 1966. pp. 167-172.

Freud, S. Some character types met with in psycho-analytic work (1916). *Standard Edition,* 14:311-333. London: Hogarth Press, 1957.

GAP Committee on Adolescence. *Normal Adolescence: Its Dynamics and Impact.* Report No. 68. New York: Group for the Advancement of Psychiatry, 1968.

Holzman, P., and Grinker, R.R., Sr. Schizophrenia in adolescence. In: Feinstein, S.C., and Giovacchini, P.I., eds. *Adolescent Psychiatry.* New York: Jason Aronson, 1977.

Inhelder, B., and Piaget, J. *The Growth of Logical Thinking from Childhood to Adolescence.* New York: Basic Books, 1958.

Johnson, A.M. Sanctions for superego lacunae of adolescents. In: Eissler, K., ed. *Searchlights on Delinquency.* New York: International Universities Press, 1949.

Kohut, H. *The Analysis of the Self.* New York: International Universities Press, 1971.

Martin, J., and Fitzpatrick, J. *Delinquent Behavior.* New York: Random House, 1964.

Masterson, J.F., Jr. *The Psychotic Dilemma of Adolescence.* Boston: Little, Brown, 1967.

Menkes, M.L.; Rowe, J.S.; and Menkes, J.H. Twenty-four year follow-up study on the hyperkinetic child with MBD. *Pediatrics,* 39:393-400, 1967.

Miller, W.B. Lower class culture as a generating milieu of gang delinquency. *Journal of Social Issues,* 14:15-19, 1958.

Millichap, J. Drugs in the management of minimal brain dysfunction. *Annals of the New York Academy of Sciences,* Vol. 205, p. 321, 1973.

Offer, D., and Offer, J. Three developmental routes through normal male adolescence. In: Feinstein, S.C., and Giovacchini, P., eds. *Adolescent Psychiatry.* New York: Jason Aronson, 1975. pp. 121-141.

Rapaport, J.L.; Quinn, P.; and Lamprecht, F. Minor physical anomalies and plasma dopamine-beta-hydroxylase activity in hyperactive boys. *American Journal of Psychiatry,* 131:386-391, 1974.

Rapaport, J.L.; Lott, I.T.; Alexander, D.F.; and Abramson, A.U. Urinary noradrenaline and playroom behavior in hyperactive boys. *Lancet,* 2:1141, 1970.

Rotnem, D.; Genel, M.; Hintz, R.L.; and Cohen, D.J. Personality development in children with growth hormone deficiency. *Journal of the American Academy of Child Psychiatry,* 16:412-426, 1977.

Sandler, J. On the concept of the superego. *The Psychoanalytic Study of the Child*, 15:153-154, 1960.

Satterfield, J. EEG issues in children with MBD. *Seminars in Psychiatry*, Vol. 5, 1973.

Satterfield, J.; Cantwell, D.; and Satterfield, B. The pathophysiology of the hyperkinetic syndrome. *Archives of General Psychiatry*, 31(9):839-846, 1974.

Sours, J. The anorexia nervosa syndrome: Phenomenologic and psychodynamic components. *Psychiatric Quarterly*, 45:240-256, 1969.

Sutherland, E. *Principles of Criminology*. 4th Ed. New York: J.B. Lippincott, 1947.

Sylvester, E. Analysis of psychogenic anorexia and vomiting in a four year old child. *The Psychoanalytic Study of the Child*, 1:167-187, 1945.

Tanner, J.M. *Growth at Adolescence*. 2nd Ed. New York: Lippincott, 1962.

Waldrop, M., and Halverson, C. Minor physical anomalies and hyperactive behavior in young children. In: Hellmuth, J., ed. *The Exceptional Infant*, Vol. 2. New York: Brunner/Mazel, 1971. pp. 343-389.

Wender, P. Platelet serotonin level in children with "MBD." *Lancet*, 2:1012, 1969.

Werry, J.S.; Minde, K.; Guzman, A.; Weiss, G.; Dogan, K.; and Hoy, E. Studies on the hyperactive child—VII: Neurological status compared with neurotic and normal children. *American Journal of Orthopsychiatry*, 15(3):441-452, 1972.

Wood, D.; Reimherr, F.; and Wender, P. Diagnosis and treatment of MBD in adults: A preliminary report. *Archives of General Psychiatry*, 33(12):1453, 1976.

The Course of Life: Psychoanalytic Contributions
Toward Understanding Personality Development.
Vol. II: Latency, Adolescence, and Youth.
S.I. Greenspan and G.H. Pollock, editors.
NIMH 1980

Adolescent Development: A Normative Perspective[1]

Daniel Offer, M.D.

Introduction

Jones (1961, p. 7) stated that "psychopathology opened a route to psychology in general, perhaps the most practical route." It is based on Freud's (1937, p. 209) earlier comment that: "A normal ego is like normality in general, an ideal fiction." It reminds one of the philosopher Kaplan's (1967) concept of "trained incapacity." Trained to recognize the abnormal (defenses, conflicts, and the six metapsychological points of view), the psychoanalyst and his teacher (in the office via the couch, or in the training institutes via supervision) have difficulty in recognizing, let alone conceptualizing, the normal.

The purpose of this chapter is to stimulate interest and discussion in concepts of normal development and to share with you what we consider the four basic perspectives of normality (Offer and Sabshin 1974). In the process we also mention briefly some of the highlights of a 10-year study of normal adolescents. Finally, we make some comments concerning the knotty problem of the relationship between clinical research and normal development.

---

1. The longitudinal research program has been supported by the following USPHS grants: First, with Mental Health Career Investigators Grant #4870 of the NIMH (1961–1964); Second, with Grant #08714 of the NIMH (1964–1966); and Third, with Grant #02571 of the NICHHD (1966–1969). The major findings have been reported in two monographs: *The Psychological World of The Teenager* (Offer 1969), and *From Teenage to Young Manhood* (Offer and Offer 1975).

The Four Perspectives of Normality

A review of the psychoanalytic, social, and behavioral science literature on normality led to a categorization of views on normality as belonging within four functional perspectives (Offer and Sabshin 1974). Although each perspective is unique and has its own definition and description, the perspectives do complement each other, and together they represent the total behavioral, psychological, and social science approach to normality.

Normality as Health

The first perspective is basically the traditional medical approach to health and illness. Most physicians equate normality with health and view health as an almost universal phenomenon. As a result, behavior is assumed to be within normal limits when no manifest psychopathology is present, as if one were to put all behavior on a continuum and abnormality would be the small remainder. This definition of normality correlates with the traditional role model of the doctor who attempts to free his patient from grossly observable signs of illness. To this physician, the lack of pathological signs or symptoms indicates health. In other words, health in this context refers to a reasonable rather than an optimal state of functioning. In its simplest form, this perspective is illustrated by Romano (1950), who stated that a healthy person is one who is reasonably free of undue pain, discomfort, and disability.

Normality as Utopia

The second perspective conceives of normality as that harmonious and optimal blending of the diverse elements of the mental apparatus that culminates in optimal functioning. Such a definition emerges clearly when psychiatrists or psychoanalysts talk about the ideal person or when they grapple with a complex problem, such as criteria of successful treatment. This approach is characteristic of a significant segment of psychoanalysts, but it is by no means unique. It can also be found among psychotherapists of quite different persuasions, for example, Rogers (1959).

Normality as Average

The third perspective is commonly used in normative studies of behavior and is based on a mathematical principle of the bell-shaped curve. This approach conceives of the middle range as normal and of both extremes as deviant. The normative approach based on this statistical principle describes each person in terms of general assessment and total score. Variability is described only within the context of groups and not within the context of one person. Although this approach is more commonly used in psychology and biology than in psychiatry, psychiatrists have recently been using pencil-and-paper tests to a much larger extent than in the past. Not only do psychiatrists use the results of I.Q. tests, Rorschach, and Thematic Apperception Tests, but they also construct their own tests and questionnaires. In developing model personalities for different societies one assumes that the typologies of character can be statistically measured.

Normality as Transactional Systems

The fourth perspective stresses that normal behavior is the end result of interacting systems. Temporal changes are essential to a complete definition of normality. In other words, the normality as transactional systems perspective stresses changes or processes rather than a cross-sectional definition of normality. Investigators who subscribe to this approach can be found in all behavioral and social sciences. Most typical are Erikson (1968) and Grinker (1956) whose thesis of a unified theory of behavior encompasses polarities within a wide range of integration. The recent interest in general system theory (Von Bertalanffy 1968; Gray et al. 1969) has further stressed the general applicability of the general system research for psychiatry. Normality as transactional systems encompasses variables from the biological, psychological, and social fields, all contributing to the functioning of a viable system over time. The integration of the variables into the system and the loading or significance assigned to each variable will have to be more thoroughly explored in the future.

Research in the Field of Normal Development

Research on normal or nonpatient populations is not exclusively of recent origin. Anthropologists have been observing cultures other than their own for more than 70 years. Social psychologists and child psychologists have worked with people in experimental and testing situations ever since psychology began functioning as a scientific discipline. Psychoanalysts, although primarily studying patients who come to see them for psychoanalytical therapy, have extended their theories to include concepts applicable to the personality development of normal children and adults. Psychiatric and clinical studies on normal populations have been undertaken during the past decade, when there has been a steady increase in outpatient studies of normal populations. What has been lacking, however, are the systematic studies by longitudinal or followup investigations of normal populations. The clinicians' experience and abilities need to be integrated with the researchers' tools and methods (Offer, Freedman, and Offer 1972).

It is almost by definition that we cannot do indepth psychoanalytic research on normal subjects (they would not have the motivation among other things and resistance will be too high). (See, for example, Eissler 1960; Gitelson 1954).

On the other hand, to assume that normal functioning of feelings and behavior is simply the antonym of neurosis can be just as misleading. As cursory and superficial (from a psychoanalytic point of view) as studies of normal people are, they are surely better than no studies at all. Let me briefly summarize our 10-year (Offer and Offer 1975) study of normal adolescent males. We have to keep in mind that there are very few longitudinal studies on normal populations. The interesting thing is that their findings are very similar. (See, for example, Symonds and Jensen 1961; Cox 1970; Block 1971; Vaillant 1977; Kagen and Moss 1962; Holmstrom 1972.)

The most intriguing finding was that there was no one developmental route which typifies our subject population. We had three distinct subgroups, all under the general rubric of normal development (those who are interested in more methodological, as well as clinical, detail should look at our recent book title, Offer and Offer 1975).

The three groups are:

1. Continuous Growth (23 percent of the total group)
2. Surgent Growth (35 percent of the total group)
3. Tumultuous Growth (21 percent of the total group)

Twenty-one percent of the subjects could not be classified; they had mixed scores and did not fit into any of the subgroups, statistically or clinically. They also did not make for a fourth group. Clinically they can be best described as being closest to the first two groups.

The psychodynamics of the three groups were as follows:

I. Continuous growth (23 percent of the total group). The subjects described within the continuous growth grouping progressed throughout adolescence and young manhood with a smoothness of purpose and a self-assurance of their progression toward a meaningful and fulfilling adult life. These subjects were favored by circumstances. Their psychogenetic and environmental backgrounds were excellent. Their childhood had been unmarked by death or serious illnesses of a parent or sibling. The nuclear family remained a stable unit throughout their childhood and adolescence. The continuous growth subjects had mastered previous developmental stages without serious setbacks. They were able to cope with internal and external stimuli through an adaptive general cultural combination of reason and emotional expression. These subjects accepted general cultural and societal norms and felt comfortable within this context. They had a capacity to integrate experiences and use them as a stimulus for growth.

The parents were able to encourage their children's independence; the parents themselves grew and changed with their children. Throughout the 10 years of the study there were basic mutual respect, trust, and affection between the generations. The ability to allow the sons' independence in many areas was undoubtedly facilitated by the sons' behavior patterns. Since the young men were not behaving in a manner clearly divergent from that of the parents, the parents could continue to be provided with need gratifications through their sons. The sense of gratification was reciprocal, with the sons gaining both from the parents' good feelings toward them and the parental willingness to allow them to create their own individual lives outside of the household. The value system of the subjects in this group dovetailed with that of the parents. In many ways the young men were functioning as continuations of the parents, living out not so much lives the parents had wished for but not attained, but rather lives similar to those of the parental units.

In their interpersonal relationships the subjects showed a capacity for good object relationships, as measured in the clinical interview, rating scales, and the psychological testings. They had close male friends in whom they could confide. Their relationships with the opposite sex became increasingly important as they reached the post-high school years. By the subjects' 4th year, post-high school, intimacy in the Eriksonian sense was being developed and was a goal toward which these subjects strove.

Subjects described by the continuous growth pattern acted in accordance with their consciences, manifesting little evidence of superego problems and developing meaningful ego ideals, often identifying with persons whom they knew and admired within the larger family or school communities. These subjects were able to identify feelings of shame and guilt and proceeded to explain not only how the experiences provoking these responses had affected them, but also how they brought closure to the uncomfortable situations. A second similar experience might be described then by these young men, but one which they had been prepared to handle better, putting the earlier upsetting experience into a past time frame of immaturity conquered.

The young men's fantasy lives were relatively active; they were almost always able to translate their fantasy into reality and action. They could dream about being the best in the class academically, sexually, or athletically, though their actions would be guided by a pragmatic and realistic appraisal of their own abilities and of external circumstance. Thus, they were prevented from meeting with repeated disappointments.

The subjects were able to cope with external trauma, usually through an adaptive action-orientation. When difficulties arose, they used the defenses of denial and isolation for protecting their ego from being bombarded with affect. They could postpone immediate gratification and work in a sustained manner for a future goal. Their delay mechanisms worked well, and, together with temporary suppression rather than repression of affect, they were generally successful in responding to their aggressive and sexual impulses without being overwhelmed or acting out in a self-destructive manner. They did not experience prolonged periods of anxiety or depression, two of the most common affects described by the entire subject population, including this subgroup.

The qualities which were common to members of this group were many of those which appear when mental health is viewed in an ideal sense. The individuals of the continuous growth group would, of course, never portray all of these qualities but would have some difficulties in one or another area. What was most distinctive about members of the continuous growth group was their overall contentment with themselves and their place in life. When compared to the other two groupings, this group was composed of relatively happy human beings. They generally had an order to their lives which could be interrupted but which would not yield to states of symptomatology or chaotic behavior as these young men progressed through the adolescent years and matured cognitively and emotionally.

None of the subjects in this group had received psychotherapy or was thought by the researchers to need treatment. This is not surprising since the person seeking psychotherapy as an adolescent or young adult would be unlikely to be characterized by belonging in the category of continuous growth. The significance of the data, that these subjects were not seen by psychotherapists or counselors from the health services of the schools or communities, lies in the fact that they then are least likely to be the young adults from whom members of the helping professions build their studies or make their generalizations about youth populations.

II. Surgent growth (35 percent of the total group). The surgent growth group, although functioning as adaptively as the first group, was characterized by important enough differences in ego structure, in background, and in family environment to present a different cluster and be defined as a different sub-group. Developmental spurts are illustrative of the pattern of growth of the surgent growth group. These subjects differed in the amount of emotional conflict experienced and in patterns of resolving conflicts. There was more concentrated energy directed toward mastering developmental tasks than was obvious for members of the continuous growth group. At times these subjects would be adjusting very well, integrating their experiences and moving ahead, and at other times they seemed to be stuck at an almost premature closure and unable to move forward. A cycle of progression and regression is more typical of this group than the continuous growth group. The defenses used, anger and projection, represent more psychopathology than the defenses used by the first group.

One of the major differences between the surgent growth subjects and those in the continuous growth group was that their genetic and/or environmental backgrounds were not as free of problems and traumas; the nuclear families in the surgent growth group were more likely to have been affected by separation, death, or severe illnesses.

Although subjects in this category were able to cope successfully with their "average expectable environment" (Hartmann 1939), their ego development was not adequate for coping with unanticipated sources of anxiety. Affects which were usually flexible and available would at the time of crisis, such as the death of a close relative, become stringently controlled. This, together with the fact that they were not as action oriented as the first group, made them slightly more prone to depression. The depression would accompany or openly follow the highly controlled behavior. On other occasions, when their defense mechanism faltered, they experienced moderate anxiety and a short period of turmoil resulted. When disappointed in themselves or others, there was a tendency to use projection and anger.

These subjects were not as confident as were the young men in the continuous growth group; their self-esteem wavered. They relied upon positive reinforcement from the opinions of important others such as parents and/or peers. When this was not forthcoming, they often became discouraged about themselves and their abilities. As a group, they were able to form meaningful interpersonal relationships similar to those of individuals in the continuous growth group. The relationships, though, would be maintained with a greater degree of effort.

For subjects described under the surgent growth category, relationships with parents were marked by conflicts of opinions and values. There were areas of disagreement between father and mother concerning basic issues such as the importance of discipline, academic attainments, or religious beliefs. In several cases the parents came from different backgrounds. The mothers of some of these subjects had difficulty in letting their children grow and in separating from them.

The subjects might work toward their vocational goals sporadically or with a lack of enthusiasm, but they would be able to keep their long-range behavior in line with their general expectations for themselves.

There were subjects in this group who were afraid of emerging sexual feelings and impulses. For these young adults, meaningful relationships with the opposite sex began relatively late, except for a small subgroup who started experimenting with sexuality early in high school, possibly owing to a counterphobic defense. These early sexual relationships were not lasting, although they could be helpful in overcoming anxiety concerning sexuality.

The group as a whole was less introspective than either the first or the third group. Overall adjustment of these subjects was often just as adaptive and successful as that of the first group. The adjustment was achieved, though, with less self-examination and a more controlled drive or surge toward development, with suppression of emotionality as characteristic of the subjects in the surgent growth group.

III. Tumultuous growth (21 percent of total group). The third group, the tumultuous growth group, is similar to the adolescents so often described in psychiatric, psychoanalytic, and social science literature. These are the students who go through adolescence with internal turmoil which manifests itself in overt behavioral problems in school and in the home. These adolescents have been observed to have recurrent self-doubts and braggadocio, escalating conflicts with their parents, and debilitating inhibitions, and often respond inconsistently to their social and academic environments.

Subjects characterized by a tumultuous growth pattern were those who experienced growing up from 14 to 22 as a period of discordance, as a transitional period for which their defenses needed mobilizing, and ego-adaptations needed strengthening.

The subjects demonstrating tumultuous growth patterns came from less stable backgrounds than did those subjects in the other two groups. Some of the parents in this group had overt marital conflicts, and others had a history of mental illness in the family. Hence, the genetic and environmental backgrounds of the subjects in the tumultuous growth group were decidedly different from those of the other two groups. Also present was a social class difference. Our study population was primarily middle class, but this group contained many subjects who belonged to the lower middle class. For them, functioning in a middle and upper middle class environment might have been a cause for additional stress.

The tumultuous growth group experienced more major psychological traumas. The difficulties in their life situation were greater than their satisfactions, and defenses were not well developed for handling emotionally trying situations. A relatively high percentage of this group had overt clinical problems and had received psychotherapy.

Separation was painful to the parents, and it became a source of continuing conflict for the subjects. The parent-son relationships characterizing this group were similar to those of many of the neurotic adolescents seen in outpatient psychotherapy. Further, parent-son communication of a system of values was poorly defined or contradictory.

Strong family bonds, however, were present within the tumultuous growth route subjects, as they were within each of the route patterns. We utilized the revealed difference technique for evaluating strength and openness of family communication. This method clearly differentiated between families of delinquent adolescents and our modal subjects. The method also differentiated the family of our modal sample along the three developmental routes. Best understanding between the generations was observed among the continuous growth group and least in the tumultuous growth group, with the surgent group in between (Offer, Marohn, and Ostrov 1979).

The ability of this group to test reality and act accordingly was relatively strong in contrast to patient populations, but disappointment in others and in themselves was prevalent when contrasted to other nonpatient populations. Action was accompanied by more anxiety and depression in this group than in the other two groups. Emotional turmoil was part of their separation and individuation process. Without the tumult, growth toward independence and meaningful interpersonal relationship was in doubt. Wide mood swings indicated a search for who they were as separate individuals and concern about whether their activities were worthwhile. Feelings of mistrust about the adult world were often expressed in this group. Affect was readily available and created both intensely pleasurable and painful experiences. Changes in self-concept could precipitate moderately severe anxiety reactions. These subjects were considerably more dependent on peer culture than were their age-mates in the other groups, possibly because they received fewer gratifications from their relationships within the family. When they experienced a personal loss, such as the ending of a relationship with a good friend, their depression was deeper, though only very rarely associated with suicidal feelings and impulses.

The tumultuous growth subjects had begun dating activities at a younger age than had their peers described in the first two groups. In early adolescence their relationship with females was that of a dependency relationship, with the female being a substitute for a mothering figure. In late adolescence, for some, their heterosexual relationships gained meaning, and they were able to appreciate the personal characteristics of their female friends.

Many subjects in the tumultuous growth group were highly sensitive and introspective individuals. They were usually aware of their emotional needs. Academically, they were less interested in science, engineering, law, and medicine. They preferred the arts, the humanities, or the social and psychological sciences. However, business and engineering careers remained the most usual choice for this group as well as for the first two groups.

As a group these subjects did not do as well academically during their high school years as subjects from the first two groups, although it is possible that in the long run they will do just as well as subjects in the other two groups. As with other variables, academic success differentiated the groups, but honor students and average students or workers could be found within each group. The academic or work failures were more likely to be found in the tumultuous group, as they would find the tasks upon which they had embarked to be incompatible with their need or abilities only after having assayed them.

Those adolescents in this grouping experienced more psychological pain than did the others, but as a result were no less well adjusted as a group in terms of their overall functioning within their respective environmental settings than were the persons in the continuous and surgent growth groups. They were less happy with themselves, more critical of their social environment, but just as successful academically as vocationally.[2]

Data Gathering With a Psychoanalytic Bent

The question will undoubtedly be raised by many of you: This is interesting phenomenological-descriptive work—but how were psychoanalytic technique and theory useful in this research? What do we really know about the internal world of these adolescents and their development through the 8 years that we studied them? We can best compare our work to an anthropologist doing field research (including depth interviews) in a strange (foreign) culture. The sub-

---

2. We are now embarking on a parallel study on the development of psychology of adolescent girls (Petersen, Offer, Gitelson, and Solomon 1978).

jects with whom we worked were seen but not studied or treated by mental health professionals. They would not seek psychoanalytic therapy. They were not the type to be studied by social scientists because they were deviant. And yet, they were there all ready to be studied and to help us understand the process of adolescence.

We believe that our knowledge of depth psychology helped us to better understand these subjects because we listen to psychological material with a psychoanalytic perspective—taking into account resistance, defenses, unconscious communication, and the fantasy life of the individual. But how? First, we developed "an alliance" with our subjects which made it easier for us to make interpretations concerning resistance of an episode in each subject's life, without promising too much in the psychotherapeutic sense or shying away from asking probing questions when indicated (Offer 1973). And second, we utilized the psychoanalytic tools of empathy and introspection to both facilitate and comprehend the subjects (Kohut 1971, 1977).

A few examples will help you understand how we used the interpretive road in our group of subjects. Why, for example, were some students, who impressed us as immature, resistant to the project, while others were almost too cooperative? Robert, for example, was worried about losing his parents and seemed afraid of what we might "force" him to reveal, so he talked little to us. He was the one who most often refused to answer our questions. He did not, for instance, want to tell us what he felt were the problems of adolescents, what his wishes were, or what he would do with a million dollars. Whom would he like to be with on a desert island? "I'd like to have my parents with me because then it would be safe and secure." Was he aware of his immaturity and afraid to join in a research alliance with us because of what his direct answers might reveal? He did frequently volunteer the subject of his mother's working for a particular firm. He liked neither the firm nor the idea of his mother's working. Robert himself was worried about not being able to succeed in carrying out his wishes. This fear he showed us in other ways throughout the interviews and also, perhaps, by his refusal to mention the wishes. We can make this interpretation of his refusal to cooperate on the basis of a series of other responses. He wanted to go to a particular university with high admission standards, but he did not think he could be accepted because, as he regretfully reported, he had only a "C" average. If rejected by the university, maybe he would become a pilot. He felt shame when he had bragged. He could not really achieve what he had claimed to have done. Robert's guilt was aroused when he did not study enough and then did poorly on an exam. We can gain insight into Robert's problems by the answers he did give and also into at least one of his ways of handling them—camouflage—by his refusal to answer several questions. Robert formed a beginning of a research alliance by attending; but by refusing full cooperation, he was protecting himself.

There was one other boy, Gerald, who came but refused to discuss several issues with us. He had difficulty forming the research alliance in the beginning.

He seemed to have problems with forming most meaningful relationships. He refused to tell us his wishes. "What would you do with a million dollars?" "That is part of wishes, so I won't discuss it. Besides, I can't think of anything." "Whom would you like to have with you on a desert island?" "I'd like to be alone because alone, under pressure, I think better." By the Third Psychiatric Interview, we were able to involve this boy. He said he was glad to see the interviewer, and he was answering all the questions. He closed the Fourth Psychiatric Interview with: "I'd like to see you more often." Was this a mood shift, a heightened self-confidence, or a development of an alliance? Although the former two may also be true, his plea for more sessions tended to support the theory of a growth of the alliance. From this material any of you, as well, can realize that an analytic stance is simply not the same as a routine interview.

Phillip read a story in the newspapers that it is dangerous to poke around people's feelings, and especially their heads. He added very quickly after he made this critical statement, "I didn't mean any offense, mind you. People who don't know much about psychology should not go around asking people questions. Psychology is really very similar to philosophy and isn't a science at all." In a later interview, Phillip was quite cooperative and said he had enjoyed the interview. He wanted to know how many had dropped out and why. After much probing, he admitted that he had considered dropping out, but because the interviewer had become personable, and because he was curious each time before he came to see us, he was staying on.

Thomas gives us an example of a form of alliance that failed, not in the sense of its strength to provide cooperation, but in that it became more of a therapeutic alliance than a research alliance. Thomas caused us to feel slightly uneasy about our explicit intention not to do psychotherapy. This subject, who had been particularly uncooperative during the first two sessions, settled down and developed a meaningful research alliance with us. There was a 7-month interval between the Fourth and Fifth Psychiatric Interviews. When the subject came to the Fifth Psychiatric Interview, in his senior year of high school, he told us that during the preceding fall he had developed a strong urge to scream out in church. He had the urge almost every Sunday. At times, he had it in school, too. He also felt like running away from home. He had done neither of the two things. But the urges continued to bother him. During Christmas vacation he received a letter from us, as did every subject, thanking him for his past cooperation, stating that we would see him in the spring, and wishing him a Merry Christmas and a Happy New Year. The subject told us that he was very pleased to receive the letter and planned to tell us about his special feeling; but amazingly the urge had disappeared since his receipt of the letter.

Naturally, there were degrees in which we were used as therapists. Some subjects had difficulty in breaking away from their families. In forming outside relationships, they reacted not by fear of us but by leaning upon us and the alliance. Some of these subjects who we felt were immature, to judge by a series of responses, formed such a strong relationship with us that they had difficulty leaving at the end of an interview. One such boy, Kenneth, who was having problems of control, came to see us on a day when he had cut classes in order to go to the movies with a couple of girls from a different town. He told us that he enjoyed coming to see us. "I get a lot of things off my chest when I come here."

Eugene began to develop his research alliance or trust in us at the First Psychiatric Interview. After answering many questions, he remarked just before leaving: "I thought you might want to know that my parents have been separated for the past 2 years." He must have felt defensive about this, because he had not mentioned it when asked questions about his family. Can we credit the alliance we formed with having made him comfortable enough to add this "afterthought"?

Not all were anywhere nearly so cooperative; more usually they would cooperate with hesitation. "Your questions are probably important," was not infrequent commentary on the project. These subjects were not too sure. Jack wondered if people were really telling us what they felt. He felt that he was, but he wondered if the others would. Certainly we, as psychoanalysts, cannot view "cooperation" as a routine issue in interviewing but rather as a significant form of resistance that only the "Interpretive road" can help understand.

Michael thought that by now, the junior year of high school, we had lost at least one-half of our subjects. He said he came out of curiosity. When told that only a few had dropped out, he was surprised but said, "I guess they have nothing better to do. I will probably drop later." This boy continued. The above conversation came after he had said that his father scared him. He seemed a little afraid that we would repeat this to his parents. In the opening interview, Michael had said that he was bigger than both his parents, but 2 years later he still felt that his father could beat him. As with so many of the subjects, his resistance to the project was a part of his general pattern of functioning. He proceeded with fear, but he proceeded nonetheless and responded to our questions.

Timothy said he objected to the project only when it took him away from athletic practice. When we pointed out that the interviews had never conflicted with his sports activities, he responded: "Oh, yeah. I guess, then, I like it." Another subject said: "I think other people might be sensitive about this interview, but I didn't mind it. I think maybe I can learn something from the interviews."

The nonchalant attitude was best epitomized by John. "Would you like to participate, John?" "Not emphatically" "Drop out?" "Not exactly." "Continue?" "Probably." This boy proved to be open and talkative. His commitment to the project, despite the unconcerned surface, was sufficient to motivate him to continue even after he later changed high schools. Here again, this boy's verbalized attitude toward the project was indicative of his attitudes toward many things. There was a combination of an "I don't care" attitude with a "But I really do." He thought school and vacations were boring, but he liked hunting and fishing and wanted to be a better student.

Several of the examples presented are illustrative of only the individuals cited. At the least, each example shows part of an individual pattern and also indicates just why we enjoyed seeing the teenagers. Although psychological patterns of statistical clusters might make the "normal students" sound uninteresting, the individual was not. As may sometimes be forgotten, the statistically "typical" student is not to be found.

These examples were not the mode; however, they will suffice in sharing with you our utilization of object relations, transference, and unconscious meaning of behavior. It is in the latter area that psychoanalytic theory was extremely helpful in enriching our understanding of these subjects. In addition, we were confident of the validity of our data once we understood the subjects in terms of their relationship with us. The subjects' responses, on a minor scale, were really not different from patients we see in therapy. The main difference was and is that there was a group whom we, as psychoanalysts, would never have been able to study by definition.

Creativity: A Comment

Can creative people be normal? It is essential that psychological conflict precede a creative outpouring. Is depression a necessary precondition for originality? And how about regression in the service of the ego in artists? All the above psychological issues have been discussed extensively in the psychological and psychoanalytic literature. It is not our purpose here to review this extensive and complex literature. It is only our purpose here to comment briefly on the nature of the Rorschach in the three groups described above.

We were wondering whether our continuous growth group varied in relation to the other two groups in terms of the adolescent fantasy life as depicted in the projective tests. The adolescents from the first group, who went through adolescence relatively easily, shifted to adulthood with values similar to their parents and were action oriented, had a rich fantasy life, and showed great flexibility of their defenses. They in no way shied away from their own internal aggressive impulses.

We examined our Rorschach data from this perspective for the first time for this paper.[3] We have collected Rorschach data twice on our subjects. First, at age 15 and later at age 21 (see Offer 1969; Offer and Offer 1975). We have found that the three growth groups differed significantly along the lines which usually are associated with creativity.

The continuous growth had the highest Movement Responses. That means that they had the most ability to depart from the strict form quality of the card

---

3. Dr. S.I. Greenspan suggested this analysis.

and bring a sense of feeling and loneliness to the responses. The surgent growth group was the most accurate in its perception of Form. This shows greater intolerance for departure from strict interpretation of reality. The tumultuous growth group was lowest in Movement and Form Responses. They were highest in Shading Responses. The latter means that they could depart from reality, but it associated with considerable emotional turmoil. It is also less in the service of the age.

The above summary statements concerning the Rorschach of our subjects are presented only as indications of an interesting finding. The findings are all statistically significant, but they represent psychological test reports and studies of creativity in vivo. Nonetheless, they are of interest in the sense that they follow the general tenor of our presentation. They challenge the common conception that psychological conflict is *necessarily* related to creativity.

Hypothesis Derived From the Research

The three developmental routes through adolescence were obtained from careful behavioral observations, psychological testing, teacher and parent ratings, the self-perception of the teenagers through the 8 years of the study, and our own empathic tool, so central to psychoanalytic psychology. What can we, as psychoanalysts, learn from such a research?

First, it is feasible to study normal (nonpatient) populations utilizing, in part, psychoanalytic principles and thereby enriching our psychological understanding of adolescence.

Second, since the process of development is a continuous one, only longitudinal research will help us understand the interaction of multiplicity of variables over time. Inasmuch as there is more than one normal development process from childhood to adulthood, the various routes need elucidation. This is particularly true in adolescence where the turmoil route has often been described at the sine qua non developmental pattern from childhood to adulthood.

Third, adaptation to the environment is crucial in adolescents as in any stage of life. The healthier adolescents are more adaptable to their family and their environment. They also come from basically healthier families (as defined by our criterion).

Fourth, harmonious blending of the diverse structures of the psychic apparatus (ego, id, superego, and ego-ideal) is essential for normal functioning. If a person has serious difficulties in one area of his or her internal psychological world, how does the person adjust to reality. We do believe that behavior encompasses the epiphenomena of the person's psychology. One cannot have reasonable adjustment to the external world without having matured psychologically (e.g., never having gone through adolescence and the separation it entails from internal parental imagoes). Our data have shown that the normal subjects we studied are definitely not infantile (or underdeveloped) adolescents. The additional data we obtained from psychological testing and parent and teacher rating conclusively point to young adults who are on the road to emotional maturity. Their internal and external adaptation is, in our opinion, not a sign of mediocrity, but a different growth pattern. We will enrich our psychoanalytic theory of adolescent development if we pay more attention to these subjects whom we do not see as patients. It is also extremely useful for longitudinal research of normal subjects to utilize the psychoanalytic method with populations which we would never otherwise come into contact with.

Fifth, the ability to interpret unconscious material to a research subject is just as important and helpful as are interpretations to our neurotic patients. There is, however, a distinct difference between neurotic patients and normal subjects as illustrated above, although we have to keep in mind that the differences are relative and not absolute.

Conclusion

Is a profile emerging that reliably describes the normal man or woman? Definitely not. The more one studies normal populations, the more one becomes aware that healthy functioning is as complex, and coping behavior as varied, as the psychopathological entities. Normality and health cannot be understood in the abstract. Rather, they depend on the cultural norms, society's expectations and values, professional biases, individual differences, and the political climate of the time which sets the tolerance for deviance.

The four perspectives of normality make it possible to differentiate between different kinds of normality. There are different typologies of normality. During the past decade, increased studies of normal populations, using a variety of psychological methods, show that we have taken an important step in the right direction. Continued empirical investigations will lead to a better understanding of the complexity of healthy development. Psychiatrists and psychoanalysts are presently shifting from deduction and theorizing about normal development to empirical investigations of the relationships among the multiplicity of variables that contribute to the healthy or normal development of people. The study of normal (i.e., nonpatient) populations has taken a very healthy turn in recent years.

It is particularly important to integrate clinical observations with developmental research. Only by understanding normal development can we understand its deviations. For example, by comparing factors involved in normal development with those in delinquency or psychopathology we may learn how problems develop and hence be better able to plan effective interventions. Similarly, the study of psychopathology or delinquency will point to problem areas and will greatly enhance our understanding of the significant aspects of normal development.

References

Block, J. *Lives Through Time.* Berkeley, Calif.: Bancroft, 1971.

Cox, R.D. *Youth into Maturity.* New York: Mental Health Materials Center, 1970.

Eissler, K.R. The efficient soldier. In: Muensterburger, W., and Axelrod, S., eds. *The Psychoanalytic Study of Society.* New York: International Universities Press, 1960.

Erikson, E.H. Identity psychosocial. In: *International Encyclopedia of the Social Sciences.* Vol. 7, p. 61. New York: Crowell, Collier, and MacMillan, 1968.

Freud, S. Analysis, terminable and interminable (1937). *Standard Edition.* 23:209–253. London: Hogarth Press, 1964.

Gitelson, M. The analysis of the 'Normal' candidate. *International Journal of Psycho-Analysis,* 35:174, 1954.

Gray, W.; Duhl, F.J.; and Rizzo, N.D. *General Systems Theory and Psychiatry.* Boston: Little, Brown, 1969.

Grinker, R.R., Sr. Towards a Unified Theory of Human Behavior. New York: Basic Books, 1956.

Hartmann, H. Psychoanalysis and the concept of health. *International Journal of Psycho-Analysis,* 20:308, 1939.

Holmstrom, R. On the picture of mental health. *Acta Psychiatrica Scandinavia,* 231:1, 1972.

Jones, E. Listed in Martin Birnbach: *Neo-Freudian Social Philosophy.* Stanford, Calif.: Stanford University Press, 1961.

Kagen, J. and Moss, H. *Birth to Maturity.* New York: John Wiley and Sons, 1962.

Kaplan, A. A philosophical discussion of normality. *Archives of General Psychiatry,* 17:325, 1967.

Kohut, H. *The Analysis of The Self.* New York: International Universities Press, 1971.

——. *The Restoration of The Self.* New York: International Universities Press, 1977.

Offer, D. *The Psychological World of the Teenager: A Study of Normal Adolescent Boys.* New York: Basic Books, 1969.

Offer, D., and Offer, J.B. *From Teenage to Young Manhood.* New York: Basic Books, 1975.

Offer, D., and Sabshin, M. *Normality: Theoretical and Clinical Concepts of Mental Health.* New York: Basic Books, 1974.

Offer, D.; Freedman, D.X.; and Offer, J.B., eds. *The Psychiatrist and Clinical Research.* New York: Basic Books, 1972.

Offer, D.; Marohn, R.C.; and Ostrov, E. *Psychological World of the Juvenile Delinquent.* New York: Basic Books, 1975.

Petersen, A.L.; Offer, D.; Solomon, B.; and Gitelson, I. "A Study of Normal Adolescent Girls." Unpublished paper, Chicago, 1978.

Rogers, C.R. A theory of therapy, personality and interpersonal relationships as developed in client-centered framework. In: Koch, S., ed. *Psychology: A Study of a Science.* Vol. 3, p. 184. New York: McGraw-Hill, 1959.

Romano, J. Basic orientation and education of the medical student. *Journal of the American Medical Association,* 143:409, 1950.

Symonds, P.M., and Jensen, A.R. *From Adolescent to Adult.* New York: Columbia University Press, 1961.

Vaillant, G.E. *Adaptation to Life.* Boston: Little, Brown, 1977.

Von Bertalanffy, L. *General Systems Theory.* New York: Braziller, 1968.

*The Course of Life: Psychoanalytic Contributions
Toward Understanding Personality Development.
Vol. II: Latency, Adolescence, and Youth.
S.I. Greenspan and G.H. Pollock, editors.
NIMH 1980*

Adolescents, Age Fifteen to Eighteen: A Psychoanalytic Developmental View

Eugene H. Kaplan, M.D.

Introduction

Among the variables influencing the spate of theoretical controversies about adolescence are the populations studied, the methods of observation, and the observer's theoretical orientation. Barglow and Schaefer (1976) note that analysts disagree on the value for psychoanalytic theory of data derived from neighboring disciplines somewhat removed from the psychoanalytic situation. They doubt that test batteries composed of psychological tests, questionnaires, and a limited number of interviews can meaningfully identify motivations, character traits, and conflicts.

Criteria for analyzability exclude the sickest as well as the healthiest patients. Moreover, Levenson et al. (1976) characterize the adolescent patients seen in private practice as children of permissive middle or upper class parents who can afford and approve of therapy and who are willing to relinquish their authority to an expert. The solipsistic danger in psychoanalytic theorizing about adolescence is to restrict the data base to the unrepresentative sampling of analyses and then consider the inferences drawn as universally applicable. This pitfall must be guarded against.

Not only do much relevant data escape through the coarser net of the nonanalytic studies, but also the workings of psychic structure and interpersonal relationships are more difficult to discern in healthier individuals. Conditions of crisis, conflict, and pathology make structures and functions more detectable.

The rational response is integration along the lines of Barglow and Schaefer's conclusions—that nonanalytic research can provide critical evaluation or validation of some psychoanalytic hypotheses, provided the studies are reproducible, utilize controls, and have demonstrable validity. Longitudinal studies are especially useful (Cramer 1976).

In the evolution of the psychoanalytic study of adolescence, the focus has shifted from the drives to the structural viewpoint, with an emphasis on the ego and its defense mechanisms, and more recently to the developmental point of view (Neubauer 1976). Contemporary psychoanalytic opinion disagrees with Spiegel's (1958) position that it is impossible to ascertain way stations over the course of adolescent development. The adolescent subphases with their specific developmental conflicts and tasks can be distinguished in a recognizable orderly sequence (Blos 1962).

The adolescent process involves the developmental tasks of adapting to physical and sexual maturation, attaining independence from parents, achieving heterosexual love relationships, planning and committing oneself to a future. These require intrapsychic restructuring and growth in a combination of regression and progression accompanied by anxiety and mourning. These intrapsychic events occur with—or without—varying degrees of overt manifestations of behavioral and emotional stress.

Psychopathology should not be confused with the adolescent process. What Geleerd (1961) mistakenly equated as paradigmatic for normal adolescence, Masterson (1967) has demonstrated to hold for the borderline adolescent alone.

Based on their longitudinal studies, Offer and Offer (1975) have described three developmental routes through normal male adolescence. The "continuous growth" group went from 14 to 22 smoothly and with self-assurance. Their genetic and environmental backgrounds were excellent, their families stable, and they had suffered no serious illness or object loss in childhood. Their parents encourged independence and seemed to grow themselves with their adolescent's growth, with a reciprocal sense of gratification.

The second, "the surgent growth" group, was characterized by developmental spurts. More concentrated energy was directed to mastering developmental tasks than in the first group. Their backgrounds were not as free of problems and trauma; their families were more likely to have experienced separations, deaths, or severe illnesses. Though they could cope with average, expected emotional challenges, the surgent group's ego development was not equal to major challenges, e.g., the death of a close relative. This group was more prone to depression, anxiety, and self-esteem problems, with greater reliance on parents or peers. There were conflicts between these adolescents and their parents and between the parents themselves, over values.

The third group, with a tumultuous psychological growth pattern, went through adolescence with an inner turmoil that often showed as overt behavioral problems at home and at school. Their backgrounds were less stable and contained more lower middle-class members than the other two groups. Their strong family bonds, however, distinguished them from delinquent adolescents. They had recurrent self-doubts, escalating conflicts with parents, and delibitating inhibitions. Their separation-individuation process was accompanied by emotional turmoil.

The Offers' "tumultuous growth" group seems to correspond with the psychoanalytic models of adolescent development adumbrated by Blos (1962), Deutsch (1967), and A. Freud (1958). Going beyond the refutation of turmoil as a prerequisite of healthy adolescent development, the Offers' followup findings suggest it to be the least desirable route. At age 22, the continuous growth group showed optimal functioning and the absence of clinical psychiatric syndromes, the surgent growth group had the same percentage of such syndromes as would be expected by the normal group distribution, while the tumultuous growth group had twice as many clinical psychiatric syndromes as would be expected by chance.

Ideally, the adolescent process simultaneously embraces transformation and continuity. The obligatory loosening, disruption, and reorganizing of psychic structure are not inevitably accompanied by significant emotional and behavioral disruption. The nature of the earlier structuralization is quintessentially important, based on successful negotiation of the previous developmental stages through surmounting their phase-specific tasks. While inner stress is unavoidable in this progression, an empathetic, synchronous, collaborative family and sociocultural context minimizes stress without thwarting the developmental process. The principle of appropriate dosage of stress, anxiety, and frustration holds not only for childhood, but for all developmental stages of life.

Gratification devoid of parental expectations of productions and contributions deprives the child of the pleasure in achievement and mastery, and of the related sense of competence and ability to deal with stress. Insufficient exposure to frustration and delay interferes with the development of the sublimatory mechanisms, with failure in impulse control and self-esteem regulation (Settlage 1969). On the other hand, our emphasis on the developmental task of freeing himself from the infantile tie to the original objects should not obscure our appreciation of the adolescent's need for stable, reliable parents. Lidz et al. (1976) suggest that latency peer involvement and adolescent essays in independent action also be considered "practicing periods" during which the parents continue to provide a delimiting influence and a source of shelter and security for moments of anxiety and failure.

Subphases of Adolescence

Freud analogized analysis to chess in contrasting the ease of describing the beginning and end games with the difficulty in conceptualizing the middle.

Most authors identify the biological event of puberty as the beginning of adolescence. The literature has focused increasingly on the end-game, late adolescence, with attempts to clarify and more precisely define in metapsychological terms the vicissitudes, modifications, transformations, and consolidations within the psyche.

In the West, successive generations have been getting taller and attaining puberty at progressively earlier ages. In Norway, where records have been kept since 1840, the age at menarche has dropped 4 months per decade, from 17 to 13. This secular trend seems to have ended in the past 10 to 30 years (Khatchadourian 1977). Although this biological shift may have halted, there is a social tendency to lower the age at which various milestones are passed, in part a diffusion of lower class practices upward to the middle and upper classes (Stone and Church 1957).

It is commonplace to contrast the biological initiation of adolescence with its socially defined termination. The end seems to be getting progressively later and increasingly blurred, at least for western middle class youth. The prolongation of education postpones the entry into vocation; among the more recent social trends, cohabitation without marriage and delay or abjuration of parenthood have rendered the delineation between adolescent and adult more indistinct.

Stone and Church (1957) hold that the psychological events of adolescence in our society are not a necessary counterpart of the physical changes of puberty, but are a "cultural invention," a product of the increasing delay in the assumption of adult responsibilities. In support of this position, Trent and Medsker (1968) found that full-time employment after high school and early marriage combined with full-time homemaking were associated with early identity closure, constriction of flexibility and autonomy, lowered intellectual curiosity, low tolerance for ambiguity, and a relative disinterest in new experiences. However, early closure does not invariably result in these sequelae. Healthy and outstanding adolescents may make definitive object and career choices which are chronologically precocious but psychologically appropriate.

Acknowledgement of the great importance of social factors should not cause neglect of the biological. Psychological growth is as rooted in biology as physical growth. Spruiell (1971) proposes the achievement of physical maturity as the biological demarcator of late adolescence, initiating psychological events which comprise a rapid restructuring within the ego of a new and more unified body image, and more mature self-and object-representations, along with the structuring of a more or less stable drive and defense hierarchy. Kestenberg (1968) believes that the hormonal increases in adolescence are paralleled by the surgence of clearly genital drives, increased depth of feeling, and augmented creativity. The most rapid increase in plasma testosterone levels occurs between 12 and 16 in boys, correlating statistically with onset of nocturnal emission, masturbation, dating, and first infatuation (Khatchadourian 1977).

Piaget and Inhelder (1958) have demonstrated a significant developmental advance from concrete to abstract thinking between 12 and 16, which they believe to depend on central nervous system maturation. The brain attains 95 percent of adult weight by age 10, and whether concomitant generalized or localized cephalic growth accompanies the advance in thinking is unknown. It is established, however, that children physically advanced for their age score higher in mental tests than those who are less mature physically but of the same chronological age (Tanner 1962). Another neuropsychological finding supporting neural maturation is that the critical period for retaining the ability to perceive phonetic contrasts may range up to age 16. Kolata (1975) cites Eimas' finding that Japanese exposed before age 16 to a language (English) which distinguishes (ra) and (la) could later hear this phonetic contrast.

The years from 12 to 15, 15 to 18, and 18 to 22 are convenient subdivisions of the adolescent years, corresponding to the ages in junior high school, senior high school, and college or work. These helpful socially defined landmarks are manifestly inadequate alone in classifying adolescents as early, middle, or late. Blos (1976*b*) states that, developmentally speaking, it is the degree of coordination and integration of ego functions, old and new, that spells out the completion of any developmental stage. Physical, sexual, and social status and cognitive level are unreliable indices.

In this developmental context we have noted Spruiell's thesis that the attainment of adult stature and procreative capacity initiates psychological changes in the ego characterized by synthesis, with a rather abrupt transition from middle to late adolescence. Prior to this inference, he notes the agreement of most psychoanalytic authors that therapeutic work in late adolescence, explicitly or implicitly assumed to be from about age 16, is different from earlier stages. In contrast to the action-language of the early adolescent who barely tolerates his "instinctual anxiety" and whose feelings remain inchoate, middle- and late-stage adolescents can express themselves in language and may even ask for help directly, with words rather than action.

In support of his proposition that integration of ego operations occurs around the age of 16, Spruiell cites Wolfenstein (1966) and Piaget and Inhelder (1958). Wolfenstein found that a true state of mourning, implying a new capacity to both relate to and separate from objects, does not develop until at least midadolescence. Spruiell claims that Piaget and Inhelder showed that fully operational thinking develops only at the age of 16 or 17; they actually date the onset from age 12.

Thinking

According to Piaget, the child from 8 to 12, in the stage of concrete operations, can deal with classes and relations as long as he has the objects present. While he does have semantic conceptions, they are more or less stimulus-bound, dependent on sensory input. As Wolfenstein (1958) puts it, the child before 12 has difficulty in understanding the figurative sense of words, adhering to a concrete visual image evoked by words, which precludes a shift of meaning. Therefore, proverbs cannot be understood. Riddles are enjoyable because the answer involves word play, while the original question remains unanswered and is forgotten.

In the stage of formal operations from age 12 on, the child no longer depends upon perceived data. Freed from the here and now, he deals with timeless, spaceless information. He can think of the possible, the potential, and he is ready to try to re-form data. Furthermore, he can think about propositions. In addition to ideas of negation originating in the previous stage of concrete operations, he now has ideas of reciprocity, i.e., how one cause acting upon a thing can nullify another cause. He can think in terms of variables and multiple determination of events. A puzzling phenomenon will touch off numerous hypotheses. Generating abstract hypotheses involves the cognition and production of implications. The adolescent in the stage of formal operations exhibits four kinds of transformations of propositions: identity, negation, reciprocity, and correlation. These transformations are necessary for dealing with proportionality and analogies and imply an increasing ability for dealing with complexity (Guilford 1967).

To recapitulate, this developmental advance in thinking between 12 and 16 is from the more concrete, present-oriented, simplistic right-good vs. wrong-bad to the general, formal, logical, and abstract. Dulit (1972) points out that Piaget's genetic epistemology focuses on cognition (problem solving, directed thinking) and not on a broader definition of thinking which encompasses motivations, affects, or fantasy. In the broader view, by middle adolescence, the capacity to think about thinking, work with ideas not immediately tied to concrete examples, leads to a greater appreciation of cause and effect, and antecedent causes. Thus the historical view appears—a sense of the causal significance of the past in viewing the present.

Meeks (1971) believes that the developmental advance in the cognitive area reinforces the predisposition to narcissism during adolescence. "The omnipotent, messianic preoccupations in the thought of the adolescent may be determined not only by his narcissistic withdrawal from the real world and internal objects, but also by the parallel developments in the unfolding of the cognitive apparatus" (p. 18).

Dulit (1972) replicated two of the formal stage experiments of Piaget and Inhelder with groups of average and gifted adolescents, ages 14 and 16–17. Contrary to the impression given by the Piaget-Inhelder work, he found that fully developed formal-stage thinking is not at all commonplace among normal or average adolescents. Dulit concludes that a unitary model of cognitive development is inadequate beyond the stage of concrete operations. He conceptualizes formal-stage thinking as a potentiality only partially attained by most and fully attained only by some.

Blos (1962) cites Spiegel's (1958) view that aesthetic conceptualization develops at this time and refers to Bernfeld's (1924) observations of adolescent achievements in thought and artistic creativity. He adds that the striking decline of creativity at the end of adolescence indicates it to be a function of the adolescent process. On the other hand, Grinker's (1971) group of healthy "homoclites" did not use fantasy as a defense against anxiety, manifested no marked capacity for abstraction, and were not very creative.

Physical Maturational Landmarks

Reviewing the data of physical development as compiled by Khatchadourian (1977), the average age of puberty onset is 10 to 11 for girls, 11 to 12 for boys. The average girl of 14 and boy of 16 have attained 98 percent of their adult heights. Continuing with the average, menarche at 12.8 years will be followed by the capacity for normal pregnancy by 14 to 15; 90 percent of boys experience the first ejaculation between 11 and 15, approximately 1 year after rapid testicular growth; mature sperm is in evidence between 15 and 16. Plasma testosterone levels in boys increase 20-fold between 10 and 17, the most rapid increase occurring between 12 and 16.

Spiegel (1958) located ages 16–17 as the midpoint of adolescence, the period of the transition from homosexual to heterosexual object choice. Blos (1962) links "adolescence proper" (equivalent to midadolescence) with the revival of the Oedipus complex, the emotional detachment from the family love objects, and the emergence of a nonincestuous, nonambivalent heterosexual object. In distinguishing this subphase from early adolescence, he follows Deutsch's (1944) division of "early puberty" and "advanced puberty."

Another ego-psychological correlation with ages 16–17 is the beginning of resolution of omnipotentiality, which Pumpian-Mindlin (1969) considers an essential element in the maturation of certain aspects of ego development, particularly as these relate to the self-concept. Extending Spruiell's argument, is it coincidental that the omnipotentiality theme starts to ebb just as physical growth is essentially completed? While the adolescent is now accustomed to his/her physical transformation and no longer very anxious about it, the very finality of "the limits of growth" poses a reality challenge to omnipotent and omnipotential fantasies. Childhood daydreams anticipating the growth to young man/womanhood are confronted by the reality of the grownup face and body. Plastic surgery to "correct" noses and ears may be a response to the narcissistic disappointment.

Two to 3 years from the onset of puberty are required for the adolescent to make his peace with the ensuing physical transformations. Waning of the profound, secret apprehension about the body is one criterion of the entrance into middle adolescence. Increasingly, the bodily changes are integrated as aspects of the self. Losing their strangeness, they may come to be taken for granted. Adding 2 to 3 years to the average age for puberty onset, middle adolescence begins between 12 and 14 in girls, 13 and 15 in boys. If, however, the onset of midadolescence is dated from the virtual completion of physical growth and the attainment of reproductive maturity, the girl enters this sub-phase at about 14 or 15, the boy around 15 or 16.

To further adumbrate our descriptions and definitions of adolescent sub-phases, the following avowedly overschematized proposition is useful for orientation: The early adolescent must redefine himself and his relationship to his parents in the wake of his momentous physical transformation. The middle adolescent must venture from the protective scaffolding of the peer group into one-to-one heterosexual love relationships. Sexual identity is further delineated in this intimacy. The late adolescent must define his spiritual and worldly standards and goals of achievement, while initiating their implementa-tion. To summarize, these redefinitions involve: first, his body and his parents; second, sexual identity and the relationship to the opposite sex; third, goals, standards, and the relationship to society.

Psychological midadolescence begins as biological adolescence, or more precisely, puberty, comes to an end. Lidz et al. (1976) list the midadolescent, phase-specific tasks as: separation from the family, assuming control of one's own life; achieving a firm ego identity and the capacity for intimacy with a significant heterosexual extra-familial love object, while tolerating the inevita-ble anxieties and feelings of loneliness. Each of these tasks requires extensive intrapsychic restructuring and modification.

Laufer (1976) makes a tripartite statement of the overall tasks of adoles-cence: changing the relationship to parents and to contemporaries and chang-ing the attitude to one's body. The mandatory change in relationship to the internal objects would normally result in the adolescent's acceptance of the fact that he alone is responsible for his sexually mature body (Laufer 1968). Separation from the family requires the relinquishment of both external and intrapsychic childhood dependent ties, while assuming control of one's own life implies the reestablishment of self-esteem regulation on a more autonom-ous level, effectively divorced from the parental figures. The capacity for heter-osexual intimacy, fusing sexual genital strivings and tenderness, devolves upon the resolution of the Oedipus complex. The accompanying intrapsychic transformations include the alteration to a more realistic inner representation of the parents, incorporating acknowledgment of their sexual lives, and changes in the superego which now entitle the adolescent to have his own sexual life, including coitus. These modifications have reciprocal reverberating influence, e.g., the adolescent's identification with the revised, more realistic image of the parents in their adult role helps shift power to the superego, simultaneously attenuating its archaic demands (Ritvo 1971).

Heterosexual relationships at the beginning of the middle subphase are more narcissistic, with one eye on oneself and the other on the peer group. At the end, adolescents are paired off, and they should manifest considerable capacity for empathy, tenderness, and responsibility. During midadolescence, the sense of personal identity, of being one's own self and owning one's own body rather than being defined solely as the child of one's parents, is worked out much more clearly in the peer-group relationship that ideally offers support, confidence, and distancing from the original objects (Solnit 1976). During early adolescence, the peer group lacks cohesiveness because of the minimal tolerance for group situations. Group formations at this time are unstable agglomerations of individuals. By midadolescence, the abatement in the narcissistic body preoccupation permits the turn to the peers. This investment is not a simple shift from the self to objects but is heavily laden with narcissism initially, insofar as the peer group takes over from the parents in serving as the ideal standard, the self-esteem regulator, and the controller of impulses.

The peer group serves as the mirror for defining the body image and sense of identity. Greenacre (1975) points out that the sense of identity involves both a feeling of uniqueness and of similarity and that the individual needs at least one other similar person to preserve the sense of identity. Identifications, which in early adolescence have a holistic imitative quality, become more selective and partial by the middle phase as the adolescent continually borrows and experiments in the reshaping of the self.

By the end of midadolescence, the individual should be more or less at ease in his sense of self and identity, self-esteem, self-regulation, independence from his parents, and heterosexual love relationships. Yet the adolescent process is far from complete. The restructuring and synthesis of late adolescence, the period of consolidation and implementation, involve further changes in superego and ego ideal with the coalescing of the hierarchy of defenses and character. The midadolescent's unfinished quality is reflected in his mood swings and open emotional display. He is still incapable of sharing his emotions with intimates and hiding them from public display without feeling divided; he still lacks a life plan, a purposive striving toward reasonable goals, an obligatory feature of adolescent closure (Blos 1976b). Identity does not incorporate definitively the sense of where he belongs in his particular society. The move to college or a job at around age 18 is the beginning of the period of implementation (Gould 1972). With the move out of the parental home, the adolescent's self-reliance will be tested. He must be able to stand alone in a secure and adaptive relationship to his new environment.

With this review of the years from 15 to 18, roughly equivalent to midadolescence, the period after the end of puberty and before consolidation and implementation, let us consider some of the features of this subphase in more detail.

Family

As the adolescent distances and defines himself in opposition to his parents, his denial of the continuing need for the limits and support of the family matrix may obscure our appreciation of its essential role. Solnit et al. (1969) view psychological growth as a consequence of the innate maturational developmental thrust plus the interaction between the less developed, less integrated psychic structure of the child and the more developed psyche of the adult. The adolescent still requires this interaction with adults.

The family itself must change, gradually relinquishing control of the young person, while maintaining a veto against excess and danger. This relinquishment causes intrapsychic reverberations in the parent. Ravenscroft (1974) posits a temporary normal family regression during early adolescence, providing an empathetic framework which reciprocally facilitates the development of the adolescent and his family. Stierlin (1974) conceptualizes the ideal form of their conflict as a "loving fight" in which the protagonists mutually affirm the other's entitlement to existence and differentiation.

Parental narcissism is affronted by the loss of their preadolescent idealized status, by the contrast between the waxing of the adolescent's sexuality and strength as their own is on the wane, by the gap between their grandiose expectations of their child as a narcissistic extension of themselves, and by the challenge to their values and ideals which earlier held their child's unquestioning adherence. Furthermore, the child's passage through the successive phases of development revives in his parents their unresolved conflicts specific to each phase (Kaplan, 1979). These assaults on parental self-esteem cause mourning for the latency child lost to adolescence and for the exalted status lost in its train. If parental depression or hostility is too great, one of a number of pathological outcomes in the relationship with the adolescent will ensue: attempts to thwart or abort the growth process, abdication, or extrusion.

Winnicott (1972) holds that many of the adolescent difficulties for which professional help is sought derive from environmental failure. Miller (1973) believes that the usual cause of failure of psychological maturation is isolation from extraparental adults. Without adult support, middle- and late-stage adolescents who are psychologically disturbed find it increasingly difficult to surmount their regressive dependency needs and to free themselves from the childish component of the tie to the original objects. While a stable network of extraparental adults will protect healthy adolescents from current disturbances in the parental relationship, it is a much less effective counter to earlier effects. In a related field, life-events research indicates that the availability of "social support systems" (enduring interpersonal ties providing emotional sustenance, assistance, and resources when needed, with shared values and standards) significantly reduces adult susceptibility to physical illness in the wake of stressful life changes (Rabkin and Struening 1976). Unfortunately, the deterioration of social networks has reduced the availability of suitable adults for individual adolescents. The lack of valid authority figures makes some adolescents excessively anxious about impulse control, fostering rigid defenses and a punitive superego. As adults, they may find it difficult to exercise authority at work and at home (Smarr and Escoll 1973).

Stable, healthy families deal with the problems and conflicts without damaging the adolescent or the family equilibrium, by dint of sensitivity, empathy, tenderness, and self-confidence. The marital relationship is a critical factor.

When parents were mutually secure and gratifying, the adolescents were healthier, even if the parents evidenced some psychopathology (King 1971). King's observations agree with those of Offer and Offer (1975), previously cited, on different routes through adolescence. Healthy parents respond to the adolescent with self-esteem intact. Their own realistically muted narcissism is reflected in the sense of competence with which they view themselves and their adolescing child. They can take pride in his developmental advances, empathize with his labors to achieve those advances, and challenge him without fear of losing his affiliation or guilt about thwarting his growth.

The function of the older generation is to provide continuity. In response to the individuating midadolescent's contesting the values of his parents and society, the most important strand of parental continuity is the maintenance of standards of value and morality (Ritvo 1971). The parents are not devalued in toto but continue to be important identificatory models. The adolescent's questioning of the validity and sincerity of the older generation's beliefs must be taken seriously. The forced reexamination of values in the face of challenge is stressful but ultimately rewarding for both sides. In Offer's (1969) study, rebellion was manifested mostly in early adolescence, between 12 and 14, and almost never concerned significant differences in values or standards. Rebellious teenagers broke rules at school and at home but were not delinquent or blatantly antisocial. This behavior gradually abated with increasing involvement in social activities later in high school. Offer sees the rebellion as part of the emancipatory process, accomplished without loss of love or respect for the parents. Katz et al. (1968) were impressed by the extent to which a sampling of late adolescent college students felt and behaved in conformity with their families in values, occupational choice, and social expectations.

Thus the teenager's equation of his repudiation of parental values with differentiation and independence should not be elevated uncritically to become one of our own criteria for successful passage through adolescence. Here the theoretician's values and experience of his own adolescence may introduce a bias. If his adolescence involved a successful overthrow of his parents' values in leaving a traditionalist group of origin behind, the theorist may tend to view the lack of repudiation as indicative of failure of the adolescent process. Acceptance or repudiation stemming from submission or defiance is a clear indication that genuine autonomy has not been achieved. However, parental values, adopted, worked over, and integrated as the adolescent's own in the course of emotional disengagement and conflict resolution, synthesize individuation and continuity. "If you are to possess what you inherited from your forefathers, you must first earn it" (Goethe, quoted by Mitscherlisch 1970).

Complementing Winnicott and Miller on environmental failure, King's typology of adolescent development differentiates a sensitive and vulnerable subgroup under the healthy category. This subgroup goes through adolescence with significantly greater distress than the other two healthy subgroups (modal-average and highly competent) but differs from the pathological categories in several important respects, including the time-limited nature of distress. It is a true adolescent phase upheaval. Despite their clear capabilities for meaningful object relationships, they tend to be loners. Their complaints about lack of parental understanding struck the observers as valid. Provided with an extraparental adult relationship through mental health services or other sources, these college students responded well to emotional support and advice, which enabled them to continue their developmental advance.

The erosion of cohesiveness in neighborhood and extended family has unquestionably limited the possibilities for relationships with adults outside the reduced family nucleus. In viewing this loss, we may tend to neglect an important channel open to the midadolescent—through his peer group to their parents.

The move to the peer group also opens the door to their homes and families. This exposure to other parents provides the teenager with reality-testing opportunities to compare their attitudes and relationships with his own. These observations alone may give enough confirmation to the adolescent challenging the idiosyncratic worldviews of his family to strengthen his sense of conviction and resolve. While the upper limits of development of ego function prior to adolescence are determined by the level attained by the family caretakers, reality testing is especially open to modification by extrafamilial influences, peer and adult, during adolescence.

Beyond this point, the relationship to the parents of friends may thicken so that they become parent surrogates. Where the adolescent's relationship with his own parents is especially troubled, the mantle of idealization may be transferred to his friend's mother and father, with effects paralleling King's sensitive-vulnerable groups' response to extraparental adults. For others, on better terms with their own parents, the friend's family is an enriching supplement, an additional source of identifications promoting ego interests; the split between the good and bad parent images isn't as marked in this instance. Both cases require a capacity for object relationship, implying a significant degree of earlier closeness to one or both of the parents. While this effectively eliminates a large number, it is surprising how many individuals who attain relatively healthy adult functioning despite psychotic parents had been able to enlist friends' parents as surrogates during adolescence.

In sum, the ideal phase-specific parental response to the midadolescent is a gradual ceding of control and power with a self-confident maintenance of one's own standards and values, with pride in their child's growth and with empathy for his struggle to achieve it, based on the realization that the advance to maturity requires the emotional disengagement and resolution of inner conflicts (Blos 1972 a). The penultimate parental wisdom is the understanding that the adolescent's defensive opposition and withdrawal do not obviate his continuing need for the parental framework during his restructuring, i.e., the parent understands that the adolescent does not want to be understood (Winnicott 1972).

Peer Relations

The psychological predicament of the early adolescent, burdened with the consequences of withdrawal from the parents and rejection of the comforting parental introjects, physical maturation, and the surgence of frightening and unacceptable impulses, prepares the way for the phase-specific shift to the peer group. Blos (1962) contrasts the "uniformism" of American middle class youth, based on this overriding shift to peers, with a much diminished tendency to seek out and identify with extraparental adults compared to European youth. At this point, the adolescent's needs are primarily narcissistic, with a touchy need for total approval from peers suitable for idealization in order to shore up fallen self-esteem. These peer involvements are quasi-relationships in a self-created social milieu, used intrapsychically to modulate and synthesize the tenuously integrated split parental images; by thus overcoming the sense of divisiveness and disharmony, a sense of basic inner unity is attained (Blos 1976a). Identification with the idealized peer or group at this stage is a regressive substitute for a libidinal object tie; when disillusionment sets in, they are dropped without a backward glance or a trace of mourning (Freud 1921), giving group formation at this stage its fickle, unstable character.

In the train of the inevitable devaluations of idealized figures, allegiance is transferred to another group or back to the family temporarily. Youth with more psychopathology are unable either to make the initial peer involvement or quickly withdraw for good. Alternately, such a disturbed youngster may attach himself to a "pseudogroup," in which some clearly defined stereotyped behavior, e.g., drug abuse, delinquency, or fighting with other gangs, confers a sense of belonging and identity, while intimacy is avoided (Meeks 1974).

The shift to contemporaries is a phase-specific accompaniment of a developmental progression; the normative adolescent launches himself outward from the stable empathetic family. By contrast, when supports are removed by death, divorce, parental pathology, or social upheaval, the youngster abandons the sinking ship and turns to his age mates as a substitute family. Precocious peer-group formation is an outgrowth of deprivation and family disorganization (Bronfenbrenner 1974) typical of the impoverished families of the inner city (Minuchin et al. 1967). With the increase of separation and divorce, this phenomenon is becoming more prevalent among middle class youth as well.

As the young person feels more secure with his body and his impulses in midadolescence, peer relations tend to jell. The peer group becomes the mirror of the body image, the social monitor, and behaviorial arbiter. The midadolescents are preoccupied with living up to the group ideal of masculinity or femininity and concerned with whether the opposite sex finds their behavior and appearance attractive (Hofmann et al. 1976). Only gradually are peers perceived more realistically as separate, distinct, and imperfect individuals whose friendship is valued notwithstanding; only gradually does the capacity for intimacy evolve.

Sexuality and Love

Sexuality is a central theme in the psychic reorganization of adolescence. In the past 15 years, sexual attitudes and behavior have changed significantly, notably among large segments of middle and upper class youth. Adolescents of both sexes in consultation or treatment speak about their sexual experiences, including menstruation, masturbation, contraception, and coitus, with much greater openness and ease today than when I began practice over 20 years ago. This does not signal the disappearance of the phase-specific need to keep optimal distance from adults, which does interfere with intimate discussions of sex (Clower 1975). Chess et al. (1976) found that sex was a closed topic with teenagers by the age of 16 with their parents, but not with the interviewers. Homosexuality and the content of masturbation fantasies are the exceptions, remaining too conflicted for easy discussion. The trend toward earlier sexual relationships, with or without emotional involvement, has provoked much disquietude with many authors echoing Deutsch's (1967) concerns that the inner transformation of narcissism into the capacity for genuine, enduring, heterosexual love relationships might be thwarted.

The truism still holds that all behavior must be evaluated in terms of its significance for the individual. While objections to earlier coitus are based on the developmental point of view, they overlook the change and even disappearance of certain taboos. Just as the younger generations use the four-letter obscenities casually and unconflictedly in contrast to their elders' twinge of discomfort at superego defiance, so also have the taboos around virginity eroded for certain youth. The superego sanctions provoked by sexual activity seem less intense than before and are no longer reinforced by harsh social condemnation. Therefore, while early coitus may well serve regressive or defensive functions, developmental interference is neither inevitable nor irrevocable. A Sicilian brought up in a tradition which sanctions death or literal castration of a seducer by the dishonored family has a different superego attitude and level of castration anxiety than a Parisian youth who learns that his friend's parents are having affairs also.

This changing valence of coitus strikingly influenced two young, white, middle class victims of black rapists. Both were involved in protracted intimate heterosexual relationships when raped. Despite the clear evidence of traumatization (gradually diminishing startle reactions, recurrent anxiety dreams, and anxiety in situations reminiscent of their victimization), neither girl's capacity for heterosexual object relationships or sexual responsiveness, including orgasm, suffered appreciably. The midadolescent's great concern about peer response was mitigated when her family moved, and she became involved with a new boyfriend within a couple of months. The late adolescent expressed no such concerns; her relationship evolved into engagement within 6 months.

Some 15 years ago, a high school senior complained that a group of junior girls were using him in common as the tool of their defloration. At first he had been flattered by this confirmation of his attractiveness and popularity, but when he realized that each girl would have intercourse with him only once and that the relationships were confined to the girl's peer group, excluding him, he cooperated no longer. Shortly thereafter, he fell in love with a girl outside of this group, amply demonstrating the fusion of tenderness and sexuality in an enduring relationship.

In the wake of changing sexual mores, a recent phenomenon highlighting the girls' biopsychological maturational lead has come to my attention. In three instances, a 17- or 18-year-old virginal youth was initiated into coitus in the context of a tender loving relationship by a girl his age, sexually experienced through a series of brief liaisons devoid of significant object relationship. These earlier sexual experiences had been undertaken by the girls to explore and prove their femininity. These narcissistic trends were succeeded by and integrated with the object relationship in a phase-appropriate evolution.

Chess et al. (1976) found in their longitudinal study a progression from friends of the same sex, to companions of both sexes, to dating, to steady dating, and finally to sexual intercourse, either as an affair or as casual sex. Offer's (1973) Model Adolescent Project data, from a group whose high school years spanned 1962–1966, do not reflect the adolescent sexual revolution; how widespread these changes are today is unclear. For boys, the dating experience was not a critical one for the first 2 years of high school. In the interviews, rationalizations for not dating were often followed by inferentially oedipal associations to their mothers. Their progressively increasing dating began as a sortie from the same-sex peer group, returning to the group to share the experience in detail almost immediately after bringing the girl home. Eventually, with diminishing anxiety, the relation to the girl became central. As boys became more at ease in the dating relationship, the ambivalence in their relationship to their mothers diminished significantly. Offer states that early and midadolescent boys appear less concerned than the girls about sexuality; the boys' more important preoccupation was curbing their aggression. The girls began dating much earlier, by the end of ninth grade; all in the sample were dating by eleventh. By contrast, only 30 percent of the eleventh grade boys dated actively; half of these petted heavily; only 10 percent had coitus. More than 90 percent of the boys daydreamed about girls, but only 25 percent about a girl they knew personally. Often, it was an older woman the boy knew. The nondating groups' daydreams were almost never about a girl known personally.

Masturbation. According to Francis and Marcus' (1975) review, adolescent masturbation assists the forward movement of the drives (the phase-adequate function) and helps to bring the pregenital drives under the regulation of the genital function (the phase-specific function). It functions adaptively in assisting further delineation of inner and outer reality, the development of psychic structure, furthering the development of the self-concept, with integration of all body parts into the body image. The integrative function of masturbation, like dreams, shows the adolescent's preferential methods for the control and discharge of tension. Masturbation fantasies help further object relatedness by bringing early autoerotic experiences into opposition with objects through fantasy. Masturbation utilizing the opposite sex as an object in fantasy is reached slowly, culminating in midadolescence.

Clower (1975) states that individual patterns of masturbatory behavior do not change much from latency to adolescence in girls with normative phase-specific conflicts. What does change is the psychological basis for the behavior. Serving as a defense against internal genital sensations and the wish-fear of vaginal penetration early, it becomes the trigger and focal point of spreading genital excitement which heralds and augments the readiness for coitus. The repeated experiencing of the body and growing capacity for sexual gratification, and the growing sense that the body belongs to the self, help complete dissolution of symbiotic infantile ties and support autonomy against the regressive fears of the symbiotic mother who won't let go, the castrating mother who left her maimed and bleeding, and the oedipal mother who brooks no rivals.

Borowitz (1973) finds that early disturbances in object relationships may lead to inadequate development of the capacity to tolerate and integrate drive discharge and an incapacity to masturbate alone in adolescence. In some cases, an external object is used to tolerate and/or defend against fantasy. He believes that the capacity to masturbate alone in adolescence is a developmental achievement, a way station in the transition from infantile sexuality to adult genitality and from narcissism to object relations.

Laufer (1976) posits that the central masturbation fantasy, a universal phenomenon, is fixed by the resolution of the Oedipus complex. With this resolution, the main sexual identifications become fixed and the core of the body image established. Only during adolescence, however, does the content of the sexual wishes and the oedipal identifications become integrated into an irreversible sexual identity. During adolescence, the oedipal wishes are tested in the context of the possession of mature genitalia. The function of adolescent masturbation is both a trial action experienced within one's own thought and a way of testing which sexual thoughts, feelings, or gratifications are acceptable to the superego. A compromise solution is found which defines the person's sexual identity. Late adolescence ushers in the consolidation phase in which this irreversible sexual position should be achieved and masturbation relinquished for true object attachment.

All mating behavior originates in mother-child behavior. Sarlin (1970) more specifically identifies the mother-child nursing dyad as the prototype of lovemaking. Ritvo (1971) reminds us that with the establishment of genital primacy, the individual becomes dependent upon the body of the object in a way that has not existed since infancy. This causes a shift in the balance between the reality-and-pleasure principle, from gratification and discharge associated with fantasy and the autoplastic activity of masturbation, to gratification in the context of the alloplastic relationship to the external object. For the late adolescent, the new object serves functions at a higher level, resembling those served by the object of infancy and early childhood, as a stabilizer of physiological and affective processes.

Adolescent Love. In view of these implications of intimacy and its anxiety-laden regressive potential, falling in love is a developmental crisis. Williams (1973) draws attention to the obstacles to this phase-specific attainment in a sociocultural and familial context, emphasizing achievement and performance which foster a competitive narcissistic ego identity. Following the initial mother-child symbiosis, Williams sees little further experience with intimacy. Yet, at 18, the adolescent is expected to somehow tap that early experience and apply it to love relationships.

Kernberg (1974) deals at length with the question of ego identity as the general prerequisite for falling in love. Ego identity, the overall organization of identifications and introjections under the ego's synthetic function, reflects the capacity for intimacy (Erikson 1956), defined as a total relation with a heterosexual object, including tenderness, full genital gratification, and human depth. Ego identity is established gradually throughout infancy and childhood, as the primitive ego organization's splitting evolves into an integrated ego employing repression and related higher level defense mechanisms. Such ego functioning, in the context of integration of total object relations, reciprocally reinforces ego identity.

In disagreement with Erikson, Kernberg's position that the establishment of ego identity is not a universal issue in normal adolescence is supported by the findings of Jacobson (1964) and the group studies of Masterson (1967), Offer (1969), and King (1971). In Kernberg's view, identity crises are normative for adolescence; identity diffusion is not. The crisis involves a loss of correspondence of the internal sense of identity with the confirmation provided by the psychosocial environment. Diffusion, characterized by mutually dissociated ego states with disintegration extending to the superego and internalized object relations, occurs in neurotics with specific narcissistic conflicts, borderline and psychotic patients.

The typical clinical manifestations of sexual conflicts in adolescence are: dissociation of tenderness from sexual excitement, dichotomy of asexual idealized objects and sexually devalued objects (Madonna vs. whore), and the coexistence of excessive guilt and impulsive expression of sexual urges. These symptoms, Kernberg warns, do not give a diagnostic clue to the severity of psychopathology. Falling in love produces an experience of transcendence in the normal adolescent. Going beyond Frosch (1966), Kernberg agrees that reality constancy is closely interwoven with object constancy, but that the former evolves beyond the limit of love-object constancy. The capacity to experience indepth the nonhuman environment, to appreciate nature and art, and to experience the self within an historical and cultural continuum are intimately linked with the capacity for being in love.

Psychic Restructuralization

It will be helpful in our consideration of the revisions, additions, and reorganization of psychic structure in adolescence to review preceding development. Object-relations theory, as explained by Kernberg (1976), provides a congenial heuristic framework which more adequately conveys the gradualistic continuity of normal development. The progressive evolution of the mind is characterized in terms of gradual reciprocal interactions and mutual influences: Through the reshaping of experiences with external objects in the light of internal object representations and of these object representations in the light of real experiences with others, ego identity (the organized processes of internalization of object relations) evolves; simultaneously the self-concept is continuously reshaped in the context of experiences with others and of experiences with the inner world of object representations. The more integrated the self-representations, the more self-perception corresponds to the reality of the interpersonal interaction; the more integrated the object representations, the greater the capacity for realistic assessment of others, and of revising the internal representations on the basis of realistic assessments. The processes of integration, depersonification, and individualization are structural outcomes of the internalization of object relations in all agencies of the mind. Individualization refers to the gradual replacement of primitive introjections and identifications with partial, sublimatory identifications compatible with the self-concept.

In Kernberg's view, the consolidation of the ego, presupposing the supersession of splitting processes by regression, probably occurs in the second and third years. With its fusion of positive and negative introjections, there is the formation of the ideal self-image, representing the striving for the reparation of guilt and for the reestablishment of an ideal, positive self-object relationship; its counterpart, the ideal-object image, represents the unharmed, all-loving, all-forgiving object (Jacobson 1964; Sandler et al. 1963). Superego components form between the second and fifth years, with definite integration mainly between the fourth and sixth, followed by depersonification and abstraction between the fifth and seventh. With integration, the absolute, fantastic nature of primitive idealization (the early ego ideal, condensed from the ideal self- and ideal-object representations), and of the sadistic forerunners of the superego (extremely hostile and unrealistic object images derived from projected and reintrojected "bad" self-object representations) is mitigated, along with a decrease in the projection of such sadistic and idealized superego nuclei.

With the decrease in the projective processes, the internalizations of the parental demands and prohibitions during the oedipal phase can occur on a more realistic level. Kernberg cites Jacobson's theoretical clarifications and adumbrations of structural evolution repeatedly, as do Ritvo (1971) and Blos in their considerations of the ego ideal in adolescence.

The ego ideal is the goal- and aspiration-setting agency of the mind, conceptualized variously as a component of the superego or separate from it. Originating in infantile narcissism, it remains closely related to self-esteem regulation, need satisfaction, and wish fulfillment throughout life (Lampl-de Groot 1962). Shame is the characteristic affect of disharmony between ego and ego ideal; guilt typifies the tension between ego and the prohibiting agency, the superego (Piers and Singer 1953). Genetically, the ego ideal operates with positive libidinal strivings; aggression prevails in the superego (Bibring 1964). While superego demands can be fulfilled with a subsequent sense of well-being, ego ideal demands for perfection can never be fulfilled (Blos 1974).

According to Blos, the function of the early ego ideal is to eradicate narcissistic mortification through recourse to a state of illusory self-perfection. In the oedipal phase, the oedipal realization of physical immaturity is mitigated by borrowing perfection from the idealized parents and from their narcissistic overestimation of the child. The normal childhood ego-ideal state of partial integration and external regulation undergoes a radical and lasting change with the second individuation process of adolescence. The emotional disengagement from the internalized love and hate objects of early childhood leads to the heightened narcissistic state, idealizations, and rebellious self-assertion typifying adolescence.

In the final stages of adolescence, Jacobson finds a hierarchical reorganization and final integration of value concepts, arising from both ego and superego into a new coherent structure and functional unit, the ego ideal. Ritvo states that the ego ideal as a structuralized institution of the mind is a development of adolescence. Blos holds that the structuralization of the ego ideal renders it qualitatively different from antecedent developmental stages and determines the end phase of the adolescent process. In the intersystemic reapportionment, the ego expands at the expense of the id and superego and cedes certain value functions to the ego ideal; the superego is encroached upon by both ego and ego ideal.

Qualitatively, the striving after perfection of the ego ideal becomes a partly independent, direction-giving function, relatively independent of objects and of instinctual processes (Hartmann and Loewenstein 1962). From dependent, personalized, and concretized, the ego ideal becomes autonomous, impersonal, and abstracted. Excessive self- and object idealization are reduced to more realistic appraisals as the ego ideal loses its more primitive wish-fulfillment quality and comes under the hegemony of ego identity.

Ritvo (1971) believes that one of the main genetic roots of the ego ideal is in the passive feminine homosexual orientation of the negative Oedipus complex (Freud 1914); that reinstinctualization of the ego ideal by predominantly homosexual libido is a normative aspect of the adolescent process; and that the ego-ideal's evolution into a structuralized institution of the mind is an adolescent development.

Summarizing Blos' thesis, in essential agreement with Ritvo, definitive resolution of the Oedipus complex, involving the total renunciation of infantile object ties to both parents as sexual objects (the positive and negative components), is the inherent task of adolescence. Since the bisexual position is less conflictual for the child, the negative Oedipus complex seems less stringently affected than the positive at the end of the oedipal phase. Bisexuality in women, less conflictual throughout life, is never repressed or resolved as definitively as for men. Stabilization of femininity and attainment of the mature, desexualized, impersonal ego ideal by the late adolescent girl involve supplanting the regressive incorporation of the paternal phallus as the narcissistic regulator of the sense of completeness and perfection by an enduring identification with her mother. Even if this development is achieved, the woman's ego ideal retains the potential for reenmeshment with object relations.

Blos views the boy's development as following a different course. In early adolescence, the regressive revival of the preoedipal, omnipotent phallic mother image intensifies both his castration anxiety and his narcissistic identification with his maternal representation. Fearing mother and women, he idealizes father, bolstering his self-esteem by identification and defending against castration anxiety by the relationship. When the sexual impulse threatens the arousal of homosexual object libido toward the father, this defensive solution is terminated. Object displacement, leading to overt homosexuality, is unacceptable; the obligatory development is the resolution of the negative Oedipus complex and the deinstinctualization of the narcissistic homosexual object tie. In the process, all ego-ideal trends coalesce into final unalterable form in the terminal stage of adolescence. The male ego ideal enshrines its history, from primary narcissism to the merger with maternal omnipotence to the oedipal love for the father. This last stage is transcended in the mature ego ideal, the heir of the negative Oedipus complex as the superego is the heir of the positive (Blos 1965).

Blos' masterfully evocative exegesis has a number of shortcomings, including excessively heavy reliance on libido theory, a tendency to metapsychological reification, and speculative assertions about cause and effect in intrapsychic evolution. Moreover, his views on normative development, based avowedly on extrapolations from psychopathology, overemphasize the punctate crisis and lurching advance or failure. The complementary neglect of the linear gradualism, which I find typical of outstanding and normal development, blurs its delineation from abnormal in Blos' conceptualization. Therefore, while joining the cumulative consensus that changes in both quality and content of ego ideal and superego occur in adolescence, I would take exception to the notion that the ego ideal is born as a structure at late adolescence or that the transition from its personalized, dependent, and concretized qualities to impersonal, autonomous, and abstracted is confined to this phase. Restructuralization is a better term.

Summary

The early adolescent must redefine himself and his relationship to his parents in the wake of his momentous physical transformation. The middle adolescent must venture from the protective scaffolding of the peer group into dyadic heterosexual love relationships. The late adolescent must define his spiritual and worldly standards and goals of achievement, while initiating their implementation. These developmental redefinitions involve: first, his body and his family; second, sexual identity and intimacy; third, standards, goals, and the relationship to society.

Psychological midadolescence begins as biological growth ends. Physical growth is virtually complete and reproductive maturity attained by age 14 or 15 in the girl; 15 or 16 in the boy. Successful negotiation of the midadolescent subphase between 17 and 19 finds the young person at ease in his/her sense of self and identity, with relatively stable and autonomous self-esteem and self-regulation, emotionally emancipated from childish dependence on family and capable of heterosexual intimacy.

The developmental tasks of midadolescence require extensive intrapsychic reorganization. Further restructuring, notably of superego and ego ideal, and the coalescing of character and the defense hierarchy take place before the final closure at the end of late adolescence.

References

Barglow, P., and Schaefer, M. A new female psychology? *Journal of the American Psychoanalytic Association,* 24:305–350, 1976.

Bernfeld, S. *Vom dicterischen Schaffender Jugend.* (On Poetically Creative Youth) Vienna: Internationaler Psychoanalytischer Verlag, 1924.

Bibring, G. Some considerations regarding the ego ideal in the psychoanalytic process. *Journal of the American Psychoanalytic Association,* 12:517–521, 1964.

Blos, P. *On Adolescence: A Psychoanalytic Interpretation.* New York: Free Press of Glencoe, 1962.

——. The initial stage of male adolescence. *The Psychoanalytic Study of the Child,* 20:145–164, 1965.

——. The second individuation process of adolescence. *The Psychoanalytic Study of the Child,* 22:162–186, 1967.

——. The function of the ego ideal in adolescence. *The Psychoanalytic Study of the Child,* 27:93–97, 1972*a.*

——. The generation gap: Fact and fiction. *Adolescent Psychiatry,* 1:5–13, 1972*b.*

——. The genealogy of the ego ideal. *The Psychoanalytic Study of the Child,* 29:43–88, 1974.

——. When and how does adolescence end? *Journal of the Philadelphia Association for Psychoanalysis,* 3:47–58, 1976*b.*

——. The split parental image in adolescent social relations: An inquiry into group psychology. *The Psychoanalytic Study of the Child,* 31:7–34, 1976*a.*

Borowitz, G.H. The capacity to masturbate alone in adolescence. *Adolescent Psychiatry,* 2:130–143, 1973.

Bronfenbrenner, U. The origins of alienation. *Scientific American,* August 1974, p. 231.

Chess, S.; Thomas, A.; and Cameron, M. "Sexual attitudes and behavior patterns in a middle-class adolescent population." Paper presented at American Orthopsychiatric Association Annual Meeting, Atlanta, Ga., March 1976.

Clower, V.L. Significance of masturbation in female sexual development. In: Marcus, I.M., and Francis, S.J., eds. *Masturbation from Infancy to Senescence.* New York: International Universities Press, 1975.

Cohen, R.S., and Balikov, H. On the impact of adolescence upon parents. *Adolescent Psychiatry,* 3:217–236, 1974.

Cramer, B. Outstanding developmental progression in three boys: A longitudinal study. *The Psychoanalytic Study of the Child,* 30:15–48, 1976.

Deutsch, H. *The Psychology of Women.* Vol. I. New York: Grune and Stratton, 1944.

——. *Selected Problems of Adolescence.* New York: International Universities Press, 1967.

Dulit, E. Adolescent thinking à la Piaget: The formal stage. *Journal of Youth and Adolescence,* 1:281–301, 1972.

Erikson, E.H. The problem of ego identity. *Journal of the American Psychoanalytic Association,* 4:56–121, 1956.

Francis, S.J., and Marcus, I.M. Masturbation: A developmental view In: Marcus, I.M., and Francis, S.J., eds. *Masturbation from Infancy to Senescence.* New York: International Universities Press, 1975.

Freud, A. Adolescence. *The Psychoanalytic Study of the Child,* 13:255–278, 1958.

——. Adolescence as a developmental disturbance. In: Caplan, G., and Lebovici, S., eds. *Adolescence; Psychosocial Perspectives.* New York: Basic Books, 1969.

Freud, S. On narcissism (1914). *Standard Edition.* 14:73–102. London: Hogarth Press, 1957.

——. Group psychology and the analysis of the ego (1921). *Standard Edition.* 18:69–143. London: Hogarth Press, 1955.

Frosch, J. A note on reality constancy. In: Loewenstein, R.M.; Newman, L.M.; Schur, M.; and Solnit, A.J.; eds. *Psychoanalysis: A General Psychology.* New York: International Universities Press, 1966.

Geleerd, E. Some aspects of ego vicissitudes in adolescence. *Journal of the American Psychoanalytic Association,* 9:394–405, 1961.

Gould, R.L. The phases of adult life: A study of developmental psychology. *American Journal of Psychiatry,* 129:521–531, 1972.

Greenacre, P. Differences between male and female adolescent development. *Adolescent Psychiatry,* 4:105–120, 1975.

Grinker, R.R., Sr.; Grinker, R.R., Jr.; and Timberlake, J. "Mentally healthy" young males: Homoclites. *Adolescent Psychiatry,* 1:176–255, 1971.

Guilford, J.P. *The Nature of Human Intelligence.* New York: McGraw-Hill, 1967.

Hartmann, H., and Loewenstein, R.M. Notes on the superego. *The Psychoanalytic Study of the Child,* 17:42–81, 1962.

Hofmann, A.D.; Becker, R.D.; and Gabriel, H.P. *The Hospitalized Adolescent.* Riverside, N.J.: The Free Press, 1976.

Jacobson, E. The self and the object world. *The Psychoanalytic Study of the Child,* 9:75–127, 1954.

——. *The Self and the Object World.* New York: International Universities Press, 1964.

Kaplan, E.H. Unfinished business: Revival of the parent's unresolved conflicts during the adolescence of his child. In: Orgel, S., and Fine, D., eds. *Clinical Psychoanalysis.* Vol. III. New York: Aronson, 1979.

Katz, J., and Associates. *No Time for Youth.* San Francisco: Jossey-Bass, 1968.

Kernberg, O. Mature love: Prerequisites and characteristics. *Journal of the American Psychoanalytic Association,* 22:743–768, 1974.

——. *Object-Relations Theory and Clinical Psychoanalysis.* New York: Jason Aronson, 1976.

Kestenberg, J. Phases of adolescence, with suggestions for correlation of psychic and hormonal organization. Part 3. Puberty growth, differentiation and consolidation. *Journal of the American Academy of Child Psychiatry,* 7:108–151, 1968.

Khatchadourian, H. *The Biology of Adolescence.* San Francisco: W.H. Freeman, 1977.

King, S.H. Coping mechanisms in adolescents. *Psychiatric Annals,* 1:10–45, 1971.

Kolata, G.B. Behavioral development: Effects of environments. *Science,* 189:207–209, 1975.

Lampl-de Groot, J. Ego ideal and superego. *The Psychoanalytic Study of the Child,* 17:94–106, 1962.

Laufer, M. The body image, the function of masturbation, and adolescence: Problems of the ownership of the body. *The Psychoanalytic Study of the Child,* 23:114–137, 1968.

——. The central masturbation fantasy, the final sexual organization and adolescence. *The Psychoanalytic Study of the Child,* 31:297–316, 1976.

Levenson, E.A.; Feiner, A.H.; and Stockhauer, N.N. The politics of adolescent psychiatry. *Adolescent Psychiatry,* 4:84–100, 1976.

Lidz, T.; Lidz, R.W.; and Rubenstein, R. An anaclitic syndrome in adolescent amphetamine addicts. *The Psychoanalytic Study of the Child,* 31:317–348, 1976.

Masterson, J.F., Jr. *The Psychiatric Dilemma of Adolescence.* Boston: Little, Brown, 1967.

Meeks, J.T. *The Fragile Alliance.* Baltimore: Williams and Wilkins, 1971.

——. Adolescent development and group cohesion. *Adolescent Psychiatry,* 3:289–297, 1974.

Miller, D.H. The drug-dependent adolescent. *Adolescent Psychiatry,* 2:70–97, 1973.

Minuchin, S.; Montalvo, B.; Guervey, B.C., Jr.; Rosman, B.L.; and Schumer, T. *Families of the Slums: An Exploration of Their Structure and Treatment.* New York: Basic Books, 1967.

Mitscherlisch, A. *Society Without the Father* (1963). Translated by E. Mosbacher. New York: Shocken, 1970.

Moore, W.T. Some economic functions of genital masturbation during adolescent development. In: Marcus, I.M., and Francis, S.J., eds. *Masturbation from Infancy to Senescence.* New York: International Universities Press, 1975.

Neubauer, P. *The Process of Child Development.* New York: New American Library, 1976.

Offer, D. *The Psychological World of the Teenager.* New York: Basic Books, 1969.

——. The adolescent sexual revolution. *Adolescent Psychiatry,* 2:165–171, 1973.

Offer, D., and Offer, J. Three developmental routes through normal male adolescence. *Adolescent Psychiatry,* 4:121–141, 1975.

Piaget, J., and Inhelder, B. *The Growth of Logical Thinking from Childhood to Adolescence.* New York: Basic Books, 1958.

Piers, G., and Singer, M.B. *Shame and Guilt.* New York: Norton, 1953.

Pumpian-Mindlin, E. Omnipotentiality, youth and commitment. *Journal of the American Academy of Child Psychiatry,* 4:1–18, 1965.

——. Vicissitudes of infantile omnipotence. *The Psychoanalytic Study of the Child,* 23:213–226, 1969.

Rabkin, J.G., and Struening, E.L. Life events, stress and illness. *Science,* 194:1013–1020, 1976.

Ravenscroft, K., Jr. Normal family regression at adolescence. *American Journal of Psychiatry,* 131:31–35, 1974.

Ritvo, S. A psychoanalytic view of the family: A study of family member interactions. *Psychoanalytic Forum,* 3:13–27, 1969.

——. Late adolescence: Developmental and clinical considerations. *The Psychoanalytic Study of the Child,* 26:241–263, 1971.

——. Adolescent to woman. *Journal of the American Psychoanalytic Association,* 24:127–138, 1976.

Sandler, J.; Holder, A.; and Meers, D. The ego ideal and the ideal self. *The Psychoanalytic Study of the Child,* 18:139–158, 1963.

Sarlin, C.N. The current status of the concept of genital primacy. *Journal of the American Psychoanalytic Association,* 18:285–299, 1970.

Smarr, E.R., and Escoll, P.J. The youth culture, future adulthood, and societal change. *Adolescent Psychiatry,* 2:113–126, 1973.

Solnit, A.J. Adolescence and the changing reality. In: Marcus, I.M., ed. *Currents in Psychoanalysis.* New York: International Universities Press, 1971.

——. Inner and outer changes in adolescence. *Journal of the Philadelphia Association for Psychoanalysis,* 3:43–46, 1976.

Solnit, A.J.; Settlage, C.F.; Goodman, S.; and Blos, P. Youth unrest: A symposium. *American Journal of Psychiatry,* 125:1145–1159, 1969.

Spiegel, L.A. Comments on the psychoanalytic psychology of adolescence. *The Psychoanalytic Study of the Child,* 13:296–308, 1958.

Spruiell, V. The transition of the body image between middle and late adolescence. In: Marcus, I.M., ed. *Currents in Psychoanalysis.* New York: International Universities Press, 1971.

Stierlin, H. *Separating Parents and Adolescents.* New York: Quadrangle, 1974.

Stone, L.J., and Church, J. *Childhood and Adolescence.* New York: Random House, 1957.

Tanner, J.M. *Growth at Adolescence.* 2nd. ed. Oxford: Blackwells, 1962.

Trent, J.W., and Medsker, L.L. *Beyond High School.* San Francisco: Jossey-Bass, 1968.

Williams, F.S. The adolescent sexual revolution. *Adolescent Psychiatry.* 2:162–165, 1973.

Winnicott, D.W. Adolescence: Struggling through the doldrums. *Adolescent Psychiatry,* 1:40–50, 1972.

Wolfenstein, M. Children's understanding of jokes. *The Psychoanalytic Study of the Child,* 13:296–308, 1958.

——. How is mourning possible? *The Psychoanalytic Study of the Child,* 21:93–123, 1966.

The Course of Life: Psychoanalytic Contributions
Toward Understanding Personality Development.
Vol. II: Latency, Adolescence, and Youth.
S.I. Greenspan and G.H. Pollock, editors.
NIMH 1980

The Tides of Change
in Adolescence

Henry P. Coppolillo, M.D.

Comprehensive statements about adolescence are difficult because adolescence can be scrutinized from a number of perspectives and vantage points. Viewing it in the past, we can note how events in history have influenced the role of adolescents in society. Anatomical and physiological changes can be contemplated as important areas of concern. The adaptive point of view highlights the tasks the youngster must muster to pick a vocation and choose a mate. The vicissitudes of libido and aggression have been studied and described, and ego psychology has given us a framework in which we can contemplate how changes in body image can be integrated into an image of the total self. In this essay I should like to invite your attention to some areas that seem to have evoked relatively less curiosity and comment in psychoanalytic thinking than other considerations. These are the areas of integration, organization, and regulation of ego functions during adolescence.

Integration can be conceptualized as the fusion of two or more functions of lesser complexity to produce a number of functions of greater complexity. The repertoire of behavior or the number of functions available to the individual after integration has taken place is greater than the sum of the individual functions prior to integration.

For our purposes, the organization of the ego is the manner in which ego functions are deployed or grouped at any given period to meet the requisites of the individual and of the environment or to relieve the strain between environmental constraints and individual wishes.

Regulation can be considered to be the process of first perceiving the need for a change in the deployment of ego functions (or the need to maintain them in an unchanged state) and then the process of undertaking these changes or stabilizing maneuvers.

With these definitions, we may construct a model that demonstrates the processes of integration, organization, and regulation.

Where better to begin to look at adolescence than Shakespeare's great ode to youth in *Romeo and Juliet?* Romeo, after crashing the Capulet party, goes to his confidant and teacher Friar Laurence to exult about his love for Juliet. The Friar is astounded since only the day before Romeo had been desperately in love with Rosaline. Romeo breezily states that his passion for Rosaline has passed and he now loves another. The Friar continues to be amazed that so desperate a love could have passed so quickly. Romeo is irritated with so much reasonable perplexity and reminds the good friar that he had chided Romeo for loving Rosaline intensely and that while Juliet returns his love, Rosaline had never done so. The friar, with wisdom and insight, explains Rosaline's reticence with the line, "O, she knew well thy love did read by rote and could not spell."

Apparently, the adolescent's tendency to assume an attitude, experience a feeling, or immerse himself in a state for the sake of the state, attitude, or feeling was well known as far back as we care to look. In addition, adult perplexity and amazement at adolescents' turbulent emotions and apparently quixotic behavior are not new. Despite the fact that it has been described and redescribed by master observers of the human condition, such as Shakespeare, it would be difficult to find today an adult who has not been charmed, seduced, perplexed, and even victimized by the storms of emotion and the vagaries of behavior that characterize young people who are traversing that brief but critically important span of life called adolescence.

To pass from the romantic to the commonplace, imagine the father of an adolescent boy settling into his chair in front of the television after a grueling day with the conviction that he has earned his preprandial drink and a half-hour's peace. His son, with whom he has been on surprisingly good terms for several days, slouches into the room and in response to father's greetings mutters something that might have been equally well understood as "Hello" or "Heck, No!" Ten minutes or so go by in silence when in response to the news commentator's remark on the energy crisis, the son begins to mutter angrily. Father, thinking that the boy's vocalizations were an invitation to conversation, says something viciously provocative such as, "It looks as if we'll be facing some pretty tough problems in the next few years." In response the boy begins with a condemnation of father's entire generation. As he warms to the task, he becomes more pointed and specific, reminding father that if he were only willing to walk or bicycle the 7 or 8 miles to work instead of driving the gas guzzling Volkswagen, the energy shortage would be resolved. But no! The hedonistic, materialistic and self-indulgent orientation displayed by father and all his contemporaries is robbing the boy's generation of any hope of physical warmth, mobility, and perhaps even survival.

To emphasize his disgust with the situation, the boy announces he is going to go find his mother. If dinner isn't ready, he plans to raise hell. If it is ready, he won't eat. Father once more is left feeling that whenever he interacts with his son, he misses some crucial point that would explain the whole interchange. The son is indeed not at dinner, and rather than face another crisis, father decides to let the boy maintain his posture of righteous asceticism. An hour or 2 later the father is startled by a cheerful "Hey, Dad" voiced by his persecutor of a short time before. The greeting is followed by a request to use the family car to take his girl to a pizza parlor across town. Father points out that there is a pizza house within two very walkable blocks of his girlfriend's house and if he really wants to save gas for posterity, he can walk. No! That just won't do! The pizza across town is just what he has a taste for at that moment. All other considerations are unimportant. He must have that particular pizza with his girl at this moment. He needs the car and nothing else will do. The father is not quite sure what appetite his son is driven to indulge, but he is sure that in the space of a few short hours the boy has passed from a trappist-like asceticism to a hedonism that would make Henry the VIII seem inhibited by comparison. He cannot understand how the boy can reconcile the position of 2 hours before with the requests that he has just heard. Father concludes that adolescence is indeed a period of "normal psychosis" through which all human beings must pass and turns to something infinitely more predictable than his son, like the stock market, and puts the event out of mind.

From his point of view, the son simply cannot understand what the problem with his father is. What does wanting to take your girl to a pizza parlor have to do with what went on before? Life seems complicated enough when he contemplates girls and dating without the added burden of being held responsible for what occurred in a different time and under other circumstances. He is sure that father's demand for such ridiculous consistency is only a ploy to deny him the car.

Stories of these quick emotional changes, contradictory attitudes standing side by side, and behaviors that belie verbal communications are legion when adults describe their exchanges with adolescents. Gradually, however, we are beginning to understand some of the phenomena that are responsible for these paradoxes. I would like to present a model—a way of conceptualizing adolescence that may help us to explain a little bit and allow us to ask questions about a good deal more, regarding these developmental three-ring circuses.

My interest in this topic evolved from curiosity about psychological functions that could be used by individuals to raise their thresholds to certain stimuli. In the course of attempting to understand threshold phenomena, I found two papers written by D. Rapaport (1951, 1958) particularly helpful. In discussing the ego's autonomies, Rapaport emphasized that the ego was neither totally vulnerable to intrusions (or stimuli) from the outside world nor completely at the mercy of the instinctual drives. If one kicks a stone (i.e., applies stimuli from outside its structure), the stone has no choice but to react according to the laws of physics. In contrast, stimuli which impinge on living matter can be reacted to in a variety of ways. This capacity for alternative responses to stimuli that impinge from without, Rapaport called "the autonomy of the ego from the environment." He stated that the drives were primary guarantees that the ego would not, like the stone, become a slave to external stimuli.

Conversely, the ego is not at the mercy of the drives. A drive can be deflected, inhibited, ignored, or partially indulged. This capacity Rapaport termed "the autonomy of the ego from the id." He postulated that the capacity to perceive the external world, to take action, to think, to reevoke memory traces, to synthesize perceptions, etc., in a word, to use the primary autonomous functions of the ego, was the guarantor of the ego's autonomy from the id.

Finally, perhaps the most elegant part of the conceptualization, he argued that these autonomies of the ego are in reciprocal, inverse relationship to each other.

Thus the ego can be thought to have two areas of sensitivity: One faces and is sensitive to stimuli from the external world; the other sensitivity is to stimuli that impinge on it from the internal environment. By virtue of their inverse, reciprocal relationship, any change in one area of sensitivity is accompanied

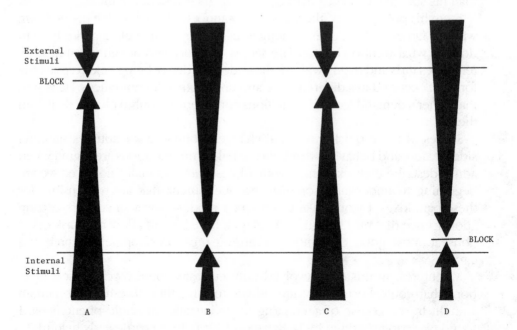

Figure 1. Graphic representation of the reciprocal "autonomies" of the ego.

by an inverse change in the other. If, for example, the ego is forced into a state of autonomy or insensitivity to the external environment by sensory deprivation, it quickly becomes extremely permeable to wishes and impulses from within (figure 1A). In a matter of a few hours or a few days, depending on the individual, the individual begins hallucinating gratifying or terrifying internal states or wishes and may also become delusional. Conversely, if the environmental stimuli become so compelling that they cannot be ignored, as in brainwashing techniques, the individual becomes virtually incapable of attending to his or her own internal states and wishes (figure 1B).

Clinically what we see more frequently is the opposite of that which has just been described. Increased drive impetus, whether is is due to adolescence, climacterium, or pathology (figure 1C), is accompanied by reduced sensitivity to the environment. An example of this state, drawn from early childhood, is the temper tantrum, during which attendance or responsivity to the external environment is grossly impaired. Conversely, self-imposed blocking of drive activity—for example, that which occurs in obsessional states or in schizophrenia—may result in endless, ruminative attention to the details of environmental stimuli, or even in extreme circumstances in an inanimate-like responsivity to the environment, as is seen in waxy flexibility (figure 1D).

Thus the ego actively processes and adapts to stimuli by raising or lowering its thresholds to stimuli from within or from without, and the state of these thresholds will often determine the intensity if not the nature of the individual's response to stimuli.

If one ponders Rapaport's elegant ideas and formulates some explanations of clinical situations in these terms, it becomes evident that while he had focused on two areas of sensitivity and responsivity in the ego, clinical observation forces us to acknowledge that there are at least three such areas. These include the two that Rapaport described (namely, the ego's sensitivity to external and internal stimuli) and the ego's capacity to observe and be sensitive to itself and to that totality of wishes, capabilities, convictions, identifications, values, ideals, prohibitions, liabilities, sensitivities, and talents that are called the "self."

With these three areas of sensitivity in mind we can now describe things that happen in the phase of human development that we call adolescence. This treatment of the topic of adolescence is, of course, focal and makes no pretense at being exhaustive. But its focus may allow us to scrutinize certain phenomena in a more microscopic way.

In many discussions the period of adolescence is described as a period of transition. There then follows a description of different states at the beginning and at the end of adolescence; or in some instances the description may be of an early, middle, and late adolescent state. The process by which the youngster moves from one state to another may be ignored or left to be inferred. While the description of various states is legitimate and necessary, it may deflect our attention from an equally important and legitimate scrutiny of the *process* by which one state merges into another. Below, adolescence is first described by comparing certain aspects of ego organization at puberty with these same aspects at maturity. In addition, some ideas are discussed regarding the process by which the adolescent proceeds from one state to another. To begin, we must explore some antecedents of adolescence.

In prepuberty, the child has lived through a period in which he or she invested the external world with a tremendous amount of authority and attention. By establishing a workable equilibrium between the push of individual strivings and wishes and the immovable rigidities of the external and internal realities that oppose them, the child has achieved enough internal serenity so that he can, between the ages of about 2 and 12, begin attending to all manner of issues in the external world. During this time, the amount of substantive information the child absorbs from the external world is enormous. The child's orientation to this information is, however, relatively indiscriminate and uncritical. There seems to be no capacity to address what the significance of the information might be to his or her own state or situation. About the time of puberty, relevant information is just beginning to be turned into usable knowledge, and the child must await further development before this knowledge can begin to become wisdom. Note, for example, that one of the most frequently found books on the bookshelf of the latency-age child's home (or perhaps more accurately under the couch in his home) is the *Guinness Book of World Records.* More recently the *Book of Lists* is popular with the younger set. When the school age child is not intrigued by the disconnected facts contained in these books, he can always turn to knowing the batting averages of most of the players in the major leagues or to knowing the vital statistics of nearly every actor and actress in Hollywood or on TV.

This capacity to absorb and process information and stimuli from the external world is not matched in the child by equal sensitivity to the inner world of wishes, impulses, appetites, and striving. Following his or her brush with sexual and aggressive impulses during the oedipal period, the post-oedipal child finds evidence for the existence of these impulses in the external world and perceives them only dimly in himself.

The child's sense of self is even more discontinuous and inconsistent. While it may seem at times that the child may have a relatively well-developed sense of self, closer scrutiny reveals that in most instances the identity and the traits that the child ascribes to himself are *assigned* by the environment rather than developed or evolved by self-awareness. One can hear at any time from the prepubertal child phrases like: "I am Daddy's son"; "I am Mrs. Jones' third grade student"; or "The gym teacher says I am the best runner in the class." It is a time for self-images that children perceive as assigned to them by the environments in which they live.

Due to the relatively indiscriminate and uncritical manner by which the child absorbs information, the clinician can, on occasion, see the destructive-

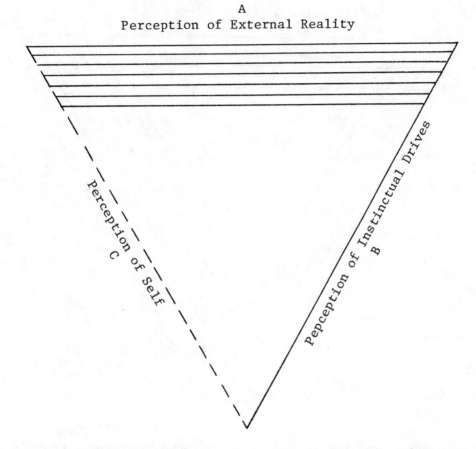

Figure 2. Deployment of ego functions in the prepubertal child (description in text).

ness which can be wrought by depreciated identities assigned to children by an environment that may be ignorant, prejudiced, or mischievous.

Graphically, the ego of the child could be depicted as having a relatively well-developed system for perceiving and organizing external events (figure 2A), a poorly developed and relatively thin capacity to perceive internal strivings and states (figure 2B), and a set of spotty, inconsistent glimpses of the self (figure 2C). Both of these latter percepts the child frequently feels are elicited or evoked by his environment.

Continuing to use this model, one could say that the child moves in adolescence from an ego organization as is depicted in figure 2, to a more evenly balanced and adaptively more efficient configuration such as that depicted in figure 3. Here we may conceive of a person with excellent sensitivity to environmental stimuli, experienced as objective phenomena as in A_2; or as potential

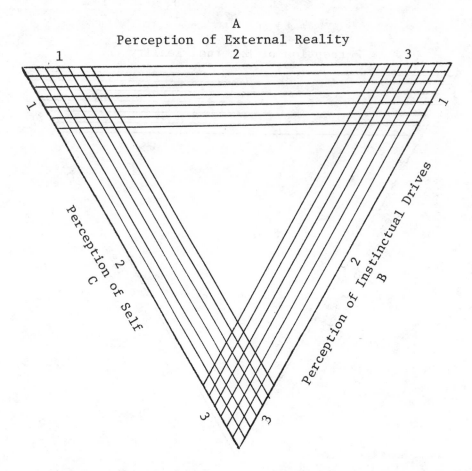

A
Perception of External Reality

Figure 3. Deployment of ego functions in the adult (description in text).

recipients of drive investment, as in A_3; or as an amalgam of the interactions between the self and the object world as in A_1. Internal states in turn can be perceived relatively comfortably, in relationship with environmental percepts as in B_1; as pure internal states or wishes as in B_2; or as part of the self system as in B_3. Similarly, the self-system can be experienced in relationship to one's surroundings (C_1); in relatively isolated self-contemplation (C_2); and in relationship to aspirations, wishes, and drives (C_3). Integrations have occurred that place the mental images of the individual's drives and derivative appetites in the context of a self-system that interacts with an environment that is perceived both in its own right as well as for its potentially gratifying objects. As our adolescents would say, the individual has "gotten it all together."

In this context I would like to address the manner in which the ego develops into the full and balanced agency of the adult from the relatively incompletely integrated and unevenly developed configuration that it presented in childhood. Clinical evidence presented by adolescents suggests that the development of the various clusters of ego functions (i.e., those that perceive and regulate external reality; those that experience and integrate impulse life; and those that monitor the self) appears to be discontinuous. Now one component, now another, occupies center stage, appearing to develop independently and perhaps even at the expense of the other two. This, of course, is more apparent than real, since any change in one group of ego functions will alter other clusters of ego functions. But it appears that the adolescent is at one moment invested in relating to a particular aspect of the environment, ignoring consideration of the self or the drives. At another moment, he seems to be captivated almost entirely by his drives, wishes, or appetites, ignoring the external environment or his self-representations. At still another time, he or she seems lost in contemplation of the self, oblivious to his or her drives or wishes and to the stimuli or reactions of the external world.

In addition, clinical observation suggests that when the development of one component of the ego reaches a certain level of competence, this same new-found competence acts as a trigger for the beginning of a new phase of development of ego functions in another of the ego's components.

Thus, the process of change is ushered in by the well-known need of the early adolescent to leave the shelter of his family. Compelling and dimly perceived sexual and aggressive stirrings as well as changed environmental expectations demand that the youngster venture out into the world of his or her peers. Blos describes this time as the second separation individuation phase (1967). Behaviorally, this thrust is manifested as a quest for more freedom and independence than the family usually affords and a rejection by the adolescent of some of the family standards and values. This desire to overthrow strict regulation is more apparent than real, however. If one looks closely, children disavow parental regulation and their values, often in a truculent manner. At the same time, they declare their autonomy and independence as they move into their peer group. They are going to dress as they like, talk about what they like, and think as they like. A look at an adolescent peer group, however, reveals that the freedom in it is in part illusory. The group prescribes dress, behaviors, and standards that are sometimes more intransigent than the parents ever dreamed of being. In many instances, the child finds comfort in this rigidity, since he comes into the group equipped to perceive and understand their ground rules with his well-developed equipment for perceiving and processing external cues. The regulatory function of the early teenage group uses equipment that children have already developed to protect and buffer them from intrusion of sexual and aggressive impulses with which they have had only limited experience.

Gradually, however, this new adaptation is in its turn disrupted. Johnny, who has used the peer group to make new adjustments, one day cannot help noticing that Mary fills out her jeans and T-shirts in a manner that is disturbingly different from the way that he and his male friends fill out theirs. Despite his attempts to distract himself and others through horseplay, pseudo-male chauvinism, and other ploys, thoughts of Mary's curves and contours intrude at the most inopportune times and occasion embarrassing and perplexing reactions.

Looking at this sequence of events reveals how the organization of the ego in prepuberty (figure 2) was helpful in allowing our young man to adapt to his group. Yet, as this ego state (or this profile of deployment of ego functions) became more sensitive to the external environment filled with Mary's curves and also catalyzed by hormonal changes in Johnny, he was catapulted by the stimulation into a situation in which he could not escape the perceptions of wishes and stirrings that came from within him (figure 4A).

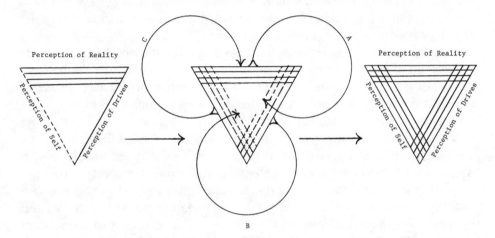

Figure 4. Depiction of shifting investments in the process of moving from a prepubertal ego organization through adolescent organization, to the organization of adulthood: the shift from attention to external stimuli to attention to instinctual drives; the shift from perceiving instinctual drives to perception of self; and the shift from perceiving the self to perception of external reality.

A number of children experience these stirrings and impulses as if they were imposed on them from the external world (Spiegel 1961). Time and repeated experiences, however, convince the youngster that the impetus for sexual strivings come from within him.

Let us suppose then that young Johnny struggles with his sexual arousal for a time. Old prohibitions against sexual expression which had acquired mental representation during the days of oedipal strife, as well as new ones in the image of a coach[1] who promises instant brain rot to the boy who masturbates,

---

1. I am not suggesting that our coaches and teachers are insensitive and psychologically punitive regarding adolescent striving. I am suggesting that transference of past prohibitions occurs during this period, and adults in the adolescent's current world are often the reluctant recipients of these transferences.

vie against sexual feelings. In adolescence, however, sexual strivings are not readily stifled by repression as during the oedipal phase (Lidz 1968). They are bolstered by a physiologically generated impetus and sooner or later must be integrated. And so Johnny may toss and turn in bed for awhile and finally decide that a bit of brain rot would never be detected by the coach and indulge in masturbation. In so doing and with each subsequent experience with sexual or aggressive strivings and their derivatives, the ego deploys functions which perceive and understand sexual and aggressive wishes and attempt to integrate these strivings on the one hand with external reality and, on the other, with a sense of self.

Before we move on, we must think of the state of the young person who indulges his sexual wishes with a fantasy or in masturbation. The mentation and activity involved in indulging sexual striving in such a psychologically undisguised manner are new and reevoke the reactions of shame and guilt that belong both to a past era and to the values and standards of the adolescent's current life. These evocations are enough to precipitate a more contemplative state of personality organization in which he begins to consider and scrutinize himself and his values (figure 4B). In part because of the shame and humiliation at having fantasized or masturbated and perhaps because of the exuberance and excitement of the sexual wish itself, the adolescent begins to ponder the questions of who he is, what he stands for, and to review his own attributes. Questions like "Who am I?" or "Do normal kids do what I do?" are common preoccupations during this phase of the cycle. Other preoccupations include comparisons of one's size with others, assessment of talents and liabilities, and often painful reviews of past identifications.

Even if the prepubertal child came into adolescence with some stable sense of self, changes in body image occasioned by the growth spurt, as well as other physiological changes that accompany puberty, disrupt these islands of self-awareness and make this phase of the adolescent process important and poignant. As the adolescent struggles with the questions and issues germane to the self, inevitably he or she eventually turns to the environment to check percepts and also to put a stop to painful ruminations. As they move back into their peer group (figure 4C) to compare themselves and to be comforted by their friends, one cycle follows another, with perhaps a different sequence but always shifting from one mode to the other in the constant scrutiny of self, the drives, or external reality. It would appear from clinical observations that in the shuttle between attending to external realities as represented by, among other sources, friends and the adolescent group, attending to drives and wishes, and attending to the emerging images of the "self," the adolescent achieves another important task. In this process the harsh, prohibitive cast of the superego of the oedipal phase and of latency is leavened. As Lidz points out (1968), the superego becomes an agency that channels and helps to shape the appropriate form for the expression of the drive rather than simply prohibits and threatens the child with guilt. And so the ego functions organize themselves now into one state, now into another, and we who observe see Narcissus at the pond one moment, Don Juan the next, and a modern-day Saint Thomas Aquinas at still another time.

To return to the young man we described earlier, one could say that while upbraiding his father he was almost totally oriented toward resonance and sensitivity toward the external environment. In this majestically ascetic state his own drives and appetites became unimportant, even to the extent of going hungry to make his point. Later in the evening, however, his outwardly directed focus, aided by a grumbling stomach, made him think of his girlfriend and triggered the shift to more hedonistic pursuits. Once the shift took place, he, like most people of his age, committed himself to it with a vengeance. It would not be at all surprising if, after being satiated by the pizza and by his girlfriend, our young man might make still another shift in his attention and begin to wonder what he really stood for and who he was or wanted to be.

Children are ripe for these processes in adolescence. Buffeted as they are by the storms of change, young people have no choice but to re-adapt. Not only are there compelling physical changes taking place within them, but as Benedek and Rubinstein have observed, their endocrinological state occasions new thoughts and fantasies (1942). Both the inchoate feelings engendered by the altered anatomy and physiology, as well as the structured mental represen- tations of new wishes and desires, are experienced by the pubertal child as something thrust upon him over which he has little or no control or regulatory mastery. Shifting ego states are necessary to attend to the perception of these wishes and to master the effects of these percepts.

In addition, new cognitive capacities begin to make their appearance during this phase. Piaget calls this new ability to think in abstract terms and to make logical deductions from hypothetical propositions the stage of formal opera- tions (1957). These new cognitive tools permit youngsters to take an image of the self and place it in the context of the world of their reality. In the compara- tive safety of private thoughts, rehearsals for living or trial actions may thus be undertaken. And so, pushed by physical and emotional changes and pulled by new-found capacities, our adolescents move to implement new levels and methods of integration, adaptation, and self-regulation. Gradually, using pro- positional thought as well as direct experience, the youngster's next step is to begin to experience control of these cycles as existing to some extent within his own ego rather than being totally dependent on external events. One would imagine that the first time Johnny sees Mary watching him play football, his attention feels drawn irresistibly to her. As he commits himself to doing his best to impress her, he finds that he must learn to concentrate on the game if he is to be effective and win her admiration. This involves barring certain external stimuli from reaching awareness so that he can more effectively attend to certain other stimuli regarding the ball game. Looking at the same phe- nomenon from Mary's point of view, she may be distracted from her studies by her reactions to Johnny's presence in the classroom but gradually finds that she can impose concentration on herself for an hour and organize her mental apparatus in a way that will permit her to attend to the external issues presented by that which she is studying. When the hour is over, she can voluntarily turn her attention inward to enjoy or struggle with her reactions. This passage of the regulatory functions from their being perceived as externally imposed to being perceived as an internal process is once again an important developmental step and requires that the adolescent be more aware of his drives and wishes, as well as noninstinctual aspects of the self, than he has ever been before.

This internalization is important "once again" because it is not the first time the child has used this psychological mechanism to help develop a regulatory mechanism for mastering his inner world. Let us recall the vignette of the toddler who has been admonished not to touch or pluck the petals from mother's favorite fern. One day he finds himself in the vicinity of the fern, and the little fingers are already on their way to the leaves before he can evoke the concrete image of mother to help him control his disastrous though delightful intentions. In a voice that has almost uncanny similiarities to that of mother's, we may hear him say "No! No! Johnny!" If the internal plea for help is successful, he swells with pride at being a good, big boy. If the evoked image and voice of mother came too late, Johnny may go on to spank his own hand. In so doing he has externalized the deed but internalized the regulatory quality of mother. It is not surprising to see Johnny become the primary defender and protector of the plant in a few weeks. This mechanism of internalizing standards and values from the external world to help manage internal strivings and to help form self images is an old friend by the time one is an adolescent. The issues that are being struggled with are different, of course, and they come into awareness in a different form, but the nature of the struggle is not new.

Awareness is, of course, necessary to perceive change or the need for change or sameness in any system. Without this perception it would be difficult to imagine adaptive shifts of state or organization in the personality. In a personal communication (1978), Sander suggested that a compelling need in our field is to develop ways of studying the ontogenesis of awareness. Perhaps as one group such as neonatologists view the phenomenon during infancy, another group may look at it during various phases of the life cycle to see how it is integrated with other functions of the mental apparatus.

Introspection and clinical evidence suggest that as the regulatory functions become internalized, the self-system begins functioning in two ways. One portion of it represents the subjective sensor. The other portion groups together traits, values, beliefs, and experiences to serve as the composite mental representation of the self as the person interacts with the external world or seeks to regulate his own drives and their derivatives. Thus the subjective "I" of the self-system observes and evaluates the particular objectified qualities, traits, and equipment that are marshaled to achieve a task and that represent at that time and in those circumstances the composite "me." The composite "me" is a constantly changing melange of qualities and traits that present themselves to the subject.

In conclusion, this model of adolescent development could be scrutinized from the point of view of its utility. While the Eriksonian model and the classical developmental concepts of adolescence give an important overview of the changes that occur during this phase, they use as a time reference the period that begins with puberty and ends with adulthood. The changes thus are described over a number of years, whereas this model attempts to supplement the broad sweep by scrutinizing the changes that occur on a day-to-day and hour-to-hour basis. It attempts to contemplate that which has been variously called the normal turbulence of adolescence or the natural lability of the period.

Epistemologically, the use of such a model permits us to ask questions that would be more difficult to ask without it, such as those which might be asked regarding the relationship of ego functions that foster self-awareness to ego functions that sensitize the individual to his environment. Another question might have to do with whether an ego function that may be deficient when employed in one area, as for example perception in reading subtle cues in a social situation, is also deficient when the youngster attempts to perceive his own internal strivings or evaluate himself.

Finally, I believe this model could provide a more accurate assessment of where the child is on the road from puberty to adulthood. Currently we have made some attempts to do this by dividing the period into early, middle, and late adolescence. Remembering how uneven the process of development can be, we can easily conceive of a child who has made great strides in experiencing the external world and his sexual desires in a sophisticated way, but may be quite slow in the development of an internally generated sense of self. By meticulous descriptions of the organization and flexibility of the child's capabilities, we can come closer to an accurate representation of the richness, variety, and wonder of adolescence in the human condition.

References

Benedek, T., and Rubinstein, B. The sexual cycle in women: The relation between ovarian function and psychodynamic processes. *Psychosomatic Medicine Monograph,* Vol. 3, Nos. 1 & 2. National Research Council, 1942.

Blos, P. The second individuation process of adolescence. *The Psychoanalytic Study of the Child,* 22:162–186, 1967.

Lidz, T. *The Person.* New York: Basic Books, 1968.

Piaget, J. *Logic and Psychology.* New York: Basic Books, 1957.

Rapaport, D. The autonomy of the ego. *Bulletin of the Menninger Clinic,* 15:113–123, 1951.

———. The theory of ego autonomy. *Bulletin of the Menninger Clinic,* 22:13–35, 1958.

Spiegel, L. Identity and adolescence. In: Lorand, S., and Schneer, H., eds. *Adolescents.* New York: P. Hoeber, 1961.

The Course of Life: Psychoanalytic Contributions
Toward Understanding Personality Development.
Vol. II: Latency, Adolescence, and Youth.
S.I. Greenspan and G.H. Pollock, editors.
NIMH 1980

The Influence of Development
Upon Career Achievement

Irwin M. Marcus, M.D.

It may be of value to our understanding of late adolescence and early adulthood to examine the vicissitudes of personality development fantasy and conflicts of significance to career achievement.

Even in Anna Freud's (1965) systematic and unique studies of normality, the concept of developmental sequences is limited to particular, circumscribed parts of the child's evolving personality. The basic interactions between intrapsychic phenomena at various developmental levels and environmental influences appear to be far more complex than some behaviorists would admit. The variables are myriad as the young child evolves from an egocentric view of life and autoerotic play, through games, hobbies, and school activities, to arrival at a career.

Available evidence indicates that, prior to puberty, the child's concept of work is in terms of adult activities and that whatever vocational interests are expressed are linked to wishes to grow up. Ginzberg (1951) and others agree that the young child's ideas of work are in the realm of fantasy and are unrelated to either actual interests or abilities. Males and females have characteristically different developmental lines in their life histories, so that understanding factors in the transition from academic activities to a career necessarily involves concepts that are not equally relevant to both genders.

Tiedeman et al. (1963) and his associates have shown that sex role and family status are no less significant than self-concept in influencing occupational choice. Their studies indicate that interest and personality inventories

---

are more effective predictors of choice of work than are aptitude tests. They confirmed Ginzberg's impression that self-concept in boys is in the process of consolidation during the high school years. The interests stage during the sophomore year of high school is followed by the development of work values by the senior year. Rather than attempting to predict vocational choice, many of the serious researchers in this field are turning their attention to studying the vicissitudes of personality-environment interaction which crystalizes into a vocational or career identity.

Searching out the components which constitute a self-concept can be thorny and much too complex for practical counseling. Note the variation even in conceptualizing self-concept: Eissler (1958); Erikson (1959); Fenichel (1953); S. Freud (1914); Greenacre (1958); Hartmann, Kris, and Loewenstein (1946); Jacobson (1964); Josselyn (1954); Kohut (1966); Levin (1969); Spiegel (1959); Sullivan (1953); and Wheelis (1958). The transition leading to a career commitment may be viewed as a multifaceted form of behavior which evolves over 8 or 10 years, passing through a series of stages. This process has a degree of irreversibility in that earlier decisions limit the options for later decisions. Compromise is also a prominent feature. Therefore, to a large degree, personal attributes are in interaction with environmental circumstances, and the work direction during maturation is channeled by the total situation, not just by the self-concept. The transition from school to career seems to go through an initial fantasy phase between 10 and 12 years of age, followed by a tentative period from puberty into middle adolescence to about 17 years of age, and finalized by the realistic stage which extends into early adulthood. The fantasy phase is self-explanatory. In the tentative period, the adolescent begins to consider personal abilities and interests more seriously. Those who have done poorly in mathematics and science are less prone to speak of careers requiring facility in these areas; however, the subjective approach is still predominant. The adolescent's preoccupation gradually shifts from individual interests to an impression of capacities and to values such as those vested in job status. The realistic stage goes one step further and includes the necessary compromises with environmental opportunities and actual awareness of skills, ability, and other factors, as mentioned above. In late adolescence, the exploratory activity with its associated inquiries varies with the initiative, curiosity, and aggressiveness of the individual. I have had boys in this age group call me to discuss the field of psychiatry specifically, as well as medicine in general. Similarly, girls have asked me about social work as a career.

The significant issue in the sequential phases is the irreversibility feature; namely, the academic selections along the road continuously limit the available options for later decisions. Thus, the time factor during this transition period is such that the later the decision, the less freedom for a change in direction. The "identity crisis" as described by Erikson is complex in its dynamics derived from both the intrapsychic and multi-environmental factors. Progress throughout schooling becomes a key issue in the vocational goals and identity which can be established by an individual. Where "work identity" becomes a pillar in the self-esteem structure, positions of less gratification and status, as well as later retirement, can—and often do—trigger a depressive reaction or another form of mental disturbance. Therefore, therapists and counselors in general should understand these work-identity interactions and related problems when confronted in patients.

Neff (1968) considers the "work personality" as having a "semiautonomous" function. This is consistent with my own observations (Marcus 1971) that individuals with severe character problems can continue to function effectively in skilled and complex occupations. The transition toward a career occurs within the matrix of total personality development. It is academic and possibly philosophical to argue that the sexual and aggressive needs and feelings are the primary drives, and the vicissitudes of these "instincts" lead to interest and pleasure in mastery, or rather that mastery is a separate basic drive (Hartmann 1958; Hendrick 1943). Motor patterns and their associated pleasure are seen by Mittelmann (1954) as independent urges intimately connected with almost all other functions of the individual. Lantos (1943) identifies the latency period as the time when the transition from pleasure in motor activity to pleasure in mastery occurs. Erikson (1959) similarly places the shift in stages at this period when the child wants to learn to do things and to enjoy accomplishment. He calls this phase the "sense of industry," when the child enjoys recognition and prestige from "producing things." During this stage, the child may feel inadequate and inferior when confronted with his unresolved conflicts and when comparing himself unfavorably with people in the adult world of parents and teachers or with more effective children.

Perhaps the concept of the superego or conscience may be expanded to include internalization of "other" social and cultural demands in addition to the earlier childhood precepts of parental prohibitions. Thus, the compulsion to work, or the "workaholic," may be viewed not only as a superego demand, but also as a drive influenced by the ego ideal with its images of the level of achievement strived for. In my practice, I have found the entire transition phase influenced by such conflicts.

One man in his late twenties was having great difficulty maintaining a consistent work level. He was about to lose a crucial position in his employment because he acted out his rage toward authorities. His hostility to his parents was rooted in considerable parental neglect throughout his childhood. The treatment uncovered his association of knowledge with power, an association which apparently had affected his long history of a partial learning disability. This serious symptom was related to his guilt-ridden defenses. He wished to avoid integrating knowledge and thus prevent the destructive revengeful fantasies he harbored and feared would emerge if he approached any degree of successful achievement. He was in constant fear that he would be unable to answer pertinent questions by superiors regarding his work activities. He had a history of changing schools and an urge frequently to alter his place of living.

If this pattern had continued during his education and into his career, his record of being an unreliable, transient, and unstable worker would have fulfilled his father's dreaded prophesy that he would end up "a bum."

The foregoing example emphasizes the importance of unconscious conflictual factors which influence career achievements adversely. Obviously, to arrive at a successful level of work ability, individuals must be capable of cooperative relationships with their superiors and peers and not be blocked by intrapsychic conflicts in achieving their capacity for competence.

The following is a brief example of the complex interaction between personality factors and vocational attitudes. This example, in contrast to those related to inhibitions in work, is in the area of work compulsions as a style of living. I analyzed a man in his mid-thirties who worked from about 7:00 a.m. to about 10:00 or 10:30 p.m. weekdays, with another 5 or 6 hours on Saturday and Sunday. His work style was similar to that of many physicians, attorneys, and businessmen I have treated. Some of these patients were single; others were married. The avoidance of a wife and/or children at home did not appear to be a determining feature of their pattern. With specific individual variations, each of the men in this category felt deprivations in reaction to the type of mothering he experienced in his childhood. In one instance, the patient's mother was depressed, withdrawn, and bedridden; in another, the mother died early in the man's childhood; in a third case, the mother was depressed, worked outside the home, and ultimately remarried following the father's death. The patient felt rejected by his mother's attention to her new husband. The deprivations were experienced as oral needs and threats to survival. All of the above patients had problems of overweight from overeating and/or difficulty in controlling their alcohol consumption.

The patient in this example had learning problems all the way through his schooling and into his college education. He flunked out of one college and held on marginally in another. He was superior intellectually and ingested considerable information but refused to give it back when confronted with examinations. His toilet training had been traumatic; he was subjected to enemas and had to show his defecated products before he was allowed to flush the toilet. The therapy revealed the association in his mind of academic examinations with having his bowel irrigated and his product checked over. Furthermore, in his compulsive work pattern, he unconsciously associated his vocational activities with his mother's demands and the financial compensation with her feeding him. He felt close to his mother and happy and secure while working, but he felt depressed and anxious when away from his occupational activities. This patient was not an example of the "Sunday neurosis" phenomenon described by Ferenczi (1919) or the sublimation of aggression and hostility through work suggested by Menninger (1942). Anxiety is aroused when the person is faced with inactivity, and defense mechanisms are utilized to contain the anxiety, with resulting symptom formation.

The developmental transition toward a career involves much more than a mere change in environment. It is also a change from supportive, friendly relationships with parental and school authorities to those with impersonal work authorities—the institution, company, or corporation. There is a change in living style and often in community environment. The necessary reorganization of personality orientation to one's self and others may produce a postadolescent identity crisis or a self-image crisis, to use Wittenberg's (1968) concept. The anxiety level may be of sufficient intensity to create a variety of symptoms, including a transient depersonalization. The latter may occur not only in borderline character pathology but also in the neurotic and even so-called normal or healthy personality. The feeling is one of confusion about one's self-image; the familiar continuity of one's personality seems lost, and the ability to feel comfortable and oriented toward the environment is similarly changed. I have seen this phenomenon in people who changed from high school to college, in others who changed jobs in the same city or who changed cities in the same corporation, and in a number of immigrants from such varied origins as Germany, England, France, South America, and Asia. Many of these disturbances may be treated without drugs or hospitalization. I explore the patients' memories of their previous more secure environment and orientation and foster the reintegration from that point forward. So far, this brief psychotherapeutic technique has been successful.

The adolescent's revolt against his or her own superego, which is identified with the parental and authority restrictions, allows the individual to feel more independent in the reorganization of the personality. However, in the transition to the occupational world, which in the young adult may be characterized as the postadolescent phase, the conflict is somewhat different. Establishing an equilibrium between ego ideals and superego is precipitated by the necessity of making significant, serious decisions for the adult life. Space does not permit a theoretical discussion of whether superego and ego ideal concepts are to be viewed as a single functional unit or as separate concepts (Arlow and Brenner 1964; Erikson 1959; Jacobson 1964).

Conflicts between ego ideals and superego stir the self-image crisis. If one distinguishes the pseudo-ideal from the true ego-ideal, the former would be linked with the grandiose, omnipotent fantasies of childhood. Learning problems in the college years in certain instances may be a result of such impossible expectations and of a rigid, cruel superego demand for fulfillment of the "superman" achievements. The ensuing feelings of discontent, failure, severe self-hatred, and projected or real perception of disappointment in the parents have led some students to drop out of school and run away. It has led others to the sad situations of suicide or serious drug or alcohol usage or other "cop-outs." Understandably, psychiatric work with young men and women during their self-image dilemmas is difficult and must be done with thoughtfulness, kindness, and as much understanding as one can muster from training and experience. A rigid, harsh superego that demands fulfillment of unrealistic ego ideals can be a constant source of conflict and symptom formation, particularly depression. For example, to be a good parent and spend time at home with one's children and spouse may run counter to the wish to be dedicated to one's career and achieve success according to whatever values are used in measuring that goal. The conscience can lash out at the self-image either way, producing a continuous state of discontent, irritability, and a sense of failure. One defensive maneuver which emerges as a solution to a superego-ego ideal or superego-pseudo-ego ideal conflict is to attack the representatives of the superego. A 19-year-old girl who dropped her educational pursuits to live in a "free spirited" style was intent on humiliating her parents and thus downgrading their values and diminishing their influence on her. However, when the superego is projected against the society or government, then the hostility is vented in that direction. Provocations are brought to a point where attacks from those sources are unconsciously welcomed to rationalize the conclusion that authorities are indeed bad or stupid and the "system" must be totally revised. The desperate effort to cling to waning youth in the transition from adolescence to adulthood is revived when people have delayed consolidation of their personalities. I have seen an incomplete transition lay dormant for many years and suddenly disrupt many years of a seemingly happy marriage and career. People in this situation attempt to look, act, and think young. The reality of the "adult world" appears boring, and they seek the "last chance" to live an exciting life and recapture or develop a sense of individuality and identity. Both groups—the young people in transition and the older ones who try to return to a new transition—have in common an aggressive, firm, and anxious desire to return to living by the pleasure principle. There is a wish for fulfillment of their self-images and an underlying depressive longing for "freedom" and happiness without the burden of responsibilities to anyone but themselves.

The adolescents in transition are alert to the effect of their behavior, achievements, and goals upon their parents' self-image. They have difficulty at times deciding whether they are gratifying themselves or their parents when they are progressing in an acceptable direction. Similarly, if hostility and parental conflict are high, they feel mingled pleasure and guilt when their parents are embarrassed or enraged at unacceptable directions. I reported a study of learning problems in adolescents where these conflicts unconsciously influenced the school failures (Marcus 1967). In another study of 110 student nurses, I found that the autonomy need—to "handle their own problems" and make their own decisions regarding the pursuit of nursing as a career or to drop out and explore other work goals—prevented many girls from consulting others about their problems. They avoided not only the available student advisors but also their own peer group. The fear of outside influence upon their identity struggles, combined with sensitivity regarding their self-images, led to impulsive decisions to drop out of a nursing career. The student nurses presented false excuses to the director of their school to rationalize their actions. As a result, the school did not know how to approach or to solve the real problem of their relatively high dropout rate. My study of this group of late adolescents led to an approach which favorably influenced the problem (Marcus 1969).

In conclusion, the developmental influence upon career achievement does involve unconscious processes in interaction with academic, social, and economic factors. These personality factors can enhance or disturb the development of career performance. However, the crystallization of a work personality allows for semi-autonomous functioning. Thus, upheavals in nonwork areas of the personality may not necessarily influence work patterns. On the other hand, developmental disorders influencing the transition from academic life to the adult world cannot be solved by simply guiding the person toward a new commitment.

Psychotherapeutic work, either brief or long-term, when indicated, can be crucial to the futures of those who present serious transition problems.

References

Arlow, J., and Brenner, C. *Psychoanalytic Concepts and the Structural Theory.* New York: International Universities Press, 1964.

Eissler, K.R. Problems of identity. In: Panel reported by D.L. Rubinfine, *Journal of the American Psychoanalytic Association,* 6:131–142, 1958.

Erikson, E.H. The problem of ego identity. *Identity and the Life Cycle. Psychological Issues,* Monograph 1. New York: International Universities Press, 1959. pp. 101–164.

——. Growth and crises of the healthy personality. *Identity and the Life Cycle. Psychological Issues,* Monograph 1. New York: International Universities Press, 1959. pp. 50–100.

——. *Childhood and Society,* Second Edition, New York: W.W. Norton, 1963.

Fenichel, O. Identification. *The Collected Papers of Otto Fenichel.* 1:97–112. New York: W.W. Norton, 1953.

Ferenczi, S. Sunday neurosis (1919) In: *Further Contributions to Psychoanalysis.* Second Edition, London: Hogarth Press, 1950, pp. 174–176.

Flanagan, J.C.; Dailey, J.T.; Shaycost, M.S.; Gorham, W.A.; Orr, D.B.; and Goldberg, I. *Design for a Study of American Youth.* Boston: Houghton Mifflin, 1962.

Freud, A. *Normality and Pathology in Childhood.* New York: International Universities Press, 1965.

Freud, S. On narcissism: An introduction (1914). *Standard Edition,* 4:30–59. London: Hogarth Press, 1948.

Ginzberg, E.; Ginsburg, S.W.; Axelrad, S.; and Herma, J.L. *Occupational Choice: An Approach to a General Theory.* New York: Columbia University Press, 1951.

Greenacre, P. Early physical determinants in the development of the sense of identity. *Journal of the American Psychoanalytic Association,* 6:612–627, 1958.

Hartmann, H. *Ego Psychology and the Problem of Adaptation.* New York: International Universities Press, 1958.

Hartmann, H.; Kris, E.; and Loewenstein, R.M. Comments on the formation of psychic structure. *The Psychoanalytic Study of the Child,* 2:11–38, 1946.

Hendrick, I. Work and the pleasure principle. *Psychoanalytic Quarterly,* 12:311–329, 1943.

Holland, J.L. Some explorations of a theory of vocational choice. *Psychological Monographs* 76, 1962.

——. Explorations of a theory of vocational choice and achievement. *Psychological Reports,* 12:547–594, 1963.

Jacobson, E. *The Self and the Object World.* New York: International Universities Press, 1964.

Josselyn, I. Ego in adolescence. *American Journal of Orthopsychiatry,* 24:223–237, 1954.

Kohut, H. Forms and transformations of narcissism. *Journal of the American Psychoanalytic Association,* 14:243–272, 1966.

Lantos, B. Work and instincts. *International Journal of Psycho-Analysis,* 24:114–119, 1943.

Levin, D.C. The self: A contribution to its place in theory and technique. *International Journal of Psycho-Analysis,* 50:41–51, 1969.

Marcus, I.M. The marriage-separation pendulum: A character disorder associated with early object loss. In: Marcus, I.M., ed. *Currents in Psychoanalysis,* New York: International Universities Press, 1971. pp. 361–383.

——. Learning problems. In: Usdin, G., ed. *Adolescence.* Philadelphia: J.B. Lippincott, 1967. pp. 94–110.

——. From school to work: Certain aspects of psychosocial interaction. In: Caplan, G., and Lebovici, S., eds. *Adolescence—Psychosocial Perspectives.* New York: Basic Books, 1969. pp. 157–164.

Menninger, K. Work as sublimation. *Bulletin of the Menninger Clinic,* 6:170–182, 1942.

Mittelmann, B. Motility in infants, children, and adults. *The Psychoanalytic Study of the Child,* 9:142–177, 1954.

Neff, W.S. *Work and Human Behavior.* New York: Atherton Press, 1968.

O'Hara, R.P. Roots of careers. *Elementary School Journal,* 62:277–280, 1962.

Roe, A. Personality structure and occupational behavior. In: Borow, H., ed. *Man in a World at Work.* Boston: Houghton Mifflin, 1964.

Spiegel, L.A. The self, the sense of self, and perception. *The Psychoanalytic Study of the Child,* 14:81–109, 1959.

Sullivan, H.S. *Conceptions of Modern Psychiatry.* Second Edition, New York: W.W. Norton, 1953.

Super, D.H. *Appraising Vocational Fitness by Means of Psychological Tests.* New York: Harper and Row, 1949.

——. A theory of vocational development. *American Psychologist,* 8:185–190, 1953.

——. *The Psychology of Careers: An Introduction to Vocational Development.* New York: Harper and Row, 1957.

——. The critical ninth-grade: Vocational choice or vocational exploration. *Personnel and Guidance Journal,* 39:106–109, 1960.

Super, D.H., and Overstreet, P.L. *The Vocational Maturity of Ninth-Grade Boys.* New York: Bureau of Publications, Teachers College, Columbia University, 1960.

Super, D.H.; Starishevsky, N.M.; and Jordaan, J.P. *Career Development: Self Concept Theory.* Princeton, N.J.: College Entrance Examination Board, 1963.

Tiedeman, D.V.; O'Hara, R.P.; and Baruch, R.W. *Career Development: Choice and Adjustment.* Princeton, N.J.: College Entrance Examination Board, 1963.

Wheelis, A.B. *The Quest for Identity.* New York: W.W. Norton, 1958.

Wittenberg, R. *Postadolescence.* New York: Grune and Stratton, 1968.

The Course of Life: Psychoanalytic Contributions
Toward Understanding Personality Development.
Vol. II: Latency, Adolescence, and Youth.
S.I. Greenspan and G.H. Pollock, editors.
NIMH 1980

Mid-Adolescence—Foundations for Later Psychopathology

Aaron H. Esman, M.D.

Adolescence is, by definition, a transitional phase of human psychological development. Whether its duration be brief, as in traditional and "primitive" societies (Muensterberger 1961), or unnaturally extended, as in ours, it looks, Janus-like, back to the childhood past and forward to the adult future. To the extent that it carries the seeds of future pathology, these derive in part from its phase-specific conflicts and developmental issues, and in part from the unresolved problems of early childhood and latency phases and the shadows they cast on the adolescent process.

To understand the foundations and precursors of future psychopathology inherent in the midadolescent period, it is desirable to reconsider the salient issues (or, speaking teleogically, "tasks") of this phase as they occur in industrialized societies. The 15–18-year-old has, in most cases, experienced the major impact of the physiological changes of puberty. He (or she) has experienced the the rebelliousness and turmoil which Offer (1969) acknowledges are characteristic of most early adolescents and which Anna Freud (1958) maintains are a necessary aspect of the adolescent experience. He is well into the throes of object removal and has, in his first postpubertal forays, shifted his major object investments to his peers and to idealized "crush" figures, typically from the world of sport or show business. In his early gropings toward sexual objects he may have enjoyed some experimental homosexual play but is by now reaching out to heterosexual partners, however tentatively. These heterosexual objects are, however, perceived largely on narcissistic lines—"I love what I would like to be," as Blos (1962) formulates it. Life is lived locally and for the moment, although the growth of operational thought (Piaget 1969) is preparing the way for experimentation with abstract concepts and for a wider view of life and its future possibilities.

The passage into mid-adolescence is in many ways analogous to that from Mahler's "hatching" subphase of separation-individuation to the "practicing" period. The 15–18-year-old has acquired an impressive array of new capacities and resources—biological and psychological—which he is now ready to deploy in his interactions with the world around him and in the enhancement of his inner world as well. Erikson (1956) has subsumed much of the work of this subphase under the process of "identity formation." This includes such matters as the establishment of a sexual identity as masculine or feminine (as opposed to gender identity as male or female, which is settled in early child-hood) and of a capacity for mutuality in relations with others, particularly with heterosexual partners.

A further component of this process is the development of an orientation to the future, in particular, toward vocational opportunities and choices. This may involve the trying out, either mentally or physically, of alternatives, an aspect of the critical tendency of mid-adolescents to test the possibilities that the world offers them. Not the least important among these is the range of possible value orientations; both the aspirations and aims of the ego ideal and the prohibitions of the superego are subject to review and reorganization during adolescence.

All of these phenomena occur in the context of the major task of adolescent development—the process of object removal. Made urgent by the reactivation of oedipal wishes and fears, this process entails the ultimate resolution of dependence-independence conflicts as well as of the incestuous longings and castration anxieties that inhere in the oedipal triangle. In a large sense, it is in the arena of this struggle that many of the aforementioned concerns are settled. By age 18, most of this work will normally have been done; it is left to the stages of late adolescence and (that artifact of our times) "youth" to consolidate the advances that have occurred during the high school years. And it should not be forgotten that for many—perhaps, still, most—young people, high school graduation marks the end of adolescence in most respects and the initiation of adult life.

Unfortunately, as Winnicott (1965) has said, "...some individuals are too ill (with psychoneurosis or depression or schizophrenia) to reach a stage of emotional development that could be called adolescence or they can reach it only in a highly distorted way." For these, the roots of future psychopathology lie in the unresolved conflicts and developmental deviations of earlier periods. For others, the normative developmental events of adolescence proper offer the potentiality for faulty resolution and maladaptive solutions. It is these situations we shall examine here, seeking to delineate some of the intrinsic, the familial, and the social factors that may contribute to such deviant outcome. It must be understood, however, that development is a continuous process; the seams in its web are imposed by the observer seeking to order his data into conceptual segments.

Maturational Delays and the Body-Image Problem.

By age 15, most adolescents will, as mentioned earlier, have passed through puberty as a physiological process. Especially this is true of girls; some boys on the slow side of the bell-shaped curve may still experience pubertal changes in their 16th year. For them, however, as for that small number whose puberty is delayed beyond the norm, substantial problems arise with both short-term and long-term consequences.

Schoenfeld (1969) has set forth in detail the bodily changes in adolescence and the immediate consequences for body-image formation of deviations from the norm. He stresses the fact that, for adolescents, "to be different is to be inferior." The 15-year-old boy who is forced into invidious dressing-room comparisons of his genital size and pubic hair development with his more biologically favored peers is likely, in order to protect his self-esteem, to withdraw from such situations; he thus risks further stigmatization as a "faggot" or a "bookworm." At least a measure of social awkwardness, at most a pattern of detachment and discomfort in social intercourse may be psychological consequences of such physiological disparity.

The problem of body-image disturbance is even greater among adolescent girls. This can be accounted for by a variety of factors, both sociocultural and intrapsychic. Ours is a culture that imposes on young women, through the mass media, demands for conformity to thoroughly unrealistic standards of bodily form—long-legged, pencil-thin, large-bosomed—that are the despair of most adolescent girls and the delight of the magazines they devour to advise them in their desperate efforts to achieve the unachievable. (The prevailing ethos is manifest in the slogan "There are two things it's impossible to be—too rich or too thin.") At the same time, the normal secondary sexual characteristics are consciously or unconsciously associated with burgeoning sexuality which may, particularly in certain family contexts, be a source of intense shame and/or guilt.

Such conditions may pave the way for one of the most flamboyant disorders of young women—anorexia nervosa. Often setting in during the midadolescent phase, it occurs with equal frequency in late adolescence or young adulthood. Bruch (1973) has defined the multiple determinants of this complex and baffling disorder; prominent among them are disturbances of body image and self-perception (often related to earlier traumata as well as adolescent irregularities). The role of sexual conflicts has been less stressed in Bruch's work than in earlier discussions (Waller, Kaufman, and Deutsch 1940) but should not be overlooked. Unconscious equation of "fat" and "pregnant" and oral impregnation fantasies are common findings in such cases and interdigitate with the separation-individuation and body-image issues emphasized by Bruch and by Sours (1969).

The counter part of such conflictual disturbances in body image is the narcissistic overinvestment characteristic of certain hysterical character types. Here, although crucial predispositions may be laid down in earlier phases, adolescence may be the point of crystallization. The adolescent girl requires affirmation of a femininity which is an aspect of her total personality development. In particular, she requires acceptance and encouragement from the primary male figures in her life, especially a father who can respond to her growing sexuality with neither defensive withdrawal nor seductive acting out. The integration of sexuality as but one element in a total self-system allows for the enlargement of self-esteem from a variety of intellectual, interpersonal, and conflict-free sources. Where such alternative sources are lacking, the adolescent girl may seek reassurance from excessive (at times monolithic) attention to her appearance and in the development of styles of seductive exhibitionism. Should this be consolidated by parental support or peer approval, the nucleus for later character pathology will be well formed by the end of high school.

Depression and Its Analogs

If the central theme in midadolescence is the pursuit of object removal, it follows that at certain points, a state of relative objectlessness will prevail in the adolescent's mental life. Detaching his emotional engagement from ("decathecting") the mental representations of his parents, he has not yet succeeded in replacing them with stable alternative figures. Much of his activity during these years is devoted to the quest for such attachment objects; for some, this process is fraught with difficulty and frustration. For the adolescent who is shy or temperamentally slow to warm up (Chess, Thomas, and Birch 1967) or for whom early oral disappointments have led to impairments in "basic trust" (Erikson 1950), or whose characterological style is passive, rather than active (Rapaport 1953), the restoration of abandoned object ties may prove an insuperable task. Chronic and lifelong feelings of loneliness and isolation may ensue with a depressive orientation toward life. The fragility of those attachments that are established, and the overinvestment in them as sources of refuge from feelings of loneliness, may lead to major depression and suicidal acts when and if they are disrupted by circumstance or by active disengagement by the partner.

The more-or-less ubiquitous depressive potential in adolescence is normally warded off in a variety of ways. Among these are frenetic hypermotility and social hunger with overtones of hypomanic denial and the use of chemical agents—alcohol and drugs. For most adolescents, these activities are transitory, experimental, and self-limited. For the most vulnerable ones, however, the use of alcohol and drugs may serve as permanent anodynes against the pains of objectlessness. Addiction or drug abuse may, therefore, be among the potential pathologies resident in the miscarried process of object removal (Wieder and Kaplan 1969).

Sexual Identity

Although as noted earlier, gender identity appears to be laid down in the pre-oedipal years, a clear sense of self as masculine or feminine and one's mode of function in one's sexual life are a product of the adolescent process. Several currents contribute to the ultimate emergence of this configuration. Important among these is the fortification of early identifications by new ones, especially with peer-group members and idealized parent surrogates (not least, those supplied by the mass media). In the resolution of recrudescent oedipal conflicts, such fortifying identifications are crucial, both in promoting the movement toward nonincestuous objects and in buttressing the negative oedipal identification with the same-sex parent.

A crucial aspect of sexual development and of the formation of sexual identity is masturbation. Masturbation is the primary sexual experience of adolescents in our culture, even in this period of "sexual revolution" (Esman 1979). It is vital resource in aiding the adolescent in organizing his sexual fantasies and in permitting experimentation with the pregenital and perverse wishes that can ultimately be integrated into the foreplay of genital heterosexuality. The capacity to masturbate alone and with relative freedom from guilt is, as Borowitz (1973) has pointed out, an essential acquisition in the adolescent's progress toward maturity (cf. the case of Mike, p. 22).

Potentialities for deviant outcome abound, of course, in so complex a process. As with other aspects discussed here, earlier predispositions play a critical role in determining the outcome of the phase-specific conflicts. Deviant early identifications, particularly those involving intense bisexual ties, will tend to skew the picture and leave the adolescent open to current influences that may have critical shaping force.

Don F. had emerged from latency with clear male identity but with a complex pattern of identifications with a powerful, overbearing, "phallic" mother and remote critical father who offered him little protection or support. His longing for an internalized sense of masculine power could be gratified only by oral incorporation. Seduced in early adolescence by an older male friend of the family into performing fellatio, he came to use this means to seduce his peers from whom he sought not sexual gratification per se, but friendship and acceptance. This pattern became consolidated during his high school years so that by 17 he was a confirmed, though highly conflicted, homosexual. Fantasies of biting off the penis represented not only his wish to incorporate the phallus and to gain its power, but a persistent identification with the devouring, castrating mother.

Leslie T. was a depressed, somewhat bewildered 21-year-old girl, fresh out of a prestigious women's college and uncertain about her direction in life. Her sadness was a reaction to the departure for Europe of a young woman who had been her homosexual lover through 3 college years. Leslie's family situation was bizarre. Her father lived and worked in a midwestern city. Her mother had taken Leslie and her 2-year older brother to live in Florida when Leslie was 12, and the father came for occasional visits and vacations. Mrs. T. was a vain, narcissistic woman who was completely idle and emotionally detached from her children. Leslie grew up an unhappy, object-hungry girl who at 15 formed a homosexual liaison with a classmate, which coexisted with heterosexual friendships and dates. In this relationship, and in the subsequent one in college, her aim was clearly to be cared for and mothered by a warm, dominant lover.

On the other hand, Blos (1957) has described the type of adolescent girl who takes flight into precocious and promiscuous heterosexuality from the unconscious pull toward an erotized tie to the pre-oedipal mother. In her eagerness to disavow such longings, tinged as they are with homosexual and infantile dependent meanings, such a girl becomes, Blos says, a "Diana," intent on pursuing her masculine prey with pseudosexual seductions. Others, with conflicts and motives similar to Leslie's, will turn their erotic attention to males as well, seeking from them maternal care rather than mature heterosexual mutuality. In adult life such women are likely to experience repeated failures in their love lives or to immerse themselves in masochistic dependence on men to whom they remain attached, despite repeated disappointments and/or sadistic manipulation, out of their terror of abandonment and loneliness. Beating fantasies may appear in such women; behind the sadistic male figure in such fantasies is the rejecting angry mother of pre-oedipal times.

Future Orientation and Work Goals

Prior to mid-adolescence, children are essentially present oriented, at first because of the immaturity of their cognitive organization and their dependence on adults and, in early adolescence, because of the intensity of their narcissism and their primary preoccupation with puberty and its consequences. In the high school years this begins to change. The cognitive development described by Piaget (op. cit.) permits a broader awareness of the nature of the world and the possibilities it affords, and the realities of adult life. The emergence from pubertal narcissism in the direction of more substantial object attachments serves further to foster anticipation of adult social-role requirements. And the growing consolidation of identifications, positive or negative, engenders vocational interests attuned to them as well as to emerging intrinsic interests and talents.

Here, too, there is a field for potential problems. For the middle class adolescent, at least, the range of vocational possibilities is broad and allows for the accommodation of individual tastes, interests, and special capacities. Premature closure, unreflective decisions based on defensive identifications or avoidance intended to obviate anxiety, or due to ideological commitments attendant on ego-ideal reshaping (Erikson's "absolutism"), or submissive conformity to parental demands and pressures—all may lead to lifelong dissatisfaction or to repeated changes of vocational role in later life.

Alternatively, the adolescent who is too closely tied to his primary objects, who fears detaching himself and establishing his own identity, or who, due to parental overindulgence, is unwilling to relinquish the infantile dependent position may avoid engaging in the business of experimentation with and exploration of work possibilities. Locked into a passive posture, he may either defer such choices endlessly and assume the position of "prolonged adolescence" described by Bernfeld (1938) or he may settle submissively into a predetermined situation unrelated to his own gifts.

It must be acknowledged that forces exist in the contemporary world that promote such prolongation of adolescence. What Erikson has called the "psychosocial moratorium"—that period during which society allows for experimentation and deferral of commitment—has been further and further extended in recent decades, with the prolongation of the period of education demanded of young people and with the need to keep at least the more affluent among them out of the labor force as long as feasible. For some, the absence of external pressure to end this moratorium resonates with inner passivity and dependency wishes to produce a type of prolonged adolescence characterized by the "hippies" of the 1960s, the peripatetic remittance man, and the interminable graduate student. If to this is added the failure to resolve the renascent oedipal conflicts, potency difficulties and/or flight from commitment to sexual objects will complete the syndrome.

Ego Synthesis and the Management of Regression

The traditional picture of normal adolescent development would have it that puberty initiates a prolonged period of instability and turmoil, marked by multiple and shifting regressions and progressions in drive and ego organization until, somewhere in late adolescence, a process of synthesis and coalescence takes place that engenders the stable ego and character organization of adult life. Only in recent years have workers such as Masterson (1968) and Offer (op. cit.) challenged this view, setting forth evidence suggesting that the turmoil-ridden adolescent is a disturbed adolescent and that most young people negotiate the high school years without major disruption of personality integrity.

That this is the case does not, of course, minimize the stresses of the mid-adolescent period; it suggests, rather, that most young people bring to them a system of defenses and coping capacities that enable them successfully to weather these stresses. It is well known, however, that a significant number cannot do so. For those that bring to this phase a fragile ego, the burdens of individuation on the one hand (Masterson 1973) and the establishment of intimate object ties on the other (Erikson 1950) may prove insuperable.

The vulnerable adolescent faced with such threats may break down completely, evidencing an acute psychotic disorder which may, or in rare cases may not, be the prelude to long-term schizophrenic illness. In order to maintain a semblance of integrity, however, he will more frequently protect his tenuous psychic structure by withdrawing into a schizoid isolation, communing in dereistic fantasies with the introjected—and at times, projected—figures of his infantile objects.

Jim R., 16 years old, was referred to me after he had just dropped out of college during the Christmas vacation of his freshman year. For the month before the break he had been avoiding classes, sleeping during the day and awake at night, preoccupied with ideas about precognition and psychokinesis.

Mathematically gifted, he was determined that he could find a way to forecast the vagaries of the stock market and predict the winners of horse races—indeed, to determine these events by the power of his own thoughts. By the time he came to see me he had some awareness of the irrationality of these ideas, but he was still occupied with them and oscillated between belief and skepticism.

Jim was the only child of relatively elderly parents, who doted on him and were gratified by his intellectual precocity. He had been overprotected in early childhood, and his earliest memory was of his acute anxiety and tearfulness when he was put on a bus to go to day camp at age 5 or 6. Academically, school had posed no problems for him and he coasted through quickly with little or no effort; his grades declined in his last year in high school but not enough to preclude his admission to a high-prestige college. His matriculation there marked the first time he had ever been away from home for any extended period. He had always "hung out" with peer groups in his neighborhood, but had no intimate friends. Though fascinated by girls and involved in ruminations about social and sexual triumphs, he had never really dated a girl before he left for college.

Thus Jim was confronted by a succession of stressful circumstances on entering college. Not only did he have to cope with separation from his overinvolved parents, but he was thrust into dormitory life, which imposed on him demands for closeness with peers and simultaneously threatened his shaky sexual identity. Further, his somewhat grandiose narcissism felt the shock of the more stringent academic pressures and his rapid realization that he was no longer the boy wonder he had been in high school.

The result was a breakdown and regression in multiple areas of ego function; his emergency defense was largely that of intellectualization and a reinforcement of other obsessive-compulsive defenses—a desperate effort to control his world by means of thought. Removal from the traumatic situation and return home provided rapid relief, but it was only after several months of intensive therapy that his thinking became more reality-bound and that he was able to take a job preparatory to returning to a local university the next year. He lost one job because of persistent lateness and lack of commitment, and his first return to college was similarly unsuccessful. The second time he set up an easy schedule and seemed able to function at adequate but marginal level. He continued in therapy until he was almost 19. Although there was no indication of further psychotic thinking or behavior, his character became consolidated into a rather shallow, narcissistic one with a focus on the quick solution and the "easy buck."

Ego Ideal and Superego Development

As Blos (1974) and Esman (1972) have recently pointed out, adolescence affords an opportunity for the reshaping of the ego ideal and a readjustment of the superego. More closely attuned to current reality, closer to consciousness, and normally less peremptory in nature, the former is likely to undergo more extensive reorganization on the basis of new identifications. Much of the psychological activity of adolescence is related to the revamping of the value system; the constant experimentation of adolescents with values alternative to or in conflict with those of their parents or of the dominant cultural ethos reflects not merely "rebellion" but a genuine effort to find and formulate a self-syntonic system of values. The oft-described decline in the credibility of traditional sources of values (cf. e.g., Esman 1977) makes this process all the more urgent and all the more difficult.

The superego (in the restricted sense as the store of prohibitive and self-critical values) also undergoes some modification. Certainly, it loses its categorical, all-or-none quality, as the evolving cognitive system allows for more shadings and concessions to reality (Nass 1966). The earlier absolute prohibitions against sexual activity, for instance, are adjusted to the adolescent's new needs and capacities. Normally the incest taboo is not only maintained but fortified, although incestuous fantasies are not unusual, even in consciousness.

It is precisely with regard to this adaptation to current and future reality that the potential for later pathology resides. Although the ultimate consolidation of the ego ideal and superego is the work of late adolescence, the way is paved during the midadolescent period. Preservation of archaic value-centered introjects (Sandler 1960) threatens the maintenance of self-esteem under conditions of stress, with both shame and guilt as irrational and potentially self-damaging consequences. Thus the failure to adjust narcissistically tinged introjections of overevaluated parent figures may induce totally unrealizable grandiose or omnipotent goals. The college student who fails to achieve in conformity with such goals (or even worse, who fails in the course of his desperate efforts to do so) may react with acute depression, feelings of hopelessness, and even suicide. Similarly, adolescents who fail to resolve sexual prohibitions, including those against masturbation, may emerge with lifelong sexual conflicts which may lead to acting out of perverse or deviant fantasies in ostensibly nonsexual ways.

Mike, a 19-year-old college junior, came to treatment because of chronic feelings of self-doubt and inferiority and intense social and sexual anxieties. Born to a rich family, reared in an exclusive suburb, educated in expensive private schools, he appeared slovenly and unkempt, with holes in his trousers, long shaggy hair, and a droopy blond moustache. He was a former drug user, having had 3 or 4 years' regular experience with marijuana and LSD and the values attending them before abruptly abandoning them completely after a "bad trip" during which he almost jumped out of a window.

Mike's sexual inhibitions were profound. He was extremely shy with women, constantly concerned about sexual performance, and generally experienced premature ejaculation in coitus. He elaborated complex, compensatory fantasies of sexual triumph associated with situations in which, as a radical political leader, he would be jailed or hospitalized, achieving through his martyrdom reconciliation with his conservative parents and amatory successes with beautiful young women devoted to his political cause. For a long period during his analysis, Mike insisted that he had never masturbated before he was 17. Gradually, however, it became clear that he was referring to manual masturbation. In fact, from age 14 he had masturbated by rubbing his genitals against his bed sheets while in a prone position. This, however, he did not consider masturbation, i.e., he was able to carry on this activity while at the same time denying what he was doing because of his profound feelings of guilt and shame, related in part to conscious incestuous fantasies about his sister. The inhibitions implicit in this pattern were clearly expressed in his sexual symptoms. His fantasies, however, with their passive, masochistic character, similarly served as continuing expressions of the masturbatory fantasies of his early and mid-adolescent years.

In contrast, Johnson (1949) described situations in which parental sanction or complicity generated superego defects or "lacunae" that may portend long-lasting character pathology. "The child's superego lacunae correspond to similar defects of the parents' superegos which in turn were derived from the conscious or unconscious permissiveness of their own parents." Such persons will demonstrate focal deviation from culturally shared norms of behavior *without* intrapsychic conflict.

It is apparent, then, that the mid-adolescent period is of crucial significance in the evolution of adult personality. As Giovacchini (1973) puts it, "...the adult personality is psychopathologically constructed insofar as it is the outcome of reactions against what has been *experienced* as a traumatic adolescence." (italics mine) The person's *experience* of adolescence will reflect not only the observable realities of his life situation, but also the personality structure and characteristics he brings to them. It is, of course, commonplace for patients— and nonpatients—to ascribe the "traumatic" or stressful quality of their adolescence, whether current or remembered, to external circumstances—not least, parents, teachers, or other adults. It is well to recall that the picture one receives is filtered through the veil of retrospective distortion and influenced by the persistence of primitive object representations and of introjective-projective defenses that make the reconstruction of adolescent experience particularly difficult in adult analysis. "We fail," says Anna Freud (1958), "to recover...the atmosphere in which the adolescent lives..." What remains for most adults is a profound sense that it was a period they would not want to live through again. "Experience tells us," says Blos (1977), "that unresolved psychological issues are always bound to remain; it is, however, their stable integration into the adult personality that gives these persistent issues a pattern and rather irreversible structure." For some, unfortunately, this pattern, this irreversibility, takes on pathological form.

References

Bernfeld, S. Types of adolescents. *Psychoanalytic Quarterly,* 7:243–253, 1938.

Blos, P. Preoedipal factors in the etiology of female delinquency. *The Psychoanalytic Study of the Child,* 12:229–249, 1957.

———. *On Adolescence: A Psychoanalytic Interpretation.* New York: Free Press of Glencoe, 1962. 269 pp.

———. The genealogy of the ego ideal. *The Psychoanalytic Study of the Child,* 24:43–88, 1974.

———. When and how does adolescence end? In: Feinstein, S.C., and Giovacchini, P., eds. *Adolescent Psychiatry.* Vol. 5. New York: Aronson, 1977. pp. 5–17.

Borowitz, G. The capacity to masturbate alone. In: Feinstein, S.C., and Giovacchini, P., eds. *Adolescent Psychiatry.* Vol. 2. New York: Basic Books, 1973.

Bruch, H. *Eating Disorders.* New York: Basic Books, 1973.

Chess, S.; Thomas, A.; and Birch, H. Behavior problems revisited: Findings of an anterospective study. *Journal of the American Academy of Child Psychiatry,* 6:321–331, 1967.

Erikson, E.H. Growth and crises of the healthy personality. In: Senn, M.J.E., ed. *Symposium on the Healthy Personality, Supp. II. Transactions of the 4th Annual Conference on Problems of Infancy and Childhood.* New York: Josiah Macy Foundation, 1950. pp. 91–146.

———. The problem of ego identity. *Journal of the American Psychoanalytic Association,* 4:56–121, 1956.

Esman, A.H. Adolescence and the consolidation of values. In: Post, S.C., ed. *Moral Values and the Superego Concept in Psychoanalysis.* New York: International Universities Press, 1972.

———. Changing values: Their implications for adolescent development and psychoanalytic ideas. In: Feinstein, S.C., and Giovacchini, P., eds. *Adolescent Psychiatry.* Vol. 5. New York: Aronson, 1977, pp. 18–34.

———. Adolescence and the "New Sexuality." In: Karasu, T., and Socarides, C.R., eds. *On Sexuality: Psychoanalytic Observations.* New York: International Universities Press, 1979. pp. 19–28.

Freud, A. Adolescence. *The Psychoanalytic Study of the Child*, 13:255–278, 1958.

Giovacchini, P. The adolescent process and character formation: Clinical aspects. In: Feinstein, S.C., and Giovacchini, P., eds. *Adolescent Psychiatry*. Vol. 2. New York: Basic Books, 1973. pp. 269–285.

Johnson, A. Sanctions for superego lacunae of adolescents. In: Eissler, K.R., ed. *Searchlights on Delinquency*. New York: International Universities Press, 1949. pp. 225–245.

Masterson, J. The psychiatric significance of adolescent turmoil. *American Journal of Psychiatry*, 124(11):1549–1554, 1968.

———. The borderline adolescent. In: Feinstein, S.C., and Giovacchini, P., eds. *Adolescent Psychiatry*. Vol. 2. New York: Basic Books, 1973.

Muensterberger, W. The adolescent in society. In: Lorand, S., and Schnees, H., eds. *Adolescence*. New York: Paul B. Hoeber, 1961.

Nass, M. The superego and moral development in the theories of Freud and Piaget. *The Psychoanalytic Study of the Child*, 21:51–68, 1966.

Offer, D. *The Psychological World of the Teenager*. New York: Basic Books, 1969.

Piaget, J. The intellectual development of the adolescent. In: Caplan, G., and Lebovici, S., eds. *Adolescence, Psychosocial Perspectives*. New York: Basic Books, 1969. pp. 22–26.

Rapaport, D. Some metapsychological considerations concerning activity and passivity (1953). In: Gill, M.M., ed. *Collected Papers of David Rapaport*. New York: Basic Books, 1967.

Sandler, J. On the concept of superego. *The Psychoanalytic Study of the Child*, 15:128–162, 1960.

Schoenfeld, W. The body and the body image. In: Caplan, G., and Lebovici, S., eds. *Adolescence, Psychosocial Perspectives*. New York: Basic Books, 1969.

Sours, J. Anorexia nervosa: Nosology, diagnosis, development process and power-control mechanisms. In: Caplan, G., and Lebovici, S., eds. *Adolescence, Psychosocial Perspectives*. New York: Basic Books, 1969.

Waller, J.V.; Kaufman, M.R.; and Deutsch, F. Anorexia nervosa: A psychosomatic entity. *Psychosomatic Medicine*, 2:3–16, 1940.

Wieder, H., and Kaplan, E. Drug use in adolescents: Psychodynamic meaning and pharmacogenic effect. *The Psychoanalytic Study of the Child*, 14:399–451, 1969.

Winnicott, D. Adolescence: Struggling through the doldrums. In: *The Family and Individual Development*. New York: Basic Books, 1965.

The Course of Life: Psychoanalytic Contributions
Toward Understanding Personality Development.
Vol. II: Latency, Adolescence, and Youth.
S.I. Greenspan and G.H. Pollock, editors.
NIMH 1980

The Sleeping Beauty:
Escape From Change

Hilde Bruch, M.D.

When the little princess, on her 15th birthday, examined the spindle of a spinning wheel, she pricked herself and began to bleed; thereupon she fell into a deep sleep. A hedge of roses grew around the castle, and she kept on sleeping until finally awakened by a prince who had cut through the hedge of thorns. The fairytale conveys the idea that adolescence and growing up have always confronted youngsters with challenges and tasks from which some would withdraw. The fairytale explains the princess's long sleep as caused by a curse at the time of her birth. We are inclined to relate such reluctance to face new tasks to developmental disturbances. The fairytale gives modern sounding information along this line. The princess was an only, late-born child, excessively loved and overvalued by her parents and everyone else, a paragon of virtue and obedience during her childhood.

Escape from adolescence takes many forms and, as Bettelheim points out (1976), a certain passivity may be a normal reaction; the transition to abnormal states may be vague. Some, when they feel the pressures and demands are too much, may change the meaning of their experiences, create a different symbolic reality for themselves, and suffer a schizophrenic breakdown. Others use drugs or stimulants to change the way their mind experiences reality; this too may lead to withdrawal from ordinary living. Still others, in a counterphobic declaration of independence, make the social demands the scapegoat, fight them openly, break the rules and mores, and become delinquent, or they join radical political groups or strange religious cults.

I shall focus here on adolescents who in this struggle for specialness change their own body and thus set themselves apart and avoid demands which to them are unacceptable. By excessive food intake they will increase their size, or they accomplish the opposite, severe emaciation with the undoing of the biological pubescence, through rigid discipline, hyperactivity, and severe dietary restrictions (Bruch 1973*a*). Such youngsters carry the badge of their incompetence and suffering in an externally visible way.

The conditions are referred to clinically as *developmental obesity* (Bruch 1957*a*) and *anorexia nervosa.* Though they look like extreme opposites, they have many features in common. The eating function is misused in an effort to solve or camouflage problems of living that appear otherwise insoluble. If this fails or is interfered with, be it by premature reducing in obesity or forced feeding in anorexia, the symptomatology of borderline states of schizophrenic disorganization may become manifest, a measure of the severity of the underlying psychological disturbance (Bruch 1957*b,* Bruch 1973*e*).

In both conditions severe disturbances in body image and self-concept are dominant. These youngsters do not feel identified with their bodies but look upon them as external objects over which they must exercise rigid control (anorexia nervosa) or in relation to which they feel helpless (obesity) (Bruch 1973*d*). Though stubbornness and negativism are conspicuous in the clinical picture, these youngsters suffer, behind this facade, from a devastating sense of ineffectiveness. They feel powerless to control their bodies and also to direct their lives in general. They experience themselves as empty and as controlled by others. They are helpless and ineffective in all their functioning, neither self-directed nor truly separate from others, and they lack a sense of ownership of their own bodies. They act and behave as if they were the misshapen and wrong product of somebody else's action, as if their center of gravity was not within themselves. They lack discriminating awareness of bodily needs; specifically they are inaccurate in identifying hunger. They also are inaccurate in recognizing other states of body discomfort, such as cold or fatigue, or in discriminating bodily tensions from anxiety, depression, or other psychological stress.

These deficits in the sense of ownership and control of the body color the way these youngsters face their problems of living, their relationships to others. With approaching adolescence they are poorly equipped to become self-sufficient and to emancipate themselves from their dependency on their mothers and families. Frequently, they feel deprived of the support and recognition from their peers which help normal adolescents in this process of liberation.

A number of questions offer themselves. Why are these youngsters so unprepared to meet the challenge of adolescence and to engage in relationships with their age group? What goes on in families who fail to transmit an adequate sense of competence and self-value to a child? How is it possible for a bodily function as basic as eating to develop in a way that it can be misused to camouflage other problems and lead to abnormal changes in bodily size?

Biological Aspects

The bodily deviations are so dramatic that there has been a continuous search for some constitutional or physiological explanation (Bruch 1973*b*). The quest for some endocrine factor which would explain the conditions has stood in the foreground. This was pursued in the hope of discovering some substance the injection of which would cure the abnormal weight and do away with all problems. Though the methods of study have become much more refined and many neuroendocrine changes have been described, there is no evidence that endocrine factors precipitate the condition. On the other hand, the abnormal nutritional states are associated with secondary changes, including the neuroendocrine pathways and metabolic transformations. Many of the physiological abnormalities that are often quoted to explain the disorders are the consequence of the abnormal nutrition. Once abnormal metabolic patterns have been developed, in particular those due to overnutrition, they have a tendency to become self-perpetuating. Obesity becomes treatment resistant, scarcely influenced by short-term diets.

Psychological Development

Psychoanalysis has played a significant role in the effort to understand the psychological development of these youngsters. It was a revolutionary step when Freud, at the turn of the 20th century, drew attention to the importance of psychic forces within human nature. Expressed in the simplest possible language, his outstanding contribution to psychiatry and to the science of human behavior was the recognition that mental illness was related to the way an individual had functioned before he became manifestly sick.

He was biological in his basic orientation when he pointed out that human behavior and psychological development, and their neurotic or psychotic distortions, were related to the way biological need (which he called *Triebe,* a word subsequently translated as *instinct*) was met and satisfied (Freud 1905). He traced the whole gamut of emotional development, character, and symptom formation to the instinctual drives and the more fortunate or hapless ways in which they developed.

Throughout his life Freud struggled to revise his theory, and he remained critical of all his efforts to formulate a fixed theory of instinct. He defined instinct as "a borderline concept between the mental and the physical, being both the mental representative of the stimuli emanating from within the organism and penetrating to the mind, and at the same time the measure of the demands made upon the energy of the latter in consequence of its connection with the body" (Freud 1915).

When Freud defined his concept of "libido," he did it as a parallel to "hunger" which he thought of as the instinct of nutrition. "Everyday language possesses no counterpart of the word 'hunger' but science makes use of the word 'libido' for that purpose."

Hunger is such a common word that it is easily overlooked as a rather complex concept with many different meanings. Hunger is used to refer to the physiological state of nutritional depletion or severe food deprivation, or to long continued starvation, or to widespread famine. Hunger denotes also a psychological experience, namely the complex, unpleasant, and compelling sensation an individual feels when deprived of food, resulting in searching, even fighting, for food to relieve torment. In the more pleasant form of desire for a particular food it is called "appetite," and it plays an important role in our eating habits (Bruch 1969).

There is a third way in which the word "hunger" is used, namely as a symbolic expression of a state of need in general, or a simile for want in other areas. In analytic explorations the emphasis has been mainly on the symbolic significance of the abnormal food intake. In anorexia nervosa it had been a standard explanation that the food refusal and weight loss symbolized unconscious fear of oral impregnation (Waller, Kaufman, and Deutsch 1940). It was felt that this explained why these youngsters shied away from adolescence. In obesity too many different symbolic meanings of the abnormal food intake were recognized. Food may symbolically stand for an insatiable desire for unobtainable love, or an expression of rage and hatred; it may substitute for sexual gratification or indicate ascetic denial; it may represent the wish to be a man and possess a penis, or the wish to be pregnant, or the fear of it (Hamburger 1951). It may help to achieve a spurious sense of power and self-aggrandizement, or it may serve as a defense against adulthood and responsibility. This incomplete list indicates that food may carry an enormous variety of different, often contradictory, connotations.

Traditionally it had been assumed that bringing such underlying conflicts into consciousness would result in the abandonment of the abnormal symptoms. Neither in obesity nor in anorexia nervosa does insight into the various symbolic conflicts bring about improvement or affect the way these youngsters approach life and view themselves (Bruch 1970). They may talk fluently about the unconscious meaning of their behavior. Such insight is only a thing they passively accept from their therapists, but which they are unable to assimilate for their own living. It was recognized that patients with eating disorders suffer from a basic disturbance in the way the sensation of hunger is experienced, and this is closely interrelated to the broad spectrum of their other psychological disturbances. Pursuit of this question led to the formulation that hunger, the ability to recognize nutritional need, is not an innate capacity of the organism but something that contains important elements of learning (Bruch 1969). In patients with eating disorders something has gone wrong in the experiential and interpersonal processes surrounding the satisfaction of nutritional and other bodily needs. As a result, such individuals are incorrect and confused in recognizing "hunger," the need to eat, and in differentiating it from signals of bodily discomfort or emotional tension that have nothing to do with food deprivation and may be aroused by the greatest variety of conflicts and problems.

Once the question was formulated in this way, evidence of a deficit in hunger awareness rapidly accumulated. Anorexic patients will spontaneously declare, "I do not need to eat," and seem to mean it literally. Actually they have taught themselves to disregard the sensation or to transform it into something pleasurable (Bruch 1978). Basically they suffer from the fear of having no control over their eating; at times they are overpowered by the urge to gorge themselves, and bulimia with vomiting become troublesome symptoms. Fat people, when questioned on this point, will answer with an immediate sense of recognition that all their lives they had suffered from an inability to know whether or not they needed food or had enough.

Corroborative Observations

Direct observations on the ability to recognize correctly the nutritional state have given support to these theoretical considerations. Measured amounts of food were introduced into the stomachs of subjects of normal and abnormal weight. Marked individual differences were observed in the accuracy of recognizing whether or not, and how much, food had been received. Some healthy normal subjects were consistently accurate; others, though of normal weight, were less so. However, obese and anorexic patients were significantly more inaccurate (Coddington and Bruch 1970). Stunkard (1969) reported that, during the presence of stomach contractions, fasting obese women usually failed to report awareness of hunger, or epigastric emptiness, or a desire to eat, whereas nonobese women usually would report such sensations.

Through a series of ingenious experiments in which external factors were manipulated, Schachter (1968) showed that obese subjects were affected in their eating habits by external cues, such as the sign of food, its availability, apparent passage of time, whereas subjects of normal weight eat according to enteroceptive determinants. Physiologists have been familiar with this for some time. Hebb (1949), summarizing his experiences and those of others, concluded that the sensation of hunger was not inborn, that the state of nutritional deprivation was apt to be disruptive of food-seeking behavior. Wolff (1966) observed in neonate infants that hunger has a disorganizing effect on goal-directed activities, after an initial augmenting phase.

Many observations on the functional deficits of animals reared in isolation point in the same directions. Monkeys raised on cloth-covered wire dummies, referred to as "mothers," but without access to other live monkeys, were grossly abnormal when fully grown, apathetic, stereotyped in their responses, suffering from abiding affectional deficiency, incapable of grooming behavior, exhibiting many bizarre mouthing habits, and inadequate in sex behavior, though having undergone physiological puberty (Harlow and Harlow 1966).

Infancy

The older psychoanalytic vocabulary has the implication that the infant in some fairly adequate though not necessarily conscious ways knows how he feels and what he wants, and furthermore that, unless he is forced to repress this knowledge by specific prohibitions from the environment, is perfectly capable of utilizing whatever opportunities the environment presents for the satisfaction of his needs. But there is no evidence that the infant knows that his actions are his own, that he has initiated them, or that they are in any way related to his finding satisfaction. It must be assumed that the human infant starts life, in his subjective experience, unable to differentiate himself from others, and his biological needs are unidentified and unidentifiable states of tension and discomfort. The achievement of the sense of separateness is the outcome of developmental experiences which are of crucial significance for the later sense of effective identity. How does a normal child learn an integrated concept of his bodily existence as separate from the outside? And how does he become aware of his having control over his own sensations and impulses and mastery in his interpersonal and social relationships? And what miscarries in the development of those who fail to achieve this?

Another tradition has it that the infant is utterly helpless, completely dependent on the environment. This model of infantile development neglects the fact that there are intraorganistic processes that need to become distinct to him. A one-sided concept of the child being a helpless receiver of the adult's administration neglects that the infant, though immature, gives the clues and signals indicating his disequilibrium, wants, and needs. How they are responded to, fulfilled, or neglected appears to be the crucial point for his becoming conscious of his needs and for developing a sense of separate identity and control over his body (Bruch 1973c).

Two basic forms of behavior, namely behavior initiated in the infant and behavior in response to stimuli from the outside, need to be differentiated from birth on. This distinction applies to both the biological and the social-emotional field and also to pleasure or pain-provoking states. The mother's behavior in relation to the child is either responsive or stimulating. The interaction between the environment and the infant can be rated as appropriate or inappropriate, depending on whether it serves the fulfillment of his factual need or whether it disregards or distorts his clues. These elemental distinctions permit the dynamic analysis, irrespective of the specific area or content of the problem, of an amazingly large variety of clinical situations.

Appropriate responses to clues coming from the infant, in the biological field as well as in the social and emotional field, are necessary for the child to organize the significant building stones for the development of self-awareness and self-effectiveness. If confirmation and reinforcement of his own initially rather undifferentiated needs and impulses have been absent, or have been contradictory or inaccurate, then a child will grow up perplexed when trying to differentiate between disturbances in his biological field and emotional and interpersonal experiences, and he will be apt to misinterpret deformities in his self-body concept as externally induced. Thus he will become an individual deficient in his sense of separateness, with "diffuse ego boundaries." He will also feel helpless under the impact of his bodily urges, like controlled from the outside, and like not owning his own body.

The confusion in hunger awareness, the deep fear of having no inner controls from which patients with eating disorders suffer, can be related to these early experiences. These children were well cared for in every physical detail, but things were done according to the mother's decisions and feelings, not according to the child's expressions of need. A mother who is sensitively attuned to her child offers food when he shows signs of nutritional deprivation; gradually the child learns to recognize "hunger" as a distinct sensation. If a mother's reactions are inappropriate or contradictory—neglectful, oversolicitous, or inhibiting—the child fails to learn to differentiate between hunger and other sources of discomfort, and he grows up without discriminating awareness of his bodily sensations, without having the conviction of having control over them.

If a mother's concepts are not out of line with the child's physiological needs, everything may look normal on the surface. When she overestimates the child's needs, or when she uses food indiscriminately as a universal pacifier, she will produce a fat child (Bruch 1940). In normal-looking children with this background, the gross deficit in initiative and active self-awareness becomes manifest only when confronted with new situations and demands. If every tension is experienced as "need to eat" instead of arousing anxiety, anger, or other appropriate reactions, he will become progressively obese. The anorexic tries to compensate for these deficits in inner control in an exaggerated way by overrigid discipline and denial of hunger.

The early feeding histories of many fat and anorexic patients have been reconstructed in great detail. Often they are conspicuous by their blandness. The parents feel there is nothing to report: The child never gave any trouble, ate exactly what was put before him; the mother was the envy of her friends and neighbors because her child did not fuss about food, nor was he difficult in other ways. Others will report with pride that they always "anticipated" their child's needs, never permitting him to "feel hungry."

Evidence from Studies of Child Development

It would be impossible to include in this brief discussion any of the wealth and detailed observations of child development that have bearing on the problem under discussion. The model of development as circular, reciprocal transactions between parent and child is in good agreement with other studies of infancy, though, as far as I know, no one has expressed this in quite such simple and general terms. Discussions of the psychological events of the first year of life have become much more detailed and clearly defined. They no longer focus on a particular "trauma" during one or the other specific phases, but on the steps necessary for progressive maturation and on the ongoing interpersonal patterns that encourage or hinder this progress.

Piaget (1954) spoke of these reciprocal processes as "accommodation," the transformation induced in the child's perceptual schemata and behavior patterns by the environment, and "assimilation," the incorporation of objects and characteristics of the environment into the child's patterns of perceptual behavior, with corresponding transformation of these objects. He thinks of the total developmental growth of biological adaptation as a dynamic equilibrium between the processes of accommodation and assimilation. The organization of the stimuli from the infant's own biological needs into recognizable patterns is here considered as part of the mode of experience Piaget calls assimilation.

Spitz (1945) stressed the importance of adequate maternal care for proper physiological and mental development when describing the poignant fate of neglected infants. The earliest mode of experience which he called "coenes-thetic" perception, he considered to be present at birth (Spitz 1965). Escalona (1963) speaks of the infant's experience as the matrix of his psychological growth and gives many details of the transactions between mother and child as reciprocal. She considers such experiences, with their countless and successive adaptations, essential for normal as well as disturbed development. However, she considers "hunger" an innate biological given. Mahler (1963) describes in detail the individuation-separation processes as circular, when infants were observed in the actual presence of their mothers. She considers the earliest period of infancy as a "symbiotic phase," during which the mother needs to strike a balance between frustration of and intrusion on the infant's "inborn wisdom" of his needs.

An interesting example of pathogenic, nonappropriate transactional patterns between a mother and her two small children was described by Henry (1961) in his naturalistic observation of the families who had produced a hospitalized schizophrenic child. His overall summation of her attitude toward the feeding of the children was that it was "biologically markedly inappropriate." They showed a series of patterned elements, of the mother overpowering the children with food when they rejected it after they had been left to cry to a high pitch of exhaustion, or her disregarding defensive maneuvers against this forced feeding, often in terms that seemed inappropriate.

In a study aimed at defining factors involved in the development of a child's attachment to his mother, Ainsworth and Bell (1969) observed that the differentiating factors in the feeding situation during the first 3 months of life were not related to the technique of feeding, such as schedule versus demand, or breast versus bottle feeding, but to the relevance of the mother's responses to the signals of the child's needs. When observed at 1 year of age, the child's trusting attachment to the mother but also readiness to explore were related to the sensitivity and appropriateness with which the mother had interacted with her child. Some mothers would overfeed the baby, either by treating too broad a spectrum of cues as signals of hunger; others, in an effort to produce a baby who would demand little attention and would sleep for long periods. Such babies, who were rated "overweight" by their pediatricians at age 3 months, continued to be overweight at age 1. Yet they differed in the security of their attachment to the mother and readiness to separate, depending on the intent of the overfeeding.

Erikson's model (1968) of the "epigenesis of identity" is that of a continuous interaction between the individual and his surroundings, with a special task at each developmental phase of the life cycle. He considers the most fundamental prerequisite of mental vitality the experience of a sense of basic trust, a pervasive attitude toward oneself and the world derived from the experiences of the first year of life, with a fundamental sense of one's own trustworthiness. He did not specifically mention one's awareness of and control over one's biological functions as part of this basic trust, nor does his formulation exclude this. His emphasis is on psychological awareness; but without the sense of "ownership of one's body," the sense of being "all right" probably cannot be experienced. Erikson postpones the development of the sense of autonomy to the next phase in development which includes toilet training. He feels that the mutual regulation between an adult and child is severely tested during this phase. Actually this mutual regulation has been operative since the first day of life in the feeding situation where one child learns to demand or reject food according to his need, while another child will fail to acquire this discriminating awareness, unable to reject the feeding his mother superimposes on him. Lack of control over eating is associated with a devastating deficit in having an autonomous and self-directed self.

Early Childhood

The leit motif in the reconstructed developmental histories of these youngsters is supergoodness, "never any trouble." Parents will report with gratitude and pride how easy it had been to raise this particular child who had been clean, obedient, and considerate. Not one expressed concern about the lack of initiative and autonomy that this type of obedient behavior implies. In anorexia nervosa oppositional behavior during the classical period of resistance is conspicuously absent. Instead of testing out their capacities for self-reliance and a will of their own, these children slavishly adhere to the rules and concepts laid down by their parents. The youngsters themselves describe later their relationships to their parents, particularly their mothers, as unusually close, that they always knew what the other was thinking. This mind-reading quality continues to the time of the illness. During family sessions it is often difficult to determine in whose name anyone is speaking, something I have called "confusion of pronouns."

The individuation and separation of the child from the mother that are expected to occur during late infancy and early childhood (Mahler, Pine, and Bergman 1975) take place only to a limited extent. The one-sidedness with which care was superimposed during infancy has left the child deficient in self-trust and capacity for self-assertion. Efforts at separation will be weak at best. A mother who needs this child to feel complete or as proof of her own perfection might show displeasure when the child makes attempts to move away and will not encourage expressions of individual initiative. Overconformity remains the pattern of childhood behavior. In the few instances where there had been a psychiatric consultation before the manifest illness, the reason was a change away from overcompliance, as if that were the norm; efforts at self-assertion were treated as disturbances. The outcome is a serious deficit in the sense of self, of being a self-directed, unified person. They take all clues and rules from the outside, continuously worrying how they look in the eyes of others with strained efforts at outguessing what the grownups expect them to do or to be (Bruch 1977).

The early disturbances in inner representation of the self and objects interfere not only with the emotional but also with the whole conceptual development. We have learned from Inhelder and Piaget (1955) that conceptual development goes through definite phases which are partly innate but need, for appropriate development, interaction with an encouraging environment. Potentially anorexic youngsters cling to the style of thinking of early childhood, the period of egocentricity, of preconceptual and concrete operations. The next steps culminating in the capacity for formal operations, the ability to perform new abstract thinking and evaluations that are characteristic of adolescent development, are deficient in them or completely absent.

The discovery of real defects in conceptualization came as a surprise since anorexic patients usually excel in their school performance, and this has been interpreted as indicating great ability and intelligence. Not uncommonly, the excellent academic achievements are the result of great effort which becomes even greater after they become ill. Sometimes it comes as a shocking surprise that performances on college aptitude tests or other evaluations of general ability fall short of what the excellent school grades had suggested. As a group, these patients are what one might call academic overachievers.

A much more serious indication of a disharmonious development is found in their everyday thinking and in the rigid interpretation of human relationships, and in their defective self-evaluation and self-concept. A symptom that has been puzzling for a long time is a nearly delusional disturbance in their "body image," that they are unable to "see" themselves and their severe emaciation or obesity realistically (Bruch 1973; Garner and Garfinkel 1977). This distortion must be viewed as part of misperceptions on a much wider scale.

They continue to function with the morality of a young child, remaining convinced of the absolute rightness of the grownups and of their own obligation to be obedient. Following their own inclinations or expressing desires of their own has never occurred to them. This overcompliance extends to minute details in everyday living. They accept presents of their parents' choosing, what they are "supposed" to get, and dare not express wishes of their own, either because they do not have independent wishes or because they do not want to disappoint the giver by expressing a wish for something different.

Prepuberty

The excessive closeness with the parents persists or increases throughout childhood. Not uncommonly each parent seeks affection and confirmation from this, their perfect child, who may function as a go-between and compensate them for their deep dissatisfaction with each other (Selvini 1974). A child's feelings of worth and importance may derive from being needed by each parent, and the recognition they get outside the home seems less rewarding. With all efforts going into satisfying the parents, little energy is left for their own personal development. With the new demands of puberty and adolescence, their inner emptiness is laid bare (Bruch 1971).

Distortions in self-concept are also expressed in their behavior outside the home. They usually are hard-working students who are praised for their devotion to work and for being helpful with less advantaged students. School is the place where they receive measurable acknowledgment for their efforts, and this may be a positive and sustaining experience. Others, even when praised for excellent work, are not satisfied. They may compare themselves to a sibling or friend who is more gifted in a certain field, or they belittle what they themselves achieve because it comes easy. As time goes on the demands they make on themselves become more and more unrealistic; only the most exhausting work is adequate. Some are in competition with themselves, living in fear of performing less well when they continue with work in which they have been successful and therefore give it up.

Friendship patterns reveal the same overcompliant adaptation to others that characterizes their whole life. They may have a whole series of friendships, only one friend at a time. With each new friend they will develop different interests and a different personality. They conceive of themselves as blanks who just go along with what the friend wants and enjoys to do, like not having anything of their own individuality to contribute. One such anorexic girl, who later in college became quite popular, was disturbed by not feeling like her own person in relation to others. She described one episode: "I was sitting with these three people but I felt a terrible fragmentation of myself. There wasn't a person inside at all. I tried with whoever I was with to reflect the image they had of me, to do what they expected me to do. There were three different people and I had to be a different person to each, and I had to balance that. It was the same when I was a child and had friends. It was always in response to what they wanted."

Some take care of the newcomers in school or of others who are in some way handicapped and do not belong to any particular group. Over and over they repeat the painful experience that these lameduck friends gain a position in some group and leave them behind. If they have one particular friend, they are invariably in the role of the follower. Even a seemingly active social life may be an expression of overcompliance with continuous concern: "What do they say about me? Do they like me, do they think I'm right?"

Social isolation is part of the picture of adolescent obesity and anorexia and is usually explained as being due to the abnormal state. Actually they have begun to isolate themselves much earlier. Some will explain that they withdrew from their friends, others that they felt they were being excluded. Some are critical of the social activities of the others, particularly of the girls who are interested in dating and parties, and express their disagreement with the values of their peers in rather condescending and judgmental terms. They complain that the others are too childish, too superficial, too much interested in boys, or in other ways do not live up to the ideal of perfection according to which they themselves function and which they also demand from others. These youngsters cling with superstitious fervor to the rules of living they had accepted for themselves when they were quite young. The new ways of acting and thinking of normal adolescents are strange and frightening to them. Increasingly they grow out of step with their age group and the illness becomes manifest.

Adolescence

Puberty signals the end of childhood, and it is associated with marked changes in appearance and bodily functions, in psychological awareness and social demands. A childhood of compliant accommodation and of fulfilling other people's expectations has left these youngsters ill prepared for positive self-assertion which becomes unavoidable with adolescence when an attitude of "fitting in" is no longer appropriate. They are least prepared for the bodily changes of pubescence, which they consider alarming and unacceptable. The rapid growth, the new body configuration, the onset of menstruation, and most of all the increase in weight are frightening experiences. The increased appetite that accompanies the growth spurt convinces them that their body is out of control.

All adolescents, particularly girls, are preoccupied with the attractiveness of their appearance, specifically their weight. Those with early deficits in hunger awareness become obsessed with the problem of size and seem unable to solve it in a realistic way. They do not feel identified with their body, but consider it an ugly thing which they are condemned to carry through life. Deeply dissatisfied with their appearance, they are hypercritical about any flaw in perfection and ashamed of their appetite which they condemn as greediness. Those who become obese give in to the desire to eat, without self-regulation and inner control; and by misinterpreting any dissatisfaction and mood disturbance as "need to eat," they become progressively heavier, feel despised for being fat, and withdraw from the activities of their age group. Anorexics exercise discipline and control in an exaggerated way, but however low a weight they reach, they still feel "too fat" and become withdrawn and socially isolated. Whether fat or thin, they do not "see" themselves realistically and suffer from serious disturbances in body image and body concept. Their obsessive concern with their appearance reflects their conviction of inner inadequacies and ugliness. At the same time they indulge in dreams of unheard-of achievement and superspecialness. These dreams include the hope that one day they will be magically released from their isolation and inner ugliness and despised body. This point needs to be clarified before they will be ready to engage in meaningful therapy.

References

Ainsworth, M.D.S., and Bell, S.M. Some contemporary patterns of mother-infant interaction in the feeding situation. In: Ambrose, A., ed. *Stimulation in Early Infancy.* New York: Academic Press, 1969.

Bettelheim, B. *The Uses of Enchantment: The Meaning and Importance of Fairy Tales.* New York: Knopf, 1976.

Bruch, H. Obesity in childhood. III. Physiologic and psychologic aspects of the food intake of obese children. *American Journal of Diseases of Children,* 58:738–781, 1940.

——. Developmental obesity. In: *The Importance of Overweight.* New York: Norton, 1957 a.

——. Weight and psychosis. In: *The Importance of Overweight.* New York: Norton, 1957 b.

——. Hunger and instinct. *Journal of Nervous and Mental Disease,* 149:91–114, 1969.

——. Psychotherapy in eating disorders. *International Psychiatry Clinics,* 7:335–351, 1970.

——. Family transactions in eating disorders. *Comprehensive Psychiatry,* 12:238–248, 1971.

——. Eating Disorders: *Obesity, Anorexia Nervosa and the Person Within.* New York: Basic Books, 1973 a.

——. Biological basis of eating disorders. In: *Eating Disorders: Obesity, Anorexia Nervosa and the Person Within.* New York: Basic Books, 1973 b.

——. Hunger awareness and individuation. In: *Eating Disorders: Obesity, Anorexia Nervosa and the Person Within.* New York: Basic Books, 1973 c.

——. Body image and self-awareness. In: *Eating Disorders: Obesity, Anorexia Nervosa and the Person Within.* New York: Basic Books, 1973 d.

——. Obesity and schizophrenia. In: *Eating Disorders: Obesity, Anorexia Nervosa and the Person Within.* New York: Basic Books, 1973 e.

——. Evolution of a psychotherapeutic approach. In: *Eating Disorders: Obesity, Anorexia Nervosa and the Person Within.* New York: Basic Books, 1973 f.

——. Psychological antecedents of anorexia nervosa. In: Vigersky, R., ed. *Anorexia Nervosa.* New York: Raven Press, 1977.

——. *The Golden Cage: The Enigma of Anorexia Nervosa.* Cambridge: Harvard University Press, 1978.

Coddington, R.D., and Bruch, H. Gastric perceptivity in normal, obese and schizophrenic subjects. *Psychosomatics,* 11:571–579, 1970.

Erikson, E.H. *Identity, Youth and Crisis.* New York: Norton, 1968.

Escalona, S.K. Patterns of infantile experience and the developmental process. *The Psychoanalytic Study of the Child.* 18:197–244, 1963.

Freud, S. Three essays on the theory of sexuality (1905). *Standard Edition,* 7:123–245, London: Hogarth, 1953.

——. Instincts and their vicissitudes (1915). *Standard Edition,* 14:111–140. London: Hogarth, 1957.

Garner, D.M., and Garfinkel, P.E. Measurement of body image in anorexia nervosa. In: Vigersky, R., ed. *Anorexia Nervosa.* New York: Raven Press, 1977.

Hamburger, W.W. Emotional aspects if obesity. *Medical Clinics of North America,* 33:483–491, 1951.

Harlow, H.F., and Harlow, M. Learning to love. *American Scientist,* 54:244–272, 1966.

Hebb, D.O. *Organization of Behavior.* New York: Wiley, 1949.

Henry, J. The naturalistic observation of the families of schizophrenic children. In: Ojemann, R.H., ed. *Recent Research Looking Toward Preventive Intervention.* Iowa City: State University of Iowa, 1961.

Inhelder, B., and Piaget, J. *The Growth of Logical Thinking from Childhood to Adolescence: An Essay on the Construction of Formal Operational Structures.* New York: Basic Books, 1955.

Mahler, M. Thoughts about development and individuation. *The Psychoanalytic Study of the Child.* 18:307–327, 1963.

Mahler, M.; Pine, F.; and Bergman, A. *The Psychological Birth of the Human Infant.* New York: Basic Books, 1975.

Piaget, J. *The Construction of Reality in the Child.* New York: Basic Books, 1954.

Schachter, S. Obesity and eating. *Science,* 161:751–756, 1968.

Selvini, M.P. *Self-Starvation: From the Intrapsychic to the Transpersonal Approach to Anorexia Nervosa.* London: Chaucer Publishing, 1974.

Spitz, R.A. Hospitalism. An inquiry into the genesis of psychiatric conditions in early childhood. In: Freud, A.; Hartmann, H.; and Kris, E., eds. *The Psychoanalytic Study of the Child.* 1:53–74, 1945.

——. *The First Year of Life.* New York: International Universities Press, 1965.

Stunkard, A. Obesity and the denial of hunger. *Psychosomatic Medicine,* 21:281–290, 1969.

Waller, J.V.; Kaufman, M.R.; and Deutsch, F. Anorexia nervosa: A psychosomatic entity. *Psychosomatic Medicine,* 2:3–16, 1940.

Wolff, P.H. The Causes, Controls, and Organization of Behavior in the Neonate. In: *Psychological Issues,* Vol. 5, No. 1, Monogr. 17. New York: International Universities Press. 1966.

*The Course of Life: Psychoanalytic Contributions
Toward Understanding Personality Development.
Vol. II: Latency, Adolescence, and Youth.
S.I. Greenspan and G.H. Pollock, editors.
NIMH 1980*

Contributions of an Innovative
Psychoanalytic Therapeutic Program
With Adolescent Delinquents
to Developmental Psychology

Milton F. Shore, Ph.D., and Joseph L. Massimo, Ed.D.

I

In the United States the major concern with adolescence as a specific bio-psychosocial developmental phase distinct from childhood and adulthood can probably be traced to the well-known work of G. Stanley Hall in 1904. The breadth and scope of Hall's interests can be seen in the title of his classic work, *Adolescence: Its Psychology and Its Relation to Physiology, Anthropology, Sociology, Sex, Crime, Religion and Education* (1904). In addition to his magnum opus, one of Hall's most significant contributions can be considered to be the link he forged between his own work on the psychology of adolescence and that of psychoanalysis, for it was Hall who was most instrumental in bringing Freud to the United States (Worcester, Mass.) in 1909.

Since that early contact between developmental psychology and psychoanalysis there have been a number of significant psychoanalytic contributions to the understanding of adolescent development. A. Freud (1958) and P. Blos (1961) have published basic works in the area. In this article we shall not review the unique characteristics of psychoanalytic theory or the ways in which it offers a creative indepth understanding of adolescent behavior. Rather, what we

shall attempt to do is to relate some psychoanalytic concepts to the planning
and implementation of a special clinical program for traditionally hard-to-reach
chronic delinquent adolescents and describe the way the evaluation of the
program, using psychoanalytic concepts, has contributed to our knowledge
about adolescent development in general, and characterologically disturbed,
acting-out youth in particular.

A number of psychoanalysts have made theoretical and clinical contributions to the understanding of antisocial disorders in adolescence. Eissler
(1950), Schmideberg (1935), and Friedlander (1945) have written detailed
clinical studies. Johnson and Szurek (1952) have identified and described what
they call superego lacuna in that group. Erikson and Erikson (1957) have
formulated and refined the concept of negative identity. Redl and Wineman
(1951, 1952) have vividly detailed the ego maneuverings of antisocial youth.

But one of the pioneers in psychoanalytic treatment of delinquent youth was
August Aichorn, whose highly original work is still extremely relevant to our
thinking about this area. Aichorn (1935) developed a combined clinical and
educational approach for characterologically disturbed antisocial youth in a
residential setting which he based on psychoanalytic principles.[1]

One of the major themes of psychoanalytic literature on adolescence has been
the new opportunity the psychosocial stage offers for working out early developmental problems. The intense maturational pressures resulting in part from
pubescent development (often described as a "developmental crisis") are
believed to create major disequilibria offering a unique opportunity for personality change. Psychoanalytic theory has stressed how any given developmental phase has its own special features forming the arena around which
various earlier unresolved conflicts are played out and, given certain corrective
opportunities, may even be resolved.[2] For the adolescent, issues of individuation are, for the first time in life, expressed in attempts to separate psychologically from the family unit and relate more closely to the broader context of
society. One of the most vivid descriptions of this task is presented by Erikson
(1968) who expanded and broadened psychoanalytic theory so as to weave
together more closely our knowledge of the intrapsychic forces in the adolescent with the social and cultural forces resulting in the final formation of a true
ego identity. The significance of Erikson's views for undertaking new strategies
of psychoanalytic intervention for certain groups of adolescents has not been

---

1. Unfortunately, the close ties between the disciplines of psychoanalysis and education,
exemplified by such notable figures in both fields as Aichorn and Anna Freud, have often been
ignored or underplayed in recent psychoanalytic work, while the ties to medicine, particularly
in the United States, have been emphasized and fostered.

2. In Shore and Massimo (1968), theories of adolescent development were classified in two
categories: those that focus on the repetition of earlier developmental issues during the adolescent phase (recapitulative theories); and those that stress the emerging elements of the
period (emergent theories). This theoretical dimension, the authors believe, is most important
for determining how the intervention program is planned and implemented.

adequately recognized. Some psychoanalysts, such as Laufer (1973) in a drop-in clinic in London, have attempted to adapt psychoanalytic techniques in a creative way to reach adolescents who have not been reached by the more traditional psychoanalytic techniques. This paper will deal with a further adaptation of psychoanalytic ideas for treating characterologically disturbed adolescent delinquents in the community.

As mentioned earlier, one area of great importance in the adolescent is the beginning of his/her adaptation to the broad sociocultural world, its values and expectations. One way such an adaptation can take place in young people is through employment and work experiences. The implications of such experiences have yet to be explored in theory, research, and practice.

Although Freud recognized work as a major area of functioning in adults, little has been written in psychoanalysis about the profound meaning and significance of employment for adolescents. In many ways, work experience in modern society can be viewed increasingly as an important avenue for working through a number of psychological developmental problems of adolescence. Many clinicians who had had either professional or personal contact with adolescents employed in human service organizations such as crisis centers, homes for the aged, medical hospitals, or educational institutions have frequently seen remarkable growth in these young people when they have been in positive work environments. Dropouts from high school, after a meaningful experience on a job, have often decided to return to school with clear direction as to career choice and some resolution of the relationships to their families, other adults, and peers. Unlike adults, whose work can often be isolated from other areas of their daily lives, with compensatory satisfactions sometimes gained from other activities, employment for the adolescent appears to be extremely important as a door to the world of adulthood and the development of social and personal responsibilities, both major factors in the formation of identity. It seems that, through concrete job experiences, the skills gained during the latency period are consolidated and broadened in such a way as to prepare the youth for dealing with issues tied to functioning within the historical context of the society. The opportunity to interact with adults outside of the family, the need to develop and expand effective skills valued and rewarded by society through payment, and the necessity to interact successfully with peers in a team situation are some of the areas that play a significant role in defining oneself and one's social and personal boundaries as described by Erikson. In some ways, the role of work in an adolescent's life may be seen as equivalent to that of the role of play in the life of a child. While the value of play has been recognized by society as appropriate, even necessary for adequate psychological development, the importance of work, for a number of reasons, has tended to be valued less. Thus, in our society jobs are often not available for youth, rewards are few, and those jobs that are available are frequently meaningless in terms of assisting in personal growth.

Although jobs in themselves may offer positive, constructive experiences, there is a second contribution they can make. Specific experiences on jobs can serve as contexts not only for new experiences but also as an opportunity for specially planned corrective, educational, and emotional experiences. Via employment one can add therapeutic learning and psychotherapy so that previous areas of major psychological difficulty may be worked out and clarified. Aichorn (1935) was well aware of the value of work within a treatment setting when he described in one case: "If a change could be brought about in his relationship to his mother and sisters, and if he could find suitable (sic) work, it seemed likely that great improvement would result. Mother was easily dissuaded from her plan to force the boy out of the house to seek work as a laborer. I was able to arrange that he be given credit for his first year of apprenticeship and go on with learning carpentry. He began work two weeks after our first meeting and did well. He gave no indication of laziness" (p. 65).

Although some psychoanalysts have recognized how work experiences can serve to gratify, sublimate, and assist in working out conflicts, the use of employment as an intervention tool in psychoanalytic therapy has not been given the consideration it merits. For many groups of young people, work in itself cannot and does not resolve problems. Rather, it is through the work experience that one can identify the academic difficulties and ego deficiencies which, in the context of the concrete work experience, can become part of a meaningful, comprehensive psychotherapeutic intervention program. How work was used in this way to assist antisocial youth will be illustrated below.[3]

II

The features of the ego functioning of characterologically disturbed, delinquent adolescents have been well described in the literature: low frustration tolerance, excessive narcissism, minimal expression of anxiety and guilt, stress on action with little use of verbal symbolization, high impulsivity with immediate gratification sought, concrete thinking, little or no long-term planning, minimal impairment of perception and reality testing, and extreme manipulation of others in terms of self-satisfaction.

Since the planned project aimed at studying the treatment of a specific disorder, it was important that the group selected for participation be homogeneous. For a number of reasons it was not appropriate to do the usual careful individual and family diagnostic workups. These youth were too resistant and were neither available nor motivated for diagnostic study. Therefore, a homo-

---

3. This view of the importance of work in personality development has been seen by some as reflecting the Protestant ethic where, simplistically, it was believed any work inherently built character. Such is not the case. Little attention was given years ago to the psychological needs of the individual at a given developmental phase and the relationship between the kind of meaningful work experience that was necessary for personality development to take place. Instead, the needs of the market place were considered paramount rather than those of the individual. It is for that reason that child labor laws were instituted so as to protect young people from the exploitation that inhibited rather than fostered their growth.

geneous group had to be obtained by using all information available from the cumulative school files and from those in the school who knew the youth (usually well-known to school personnel because of his provocative acting-out behavior). The information gathered from these two sources, when evaluated, insured relative homogeneity. The criteria used for selection were: The youth had to be 15 to 17 years of age so that employment would be possible (State and Federal laws regulate the age and type of employment for youth). The measured intellectual functioning on a standard intelligence scale should be above 85 (to eliminate mental retardation or severe organic impairment). From the material gathered by school and police officers, there should be evidence of a long history of antisocial behavior with repeated truancies from school (the youth had to have been on probation at least once). The youth also had to have longstanding problems in school adjustment and severe academic performance difficulties not diagnosed as caused by neurological dysfunctioning. The youth also had to have been suspended or expelled from school or to have voluntarily dropped out of school because of a combination of poor school performance and antisocial behavior. There should also have been no observable psychotic behavior. In addition, there should have been no previous psychotherapy for the boy or members of his family that lasted for longer than a month. It was on the basis of these criteria that the youth were called character-disordered delinquents.

The youth in this study were living in a suburb outside the Boston area. Twenty boys were selected according to the criteria by the attendance officer at the school. By random assignment 10 were in the treatment program, and 10 were left to the resources available for help in the community. The program that was developed was called "Comprehensive Vocationally Oriented Psychotherapy" (Massimo and Shore 1967). It lasted 10 months with each youth aware of the program's duration.

With the desired group selected, a treatment plan was developed consonant with psychoanalytic theory and with previous experience in the outpatient treatment of characterologically disordered adolescent delinquents. The plan was, of course, adapted to individual needs, and the strategies varied with the specific clinical issues being dealt with at a given time. Nevertheless, there were certain general principles that formed the basis of intervention:

Principle 1. These antisocial young people by definition are characteristically resistant to help. Therefore, one major initial task is how to arouse anxiety and motivation. We asked, could there be a time when they might be amenable to help? Although it may not be considered a crisis of major proportions, we felt that when any youth either left school or was expelled from school permanently, it was necessary for him to reevaluate himself, rethink his direction, and develop new patterns of behavior. The need for these new adaptations to a life without school, we believed, might be considered a situation which produced some anxiety. Contact was made within 24 hours after the boy had left school. This immediate contact was to avoid any possibility that he might resolve the discomfort and harden his characterological defenses. The use of "crisis" in this way is not what is called "crisis intervention," i.e., as an end in itself. Instead, the crisis was used to make contact with the youth in the hope that he could be involved in intensive and lengthier therapeutic contact. Most crisis intervention work seems to be short-term in duration, aimed at alleviating the immediate disequilibrium. Thus, a crisis can either be used as a strategy for getting some-one into therapy or as brief therapy itself. It was the former way that was used here. At the conclusion of the therapeutic program, many youth reflected on this first contact. They remembered that they were indeed in a state of discom-fort, needed to reevaluate their lives, and were most vulnerable to therapeutic contact.[4]

Principle 2. These disturbed youth had experienced a number of unsuccessful contacts with community agencies. Therefore, it was important that the thera-pist separate himself from any of the agencies such as school, police, courts, social agencies, or government groups. Although many of the youth soon asked, "Who the . . . . do you work for?" the program, which was independently financed, could honestly be described as not connected with any known organ-ized community agency or group. The absence of the usual organizational restraints of a formal agency base permitted a great deal of flexibility and autonomy, a major element in implementing the program.

Principle 3. Outreach into the community offered an opportunity for the youth, who were nonverbal, to show the therapist their world rather than be forced to verbalize prematurely about their lives. Therefore, initial contact was made away from an office and took place in the community—in a car, at a restaurant, or on a streetcorner—depending on the youth's particular preference. These youth were comfortable having the therapist "on their own turf," rather than their having to come to the therapist's office. Sometimes they chose to have friends with them as their "protection."

Principle 4. Initial contact was made in terms of opportunities to look for a job, with other "help" available, if needed. These youth appeared particularly attracted by the notion of a job. In line with adolescent expectations, as well as with their fantasies of wealth and power, they were often eager at least to take a chance in exploring the possibilities of employment. The wish for a job offered an avenue for discussion of many other activities, including the youth's background. Their very severe limitations in learning and interpersonal skills were manifested early in the contact. At the beginning, efforts were made to encourage accep-tance of any type of work that offered financial compensation and was in line with the boys' dynamics and desires. One could then move to other jobs as skills and opportunities increased. In order to sustain motivation, the jobs could not be dead-end positions. Throughout treatment there was discussion about moving up.

---

4. Such immediate contact at vulnerable times has been compared to the manner in which adult criminals are often able to "capture" young people and direct them to criminal activity (e.g., drug use, prostitution, etc.). Mental health people have characteristically missed such opportunities.

Principle 5. From previous clinical experience we had learned that these young people, once they made "contact," indulged in detailed descriptions of sado-masochistic orgies, some of which were real and some fantasy. Given the primitive ego structure of these young people with the focus on manipulation, we soon learned that permitting them to indulge in these descriptions too soon in the contact was anti-therapeutic. We knew from experience that they could be overwhelmed by the material and never return. Therefore, although some information was obtained in the first interview, the emphasis was on the goal of exploring concrete tasks—job interests, job possibilities, job skills, and the fears that might be related to taking some clear initiative with the therapist toward finding employment. This task orientation seemed to bind the desire to indulge in omnipotent fantasy and turned out to be a major factor in keeping these youth in treatment.

Principle 6. The therapist was available for contact at any time of day or night. Each youth was given the therapist's telephone number to call if he wished.[5] To test the availability of the therapist, calls at first were made at 3 or 4 in the morning. The therapist made clear that his role was not to rescue young people who might be in trouble, but instead to help figure out, over the telephone, ways in which the youth could handle a situation. The therapist would help in considering the realities of the situation, the choices that were made, what had happened, why, and the consequences; the youth would have to make the decisions. In some ways, the approach could be compared to the life-space interview of Redl and Wineman (1952). Besides availability at night, there were few restrictions on time during the day. Sometimes a young person was seen for 3 or 4 hours at a time, sometimes not for an extended period. Characteristically, contacts took place in the community, at home, or in the car.

Principle 7. Where possible, the jobs were selected in terms of the particular needs of the youth. Thus, an extremely uncontrolled, aggressive youth was able to find a job on a housewrecking crew. A boy who wished to control his weight was found a job in a frozen food factory where he could see the food but could not eat it immediately. None of the jobs were preselected. In fact, part of the therapeutic contact was for the therapist and the youth to explore together what was available in terms of the youth's interests, his limited skills, and the job market. This was done through such activities as looking at newspaper ads and visiting various business establishments. It was clearly understood that any jobs had to be meaningful and rewarding, personally and financially. Following the preparation for seeking a first job, the therapist went with the youth to the job interviews. After the job was found, the focus of therapy switched to on-the-job problems, both academic and personal.

---

5. The importance of diagnosis is highlighted in determining when to give someone a telephone number. Facetiously, it has been said that one offers one's telephone number to those least likely to call. Highly dependent individuals would misuse the opportunity and call frequently. In this group, where dependency was constantly denied, any call to the therapist would be an acknowledgement of the need for help and thus be a sign of progress.

Principle 8. The therapist entered all aspects of the youth's life. He went with him to court appearances, to initial job interviews, to shop, helped him to open a bank account and to get a license to drive a car. The therapist used role play to anticipate with the youth some of these situations prior to their actual occurrence. The concrete goal-directed focus was extremely important, always within the context of understanding dynamically what was going on at a given time. The youth was constantly encouraged to take his own initiative. Dependency was not fostered, although the emphasis was on working together. That is, the therapist could be counted on for support and assistance in specific ways such as being with the youth in situations where it was clear such support would be therapeutically useful.

Principle 9. Because of these youths' poor learning skills (despite being in high school, their average reading level was third grade), an integral part of the therapeutic program was to develop and implement an individual learning program. No youth was encouraged to return to regular high school unless he chose to do so.[6] Instead, alternative learning resources were found, such as night schools, correspondence courses, and on-the-job training. Individual tutoring with the therapist was also part of the program. The therapist developed unique techniques by which the youth could improve his skills in reading, vocabulary, and arithmetic through the use of automobile driver's manuals, restaurant menus, and automotive magazines. Often it was difficult for the youth to recognize his academic deficiencies, since his omnipotent fantasies were used to deny his basic feelings of inadequacy and fears of humiliation. However, on the job these deficiencies soon became evident. Instead of permitting self-pity, regression, or counterphobic acting out, the therapist used the opportunity to improve the youth's learning skills and understanding. Academic materials were always made relevant to the youth's concrete job goals and activities.

Principle 10. Dependency, homosexuality, and primitive fears related to their overt behavior were discussed openly and bluntly with these youth when appropriate. As Redl and Wineman (1952) have suggested, the ego structure of many antisocial young people makes it possible to deal with these areas directly and frankly. Unlike the borderline or psychotic individual, whose ego structures are fragile, confrontation is possible in treating these youth once some minimal trust has been established (in fact, such frankness also serves to build trust).

Principle 11. Because of the severe manipulative tendencies in these young people, the establishment of separate, discipline-bound agency "departments"

---

6. Many school dropout programs have, as a major goal, the return to high school. Often what happens is that the persons drops out of school again. What needs to be recognized is that school personnel are often relieved when an antisocial youth leaves school, since he has been a source of frustration and difficulty to school personnel and administrators. Returning to a situation where the youth has been labeled "a troublemaker" can only result in those types of pressures that inevitably force him out again.

where different individuals are used for academic help, job counseling, and psychotherapy was rejected. A study using separate administrative units found that these youth, because of their ability for environmental manipulation, were very clever at creating staff dissension, disruption, and anger. Therefore, it was felt that all components of the program should be the responsibility of one individual who would be responsible for all aspects of work with a youth. The therapist, thus, would play the role of educator, job counselor, psychotherapist, or any other that was needed at a given time.

Although the therapist was deeply involved in all aspects of the young person's life, no efforts were made to foster a true transference neurosis, since the aims of the study were limited. The belief was that by producing certain changes at a sensitive time in life, processes of change might be mobilized that would continue when the youth were on their own. Despite the severity of the disturbances of these youth, it was felt that the forces of change in adolescence were on our side, and that, given the normal disruptions of this developmental phase, effective intervention could bring about major long-lasting change.

Principle 12. Throughout treatment, motility and action were stressed. Field trips were made and a great deal of therapeutic work was done over coffee, in automobiles transporting the youth, or through casual, informal contacts at the job site.

Principle 13. Natural crises on the job site offered opportunities for major therapeutic interventions. The arrangement with the employer was that the youth had to meet the same standards as the other employees. If he did not, the employer could discharge him. However, the employer agreed to contact the therapist if such an event occurred so that it could be used in therapy.

Principle 14. The focus of treatment was on the individual youth. The family was not seen. It was our belief that, unlike the usual close-knit family interactions of neurotics, these youth were isolated from their parents who were primarily involved in meeting the overwhelming economic needs common to large families of lower social class. The parents were grateful that they would not need to take a day off from work to appear at school or in court. The youth, when given an opportunity to earn money, soon began to think of ways to move out of their parents' homes.

III

One of the major methodologies used in research in psychoanalysis is to generate understanding about personality development and functioning through careful study of the therapeutic intervention process. The aim of this study was to use that methodology and determine what changes, if any, occurred during the 10-month treatment period and the significance of those changes.

Three approaches were used to study the nature and degree of change resulting from treatment. The first was a multilevel analysis of change over the 10-month treatment period. Three levels were used: (1) overt behavior—legal situation, employment situation, school situation, and other descriptions of general observable behavior; (2) academic cognitive functioning—standard achievement tests were administered in vocabulary, reading, arithmetic problems, and arithmetic fundamentals; (3) changes in ego structure—to determine changes in specific aspects of ego functioning, a group of clinical psychologists selected TAT-type pictures that they believed would elicit material in three areas—attitude toward authority, control of aggression, and self-image. It was assumed that the way the youth handled the instructions to make up a story to the stimulating conditions of the specific picture shown him would be a valid measure of ego functioning.

A second methodology used in this study was a followup study of all youth in the program. In this way, we would be able to determine if the changes that took place were merely efforts to please the therapist or were indeed substantive alterations in personality functioning. Followup evaluations were done 2, 5, and 10 years after the program ended.

The third technique was to find a random group of suburban adolescent youth of the same social class who had no history of characterological delinquency problems. These youth were tested twice on the same measures as the delinquent youth over a 10-month period in order to compare their functioning with the acting-out group. The contents of all the stories to the pictures for the three groups were analyzed for specific ego functions such as guilt, object relations, and verbalization.

General Findings

Comparisons were made between the overt behavior of the treated and untreated group before and after the 10-month program. Descriptive tables were used to make comparisons because there are no adequate ways of quantifying areas such as legal difficulties or job performance. Since these acting-out youth had been identified in the community as sources of trouble, they would also be the first picked up by the police whether or not they had actually committed an antisocial act.

To measure cognitive changes, the scores on the achievement tests were compared for the treated and untreated group at the beginning and end of the 10 months.

To measure personality changes, a special rating guide was devised based on test material taken from the files of known delinquents with character disorders who were not part of the study. Criteria were developed to determine what should be considered a sign of positive or negative change in the handling of the stimulating situation, i.e., where stories were requested to certain pictures of known stimulus value. The stories told before and after treatment were paired, and a highly experienced clinical psychologist was asked to make judgments of improvement or deterioriation on the basis of criteria described in the rating guide. Since his global judgments of change showed 90 percent agreement with two other psychologists who were asked independently to rate a randomly selected group of story pairs, the results of his ratings were considered reliable.

In all areas (overt behavior, cognition, and ego functioning), highly significant positive changes were found in the treated group; that is, although the treated and untreated delinquent group (who had been selected randomly) showed no differences prior to treatment, at the end of treatment in every area (other than attitude toward authority) the treated group had significantly improved.[7] Thus, comprehensive, vocationally oriented psychotherapy was effective in bringing about significant improvement in this group of hard-to-reach antisocial youth (Massimo and Shore 1963).

The information and test material collected on the treated and untreated delinquent group and on a group of nondelinquents offered an opportunity to explore further significant dimensions of personality functioning, particularly in light of psychoanalytic theory. Some of these issues will now be discussed.

Object Relations

The concept of object relations in psychoanalytic theory is an extraordinarily difficult one, not only to define, but also to quantify. Nevertheless, it remains an extremely important theoretical concept. Object relations might be defined as "the inner world of a person's feelings to others which determines in a fundamental way the individual's relationship to people in the external world" (Phillipson 1955, p. 7). Building on the work of Phillipson at the Tavistock Clinic in London, the stories given by the youth to the selected picture cards were analyzed using the Leary Scale of Interpersonal Analysis (1957). The scale divides all interactions along two dimensions: affect and activity. Four interpersonal categories are obtained: positive active (leading, teaching, directing); negative active (aggression, destruction, criticism, attack); positive-passive (joining, agreeing, accepting), and negative-passive (hesitating, delaying, and passively resisting). Using this scale to analyze the preconscious fantasy material obtained from the stories, we felt, would be one way of measuring object relations. The Leary scores on these stories before and after treatment were then correlated with the other tests (achievement tests and IQ). The results were remarkably consistent with expectations from psychoanalytic theory (Shore et al. 1966; 1968).

In successfully treated adolescent delinquents there was a significant improvement in object relations from negative to positive. No change was found in the active-passive dimension; that is, the youth continued to focus on action and

---

7. The finding that attitude toward authority was the area that changed the least adds to the internal validity of the study, since adolescence, by its very nature, is a time when opposition to authority is not only common, but expected.

activity. Thus, the *quality* of the activity was changing rather than the *degree* of the activity. What appeared to be taking place was socialization, with interactions with others perceived as more gratifying, satisfying, accepting, and constructive. Open defiance, opposition, and resistance were no longer necessary. Positive, active interactions took their place.

It should be remembered that this program did not foster passivity but rather focused on the individualized aspects of the youth's ability to make independent decisions and take the consequences of his decisions. The changes found, therefore, were consistent with the nature of the program itself. However, one may wonder how much passivity should be encouraged in mental health treatment of adolescents in general. Could we, in our therapeutic approaches, perhaps be focusing too much around the acceptance or rejection of passivity, rather than encouraging adolescents to become more constructively active?

Correlations with the achievement tests showed highly significant association between the quality of object relations and academic performance in all areas (arithmetic, vocabulary, and reading). Learning was highly correlated with increased socialization. Consistent with psychoanalytic theory, the learning difficulty in this group was not associated with symbolic meanings and the problems one often sees in neurotics, nor with the difficulties in processing information found in brain-damaged or intellectually limited individuals. Rather, learning difficulty resulted from a rejection of school and school-associated material as a socializing force. Once this rejection of socialization has been altered through appropriate therapeutic intervention, major learning can then take place.[8]

Guilt

Kohlberg (1964) has written a great deal about the development of stages of guilt, expanding and elaborating on the work of Piaget (1932). Concurrently, psychoanalytic theory has focused on the development and growth of the superego. As noted by Johnson and Szurek (1952), one of the major disturbances in youth with characterological acting-out difficulties is in superego functioning. In this study, the stories given to pictures of aggressive activity were analyzed using a guilt scale constructed in line with developmental principles. Thus, the early stages of outside control, expressed as fear of retaliation and revenge, were given very low scores, while stories dealing with remorse, concern, desires for self-control and restraint were given higher scores. The results

---

8. An analogy has been drawn between the therapeutic program for adolescents described here and the struggles of the toddler during the separation-individuation stage as described by Mahler (1974). The toddler, in relation to one person (mother), has to learn to develop object constancy. Nonverbal behavior and limited symbolization predominate. As coping improves and greater individuation occurs, thought processes (abstract thinking), delay, and words all arise to deal with aggression. All this is done within the basic narcissistic orientation of the first nonautistic interpersonal object relationships (beginning with symbiosis and continuing until some individuation has taken place).

showed a significant increase in more highly developed levels of expression of guilt in the successfully treated group (Shore, Massimo, and Mack 1964; Shore et al. 1968). These changes were associated with independently judged changes in overt behavior (marked reduction in overt aggression), and a marked improvement in academic functioning. Thus, internalization of controls was taking place with major improvement in superego functioning.

Verbalization

One goal in working with acting-out youth therapeutically, according to psychoanalytic developmental theory, is the fostering of vicarious rather than direct ways of impulse expression. Words serve such a function. This study was able to offer some insight into this area. Since the youth were requested to tell stories to pictures, it was possible to look at the number and quality of the words used before and after treatment for each picture stimulus. Posttreatment results showed a significant increase by the successfully treated group, as compared with the untreated delinquents, in word use in response to stimuli that aroused aggression (Shore and Massimo 1967). This increase in use of words was associated with reduced acting-out behavior. In fact, the number of words used was greater in the treated delinquents than in the nondelinquents who were tested. What seemed to be occurring was that the treated youth were overusing words as a way of controlling impulses, a common occurrence in clinical work where one often sees over-responsiveness, overreaction, and overuse of new behavior patterns before they become well integrated and more flexibly used in personality functioning.

Cognitive Functioning in Delinquents

The opportunity was available to study the cognitive structure of the characterologically disturbed delinquent adolescents by comparing their test results to the group of nondelinquents of the same social class. In this way one might be able to determine the nature of the character structure in these youth. When stories of the delinquent and nondelinquent youth scored on the Leary Interpersonal Analysis Scale were compared, many of the beliefs about the cognitive structure of antisocial youth derived from clinical observations were confirmed (Shore, Massimo, and Moran 1967). For example, although the number of words used by delinquent youth in telling stories was almost identical to that used by nondelinquent youth, the number of interpersonal action-oriented events in the stories was significantly greater. The events described by delinquent youth were significantly more attuned to manipulation, action, aggression, and significantly less to elaborations, descriptions, and symbolic elaborations commonly used in communication with others. The cognitive structure, therefore, reflected the clinical descriptions of these youth as hyperalert and oversensitive to opportunities for manipulation within the context of a sadomasochistic orientation. Such a cognitive focus was at the expense of more elaborate and developmentally higher level symbolic activities.

Time

A very important area of ego functioning is the personal conception of time. It is through the development of a sense of personal time that one can begin to plan, organize, and reflect. Indeed, the use of time may be closely tied to reduced impulse gratification and restraint over overt behavior. The tasks of telling stories to pictures permitted the evaluation of perceived time in a very subtle way, the evaluation of the time frame in which stories were told. Were they told in the past or the future? If so, how far in the past or the future? This measure of ego functioning showed very significant results in the treated delinquent youth (Ricks, Umbarger, and Mack 1964). But the findings are of still greater interest. There was no increase in the use of the past time frame after treatment. However, the treated and untreated groups significantly differed at the end of treatment in future time orientation. Two reasons might explain this finding: (a) Perhaps adolescence, by its very nature, should be seen as a developmental phase geared toward the future. Those with existential views have recognized the issue of "becoming" in the adolescent phase rather than looking at earlier childhood experiences; and (b) the program focused around consequences of acts rather than any attempts to stress the origins of behavior and their roots in the past. It was our strong belief that attempts to tie the past to current behavior would have limited success in this particular diagnostic group. The results on perceived time certainly indicate its relevance as a meaningful dimension of ego functioning, especially in relation to acting-out behavior.

Adolescence as a Unique Opportunity for Intervention

The followup studies, completed 2, 5, and 10 years after the program ended, found major differences between the treated and untreated youth. These findings reinforce the importance of adolescence as an opportunity for major changes to occur (Shore and Massimo 1966; 1969; 1973). The optimistic view that adolescence is a second chance for the basic reorganization and restructuring of the personality appears to be substantiated by the current study. Over the 10-year period, the 20 youths in the program (10 treated and 10 untreated) showed no reversal of direction; that is, those who showed improvement over the 10-*month* treatment period in adolescence continued to improve over 10 *years;* those who dropped continued to deteriorate. The findings are remarkably consistent with Erikson's theory of the importance of the formation of identity in adolescence. Adolescence seems to be a developmental period in which appropriate interventions can have major consequences. In fact, even interventions that are brief may end up having major effects during that time. The openness to change of most young people in the throes of adolescence offers a chance to bring about some major change in a short period of time, provided we are aware of what is needed and provided we are able to develop the flexible strategies and innovative techniques for bringing about such change.

IV

Case Illustration

Mark, aged 15, was expelled from high school in his sophomore year because of his overt, hostile, destructive behavior. He was not only preoccupied with violence but participated in any physical fights he heard about. Although considered above average in intelligence, he did not work in school and was failing in all his subjects. Mark was reading at a fifth-grade level. He was in trouble with the police, having been put on informal probation for drinking, later on formal probation for car theft.

Mark's mother would probably be diagnosed as a paranoid schizophrenic. His father was a severely disturbed man. He was an outstanding draftsman who, despite his education, had not done well financially. Mark's father had left the family when Mark was 9 years old. Two years later the divorce was finalized. Mark was the oldest of four children in the family.

The initial interview revealed that Mark's destructive impulses were so overwhelming that he could talk only about his desires to destroy everything and anything. Since it was not possible initially to deal with Mark's psychological conflicts, the therapist attempted to redirect Mark's hostile behavior into more constructive channels.

In each initial interview, the focus was not only on jobs that were available if the boys wanted them but that were also in some way related to the psychodynamics. For example, only after much discussion did the therapist realize that Mark might be interested in working for a construction company that did housewrecking. The job was found by the therapist and Mark when they combed through newspaper advertisements. They then visited the firm, where Mark was immediately employed as a helper in demolishing houses.

The therapist spent many hours with Mark discussing housewrecking, as Mark would relate intimate details of demolition and destruction. As a change, they attended a few stock car races. One day the firm decided to move a house that had been slated for destruction. Mark seemed angry over the change. It was this event that led to one turning point in his treatment. The therapist discussed with Mark how his life had been focused only on destruction. Exploring this further, he exposed Mark's use of aggression to hide, among other things, his own fears of attack and his use of omnipotence as a defense. Not long after, Mark began to show increased interest in cars and changed to a job with an automobile salvage company where parts from cars were saved prior to the destruction of the car.

In this auto salvage job Mark did very well. He enjoyed going to scenes of death and destruction in order to obtain the wrecked cars. As his performance improved on the job, Mark was given more responsibility. This required taking phone calls, reading auto sections of books, and writing orders. It was at this point that remedial education became essential, and the therapist and Mark worked on spelling and reading. Because of Mark's high native ability, he was able to learn rapidly.

Following his job in salvage work, at the eighth month of treatment, Mark became interested in auto body mechanic work. This meant further involvement in terminology, catalogs, and other educational pursuits. The therapist and Mark visited auto body shops to find out about the necessary requirements for a mechanic job. Mark even learned to handle an oxyacetylene torch.

After 9 months of treatment Mark was able to talk about some of the origins of his rage. He began to see how his feelings of helplessness during some of his early experiences affected his total view of life as a primitive fight for survival.

During the 3 years following treatment, Mark took a correspondence course from the Department of Education of the State of Massachusetts and completed his high school equivalency for a diploma. He had some minor traffic violations, but none serious enough to place him on probation.

In the years prior to the 5-year followup he had married and had become a mechanic. Ten years later he had become a specialized diesel mechanic and had two children. He is currently the coach of a Little League team and is described as a "solid citizen." He has had no legal problems for over 7 years.

Some of the youth who were having marital problems were able to get help from family agencies in the community. Such help would not have been sought prior to the program.

V

Summary

Psychoanalytic understanding of the development of characterological acting-out behavior in adolescents formed the basis for establishing and evaluating a special treatment program. Treatment techniques were undertaken based on the theoretical understanding of the ego structure of antisocial youth, as well as on the understanding of some of the developmental issues of adolescence. One major feature was the role of work in the adolescent's life as a tool for initiating and fostering a therapeutic program in which comprehensive educational and therapeutic assistance could be offered by a single therapist within the context of real-life issues and concrete activities. The adolescent struggle offered a unique opportunity for the resolution of a number of earlier problems. Data on the nature of the changes that occurred in the successful therapeutic program were consistent with many of the psychoanalytic concepts of the development of ego functions in acting-out youth and their relationship to areas of academic learning, socialization, and acting out.

Above all, the study shows the relevance of psychoanalytic theory to new treatments within a community context. Psychoanalytic theory need not be confined to traditional settings but can be used to form the basis for establishing social policy which stresses new ways of working with hard-to-reach individuals who have major social problems. The significance of psychoanalytic theory for social policy is exemplified by the work of Robertson (1958) whose psychoanalytic insights on hospitalized young children have lead to a number of revolutionary changes in medical settings in Great Britain, the United States, and other parts of the world. It is indeed possible that the psychoanalytic insights derived from work on characterologically disturbed adolescent delinquents will offer us insights into the types of programs necessary for adequate development to occur in adolescence, as well as for new treatment approaches for highly distressed youth. The saddest finding in this study was how those young people who were not in comprehensive, vocationally oriented psychotherapy, but who were left to the available community resources, had great difficulty in later life, many ending up as adult criminals (Shore and Massimo 1973).

References

Aichorn, A. *Wayward Youth*. New York: Viking Press, 1935.

Blos, P. *On Adolescence*. Glencoe, Ill.: Free Press, 1961.

Eissler, K.R. Ego psychological implications of the psychoanalytic treatment of delinquents. *The Psychoanalytic Study of the Child*, 5:97-121, 1950.

Erikson, E.H. *Identity: Youth and Crisis*. New York: W.W. Norton, 1968.

Erikson, E.H., and Erikson, K.T. The confirmation of the delinquent. *The Chicago Review*, 10:15-23, 1957.

Friedlander, K. Formation of the antisocial character. *The Psychoanalytic Study of the Child*, 1:189-204, 1945.

Freud, A. Adolescence. *The Psychoanalytic Study of the Child*, 13:255-279, 1958.

Hall, G.S. *Adolescence: Its Psychology and its Relation to Physiology, Anthropology, Sociology, Sex, Crime, Religion and Education*. New York: D. Appleton, 1904.

Johnson, A.M., and Szurek, S. The genesis of anti-social acting out in children and adults. *Psychoanalytic Quarterly*, 21:323-343, 1952.

Kohlberg, L. Development of moral character and moral ideology. In: Hoffman, M.L., and Hoffman, L.W., eds. *Review of Child Development Research*, Vol. 1. New York: Russell Sage, 1964.

Laufer, M. Studies of psychopathology in adolescence. In: Feinstein, S.C., and Giovacchini, P.L., eds. *Adolescent Psychiatry*, Vol. II, New York: Basic Books, 1973, pp. 56-70.

Leary, T. *Interpersonal Diagnosis of Personality*. New York: Ronald Press, 1957.

Mahler, Margaret S. Symbiosis and individuation. *The Psychoanalytic Study of the Child*, 29:89-106, 1974.

Massimo, J.L., and Shore, M.F. The effectiveness of a vocationally oriented psychotherapy program for adolescent delinquent boys. *American Journal of Orthopsychiatry*, 33:634-643, 1963. Reprinted in Riessman, F., Cohen, J., and Pearl, A., eds. *Mental Health of the Poor*. Glencoe, Ill.: The Free Press, 1965.

——.Comprehensive vocationally oriented psychotherapy: A new treatment technique for lower class adolescent delinquent youth. *Psychiatry*, 30:229-236, August 1967.

Phillipson, H. *The Object Relations Technique*. Glencoe, Ill.: The Free Press, 1955.

Piaget, J. *The Moral Judgment of the Child* (1932). Glencoe, Ill.: The Free Press, 1948.

Redl, F., and Wineman, D. *Children Who Hate: The Disorganization and Breakdown of Behavioral Controls*. Glencoe, Ill.: The Free Press, 1951.

——.*Controls from Within: Techniques for the Treatment of the Aggressive Child*. Glencoe, Ill.: The Free Press, 1952.

Ricks, D.; Umbarger, C.; and Mack, R. A measure of increased temporal perspective in successfully treated adolescent delinquent boys. *Journal of Abnormal and Social Psychology*, 69:685-689, 1964.

Robertson, J. *Young Children in Hospitals.* New York: Basic Books, 1958.

Schmideberg, M. The psychoanalysis of asocial children and adolescents. *International Journal of Psycho-Analysis,* 16:22-48, 1935.

Shore, M.F., and Massimo, J.L. Comprehensive vocationally oriented psychotherapy for adolescent delinquent boys: A follow-up study. *American Journal of Orthopsychiatry,* 36:609-616, 1966. Reprinted as a Monograph of the Harvard Research and Development Center on Educational Differences (Reprint #11).

_____ Verbalization, stimulus relevance, and personality change. *Journal of Consulting Psychology,* 31:423-424, July 1967.

_____ The chronic delinquent during adolescence: A new opportunity for intervention. In: Caplan, G., and Lebovici, S., eds. *Adolescence: Psychosocial Perspectives.* New York: Basic Books, 1968.

_____ Five years later: A follow-up study of comprehensive vocationally oriented psychotherapy. *American Journal of Orthopsychiatry,* 39, 5:769-774, October 1969.

_____ After ten years: A follow-up study of comprehensive vocationally oriented psychotherapy. *American Journal of Orthopsychiatry,* 43, 1:128-132, January 1973. Reprinted in Strupp, H.; Bergin, A.E.; Lang, P.J.; Marks, I.M.; Matarazzo, J.D.; and Patterson, G.R., eds. *Psychotherapy and Behavior Change,* 1973. Chicago: Aldine, 1974.

Shore, M.F.; Massimo, J.L.; and Mack, R. The relationship between levels of guilt in thematic stories and unsocialized behavior. *Journal of Projective Techniques,* 28:346-349, 1964.

_____ Changes in the perception of interpersonal relations in successfully treated adolescent delinquent boys. *Journal of Consulting Psychology,* 29:213-217, June 1965.

Shore, M.F.; Massimo, J.L.; and Moran, J.K. Some cognitive dimensions of interpersonal behavior in adolescent delinquent boys. *Journal of Research in Crime and Delinquency,* 4:243-248, July 1967.

Shore, M.F.; Massimo, J.L.; Kisielewski, J.; and Moran, J.K. Object relations changes resulting from successful psychotherapy with adolescent delinquents and their relationship to academic performance. *Journal of the American Academy of Child Psychiatry,* 5:93-104, January 1966.

Shore, M.F.; Massimo, J.L.; Mack, R.; and Malasky, C. Studies of psychotherapeutic change in adolescent delinquent boys: The role of guilt. *Psychotherapy,* 5:85-89, June 1968.

Shore, M.F.; Massimo, J.L.; Moran, J.K.; and Malasky, C. Object relations changes and psychotherapeutic intervention: A follow-up study. *Journal of the American Academy of Child Psychiatry,* 7:59-68, January 1968.

The Course of Life: Psychoanalytic Contributions
Toward Understanding Personality Development.
Vol. II: Latency, Adolescence, and Youth.
S.I. Greenspan and G.H. Pollock, editors.
NIMH 1980

Late Adolescence to Early Adulthood

Carl P. Adatto, M.D.

Late adolescence and early adulthood are characterized by restructuring and integration of the mind. The adolescent upheaval is brought to a close, and adult structures are laid down. This paper will deal with the vicissitudes of the mental apparatus formed in childhood and adolescence, the metamorphosis during the 18- to 23-year-old period, and the significance of these changes for future development.

Developmental processes can best be examined through the changes in mental structures and object relationships. The id, ego, and superego undergo modifications and functional changes, finally reintegrating into adult patterns. Object relationships are the medium through which stimulation of mental development and the effects of social determinants take place. In the conduct of an analysis a special form of object relationship—the transference—provides a window into the derivatives of the unconscious workings of an individual's mind and also a means by which psychic development can be catalyzed. The point of view presented here primarily comes from the experiences of psychoanalyzing patients in this age group, describing and explaining the mind as a phenomenon observed in the analytic situation. No attempt will be made to cover all of the literature in this area.

Developmental Concepts

Freud (1905*b*) introduced his concepts of puberty in a psychosexual developmental framework and in so doing brought into perspective the importance of the impact of the infantile period on structuring the mind. Puberty was described as a time when the infantile life was given its final shape centered

---

around the primacy of the genital zone and the finding of new sexual aims and objects. Some time elapsed before adolescence was given more attention in the psychoanalytic literature (Jones 1922; Bernfeld 1923; Aichorn 1925). Not until much later was special designation given to late adolescence or early adulthood as specific phases, even though some of the early cases which shaped analytic theory fell into this age group: Anna O., age 21; Katharina, 18; Elisabeth von R., 24 (Breuer and Freud 1893-1895); Dora, 18 (Freud 1905*a*); Wolf-Man, 23 (Freud 1918); and Homosexuality in a Woman, 18 (Freud 1920).

Jones (1922) stated that in adolescence "the individual *recapitulates and expands* in the second decennium of life the development he passed through during the first five years of life, just as he recapitulates during these first five years the experiences of thousands of years in his ancestry, and during the pre-natal period those of millions of years" (p. 398). Wittels (1949) included a second phallic and latency period in his four subdivisions of adolescence. Jones's recapitulation theory corrected the neglect of infantile sexuality in adolescence, but it also needed further emendation to introduce the qualitative changes in adolescence as espoused by Anna Freud.

While the importance of the infantile period is central in psychoanalytic theory, its mutability and differentiation in adolescence are still actively under study. Recently the fate of the separation-individuation phase of infancy (Mahler 1968) as it relates to adolescence and early adulthood has been a focus of interest. Blos (1967) views adolescence as a second separation-individuation period. Furman (1973) and Schafer (1973) point out the great differences between toddler and adolescent, bringing into question the limits of use of individuation as an explanatory concept for adolescence. Spiegel (1973) attempts to bridge this gap in correlating early phallic and later genital drives in individuation. One can view the importance of the processes of separation and individuation in both periods of life, but the maturation of the psychic apparatus and changes in object relationships bring new forces and tasks into play.

Characteristics of Late Adolescence and Early Adulthood

Most authors place the age span for late adolescence and early adulthood between 18 and 25 years. Individual differences and socioeconomic factors influence the transition between the two phases. For instance, graduate education may prolong the transition, while early marriage or economic demands may shorten it. Social factors will be touched upon later in the presentation.

By the time an individual reaches 18, most of the storm of puberty and the physical and physiological changes have taken place; individual physical and psychic patterns have become relatively stable. However, even physical maturation is incomplete, as evidenced by continuing epiphyseal closure in some individuals. Studies of these phases emphasize both the radical changes and the fixations that take place at this time in life. Small qualitative changes,

intrapsychic and interpersonal, can realign already established psychic structures and patterns. It is erroneous, however, to view this period as definitive, for
considerable change, especially following developmental crises, occurs in
many individuals.

The characteristics of these phases are ill defined, and the transition from late
adolescence to adulthood is by no means easily ascertained. Psychoanalysts
who have described these periods use many criteria for differentiating between
the two. Jones (1922) uses differences in intellect, integration, egocentricity of
fantasy life, dependency, and sexual maturity as distinguishing characteristics.
Erikson (1968) describes the psychosocial crises in adolescence as identity vs.
identity confusion; in the young adult, intimacy vs. isolation. Fountain (1961)
lists five qualities of adolescence: intensity and volatility of feeling, need for
frequent and immediate gratification, ineffective reality testing, failure of self-
criticism, and lack of concern for worldly affairs and other people. He states that
most or perhaps all of these qualities owe their existence to the oedipal struggle and that adulthood is reached when the intensity of cathexis to the oedipal
figures is diminished. Blos (1976) described four developmental tasks leading
into adulthood: second individuation process, ego continuity, residual trauma,
and sexual identity. Laufer (1976) considers that adulthood (ages 22 to 25 "or
so") is reached when the late adolescent (ages 18 to 21) establishes his final
sexual organization. He views the distinction between the two phases to be
important clinically and theoretically.

The multiplicity of characteristics chosen by different analysts reflects the
complexity of the underlying psychic process and the continuing search for
more knowledge about these phases. Recently considerable attention has been
given to this age group with resultant exploration of subtle but definite difference from other groups. These differences will now be discussed under various
headings.

Changes in Object Relationships

Late adolescence is characterized by the end phases of removal (Katan-Angel
1937) from infantile object relationships and the beginnings of establishment
of adult love objects. By early adulthood, the instinctual aims toward parents
are defused, and newly formed need-gratifying relationships offer a stability to
the individual.

Anna Freud (1958) compared the reactions of adolescents in analysis to
unhappy love affairs and mourning, characterized by the mental pain in giving
up a relationship which offers no further hope for return of love. The renunciation of parental ties in late adolescence is in many ways a welcome relief. The
threat of regression to early ties and the uncertainty of commitment to new
ones are characteristic of the 18- to 23-year-old youth. Considerable experience
and working through of adult relationships are necessary before a constancy in
relationships can be achieved.

The process of changing object relationships is different than in previous development because the emphasis is now toward permanency of a love relationship rather than gradual detachment from old ones. Individuation, in some form, has been achieved; the aim is now to secure its certitude, a prerequisite for stable, adult relationships.

Intermediary objects, such as temporary love relationships or idealizations made in late adolescence, often are important as catalysts to change in the formative period. Winnicott (1953) described the transitional object—an inanimate object such as a blanket or toy—in infancy as acting as an intermediate area of experience between the infant himself and his mother. During late adolescence the new object—a human being—while encompassing narcissism, acts as the transition between infantile and adult love objects. Ritvo (1971) suggests that a new object in late adolescence can become an organizer in a way similar to those objects of infancy and early childhood. He views the new object as helping the adolescent make the transition from narcissistic to object cathexis required for adult love relationships. Pederson (1961) observes that the first loves of youth often provide an important impulse toward psychic transformation, while owing their fascination to a revival of some special phase of the oedipal constellation.

The revival of the infantile object relationships through new objects creates a fresh opportunity for more definitive resolution of the infantile neurosis and its revisions made during adolescence. The individual now has sufficient ego capacity to deal with his conflicts and engage in the self-observation needed to reexamine and update his infantile and recently experienced ties. New love objects act as relief from the adolescent storm; however, in addition to their benefits they also pose the problem of acting as a defense against continued resolution of the infantile and adolescent conflicts.

The duality of maturation and defense was observed (Adatto 1958) in analysis of late adolescents whose motivation to continue analysis was diminished once sufficient resolution of the infantile neurosis was achieved to form new love relationships. The analyst, earlier sought out for gratification of unfulfilled instinctual aims as a transference object, now became a threat to regression to infantile ties. The same individuals reanalyzed as adults were able to analyze the transference, once sufficient psychic maturation was achieved to view the analyst with more detachment (Adatto 1966).

The course and development of an individual's object relationships are observed during analysis in the manner by which he views the analyst. The analysis of the transference to the analyst is a reliving of neurotic conflicts and thus a central aim of the analysis. The patient's use of the analyst as an intermediary object becomes a stabilizing force in the analysis and not subject to analysis unless it becomes "conflictualized." Thus the analyst is able to observe the force of the residual conflicts connected to the infantile objects and also the progress being made toward achievement of a mature relationship. Connection of the nature of the relationship to the analyst with derivatives of the unconscious fantasies facilitates the process of derepression of psychic conflicts. Through this route the patient is able to experience and observe the nature of the obstacles standing in the path of achieving adult relationships.

Developments of a sense of self or identity and of object relationships are reciprocally interrelated and difficult to separate clinically. The totality of the psychic apparatus reflects the narcissism of an individual which is vital to a person's functioning and reflected in the kinds of object relationships formed. The adolescent's object choice invariably contains elements of narcissistic and infantile object identifications. A task of youth is to resolve these identifications in a manner to create a situation in which needs of self and for objects are satisfied. Sacrifice of one for the other creates an imbalance which leads to crisis or pathological formations.

Late adolescence in many ways resembles the narcissistic personality disorders described by Kohut (1971), characterized by vague feelings of emptiness and depression while struggling with feelings of grandiosity and intense object hunger. While some adolescents indeed have pathological disorders, most are working through the last vestiges of separation from infantile objects and taking stock of themselves. In contrast, young adults emerge from regressions which accompany psychic transformations and are more clearly object oriented, with narcissistic conflicts less in evidence. Pumpian-Mindlin (1965) describes the omnipotentiality of the 16- to 22-year-old—an outgrowth of earlier omnipotence, characterized by the feeling and conviction that at this age one can do anything or resolve any problem in the world. He characterizes the young adult as engaged in commitment. The differences in tasks reflect the normal developmental shift from considerable preoccupation with the self in adolescence to newly found relationships in the young adult.

Establishment of Sexual and Aggressive Organization

Integration of pubertal changes with other aspects of the personality is a significant task of this period, requiring a resolution of residual sexual and aggressive conflicts, establishment of sexual identity, the determination of gender preference, and the formation of an adult sexual pattern. Unconscious fantasies condense the past and current aim, object, and direction of the sexual and aggressive drives and act as a force directing instinctual organization.

Laufer (1976) attaches considerable importance to a central masturbatory fantasy whose contents contain the various regressive satisfactions and the main sexual identifications. He states that a final sexual organization is established at the end of late adolescence, and diagnostic criteria for late adolescence and early adulthood can be assumed through whether or not the libido is object directed, the individual is able to integrate his physically mature genitalia, and if thoughts and behavior show some detachment from the central masturbatory fantasy. Some patients report this type of fantasy in preparation for or during sexual activity with partners. It is not the detachment from the fantasy that is significant but the resolution of the conflictual elements embodied in the fantasy. Sexual fantasies are reported by most analysands, and often psychic transformation can be measured through changes of the fantasies.

Blos (1962) views masturbation with its accompanying fantasies as facilitating forward movement of the instinctual drives, leading to definitive consolidation of the self. He considers that adulthood is marked by formation of an irreversible sexual position. Moore (1975) considers the masturbatory-complex fantasy to be a significant part of psychological growth during adolescence and its successful conclusion essential to the final sexual identity and establishment of adult relationships. Eissler (1958) maintains that orgasm is endowed with the power to confirm, create, and affirm convictions and that during adolescence convictions are decided which ultimately become associated with orgasm in later life.

The choice of sexual partner reflects the vicissitudes of preferences developed from infancy through adolescence. The interaction of drive gratification or lack of it during sexual encounters often reveals an individual's conditions for sexual gratification. Vacillation of sexual preference observed in some late adolescents often can be traced to identifications with infantile objects as well as to conflicts which are accompanied by castration anxiety. During late adolescence sexual preferences are much more open to change than in early adulthood. The relative psychic stability of early adulthood encompasses stability of sexual organization. The fate of the oedipal conflicts and their revision during adolescence is reflected in the choice of sexual partners.

A panel on the psychology of women in late adolescence and early adulthood (Galenson 1976) reflects the current revised interest in female psychology. Further clarification is much needed in order to understand the processes of becoming a man or a woman.

In contrast to sexuality, changes of aggressive drives in youth are relatively obscure; there is a paucity of literature in this area. Studies in delinquency (Aichorn 1925; Eissler 1949) have dealt with aggression in the younger adolescent. Friedman et al. (1972) have studied attempted suicide and self-mutilation in adolescence. Rebellion and violence in youth have been approached through application of psychoanalytic theory to social phenomena. Few patients with overt aggressive conflicts present themselves or are suitable for psychoanalysis, thus adding to the paucity of psychoanalytic data.

Ego Changes

Widening and consolidation of ego functioning characterize development into adulthood. Changes occur as the result of maturation, freeing of ego from its defensive activities as the earlier conflicts are more fully resolved, and catalytic activity prompted by new objects.

A. Freud (1958) describes adolescence as an interruption in peaceful growth in a state of disequilibrium; peaceful growth and equilibrium are restored only in early adulthood. Reliance on reality testing, self-observation, introspection, as well as other ego functions is necessary to do analytic work. Effectiveness of analysis often is increased as the patient reaches early adulthood and the ego reintegrates. For instance, amnesias of early childhood observed in late adolescent analyses are lifted in adulthood as the result of conflict resolution and the strengthening of memory function. Ego activity becomes more autonomous or conflict free in early adulthood, permitting synthetic functioning to prevail. Concurrent with increase of mutability of the ego is an increased capacity to cope with adaptational problems. Especially significant is the capacity to integrate and cope with instinctual demands which increased anew during adolescence.

What of the fate of the adolescent ego defenses against infantile object ties and impulses (A. Freud 1946; 1958)? Residues of the defenses of reversal of affect, displacement, withdrawal of libido to the self, asceticism, and uncompromising attitudes are still in evidence in late adolescence, but are considerably attenuated. Intellectualization, a common defense of puberty, has an unusual fate in many youths who engage in graduate education; the need to use intellect in actively pursuing studies often increases its use defensively, thus delaying conflict resolution. Spiegel (1958) notes that toward the end of adolescence there is a greater directedness of thinking; he feels the interruption of dramatic writing toward the end of adolescence is due to increasing psychic consolidation. One can observe that the intellect and thinking processes, while still serving defensive purposes, also change in function.

Geleerd (1961) observed that real-life traumata in adolescence often have serious impact and may lead to neurosis in adult life because of ego vulnerability. Trauma in late adolescence, such as death of a parent or sibling, while less crippling than before, still can have the effect of delaying resolution of the adolescent phase or leave the individual in early adulthood with a new revision of an old neurotic problem. Thus, while the ego is considerably more effective, the gains can be tenuous.

Character formation, the result of ego activity and compromises, is shaped more definitively in late adolescence. Analysis of young adults reveals that character traits formed during the infantile period often take adult form only recently. Newly acquired, stable ego activity has the advantage of permitting the psyche to function more economically; however, there are also economy of defense and containment of neurotic structure. Gitelson (1948) viewed character synthesis as an essential task of adolescence. Blos (1968) associates the outcome of character in adolescence with psychic restructuring and considers character to stabilize the newly attained personality of adulthood.

Superego and Ego Ideal

During adolescence external changes in relationship to infantile objects are paralleled by inner changes in the superego. Revival of oedipal conflicts creates a disruption in superego regulatory and stabilizing functions. Not only are the oedipal conflicts revived, but also the pre-oedipal and post-oedipal determinants modified and condensed into the current version of the superego. It is necessary to reinstinctualize the infantile objects for the adolescent to form his adult instinctual patterns. Without this shift, adult sexuality is greatly impaired. The adolescent of both sexes must work through castration anxiety and anxiety of genital mutilation in order to achieve satisfactory object relationships. Spiegel (1958) states that during analysis one no longer has the superego as an ally and that marked castration anxiety and less superego anxiety frequently dominate the scene. Guilt, formerly observed, is often overtly diminished as the adolescent integrates his newly found experiences.

By late adolescence, the individual has revised his internal distorted version of parental objects, bringing them into harmony with the reality of what adults are like, himself included. The primitive, controlling, along with the omnipotent, protective concepts of the parents are modified, together with the concept of the self. The individual senses freedom from restriction and sadness from loss of parental presence as the internalized parents are updated.

Freud (1923) described the superego as a precipitate of the ego, consisting of father and mother identifications and reactions against them, and as having the task of repression of the Oedipus complex. The superego gives permanent expression to the influence of the parents and of society; as the child grows up, the parental roles are carried on by teachers and others in authority. Freud considers self-judgement, injunctions and prohibitions, moral censorship, a sense of guilt, and social feelings and identifications to be subsumed under superego. Later Freud (1933) defined the ego ideal as a function of the superego, a vehicle "by which the ego measures itself, which it emulates, and whose demand for ever greater perfection it strives to fulfill" (p. 65). He stated that the ego ideal is a precipitate of the old picture of the parents and the child's expression of admiration of their perfection which he attributed to them. A. Freud (1946) described the repeated internalization involved in superego formation which changes with development.

Some analysts consider the ego ideal to be a function separate from the superego. However, Hartmann and Lowenstein (1962), using a functional and genetic framework, hold the prevailing view that the ego ideal is part of the superego, that it originates in oedipal conflicts and differs from earlier identifications. They consider that in postadolescence there is prolonged superego development along with that of the ego and that ideally there is a workable equilibrium and tension between the two. Jacobson (1961) notes that the adolescent has no new psychic system to help him break away from his infantile love objects, but the modification and restructuring of the superego give him support in this endeavor. Lampl-de Groot (1960; 1962) views the ego ideal as an agency of wish fulfillment, and the superego a restricting agency, noting that adolescents have difficulty in coping with the narcissistic injury engendered by clinging to the superego objects and that giving them up implies giving up part of oneself. Laufer (1964; 1965) maintains the content of the superego does not change, but the interrelationship of superego functions and that of ego and superego change through new identifications, especially with contemporaries. Ritvo (1971) states that the ego ideal attuned to reality is a development of late adolescence and necessary for the adaptive tasks of adult life, and that crises of this period are marked by failures of adequate ideal formation and insufficiently reality-attuned ego ideals. Settlage (1972) considers the ego ideal compensates for infantile narcissistic losses and that early aspirations influence the later content of the ego ideal, regardless of familial or cultural influences. He considers the feasibility for superego change in late adolescence to be a potential for constructive change in individual and society.

The ego ideal, thus, can be viewed in a developmental continuum with mutability of its functions. Clinical observations in analysis of late adolescence as compared to early adulthood verify the rapidity of these structural changes and the ease with which the developmental antecedents can be evoked, especially in areas of pathological conflict. When there is relative stability of the psychic apparatus with ego, id, and superego functioning in harmony, the unconscious meanings and origins are difficult to evoke.

Societal Influences

At no time in life does society have as direct an influence on personality development as it does during youth. Social values and ideals originally are transmitted through parents, later by siblings and others such as teachers and relatives. The separation from the infantile objects and formation of new ones create a vacuum in which the individual is receptive to social forces transmitted through contemporaries and newly discovered (or rediscovered) people— teachers, religious leaders, politicians, and celebrities are among the many possible new objects chosen to emulate. These identifications, while not creative of basic psychic change, give shape and direction, especially to the superego and ego ideal.

Aries (1962), a cultural historian, has described how adolescence had no special social recognition until the 19th century. The continued rapid redefinition of youth's role in current society has been an area of psychoanalytic study. A panel which explored the genetic, dynamic, and adaptive aspects of dissent (Gillman 1971) seemed to generally agree that dissent was an essential feature of youth in his transition from adolescence to adulthood, and that social institutions can transcend individual motivation and help define behavioral roles and moral standards. Deutsch (1976) has described her experiences in brief contact with patients, covering both psychic and group phenomena in campus life. Lustman (1972) observed that during a year of campus confrontation two groups emerged: one engaged in caretaking of adults and children in an apolitical way, and another radical group primarily interested in the events. His study has the sobering effect of avoiding generalizations about the kinds of identifications a student might make in times of unrest. Solnit (1972) has suggested that changes in the biological timetable in the direction of more rapid and elaborate maturation intensify the conflicts and dilemmas of the adolescent in our society.

The extensive literature in this area emphasizes the interrelationship between societal forces and psychic development. Erikson (1968) described the importance of a psychosocial moratorium for adolescents in their psychic restructuring and consolidation. However, there is no moratorium of the mind. Psychic activity and change are intense during this period, challenging one to understand the rapid shifts observed in a youth undergoing analysis.

Pathology

Because late adolescence is characterized by psychic upheaval together with reorganization, the separation of pathological from normal activity is a difficult task. Upsurge of instinctual activity, revival of infantile conflicts, change in the stability of superego, and vulnerability of ego can lead to alarming behavior. Assessment of mental activity, rather than of behavior alone, is a requirement for understanding a given individual; generalizations can easily lead to misdiagnosis.

Especially common is the difficulty in differentiating psychotic or severe neurotic states from normal disruption. Late adolescents entering analysis with the appearance of being overtly psychotic often, in a short time, with resumption of psychic equilibrium, show remarkable restoration of functioning. Because of the mercurial behavior changes, one must exercise caution in diagnosis and give the patient an opportunity to restore functioning in a way that is the least disruptive to his life. For instance, at times a decision to hospitalize a patient might have the effect of reinforcing pathological defenses rather than resolving them. Decisions of this type are difficult to make, especially when symptoms, such as depression, are intense.

There is a need to take into account the special characteristics of this age group— structural and object relationship changes—and use them as diagnostic guideposts. A. Freud (1958) notes the etiological elements characteristic of adolescence to be the danger felt not only in the id impulses and fantasies, but also in the existence of love objects of the individual's past. One observes intense reactions to parents when they are being treated as the archaic figures of the past rather than as they presently exist. New relationships in which the transference to earlier objects surfaces also become threats to be defended against. In the course of an analysis some patients seem to be besieged on three sides—by the living parents, new love objects, and the analyst. All three, including the parents, can become objects of transference revivals of the infantile past. Narcissistic retreat, a part of regression necessary in route to progression, also creates anxiety in the youth and his family.

Changes in the superego, with resultant weakening or strengthening of controlling function, can lead to delinquent or asocial behavior with lessening of overt guilt or to masochistic symptoms accompanied by intensification of guilt. The ego ideal, instead of functioning in the service of maturation, can act as a barrier to change. The entire range of the infantile neurosis can be revived. Clinical experience reveals that intensification of pathology can be a part of the process of mastery of old problems, much in the manner of play, only with less pleasure in the activity.

The shift from late adolescence to early adulthood creates a stability which makes the differentiation of pathology from normality more easily recognizable. Blos (1972) believes that the consolidation process of early adulthood structures the adult neurosis into its definitive form. Laufer (1976) maintains that because a person's final sexual organization is established by the end of adolescence, it is essential to determine if the adolescent developmental process is either seriously interfered with by internalized conflict or has stopped as a result of breakdown of functioning. Treatment aims to restore progressive development. He believes treatment of young adults should be directed toward understanding and working through the traumata and pathological solutions made in adolescence.

Because of vulnerability to pathology during late adolescence, it becomes imperative to give the individual an opportunity for sorting out and evaluating his mental functioning. It is a time in life when considerable change can occur as a result of analytic assistance.

Technique

Technique of analysis of youth follows the basic principles of analytic technique: analysis of the transference and resistance, and the resolution of the transference neurosis. The unique characteristics of youth shape the special technical interventions and act as a guide in evaluation of psychic change.

Current interest in developmental defects and their effect on later pathology has evoked considerable discussion on the need for change in technique. Eissler (1950) dealt with differences in kinds of technique required in the psychoanalysis and therapy of delinquents. Knowledge of deprivations in infancy and childhood and their effects on later development has called for reassessment of the efficacy of different techniques. However, such changes would alter the aim of standard analytic technique from the analysis of conflict to attempts to create psychic functioning which never fully developed. Little has been written about this type of change of technique as it relates specifically to youth.

Analysis of the transference is essential in youth as it is in other phases. Freud (1905a) attributed failure in mastery of the transference as a reason for Doris's early interruption of her analysis. A feature differentiating late adolescence and adulthood is the quality of the transference neurosis—the new edition of the infantile neurosis directed toward the analyst (Adatto 1971; Blos 1972; Ritvo

1974; Sandler 1975). The late adolescent, because of the threat of regression experienced in the relationship to the analyst and the vulnerability of his psychic apparatus, evidences an attenuated or sporadic transference neurosis as compared to its full expression as an adult. The incompleteness of the transference neurosis is reflected in the inability to fully explore the infantile neurosis and its later versions during analysis. Thus, one observes that many late adolescents interrupt their analysis once satisfying love relationships are made and sufficient analysis is accomplished to achieve adult stability. Often as adults they resume their analytic work.

There is also a focus on the importance and difficulties of reviving the adolescent period in the analysis of adults, and especially of the attitudes toward parents during adolescence (A. Freud 1958; Lampl-de Groot 1960; Hurn 1970; Feigelson 1976). The reconstruction of childhood has always been taken as a given in adult analysis; the understanding of the adolescent phase now also is recognized as necessary. No doubt the vagueness and secrecy as well as the psychic discomfort of adolescence have contributed to the paucity of information one gets about adolescence in adult analyses. Even in the analysis of late adolescents, it is difficult to revive the earlier adolescent period which often was crucial in determining the structuring of the psyche.

Summary

Late adolescence and early adulthood are characterized by the final upheaval of adolescence and the tenuous structuring of the adult mind. Processes of psychic transformation are presented in a developmental framework with emphasis on changes in mental structures and object relationships. The infantile neurosis is formed during the first years of life; during late adolescence and early adulthood the infantile neurosis is given more definitive shape, and qualitative changes reflect continuing psychic development. Attention is also given to mental characteristics, problems of psychoanalytic technique, and assessment of psychopathology of youth.

References

Adatto, C.P. Ego reintegration observed in analysis of late adolescents. *International Journal of Psycho-Analysis,* 39:172-177, 1958.
____On the metamorphosis from adolescence into adulthood. *Journal of the American Psychoanalytic Association,* 14:485-509, 1966.
____Developmental aspects of the transference neurosis. In: Marcus, I.M., ed. *Currents in Psychoanalysis.* New York: International Universities Press, 1971.
Aichorn, A. *Wayward Youth* (1925). New York: The Viking Press, 1948. 236 pp.
Aries, P. A social history of adolescence (1962). In: Esman, A.H., ed. *The Psychology of Adolescence: Essential Readings.* New York: International Universities Press, 1975.
Bernfeld, S. Uber eine typische Form der mannlichen Pubertat. [On a typical form of male puberty] *Imago,* 9:169-188, 1923.

Blos, P. *On Adolescence: A Psychoanalytic Interpretation.* New York: The Free Press of Glencoe, 1962.

——.The second individuation process of adolescence. *The Psychoanalytic Study of the Child,* 22:162-186, 1967.

——.Character formation in adolescence. *The Psychoanalytic Study of the Child,* 23:245-263, 1968.

——.The epigenesis of the adult neurosis. *The Psychoanalytic Study of the Child,* 27:106-135, 1972.

——.When and how does adolescence end? Structural criteria for adolescent closure. *Journal of the Philadelphia Association for Psychoanalysis,* 3(3):47-58, 1976.

Breuer, J., and Freud, S. Studies on Hysteria (1893-1895). *Standard Edition.* Vol. II. London: Hogarth Press, 1955.

Deutsch, H. *Selected Problems of Adolescence: With Special Emphasis on Group Formation.* New York: International Universities Press, 1967.

Eissler, K.R. Some problems of delinquency. In: Eissler, K.R., ed. *Searchlights on Delinquency: New Psychoanalytic Studies.* New York: International Universities Press, 1949.

——.Ego-psychological implications of the psychoanalytic treatment of delinquents. *The Psychoanalytic Study of the Child,* 5:97-121, 1950.

——.Notes on problems of technique in the psychoanalytic treatment of adolescents; with some remarks on perversions. *The Psychoanalytic Study of the Child,* 13:223-254, 1958.

Erikson, E.H. Identity and the life cycle: Selected papers. *Psychological Issues,* 1(1):1-171, 1959.

——. *Identity: Youth and Crisis.* New York: Norton, 1968. 336 pp.

Feigelson, C.I. Reconstruction of adolescence (and early latency) in the analysis of an adult woman. *The Psychoanalytic Study of the Child,* 31:225-236, 1976.

Fountain, G. Adolescent into adult: An inquiry. *Journal of the American Psychoanalytic Association,* 9:417-433, 1961.

Freud, A. *The Ego and the Mechanisms of Defense.* New York: International Universities Press, 1946. 196 pp.

——.Adolescence. *The Psychoanalytic Study of the Child,* 13:255-278, 1958.

Freud, S. Fragment of an analysis of a case of hysteria (1905*a* [1901]). *Standard Edition.* 7:7-122, London: Hogarth Press, 1953.

——. Three essays on the theory of sexuality (1905*b*). *Standard Edition.* 7:130–243, London: Hogarth Press, 1953.

——.From the history of an infantile neurosis (1918 [1914]). *Standard Edition.* 17:7-120, London: Hogarth Press, 1955.

——.The Psychogenesis of a case of homosexuality in a woman (1920). *Standard Edition.* 18:147-172, London: Hogarth Press, 1955.

——.The ego and the id (1923). *Standard Edition.* 19:12-66, London: Hogarth Press, 1961.

——.New introductory lectures on psycho-analysis (1933 [1932]). *Standard Edition.* 22:5-182, London: Hogarth Press, 1964.

Friedman, M.; Glasser, M.; Laufer, E.; Laufer, M.; and Wohl, M. Attempted suicide and self-mutilation in adolescence: Some observations from a psychoanalytic research project. *International Journal of Psycho-Analysis,* 53:179-183, 1972.

Furman, E. A contribution to assessing the role of infantile separation-individuation in adolescent development. *The Psychoanalytic Study of the Child,* 28:193-207, 1973.

Galenson, E. Panel report: Psychology of women: Late adolescence and early adulthood. *Journal of the American Psychoanalytic Association,* 24:631-645, 1976.

Geleerd, E.R. Some aspects of ego vicissitudes in adolescence. *Journal of the American Psychoanalytic Association,* 9:395–405, 1961.

Gillman, R.D. Panel report: Genetic, dynamic and adaptive aspects of dissent. *Journal of the American Psychoanalytic Association,* 29:122-130, 1971.

Gitelson, M. Character synthesis: The psychotherapeutic problem in adolescence. *American Journal of Orthopsychiatry,* 18:422-431, 1948.

Hartmann, H., and Lowenstein, R.M. Notes on the superego. *The Psychoanalytic Study of the Child,* 17:7-122, 1962.

Hurn, H.T. Adolescent transference: A problem in the terminal phase of analysis. *Journal of the American Psychoanalytic Association,* 18:342-357, 1970.

Jacobson, E. Adolescent moods and the remodelling of psychic structures in adolescence. *The Psychoanalytic Study of the Child,* 16:164-183, 1961.

Jones, E. Some problems of adolescence (1922). In: *Papers on Psycho-Analysis.* 5th ed. London: Bailliere, Tindall & Cox, 1948, pp. 389-406.

Katan-Angel, A. The role of displacement in agoraphobia (1937). *International Journal of Psycho-Analysis,* 32:41-50, 1951.

Kohut, H. *The Analysis of the Self.* New York: International Universities Press, 1971.

Lampl-de Groot, J. On adolescence. *The Psychoanalytic Study of the Child,* 15:95-103, 1960.

——.Ego ideal and superego. *The Psychoanalytic Study of the Child,* 17:94-106, 1962.

Laufer, M. Ego ideal and pseudo ego ideal in adolescence. *The Psychoanalytic Study of the Child,* 19:196-221, 1964.

——.Assessment of adolescent disturbances: The application of Anna Freud's diagnostic profile. *The Psychoanalytic Study of the Child,* 20:99-123, 1965.

——.The central masturbation fantasy, the final sexual organization, and adolescence. *The Psychoanalytic Study of the Child,* 31:297-316, 1976.

Lustman, S.L. Yale's year of confrontation: A view from the Master's house. *The Psychoanalytic Study of the Child,* 27:57-73, 1972.

Mahler, M. *On Human Symbiosis and the Vicissitudes of Individuation. Vol I: Infantile Psychosis.* New York: International Universities Press, 1968.

Moore, W.T. Some economic functions of genital masturbation during adolescent development. In: Marcus, I.M., ed. *Masturbation: From Infancy to Senescence.* New York: International Universities Press, 1975.

Pedersen, S. Personality formation in adolescence and its impact upon the psycho-analytical treatment of adults. *International Journal of Psycho-Analysis,* 42:381–388, 1961.

Pumpian-Mindlin, E. Omnipotentiality, youth, and commitment. *Journal of the American Academy of Child Psychiatry,* 4:1-18, 1965.

Ritvo, S. Late adolescence: Developmental and clinical considerations. *The Psychoanalytic Study of the Child,* 26:241-263, 1971.

——.Current status of the concept of infantile neurosis: Implications for diagnosis and technique. *The Psychoanalytic Study of the Child,* 29:159-181, 1974.

Sandler, J.; Kennedy, H.; and Tyson, R.L. Discussions on transference: The treatment situation and technique in child psychoanalysis. *The Psychoanalytic Study of the Child,* 30:409-441, 1975.

Schafer, R. Concepts of self and identity and the experience of separation-individuation in adolescence. *Psychoanalytic Quarterly,* 42:42-59, 1973.

Settlage, C.F. Cultural values and the superego in late adolescence. *The Psychoanalytic Study of the Child,* 27:74-92, 1972.

Solnit, A.J. Youth and the campus: The search for social conscience. *The Psychoanalytic Study of the Child,* 27:98-105, 1972.

Spiegel, L.A. Comments on the psychoanalytic psychology of adolescence. *The Psychoanalytic Study of the Child,* 13:296-308, 1958.

——. In: Marcus, I.M. Panel Report: The experience of separation-individuation in infancy and its reverberations through the course of life. *Journal of the American Psychoanalytic Association,* 21:155-167, 1973.

Winnicott, D.W. Transitional objects and transitional phenomena. *International Journal of Psycho-Analysis,* 34:89-97, 1953.

Wittels, F. The ego of the adolescent. In: Eissler, K.R., ed. *Searchlights on Delinquency: New Psychoanalytic Studies.* New York: International Universities Press, 1949.

*The Course of Life: Psychoanalytic Contributions
Toward Understanding Personality Development.
Vol. II: Latency, Adolescence, and Youth.
S.I. Greenspan and G.H. Pollock, editors.
NIMH 1980*

Bridge to Adulthood:
Years From Eighteen to Twenty-three

Herman D. Staples, M.D., and Erwin R. Smarr, M.D.

Introduction

The years between 18 and 23 may properly be claimed by both late adolescence and young adulthood; likewise, they may be considered a bridge between these two developmental stages. Interest in late adolescence and early adult years has been stimulated recently by several factors, among these the ascendancy of the psychoanalytic developmental perspective to its present position of central importance in the entire lifespan of the individual. The contributions of many authors, most notably Erikson and Blos, have expanded our understanding of all phases of adolescence. On the basis of intrapsychic forces, Blos (1962) demarcated five subphases of adolescence: preadolescence, early adolescence, adolescence proper, late adolescence, and postadolescence. The last two of these are especially pertinent to our topic.

It has often been said that the end of a developmental stage is harder to recognize than the beginning. Since our task is to examine both the resolution of adolescence as well as the transition to adulthood, we have a dual problem. No discrete physiological or hormonal event characterizes the end of adolescence (in contrast to the menarche or the first seminal ejaculation that signals the advent of puberty). By 18 or 20 years of age, the individual's physical growth potential has been reached, and all the physiologic equipment is present for the remainder of life's journey. Young adulthood is then more a psychocultural status than a distinct physiological stage.

In the realm of cognitive development, as brilliantly elaborated by Piaget, the changes to formal operations and abstract thinking that are characteristic of adolescence have normally occurred in early and midadolescence. No further change has been noted that is specifically associated with late adolescence or early adulthood. It is more a matter of the uses to which cognition is put, paying much greater attention to both external and internal reality and modifying of values. These tasks reside in the progressive development of ego functions, assisted by developments in the ego ideal and in the area of object relations. This survey of the intrapsychic development of this phase in the life cycle will center around these events.

Adolescence Into Adulthood

There have been essentially three approaches that have been used to delineate the interpersonal and intrapsychic factors involved in development from adolescence to adulthood. These approaches overlap in many respects and are by no means mutually exclusive. Each way of looking at the developmental changes can contribute to our total understanding. The three approaches are: (1) outlining the main psychological characteristics of the adolescent and showing how these characteristics are transformed in the adult; (2) enumerating the tasks that are expected to be completed by an adolescent before he or she may be considered an adult; and (3) tracing the changes in psychic structures, defensive operations, adaptive functions, object relations, etc., that accompany advancement into adult life. Each approach will be examined briefly by reviewing a sampling by its leading exponents.

Transformations of Adolescent Into Adult Characteristics

Fountain (1961) selected five qualities which generally were found in most adolescents but which most adults do not show. (a) Emotional Volatility—the well-known intensity and volatility of emotion and the strong urge to experience a variety of feelings in adolescence are reduced in adulthood. (b) Need for Immediate Gratification—the adolescent's intolerance of anxiety, frustration, and postponement of gratification gives way to the adult's greater tolerance and patience. (c) Impaired Reality Testing—in contrast to the adult, the adolescent is more likely to be less aware of the consequences of his actions and of the feelings of others. (d) Failure of Self-Criticism—the adolescent is less able than the adult to see himself as others see him, to judge the impact on others of his behavior, or to consider another person's point of view. (e) Indifference to the World at Large—having lived through the activistic late 1960s and early 1970s, one might question this so-called characteristic of the adolescent, although here Fountain was really referring to the adolescent's greater propensity to be preoccuppied with his personal needs and urges, whereas the world of public events belongs to adults. Conversely, adulthood could therefore be characterized by emotional stability, tolerance and patience, impulse delay, fairly reasonable reality testing and sense of reality, insight, some objective viewpoint of oneself, tolerance of criticism, and some chosen stances in relation to the public world.

Completion of the Tasks of Adolescence

The GAP Report, *Normal Adolescence* (1968), lists six tasks the completion of which ideally characterizes the "resolution" of adolescence. The list is representative of many of its genre and would probably be acceptable to most observers. The tasks enumerated are: (a) the attainment of separation and independence from the parents; (b) the establishment of sexual identity; (c) the commitment to work; (d) the development of a personal moral value system; (e) the capacity for lasting relationships and for both tender and genital sexual love in heterosexual relationships; and (f) a return to the parents in a new relationship based upon a relative equality. Attainment of each of these capacities is influenced by intrapsychic and sociocultural factors simultaneously.

Tracing the Intrapsychic Changes of Late and Postadolescence

Blos (1962) sees late adolescence as a phase of consolidation, a time of crisis, and a decisive turning point. Changes take place primarily in the ego leading to: the elaboration of "a highly idiosyncratic and stable arrangement of ego functions and interests"; an extension of the conflict-free sphere of the ego; a stable and irreversible sexual position; a relatively constant cathexis of object- and self-representations; and the stabilization of the mental apparatus. In late adolescence, three basic antitheses of mental life are accepted and more or less settled; subject-object, active-passive, and pleasure-pain.

According to Blos, postadolescence is primarily a phase of harmonizing the various parts of the personality so that the components are integrated into a functioning whole. This gradual process proceeds along with vocational choice, courtship, marriage, and parenthood. During this stage of development, internal conflicts which have not already been resolved are rendered specific and are now integrated into the ego as life tasks. Avenues are created to implement these tasks. There is much postadolescent experimentation to try to gratify instinctual needs and ego interests. The moral side of personality emerges with an emphasis on personal dignity and self-esteem. The Ego Ideal is more in evidence, compared to the idealized parent of the superego of childhood and early adolescence. The postadolescent completes his detachment from parental object representations, comes to terms with this, reaches a lasting settlement with it, and finally is able to integrate ego interests and attitudes of the parents.

In a paper on the structural criteria for adolescent closure, Blos (1977) returns to the question of when and how adolescence ends. He first acknowledges the more easily recognized phenomenological criteria defining the end of adolescence. These include: the relative stabilization of moods; the veiling of emotions; the selective sharing of the self; the attempt to understand oneself; the predictability of behavior and motivation associated with the stabilization of character formation; the achievement of ego autonomy over the childhood dominance of the superego; and the emergence of a lifestyle.

Turning to "the more reliable and crucial psychological criteria," Blos proposes four such interconnected developmental tasks and challenges. (1) The Second Individuation Process—this refers to the object disengagement through individuation at the adolescent level "especially from the internalized objects of childhood." (2) Ego Continuity—the adolescent is able to use reality testing to develop a sense of his past, present, and future. (3) Residual Trauma—the inevitable accumulation of traumas during infancy, childhood, and adolescence is dealt with and more or less mastered by the adaptive resourcefulness of the late adolescent, promoting a consolidation of adult personality. (4) Sexual Identity—ideally, in late adolescence, and after the resolution of the negative oedipus complex, the infantile narcissistic ego ideal has slowly and laboriously been transformed into the adult abstracted and desexualized ego ideal, making possible the formation of stable, adult object relations.

The "Developmental" Approach

Historically, earlier conceptualizations of adolescence tended to view this age period as a re-edition of childhood with the addition of sexual maturation. Freud (1905), in his landmark paper, "Three Essays on the Theory of Sexuality," described the adolescent changes which gave infantile sexual life its final shape. In keeping with the then-current emphasis on id development and the elaboration of the discoveries of the psychosexual stages, early psychoanalytic writers addressed the issues of disruption of latency equilibrium by drive ascendancy in puberty, bisexuality elements in early adolescence, a second confrontation of oedipal conflicts in middle adolescence, and the challenges of heterosexual object choice in late adolescence. Superego and ego ideal transformations were likewise described as they occurred throughout adolescence. With the increasing emphasis on ego psychology initiated by Anna Freud (1937), great strides were made in understanding ego defensive operations and object relations in adolescence. Hartmann (1939) led the way to our deeper appreciation of the adaptive and the autonomous functioning of the ego in adolescence. Erikson (1950, 1968) brilliantly broadened our views on adolescence into the realm of the psychosocial and the problems of identity.

Mahler's (1963, 1968, 1975) groundbreaking observational research and extension of psychoanalytic theory to the symbiotic and separation-individuation stages of development recently added a whole new framework to help us understand adolescence. Blos (1967) quickly saw this when he referred to "the second individuation process of adolescence." The American Psychoanalytic Association recognized the applicability of Mahler's ideas throughout the entire life cycle by scheduling a three-part series of panels on "The Experience of Separation-Individuation in Infancy and Its Reverberations Through the Course of Life" (Panel Reports, 1973 *a, b, c*), the second of which was devoted to adolescence.

Settlage (Panel Report 1976) and others have been explicit in saying that we must now correlate the psychosexual and the separation-individuation theories. Thus, we are now beginning to glimpse the separation and individuation processes as they evolve in the first 3 years of life and reverberate in the teen years; to see the similarities between the issues and crises of the rapprochement subphase and early adolescence, between self- (object-) constancy at the end of the separation-individuation phase and personal identity at the end of adolescence. However, Mahler (1977) herself cautions against oversimplification in making such correlations and emphasizes the possible corrective influences of other subphases. Currently, analysts are working at this integration of classical psychosexual libidinal phases, developmental perspectives, recent concepts of narcissism, and the psychosocial framework. We shall review, in a highly condensed summary, current concepts of the intrapsychic process.

Intrapsychic Processes

Object Relations and Ego Ideal

Ritvo (1971) has focused on these two principal aspects of development, using the male model. Their intertwined transformations contribute to the greater engagement of the late adolescent with the reality principle and the reality world. He begins with contributions from Jacobson and Anna Freud. Through the identifications with new realistic images, the superego and moral codes are readjusted so that the id is restricted, and there is a shift of power to the ego, to its goals, and to standards of achievement. Compelled to break the libidinal ties to infantile objects by the anxiety created by relibidinization of repressed infantile fantasies, the adolescent libido returns to a narcissistic cathexis of the self.

> In the recent film, "Saturday Night Fever," the central character is depicted as a late adolescent in the process of breaking away from an engulfing mother and an authoritative father. In much of the movie he primps and adorns himself to prepare for his exhibitionistic solo dancing but remains impervious to the blandishments of the girls he attracts.

Reprojection of this narcissistic libido to new objects, including peers, idealizes them and permits new identifications within the ego ideal. The fact of genital primacy and the importance of orgasm in psychic life now make the adolescent dependent upon the body of the new love object. Thus, reality acquires a greater role in pleasure, while the role of fantasy is reduced to a more pragmatic and anticipatory one. However, the possibility of discharge of aggression upon the new object raises the need to erect new defenses or to flee.

> A young woman, who in late adolescence fled from her strict, narrowminded, controlling father, successively married and divorced two young men when she developed mounting but unconscious hostility as they became father-figures to her.

Problems center around issues of heterosexual approach-avoidance and homosexual reactions to choices in self-definition. The conditions of pleasure-gain having become more manifest and specific, the adolescent now becomes more aware of the limitations and distortions of his sexual life, and fantasies directed toward his objects may arouse anxiety.

The new central love object is the rerepresentation of the old central love object, mother, and now functions similarly as the organizer of the psyche in effecting new identifications. Besides re-arousing old, repressed oedipal conflicts due to death wishes toward the rival, threats to the self also arise from the regressive merging and fusion fantasies that originate from both narcissistic and anaclitic aspects of object choice. The fear of engulfment as the result of passive wishes, which conflict with phallic active aims, arouses ambivalence and hostility, which, projected, re-arouse the phallic woman imago of primitive superego introjects. There is oscillation between the urgency of need for her, the threat of her demands, and the hostility aroused by any narcissistic wound.

The ability to progress from the narcissistic aspects of object choice to toleration of the anaclitic ones marks the steps toward the eventual attainment of intimacy. Attaining both heightens self-esteem, which enhances the consolidation of the ego and the changes in the ego ideal. Through realizing some parts of his own ego ideal in both the self and love object, and in providing for the loved one, a pleasure-gain is accrued to work functions. The need to commit the self to a love object and the need to prove oneself are links to the tasks of commitment to adult love and work life, and part of the specific delimited identity formation of the self that must replace youth's omnipotentiality (Pumpian-Mindlin 1965). The problem solving of the new central object love, like that of the old central object love, releases new resources of now neutralized energy. However, the new object has to merge and blend with the old, and early impairment of the ego and object relationships can cause severe difficulties in making the way back from the ego regression of early adolescence.

One of the main roots of adolescent structuralization of the ego ideal also lies in the passive-feminine orientation of the negative Oedipus complex (Freud 1923; Blos 1977). Libido, freed from infantile object ties, can be displaced readily from the self to a grandiose compensatory self-image, when feeling failure of other narcissistic wounds, and can easily attach itself to an object who represents his own ideal by regression to the negative oedipal position. Acting out may occur, and identification attempted with the idealized qualities of a homosexual object choice. On the other hand, the adolescent's capacities for abstraction and sublimation permit displacement of narcissistic libido to the idealization of the intellect in general, which may include moral and ethical values and concepts, religious beliefs, philosophies, etc. These idealizations and identifications provide directions for aim-inhibited pursuits, utilizing the neutralized energy thus released, toward choice of work and mastery of other portions of reality.

Recent Modifications About Female Development

Psychoanalytic theories of feminine development are in the midst of undergoing modifications from three sources of influence: (1) the direct observational studies of early childhood; (2) the separation-individuation theories; and (3) the changes in women's adult-role expectations caused by reduced procreation and increased career emphasis. There is occurring a reevaluation of classical analytic theory in an attempt to integrate these new aspects. Currently, there is considerable lack of agreement, but a great deal can be said about the psychology of adolescent female development from the attention recently focused on the whole subject (Panel Report 1976).

What has already been said here about object relations and ego ideal applies to the female, especially as regards reactivation and recapitulation of the Oedipus complex and the regression to pregenital conflicts. Certain features, however, are unique for the female. Whereas the male, in approaching heterosexuality, returns to the original love object, the nurturant female, the girl must make the transition from mother to father as prime object. Classical theory accounted for this as arising during the phallic phase from narcissistic disappointment in the inferior genital, thus making penis envy central to identification with the father both narcissistically and competitively. In order to reach a postambivalent positive acceptance of femininity and childbearing, resolution of penis envy and the oedipal rivalry with the mother, with subsequent positive identification with the maternal-receptive orientation, were held to be developmental tasks of late adolescence and young womanhood.

Current thinking recognizes an early genital stage in the toddler girl during the second half of the second year, with penis envy arising then, but very likely resolved by the oedipal period, persisting only pathologically, and easily reactivated during the early adolescent regression to pregenitality. The place of penis envy in the adult woman is now a controversial idea. Blum (1976) articulates a present view that it plays no important part normally. On the other hand, separation-individuation theory attributes a greater emphasis to the role of the first heterosexual love object (father and his successors) as replacements for the mother, to whose tie the libido has been loosened by the threatened regression to pregenitality ushered in by the menarche. The principal problems of sexual development for the girl are now seen to be in the feminine aspects of her self- and body-image.

Ritvo (Panel Report 1976) has reviewed classical analytic understandings of adolescence in general. Among other tasks, there is the need to integrate childbearing functions with other life goals. Ego-ideal formation has both a biological and a social aspect; from the identification with the mother and from body-image experiences, it is related to nurturing, mothering, and comforting. Sociocultural emphasis upon careers now puts strain on the young woman's ego to integrate the biological and career roles and timetables. Settlage (Panel Report 1976) put it that an adult sense of female gender identity does not require, but is augmented by, the experiences of childhood and mothering. The complexity of achieving psychosexual and social independence within an intimate relationship occupies a central focus of other writers. These developmental tasks, completed, obtain integration and consolidation through the experiences of childbearing and childrearing.

As to the role of masochism, once thought to be crucial to feminine psychology, Blum (1976), among others, now rejects this completely. Young women have to integrate, with their whole self-accepting maternal images, inner fluctuating feelings and sensations, rhythmicity (Benedek 1963), their "inner space" (Erikson 1968), and their "inner genital" (Kestenberg 1968). Newer concepts recognize that both clitoral and vaguer vaginal sensations are likely to occur early, though either or both may be repressed. Gradual discovery of the vagina, and its blending with clitoral components, is a task of late adolescence. The passive-receptiveness of vaginal sexuality is no longer seen as necessarily rooted in sadomasochism.

Thus, female development is coming to be better understood and more clearly differentiated from its parallels in the male adolescent. Indeed, it is during adolescence and its last phase, youth, that the psychosexual identification as male or female and the capacity for intimacy must be basically established for adulthood to occur.

While this section has focused on the intrapsychic processes of self-and object-transformation, none of this takes place without the influence of the sociocultural reality world in which the evolving personality must find further adult role models and fitting self-roles. We have seen that the new central love object, in reality as well as fantasy, can play an organizing role in this transition. The outcomes of adolescent love are important events for what follows. But there are wider influences that also affect the outcome of development.

Psychosocial Influences and Identity Consolidation

Erikson (1956) speaks of youth as the time of life when there is a simultaneous demand to accomplish commitments to physical intimacy, to decisive occupational choice, to energetic competition, and to psychosocial self-definition. All of these are elements of adult role identity. Keniston (1968) adds that even if all the developmental tasks were accomplished, adulthood would still be lacking without the achievement of a bond to society in some enduring form, whether it be through a positive identification with it or a negative, opposing one.

The various identifications must be worked out and consolidated into forms that simultaneously satisfy certain internal and external needs. They must be internally consistent with each other and with the moral value system that is chosen. Social roles must be adopted that are consistent with the predominant identifications and which provide a fulfilling lifestyle for these identifications and value systems. Moreover, these social roles must also provide reality testing of those values and be compatible enough with them. Youth is a time of encounter with the adult role models available in the external world, to accept, reject, or modify for oneself. Achieving the fit allows resolution of both preoedipal and oedipal ambivalences through conflict-free identifications with role models. One then possesses a form by which to pursue fulfillment of the ego ideal. Finding suitable role models may allow ultimate positive identification with the parent of the same sex. During periods of little historical and technological change, these models change little and are less conflictually cathected than at times such as the present.

Erikson has also described how, in such times of "historical identity vacua" (1977), youth flock to totalitarian movements for ideological renewal. These movements provide the dynamic function of ritualization that youth need to effect an induction into an adult lifestyle. More basically, however, they provide a lifestyle that will perpetuate the certainties and securities of the regressive, pregenital, omnipotent superego while giving the illusion of emancipation. It matters not whether the ideology be one of identification with the society or rebellion against it. However, in the partial regression to idolism, there occurs a sustained mutuality in affiliations of work, friendship, and love that merges into the stage of intimacy. Out of a kind of shared narcissism in the form of an elitism, there comes a fitting of respective identities, possibly promising affiliations in productive and procreative life.

When these identifications take place too wholly in positive imitation of parental models, without the self-testing and societal testing that mature identity requires, premature foreclosure may occur, at risk of later vulnerability to stress. Equally compulsive fixation upon rebellious negative identity can occur. More healthfully, youths go through a series of temporary identities, not expected to outlast their youthfulness, as part of the means of testing and dealing with their ambivalence toward society (Keniston 1968). They will ultimately lead to a chosen enduring stance toward that society, whether it be acceptance of the values and lifestyles of the parents, total or partial, and selective modification of it, warfare against it, or some idiosyncratic mode of being adult. The keystone of the adulthood is the conscious realization and acceptance of the consequences of that lifestyle and the responsibility of commitment to it in real life.

Societal turmoil distinctly influences individual turmoil of development. Many authors have documented the principal societal changes that have altered the structure of values and roles in America: loss of belief in the theological transcendance of life, the passage of Victorian and Puritan morality, the loss of paternal authority, the separation from holistic meaning of work in life, the loss of significance of the person in mass society, and the triumph over nature to the point of probable extermination of the species. When society fails to provide these supports for future identifications, youth's grapplings to find meaningful and gratifying adult roles strain the ego capacities. Deficiencies in ego development from early childhood are then laid bare upon departure from the family structure (Blos 1967).

Esman (1975) describes how the changing values of morality make consolidation of psychosexual role and object choice more diffuse, less defined, citing the prevalent value placed on male homosexuality, corresponding to the prevalent emphasis on female independence in sexuality. Mystical and exotic sects and gurus are sought in a search for certainty and embraced for their puritanical moral codes that restrict and repress drive impulses, making psychosexual definition avoidable.

Lifton (1975) characterizes the lifestyle of youth that has recently developed as "protean"—an experimenting and questing after psychological patterns in response to the breakdown of forms. It is a struggle for rituals and symbols that allow the experience of primordial emotions which approach the ecstatic rather than the prosaic.

To try to categorize these radically deviant forms as either all necessarily pathological or healthful is to misunderstand the nature of societal forms and to unjustifiably displace to the social sphere those criteria of health which arise from, and are valid only for, the individual. Even there, overt behaviors often make it difficult to judge pathological development, since the outward garb of negative identification is so uniform for all. Beneath it any individual may be anywhere along a range, from very healthy reality testing, making effective use of his moratorium to test himself and life, to psychotic, borderline, or narcissistic personality structure.

Identity crisis, even with transient anxiety, depression, and confusion, may be normal, as is the moratorium on commitment, whether institutionalized or unique. It is identity diffusion which is pathological. Because choices in sexuality, competition, intimacy, and occupation are required, repudiations must be made. The inability to do so, or excessive avoidance, exposes one to the regressive pull which can become pathological if more than transitory.

Kernberg (1975) emphasizes the sharp delineation between the normal identity crisis and pathological identity diffusion which comes only from early developmental vicissitudes, not from contemporary moral changes. The difference lies in the primitive superego nuclei which are reprojected in borderline and narcissistic structures. He offers the following criteria for discerning the difference: the capacity for experiencing guilt and concern and a genuine wish to repair the damage from aggressive behavior; the capacity for establishing lasting nonexploitative relationships and the relatively realistic, indepth assessment of such persons; and a consistently expanding and deepening set of values, regardless of whether in conformity or opposition to the prevalent culture. In contrast to those who lack depth but give only lipservice, healthy adolescents have an internal consistency between their values and their behavior and relationships to others.

Healthy Development

At a later point, we will deal with pathological results of adaptive failures to negotiate this transition. At this point, it would be useful to summarize the features of healthy development identifiable from a psychoanalytic perspective, as well as to note the roles of defensive operations of the ego under normal circumstances.

It is not to be expected that anxious and painful periods of separating from parental ties and reinvesting in new loves, friendships, and models should be without traumas. Indeed, depth and growth require some. Optimally, they will not result in lasting regressive retreats or elaboration of too-restricting protective defenses, emphasizing constriction of the ego, repression of drives, narcissistic rescue by excessive projection and rationalization, retreat to sadomasochism, somatizations, or withdrawal to fantasy replacement of the object world. The attainment of gratifying love relationships is crucial to consolidating the self-identity positively related to the real world. Its achievement frees emotional energy from conflict to address the other conflict-free areas of ego development: learning the ways of the world, formal education and apprenticeship, and moral value delineation. This ability to use cognition to learn accurately about oneself and others develops insights that are important in selecting goals authentic to one's own future needs and to pursuing them. Lack of these capacities is found in identity diffusion.

Defenses are not without a role in attaining this healthy state. Normally the deeper aspects of the regressive pull of adolescence remain unconscious by virtue of protective repressions. Anxieties, depressions, even somatizations that accompany the transient crises of developmental flux are normally repressed when successful shifts to new objects, identifications, and interests supervene. The late adolescent's capacity to undergo these rapid changes of mood with new identifications is legend. In fact, identification is itself one of the principal normal defenses employed, fostering repression and externalization of the old repudiated traits that are superseded.

Likewise, needing to be outgrown are the anxieties arising not only from separation and castration but their associated fears of existential mortality. A comfortable engagement with adult life requires enough sense of trust in the future. This is abetted by a certain amount of selective denial of potentially present reminders of mortality, reinstituting, in the service of adaptation, a piece of magical omnipotence in concert with whatever form of transcendental

or supernatural omnipotence becomes most appealing as superego replacement. Intellectualization, a defense highly developed at this stage, provides the
pathway to the moral, ideological, or philosophical sublimation frequently
seen at this stage. No doubt reaction-formations closely interdigitate with sublimations in attaining ethical and moral controls over sadistic and narcissistic
impulses and furthering socialization if not altruism. These defenses play their
part, along with the capacity for identification, in allowing for compassion
and empathy, qualities that are ultimately necessary for a mature loving relationship and parenting, but not possible while narcissistic needs predominate.

Not all regression is pathological. Sufficient flexibility needs to prevail to
enjoy healthy regressions, socially sanctioned, to play, relax, sleep, and to
create artistically. All these call upon sublimation to provide the ego with
satisfying expressions from the id, lastly, to play with life and self with jest, in
forms that outgrow the immature sadomasochism of earlier stages and contribute to the well-being of people at no one else's expense.

There is a psychosocial question about identification with the parent of the
same sex at the point of completion of late adolescence that calls for some
consideration. In the section on "Adolescence into Adulthood," we have quoted
the GAP Report criterion that describes a return to the parents in a new relationship of greater equality, implying that sufficient resolution of the ambivalence
should take place to allow both generations to respect each other's humanity
and adulthood, including tolerance for their individual differences and fallibili-
ties. This is a product of resolution of earlier demands for absolutism, perfection, or sameness, and is part of the capacity to accept people as well as the
world for what they are. The experiences of "settling down," finding a home,
persevering in work, arranging a wedding, mixing socially with older people,
etc., all promote greater identification with the parents. Nevertheless, during
periods of rapid social changes in values, roles, and style, it becomes an additional problem to accomplish this rapprochement if the younger generation
adopt lifestyles too radically different from their parents. What seems to be a
pivotal time, even then, however, is the experience of their becoming parents
themselves, assuring the role responsibilities, cares, and interests of nurturing
another generation. This has the effect of integrating part self-images with
internalized parental images, both conflictual and conflict-free. Problems there
after often center around the necessity to resolve those internal conflicts. The
ultimate effect, if successful, is to achieve a still healthier identity as adult-parent.

Early Adulthood

Several studies have appeared recently chronicling the longitudinal life
courses of people from their youth through stages of adulthood. They are
interesting because they are the first long-term, organized, clinical studies of
"normal" adults. They highlight some of the features of change from youth to

young adulthood. In Sheehy's *Passages* (1974), there is a graphic description of the identity struggles of a black ghetto youth as he encounters, accepts, and rejects a multiplicity of identifications and role models, loyalties, and roles until an adult synthesis suitable for him can be created.

Levinson et al. (1978) find that the process of entering manhood runs from around 17 to around 33. They call this the "novice phase," composed of the "early adult transition" (17 to 22±), "entering the adult world" (22 to 28±), and the "age-30 transition." Four developmental tasks were most important: forming a Dream ("a vague sense of self-in-the-adult-world") and giving it a place in the life structure; forming mentor relationships; forming an occupation; and forming love relationships, including marriage and family. Whether or not a young man's early life is consonant with, and infused by, the Dream or opposed to it affects his growth a good deal. If too many forces oppose it, externally or within himself, he may abandon or betray it, but this affects his sense of aliveness and purpose in his vocational life. The mentor is necessary as teacher, sponsor, host, guide, etc., who helps define the Dream and create a space for the young man. From the apprentice role he gradually gains a fuller sense of his own authority and capability of autonomous action, gradually transcending the father-son, man-boy division. Lasting about 2 to 10 years, the mentor relationship is a love relationship and often ends with strong conflict and bad feeling. As in all object loss, there are internalization and identification, furthering adulthood. Even the process of "forming" an occupation is a complex one that extends over the novice phase and often beyond. It requires not only suitable choices and changes but acquisition of skills, values, and credentials. Even for working-class men, the same prolonged process was involved, with periods of crisis. By the age-30 transition, more enduring choices must be built on the groundwork established.

Half of Levinson's men married during the early adult transition, having had little experience in forming peer relationships with adult women. He describes how the wife, whose attraction for him was in part because she seemed to lack the qualities he feared and resented in his image of his mother, nevertheless became the recipient of his various pregenital and genital fantasies he then struggled to both express and control. There are often many aspects of the mother-son interaction which will later become the more problematical. Levinson draws attention, however, to the Special Woman, who is also a mentor, animating the part of him that contains the Dream and helps him attain it. She too is a transition figure whom he will later outgrow as he becomes more complete. A man's wife may be his Special Woman or not. Whether or not their Dreams are the same may well affect the marital future.

While parallel studies of the same sort have not been carried out in women, Sheehy gives us very useful portraits of the course of development in these same periods of life. We see in her writing the continual interplay of what she calls the merger- vs. the seeker-self, another way of speaking about the fusion-differential process of separation-individuation. Unlike the young man who usually has a societal imperative to define himself occupationally, the structure that is thereby provided is more often an optional one for the woman, requiring increasingly nowadays a struggle between the goals of career-self and pro-creative-self. The latter offers itself as a role compatible with the needs for intimacy, fulfilling, with greater or lesser ambivalence, an identification with the mother but quite possibly at the risk of closure on self-development and displacement of unresolved dependencies onto the man. In Sheehy's cases there is a frequent pattern of dysphasic growth between men, whose occupational life in the world facilitates their adulthood, and wives who take much longer to discover their identity crises and react to it in their 30s and 40s. Again, changes in social attitudes have altered patterns of mating and intimacy and family life. It is too soon to know what effects these altered adult models will have on the imagos developed by today's young children, affecting their superegos and ego ideals.

In Vaillant's (1977) long-term study of 95 college men from the classes of 1942-1944, success or failure of intimacy again emerged as important for mastery of the next stages of adulthood. He too found the role of the mentor, the successor to the adolescent hero, usually cast aside by age 40 and frequently denied. An interesting finding from this study was that personality traits of adolescence had no predictive value for the future emotional stability of the young adult. Three traits uncharacteristic of adolescence were most often diagnostic, however, of future mental health: adolescents who were seen as "well integrated, practical, and organized" were best adapted at age 50.

Psychopathology

From a descriptive standpoint, the years of late adolescence to young adulthood present a range of maladaptive disorders from mild to severe disability. There are problems of situational maladjustment which may present with anxiety, somatizations, study or work inhibitions, or depression, or may have been acted out with development of secondary situational complications. These situations may have to do with school, work, family, love, or other relationship problems. These are of a relatively acute, short-term nature, and the symptoms may alarm the young person or others out of proportion to their underlying implications for more severe illness. Other conditions of a more chronic nature also appear by virtue of the failure of the adolescent process to resolve more satisfactorily the developmental problems from earlier years. These may take the form of psychoneurosis, characterological disorders, borderline personality with affective, behavioral, or pseudoneurotic symptoms, or frank psychosis. The range of these disorders represents various degrees of adaptive failure to the requirements of psychic development for coping with and mastering life's tasks and challenges in a satisfactory and satisfying way. Some brief clinical examples will be cited to illustrate some typical forms of illnesses characteristic of this age period, progressing from relatively mild to more severe forms of maladaptation.

Normal Developmental Psychodynamics of Oedipal Resolution—Mild Depression

A 20-year-old, very intelligent, sensitive, and artistic, male college student came for help on the advice of his mother because of his confusion over relationships with girls. It became apparent that certain girls he befriended would cut him down out of their own competitive strivings, but he had accepted their derision as his own defect and had become depressed. He cathected the therapist strongly, utilizing insights and the narcissistic supports from the positive transference to grow in confidence and competence socially. It developed that he was fixated in an unresolved oedipal entanglement which burdened him, wishing his father were stronger, to remove the mother's displaced attachments from her son. As he gained insight into this, his own strivings for masculine ideals attached themselves to athletically potent peers. He identified with them imitatively. In contrast to the denial commonly used, this young man could allow himself to be aware of the sexual tinging. Identification with more adventurous models enabled him to travel and explore more on his own. He then began to approach other girls more assertively, with more self-confidence.

Hysterical Somatic Symptom in Avoidance of Adolescence

After a fall, a 23-year-old, immature, young woman developed paresis and tremor of her lower extremity, diagnosed orthopedically and neurologically as hysterical. She had not progressed developmentally beyond latency. Her parents were quite rigid, repressive, and controlling. She had remained at home in financial and conflictual dependence on them, in a state of relative sexual ignorance and innocence. Her own fear of autonomy combined with her fear of asserting her own wishes for it. When supported toward independency, she was able to leave home and subsequently developed a relationship more typical of late adolescent development.

Psychoneurosis Limiting Successful Consolidation and Adaptation

A 22-year-old, married, male, graduate student was self-referred for treatment of an obsessive-compulsive neurosis present since early adolescence. He was compelled to think, "What if I murdered my mother?" Additionally, despite high intelligence and clearly outstanding promise academically, he had failed to achieve in college up to his own reasonable superior expectations, mainly due to examination anxiety. He had had to compensate for these handicaps by very hard work, which itself was compromised by his excessively obsessive, overorganized, perfectionistic thinking, worry, and work habits.

Treatment required analysis of lifelong developmental problems. Born into an extraordinarily closely binding family, he had developed an unrecognized and untreated infantile phobic neurosis in early latency, the resolution of which was partially accomplished by repression and the development of an obsessive-compulsive character structure. When, in early adolescence, his parents' opposition to his precocious sexual wishes aroused rage within him, his repressed patricidal wishes were displaced onto the weaker maternal figure but were limited to the ego-dystonic obsessive thoughts. It was necessary to work through much unresolved infantile omnipotence, phallic grandiosity, and oedipal material, as well as a narcissistic defense of derogation of authority that, via projection, subjected him to persecutory anxiety, before he could apply himself more freely and self-confidently to his career. While burdened with his neurosis, he could not accept the role of an adult, let alone that of parent, to the frustration of his wife who wanted a child. Only after resolution of the oedipal conflicts, including both the competitive and negative sides of the oedipal relationship to the father, could he separate from his overidentification with the father imago and individuate himself as an autonomous and different person, his own man, in a new kind of adult relationship to the father. His symptoms subsided, he succeeded academically and obtained his choice of position to begin his career, which had originally been chosen unconsciously as a mode of continuing to re-experience (and hopefully to master) the residual trauma of his childhood. As the result of treatment, he will not have to go through life acting out his neurosis through his career.

Failure in Identity Consolidation with Adaptive Failure and Depression

A 22-year-old, single female, finishing college, found herself having mounting anxiety over not wanting to follow the vocational field for which she had trained. At a similar point 4 years earlier, approaching the end of secondary school, she had had a brief psychosis. She was closely, though ambivalently, identified with both parents and had a religiously moralistic superego that prohibited premarital sex. Faced with the need to terminate her moratorium and assume an autonomy for which she was unprepared, she became mildly hypomanic, fell suddenly in love, and quickly moved to engagement. This flight into premature marriage failed when her fiance withdrew, and she collapsed into a psychotic depression. During a year of subsequent therapy, she gradually worked out unresolved ambivalences to her parents and separated from them, although utilizing her identifications with them to accept a vocation like theirs. When financially able, she took her own apartment and later dealt with transferred dependencies upon men and the issues about sexuality.

(The Eating Disorders are a particular form of psychopathology frequently occurring from midadolescence to young adulthood. The severity varies from fairly superficial hysterical problems of adolescence to borderline or psychotic structures. The following two cases illustrate chronic maladaptive forms of illness.)

Bulimia

A 15-year-old girl acquired infectious mononucleosis with anorexia and weight loss, secretly prolonging the symptoms thereafter as an ego mechanism to control her ravenous appetite that made her gain weight. A year later, she learned to regurgitate her food several times and re-ingest it, thus satisfying her hunger all the more without weight gain. She preserved the figure and appearance of a prepubertal girl even when she came for treatment, resistively, at age 23. Her parents were highly competitive, successful achievers, and she developed through latency and puberty feeling inferior and defective compared to them and her athletic sister. At 15 she had identified strongly with a rebellious boy who stimulated her secret rebellion against her parents' values and lifestyle. When forced to stop seeing him, she got sick. Her rebellion continued covertly in the form of her retreat into nightly eating binges with regurgitation, a narcissistic withdrawal that constricted her social development and left her very much at the mercy of what became a compulsive ritual. Her search for an omnipotent being, so strong as to enable her to break the compulsion, took her into fundamentalist religion, where she hoped to find in God a love so strong that she would always be loved, no matter how many times she failed and disappointed Him. The roots of the problem were evident in her inability to satisfy her parents' narcissistic ambitions through her, and her need to replace them with an unconditionally loving parent whom she would repeatedly test by failing. Her fantasy was that finally He would prove Himself sufficiently that she would love Him unambivalently, identify with His strength, and thereby resist her compulsion and be "born again."

Anorexia Nervosa

A 24-year-old, childless woman of 80 pounds had become anorexic at age 16, but had gone through college and married, her condition worsening gradually. She had always resisted treatment and began it only when threatened with the breakup of her marriage. Analysis revealed a lifelong developmental history, beginning with her mother's post partum depression and surrender of this girl to the maternal grandmother who became the primary mother figure. The mother had never recovered her role in the life of this child who further formed a strong oedipal attachment and identification with her father. There had been a religiously repressive upbringing, with adolescent failure to incorporate feminine sexuality. A great deal of rivalry existed toward her two younger sisters, and her personality had acquired a very bossy, controlling character. She remained phobic about heterosexuality, marrying a man she thought she could control verbally. She existed by virtue of a calculated ritual of nocturnal nutrition to maintain a steady weight level, gorging herself with noncaloric foods. The analytic work involved a great deal of oral-aggressive drive and sadistic preoccupation, with infantile terror of abandonment to nocturnal malevolent forces.

Complete Failure of Integrative Capacity—Ego Defect and Psychosis

A 19-year-old boy was referred after 2 years of hospitalization for psychosis following several years of drug use. He was hyperintellectual and postured constantly as a fighter, a skill his father possessed. History revealed that as an infant he had been terrified by a psychotic older brother, but had in early childhood idealized this brother; between them, they had developed a secret world, private psychotic interpretations of reality, and attitudes about the father. In retrospect, he had had a severe learning problem throughout school, with possible minimal brain dysfunction. At any rate, he learned little and felt progressively inferior. In adolescence he tried to emulate his peers in the neighborhood and sought some self-worth by amateur boxing. Early attempts at sexuality brought a rejection from a girl. He began to use drugs and one afternoon suddenly felt his penis was shrinking and all his muscles were losing their bulk. These somatic delusions remained for years. Out of his psychedelic experience, he acquired an absolute conviction of his own omnipotent power to control the thoughts of others, derived from a universal power of the cosmos. He was unable to sleep because of fear and periodically became suicidally depressed.

Summary

Late adolescence and early adulthood are a phase in the life cycle marked by consolidation and integration of psychic processes and by the stabilizing and harmonizing of psychic structures. In Eriksonian terms, it is a phase of achieving a sense of identity. Blos paraphrases a well-known statement of Freud to say that "the heir of adolescence is the self."

Late adolescence is a psychosocial phenomenon rather than a physiological stage. Important intrapsychic transformations occur in object relations, conflict resolution, ego and superego functions, ego ideal, defenses, etc. There is a great deal of experimentation, testing, trying of roles, and beginnings of implementation of goals. In leaving home and family, the late adolescent is influenced by, and influences, the larger social world and current lifestyles.

Cognition does not undergo any further formal change but is deployed toward greater apprehension of the external and internal worlds. New love investments are central to the changes in object relationships, ego ideal, and sense of self, even though they bring the potentialities for regressive ambivalences associated with the earlier central love object. Earlier developmental failures constitute potential fixation points for pathological courses during this transitional stage. There is a great propensity for acting out of newly idealized identifications, intellectualized areas of religion, morality, ethics, and philosophies, as well as regressive trends. These all become the arena for repetition and further resolution of both narcissistic and anaclitic problems. Surmounting them enhances self-esteem, while at the same time the need to prove oneself promotes the commitment to the realistic world, its tasks and mastery.

The principal problems of young womanhood are seen to be consolidation of the feminine sense of self and body image within the context of new intimacy relationships. Expanded role choices for career and for procreation complicate these years of self-object development.

Whereas in stable historical times societies provide ritualizations for induction into adult lifestyles through education, apprenticeship, military life, courtship and marriage, in times of "historical identity vacua" youth seek their own forms of ritualization that may embody ideological rebellion. Temporary identifications test the societal reality, contributing to social change, leading ultimately to more enduring chosen stances toward personal and social values and lifestyles. Losses of support from traditional social roles and values put strain on young ego capacities. Faced with the necessity of responsibility for self, they become more vulnerable to pathological regression. While identity crisis at this stage is normal, identity diffusion exposes the ego to the pulls of early developmental vicissitudes, and there are potentialities for the entire range of pathological conditions. Successful development, however, is accompanied by insights that are essential to selecting and pursuing authentic personal goals and free the emotional energies for the tasks involved.

Defenses play their part in healthy development. Repression of anxieties and denial of existential threats permit a greater sense of safety and confidence. Sublimations most successfully channel drive energy into socialized, gratifying behavior, linking the drives to social reality, allowing healthy forms of regression to contribute recreatively. Resolution of narcissistic fixations allows empathic and compassionate identifications with others, including one's own parents.

Recent clinical studies have illuminated the central role played by the Special Person and the Mentor who become important love objects in pursuit of a highly individualistic Dream. While adulthood is defined by the acceptance of responsibility for an integrated lifestyle with its consequences, psychological development has by now evolved sufficiently stabilized internal structures and object relations to approach these roles. This does not mean the end of development but only a readiness for adult experience.

References

Benedek, T. An investigation of the sexual cycle in women: Methodologic considerations. *Archives of General Psychiatry,* 8:311-322, 1963.

Blos, P. *On Adolescence.* New York: The Free Press of Glencoe, 1962.

——. The second individuation process of adolescence. *The Psychoanalytic Study of the Child,* 22:162-186, 1967.

——When and how does adolescence end: Structural criteria for adolescent closure. In: Feinstein, S.C., and Giovacchini, P.L., eds. *Adolescent Psychiatry,* Vol. V. New York: Jason Aronson, 1977.

Blum, H.P. Masochism, the ego ideal, and the psychology of women. *Journal of the American Psychoanalytic Association,* 24:157-191, 1976.

Erikson, E.H. *Childhood and Society.* New York: Norton, 1950.

———. The problem of ego identity. *Journal of the American Psychoanalytic Association,* 4:56-121, 1956.

———. Womanhood and the inner space. In: Erikson, E.H., ed. *Identity, Youth and Crisis.* New York: Norton, 1968.

———. *Toys and Reasons.* New York: Norton, 1977.

Esman, A.H. Consolidation of the ego ideal in contemporary adolescence. In: Esman, A.H., ed. *The Psychology of Adolescence: Essential Readings.* New York: International Universities Press, 1975.

Fountain, G. Adolescent into adult: An inquiry. *Journal of the American Psychoanalytic Association,* 9:417-433, 1961.

Freud, A. *The Ego and the Mechanisms of Defence.* London: Hogarth Press, 1937.

Freud, S. Three essays on the theory of sexuality (1905). *Standard Edition,* 7:125-243. London: Hogarth Press, 1961.

———.The Ego and the Id (1923). *Standard Edition,* 19:12-66. London: Hogarth Press, 1961.

Group for the Advancement of Psychiatry. *Normal Adolescence,* Vol. VI, Report No. 68. New York: G.A.P., 1968.

Hartmann, H. *Ego Psychology and the Problem of Adaptation* (1939). New York: International Universities Press, 1958.

Keniston, K. *Young Radicals: Notes on Committed Youth.* New York: Harcourt, Brace & World, 1968.

Kernberg, O. Cultural impact and intrapsychic change. In: Feinstein, S.C., and Giovacchini, P.L., eds. *Adolescent Psychiatry,* Vol. IV. New York: Jason Aronson, 1975.

Kestenberg, J. Outside and inside, male and female. *Journal of the American Psychoanalytic Association,* 16:457-520, 1968.

Levinson, D.J.; Darrow, C.D.; Klein, E.B.; Levinson, M.H.; and McKee, B. *The Seasons of a Man's Life.* New York: Alfred A. Knopf, 1978.

Lifton, R.J. Proteus revisited. In: Feinstein, S.C., and Giovacchini, P.L., eds. *Adolescent Psychiatry,* Vol. IV. New York: Jason Aronson, 1975.

Mahler, M.S. Thoughts about development and individuation. *The Psychoanalytic Study of the Child,* 18:307-324, 1963.

———. *On Human Symbiosis and the Vicissitudes of Individuation.* New York: International Universities Press, 1968.

Mahler, M.S., and Kaplan, L. Developmental aspects in the assessment of narcissistic and so-called borderline personalities. In: Hartocollis, P., ed. *Borderline Personality Disorders.* New York: International Universities Press, 1977.

Mahler, M.S.; Pine, F.; and Bergman, A. *The Psychological Birth of the Human Infant.* New York: Basic Books, 1975.

Panel Report. The experience of separation-individuation in infancy and its reverberations through the course of life: 1. Infancy and childhood. Winestine, M.C., reporter. *Journal of the American Psychoanalytic Association,* 21:135-154, 1973a.

Panel Report. The experience of separation-individuation in infancy and its reverberations through the course of life: 2. Adolescence and maturity. Marcus, I.M., reporter. *Journal of the American Psychoanalytic Association,* 21:155-167, 1973b.

Panel Report. The experience of separation-individuation in infancy and its reverberations through the course of life: Maturity, senescence, and sociological implications. Sternschein, I., reporter. *Journal of the American Psychoanalytic Association,* 21:633-645, 1973c.

Panel Report. Psychology of women: Late adolescence and early adulthood. Galenson, E., reporter. *Journal of the American Psychoanalytic Association,* 24:631-645, 1976.

Pumpian-Mindlin, E. Omnipotentiality, youth, and commitment. *Journal of the American Academy of Child Psychiatry,* 4:1-18, 1965.

Ritvo, S. Late adolescence: Developmental and clinical considerations. *The Psychoanalytic Study of the Child,* 26:241-263, 1971.

Sheehy, G. *Passages: Predictable Crises of Adult Life.* New York: E.P. Dutton, 1974.

Vaillant, G.E. *Adaptation to Life.* Boston: Little, Brown, 1977.

The Course of Life: Psychoanalytic Contributions
Toward Understanding Personality Development.
Vol. II: Latency, Adolescence, and Youth.
S.I. Greenspan and G.H. Pollock, editors.
NIMH 1980

Personality Development
in the Young Adult

Graham B. Blaine, Jr., M.D., and Dana L. Farnsworth, M.D.

Introduction

In this chapter we deal with some aspects of childhood development leading up to the young adult stage. This approach is used to point out the dynamic factors which influence the resolution of the problems and dilemmas facing individuals in the age group from 18-23, which our chapter is attempting to explain. Psychoanalytic theory proposes that personality growth is determined by events and attitudes experienced over a span of time from infancy through adolescence. We have concentrated on these attitudes and events in order to show how important they are and to emphasize the necessity of recognizing and dealing with them in order to promote healthy personality development in the young adult.

Between the ages of 18 and 23, young people experience rapid transition from the status of adolescent to that of adult. The length of time required by this process depends to a considerable extent on the attitudes of parents, teachers, and other important adults around them. Some young people of 18 are as "adult" in their thinking and behavior as others in their midtwenties. Others seem hardly to have progressed beyond early adolescence. But by the end of this period, certain developmental tasks should have been accomplished and early adulthood achieved.

Early adulthood brings a set of challenges which are unique to that stage in life. It is different in many ways from the previous decade. Early adolescent struggles represent attempts to gain freedom from dependence upon parents.

The often unconscious need to get "out from under" and to feel inwardly motivated rather than outwardly guided often leads to nonconformist or rebellious behavior during adolescence. Vacillation between following the crowd (as a substitute for following parents) on the one hand and, on the other, trying to resist peer pressure without regressing to becoming mother's "model child," characterizes the high school student's attitudes and behavior. Once in college, however, or living independently in the work world, new internal and external problems present themselves. One has to feel at home as an adult in the adult world. No longer is there protection from others expressed in statements like: "He's too young to understand," or "Leave her alone; she'll grow out of it." Total responsibility for one's action must be taken. The people in the world outside expect young adults to know where they are headed and to possess convictions they can define, be sure about, and are able to defend logically if called upon.

There are many who describe college as a place and a time to experiment, but most of the students who are there feel differently. They consider themselves mature, and they look within themselves for answers to questions about sex, religion, career, loyalty to friends, and also about political and cultural morality. They are no longer content to ask advice or follow the examples of others. Disappointment and shame affect young adults who find themselves floundering over questions about career and marriage. Choices about going home for Christmas or skiing with friends instead, whether or not to date a boy friend's roommate, for instance, may cause confusion, and this confusion feels embarrassing. Erikson (1950) postulates that commitment is the primary task for the young adult. If this challenge cannot be met, an individual feels immature and inadequate and, in our opinion, experiences a developmental lag.

Events in an individual's childhood and adolescence bear importantly on ability to make healthy commitments as an adult. These need to be made in many different areas. Among the most important are: (1) problem solving, (2) sexuality, (3) career choice, and (4) intimacy. Successful commitment in these areas requires an intellectual and an emotional set of values—a ranking of internal priorities in order of importance that feels comfortable. Doing so means taking into consideration how the individuals view themselves and how they perceive that others view them.

Making such commitments and, as a result, achieving a state of internal equilibrium must include a realistic appraisal of what are reasonable goals, for everyone's goals are limited by their own capabilities. Many men can be content with a subordinate position at home and at work, for instance, if they are reconciled to the fact that their nature and temperament are best suited to such a position. Many women can become committed to goals involving career or profession exclusively if they are convinced that characterologically they have developed into or have been created in that mold. The young adult should be ready to start moving in the direction which is right for him or her. Let us examine each one of these four challenges facing the young adult singly and in depth.

Problem Solving

No matter how warm and loving our childhood or how thoroughly we may have been psychoanalyzed, life is bound to present us problems almost daily. Some are soluble, and some are not; and the manner in which we face the task of working out a solution for them or bearing the frustration of living with them is a measure of the degree to which we have developed adult maturity. The young adult who runs from a problem, denies it, or poorly defines it has not developed as he should and deserves attention. Rarely does he experience his problem in these terms. Instead, it is depression, anxiety, insomnia, or a psychosomatic symptom such as headache or a knot in his stomach which is the presenting symptom.

Preparation in childhood for healthy problem solving as an adult must rely strongly on parental permission to make choices. Areas in which it is safe to allow this are limited, but early in life it is important that a child learn to recognize a problem when one confronts him and that he has the ability to solve it correctly or incorrectly. A simple example would be a 3-year-old child standing on the edge of a mudpuddle deeper than his rubbers. Mother could carry him over it, pull him around it, or wait for him to solve the problem his own way. Clearly there are alternatives open to the mother after the fact also which will transmit messages of different qualities to the child. If he puts one foot in the puddle, she might yank him back or let him walk through, after which she might admonish him or simply let him suffer the discomfort of cold wet feet.

Children differ enough in basic nature to make it impossible to make judgments about which of the approaches described above might be the best in terms of training any one of them for problem solving, but it is fair to say that for the average child an opportunity for recognizing the existence of alternatives should be given. Mother might say, "What are you (not 'we') going to do about that puddle?" It might be necessary to restrain the child from impulsively running through or sitting down in the water, thus giving him a chance to consider alternatives. This would in most cases seem preferable to taking over the decision completely by carrying him across or pulling him around.

Once he has chosen an alternative, it is best to let him carry it out and afterward discuss the consequences and also the options which had been possible. If he splashed through the puddle, wetting the parent, and sat down in the middle soiling his clothes, it would take considerable parental control not to admonish or punish immediately, but it would be better to point out the consequences and mention the alternatives he had opted against before expressing righteous indignation. Parental displeasure should be shown clearly to be one of the consequences of the child's decision.

If a child's decision conforms with a parent's expectation (is the "right" decision), then the opportunity to point out the fact that a decision had been made and a problem solved should not be lost. It would be a good idea to say something like, "Well, I'm glad you decided to walk around that puddle rather than run through it or try to jump over it." This reinforces a child's sense of self, acknowledges that he has a degree of autonomy, and encourages him to identify ways and means by which he can validate these facts for himself in the future.

Incidents such as the one just described exemplify various parental attitudes. Their influence on the eventual development of a healthy problem solving approach in their children later in their lives is very significant. Encouragement to make choices and to define for themselves, after the choice is made, whether or not it was the correct one is the best way for parents to help their children develop skills in dealing with the decisions they will face throughout their lives.

During adolescence it is the personality structure inside the individual, rather than the adults outside, which most influences the building of the elements which will provide a basis for solving problems effectively later in life. An adolescent may deal with a problem by many different behaviors, and he may be unaware of the fact that certain behaviors are related to this kind of decision or conflict. In other words, the cause of a certain behavior may be unconscious. A high school student who is sleepy all day and unable to go to sleep at night may be unconsciously compelled to behave this way because of her inability to decide on taking a business or a college preparatory degree program. Once forced to confront her own uncertainty about this choice, she may continue her counterproductive behavior and, at the same time, feel anxious and frustrated over her inability to make a decision. Her early training in problem solving may have been inadequate, or she may simply be delayed in her personality development in this area. Whatever the reason, the most effective way of dealing with such a problem in adolescence is to provide help as parents and teachers with, first, the identification of the problem, bringing it out into the light, so to speak, and then to help the individual weigh all the factors involved for herself. Usually, once the pros and cons for pursuing each course are fully realized, a solution appears and can be worked out. If an adolescent becomes more confused, as more facts are gathered, then a serious disturbance in psychological functioning is likely to be present—either a developmental failure or an obsessive neurosis.

Piaget (1928) has shown that cognitive development in childhood relates importantly to decisionmaking, and his studies indicate that a pragmatic approach to problem solving in early childhood helps the child learn better than an abstract one. In other words, learning to choose correctly in the puddle example above would be helped more by the direct experience of feeling wet feet than by a discussion of the pros and cons of navigating, circumnavigating, or plunging into the water. Erikson (1950) makes clear that decisionmaking in adolescence depends upon clear definition from significant adults of their own point of view and their own ways of making decisions for themselves—all of this presented in a manner which does not superimpose a solution but offers an example of one person's method. The adolescent may or may not identify with this model, and this is an option which must remain open. In the instance of the girl with sleep reversal, discussion of the pros and cons of pursuing a business career as opposed to going to college with all the ramifications relating to sex stereotyping and the choice of motherhood over career, as well as the simpler choice between a prolonged or a short-term educational span, should help her identify the problem and then solve it.

The method followed by parents, teachers, and therapists in helping adolescents develop successful problemsolving must be a subtle one, for one must avoid preaching values on the one hand and being wishy washy on the other. Conversation that begins, "When I was your age . . . ," is doomed to failure from the start. One can see the film cover any adolescent's eyes at such a moment! "Knowing you as I do, I would guess you must be feeling a lot of pressure from lots of directions to do such and such" is often a good opening, or "Decisions! Decisions! You must be facing a lot of them" may prove to be another way to direct talk away from the presenting problem (sleep reversal) to what lies beneath it (a nagging uncertainty about a decision).

Once the problem is identified, the temptation is to offer solutions, and, while this helps a child make up its mind, it only irritates an adolescent. One can work for a long time to try to tease alternative solutions from the individual. "What comes to your mind? What do you see ahead?" "Tell me what it feels like to see yourself doing this, that and the other." All these leading questions and statements may lead nowhere or, more likely, to the persistent trap question from the young person, "What do you think I should do?" The answer, "Whatever you want to," begs the question, and "Go to Vassar" starts an argument.

In such instances bringing a third party into the discussion may be helpful. "Joanie Smith went to secretarial school. I don't know how she liked it"; or "I really admire Jane Doe for staying in school after she got married and had her baby." The latter brings your own values out without superimposing them. Of course the adolescent is not going to make her decision on the spot or give you any credit for influencing her solution to the problem if she does solve it later on, but your identification of the underlying conflict and your subtle presentation of solutions with some indication of your own priorities have no doubt been an important contribution to her becoming a mature problem solver herself.

The emotionally healthy young adult will have had good "training" experiences in childhood and adolescence and, as a result, will be able to make crisp, accurate, clear-cut decisions without experiencing neurotic doubting and circular obsessive rumination.

Sexual Satisfaction

A second area in which one sees emotional health or ill health is the area of sexuality—in its broad and its narrow context. For some, gender identity is never fully crystalized. There is discomfort with maleness or femaleness. This represents ill health in the general area of sexuality. Others are unable to obtain satisfying gratification in their genital relationships with their partners, and this represents pathology in the specific area of physical sexuality.

Those young adults who have problems developing a healthy maturity in the general area of sexuality may have experienced problems in childhood or in adolescence. Early in life the distinctions between the sexes are defined by parents and other caretakers (nurses, teachers, and babysitters), and the manner and method of this definition have an important impact on the later gender comfortableness of the child. In some families there are two separate value systems for sons and for daughters. What is allowed one and denied the other and what is expected of one and not of the other are clearly defined, and the difference is immediately perceived by the child. It is not simply that boys urinate standing up and girls sitting down, but boys can run around naked, while girls must cover up their torso even before breast development begins. Girls are given dolls, and boys are given trucks. Boys can shout and talk loudly, but girls must speak softly. Girls are expected to be neater and tidier than boys. It seems to us that when these distinctions are made clearly in childhood, there are less concern and anxiety in early adulthood about passivity and aggressiveness and less disturbing power struggles between men and women. Divisive competitiveness is less when the arenas are separate.

There is considerable controversy today about sexual stereotyping. The feminists feel that this practice results in the downgrading of women, but so far the evidence is in favor of helping children develop a clear-cut sense of gender rather than blurring the natural differentiation. Of course, most feminists do not believe in a "natural differentiation" (other than the anatomical one) and attribute all other differences between the sexes to the effects of cultural conditioning (the male "putdown" of women). Most studies, however, whether conducted by men or women, show that there are temperamental, characterological, and sexual arousal differences which are not culture created.

Presently there is a greater degree of encouragement for daughters to prepare for careers than was true in the past. Typical American parents do not hold out the prospect of "Kirche, Küche, Kinder" ("Church, Kitchen, Children," a German expression describing woman's lot in life) as the most desirable goal for their daughters, as they used to. They indicate that they would be pleased at a daughter's choice of a number of different options, but in regard to dress, manners, sex, and the division of labor within the home, there are still different expectations for sons and for daughters. For healthy personality development these distinctions are necessary.

Treating boys and girls differently in childhood seems clearly indicated, but we are less sure about this when these children become adolescents. The trend is now toward coeducation in private schools and colleges (it has always been more the rule than the exception in public educational institutions), and this can be seen as good evidence that identical curricular and extracurricular programs are preferred for male and female adolescents. Similarity in dress and manners in this age group does seem to foster an ease in relationships between the sexes which leads to the kind of comfortableness together to which we referred earlier. While it may be hard for traditionalists to accept women college students as rugby and ice hockey players, so far no harm seems to have come of it, and a great deal of pleasure and companionship between the sexes has apparently resulted. Despite the occasional vituperative outbursts on the part of a few militant feminists, the overall interaction between the sexes at all ages seems to us to be at a higher level of understanding and mutuality than ever before.

Of course, a satisfactory physical relationship between men and women depends almost entirely on the nature of the emotional one. Couples who are angry, distrustful, or afraid of each other are going to engage in mechanical, competitive, mutually demeaning, and unsatisfying sexual relationships. There are other factors which stem from earlier experiences with parents, siblings, and peers which can inhibit the pleasure of sex relations with a partner with whom one has a loving, trusting relationship. Early childhood experiences that can lead to later trouble in this area often have to do with parental attitudes during toilet training. Emphasis on the dirtiness, foul smelling, disgusting appearance, and even the possible contaminating effect of urine and feces tends to build feelings of revulsion for the sex organs and to lead to excessive shyness and modesty later in life when these organs are participants in what should be a happy and loving experience.

Sex play with siblings or, rarely, incestuous relationships with parents also result in inhibitions which can seriously interfere with healthy sexual relationships in adulthood. There may be little that parents can do in the way of forestalling such incidents other than being aware of their possibility and taking precautionary measures which do not cause unwarranted fears on the part of the child being protected. However, if such incidents do occur (and sex play among siblings or peers is very common in childhood), the attitude taken by parents is usually crucial in determining whether or not the incident will leave a damaging scar on the psyche of the child. A thorough discussion of the episode between child and parent or a therapist, which includes both the initiator and the complier in separate talks, should take place as soon as possible after the event with the hope that feelings of guilt about the physical enjoyment which occurred and any seduction that might have been thought to have played a part will be aired, as well as the shame, the fear, and the perplexity which are usually involved. Once this kind of catharsis has been achieved, the matter can usually be dropped, and it is unlikely that any inhibiting effect will be seen later.

Positive attitudes toward physical closeness are important also. Simply preventing or dealing with traumatic events is not enough to ensure satisfying sexual relationships in later life. Children need to know that touching, hugging, holding, and kissing between parents are an enjoyable and healthy part of being an adult. A feeling of comfort with physical contact has its developmental origins in the child's observation of what happens between their parents' bodies. Erikson (1950) has written eloquently on this subject, and Harlow's (Harlow and Zimmerman 1959) monkeys have proven the same thing—not only in terms of the attainment of mutually satisfying sexual relations but also, in the broader sense, in the development of trust in others.

Serious inhibitions in sexual functioning can result from experiences taking place in early adolescence as well as in childhood. Rape, sexual assault, sex play with siblings, incest, being required to share a bed with sibling or parent can all happen to a teenager with the same results described before for the child, and the prevention and treatment of such occurrences are much the same. In addition, however, the adolescent is forced to deal with his or her own burgeoning sexual impulses, and the manner in which these impulses are reacted to by parents and significant others influences to a considerable degree sexual adjustment as an adult.

There has been considerable controversy about where and by whom sex education should be given, and we believe that there is no clear answer to this question. Schools, churches, physicians, and parents are capable of providing the necessary education, if they are comfortable with the subject, and there are so many variations in this regard that one cannot make a general recommendation. Suffice to say that teenagers do need to know the facts about sexual anatomy and physiology as well as about pregnancy, contraception, and abortion, but these facts have to be accompanied by teaching about their emotional correlates. For instance, boys need to have their feelings about penis size understood, and girls need to have a chance to discuss feelings about size of breasts and about delayed menarche. Myths which correlate penis size with virility and ability to give satisfaction and those which suggest that women with small breasts are homosexual create feelings of fear and inadequacy which can seriously cripple sexual performance and enjoyment in early adulthood. They need to be discussed and their influence counteracted. Masturbation, thanks to some of our popular novels and sex manuals, has come to be generally understood for what is is—a healthy release for sexual tension, but there is still an aura of impurity around it which leads some adolescents to suffer from inappropriate guilt feelings. These must be dealt with by knowledgeable and understanding parents and teachers. Calderone (1970) has been a pioneer in this field, and her work by writing and lecturing has gone far toward breaking down mythology and creating relaxed and happy attitudes toward physical sex.

Career

Moving on now to the area of commitment to career—something that has always been the core of most men's midlife existence and is becoming increasingly important also for women, here again we find that occurrences and attitudes experienced, both in childhood and in adolescence, have a significant and often crucial developmental impact. Early in childhood we begin to gain a sense of our own competence and to experience feelings of success and of failure. If we grow up feeling inferior and incompetent in comparison with those around us, then it becomes more and more difficult to meet the challenges that are part of daily life and in the long run to make the commitment necessary to pursue consistently a career. Often it is children low in the birth order who fail to attain a sense of competence. They have become used to being smaller, weaker, and more stupid than their siblings, and, from the constant frustration of trying to catch up from behind, a feeling of inadequacy and a pessimism about achieving success are created which make them back away from challenges and then avoid commitment to competitive employment throughout their lives.

But it is not only low birth order that may cause children to have problems with their careers in later life. Young people whose parents' expectations are so narrow that they can praise their children for success in a very limited number of areas also fail to gain the courage and feeling of optimism which allow them to compete and to commit themselves to careers that are demanding. It is incumbent upon parents to compensate in what ways they can for the feelings of smallness in their later-born children, taking them away on trips without the older children, for instance, or having them visit relatives by themselves where they will be out from under the domination of their brothers and sisters. Parents, too, should seek out areas of competence and interest in their children and foster them. Sometimes these areas may seem "far out" or perhaps even unacceptable, but the advantage of doing something right and feeling pleased with the achievement as well as gaining some praise from respected elders means so much to the child, both in the present and for the future, that mothers and fathers should be able to broaden their focus and, in some instances, swallow their pride in the best interests of their children. We know of one individual who gained a sense of pride in himself from being the local tiddly-winks champion, another from collecting butterflies, and another, a girl, who found a new sense of self-worth from having more freckles than any other person, boy or girl, in the county!

Another important factor in the development of the ability to commit oneself to a career is the image of work projected by those in the family who are employed. Sometimes parents will blame their jobs for taking them away from home and causing them to be less adequate mothers, fathers, or spouses than they want to be. This casts careers in the role of enemy and leads to feelings in the children that they should be avoided rather than sought after. To adults, such an assumption seems silly and irrational, but we must never forget that young children are much more in tune with the feelings embodied in situations in their environment than they may be with the logic involved.

Parents who are able to give their children a sense of the value of the various jobs they are working at and, if at all possible, a sense of the enjoyment and gratification which come out of their employment are parents who are cultivating the roots of a later ability to make commitments to career in their children.

For the adolescent, the problems that arise to interfere with career commitment are different from those we find in the child. Young men and women from about 15 on begin to look within themselves for incentive and motivation. They tend to be suspicious of suggestions and even of encouragement from adults about where they should go and what they should do. The primary need in adolescence is to be sure that one's goals and ambitions are independently chosen and are unique to themselves. Often they experience an interim of neutrality labeled by Erikson (1950) a psychosocial moratorium, when they are against everything and for nothing. This is often very distressing to adolescents, but at times they seem oblivious of it or even happy with it. It is almost always frustrating and irritating to parents, teachers, and therapists, and they tend to moan about "wasted lives" and "unfulfilled potential." There is little they can do about it except to wait until it passes—which it almost always does after months or perhaps a year or 2. At this time in the lives of their children, parents must be tolerant of experimentation and not preach the old saw "Anything worth starting is worth finishing." They also must be careful not to take over when a flash of enthusiasm appears in their young son or daughter. This almost always results in the immediate dropping of the project, whatever it may be. Former President Eliot of Harvard once said regretfully, "Whenever we see a spark of genius around here we water it!" Walking the tightrope between appropriately supporting an adolescent's interest in something and taking it away from him or her through your own enthusiasm and wish to participate in it is difficult, but it is an important responsibility of parenthood.

Models are important to adolescents, more even than to children, for they are aware of the action and attitudes of the adults whom they respect and admire. They rarely can acknowledge this for, as we said before, they very much want to feel that their values and goals spring from within. But unconsciously they are identifying with those whom they respect. Over and over again we see young people lose their zest for life and become lethargic and unmotivated following the death of an older family member or admired teacher. Without knowing it, their reason for succeeding is suddenly gone. No longer can they unconsciously work toward emulating this person and gaining his praise and respect. This is beautifully characterized in Arthur Miller's (1949) play when Biff, shortly after surprising his father in a hotel room with a prostitute, says to his mother, "Gee, Mom, I can't seem to take hold. I can't get hold of a way of life."

One other eventuality which may have a deleterious effect on an adolescent's ability to commit himself to the idea of working is the death of a parent which may be attributed to overwork or the pressures inherent in his job. Such an event may set up an unconscious association between dedication to a career and death. Parents need to be careful in their assessment of the influence of employment on the health of the person who is working. Sometimes the effects can be exaggerated and adversely influence the ambition of a child. By careful encouragement of young people to seek out their own egosyntonic means of expression and an enthusiastic and optimistic attitude toward their own work, parents can help their children develop a healthy commitment to careers when they become young adults, and later this same attitude on the part of teachers will be very important. White (1975), Erikson (1950), and Vaillant (1977) have made important contributions to our understanding of what enhances the development of feelings of competence, commitment, and success in the world of work.

Intimacy

Intimate relationships with others are the healthy expression of commitment in the interpersonal area. Touching, holding, carrying, hugging in infancy have been found to be related to the development of trust, and indeed, the existence of trust as opposed to suspiciousness is the key to healthy relationships throughout life. If an infant has obtained a sense of trustingness by feeling his body supported and nourished by another, then he has a good start toward developing intimate feelings as an adult, but other factors in childhood and adolescence play a role also.

In addition to loving acceptance at home, children need and tend to develop close relationships to peers easily in play groups and at school. The importance of these friendships is often minimized by the child, either because he does not recognize them for what they are or because he does not have the vocabulary to describe his feelings. Parents must be careful to foster such friendships and do their best not to disparage these friends or to fail to take the trouble to arrange opportunities to meet and play. Also, they must be alert to the trauma involved in separation from playmates when one or the other family moves to a remote community. Special efforts need to be made in such cases to find new companions and to help the child overcome any shyness or reluctance in reaching out or responding to new friends. Attempts to help the child verbalize his sadness and his sense of loss, although not often very successful, should be made.

Adult figures need to be as consistent and as constant in the child's life as is possible. Revolving babysitters or a changing cast of spouses or lovers tends to build distrust of people in young children. It is hard for them to tolerate the disappointment which follows the disappearance of a person whom they had come to trust, and a multiplicity of such disappointments can leave vestiges of uncertainty about relationships which may inhibit the development of deep relationships later in life.

Intimacy includes a deep trust and a mutuality of feeling which allow for and even enjoy differences in opinions, taste, and values. Many experts, specifically Erikson (1950), believe that it can come only after the attainment of identity, for it is believed that intimacy threatens one's identity, because the closeness one feels to another brings to mind the possibility of merging into the other and thus losing one's own individuality. Whether this is true or not, there are many adolescent experiences which can work against the development of a capacity to be intimate. One has already been discussed in the context of career commitment—loss of or disillusionment in a respected and admired adult. As does a child, an adolescent feels angry and resentful if a loved one dies. Although it is irrational, there is always a sense that the person who died deserted the individual who was left behind and that this was a breach of faith and a breaking of trust. It becomes more difficult after such a loss to love and become intimate with another.

Behavior on the part of one person toward another which breaks trust and thereby interferes with the ability to become intimate is all too common, and much of it is not preventable. Fractured romances seem to be part of growing up, and, all too often, a truly one-sided defection on the part of a lover leads to the development of a callousness and a defensive burying of tenderness which may never change. Fortunately, the trite saying "Time heals all wounds" is (as are so many trite sayings) very true, and the individual who is hurt recovers, at least to some degree, and is once more able to feel lovingly enough toward another to develop intimacy after a period of numbness. Helping adolescents to grieve for a lost parent or lover is one of the most frequent tasks which challenge therapists and counselors of adolescents. Their help can often make the difference between permanent scarring and temporary withdrawal. Intimacy can follow successful recovery from rejection or loss, but such a recovery often requires help from older and wiser confidantes.

Conclusion

The goals of the young adult should be to work out a stable identity, decide on what one wants to do, develop independence from one's family, but retain good relationships with them, develop appropriate sexual attitudes and customs, and adopt or reject, when necessary, the ethical and moral values that are consistent with the well-being of one's society.

As we have said, the transition from adolescence to adulthood, or maturity, can be quite difficult or seemingly unlikely if the developing person has not been helped to know what to expect and what is expected of him. This depends on a value system clearly defined. It is here that one all too often finds much uncertainty on the part of older people. The young adults tend to admire and respect, as well as emulate, older persons whom they observe engaging in pleasant and rewarding activities, particularly those that help others or the general community culture. Unfortunately, many of the ideas being taught are destructive rather than constructive. This is especially true in the content of many recreational activities, most notably television. In many programs the ideals expressed in action, speech, dress, and thought are all too often expressed in terms that tend to exploit young adults rather than encourage them to develp patterns of living that are most conducive to the betterment of everyone.

This development period is the culmination of much nurturing, teaching, and coaching by a wide variety of significant persons: parents and other relatives, teachers, classmates, neighbors, religious authorities, and those whom the young person encounters through books, magazines, and television. Fortunately, the resiliency of late adolescents and young adults is such that the early positive influences can have a dramatic effect in overcoming difficulties encountered in this age span and in enabling them to live satisfying lives.

References

Calderone, M.S. *Manual of Family Planning and Contraceptive Practice.* Baltimore: Williams and Wilkins, 1970.

Erikson, E.H. *Childhood and Society.* New York: W.W. Norton, 1950.

Harlow, H.F., and Zimmerman, R.R. Affectional responses in the infant monkey. *Science*, 130:421-432, 1959.

Miller, A. *Death of a Salesman.* New York: Viking Press, 1949.

Piaget, J. *Judgment and Reasoning in the Child.* London: Harcourt, Brace, 1928.

Vaillant, G.E. *Adaptation to Life.* Boston: Little, Brown, 1977.

White, R.W. *Lives in Progress,* 3rd ed. New York: Holt, Rinehart & Winston, 1975.

*The Course of Life: Psychoanalytic Contributions
Toward Understanding Personality Development.
Vol. II: Latency, Adolescence, and Youth.
S.I. Greenspan and G.H. Pollock, editors.
NIMH 1980*

Late Adolescence: The Second
Separation Stage of Adolescence

Richard A. Isay, M.D.

The onset of adolescence is accompanied by an upsurge of libidinal and aggressive impulses, propelled largely by the physiological changes that initiate puberty. The adult-like sexual and aggressive capacities are now better organized than the instinctual impulses of childhood, which were more diffuse with regard to both their aim and origin. Puberty, following a latency period in which there has been consolidation of the development gains of childhood, finds an ego becoming more capable of tolerating, as well as controlling, an increase in drive strength. Accompanying these strong sexual and aggressive impulses are recrudescent, incestuous, libidinal fantasies and hostility toward the same-sex parent with a concomitant fear of retaliation. There is, therefore, a need for distance from the parental objects toward which these impulses are directed. We might think of the separation that the early adolescent imposes between himself and his parents in order to achieve this distance as constituting a first separation stage of adolescence.

Unlike the onset of early adolescence, that is demarcated by both physiological and psychological changes and the consequent need for emotional distance, the onset of late adolescence is initiated by a cultural expectation of independence and developmental progression. This usually occurs in our society at about the age of 17 or 18 and often, but not always, coincides with the departure for college.[1] This cultural expectation of independence initiates the

---

Copyright 1980 by Richard A. Isay.

1. In Israel the separation that marks the onset of late adolescence also occurs at 18, imposed by military training rather than by advanced education. In Israeli society this period is consciously and clearly acknowledged as an opportunity for growth and independence for their adolescents,

(Cont.)

second separation stage of adolescence known as "late adolescence." In this developmental stage there is further mitigation of the restraining parental ego and superego, in large measure a result of the loosening of parental ties. While the core superego remains, there have been at times an extensive modification and revision of values during adolescence through the influence of peers and other adults. There is another increase during late adolescence in sexual and aggressive wishes and impulses—this time, largely a result of the separation and not the cause of it—with greater opportunity than in early adolescence to express these impulses through diverse experiences in an enlarged sphere of relationships.

The separation and increased emotional distance from parents that mark the onset of this stage of adolescence normally result in some subjectively experienced depression and anxiety; however, the mood swings of this age are neither as abrupt nor as pronounced as in early adolescence, when what has been compared to a mourning process occurs (Jacobsen 1961). The discomfort is not usually as marked, since a partial working through of the loss has previously taken place and the ego is better equipped to cope with anxiety and trauma, both factors enhancing the adolescents' capacity to deal more effectively with the separation.

With the menarche, the pubescent girl, confronted by her separateness and the need to care for herself, has had separation forced on her by her physiology at the earliest stage of adolescence. A boy in early adolescence has had no comparable physiological confrontation with his own separateness, for while masturbation with ejaculation is a physiological landmark that may cause anxiety because of the new sexual and competitive prowess it represents, it does not evoke comparable feelings of separateness and aloneness, lacking the regularity, automaticity, and total body involvement of menstruation. Some adolescent boys attempt to control their anxiety by being abstemious, thereby attempting to assert the efficacy of mind over a body whose impulses and responses to impulses appear to dominate them. The adolescent girl has no such option; the onset of menstruation demands of the pubescent girl that she regularly take care of the needs of her body by herself, evoking a sense of abrupt and often profound, painful separation from the mother.

It is this abrupt and more painful separation that may contribute to making early adolescence more traumatic for a girl than for the early adolescent boy. The feelings of depression, caused by the girl's feeling of separateness, and the anxiety, evoked by the ensuing regressive pulls, may be major causes of the early adolescent girl's seeking psychological assistance. It is my impression that

although it is also a time fraught with realistic anxieties about the potential current and future dangers for these young people. The demarcation between early stages of adolescence and late adolescence is not so clear in our society. Physical separation is neither enforced nor universal; and, although the 18-year-old now has most of the legal prerogatives of the adult, most middle-class American adolescents are still dependent for support on their parents and are not perceived as nor treated as adults within the family.

girls are more likely to seek psychological help at this age than boys for problems that involve separation and the recrudescence of childhood separation conflicts. The mother's identification with her daughter, the mother's own anxiety and ambivalent involvement in her daughter's maturation often make the progress through this first adolescent separation phase particularly difficult.

We might hypothesize that, because of the girls' prior, relatively more profound and extensive experience with feelings of separateness, they would be better prepared for and less distressed by the separation at this later developmental stage than their opposite-sex peers. It is my impression, however, that this is not the case. I believe this to be explicable by a girl's identification with and attachment to her mother which to some extent must be surrendered to form the deeper and more complex heterosexual attachments of late adolescence, contributing to her sense of loss at this stage. We are also aware of those variables that may make the separation of late adolescence especially difficult for a girl, such as an intense symbiotic relation with her mother, or as frequently seen today, attending a male-dominated college that, lacking maternal surrogates and role models, increases her longing and loneliness.

All of us who work with late adolescents in analysis or psychotherapy frequently see depression, overt and masked, in both boys and girls during the first year in college. It may take the form of doleful, repetitious complaints about classmates, roommates, living accommodations, or other aspects of college life, a displacement of the anger associated with longings, loneliness, and anxiety caused by the separation. A new school for the second year may be sought—one that may be either very close to home or very distant—in an essentially futile attempt to escape these painful longings.

The increased psychological and physical space for the expression of libidinal and aggressive impulses, along with the forceful aggressive push of physiological maturation, may be frightening to many adolescents, and their behavior often demands external intervention as an unconsciously imposed means of constraining or containing these impulses. What we consider the testing of limits to help him contain impulses may also have the function of providing an external authority as a substitute for the ego and superego function of the longed-for parents. Such "limit testing," then, may be another form of expression of the late adolescent's mourning process, and these self-imposed external constraints may be unconsciously sought-after substitutes for the missed and missing parents (also see Blos 1963).

The intensity of competitive strivings with the parent of the same sex evokes in many late adolescents the resurgence of enormous anxiety, often caused by fears of retaliation. Various forms of self-injurious or self-destructive behavior may occur as a means of controlling, or magically attempting to ward off, the feared retaliation for the expression of these aggressive and sexual strivings. What appears, however, to be simply self-destructive behavior may also be an expression of the late adolescent's need to examine and test his or her own capacities in an effort to learn to deal more effectively with new aspects of external reality, a need arising from the separation and increased psychological distance from parents. A variety of experiences and relationships with peers serves this function of testing the viability and solidity of certain functions of the ego, especially those "autonomous characteristics," such as motor, language, and thinking skills that are primarily concerned with increasing mastery over the environment. These aspects of ego, of course, do no necessarily remain untouched by conflict (Hartmann 1958, p. 9). Any analyst working with adolescents can attest to the severe disruptions, distortions, and inhibitions that occur at times, especially in the spheres of language and thinking, because of conflict.

Adolescents may form close attachments to peers whom they anticipate will be unacceptable to their parents or whom they experience as being unlike anyone they had previously associated with. These relationships, "spite and revenge attachments," may be a means of placing a barrier between the adolescent and his parents. In this manner, he attempts to force a separation by causing a rupture in a relationship in which he unconsciously feels his dependency longings to be too great, or in which he experiences, again usually unconsciously, the parental attachment to be frightening. This is seen relatively frequently when a late adolescent, spending his college years at or near home, experiences the continued attachment to be too uncomfortable.

Not all late adolescents who live at home, of course, need to expand their psychological space in this manner, as the psychological distance and the independence necessary for developmental maturation at this stage may be achieved even though there is physical proximity. There are, furthermore, late adolescents who leave home during the college years, forming vindictive attachments in order to establish greater independence, and sever what is perceived as a burdensome emotional attachment to either or both parents. Physical separation itself does not insure the necessary independence for maturation at this stage, any more than physical proximity necessarily limits the capacity for emotional growth.

This traditional way of viewing such relations does not, however, do justice to their complexity. For, while their aim may be, in part, to aggravate parents and to enhance separation, they are also a means that the adolescent has of testing his capacity to deal effectively with unfamiliar types and groups of people in new and unfamiliar circumstances, just as he tests his capacity to deal with unfamiliar, and at times, dangerous situations. Such apparently vindictive attachments are thus formed not only to compel the rupture of a relationship with parents, but to test and enhance the adolescent's social competence after he has achieved a degree of separation and independence.

The late adolescent's testing of society's limits, his reckless and sometimes even dangerous behavior, and his seeking out relationships that may appear dangerous, unwise, or unhealthy do express the wish to have external forces intervene to help contain frightening internal pressures. But all these experiences also test and expand the ego's capacities to contain, control, organize, and cope with a variety of new and variegated reality situations. Largely because of such experiences, along with enhanced intellectual and motor skills that occur as a result of physiological maturation, there occurs during late adolescence a further increment in ego assets, particularly in the coping devices that enhance the capacity to deal more effectively with external reality and, in turn, with instinctual impulses.

Developmental Goals

Laufer (1976) writes that the developmental tasks of late adolescence are as follows: "the change in relationship to contemporaries; and the change in attitude to his (the adolescent's) own body." The main developmental function of adolescence, in his view, lies in the "establishment of a final sexual orientation" (pp. 298).

Blos (1962) understands late adolescence as a stage of consolidation whose goals and tasks are the "elaboration of a highly idiosyncratic and stable arrangement of ego functions and interests; an extension of the conflict-free sphere of the ego; an irreversible sexual position (identity constancy); a relatively constant cathexis of object and self representations; and the stabilization of the mental apparatuses . . . ."

Aarons (1970), Ritvo (1971), and Blos (1974) all stress that there is a final structuralization and organization of the ego ideal that occur as an outcome of the psychic reorganization of late adolescence. They see many major conflicts and difficulties of late adolescence arising out of an insufficient and inadequate ego ideal. The final structuralization of the ego ideal corresponds to the final resolution of the negative oedipal complex by freeing up, for the boy, the homosexual libidinal tie to the father and, for the girl, the libidinal attachment to the mother. Laufer (1964, 1976) feels that it is more accurate to say that the ego ideal is fixed as a more or less permanent structure from the immediate postoedipal identifications, but that there are some "realignments" and additions to the ego ideal occurring during late adolescence that reflect "the demands and expectations of contemporaries" (1964, p. 197).

My clinical work has suggested two developmental goals (or tasks) of late adolescence: (1) the consolidation of a final sexual orientation, so that there is at the conclusion of this developmental stage a reasonably consistent sexual self-image; and (2) the consolidation of a vocational goal, so that there is a more or less consistent vocational identity which is not subject to change with the tentative vacillations and shifts of interests that may occur at times of crisis, such as unexpected loss or trauma. This does not mean that for adolescence to be completed, one must know what vocation he wants to pursue. I am suggesting, however, that by the conclusion of adolescence, he or she does have a vocational as well as a sexual direction.

The successful accomplishment of these goals depends upon the adolescent's capacity to effect the psychological separation and to gain the necessary

distance from his or her parents to permit the expression of sexual and aggressive needs in a broadened scope of relationships and experiences, leading to
an ever-increasing specificity of love-object and career choice. If difficulties in
early relations with parents have made and continue to make separation difficult, then one may expect to encounter at this age symptomatic disturbances
that interfere with both goals of late adolescence. If there is not therapeutic
intervention during this period of consolidative development, then a symptomatic adult neurosis is likely to develop (see also Blos 1972*a*, p. 110).

The process leading to the consolidation of a vocational identity is inextrica-
bly tied to the formation of the ego ideal. Early ego-ideal precursors lie in the
fantasies the 2-, 3-, or 4-year-old uses to heal wounded self-esteem and to achieve
a sense of security, as he or she attempts to maintain equilibrium between his
desires and reality. Lampl-de Groot (1962) gives the engaging example of
John, age 2 years 10 months, who told his mother that "his penis would grow to
be as big as the garden hose; he would fill the ocean and a big steamer would
take him overseas" (p. 97). The ego ideal later becomes less exclusively an
agency for the healing of narcissistic wounds as a result of the identifications
and internalizations that are the outcome of the oedipal rivalry. It becomes the
agency that contains wishes to be like the parents, especially the same-sex
parent.

The late adolescents' testing of external reality, mentioned previously in the
context of enhancing and strengthening the ego, also contributes to accretions
in, modification, and solidifications of those aspects of the ego ideal that contributed to vocational interests. This occurs through identifications with an
extended group of peers and parent surrogates and the adolescents' increased
understanding of cultural expectations.

On the basis of clinical work with adults as well as adolescents, it is clear that
the ego ideal of the late adolescent contains identifications, not only with the
same-sex parent, but with the opposite-sex parent as well. In part, this may
represent residuals of the archaic, need-fulfilling, preoedipal ego-ideal precursors; restitutive identifications with the lost parent of the oedipal period; aspects,
for example, for the boy of his mother's vocational ambitions that are part of the
father's wishes and ambitions; as well as identifications with valued vocational
interests and activities of the mother. There are also identifications with the
opposite-sex parent's interests that are, of course, caused during the oedipal
period by regressive solutions of castration fears or envy of such maternal
functions as childbearing. However, the boy's identification with the vocational
interests of his mother have become increasingly common as a reflection of
society's greater appreciation of the professional and working woman in the
family.

As with the boy, a girl's vocational ambitions are in part derived from that part
of the ego ideal that is formed through attempted resolution of early narcissistic
injuries. In addition, one finds identifications with the father's vocational aims
and aspirations, which may be emphasized if she has a sense of not being equal

to her brother or father or of not having the body completeness of a man. One may find at the end of the oedipal period, a strengthened identification with the mother, which is in part an attempt to restore a sense of closeness to the lost father as well as to the mother, thereby maintaining contact with both parents through this identification. The demands and expectations of peer groups and parent surrogates, along with social expectations, lead to increments in the girl's ego ideal. Since one aspect of the solidification of the ego ideal that is concerned with vocational interest occurs through the restitutive identification with both parents, the accepted role of the working mother may make the achievement of a reasonably stable vocational identity less conflicted for many female college students who have two working parents. On the other hand, this increased freedom of vocational choice may evoke conflict in a girl from a more traditional middle-class family in which only the man works, as she may feel that by selecting a vocation she surrenders the closeness derived from identification with her mother, entering into what may be a frightening rivalry with her father (and/or brothers). (See also Jacobson 1954 and Blos 1974 for further elaboration of ego-ideal formation in girls.)

I have focused on the development of vocational identity in an attempt to emphasize an important developmental goal of late adolescence that has been attended to less than the attainment of a stable sexual identity. The consolidation of sexual identity follows a similar developmental course. It is clear that for both there must be sufficient resolution of oedipal conflicts to permit a core identification with the same-sex parent. If negative oedipal issues are still dominant during adolescence, of which one cause may be the inadequate resolution of preoedipal issues, especially during the separation and individuation stages, then anxiety may be so disabling as to interfere with the establishment of either a stable vocational or sexual choice. This is the implication of Blos's statement that "only after the analysis of the fixation in the negative oedipal complex has been accomplished, can the formation of an age-adequate, workable ego ideal take its normal course" (1974, p. 46).

The indication for the psychoanalytic treatment of the late adolescent is the presence of conflict that results in painful symptoms that interfere with the attainment of either of these developmental tasks (goals). I am stressing here not only the presence of conflict that may result in the failure of developmental progress, but the experience of pain. For, unlike the child who can be brought to the office and whose motivation can largely be supplied by the parents' distress, concern, and exhortation, the adolescent must proceed of his own volition, participating in a process that demands, among other things, passivity, acquiescence, and verbalization. All of these at times run counter to peer, other social, and, as we have seen, developmentally appropriate growth forces that demand activity in the service of mastery. In another paper I will discuss the implications of this conception of late adolescence for psychoanalytic technique. For the purpose of this paper, I am using the following cases to illustrate the types of developmental conflicts that make it both difficult and painful for a late adolescent to accomplish these tasks satisfactorily, necessitating psychoanalytic intervention to free up and facilitate development into adulthood.

Clinical Illustrations: Adam

Adam was 19 when he was referred for analysis, at the end of his freshman year at college. Although his college work had been fair, he had the continued, painful recognition that his performance was not as good as he wished, and he feared that he would be unsuccessful in any attempted vocational endeavor. He was concerned about a stammer and what he thought to be a small, inadequate penis.

Adam's father was very competitive and very successful. He viewed his father as a ruthless man, ruling a vast business empire by humiliating subordinates, as he had humiliated Adam as a child. Adam adored his mother, and they shared an articulated fear and ambivalence toward the father. Adam had no recollected overt symptomology or significant distress as a child. Although he was compliant and agreeable at home in order not to anger his father, he was successful and popular in school and in his social relations.

It is, however, important not to confuse the absence of recollected subjective distress, or of symptoms, with the absence of neurotic conflict. It is clear that there was massive inhibition of rage and of competitiveness with his father, which was expressed in compliance. Agreeable environmental factors, especially the favored support of his mother, made it possible for Adam to succeed despite these inhibitions. However, the fear and hostile ambivalence toward the father, along with the closeness to his mother, made the successful identification with his father impossible. While the origin of his neurotic conflict clearly lay in childhood, he did not become symptomatic until the onset of adolescence.

It was with the onset of pubescence, at age 12 or 13, that Adam became preoccupied with the small size of his penis and his general inadequacy. A painful and transiently immobilizing hip dislocation in early adolescence, along with a frightening upsurge of age-specific instinctual impulses, increased his need to maintain a passive posture and helped to explain the onset of symptoms at this time. He began to stammer in class. Athletically inclined, he now failed where he had previously only known success. Academically he seemed to thwart his every effort to be successful. Although admitted to a major university, he felt, and he may have been correct, that it was due to his father's connections or even his active intervention. He was totally unable and unwilling to make up his mind about what to do upon graduation or to entertain serious vocational alternatives.

In the analysis the transference took the form of Adam's needing to appear stupid to protect himself from any retaliation from me for his competitive and at times murderous impulses. He hid his ambition and rage in part behind ambiguities and obscurities of speech (Isay 1977). At the same time he made himself look small and inadequate, which gave expression to the intense repressed passive longings he had toward his father, whom he was fearful of getting close to. His difficulty in studying, his inability to decide on a vocation, his feeling of sexual inadequacy, and his occasional impotence protected him from feared retaliation for his anger and competitiveness, expressed in an unconscious desire to be taken care of by his father and a related desire to remain close to his mother. To do nothing, to be nothing was not only safe vis-a-vis his father: It was to remain his mother's child. The distance imposed by the separation of early pubescence, and now by late adolescence, entailed activity, decisions, experiences, and relationships that were perceived as dangerous.

On one occasion during his third year of analysis after I had attempted to help him understand some aspect of his complex work and sexual inhibitions, he had the following dream:

> I am driving down a highway with you. You are in the back seat. I'm driving about 90 mph. There is a lot of oil on the road. All the cars in front of me begin to fish tail, slide and crash into each other. My car is traveling straight and fine. I apologize for not slowing down, but I really didn't want to. You then point out the window and say, "Look, there's a growing tree."

His association to this dream centered about the discovery of his capabilities in the analysis. He had an occasional desire to be a racing-car driver, which his father viewed as one of his many "mindless preoccupations," but he also liked the skill and challenge of successfully maneuvering a dangerous course of action, which can be understood as the beginning enjoyment of attempts to cope with and master a frightening and dangerous external reality. Of course, he also felt that if he permitted himself to pursue a vocation or to enjoy sexual potency, he would unleash a terrible rage and kill or be killed; he did not want to be violent and competitive like his father, whom he felt and hoped his mother could not love.

The completion of his college career terminated our work after just under 3 years of analysis. This was not a complete analysis, for while we touched on most of the areas of conflict, there was not enough time for an optimal amount of working through of his conflicts in the transference, in dreams and associative material. Nevertheless, he became aware enough of many of the unconscious determinants of his inhibitions to decide upon a career related to his father's, and he experienced mitigation of his sexual inhibitions and consequent improvement in his self-perception. He also intended to continue his analysis in the city where he had acquired a job.

Benjamin

This boy entered analysis when he was 19, at the beginning of his sopho-more year of college. He felt he was inadequately masculine, was fearful of homosexual impulses, had distressing and painful psychosomatic complaints, and was unable to do his work adequately. He had had 1 year of previous psychotherapy.

Benjamin was an only child. His mother was perceived as obtrusive, over-whelming, and devouring; his father, as weak, submissive, and impotent. He was first symptomatic in early childhood as a fussy, poor eater, and later with a stutter, for which his parents sought assistance when he was 6 or 7. The early disturbances in Benjamin's relationship with his mother caused him to seek comfort and security from a less obtrusive, probably seductive father, and in later childhood he seemed comfortable only in his father's presence.

With the onset of early adolescence, Benjamin veered violently away from both parents and began to view them with contempt. His relationship with boys, who were older and admired, had a hero-worshipping quality. His inti-mate physical relationships with girls were terrifying from the time of his earliest sexual experiences at 16. His intense castration fears were aroused by the female genitals, which repulsed him and filled him with anxiety. On many occasions he was impotent. Although his grades were adequate, this seemed to be due mainly to his high intelligence, for it took enormous effort and entailed inordinate amounts of time to complete his assignments.

In his analysis, the transference first took the form of his viewing the analyst as holding him back, interfering both with his work and with satisfying sexual encounters. In a later aspect of the transference, he somewhat resembled Adam: looking silly or inadequate when his angry, competitive feelings manifested themselves. This was, as with Adam, a means of warding off retaliation, of acting out passive wishes toward the father and the desire to be mother's child again. For both Adam and Benjamin, the conflicts that made postoedipal identifica-tions with their fathers difficult and core ego-ideal formation inadequate resulted in passive fears, longings, and anxiety that interfered with scholastic perfor-mance, vocational goals, and sexual functioning.

Benjamin's analysis, like Adam's, terminated after approximately 3 years of work, which was 4 months following his graduation. It helped him to establish more satisfying relationships with women, much freer of the terrors characteris-tic of his previous relations; to become less passive, more mutual in his rela-tionships with male peers; and to achieve some mitigation of psychosomatic complaints which had interesting and complicated unconscious determinants. Both analyses were technically incomplete, as they are for many late adoles-cents if college graduation and/or vocational requirements necessitate a move. Benjamin terminated his analysis after 3 years to enable himself to pursue in another State a vocation in which he had become increasingly interested. For some late adolescents termination before completion of the analysis may be a resistance; for others such as Adam and Benjamin, immediate continuation of the analysis might have been a resistance to continued growth and progression by impeding heretofore inhibited vocational aspirations.

At the time of the onset of late adolescence, both Adam and Benjamin had been unable to achieve satisfactory emotional distance from either parent, particularly from their fathers. The result was not an expanded sphere of social relations and experiences, but a world narrowed by their fears and longings. This made the testing and mastery of new social skills, including the establishment of heterosexual attachments, extremely difficult and painful. It also limited their capacity to test and examine fantasies and wishes related to vocational ambitions, making academic success difficult and the discovery of a vocational direction temporarily impossible. Analysis resulted in sufficient conflict resolution to enable them to deal more effectively with frightening aspects of an extended reality, which, in turn, made further developmental progression possible.

Summary

Late adolescence as a developmental stage is discussed. A cultural expectation of increased independence from parents initiates this second separation stage of adolescence by prompting increased psychological distance that often involves a physical separation as well. Sexual and aggressive feelings and impulses are subsequently expressed within a widened sphere of relationships and activities, and the adolescent's attempts at mastering his or her extended world assist in the growth of ego assets and consolidation of a sexual and vocational identity during this developmental period.

References

Aarons, Z.A. Normality and abnormality in adolescence. *The Psychoanalytic Study of the Child,* 25:309-339, 1970.

Blos, P. *On Adolescence.* New York: The Free Press, 1962.

_____The concept of acting out in relation to the adolescent process. *Journal of the American Academy of Child Psychiatry,* 2:118-143, 1963.

_____The epigenesis of the adult neurosis. *The Psychoanalytic Study of the Child,* 27:106-135, 1972a.

_____The function of the ego ideal in late adolescence. *The Psychoanalytic Study of the Child,* 27:93-98, 1972b.

_____The geneology of the ego ideal. *The Psychoanalytic Study of the Child,* 29:43-88, 1974.

Hartmann, H. *Ego Psychology and the Problem of Adaptation.* New York: International Universities Press, 1958.

Isay, R.A. Ambiguity in speech. *Journal of the American Psychoanalytic Association,* 25:427–452, 1977.

Jacobson, E. The self and object world: Vicissitudes of their infantile cathexes and their influence on ideational and affective development. *The Psychoanalytic Study of the Child,* 9:75-127, 1954.

_____.Adolescent moods and the remodeling of psychic structures in adolescence. *The Psychoanalytic Study of the Child,* 16:164-183, 1961.

Lampl-de Groot, J. Ego ideal and superego. *The Psychoanalytic Study of the Child,* 17:94-106, 1962.

Laufer, M. Ego ideal and pseudo ego ideal in adolescence. *The Psychoanalytic Study of the Child,* 19:196–221, 1964.

——. The central masturbation fantasy, the final sexual organization, and adolescence. *The Psychoanalytic Study of the Child,* 31:297-316, 1976.

Ritvo, S. Late adolescence: Developmental and clinical considerations. *The Psychoanalytic Study of the Child,* 26:241-263, 1971.

The Course of Life: Psychoanalytic Contributions
Toward Understanding Personality Development.
Vol. II: Latency, Adolescence, and Youth.
S.I. Greenspan and G.H. Pollock, editors.
NIMH 1980

The Phase of Young Adulthood, Age Eighteen to Twenty-three Years

Melvin Lewis, M.B., B.S. (London), F.R.C. Psych., D.C.H.

Introduction

The phases of development that commonly occupy the years 18-23 may include late adolescence (Blos 1962), youth (Kenniston 1970), the periods of "Intimacy and Distantiation versus Self-Absorption" and "Generativity versus Stagnation" (Erikson 1956), and young adulthood (Lidz 1968). Indeed, the word "adolescence" means becoming an adult and was first used in the English language in 1430, when it referred to age 14-21 years in males, and 12-21 years in females. These phases of development in turn have biological, psychological, and social correlates and are viewed differently by society as the individual matures from a juvenile to an adult. Lastly, there are sex differences as well as sociocultural variables.

Developmental Tasks

Just as there is a stabilization of biological maturation as epiphyses close, adult stature is achieved, and drive upheaval settles, so there is an increasing stabilization of the personality. Conflict between the self and the changing milieu intérieur abates and is displaced by conflict within the self and between the self and the external world. Thus consolidation and integration of one's personality and the adaptation to a changing and unfamiliar society become the pivotal "developmental tasks" at this stage. Specific developmental tasks include the achievement of gratifying heterosexual relationships, deciding upon a career, and committing oneself to marriage or an alternative lifestyle.

Failure to resolve any of these developmental tasks may occur because of persisting difficulties arising from unresolved earlier conflicts. Moreover, current conflicts may be heightened by interaction with the existential anxiety that arises when confronted with certain challenges of society. These societal challenges, at least in western society, include attitudinal and technological confrontations. For example, changing attitudes toward sexual intercourse have been accelerated by the reduced fear of pregnancy. Modern technology of instantaneous mass communication has enabled young people to realize that they have much in common and that they now constitute the largest group in our population. The precarious control of destructive violence of a magnitude far greater than ever before possible may engender or aggravate a high level of anxiety in the adolescent, particularly at times of international crisis accompanied by the threat of nuclear attack.

Another, more immediate, variable is the socioeconomic status of the individual (Esman 1977). For example, a white, middle-class, professional person has an entirely different experience from a native American Indian. Additional variables are sex and parenthood. Recent psychoanalytic investigations during this period, however, have still focused for the most part on the affluent individual. For example, Ritvo (1971) has concentrated mostly on college students and those who have dropped out of college. Yet even among this group there is change. Thus, the striking difference in the behavior of students in the late 1960s compared to those seen in the early 1970s seems to reflect both intrapsychic development and the individual's responsiveness to the particular (historical) social context.

Yet the basic, fundamental, developmental tasks remain to be resolved, even if they are influenced by immediate or global social factors. Some of those tasks will now be discussed in greater detail.

Identity, Intimacy, and Society

By age 18-23 years, a sufficient history of personality traits and intellectual development has occurred to enable the individual to observe his or her own behavior in response to internal urges and external demands. This conscious identity, including a new decisionmaking capability, is now more fully integrated into the ego and should now be more or less independent of superego reinforcement. Moreover, decisions can now be made in the context of lengthier commitment rather than immediate wishes or superego sanctions. In addition, a greater degree of intimacy now becomes possible as independence from the family is established and a conscious sense of identity is achieved. Further, a new relationship with society emerges as the individual's horizons widen and the inequalities of society are recognized, if not tolerated. In some young adults there is an acute disillusionment with society, reminiscent of the disillusionment with parents that occurs in the postoedipal phase. Disillusionment with society may be an extension of, or a displacement from, that earlier disillusionment. However, in most instances it is a true recognition of human frailty and social reality. Thus, identity is a complex achievement, involving a sense of one's personal sameness within a comprehensible social reality and having both conscious and unconscious aspects.

Dyadic Love Relationships

Both males and females in this period are on the threshold of establishing new, long-lasting relationships that are based primarily on reality considerations. The short-lived relationships based on replication of original objects, or part-identification or overidealization, that characterize earlier adolescence are now replaced by a full sense of identification and the need to form realistic and real, lasting relationships that "fit" the now-consolidated identification. The motivations and forces acting on the formation of long-term, heterosexual relationships (including marriage) are early conscious and unconscious need fulfillment, unconscious incestuous fantasy wishes, the need for intellectual stimulation, sexual pleasure, self-esteem and narcissistic gratification, the influences of family and peer relationships, social striving, neurotic role interlocking, the wish to have children, and desire for complementarity. The degree to which any one of these components overrides the others will determine whether the relationship will succeed or fail. Since few, if any, relationships stay the same, a strong conscious commitment is usually required to resolve difficulties and misunderstandings arising from these factors. Young adults are generally capable of making this kind of commitment, particularly as they approach their midtwenties. A failure to make this kind of commitment or an overriding and interfering unconscious motivation, or even preconscious motivation that is not allowed recognition or expression, is likely to result in a failure or radical change in such relationships.

Early Parenthood Phase

During this phase the individual also becomes capable of parenthood, during which the individual's own childhood experiences are reworked (Benedek 1959). The individual's children act as stimuli and provide opportunities for this development. This in turn is a part of the individual's growing capacity for mutuality during what Erikson calls the stage of "Generativity versus Stagnation." Parenthood, however, is more than a single developmental phase; it is a series of interconnected subphases, beginning with fantasies of parenthood, through the psychological process for man and woman during pregnancy, labor and childhood (Bibring et al. 1961), to the identity changes in the parents as they experience changes in their relationships to each other and to their children as their children move from phase to phase in *their* development.

Intergenerational Experience

The period between age 18 and 23 years is often the beginning of the experience of being between two generations, one's parents and one's children. While emancipated from parents, there is a concern that one will be pulled back into the family of origin as a child and not as an adult (Gould 1972). Consequently, there is a tendency to intensify peer relationships, provided such relationships, especially in the aggregate, do not in turn threaten one's autonomy and individuality. Life is viewed mostly in terms of the present and future as the individual sets on a course that involves mastering a work skill, profession, or lifestyle.

Work

Sociocultural and family influences, sex, economic conditions, physical status, cognitive abilities, education, job opportunities, personality type and needs, specific conscious and unconscious motivations, identifications, talents and skills are some of the factors that determine an individual's work. Sometimes the choice of a particular career provides an environment in which group values can take the place of individually derived moral and ethical values. The individual superego may become dissolved in the group superego or may be reinforced by the group-ego ideal. Repetition compulsion may be another factor in determining not only the individual's choice of work, but the outcome, i.e., the degree of success or failure in that work. Work may thus be an end in itself, or a means of satisfying old urges, or a force acting upon the young adult—or all three.

Intellectual Function

By age 18 years, the individual should be capable of formal operations (Piaget 1969), wherein intellectual thought can begin with a theoretical synthesis of certain relations and then proceed to empirical data, instead of vice versa. This intellectual ability enables the normal individual to take distance on his or her thoughts, feelings and behavior, and influence the direction of all three. Cognitive fixation, on the other hand, interferes with this capacity and leaves the individual vulnerable to the repetition compulsion mentioned earlier.

Summary

In overview, the normal individual between 18 years and 23 years ideally is experiencing for the first time the consolidation of identity, the mastery of drives, the achievement of unfettered, true heterosexual object relationships, and a realistic view of the world as he or she enjoys new heights of intellectual activity. Few achieve this ideal state. Indeed, even were this state achieved, it would not last; the next phase of development would once again demand change.

References

Benedek, T. Parenthood as a development phase. *Journal of the American Psychoanalytic Association,* 7:389-407, 1959.

Bibring, G.L.; Dwyer, T.F.; Huntington, D.S.; and Valenstein, A.F. A study of the psychological processes in pregnancy and of the earliest mother-child relationship. In: Eissler, R.S.; Freud, A.; Hartman, H.; and Kris, M.; eds. *The Psychoanalytic Study of the Child,* 16:9-44, 1961.

Blos, P. Phases of adolescence. In: *On Adolescence: A Psychoanalytic Interpretation.* New York: The Free Press of Glencoe, 1962. pp. 52-157.

Erikson, E. Growth and crises of the healthy personality. *Psychological Issues,* 1:50-100, 1959.

Esman, A.H. Changing values: Their implications for adolescent development and psychoanalytic idea. In: Feinstein, S., and Giovacchini, P., eds. *Adolescent Psychiatry.* Vol. 5. New York: Jason Aronson, 1977. pp. 18-34.

Gould, R.L. The phases of adult life: A study in developmental psychology. *American Journal of Psychiatry,* 129:521-531, 1972.

Kenniston, K. Youth: A new stage in life. *The American Scholar,* 39:631-653, 1970.

Lidz, T. The young adult. In: *The Person.* New York: Basic Books, 1968. pp. 362-367.

Piaget, J. The intellectual development of the adolescent. In: Caplan, G., and Lebovici, S., eds. *Adolescence: Psychosocial Perspectives.* New York: Basic Books, 1969.

Ritvo, S. Late adolescence: Developmental and clinical considerations. *The Psychoanalytic Study of the Child,* 26:241-263, 1971.

Appendix A

Volume I. Infancy and Early Childhood
Contents

T. Berry Brazelton
Neonatal Assessment

Pirkko L. Graves
The Functioning Fetus

W. E. Freud
Notes on Some Psychological Aspects of Neonatal Intensive Care

Stanley I. Greenspan and Alicia F. Lieberman
Infants, Mothers, and Their Interaction: A Quantitative Clinical Approach to Developmental
Assessment

Lois B. Murphy
Psychoanalytic Views of Infancy

Reginald S. Lourie and Robert A. Nover
Applied Psychoanalysis and Assessment of Psychopathology in the First Year of Life

Sally Provence
Direct Observation and Psychoanalytic Developmental Psychology: The Child From 1 to 3

Margaret S. Mahler and John B. McDevitt
The Separation-Individuation Process and Identity Formation

John B. McDevitt and Margaret S. Mahler
Object Constancy, Individuality, and Internalization

Marian Tolpin and Heinz Kohut
The Disorders of the Self: The Psychopathology of the First Years of Life

Eleanor Galenson
Characteristics of Psychological Development During the Second and Third Years of Life

Henri Parens
Psychic Development During the Second and Third Years of Life

Albert J. Solnit
Psychoanalytic Perspectives on Children 1-3 Years of Age

Calvin F. Settlage
The Psychoanalytic Theory and Understanding of Psychic Development During the Second
and Third Years of Life

Peter B. Neubauer
Phase Specific Disorders of the Second and Third Years of Life

Humberto Nagera
The Four to Six Years Stage

Jeanne Lampl-de Groot
On the Influence of Early Development Upon the Oedipal Constellation

Heiman van Dam
Ages Four to Six—The Oedipus Complex Revisited

Robert J. Stoller
A Different View of Oedipal Conflict

Paulina F. Kernberg
  Childhood Psychosis: A Psychoanalytic Perspective

Clifford Yorke, Hansi Kennedy, and Stanley Wiseberg
  Some Clinical and Theoretical Aspects of Two Developmental Lines

Appendixes

Index

Appendix B

Volume III. Adulthood and the Aging Process
Contents

Stanley R. Palombo
The Archaic Adaptive Ego

Stanley I. Greenspan and William J. Polk
A Developmental Approach to the Assessment of Adult Personality Functioning and Psychopathology

W. W. Meissner
Developmental Psychopathology of Adult Disorders

Jacob A. Arlow
Developmental Aspects of Neuroses

Otto F. Kernberg
The Development of Intrapsychic Structures in the Light of Borderline Personality Organization

Arnold H. Modell
The Narcissistic Character and Disturbances in the "Holding Environment"

John Frosch
Neurosis and Psychosis

Louis A. Gottschalk
Psychoanalytic Perspectives on the Affective Disorders: Neurobiological and Psychosocial Interactions

Edward A. Wolpert
On the Nature of Manic Depressive Illness

Clarence G. Schulz
The Contribution of the Concept of Self Representation-Object Representation Differentiation to the Understanding of the Schizophrenias

Ping-Nie Pao
Schizophrenia in Terms of the Psychoanalytic Concept of Human Development

David L. Gutmann
Psychoanalysis and Aging: A Developmental View

Ewald W. Busse
Old Age

Jerome M. Grunes
Reminiscences, Regression, and Empathy: A Psychotherapeutic Approach to the Impaired Elderly

George H. Pollock
Aging or Aged: Development or Pathology

Index